All Manners of Food

All Manners of Food

Eating and Taste in England and France from the Middle Ages to the Present

STEPHEN MENNELL

Second Edition

University of Illinois Press
Urbana and Chicago

For Norbert Elias
'But civilised man cannot live without cooks'
Owen Meredith
(E. R. B. Lytton, Earl of Lytton, 1831–91)

First Illinois paperback, 1996

Manufactured in the United States of America
P 7 6 5

This book is printed on acid-free paper.

Library of Congress Cataloging-in-Publication Data

Mennell, Stephen.
All manners of food : eating and taste in England and France from the Middle Ages to the present / Stephen Mennell. —2nd ed., Illini books ed.
p. cm.
Includes bibliographical references and index.
ISBN 0-252-06490-9 (paper : acid-free paper)
ISBN 978-0-252-06490-6 (paper : acid-free paper)
1. Food habits—England—History. 2. Food habits—France—History. 3. Food habits—Social aspects. 4. Cookery, English—History. 5. Cookery, French—History. I. Title.
GT2853.G7M46 1996
394.1'094—dc20 95-2359
CIP

The first edition of this work was published in cloth (ISBN 0-631-13244-9) and paperback (ISBN 0-631-15638-0) by Basil Blackwell.

Contents

Acknowledgements

Figures 1 and 2 are reproduced from Claude Lévi-Strauss's *The Origin of Table Manners* (translated by John and Doreen Weightman), by permission of Professor Lévi-Strauss, Jonathan Cape Ltd., and Harper and Row, Publishers, Inc.

Figure 3 is reproduced from *Nature*, 1884, by permission of Macmillan Journals Ltd.

Figure 4 is reproduced from Louis Stouff's *Ravitaillement et Alimentation en Provence aux 14ᵉ et 15ᵉ siècles* by permission of Mouton Publishers.

Figure 5, a facsimile of Crown-copyright records in the Public Record Office, appears by permission of the Controller of HM Stationery Office, as do transcripts of similar material in the text.

Figure 6 is reproduced from *Carême French Cookery*, John Murray, 1836.

Figure 7 is reproduced from *L'Art culinaire*, 1883, by courtesy of the Bibliothèque Nationale, Paris.

Extracts from *State Formation and Civilisation*, the second volume of Norbert Elias's *The Civilising Process*, are reproduced by permission of the author and Basil Blackwell.

Preface

I first thought of writing this book as long ago as 1974. It arose out of the intersection of three interests. One was simply eating. For that I am particularly indebted to my wife Barbara, for her excellent and diverse cooking and ever-growing assortment of cookery books. A second interest was the work I was then doing for the Council of Europe on cultural policy in towns in thirteen countries. One could hardly visit all these countries – France most frequently and Strasbourg in particular – without becoming more conscious of the place of food and eating in cultural life. Thirdly there was my long-standing admiration for the work of Norbert Elias, whose ideas permeate this book even in those few parts where his name is not mentioned. Norbert has always encouraged his friends to do research on subjects in which they have a keen personal involvement. Since a great many other people enjoy eating too, I hope that in reading it they will share some of the enjoyment I had in writing the book. It is dedicated to Norbert in gratitude for the stimulus and encouragement he has always given me.

Other commitments prevented me from making a serious start on the research until 1979. Then three institutions jointly made it possible. The University of Exeter gave me study leave for the Lent and Trinity terms in 1980. The Warden and Fellows of St Antony's College, Oxford, kindly made me a Senior Associate Member of the College during 1980–1; I owe particular thanks to Herminio Martins who was my sponsor at St Antony's. Above all it was a grant from the Nuffield Foundation which enabled me to spend that period ransacking libraries in Oxford, London and Paris. Such was the mass of material I accumulated that it has taken me until 1984 to digest it and write it up – though I have to confess that it would have been finished earlier had I not in 1981 been unexpectedly diverted into politics.

Any number of friends have helped me in my work. In Exeter Ernest Martin was the first to encourage me to undertake this research. Colleagues in the Departments of History, Economic History and Sociology all took part in lively discussions of early drafts of parts of the book I presented to them in seminars. Professor J. R. Porter gave me some useful leads on religious influences, as did Stephen Lea for psychology, and Colin Jones and Nicholas Orme both read draft chapters in their specialist periods. Locally too, Geraldene Holt gave me her advice as a cookery writer, and Patricia Chandrasekera was my spy in two local schools. I must also thank Rodney Fry, John Saunders and James Gould who prepared illustrations.

I also learnt a great deal from discussions in seminars I gave elsewhere, beginning with the conference on 'The Civilising Process and Figurational Sociology' which Eric Dunning and I organised for the Theory Group of the British Sociological Association at Balliol College, Oxford, in January 1980. Later I had the benefit of seminars with Eric and his colleagues in Leicester, Richard Kilminster and his colleagues in Leeds, members of the Institute of Social Anthropology at Oxford, and the Figurational Sociology Section of the Dutch Sociological Association in Amsterdam.

Through Theodore Zeldin at St Antony's I met Alan Davidson, the unofficial but ubiquitous co-ordinator of research in the history of cookery in Britain, and through the four Oxford Cookery Symposia they have organised at the College I made the valuable acquaintance of dozens of cookery writers and researchers. Among them were Philip and Mary Hyman, without whose knowledge and advice my research trips to Paris would have been far less fruitful, as well as less enjoyable. Also thanks to the Davidson/Zeldin network, Jill Stone arrived in Exeter from Australia just in time to read the whole first draft and make an indispensable contribution to its improvement.

Two debts are paramount however. One is as always to my wife, who has kept me at the task, read and criticised each section as I wrote it, and helped me pour it all into the word processor. The other is to Joop Goudsblom, who has followed the work from the beginning, suggested several of the most useful lines of enquiry, and often brought me back to questions of sociological significance when I have threatened to lose myself in a welter of fascinating but not entirely relevant historical detail.

If in spite of the help of all these friends this is far from a faultless book, the responsibility is of course mine alone. Given its scope – both in time and in the many intertwined strands of argument – perhaps it is inevitable that specialists in particular fields will find errors. Nevertheless, this is the book I wanted to write, and I hope it may at least raise questions which will stimulate others to further research.

Finally I must mention two things the book is *not* about. It is about food, *not* drink – food was a big enough topic on its own, so such related topics as wine snobbery have been excluded. The book is also about *England* and France, *not* Britain and France. I have not done any research on Scotland's culinary history (or Wales's for that matter), and there are only a few incidental references to matters over the border. Scottish and Welsh readers will therefore understand why, except where in recent decades developments plainly affect Great Britain as a whole, I have spoken of 'England', not 'Britain'.

University of Exeter Stephen Mennell

1

Introduction

'One man's meat is another man's poison.' 'Chacun à son goût.' 'There's no arguing about taste.' Popular sayings such as these are symptoms of the common assumption that likes and dislikes among foods are a purely individual matter, and they are also used metaphorically about people's non-culinary 'tastes' or preferences of all sorts. The assumption is deeply rooted in the individualistic outlook which dominates modern thinking, and has become permeated with powerful ethical implications. 'A person's taste is as much his own peculiar concern as his opinion or his purse', wrote John Stuart Mill in *On Liberty* (1859:4). Or, as a well-known British journalist more recently remarked specifically about food, 'The truth is that with food, as with sex or religion, different people like different things. *It is not a moral issue*.'[1]

It is of course true that individuals do vary in their likes and dislikes. Much is not yet well understood about the psychology of taste and the precise mechanisms by which humans acquire their perceptions of and preferences among foods and flavours. Experimental psychologists have so far had to work not with the complex styles of cookery and mixtures of tastes with which we shall be mainly concerned in this book, but at the level of single foods and simple flavours. Even at that level, it is clear that in humans most likes and dislikes are learned. Innate instincts play a small part. It is thought that only a small number of taste labels are innately recognised. Sweetness is one example: there had been much discussion about whether the sweet taste was innately preferred or whether it became preferred because milk is sweet, until Steiner (1977) demonstrated that new-born infants, tested before they had been suckled or eaten anything at all, reacted with pleasure to a sugar solution. The sweet taste is thought to serve as a label for the calories the body requires. The salty taste is similarly believed to serve as an innately recognised label for the sodium ion, and perhaps also for the minerals in general necessary to health.

Beyond that, innate recognition appears to explain very little in human perception of taste. A great deal of research has been devoted to exploring the possibility that 'sweet', 'sour', 'salty' and 'bitter' constitute four basic dimensions of taste. One experiment involved a panel of people, having tasted the compound salty, sour and bitter taste of ammonium chloride, being asked to mix a cocktail of common salt, tartaric acid (sour) and quinine hydrochloride (bitter) to achieve the closest possible approximation to the ammonium chloride.[2] This revealed very wide individual differences in the cocktails chosen, implying that the panel experienced considerable problems in the perception and recognition of unfamiliar flavours. The almost random responses people make to unfamiliar flavours in this and similar experiments suggests that what they experience is not really *taste* but a sort of *pre-taste*. It is not really taste until they have learned how to interpret it. A parallel may be found in Howard Becker's classic sociological essay 'Becoming a Marijuana User' (1953), which demonstrates how the novitiate pot-smoker has to *learn* how to handle the drug's stimuli so as to produce the 'appropriate' response. Something not dissimilar may be involved in learning to like many foods and flavours, such as coffee:

> Coffee is one of the great, marvellous flavours. Who could deny that? Well, actually, anyone drinking coffee for the first time would deny it. Coffee is one of those things that [have been] called innately aversive. It is bitter and characterless; it simply tastes bad the first time you encounter it. By the time you have drunk a few thousand cups of it, you cannot live without it. Children do not like it, uninitiated adults do not like it, rats do not like it: nobody likes coffee except those who have drunk a fair amount of it, and they all love it. And they will tell you it tastes good. They like a mediocre cup of coffee, they relish a good cup of coffee, and they go into ecstasies over a superb cup of coffee. (Bolles, 1983: 68)

Research has also shown the importance in taste perception of the differing vocabulary for describing flavours available to humans in their diverse languages.[3] The role of language in taste perception is enough to point to differences in the senses between humans and other animals. Man, as J. J. G. Prick (1977) remarks, is an intellectual being who can theorise and rationalise about what he tastes and smells; without remembering that, one can hardly understand the fine discrimination developed by, say, connoisseurs of French wines or of *haute cuisine*.

That the detailed psychology of the learning and cognition of taste is not fully understood does not greatly matter for the purposes of this book. We shall be concerned mainly with a quite different problem: how social groups develop standards of taste. Such cultural standards vary in their form: some have the strength of binding 'commands', others are merely 'options' open to members of the group.[4] The overall force of these standards can best be judged not from psychological but from anthropological evidence. In most human groups, members show evident similarities to each other in food preferences, while differing dramatically from the preferences of members of other groups. These differences can only to a very limited extent be explained by which foods happen to be available to particular societies or social groups

– especially in the industrial world where in principle virtually any food produced anywhere can be made available at a price. In fact, no human social group is believed to eat everything of potential nutritional value available to it. Nor is it merely that some exotic tribes eat foods which would revolt the average European or American; equally some foods which are commonplace to us are avoided in other cultures. Apart from the well-known avoidance of beef by most Indians and of pork by Jews, Muslims and other religious groups in the Middle East, chicken and eggs are avoided in much of Africa and parts of South-East Asia. Dogs, on the other hand, are a prized meat in much of sub-Saharan Africa and in South-East Asia; camel is eaten in the Middle East; horseflesh eating has historically been centred in central Asia, and was introduced in the nineteenth century with some success into France but with little in Britain or America.[5] The Chinese do not eat milk or dairy products, fish is avoided by many cultures, insects eaten in others, and that is to say nothing of the vegetable kingdom.

People very generally have strong feelings not just about what foods should be eaten, but also about how the foods they choose should be prepared for eating. Ways of cooking become woven into the mythology and sense the identity of nations, social classes and religious groups. People take sides, and exaggerate differences. Even two such closely related cuisines as those of England and France, which have been in reciprocal contact for hundreds of years, stir the emotions in each other's protagonists. Evelyn Waugh (1942: 28) puts into the mind of one of his characters the longstanding English patriotic view of French cooking (and, by extension, of the French themselves):

A hard-boiled people, the French . . . hard-boiled; over-cooked; over-praised for their cooking. When people professed a love of France, they meant love of eating . . . She had heard a commercial traveller in the Channel packet welcome Dover and English food. 'I can't stomach that French messed-up stuff.' A commonplace criticism, thought Angela, that applied to French culture for the last two generations – 'messed-up stuff', stale ingredients from Spain and America and Russia and Germany, disguised in a sauce of white wine from Algeria. France died with her monarchy. You could not even eat well, now, except in the provinces. It all came back to eating.

Correspondingly, Grimod de la Reynière (1806: 60–1) expressed the traditional French view of English food:

England has never been famous for its *ragoûts*, and a gourmet would scarcely hazard the Channel crossing to eat roast and grilled meats. . . . English cooking is limited to boiled chickens, of extreme insipidity, and to what they call Plump Pudding [*sic*], a concoction based on breadcrumbs and Corinth raisins as a rule, though there are many variations and they throw in crowds of ingredients, which makes it a bizarre and indigestible mixture rather than a healthy and skilfully-made dish. . . . However, like every nation, even the least civilised, they have a few national dishes, of which they boast more out of patriotic spirit than conviction, . . . such as Turtle soup.

The task of this book is not to take sides, not to exaggerate differences, but to attempt to *explain* some of the real differences in the tastes of two nations and many social groups within each.

The likes and dislikes of other people are often incomprehensible to others. Waverley Root, an American gastronomic journalist long resident in France, reluctantly concluded that

> Every country possesses, it seems, the sort of cuisine it is appreciative enough to want. I used to think that the notoriously bad cooking of England was an example to the contrary, and that the English cook the way they do because, through sheer technical deficiency, they had not been able to master the art of cooking. I have discovered to my stupefaction that the English cook that way because that is the way they like it. This leaves nothing to be said, as I suppose the rule that there can be no argument about matters of taste applies to the absence of taste – in the literal sense – as well. (Root, 1958: 15–16)

But *is* that all that can be said? If food preferences are not a matter of purely individual and random variation, but are broadly shared within social groups, can nothing be said about how social groups come to like food the way they do?

One very superficial explanation frequently offered of differences in food preferences is that people like what they are used to, and conversely dislike the unfamiliar. In her book *Food in England*, Dorothy Hartley comes closest to suggesting that tastes are determined simply by the foods available in the local environment:

> Mankind always liked the food he was accustomed to, and his women cooked best the food which grew around their homes; their babies were reared on it, their stomachs learnt to cope with it. . . . Mankind enjoys a foray, and the young try out foreign fare, but the stubborn conviction that home-made is best is a natural instinct. (Hartley, 1954: 20)

And Renner puts the same argument in the opposite way:

> How is it that avoidance ends in abhorrence? Avoidance leads to the flavour or other properties of a dish becoming unknown, either partially or totally. How this operates can be guessed from the average attitude to foods that have failed to gain a place in common diet, though not because of any taboo, as, for example, medlars, quinces and topinamburs. In most countries people view such things more dubiously, and with complete aversion if the food is entirely unknown. (Renner, 1944: 78)

Such arguments are not entirely without force; for instance, human infants which after weaning are no longer given milk lose the ability to digest it, and so there is a simple physiological explanation for milk being nauseous to the Chinese, among others. Beyond that, a certain conservatism or suspicion of the unfamiliar no doubt does give a measure of inertia to food habits and culinary tastes, but essentially this sort of reasoning explains very little. To say that people like what they are used to simply pushes the problem further back: how did they have the chance to *become* used to it? Such arguments also fail to offer any explanation of why, if people like what they are used to, *changes* take place over time in what social groups like to eat; for in spite of the inertia in people's likes and dislikes, very considerable changes have taken place over the centuries, and indeed in recent decades there have been rapid changes. Social standards are not eternal: later standards obviously arise out of earlier standards.

If the argument that people like what they are accustomed to is a weak form of explanation, still weaker is any form of argument based on the inherent palatability or nutritional merits of the foods themselves. The nutritionist John Yudkin (Yudkin and McKenzie, 1964: 15–19) contends that on the whole there is a direct relationship between palatability and good nutritional value – that, for example, protein-rich animal foods are in general tastier that starch-rich vegetable foods – but he admits there are many exceptions. The difference in price between stewing steak and fillet, or between herring and salmon, is related to taste rather than nutritional value, while the often despised broiler chicken – though less tasty – is no less nutritious than the farmyard variety. Moreover, Yudkin admits that the activities of the modern food manufacturer now permit a very significant degree of dissociation between palatability and nutritional values. The high sugar content of many manufactured foods – the consumption of sugar in the industrialised world today is about twenty-five times as great per capita as it was in the mid-eighteenth century – is a striking example. The taste for sweetness has led to such perversions as manufactured baby foods containing so much sugar to attract mothers (who habitually sample them before feeding their infant) that they are harmful to the baby itself. Apart from sugar, manufactured foods now contain many other substances such as preservatives and the ubiquitous taste-enhancing monosodium glutamate which, if harmless in small amounts, are considered by many medical people to be dangerous in the total quantities which it is now possible to consume willy-nilly. The rapid acceptance and demand for manufactured foods in the countries of the Third World is an increasing social and economic problem. In the industrial world, one effect merely of large-scale food preservation is that people are increasingly able to choose to eat the same 'tasty' foods all the year round, where the rhythm of the seasons once forced them to eat some less palatable but nutritionally beneficial things.

In any case, even with all these qualifications, Yudkin's contention that there is a broad correlation between palatability and nutritional value is plausible only if the standards of palatability which prevail in the familiar world of Europe and North America are taken as a yardstick. In fact, not only are there very different ideas of palatability in other societies, but even our own taken-for-granted standards are culturally conditioned and by no means unchanging. A nineteenth-century writer made the point elegantly, linking in his discussion of 'acquired tastes' both the strange preferences of exotic societies and the refined palates of the knowledgeable eater in our own.

> Perhaps there is no such thing in persons who are grown up as a perfectly pure and natural taste. The taste may be sound and even fine, but it is always more or less influenced by custom and by association, until it breeds an Acquired taste which is not to be reasoned with and will not be denied. The Greenlander takes to tallow; the southern Frenchman glories in garlic; the East Indian is mighty in pepper. No force of reasoning can prove to them that other tastes are better; they have an Acquired taste which insists on being pampered. And precisely the same phenomenon occurs, though in a less marked way, when we get a dish which we know, which we expect, and which does not correspond to its name. A very pleasant Julienne soup can be made without sorrel; but those who look for the sorrel always feel that without it the Julienne is a failure. (Dallas, 1877: 12–13)

By no means is the 'acquired taste' the prerogative only of the fastidious gourmet. In the nineteenth century it was found that many of the British working class, after having their bread, their tea and their pickles adulterated with poisonous substances for decades, actually preferred them that way to the taste of the pure product (Burnett, 1966: 86). And today, after a generation in which instant coffee has displaced real coffee more thoroughly from British kitchens than in any other country in the world, it is not uncommon to meet people who much prefer its taste to the very different one of the genuine article.

The idea of 'acquired taste', however, goes no further than the idea that people like what they are accustomed to: a bare acknowledgement that culinary likes and dislikes are conditioned by social and cultural influences does not much advance our understanding of the subtle and complex ways in which these influences operate. As Mary Douglas has argued,

> Nutritionists know that the palate is trained, that taste and smell are subject to cultural control. Yet for lack of other hypotheses, the notion persists that what makes an item of food acceptable is some quality inherent in the thing itself. Present research into palatability tends to concentrate on individual reactions to individual items. It seeks to screen out cultural effects as so much interference. Whereas . . . the cultural controls on perception are precisely what needs to be analysed. (Douglas, 1978: 59)

That analysis is exactly what a number of social scientists tried to produce in the 1960s and 1970s.

THE STRUCTURALIST SOLUTION

The most influential writing on food habits by social scientists in recent decades has been by anthropologists like Claude Lévi-Strauss and Mary Douglas, by the semiologist Roland Barthes and the sociologist Pierre Bourdieu, all of them adherents of or – in the latter case – strongly influenced by the school of thought known as 'structuralism'. The great virtue of the structuralist approach is that it clearly recognises that 'taste' is culturally shaped and socially controlled. Its weakness is that it tends to be static, and has little to say about how tastes change and develop in society over time, which is the prime concern of the present book. But first let us look at its strong point, the attention it pays to the aesthetic – and thus pre-eminently social – patterning of food preferences.

Certainly it is essential to take account of the powerful aesthetic component of the whole business of the choice and preparation of food. Mary Douglas has argued that a clear distinction has to be made between the aesthetic and the nutritional components.

> My own preferred approach would be to take the aesthetic as distinct from the nutritional aspect of food to be that part which is subject to pattern-making rules, like the rules of poetry, music or dance. The explanation of any one such rule will only be found in its contribution to the pattern it helps to create. (Douglas, 1974: 84)

She goes on to explain that rules about the choice, the cooking or the serving of foods which people justify by reference to risks of poisoning, infection or indigestibility count as nutritional rather than as aesthetic. The distinction, she admits, is difficult to maintain, but most anthropologists concerned with food habits in recent decades have concentrated heavily on the aesthetic side.

Most influential of all anthropologists in the post-war era has been Claude Lévi-Strauss, whose writings on food – only a small part of his total work – have transfixed almost everyone working on that subject. This is not the place to discuss Lévi-Strauss's structural anthropology as a whole.[6] Suffice it to say that he was crucially influenced by the theories of structural lingistics, and in particular the idea that the recognisable 'phonemes' which constitute the units of meaning in every language are constructed by the binary opposition of contrasting phonetic sounds. In his very first venture into the field of cuisine, Lévi-Strauss (1958: 85) tackled the old question of the contrasts between English and French cooking, introducing the word 'gusteme' as an analogy in the field of taste to the phonemes of language.

> Like language, it seems to me, the cuisine of a society may be analysed into constituent elements, which in this case we might call 'gustemes', and which may be organised according to certain structures of opposition and correlation. We might then distinguish English cooking from French cooking by means of three oppositions: *endogenous/exogenous* (that is, national versus exotic ingredients); *central/peripheral* (staple food versus accompaniments); *marked/not marked* (that is, savoury or bland). We should then be able to construct a chart with + and – signs corresponding to the pertinent or nonpertinent character of each opposition in the system under consideration.

	English cuisine	French cuisine
endogenous/exogenous	+	–
central/peripheral	+	–
marked/not marked	–	+

That is to say, according to Lévi-Strauss, in an English meal the main dishes are made from ingredients native to Britain cooked in a relatively bland way, but are surrounded with more strongly flavoured accompaniments of exotic origin (he mentions tea, fruitcake, marmalade and port!). On the other hand, in French cuisine, the opposition between exotic and endogenous ingredients is not emphasised, and strong flavours are a feature of central dishes as well as of accompaniments.

A sceptic may well suspect that Lévi-Strauss is here simply giving expression in sophisticated vocabulary to the traditional Frenchman's image of the English eating boiled chicken and swilling it down with fruitcake and port wine. It certainly is not clear that he was comparing like with like: it is too easy to compare French *haute cuisine* (long eaten also by the English upper classes) with English lower middle-class home cooking. And the extensive use of exotic ingredients in 'central' dishes is an integral feature of all *hautes cuisines*.

But, setting aside such empirical quibbles for the moment, what is Lévi-Strauss trying to demonstrate? He maintains that such structures may not be confined simply to the sphere of cuisine, but may be found in transformed fashion in other spheres such as mythology, art, codes of etiquette, or political ideology. If so, 'we have a right to conclude that we have reached a significant knowledge of the unconscious attitudes of the society or societies under consideration' (Lévi-Strauss, 1958: 86).

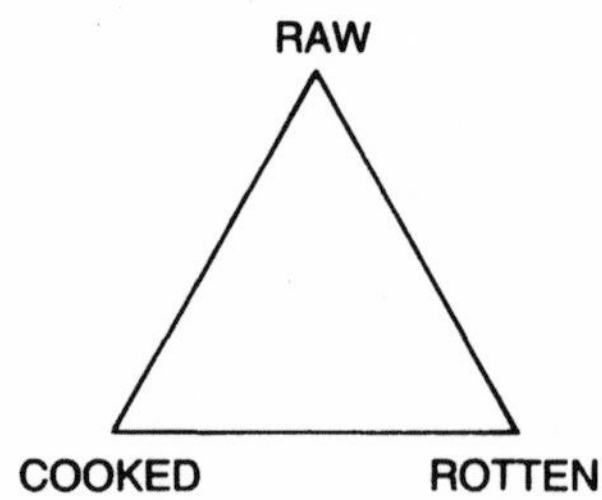

Figure 1 *The basic 'Culinary Triangle'*

The next stage in the development of Lévi-Strauss's thinking about food in fact came about in the course of his gigantic study of Amerindian mythology. In *The Raw and the Cooked* (1964), his attention shifted from 'gustemes' or tastes to the basic operations of cookery. He showed how the distinction between raw food and cooked food is linked in human thought with the fundamental distinction between *nature* and *culture*, between that which is found in a natural state and that which is transformed or elaborated by human effort. This led him to his celebrated 'culinary triangle' (Figure 1): the cooked is a cultural transformation of the raw, while the rotten (*pourri*) is a natural transformation of either the raw or the cooked (Levi-Strauss, 1965). From here, Lévi-Strauss moved to a more complicated 'triangle of recipes' (Figure 2). Already, tying in the techniques of cookery to the nature/culture distinction requires some mental gymnastics. With regard to the means employed, grilling, roasting and smoking are identified with nature, because they each require minimal equipment and bring the food quite directly in contact with the fire (grilling more than roasting, and roasting more than smoking), in contrast with boiling, which requires a man-made container and is therefore identified with culture. On the other hand, with regard to results, roasting and boiling are on the side of nature, smoking on that of culture. Why? For rather disparate reasons. Smoking transforms food into a man-made, preservable substance. Roasting brings about the least change in the food. As for boiling, it is identified with the rotten simply because certain tribes assert this relationship, but as far as European thinking is concerned the connection seems to rest entirely on the French term for a type of stew – *pot-pourri*. Finally, if techniques like frying are to be brought within the schema, it has to be transformed from a culinary triangle into a culinary tripod, by the addition of a third leg representing oil as a cooking medium in addition to air and water.

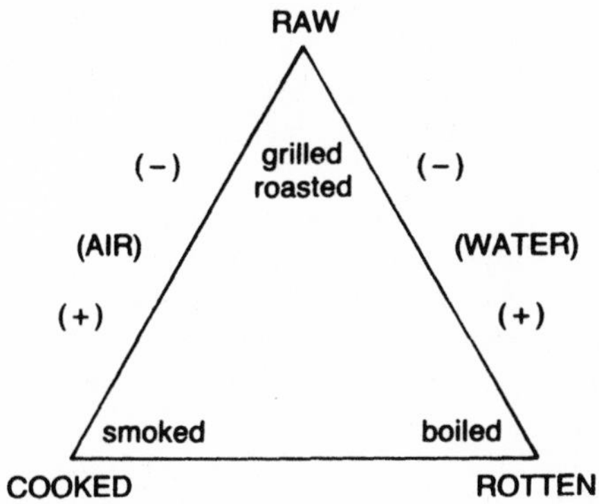

Figure 2 *The 'triangle of recipes'*

The general reader may well consider the culinary triangle a farrago of nonsense, though that has not prevented many anthropologists and sociologists taking it seriously. Lévi-Strauss is, of course, trying to discover structures underlying thinking about food as one symptom of human thinking in general. But when he attempts to explain preferences for particular kinds of food, especially in the more familiar context of European societies, his culinary triangle does not seem to help him very much, and he resorts to far more commonsensical arguments. For example, he reasons that

> boiling provides a method of preserving all the meat and its juices, whereas roasting involves destruction or loss. One suggests economy, the other waste; the second is aristocratic, the first plebeian. This aspect of the matter is obvious in societies which stress status differences between individuals or classes. (1968: 484)

He uses this argument to explain why the eighteenth-century compilers of the *Encyclopédie*, inspired by the democratic spirit, praised boiled food as 'one of the most succulent and nourishing foods available to man'; and why conversely the gastronome Brillat-Savarin (1826: 72–3) poured disdain on boiled meat. There may be a good deal of truth in this argument – certainly boiling was the main peasant way of cooking, and classes higher up the social ladder could be expected to distance themselves from it. But one hardly needs a structuralist sledgehammer to crack that empirical nut, and the argument is too crude to be of much use in explaining, say, the detailed differences between French and English food. In any case, there are deviant cases to the general social prestige of roast food; apparently the Czechs hold boiled meat in high esteem, unlike their close cousins the Slovaks and the Poles. Lévi-Strauss can only speculate that 'The reason why the Czechs look upon boiled meat as a man's food may be that their traditional society was more democratic in character than that of their Slovak or Polish neighbours' (1968: 485). That is an exercise in pure conjectural (and implausible) history. It is also worth noting that Lévi-Strauss, in his argument about the conservation of nutrients in boiling and the wastefulness of roasting, as well as about the social connotations of the two processes, blurs the distinction between the nutritional and the aesthetic which Mary Douglas believes is essential to maintain.

Mary Douglas's own work differs in a number of ways from that of Lévi-Strauss. Unlike him, she does not expect to find any universal message, valid for all mankind, encoded in the language of food, nor does she place the same reliance on the discovery of binary oppositions (Douglas, 1972: 62). Yet at the same time, since research into small remote societies 'suggests that each individual, by cultural training, enters a sensory world that is presegmented and prejudged for him', she shares Lévi-Strauss's general hope that research into the cultural aspects of food habits will eventually enable us at least 'to discover the principles and ranking of tastes and smells' (1978: 59) – but the actual segmentation and ranking will differ from one society or social group to another. Douglas has focused most attention on the task of 'deciphering a meal', or rather whole sequences of meals. It is not merely the binary oppositions within a single meal, such as those between meat and accompaniments and between main course, sweet and savoury which Lévi-Strauss pointed to in his early remarks on French and English food. It is also a matter of understanding the number of courses and composition of one meal in relation to numerous others. For, as Douglas remarks in the course of analysing the food system of her own household,

> Between breakfast and the last nightcap, the food of the day comes in an ordered pattern. Between Monday and Sunday, the food of the week is patterned again. Then there is the sequence of holidays and fast days throughout the year, to say nothing of life cycle feasts, birthdays and weddings. (1972: 62)

There is a very clear idea of what should constitute Christmas dinner; Sunday dinner provides a lesser peak during each week; and meals are ordered in scale of importance in relation to each other, by the addition or the omission of an item, through the week and the day down to the meanest pause for a snack. Fieldwork among a small number of London working-class families by one of Douglas's graduate students revealed tea and biscuits as the lowest unit in the food system (Douglas and Nicod, 1974). For the chain which links meals together gives each its meaning. Food categories encode social events, as Douglas puts it – they express hierarchy, inclusion and exclusion, boundaries and transactions across boundaries. Thus, in the Douglas household – no doubt a fairly typical British upper-middle class one – drinks were shared with strangers, acquaintances and workmen, but meals were shared only with family, close friends and honoured guests; so the meal structure serves to maintain external boundaries, and significant social thresholds are crossed when a guest is invited to share a meal. But the food system also discriminates occasions simply within the family: Douglas ascribes to its unconscious power her family's discontent at the proposal that supper be cut down for once to a single substantial dish of soup. More courses were necessary, because otherwise it wouldn't be supper.

Roland Barthes too, in his essay 'Toward a Psychosociology of Contemporary Food Consumption', proposed a search for the code or 'grammar' underlying the foods people eat:

> If food is a system, what might be its constituent units? In order to find out, it would obviously be necessary to start out with a complete inventory of all we know of the food in a given society (products, techniques, habits), and then subject these facts to what the linguists call transformational analysis, that is, to observe whether the passage from one fact to another produces a difference in signification. (1961: 168)

He gave as examples from contemporary France a changeover from ordinary bread to milk loaf, the former signifying day-to-day life, the latter a party; and the changeover from white bread to brown bread, which corresponded to a change in what was signified because, paradoxically, brown bread had become a sign of refinement. From America, Barthes takes the example of the contrast between *bitter* and *sweet* flavours (in chocolate for instance) which tends to be associated with a contrast between upper and lower classes, and also points to the interesting opposition Americans often draw between *sweet* and *crisp* foods – not logical, yet often significant. Barthes seemed to be suggesting that if an exhaustive list of all such contrasts could be drawn up, it would be possible to compare the food grammars of different countries just as the structures of their languages can be compared. But he promised more than he delivered.

Barthes was writing specifically about the *contemporary* food system and, characteristically as a structuralist, expected to be able to derive his 'grammar' without reference to history. The past was simply a place where potent meanings could be quarried, for example by advertisers. Commemoration of the French past was in fact one of the three principal groups of themes Barthes observed in food advertising in France; it appealed either to an aristocratic tradition (dynasties of manufacturers, Napoleon brandy, *moutarde du Roy*), or to a highly idealised survival of an old rural society.

In this manner, food brings the memory of the soil into our very contemporary life. . . . By way of a thousand detours, food permits [the Frenchman] to enter daily into his own past and to believe in a certain culinary 'being' of France. (1961: 170–1)

In spite of that, for Barthes it was not necessary to study the past in any systematic way in order to understand a society's grammar of food. In practice, however, like Lévi-Strauss he tended to draw constantly on 'commonsense', taken-for-granted historical knowledge, not always of a very accurate sort.

Finally, a slightly different sort of structuralist: Pierre Bourdieu. Slightly different, because the sort of structuralism which influenced Bourdieu is the Marxist variant.[7] Although most forms of Marxism are greatly concerned with patterns of social development in history – with *diachronic* theories – structuralist Marxism emphasises how the forces of capitalism are capable of blocking change. In consequence, Bourdieu's work has the same *synchronic* or static quality as Lévi-Strauss's or Barthes's.

Bourdieu's book *La Distinction* (1979), sub-titled 'Social Critique of Judgment', deals not just with food but with several other aspects of behaviour (clothes, furniture, music) which are often attributed to individual taste and yet at the same time recognised as being linked to social stratification. (People make individual choices, apparently according to their own preferences, but that does not prevent lower-class individuals being said to have 'vulgar' tastes and upper-class ones 'refined' tastes.) According to Bourdieu, each individual is assigned from the beginning to a class position, defined by the amount of economic and symbolic capital of which it disposes. Only to a very limited extent can this inheritance be modified by strategies of social mobility. Now, just as Lévi-Strauss and Barthes looked for a fixed code or grammar underlying the food preferences of different societies, so Bourdieu looks for formulae underlying the cultural preferences of each class or sub-class:

the spheres of food, clothing, and cosmetic preferences are organised according to the same fundamental structure, that of the social sphere determined by the quantity and structure of capital. In order to construct completely the spheres of styles of life within which cultural consumption is defined, it is necessary to establish for each class and sub-class, that is to say for each of the configurations of capital, the *generative formulae* of the habitus[8] which retranslates into a particular *style of life* the characteristic necessities and facilities of that (relatively) homogeneous class of conditions of existence. (1979: 230)

Bourdieu uses extensive social survey data to document these different styles of life among the classes and sub-classes of contemporary France. This snapshot of things as they are now, however, scarcely justifies Bourdieu's contention that none but the most superficial change is possible. Individuals, he contends, may be ready to adopt in the most visible part of their way of life the ways of doing things in the social stratum into which they have moved, but this conformity is only on the surface: clothes, furniture and food are aspects of social life subject to 'precocious apprenticeship' – they are not remoulded through education, and remain closely dependent on the person's class of origin (1979: 85). It is, as one commentator on Bourdieu observed, as if:

> Everything happens as though society, with no history other than the temporal unfolding of individual lives, were immobile, locked with the shackles of stratification into classes and sub-classes neatly cut up and arranged in a strict hierarchy. (Giard, 1980: 193)

THE LIMITS OF STRUCTURALISM

The search for a fixed 'code' or 'deep structure' underlying people's surface behaviour would be justified if the code thus discovered enabled us to predict a hitherto unknown surface structure – such as the behaviour of a society or social group not previously studied. 'But,' as Jack Goody observes in *Cooking, Cuisine and Class*,

> in practice there is no adequate way in which this programme could be carried out. Therefore, because the deep structure is derived from surface elements alone and is unknowable without them, it is meaningless to discuss one as expressing the other, except in a circular, Pickwickian sense. (1982: 31)

Or, as E. B. Ross puts much the same point, 'Structural and symbolic anthropologists seem largely to accept such proscriptions and avoidances [of particular animals as food] as given and justify them within an ideological domain' (1978: 1). What Goody and Ross are saying in a rather restrained way is that structuralist and cultural 'explanations' of food preferences really add little to the old argument that 'people like what they are used to' – they offer mainly a classificatory scheme, not an explanation.

The fundamental reason why structuralism is so little able to explain the origins of or changes within patterns of food preference is that the basic impulse behind the whole approach is one of what Norbert Elias (1970b: 111ff.) calls 'process-reduction'.[9] By this he means the tendency in Western thought to look behind flow and process for something which is static and constant. In the social sciences particularly, there is a widespread inclination to look for static structures underlying the flux and change of the social relations we actually observe, resulting in 'the changeless aspects of all phenomena being interpreted as most real and significant' (Elias, 1970b:

112). The structuralist preoccupation with codes and deep structures is a striking example of this: not only are the codes apparently depicted as static and unchanging but so, as often as not, are the patterns of social relations which they are supposed to 'express'.

Yet food preferences, like other cultural patterns, do change in the course of time. No one denies that. Even in the tribal societies chiefly studied by anthropologists, changes in what people like to eat have been very noticeable in recent decades. In African tribes among whom until recently all social ranks ate much the same local food, Western food is now beginning to make an impact, being eaten particularly in West Africa by an emerging literate élite (Goody, 1982); and among the Massa and Mussey of Central Africa described by Garine (1980) social differences associated with the consumption of imported foods are also emerging. But in these cases, the source of change appears to be outside the society. It may not be entirely true, but the society and its cultural patterns can be depicted as having been stable and static until there impinged some adventitious cause of change from outside. Yet in societies such as those of Europe about whose past we know far more, it is clear that 'social structures' and 'cultural patterns' have changed continuously over many centuries, not necessarily because of impinging influences from outside, but because of internal dynamics of their own. How are such processes to be explained?

The problem is seen with particular clarity in Mary Douglas's book *Purity and Danger*, where she deals not specifically with food preferences and avoidances, but with the related and more general question of dirt-avoidance, matters of hygiene and notions of pollution, which she sees as another general means of imposing pattern on an inherently untidy experience. She argues that

> Our idea of dirt is compounded of two things, care for hygiene and respect for conventions. The rules of hygiene change, of course, with changes in our state of knowledge. As for the conventional side of dirt-avoidance, these rules can be set aside for the sake of friendship. (1966: 7)[10]

Overlooking dirt for the sake of friendship is illustrated by Gabriel Oak, in Hardy's *Far from the Madding Crowd*, refusing a clean cup for his cider when drinking with fellow farm workers. But the interesting thing about Douglas's statement is the implication that changes in conceptions of dirt and pollution stem entirely from the growth of knowledge – in this case, biological knowledge. Again, the source of change is seen as originating 'outside', not geographically outside this time, but intellectually outside the social conventions in question. There appears to be no recognition that *conventional* rules, whether of dirt-avoidance or of food preference, may themselves change in a systematic and structured way. And, as a matter of fact, there is reason to doubt even Douglas's confidence that the growth of scientific knowledge has been primarily responsible for changing habits in the field of hygiene. For Elias, in *The Civilising Process* (1939), his study of the development in

Europe since the Middle Ages of such matters of social convention as table manners, blowing one's nose, spitting and behaviour in relation to urination and defecation, is able to show that changes in the direction of more 'civilised' behaviour characteristically came *first*; only later were reasons of hygiene advanced *ex post facto* as justifications for the new standards. "'Rational understanding" is not', he declares, 'the motor of the "civilising" of eating or of other behaviour' (1939: I, 116; see also Goudsblom, 1979). Elias himself advances a quite different explanation, in which changes in patterns of social convention and cultural tastes are understood in relation to broader processes of social development. Has his theory any implications for understanding the problem of people's tastes in food?

A DEVELOPMENTAL APPROACH

If the dominant structuralist approach to food preferences and avoidances does not have much to offer in understanding their origins, formation and processes of change over time, is there an alternative? If structuralism is too static, that points to the need for a developmental approach.

Certainly people's cultural tastes and 'needs' are the product of their social experience, the result of what they encounter in their tribe, their community or social class within a larger society.[11] But the social forces which shape the taste of one generation are themselves the product of long-term processes of social development running back many generations. The experience of one generation cannot be understood without looking back to that of its predecessors. To explain changing tastes, we have to look at the matter historically. That is obvious. But history is not enough, if by history we mean a chronological catalogue of ill-assorted 'factors' and episodes which from time to time have had some effect on this aspect or that aspect of what people liked and disliked to eat. To go beyond that, it is necessary to look carefully at the jumbled historical record to see if it is possible to discern not constants beneath the flux, but an order of a different kind, a sequential order constituting *structured processes of change*.

This book therefore attempts to apply to the history of cooking and eating in England and France Elias's 'figurational' or 'sociogenetic' approach. Figurational sociology is inherently concerned with processes of development. The word 'figuration' is used to denote the patterns in which people are bound together in groups, strata, societies – patterns of interdependence which encompass every form of co-operation and conflict and which are very rarely static and unchanging. Within a developing social figuration, modes of individual behaviour, cultural tastes, intellectual ideas, social stratification, political power and economic organisation are all entangled with each other in complex ways which themselves change over time in ways that need to be investigated. The aim is to provide a 'sociogenetic' explanation of how figurations change from one type to another, why some have greater potential for change than others, the consequences for people's lives and the way they perceive them.

Elias finds a major driving force of social and cultural development in conflict and competition – perhaps 'contest' is the best general word – between social groups, whether territorial units, social strata, or smaller groupings of people. The patterns of conflict and forms of competition change and develop over time and find expression in countless ways. The dominant anthropological school of thought has neglected precisely these forces in the development of food habits, exaggerating the homogeneity and uniformity of the groups they study. As Goody remarks, 'By concentrating upon the behavioural unity of specific groups, tribes or nations at a cultural level, one might neglect those important aspects of that culture which are linked with social or individual differences' (1982: 28).

One phrase which will recur repeatedly in the book is 'balance of power'. Balances of power are not to be observed only between states. Wherever people are bound together through interdependence with each other, they have power over each other – sometimes very unequal and one-sided, sometimes rather evenly balanced, usually fluctuating to some extent, and often changing in a definite direction over time. The very fact that people are interdependent with each other means that they exert forces over each other, forces which shape not just their overt behaviour but their tastes and the way they think about themselves and their activities.

That is all rather abstract. The approach must be judged not in the abstract, but in its usefulness in the chapters that follow. Like the structuralists, we shall be concerned particularly with the aesthetic, pattern-making aspect of food, cooking and culinary tastes, which is relatively autonomous from strictly nutritional considerations. But unlike them, we shall approach the subject from an historical and developmental viewpoint. Focusing particularly on England and France, we seek to show how changing structures of social interdependence and changing balances of power within society have been reflected in one particular cultural domain, that of food. It will, however, become apparent that the 'nutritional' and 'aesthetic' aspects of the development of food habits are only *relatively* autonomous from each other and cannot be studied entirely separately. One side of the story is the distribution of nourishment within society and how it has changed over time. But that is linked with an examination of the social mechanisms which have generated styles of cookery, developing and succeeding each other much as do schools and styles in the other arts.

This book therefore draws on the work of many historians, without undertaking the same task as they have done. It uses the evidence of old recipe books – where there is still huge scope for scholarly research – without pretending to be another history of cookery books. Still less would it be possible without drawing on the work of social historians and nutritionists with an historical bent: Drummond and Wilbraham's *The Englishman's Food* (1939); John Burnett's *Plenty and Want* (1966); Yudkin and McKenzie's *Changing Food Habits* (1964); Barker, McKenzie and Yudkin's *Our Changing Fare* (1966); Oddy and Miller's *The Making of the Modern British Diet* (1976); and in France the marvellous profusion of research which sprang forth in response to Fernand Braudel's call in *Annales* in 1961 for a history of food. Much of this notable research has been concerned chiefly with the history of nutrition, of food supplies, and their relation to social welfare. In this book I have not sought to present new research on the 'material' history of diet, but to link these material concerns with the aesthetics of eating.

Tastes in food, like tastes in music, literature or the visual arts, are socially shaped, and the major forces which have shaped them are religions, classes and nations. In European history, religion has been a relatively weak influence on food, class overwhelmingly the strongest. People have always used food in their attempts to climb the social ladder themselves, and to push other people down the ladder. Today it is possible to speak of élite or highbrow food, popular or mass cooking, folk cookery, even junk food. Inevitably these notions provoke controversies parallel to those between protagonists of high culture, popular culture and folk traditions.

Nations have also been a powerful influence on taste in food. Because this is a comparative study of England and France, I have possibly at times slightly overstated national at the expense of class differences – though I also show how class and nationality become entangled. Precisely because the cuisines of England and France are popularly supposed to offer striking contrasts, I shall attempt in this book to relate some of the contrasts between the two countries to differences in their social development over the past few centuries. Here a certain caution is required, for it is all too easy to compare like and unlike, the best of French professional *haute cuisine* with the most mediocre of everyday English domestic cookery. All the same, it is perhaps worth saying a little at the outset about the technical difference between what is today thought of as 'typical' French cookery and English cookery. Phillip Harben, the celebrated British 'TV chef' of the 1950s and 1960s, summed it up in this way:

> On the continent of Europe they compose dishes (and very well they do it, too). In Britain we produce, prepare and serve food. That is a very different thing. Continental cooks regard the ingredients as means to an end. They want them to be good, of course, otherwise the end cannot be. No painter uses dud paints. But a means to an end, a medium of expression is what they are. It is not so with British food. With us the foodstuff is almost an end in itself. We ask the cook to add nothing to it – all we ask is that not too much shall be taken away. (*Wine and Food*, No. 91, Autumn 1956)

The great French chef Escoffier made the same point in a still more technical way when he explained in his *Guide to Modern Cookery* that

> Except for roasts, grills and fryings, which will be described later, all culinary operations dealing with meat are related to one of the four following methods: braising, poëling, poaching and sautés.

These four methods of cooking belong, however, to the sauces, and this explains how it is that the latter hold such a pre-eminent position in French cookery. (1903: 97)

Braising, he explained, was slow cooking in a closed pot; poëling was roasting but used butter rather than merely the meat fat for basting; sautés similarly meant frying in butter or oil, not meat fat, and poaching was a boiling that did not quite boil. Each was designed to yield the basis of a fine sauce, essential to the composition of the dish, unlike the roasts, grills and fryings which predominate in English cookery.

In practice, the differences which have developed between English and French cookery and culinary tastes are more subtle and difficult to pin down than these eminent writers imply. Moreover, French and English cookery are *not* entirely separate things. They have been in mutual contact and influenced each other over a very long period. Since they are not wholly independent, the differences and similarities between them can only be understood in developmental perspective.

It will be seen that a number of themes are intertwined in this book, in a complexity reflecting that of the subject matter. First, in chapter 2, the problem of appetite is raised: what part do social controls play in regulating appetite, and can the appetite of Europeans be said to have become 'more civilised' (in Elias's sense of 'civilisation') since the Middle Ages? Spanning the whole period from medieval times to the present day, that chapter serves as a background to the more chronologically organised Chapters 3–9. These deal with the development of cookery and conceptions of 'good food' in England and France, and its relation to patterns of stratification and social competition. Chapter 3, on the Middle Ages, describes a period when differences in culinary culture between the strata of European society were far more developed than national differences. Chapters 4 and 5 deal with the period between the Renaissance and the French Revolution when different national traditions became more noticeable, though differences within society also persisted strongly. Chapter 6 traces in some detail the development of professional cookery in the nineteenth and twentieth centuries, arguing that with the rise of the restaurant, stylistic developments to a considerable extent originated through competition within the profession and in its response to changing social circumstances. The main phases of professional cookery, from the age of Carême through that of Escoffier to contemporary *nouvelle cuisine* are sketched, largely from cookery books. Chapter 7 is based on an investigation of the trade press in England and France, which has been much less studied than the cookery books; it shows some pronounced differences in the outlook of the cooking professions in England and France. Chapter 8 focuses on domestic cookery, and, besides examining England's increased culinary 'cultural dependency' on France and its complicated consequences for middle- and upper-class eating, reminds the reader that it was only in the course of the nineteenth century that a clear trend emerged towards greater uniformity in food, relatively speaking, from the top to the bottom of the social scale. Chapter 9 draws particularly on evidence from women's magazine cookery columns in the two countries (which, like the trade press, have previously been little studied), to show the continuation of that trend in the period since the end of the nineteenth century when professional and domestic cooking have become far more closely interdependent. Having thus returned once more to the present day, we take different tacks in chapters 10 and 11, which deal respectively with the role of gastronomic writings in formulating conceptions of good food, and with the patterning of the sense of repugnance – the conception of *bad* taste being inextricably bound up with that of *good* taste. Finally, chapter 12 comments on some contemporary trends, and draws some conclusions from the book as a whole.

2

The Civilising of Appetite

'A full gut supports moral precepts' (Burmese proverb)
'A hungry stomach has no ears' (La Fontaine, *Fables*)
'All's good in a famine' (Thomas Fuller, *Gnomologia*, 1732)
'There is no banquet but someone dislikes something in it' (*Ibid.*)
'There's no sauce in the world like hunger' (Cervantes, *Don Quixote*)

Hunger, appetite, taste: rough-hewn insights into the tangled connections between the three are to be found, as insights so often are, in proverbs and literature. When people are sure of enough to eat, 'taste' is important. Taste, in food as in other domains of culture, implies discrimination, standards of good and bad, the acceptance of some things and the rejection of others. Good cooking revives the jaded appetite. When food is short, people are less selective. Hunger is one of the most powerful of all drives. How have people coped with it, and how has the patterning of appetite changed in response to changing supply and social distribution of nourishment? This chapter is concerned less with changes in qualitative tastes in food – later chapters deal with those – than with the more difficult question of changes over time in the regulation of appetite in the quantitative sense. In particular, it explores the question of whether the same long-term changes in the structure of societies which Norbert Elias argues in *The Civilising Process* (1939) brought about changes in manners, in the expression of the emotions, and in personality structure were also reflected in the patterning and expression of so basic a drive as appetite.

HUNGER AND APPETITE

Appetite, it must be remembered, is not the same thing as hunger. Nor is it the same thing as eating. Hunger is a body drive which recurs in all human beings in a reasonably regular cycle. Appetite for food, on the other hand, in the words of Daniel Cappon, a psychotherapist specialising in eating disorders, is:

basically a state of mind, an inner mental awareness of desire that is the setting for hunger. . . . An individual's appetite is his desire and inclination to eat, his interest in consuming food. Eating is what a person *does*. Appetite is what he *feels* like doing, mostly a psychological state. (1973: 21)

We tend to think of hunger, appetite and eating as directly linked in a simple chain of causality. That, as Herbert Blumer has pointed out, is a marked misrepresentation of what takes place. It omits the internal processes through which a person constructs his act:

First, a person has to note his own hunger. If he didn't point it out to himself, he would be merely uncomfortable and restless and would not organise himself to search for food. Then he has to define his hunger in terms of whether it is something he should take care of. A glance at his watch may indicate that it is a half-hour before eating time and so he may decide to do nothing about it for that half hour. Or, he may remind himself that he is on a diet and say to himself, 'too bad, you will just have to skip a meal', and thus not act at all on the basis of hunger. Or he may decide he will eat. If so, he has to engage further in constructing his act. Through the use of images he points out to himself various possibilities of action – the selection of different kinds of food, different sources of food, and different ways of getting the food. In parading different objects before his mind's eye, he may fashion an intention of having a very delectable meal. Then he may recall or point out to himself the depleted state of cash in his pocket and, accordingly, map out another line of action. He may take into consideration the weather, the inconvenience of going out of doors, the food in the refrigerator, or the reading he wants to do. (1955: 95)

Blumer is right to point out how much may supervene between hunger and eating, but he makes it sound very coolly cerebral: his actor is very self-controlled. One would hardly guess how compelling a force appetite can be.

The link between hunger and appetite is provided by what is sometimes referred to as the 'appestat', by which is meant a *psychological*, not simply physiological, control mechanism regulating food intake. Just as a thermostat can be set too high or too low, so a person's 'appestat' can be set too high or too low in relation to the physiological optimum range. Too high a setting, too much food intake, is a condition of *bulimia* and excessive body weight; too low a setting represents the condition of *anorexia* and underweight.

A person's 'appestat' setting is determined not only by the underlying hunger drive, but also by often rather complex psychological processes in which social pressures can play a considerable part. Body image is a particularly notable element: how a person perceives his or her own body and its relation to what he or she perceives to be the socially approved body size and shape. Today psychologists understand more about the psychological problems which can lead individual people to have pathological 'eating disorders' and body weights deviating from what is healthy.

But what about the regulation of appetite in the 'normal' majority? Can that be studied in a long-term developmental perspective according to the model provided by Elias in *The Civilising Process*? Cappon provides a clue that perhaps it can, when he argues that his patients with eating disorders are in some sense 'immature' personalities, and that the normal mature individual today 'is able to change his eating habits at will – when he eats, how long he lingers over a meal, what he eats, and the amount' (1973: 45). In other words, Cappon is arguing that normal eating behaviour involves a capacity for considerable self-control. Has this capacity developed over the long term in European society in the same way that Elias argues other facets of self-control have done?

THE APPETITE OF GARGANTUA

The celebrated banquets of the Middle Ages and Renaissance, known to us from literary sources like Rabelais and from numerous documents throughout Europe, give a misleading image of typical eating in that period. Not only did they involve just a small minority of society – even if we allow that servants and retainers received their share – but from the spectacular bills of fare it is difficult to work out how much each individual actually ate. For example, the menu for a feast given by the City of Paris for Cathérine de'Medici in 1549 (Franklin, 1887–1902: VI, 93) lists 24 sorts of animals (mainly birds and other game, because butcher's meat was then disdained for such grand occasions), many kinds of cakes and pastry, and a mere four vegetable dishes – but we do not know how many shared the food. At the feast for the enthronement of Archbishop Nevill at York in 1465, 1000 sheep, 2000 pigs, 2000 geese, 4000 rabbits, fish and game by the hundred, numerous kinds of bird, and 12 porpoises and seals were eaten (Warner, 1791: 93ff.); but though we know the order of courses and even the seating plan for the most important guests, it is uncertain how many others took part, or indeed how long the feast lasted – it may have been several days. There is little doubt that guests *could* if they wished eat as much as they could take. The number of dishes set before the diners on such great occasions was very large – for example, *Sir Gawain and the Green Knight* (*c.* 1400: 25) mentions 12 dishes between each pair of diners – but they did not necessarily finish them, for it is known that surplus from the high table generally found its way to lower tables and eventually to the poor. Whatever the uncertainties, however, there seems little doubt that prodigious feats of appetite were witnessed on these occasions.

Yet the well-chronicled feasts are symptomatic of the period only in that there was often little to chronicle below this level, and the great mass of the people were lucky to be eating much at all; those who had the power to do so sometimes indulged in such banquets in times of widespread dearth.[1] But the great feasts were also untypical in a more important sense: they were high points of an oscillating dietary regime even for the courtiers and nobility. Even they did not eat like that all the time. Perhaps, unlike most people, they rarely went hungry, but they did not always enjoy the wide choice which (rather than the sophistication of the cooking) was the hallmark of the feast. The rhythm of the seasons and the hazards of the harvest impinged even on their diet; even they knew periods of frugality.[2] Breakfasts even in a royal household 'would not now be regarded as extravagant in a day labourer's family', and on ordinary days dinners consisted of no more than two joints of meat, roast or boiled, or fish (Mead, 1931: 114–15). Robert Mandrou recognised the significance of these fluctuations in the pattern of eating:

> without any doubt it was normal for all social classes to alternate between frugality and feasting. A consequence of the general insecurity where food was concerned, this oscillation imposed itself as a rite, some signs of which can still be found today. The festivals of the fraternities in the towns and those of the harvest, vintage or St Martin's Day in the country were always occasions for fine living for a few hours at least – and with innumerable variations in the form it took, of course. But these huge feasts, after which a man had to live on bread and water for months on end provided compensation, however meagre, for ill-fortune, and were appreciated for that reason; the very precariousness of existence explained them. The virtue of thrift, of making one's resources spread evenly over a given period, cannot be conceived of without a certain margin of supply. One other factor to be taken into account in explaining these 'orgies' is the ever-present dangers threatening the granary; what was the good of laying up large stocks if brigands or soldiers might come along the next day and carry them off? (Mandrou, 1961: 24)[3]

This oscillation between fasting and feasting runs parallel to the extreme emotional volatility of medieval people noted by Elias, their ability to express emotion with greater freedom than today, and to fluctuate quickly between extremes. And their sources are the same.

Mandrou, like Elias, Bloch and Huizinga before him,[4] notes this general psychological volatility but, curiously, relates it only indirectly to the insecurity of life in medieval and early modern Europe; he attributes it in large part to the physiological effects of inadequate and irregular feeding: 'The effect of this chronic malnutrition was to produce in man the mentality of the hunted, with its superstitions, its sudden outbursts of anger and its hypersensitivity' (Mandrou, 1961: 26). Such direct physiological effects of nutrition on psychology should perhaps not be entirely discounted, but they should equally not be overstressed; the suggestion merely adds one more complication to an already complex causal nexus. More important – as Mandrou himself seemed to see clearly when specifically discussing the fluctuation between feasting and fasting – is the link between the general precariousness and unpredictability of existence and its reflection in personality, beliefs and social behaviour. Keith Thomas (1971) has emphasised the connection between the hazards of life in the sixteenth and seventeenth centuries and the prevalence of superstition and magical beliefs, which declined noticeably with the growing security of the late seventeenth and eighteenth centuries. But it is Norbert Elias who has traced most fully the general connection between the changing emotional economy of the personality and the gradually growing calculability of social existence brought about by long-term processes of change in the structure of societies, and it is his theory we shall apply to appetite, gluttony and dieting.

The Civilising Process presents a theory of state-formation and of the internal pacification of larger and larger territories which the growth of states involved. But Elias has also made it clear that state-formation is only one of several intertwining and interdependent long-term processes of social development which gradually increased the security and calculability of life in society. Internal pacification permitted the division of labour and growth of trade – eventually increasing the security of food supplies among many other things – which in turn provided the economic basis for further expansion of the territory and the internal regulative power of states. *The Civilising Process* is also a study of the changing codes of manners and standards of social behaviour which broadly accompanied these processes. Elias gives a characteristically vivid illustration of the connection between these two aspects of his study. Travelling by road, he observes (1939: II, 233–4) was dangerous in medieval times, and it remains so today – but the nature of the danger has changed. The medieval traveller had to have the ability – temperamental as well as physical – to defend himself violently against violent attack. Today, the chief danger is from road accidents, and avoiding them depends to a great extent on high capacity for self-control in the expression of aggression, whether in overt or in disguised form. And aggression is only one of the manifestations of affect over which people came gradually to be subject to increased pressures to exercise greater self-control. Not that the expression of feeling by people in the Middle Ages lacked all social patterning and control. There is no zero-point. But in the long term the controls grew not just stronger but also more even and all-round. That is to say, they not only came to exert control more evenly over particular individual personalities, but also came to bear more nearly universally on *all* individuals in society.

Against this background, the oscillation between extremes of gluttonous gorging and enforced fasting seems all of a piece with other aspects of the medieval and early modern personality. As such it need not be seen as connected only with the insecurity and unpredictability of food supplies, but also with the more general insecurity of life.

FAMINES AND OTHER HAZARDS

Life in medieval and early modern Europe certainly was by today's standards very insecure. As late as the third quarter of the seventeenth century in England, the life expectancy of males at birth even among the nobility was only 29.6 years (Thomas, 1971: 5). Epidemic diseases including smallpox and plague periodically cut swathes through all ranks of society; the undernourished were particularly vulnerable, but poor sanitation and hygiene – reflecting deficiencies in medical knowledge and technology – also played their part. Other hazards included frequent disastrous fires, again made worse in their consequences by organisation inadequate to control them (Thomas, 1971: 15). But nothing was more bound up with the overall insecurity of life than the precariousness of food supplies. And nothing contributed more fundamentally to that than harvest failure.

The historical record of harvest failure and famine is incomplete, and the evidence not always easy to assess. However, it is clear that throughout the medieval and early modern period subsistence crises were very frequent. Even the shrinking back of the margin of cultivation onto more productive land after the Black Death did not long prevent them. During this period, the age of deserted villages and abundant pasture, production of meat rose very considerably throughout Western Europe, and in the late fourteenth and fifteenth centuries meat appears to have formed a larger part of the diet of even the humbler strata than it had done previously or was to do in the sixteenth century once more (Abel, 1935; 1937). As population rose again, the increased degree of pastoralism built into the mode of production made food even shorter when harvests failed, as they continued to do. It has been estimated that between 1375 and 1791, Florence experienced 111 poor harvests, one in four, and only 16 really good harvests (E. Weber, 1973: 194). In England, in the period 1500–1660, about one harvest in six appears to have been a serious failure (Hoskins, 1964; 1968). Conditions in France appear generally to have been worse than in England. Goubert's work on the Beauvaisis (1960) gives a striking impression of the spectre of hunger there in the seventeenth and early eighteenth centuries. A period of relative agricultural prosperity in France in the middle of the seventeenth century was broken by increasingly frequent major harvest failures in the later part of that and the early part of the next century. The consequences of harvest failures were more intense when they followed closely on each other: there were major famines in France in 1680, 1694 and 1709–10.

Sometimes whole countries or even large parts of the continent were short of food at the same time. An example is the great European famine of 1315–17. At the peripheries of Europe, whole countries continued to suffer disastrous depopulation through famine until relatively recent times: a third of the population of Finland died in 1696–7; East Prussia lost nearly half its population at the beginning of the eighteenth century, and as late as 1770 a quarter of a million people died of famine and accompanying epidemics in Bohemia – a tenth of the total (Behrens, in Rich and Wilson, 1977: 575, 614).

Often, however, only a limited region was affected by harvest failure, though before authorities were able to organise the holding of sufficient stocks of grain, and before trade and transport were adequate to remedy local shortage, they could be serious enough.[5] Inadequate transport meant that food could not be moved, or could be moved only with difficulty, from surplus to deficit areas. Shortages led to panic buying, hoarding and speculation, prices soaring and putting what food was available for sale quite beyond the means of the poor. Holding stocks could have helped to remedy this, but administrative difficulties defeated most governments before the late seventeenth or eighteenth century. On top of all this, in times of famine, vagrancy could become 'a veritable scourge', adding to the insecurity of life in already hard times.[6] And finally it has to be remembered that war too could bring about famine, as did the Wars of Religion in France from 1560 onwards.

In times of dearth, what did people eat in order to survive? Ladurie quotes a description of the people of the Vivarais countryside in 1585–6 being 'forced to eat acorns, wild roots, bracken, marc and grape seeds dried in the oven and ground into flour – not to mention pine bark and the bark of other trees, walnut and almond shells, broken tiles and bricks mixed with a few handfuls of barley, oats or bran flour' (1966: 198). Bread made from a mixture of couch grass and sheep's entrails is also recorded (Ladurie, 1966: 244). Some people forced themselves to eat bark bread from time to time even when food was plentiful, knowing that otherwise their stomachs would be unable to digest it when, the harvest having failed, they had no choice (E. Weber, 1973: 197). Indeed, differences in the digestive powers of various social classes were generally taken for granted, and it was accepted that the lower orders were capable in times of dearth of surviving on coarse foods which their superiors could not eat (O'Hara-May, 1977: 118–19).

For centuries harvest failures were inevitably followed by abrupt upward movements in mortality – 'steeples' of mortality Goubert calls them, from the appearance of the graphs. Not that even in the worst times a great proportion of people actually starved to death. But hunger made many more susceptible to disease. And others who survived the immediate famine had their lifespan curtailed by the effects of hunger and malnutrition. The direct relationship between harvest failures and soaring rates of mortality only gradually disappeared from Western Europe from the late seventeenth century onwards. By then, large grain stocks held, for example, at Amsterdam were helping to alleviate the effects of dearth not only in the Low Countries but in coastal and other areas of neighbouring countries accessible to trade. In the eighteenth century, food production increased markedly, but so did population. There was more food, though not necessarily greater consumption per capita. Food supplies, however, became gradually more reliable and shortages less frequent. After 1750, according to Braudel and Spooner (in Rich and Wilson, 1977: 396), only 'suppressed' famines ('almost bearable ones') continued to occur in Western Europe, very largely because of improvements in trade and transport, the effects of which can be seen in the levelling out of food prices plotted (as on a weather map) across the continent. In England scarcity following crop failures no longer reached famine proportions by the first decade of the eighteenth century, though food prices rose very high and death rates were still noticeably up in years of bad harvests in the 1720s and 1740s. In France, the last full nationwide famine was that of 1709–10, but regional dearths accompanied by rising mortality still happened as late as 1795–6 and 1810–12 (Cobb, 1970: 220–2).

Improved trade and transport were not altogether straightforward in their effects:

> the growth of trade, if it enabled the surplus of one region rather more often than before to relieve the dearth of another, also left a larger number of people at the mercy of market fluctuation, tended to depress or hold down real wages, and increase the gap between the rich and the poor. (Wernham, 1968: 5)

This conflict between national markets and local needs was one reason why food riots were still common in eighteenth-century England and France (Tilly, 1975: 380–455; Rudé, 1964; E.P. Thompson, 1971; Cobb, 1970).

Another reason was more important: what could not immediately disappear with general famines was the fear of going hungry engendered by centuries of experience. Mandrou observes that one of the most characteristic features of early modern Europe was 'the obsession with starving to death, an obsession which varied in intensity according to locality and class, being stronger in the country than in the town, rare among the upper-classes and well-fed fighting men, and constant among the lower classes' (1961: 26–7). The themes of starvation, child abandonment and outright cannibalism so common in European folklore are further evidence of the pervasive fear of food scarcity.[7] As late as 1828, notes Cobb (1970: 215), dearth was still being written about as a major threat to public order in France, because 'the fear of dearth was permanent, especially at the lower levels of society, and it took very little at any time for this fear to become hysterical and to develop into the proportions of panic'.

FASTING, GLUTTONY, THE CHURCH AND THE STATE

In these circumstances, self-control over appetite was scarcely a pressing problem for the vast majority of Europeans from medieval until relatively recent times.

At first glance, the large number of fasts expected of the fervent Catholic by the Church in the high Middle Ages might be seen as evidence of pressures to self-control over appetite. Fasting was in theory required on three days a week (Wednesday, Friday and Saturday), for major saints' days, for three days at each of the Quarter Days, and for the whole of Lent except Sundays. Strict fasting consisted essentially of eating only once in 24 hours, after

Vespers, and as far as possible then eating only bread and water. But, of course, for all but the most ascetic, fish was permitted, as were vegetables, but wine as well as meat and any other animal product were excluded (Franklin, 1887–1902: VIII, 124ff.; Henisch, 1976: 28–50). As time passed, the Church made more and more exceptions, such as permitting eggs to be eaten on fast days – and made the requirements less stringent, but in principle the rules still applied in Catholic countries towards the end of the eighteenth century. After the Reformation, the Protestant churches generally disapproved of fasting on specific days as an integral part of Catholic ritual. In a characteristic compromise, the Elizabethan Church of England frowned on fasting as a form of display, though it allowed that at the discretion of individuals it could be a useful adjunct to prayer; and it adjured Christians to observe fasts decreed by law, not for religious but for political reasons:

> as when any realm in consideration of the maintenance of fisher-towns bordering upon the seas, and for the increase of fishermen, of whom do spring mariners to go upon the sea, to the furnishing of the Navy of the Realm, whereby not only commodities of other countries may be transported, but also may be a necessary defence to resist the invasion of the adversary. (Anon., *Homilies*, 1562: 300; cf. O'Hara-May, 1977: 122ff.)

Yet even when and where the Church's authority fully upheld the ritual of fasting, how much difference did it effectively make to how much people actually ate? The majority of people would have considered themselves fortunate if there were meat to eat as often as four days a week. Nor did the rules of fasting do anything to impede their enjoyment of the great binges which at times of plenty relieved the monotony and sparsity of their usual diet. As for the minority for whom plenty was not exceptional, they could eat sumptuously even on *jours maigres*, breaking not the letter but merely the spirit of the fasting rules. How little abstinence a dinner on a fish day might represent is suggested by the vigil dinner set before Sir Gawain on Christmas Eve:

> Several fine soups, seasoned lavishly
> Twice-fold, as is fitting, and fish of all kinds –
> Some baked in bread, some browned on coals,
> Some seethed, some stewed and savoured with spices,
> But always subtly sauced, and so the man liked it.
> The gentle knight generously judged it a feast,
> And often said so, while the servers spurred
> him on thus
> As he ate
> 'This present penance do;
> It soon shall be offset.' (*c.* 1400: 54–5)

Much later, French courtly recipe books of the seventeenth and eighteenth centuries also show what could be achieved within the rules on *jours maigres*. In fact, the observance of fasting in the medieval and early modern period has all the hallmarks of – to use Elias's terms – 'external constraints' (*Fremdzwang*) rather than 'self-restraints' (*Selbstzwang*). That is to say, there is very little evidence of people having internalised the controls the rules embodied; few evidently felt any personal guilt or repugnance at breaking the rules. In any case, the prescribed fasts in their full severity were probably only ever observed in some religious orders.[8] And such exceptional instances of extreme abstinence are indeed a symptom of the unevenness of controls over eating.[9] Very gradually there was to take place a process of development towards more even controls and – eventually – to less marked differences in dietary regimes between strata. But in this process, the teachings of the Church seem not to have played any very significant part.

Gluttony, it is true, was always counted a sin, but the Church did not on the whole inveigh against it with the enthusiasm it brought to bear on drunkenness. This point is partly obscured, in the English sources at least, by the fact that the one word, gluttony, was used in the Middle Ages to refer to both excessive eating and excessive drinking; it acquired its modern reference exclusively to excessive eating only much later (Owst, 1933: 455). The teaching of the Church appears to have contained a strong counterpoint of 'eat, drink and be merry, for tomorrow we die' (1 Cor. XV: 32). Its authority rested on such texts as Galatians 5, in which St Paul condemns drunkenness – but not specifically gluttony in the modern sense – for its leading to a loss of self-control and thereby to the commission of various other deadly sins. It is mainly excessive drinking which Langland depicts in *Piers Plowman* (*c.* 1390: 70–2). St Augustine's earlier denunciation of the enjoyment of food (amongst all other sensual pleasures) appears, despite his general prominence in medieval theology, to have little practical influence on the Church's attitudes.[10] Gluttony in the modern sense of overeating was usually mentioned as an adjunct to drunkenness, and this continued to be the emphasis in such Protestant treatments of the subject as found in the Elizabethan *Homilies* (1562: 309–21), the Stuart divine Jeremy Taylor (1854: III, 47–55; IV, 180–206), and John Wesley (1829–31: VII, 32). The Societies for the Reformation of Manners active in England in the late seventeenth and early eighteenth centuries seem to have been concerned with drunkenness to the exclusion of gluttony (Bahlman, 1957). The reason is simple: the lower orders scarcely had the opportunity to indulge in that vice. Where gluttony in the modern sense was specifically the target of criticism from the medieval pulpit, it was because the glutton wasted the fruit of other men's labours. As Owst comments,

> This latter point proves that the vice had an important bearing on the whole social problem of rich and poor, a bearing, indeed, which those who expressly viewed society as a delicately adjusted system of mutually dependent parts could never afford to overlook. Hence the special enormity of those who 'recken not what thei spende, so that her mouth be feed deliciousli' whilst others lack. (1933: 445)

Perhaps more significant than the Church's teaching is that from the late

Middle Ages onwards the secular authorities in England, France and other countries showed their concern to discourage over-elaborate banquetting by enacting sumptuary laws. That the problem was seen as one of social display, not of sheer physical appetite, can be seen from the fact that such laws often sought to control the clothes people wore as well as the food they ate (see Baldwin, 1926; Boucher d'Argis, 1765). The enactment of these laws by royal governments and parliaments dominated by the old knightly class is possibly a sign of European society becoming somewhat more open. Enormous banquets were perhaps acceptable when given by feudal lords sharing their viands by custom and obligation with their followers and distributing remains to the poor, but were seen as excess and mere social display when copied by rising strata whose social obligations were ill-defined and dependents few. Not that sumptuary laws were ever effective. Like many other laws before the seventeenth century, the same law was often re-enacted at frequent intervals without ever being effectively enforced; the states simply did not have the power to enforce them. In France, a law of 1563 forbade even private families to have meals of more than three courses, and the number and type of dishes to constitute each course was also specified in detail. But very much the same law had to be re-enacted in 1565, 1567, 1572, 1577, 1590, 1591, and finally in 1629 (Franklin, 1887–1902: I, 102). In England, Archbishop Cranmer and his bishops agreed in 1541 on very detailed rules carefully grading the number of courses and number of dishes which the archbishops, bishops, deans, archdeacons and junior clergy might eat; but Cranmer appends a sad little memorandum 'that this order was kept for two or three months, till, by the disusing of certain wilful persons, it came again to the old excess' (1846: 491).

QUANTITY AND QUALITY

It would be interesting to know whether fatness was common and whether it carried any stigma in medieval and early modern Europe. The evidence is not entirely unambiguous. On the one hand, doctors were aware of the medical dangers of obesity, but they tended to interpret it as a result of inactivity and laziness rather than of overeating *per se*. Jane O'Hara-May (1977: 127) suggests that the frequent use of purges and the large amount of exercise which in this period even the wealthy could scarcely avoid tended to balance excessive intake. She argues that paintings show relatively few very fat people. In contrast, Kristoff Glamann draws precisely opposite conclusions from portraits, and states that corporal bulk was in all ranks of society a source not of shame but of prestige:

> Eating made one handsome. A thin wife brought disgrace to a peasant. But of a plump wife it was said that 'a man will love her and not begrudge the food she eats'. Men too ought to be stout. That this ideal was not confined to the rustic world is plain

from a glance at the magnificent amplitude of the human frame so abundantly depicted by the Renaissance painters. (Glamann in Rich and Wilson, 1977: 195)

The contradictory conclusions about average girth in paintings point to the need for more systematic studies. But on the more general question of the prestige or otherwise of bodily bulk, the most likely conclusion is that while obesity which impeded health and activity was deplored (particularly by the doctors whom O'Hara-May is studying), a healthy stoutness was widely considered prestigious.

In the sixteenth and seventeenth centuries, there were many who seem to have been noted more for their capacity than for their refinement of taste. Cathérine de'Medici was celebrated for her appetite and frequent indigestion. Diarists at the court of Louis XIV have left graphic accounts of the great king's prodigious consumption. Nor does he appear to have been untypical of his court. The Princess Palatine often describes the overeating of the French nobility, including her son the Regent, though the Duchesse de Berri's eating herself to death seems to have been even then considered an instance of a pathologically abnormal appetite (Orléans, 1855: I, 348; II, 51, 85, 131, 143).

Faint traces of the beginnings of pressures towards self-restraint in appetite can be seen a century earlier. In appetite as in so many other facets of the civilising process, Montaigne is a good witness (Mennell, 1981a). He reports that he himself has little self-restraint in eating, but bemoans the fact:

if they preach abstinence once a dish is in front of me, they are wasting their time. . . . To eat greedily as I do, is not only harmful to health, and even to one's pleasure, but it is unmannerly into the bargain. So hurried am I that I often bite my tongue, and sometimes my fingers. . . . My greed leaves me no time for talk. (1595a: 394)

By the mid-eighteenth century extreme gluttony appears to have become the exception. Louis XVI, who saw off chicken, lamb cutlets, eggs, ham and a bottle and a half of wine before setting out to hunt, without it diminishing his appetite at dinner, appears to have been considered something of a throwback:

By his appetite, and by his appetite alone did the unfortunate Louis XVI revive memories of Louis XIV. Like him, he did not bother himself with cookery, nor with any refinements; to him, always afraid of not having enough to eat, sheer quantity was more important than anything else; he did not eat, he stuffed himself, going as far as to incapacitate himself at his wedding dinner, scandalising his grandfather [Louis XV]. (Gottschalk, 1939: 232)

In England, another famous trencherman of that time, Dr Johnson, though of less exalted social rank, was also considered a coarse eater. Not only did he show so little sense of what was proper as to call for the boat containing the lobster sauce left over from the previous course and pour it over his plum-pudding (Piozzi, 1785), but he wolfed his food down in a shameful manner:

> When at table, Johnson was totally absorbed in the business of the moment; his looks seemed rivetted to his plate; nor would he, unless when in very high company, say one word, or even pay the least attention to what was said by others, till he had satisfied his appetite, which was so fierce and indulged with such intenseness that while in the act of eating, the veins of his forehead swelled and generally a strong perspiration was evident. To those whose sensations were delicate, this could not but be disgusting; and it was doubtless not very suitable to the character of a philosopher, who should be distinguished by self-command. (Boswell, 1791: I, 323)

Significantly, Boswell comments that everything about Johnson's character and manners was forcible and violent, and adds 'Johnson, though he could be rigidly *abstemious*, was not a *temperate* man either in eating or drinking. He could refrain, but he could not use moderately.' That sounds very much like a throwback to the mode of behaviour typical of medieval and early modern Europe. But by the mid-eighteenth century it was no longer considered quite the right thing in the better circles. What changes were taking place?

The civilising of appetite, if we may call it that, appears to have been partly related to the increasing security, regularity, reliability and variety of food supplies. But just as the civilising of appetite was entangled with several other strands of the civilising process, including the transformation of table manners, so the improvement in food supplies was only one strand in a complex of developments within the social figuration which together exerted a compelling force over the way people behaved. The increased security of food supplies was made possible by the extension of trade, the progressive division of labour in a growing commercial economy, and also by the process of state-formation and internal pacification. Even a small improvement was enough to enable a small powerful minority to distinguish themselves from the lower ranks of society by the sheer quantities they ate and the regularity with which they ate them. As the improvement continued, somewhat wider segments of the better-off groups in society came to be able to copy the élite. The same structural processes, however, served not only to permit social emulation but positively to promote it. The longer chains of social interdependence produced by state-formation and the division of labour tended to tilt the balance of power little by little towards lower social groups, leading to increased pressure 'from below' and to intensified social competition. The sumptuary laws, with their vain attempt to relate quantities eaten to social rank, seem symptomatic of that.

By the sixteenth or seventeenth centuries, for the nobility to eat quantitatively more than they did would have been physically impossible.[11] That was one reason for increasing demands made upon the skill of the cook in making food more palatable; as a modern expert explains,

A variety of studies demonstrates that hunger and palatability are substitutive for each other and algebraically additive in their effects. Equal amounts are eaten of a highly palatable food in a minimal state of hunger and even without hunger, and of a minimally palatable food in a state of hunger. Thus it is equally true to assume that hunger potentiates palatability and that palatability potentiates hunger in their common effect of eliciting eating. The consequence of this relationship is that the differential palatability of two foods decreases with increased hunger. (Le Magnen, 1972: 76)

Or, as a nineteenth-century classic of dietetics put it,

Appetite . . . may . . . be educated or trained to considerable deviations from the ordinary standard of quantity and quality. . . . The most common source . . . of the errors into which we are apt to fall in taking appetite as our only guide, is unquestionably the *confounding of appetite with taste*, and continuing to eat for the gratification of the latter long after the former is satisfied. In fact, the whole science of a skilful cook is expended in producing this *willing* mistake on our part. (Combe, 1846: 29–30)

Here then is the psychological basis for the elaboration of cooking in an age of plenty. And the skills of cooks had another advantage: they could be applied not simply to stimulating the sated appetites of the glutton, but also to the invention and elaboration of an endless variety of ever more refined and delicate dishes; when the possibilities of quantitative consumption for the expression of social superiority had been exhausted, the qualitative possibilities were inexhaustible.

Later chapters will explore in detail the links between the growing arts of the cook, developing conceptions of refined taste, and changing patterns of social contest. Broadly speaking, the break with medieval cookery which seems to have begun in the city-courts of Renaissance Italy and spread to the noble courts of seventeenth- and eighteenth-century France, involved a shift in emphasis from quantitative display to qualitative elaboration. By the eighteenth century the fashion for more varied and delicate ragoûts was spreading from courtly circles to the bourgeoisie. Louis-Sebastien Mercier noted towards the end of the century how fashions had changed:

In the last century, they used to serve huge pieces of meat, and pile them up in pyramids. These little dishes, costing ten times as much as one of those big ones, were not yet known. Delicate eating has been known for only half a century. The delicious cuisine of the reign of Louis XV was unknown even to Louis XIV. (1783: V, 597–8)

The tendency for courtly models of eating to be emulated by the bourgeoisie probably gave increased impetus to the movement towards greater delicacy and self-restraint. The connections are complex. We have noted that courtly fashion moved towards the proliferation of small, delicate and costly dishes, and that knowledgeability and a sense of delicacy in matters of food became something of a mark of the courtier. Now a sense of delicacy implies a degree of restraint too, in so far as it involves discrimination and selection, the rejection as well as the acceptance of certain foods or combinations of foods, guided at least as much by social proprieties as by individual fancies. No courtly gourmet would pour the lobster sauce over his plum pudding. But while the development of systems of fashionable preferences involves a degree of rationalisation, the courtly ethos was antithetical to that of bourgeois economic rationality; lavish consumption was too closely part of the courtier's social identity for him to economise like a good bourgeois. While there is plenty of evidence that, in France at least, the bourgeoisie wanted in the eighteenth century to follow courtly models of eating, it is also clear that most did not have the resources to eat on such a lavish scale; they were therefore both under more pressure than the nobility to choose and select, and also more easily able to do so. The bourgeoisie was in many ways a more appropriate *couche* for the emergence of a body of gastronomic theorising. When it did emerge, the theorists were indeed mainly members of the high bourgeoisie, and the themes of delicacy and self-restraint were prominent in their writings, the latter increasingly so as time went on.

GASTRONOMY AND MODERATION

Sociologists have argued that political security and economic surplus are prerequisites for the development of the cultural syndrome of bourgeois rationality as a whole (Elias, 1962). It seems no coincidence that gastronomic theorising as a genre first appeared during the period when the insecurity of food supplies ceased to be of catastrophic proportions, and burgeoned fully during the nineteenth century.

The notion of *régime alimentaire* began to be prominent in medical circles in the eighteenth century, and was reflected in the writings of Rousseau, who favoured moderation and pure foods (Aron, 1961: 971–7). Early in the century, both in England and France, a number of doctors advocated strict diets as a way to health.[12] Jones and Sonnenscher (1983) have described how, later in the century, the diet of hospital inmates was the subject of conflict between doctors and nurses at the Hôtel-Dieu in Nîmes. The nursing sisters had traditionally seen their role as a charitable one and, aware that many illnesses had resulted from repeated subsistence crises, saw it as their duty to feed up the poor and needy ill. One of the doctors at Nîmes complained bitterly against the overplentifulness of the patients' diet, which often impeded their recovery. 'They are always afraid in this hospital that people will die of hunger . . . they always feed the sick too much.' A colleague in neighbouring Montpellier in the 1760s documented how overfeeding by the sisters had led to patients' premature deaths, and 'gave the impression that over-eating was one of the major causes of hospital mortality!' Significantly, the doctors in eighteenth-century Montpellier also launched an onslaught on the tradition of marking the hospital's patron saint's day with feasting.

Although the social power of the medical profession was growing during the eighteenth century, it would be incautious to overemphasise the influence of advancing medical knowledge in pressuring people to exercise self-control over appetite. To reiterate Elias's argument, 'rational understanding' is not the motor of the 'civilising' of powerful drives like those which govern eating. As far back as the Salerno School medical opinion had favoured moderation in eating, and there is little evidence to suggest that their opinions had had much effect on people's daily eating habits in the past. Still less is it safe to assume that philosophers like Rousseau had great practical impact on such mundane behaviour; it is not easy to find any signs of explicit influence even on gastronomic theorising, which after the Revolution most closely reflected feelings about taste and eating in the upper strata of society.

Neither Grimod de la Reynière (1803–12) nor Brillat-Savarin (1826), the two most noted pioneers of gastronomy, entirely dismissed a large capacity as an epicurean virtue. But their writings emphasise the need for a discriminating palate and scorn as vulgar any merely quantitative display. They set the pattern for gastronomic writing in both France and England for the rest of the century. An Englishman strongly influenced by Grimod writes in 1822:

> Gluttony is, in fact, a mere effort of the appetite, of which the coarsest bolter of bacon in all Hampshire may equally boast with the most distinguished consumer of turtle in a Corporation; while Epicurism is the result of 'that choicest gift of Heaven', a refined and discriminating taste: this is the peculiar attribute of the palate, that of the stomach. It is the happy combination of both these enviable qualities that constitutes that truly estimable character, the real epicure. He is not only endowed with a capacious stomach and an insatiable appetite, but with a delicate susceptibility in the organs of degustation, which enables him to appreciate the true relish of each ingredient in the most compound ragoût, and to detect the slightest aberration of the cook; added to which advantages, he possesses a profound acquaintance with the rules of art in all the most approved schools of cookery, and an enlightened judgment on their several merits, matured by long and sedulous experience. (Sturgeon, 1822: 3–4)

A few decades later, in 1868, another writer bemoans England's lagging behind France in gastronomic *savoir-faire*, and now directly disparages the lack of discrimination masked by plenty:

> Not only our merchant princes, but our gentry and nobility, have merely a superficial knowledge of the science of cookery and the art of giving good dinners. Consider the barbarism implied in the popular phrase for ample hospitality! The table is described as groaning under the plenty of the host. (Jerrold, 1868: 5)

By the twentieth century, the theme of moderation was still more explicit. G. F. Scotson-Clark, in a book entitled *Eating without Fears* published in 1924, writes that

> Consuming large quantities of food is only a habit. What is often called a 'healthy appetite' is nothing of the sort. The only people who should eat really large quantities of food are those whose regular daily life involves a vast amount of physical exercise – like the road-mender. (1924: 65)

And André L. Simon reiterates an argument prominent in his extensive writings between the 1930s and 1960s: 'There cannot be any intelligent choice nor real appreciation where there is excess. Gastronomy stands or falls by moderation. No gourmand and no glutton can be a gastronome' (1969: 94). The theme of moderation was now becoming clearly linked to questions of health as well as discrimination. Scotson-Clark says:

Cookery plays such a large part in our life, it is really the fundamental basis of our life, our very existence, that it is foolish to belittle its importance. To take no interest in it is as bad for one's health as to take no interest in one's ablutions. An individual should cultivate his palate just as much as he should cultivate his brain. Good taste in food and wine is as necessary as good taste in art, literature and music, and the very fact of looking upon gastronomy as one of the arts will keep a man from becoming that most disgusting of creatures, a glutton. . . .

I am sure that moderation is the keynote of good health, and I contend that anyone can eat anything I mention in this book, without increasing his girth, and if taken in moderation he can reduce to normal weight. It is not necessary for one to deprive oneself of all the things one loves, for fear of getting too fat, but it is necessary to take an intelligent interest in the provender with which one intends to stoke the human furnace. (1924: 8–9)

At about the same time in France, Edouard de Pomiane, the medical doctor turned cookery writer, was developing similar themes (1922).

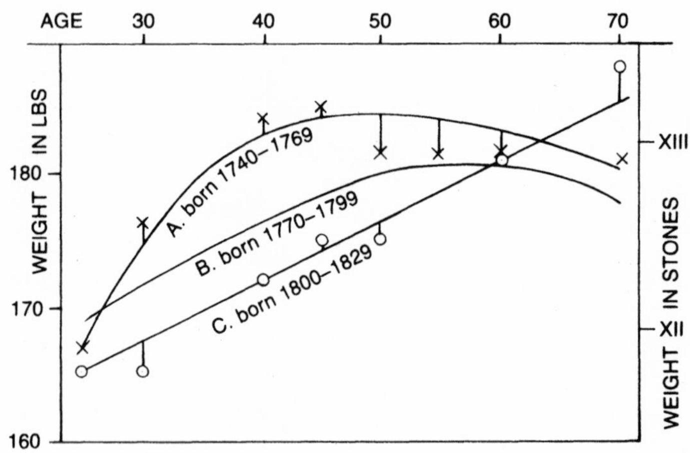

Figure 3 Mean age-weight of British noblemen in three successive generations.

The problem and the fear of being overweight seems, not surprisingly, to have started towards the top of the social scale and progressed steadily downwards. The 'magnificent amplitude of the human frame' which once constituted the cultural model was gradually replaced by the ideal of the slim figure. The changing standard of beauty among the upper strata can be seen around the time of the Romantic movement, when 'for both women and men paleness, frailness, slenderness became the vogue' (J. H. Young, 1970: 16). Burnett (1966: 80) quotes some fairly abstemious diets recommended for well-to-do ladies at that period. Exactly when the ideal began to be reflected in an actual decline in typical body weights, and how the decline progressed down the social scale, is very difficult to demonstrate. Given the complexities of relating body weights to height, age and sex, let alone to social class, little in the way of time-series data over the long period required is available or likely to become available. An interesting clue is an article by Sir Francis Galton in *Nature*, in 1884, comparing the weights of three generations of British nobleman among the customers of Berry Brothers', grocers and wine-merchants in St James's, London, from the mid-eighteenth century to the late nineteenth (see figure 3). The evidence is far from conclusive, but it does suggest that by the late nineteenth century men in the highest stratum of English society were no longer putting on weight so rapidly as young men as their fathers and grandfathers had done. They reached the same weight in the end, but possibly this is consistent with them having overeaten slightly but persistently rather than indulging in dramatically excessive over eating. Whatever happened to actual body weights, however, there is plenty of evidence of the worry that subject caused in the upper reaches of society. Gastronomic writers from Brillat-Savarin to Ali-Bab (1907) discussed obesity as a worry and affliction among gourmets. In the latter part of the nineteenth century, great innovating chefs such as Escoffier, Philéas Gilbert and Prosper Montagné, cooking for a fashionable clientèle, were beginning a trend towards simpler, lighter food and fewer courses. Yet at the same time, books were still being written on how to put on weight (for example, T.C. Duncan, *How to Become Plump*, 1878), and as will be seen in chapter 8 the cookery columns addressed to the lower-middle classes (especially in England) emphasised the need to eat fat and heavy food for body-building. The upper and upper-middle classes often commented on the greed of servants.

In towns we often observe the bad effects of overfeeding in young female servants recently arrived from the country. From being accustomed to constant exercise in the open air, and to the comparatively innutritious diet on which the labouring classes subsist, they pass all at once, with appetite, digestion and health in their fullest vigour, to the confinement of a house, to the impure atmosphere of a crowded city, and to a rich and stimulating diet. Appetite, still keen, is freely indulged; but waste being diminished, fulness is speedily induced. . . . (Combe, 1846: 217)

And, at Buckingham Palace (no less), at the turn of the century:

The plentiful meals of those days naturally enough encouraged greed, particularly among some of the servants. After a five-course breakfast those who visited the kitchens often slipped two or three hardboiled eggs into their pockets to help them last out the next few hours until it was time for morning tea. (Tschumi, 1954: 63)

It is hardly surprising if people drawn from ranks of society where the worry for centuries had been simply getting enough to eat did not immediately develop self-control when suddenly confronted with plentiful food.

Even at the present day, in the world's affluent societies the incidence of obesity is highest in the lower and poorer strata, in contrast to the countries of the Third World where it occurs only among the privileged few (Bruch, 1974: 14). Obviously the plentiful availability of food is a prerequisite for the development of obesity, but clinical evidence suggests that psychological pressures to overeat are often rooted in past hunger, perhaps in a previous generation. For instance, among the mothers of obese children in America,

Many of these women had been poor immigrants who had suffered hunger during their early lives. They did not understand why anyone should object to a child's being big and fat, which to them indicated success and freedom from want. (Bruch, 1974: 15)

Conversely, cases of *anorexia nervosa* arise disproportionately among the more well-to-do strata. There may have been instances of this affliction, which is far more common among females than males, in earlier centuries. A number of 'miraculously fasting' girls are known to have attracted attention from the sixteenth century onwards, and though several were probably frauds, some were possibly cases where psychological disturbance led to serious undereating (H. G. Morgan, 1977). The condition was however not well described, and was probably not at all common, until the latter half of the nineteenth century when it was named by Sir William Gull. Gull in England and E. C. Lasègue in France both gave clear accounts of it among their middle-class patients at that period. Today, it is a very familiar illness. Again, there appears to be a clear connection with the reliable and plentiful availability of food: apparently *anorexia nervosa* is not reported from countries where there is still danger of widespread starvation or famine, nor among blacks and other underprivileged groups in the USA (Bruch, 1974: 13).

Anorexia nervosa and obesity can be regarded as similar if opposite disturbances of the patterns of self-control over appetite now normally expected and necessary in prosperous Western societies. Though the process may not yet be complete, in the course of the twentieth century the concern with weight-watching and slimming has gradually become more widespread in all ranks of society: its progress can be observed in cookery columns in popular magazines. For example, ever since the early 1950s, the French women's magazine *Elle* has had weekly columns giving menus and recipes with calorie counts, playing on and encouraging the reader's concern with her own weight and that of her family. A typical early instance is an article in *Elle*, on 2 February 1953, entitled 'Unconscious Overeating can Threaten your Life', with a photograph of a slim girl in a swimsuit to illustrate the prevailing body image. The not-very-subliminal connection between self-control over the appetite, slimness, health and sex-appeal is one of the most salient themes in British as well as French mass-circulation women's magazines since the Second World War. Which is not to deny that persistent slight but definite overeating remains a characteristic problem among the populations of England, France and other Western industrial states. But a general anxiety to avoid obesity is very widespread, and the fitful extreme overeating of an earlier era seems less common.

CONCLUSION

Very broadly speaking, the increasing interdependence and more equal balances of power between social classes has been reflected in more equal distribution of foodstuffs, which in turn has been associated with somewhat greater similarity of cuisine, and also with less extreme differences between festival or banquet food and everyday eating, and with greater evenness of controls over appetite. Yet the process of the civilising of appetite is in detail more complex than it has been possible to depict it here. It has not been a simple linear development; in fact there have been spurts and reversals, exceptions and sub-themes. For example, the seasonal rhythm and ritual of early modern eating, the observance of festivals and eating of festival fare, persisted longer in the countryside than in the towns,[13] where the special dishes of an earlier age have become the commonplace dishes of industrialised eating. At the opposite end of the social scale, the appetite of a figure like King Edward VII might convince us that in the early twentieth century nothing had greatly changed since the carnivorous accomplishments of the medieval nobility; but within a couple of decades of his death, British royalty too was eating relatively abstemiously food which would not be very unfamiliar to most of their subjects (Magnus, 1964: 268–9, 449; Tschumi, 1954). All these points serve to remind us that the 'civilising of appetite' in the quantitative sense cannot be understood in separation from the qualitative development of cooking and conceptions of 'good food'. This will be the main concern of the next few chapters.

3

Pottages and Potlatch: Eating in the Middle Ages

Before the age of the printed book, detailed evidence of what people ate in Europe and especially of how they cooked it is scanty. A few famous manuscript lists of recipes have survived, but not only do they depict the festive dishes of a small élite, they are also too few and far between to make it possible to trace any definite pattern of change and development through the long centuries of the Middle Ages. As for the lower orders, the further down the social scale one looks, the more scanty does the evidence become. Nevertheless, the picture is sufficiently clear to make some broad generalisations about this immense period. In medieval times, differences between the strata of society in matters of food, as in many other aspects of manners, were more striking than differences between countries. At the highest level, a grand banquetting cuisine was common to the great courts of Western Europe. More characteristic of the diet of knightly class was the high consumption of meat and fish, and this changed little between the twelfth and fifteenth centuries. Equally there were great similarities in how the peasantry ate in different parts of the continent. With the increased production of meat and dairy produce following the Black Death, more changes were evident in the diet of the peasantry throughout Western Europe than in that of the nobility – something rather unusual – though they were by no means sufficient to obliterate the broad pattern of stratified diet. Afterwards, the pace of change in the countryside reverted to its normal slow pace, and the peasant diet appears to have remained virtually unaltered for centuries. In contrast, towards the close of the Middle Ages, the beginnings can be observed of what were to become rapid developments in *haute cuisine*, and the effects of these were gradually to spread socially within the growing towns. Marc Bloch contrasted the monotony of peasant food with the innovations taking place on the social heights, and remarked that 'Even on the eve of the Revolution, in contraposition to a bourgeois and even artisan diet which had already undergone appreciable development, the everyday food of the peasant remained singularly archaic' (Bloch, 1954: 231). The distinction drawn by historians of the Annales School between different modes of historical time is pertinent here: the world of food fashions and cookery books was eventually to become something to study in the context of the 'time of conjunctures'; but in the Middle Ages the food of all classes was a subject for study in the *longue durée*, and the food of the country people was long to remain so.

THE SOCIAL DISTRIBUTION OF FOOD

It is commonly accepted that the great differences which existed between social estates in the centuries of feudalism were reflected in what people ate. In particular, the prodigious consumption of meat by the secular and ecclesiastical upper classes has long been familiar, and it has generally been assumed that, in contrast, the peasantry's diet was predominantly based on cereals and vegetables, and was often sparse at that. There have long been dissentient voices. In the mid-nineteenth century, Thorold Rogers tried to demonstrate that 'the Englishman of the middle ages lived in ordinary times in coarse plenty' (1866: 63). But the orthodoxy among historians has generally been that, while some of the most prosperous among the peasants may have enjoyed 'coarse plenty', there were many more of the poor who did not. Favourite literary sources for England in the late Middle Ages are Chaucer and Langland. The description of the poor widow in the *Nun's Priest's Tale* is frequently quoted:

> And there she ate full many a slender meal;
> There was no *sauce piquante* to spice her veal,
> No dainty morcel ever passed her throat,
> According to her cloth she cut her coat.
> Repletion never left her in disquiet
> And all her physic was a temperate diet,
> Hard work for exercise and heart's content.
> And rich man's gout did nothing to prevent
> Her dancing, apoplexy struck her not;
> She drank no wine, nor white nor red had got.
> Her board was mostly served with white and black,
> Milk and brown bread, in which she found no lack;
> Broiled bacon or an egg or two were common,
> She was in fact a sort of dairy woman.
> (Chaucer, *c.* 1386: 231)

And here are Langland's Piers Plowman and his fellow peasants appeasing an allegorical Hunger:

> 'I haven't a penny left,' said Piers, 'so I can't buy you pullets or geese or pigs. All I've got is a couple of fresh cheeses, a little curds and cream, an oat-cake, and two loaves of beans and bran which I baked for my children. Upon my soul, I haven't a scrap of bacon, and I haven't a cook to fry you steak and onions. But I've some parsley and

shallots and plenty of cabbages, and a cow and a calf, and a mare to cart my dung, till the drought is over. And with these few things we must live till Lammas time, when I hope to reap a harvest in my fields. Then I can spread you a feast, as I'd really like to.'

Then all the poor folk came with peascods, and brought beans and baked apples by the lapful, and spring onions and chervils and hundreds of ripe cherries, and offered these gifts to Piers, to satisfy Hunger.

Hunger soon gobbled it all up and asked for more. So the poor folk were afraid, and quickly brought up supplies of green leaks and peas, and would gladly have poisoned him. (Langland, *c.* 1390: 89)

From more conventional documentary sources comes a matching impression of the limited range of foodstuffs eaten by country people. Bennett (1937: 235–6) summarised hundreds of lists of food provided by lords for their serfs working on the harvest and similar tasks, as consisting of bread, ale or cider, pottage, followed by a dish of fish or meat and perhaps a lump of cheese. The bread was mostly of rye or maslin,[1] the pottage 'a grewell without flesh boiled in it' and often made from peas or beans. Fish on fast days, and particularly the meat on flesh days, would have been the high point of such a meal, but Bennett cautioned that these rations 'must not be looked on as normal, but as something superior to the ordinary meals which most men were able to afford for themselves'. Poultry and (since poaching was common) rabbits and hares probably were eaten particularly on special occasions; such sources as the Glastonbury records – from which Coulton, (1926:28–30) drew a rather romantic picture – show that there were communal feasts and drinking on major religious and secular occasions such as Christmas, May Day and Midsummer Day, seed-time and harvest, Martinmas (when cattle were slaughtered) as well as for weddings and funerals. Nevertheless Bennett, while conceding that the most prosperous of the peasants may have 'lived in ordinary times in coarse plenty', argued that there were many others on the manors for whom food in general was not normally either plentiful or varied, and for whom meat in particular remained a luxury.

This view of English peasant food is broadly confirmed by the much more recent researches of Christopher Dyer (1983) on the 'maintenance agreements' recorded in manorial rolls. These were agreements usually drawn up when an elderly peasant, often a widow, retired and surrendered the holding to a new tenant, who accepted an obligation to maintain his predecessors. Dyer analysed 83 such agreements, 70 of them from before the Black Death. Though the better-off stratum of peasants is probably over-represented among these agreements, they do bear out the predominance of cereals in the peasants' diet. The agreements most commonly stipulate the quantities of the various sorts of grain and pulses that were to be supplied. In some cases, the quantities were such as to allow for the brewing of ale as well as the baking of bread; in others, they look scarcely adequate to maintain life. The only animals kept entirely for meat were pigs, and bacon was always regarded as

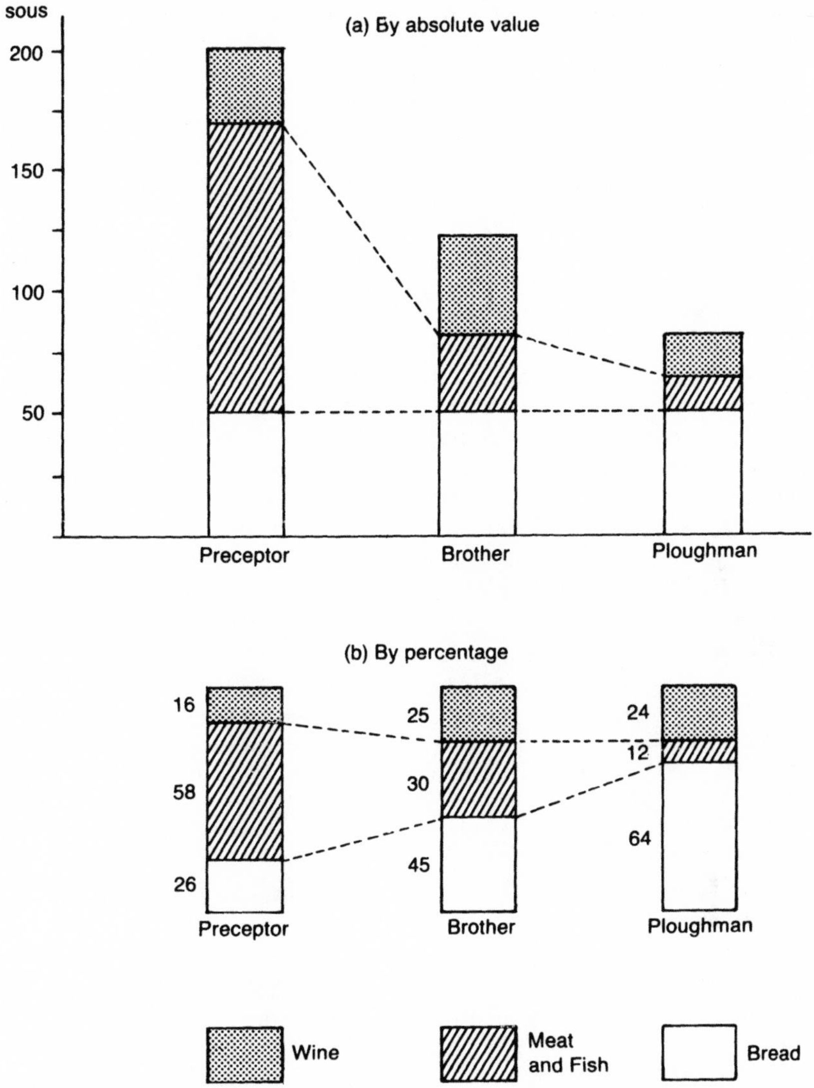

Figure 4 Food budgets in the Commanderie de Saliers, 1338

typical peasant food. So was dairy produce – 'white meat' – but since peasant households rarely owned more than one or two cows, that supplement to a cereal diet should not be exaggerated. Nor were vegetables more than a minor supplement. A small range of vegetables, principally cabbages, onions, leeks and garlic, was grown in gardens; peas and beans were the only vegetables grown in the fields.

The hierarchical differences in diet in the high Middle Ages were much the same in France. Possibly the most vivid demonstration of them is found in Georges Duby's data (1961) from the food budgets of the Knights Hospitaler at the Commanderie de Saliers in 1338. There, within the same establishment, as figure 4 strikingly shows, the budgets for the food for the ranks of preceptor, brother, and farm labourer differed greatly. Even allowing for the possibly more expensive foods purchased for preceptors, it would appear that the higher the rank, the more did people eat even in purely quantitative terms, and the larger was the percentage represented by meat; the lowest rank presumably performed the heaviest manual labour but had the smallest quantity of food, and certainly much less meat.

Although historical research now confirms socially stratified differences in diet throughout Western Europe, it was long accepted that the English peasantry were relatively well-provided with meat and fish in comparison with the French. Curiously enough, one of the principal sources Marc Bloch (1954: 231–5) cited as evidence on French diet was English – the fifteenth-century jurist Sir John Fortescue's famous description of the impoverishment of the common people of France by the imposition of taxes without the consent of the Etats-Généraux by the already incipiently absolutist French monarchy:

> They drink water, they eat apples, with right brown bread made of rye; they eat no flesh unless it be very seldom a little lard, or the entrails and hides of beasts slain for the nobles and merchants of the land. . . . Truly they live in the most extreme poverty and misery, and yet they dwell in the most fertile realm of the world. . . . But blessed be God, this land [England] is ruled under a better law; and therefore the people thereof be not in such penury, nor thereby hurt in their persons, but they be wealthy, and have all things necessary to the sustenance of nature. (Fortescue, *c.* 1471: 114–15)

Despite Fortescue's obvious polemical intent, Bloch accepted this picture of France and the implied contrasting picture of English fare. He commented that 'one of the greatest difficulties in the supply of meat in the countryside has always been that, the isolated household being scarcely able to consume whole beasts, it almost necessarily presupposes a butchery trade; it would be interesting to know how 'Merry England', where the farmer was very much earlier a beef eater, resolved the problem' (1954: 232).

Yet though a monotonous diet with little meat in it may have been typical of much of rural Europe in the high Middle Ages, and was to become so once more in the later sixteenth century, there is now considerable evidence that in the late fourteenth and the fifteenth centuries food, and meat in particular, were relatively plentiful, and that England was not unique in this respect. The pioneering researches of Wilhelm Abel (1935, 1937) showed the high level of meat production and consumption in Germany in the age of low population and deserted villages after the Black Death. And Fernand Braudel

(1967: 127–30) cites a variety of evidence from various parts of Europe to show that 'from 1350 to 1550, Europe probably experienced a favourable period as far as individual life' – including food and the consumption of meat – 'was concerned'. During these two centuries, Braudel argues, it was not only the courts at which meat abounded both in quantity and variety. We have accounts of beef, mutton, pork, poultry, pigeon, goat and lamb in butchers' shops, inns and eating houses, not to mention long lists of game available in markets as far apart as Venice, Sicily and Orléans. The variety, at least, might still be much greater in the towns than in the countryside, but again in these years Braudel is able to cite fairly lavish directions for the feeding of peasants doing statute labour in the fields of Alsace. Livestock was reared in large numbers on the now-abundant pasture of Western Europe, but was also driven over vast distances from Eastern Europe and the Balkans. The butchery trade was by then highly organised – not just in England as Bloch was inclined to think, but in other countries, and in the smaller settlements as well as in the large towns. In the most detailed regional study of late medieval food supplies and consumption undertaken to date, Stouff (1970: 171–94) demonstrates not only the large number of butchers in Provence, but their prosperity and the vast extent of the trade in animals over considerable distances.

If, however, at the close of the Middle Ages meat was not a luxury reserved exclusively for the tables of the very rich, one must not jump to the conclusion that the social distribution of nourishment suddenly became quite equal. On the contrary, hierarchical differences in what people ate remained more striking than geographical ones. In his study of Provence, Stouff examined not just the food supplies of a whole town – Carpentras – but also the food budgets mainly of clerical households, schools and monasteries. His picture of what foods people ate does not differ very greatly from that drawn by Abel for Germany, Ladurie (1966) for Languedoc, or Dyer (1983) for England. The differences between the social ranks are, however, still quite striking. The dozen clerics who constituted the household of the Archbishop of Arles in 1429 habitually consumed very large quantities of meat and also of bread. The daily ration of meat was 306 grammes (305 in 1430, 314 in 1442) and 65 kilogrammes a year (66kg in 1430, 67kg in 1442). Even reducing the figures by 30 per cent to allow for the weight of bones, Stouff points out, these are figures clearly much higher than for Carpentras, where meat consumption in 1473 was 26kg per capita per annum.

> The comparison between data for a whole town and those for a limited group of a dozen people is very revealing. The Archbishop of Arles's accounts confirm what is already apparent from the butchers' books in the county town: the inequality in the consumption of meat by the different social strata. A household where meat was eaten twice a day and five days a week was in a privileged circle. (Stouff, 1970: 236)

Evidence on the consumption of vegetables is more difficult to interpret; that such households had gardens and orchards is certain, but fruit and vegetables feature in only a very minor way in the accounts. It is sometimes argued that medieval accounting simply paid no heed to the value of home-grown garden produce eaten in the household. In the case of the Archbishop of Arles's household, there is evidence that, in addition to whatever they produced for themselves, they purchased fruit, beans and peas. Stouff feels able to infer that vegetables introduced a valuable element of variety into the diet. Dyer, studying comparable household accounts in England, disagrees. He argues (1983: 195) that such reasoning underestimates the sophistication of late medieval accounting techniques, which did involve the valuation of garden produce used in any quantity. He abides by the older view, that the quantities eaten really *were* very small. Seigneurial gardens could be large, but were often used to grow flax and hemp more than vegetables, while apples and pears from the orchard were often used for cider- and perry-making. Vegetables remained firmly associated with the tables of peasants and labourers, and indeed there is plentiful evidence of upper-class disdain of vegetables long into the early modern period.

Dairy produce also remained very much identified with the lower orders and disdained by the grand. Here Stouff does not differ from Dyer. After analysing their food in modern dietetic terms, he concludes that

> in 1429 (and this appears to be true for the rest of the fifteenth century too), the food consumed by the household of the Archbishop of Arles was excessive in quantity, but relatively well balanced. Only calcium was deficient, and it would have been necessary to reduce the consumption of bread by half and triple the consumption of cheese in order to have a diet appropriate to the norms of modern dietetics. (1970: 238)

Stouff also analysed the diet of the boys of the Studium Papal at Trets in 1364–5. It proved to be similar in composition to that of the archbishop's household, but not so huge in quantity – the boys were, of course, of humbler social status. It could in certain respects be an advantage to be humble, for the boys were well nourished and needed only a little milk, butter and an orange to meet twentieth-century standards. For that matter, one of the few ways in which peasants in the mountains of Provence had a dietary advantage over the archbishop was in their high consumption of cheese.

In short, even after taking full account of the increased production and consumption of meat after the Black Death, Stouff is able to conclude that in fifteenth-century Provence 'every element in the diet, bread, wine, meat and fish, throws the spotlight on a pattern of "class feeding"' (1970: 222). What he says of Provence seems equally true of the rest of France, of Germany and England. For, as far as the broad constituents of diet were concerened, the evidence is of great similarities throughout Western Europe. That is not to deny that there were some differences asssociated with climatic and other conditions. Of course, olive oil was much used in Provence and not in England, and there were different regional staples: merely within England there were clear regional variations in the grains grown. On the other hand, in the pre-Columbian age, the range of available crops was smaller, and the predominance of items such as cabbages, onions and leeks in both England and Provence is striking to modern eyes. The variety of available foods must have been greater in the towns and along major trade routes, but this too probably on balance reinforced the pattern of 'class feeding'. For, broadly speaking, the magnates bought their luxuries in the major ports and at large fairs, while the lesser lords patronised the smaller towns (Dyer, 1983: 197), and the peasantry remained much more restricted to what was available locally. Thus, whatever the extent of regional variations in foods eaten, the *structural* similarities in the peasant diet throughout Western Europe were very marked.

MEDIEVAL COOKERY

None of the historical evidence discussed so far tells us much about what people in the Middle Ages actually did with food when they had produced or purchased it. What happened to it in the kitchens of the great and of the poor? And what did it look like when it reached their tables? These questions are not easy to answer even for the higher strata, given the scarcity of surviving manuscripts. They are positively difficult to answer for the peasants and the urban poor, about whose means and modes of cooking we have very little direct evidence. Something at least can, however, be inferred from what we know of their kitchens and kitchen equipment – or lack of them. References in court rolls to tenant possessions suggest that virtually every peasant household owned a brass cooking pot or pan, and archaeologists find ceramic cooking pots everywhere on medieval sites: there was no problem with boiling (Dyer, 1983: 204). On the other hand, the documentary and archaeological evidence both show that baking ovens were found only sporadically, and by no means in every house or toft. Some villages had communal ovens, and in some there were specialist bakers. Most homes in the towns were no better equipped, though there would have been more specialist tradesmen there. As Alfred Gottschalk writes:

> In the towns, the rudimentary arrangements in small houses and lodgings allowed no more than soups and *bouillés* to be made; for even the most modest step beyond that, it was necessary to have recourse to the *rôtisseur*, to the *charcutier*, to the cookshop or the baker. Only the great lords and the rich bourgeois had proper kitchens and the necessary personnel. (1948a: I, 322)

The facilities available even in the kitchens of the better-off should not be exaggerated. 'Early cooking was necessarily simple,' emphasises Waverley Root, 'if only because of the limitations of contemporary kitchens.'

> It was usually not practical, in a kitchen that was in essence only the enlarged base of the chimney, to prepare dishes requiring, during their preparation, manipulations

more complicated than simple basting. Boiling, and roasting meat and poultry on a spit, ordinarily exhausted the available possibilities. (Root, 1958: 41)

In fact, the method of slow boiling dominated the cooking of all but the richest in both England and France. In the Massif Central chestnuts were a staple food, often simply boiled in water or milk (Bloch, 1954: 232). Elsewhere the poor ate cereals in the form of simple *bouillies* – in effect porridge or frumenty. Bloch described these as one of the most ancient dishes known to humanity, and accounted in part for its persistence by pointing out that by grinding cereal in primitive mortars and cooking it over the fire at home, the peasant was able to escape the double seigneurial monopoly of the mill and the communal oven. As a result, not only wheaten bread, but bread in any form, spread to certain regions of France surprisingly late – in some cases as late as the nineteeth century. Much the same is true in Britain, where the consumption of cereals in the form of porridges and as an ingredient in broths persisted in Scotland and the North of England until recent times, though bread was more clearly established as the staple in the south of England.

The method of slow boiling in an iron cauldron is particularly associated with the dominance of meals by soup.[2] Certainly there is a great deal of evidence that until into the twentieth century, soup was the staple dish at every meal (including breakfast) for the majority of Frenchmen (Claudian and Serville, 1970: 300–6), and that this trait was of very ancient origin. Stouff writes of fifteenth-century Provence: 'For the majority of people of that time, there was no distinction in a meal between the soup and the plate of meat; the two were but a single thing and, in many cases, it was the only dish of the day' (1970: 258). Scarcely any detail is known about the techniques of making soups; onions, along with cabbage or beans, are thought to have been frequent ingredients, as was parsley.

Even Stouff's very detailed research in Provence revealed very little about the recipes people used, though he speaks of friars cooking meat *à la broche* in the oven, of meat being prepared in a *marmite* with spices, and for Christmas and other special occasions, beef with a pepper sauce. Fish could also sometimes be served with a sauce, but were normally fried, as also were eggs and beans. Of course, no town lacked a *pâtissier*, and pastries made from butchers' meat, poultry and game were very popular. The Pope had them every week, perhaps every day, the bishops ate them frequently, the minor canons on feast days. But they were expensive, and again not easily made in private homes which lacked ovens.

In fact, little is known of domestic cookery in the Middle Ages. Yet what did come to light of it in the course of his study of Provence enables Stouff to give a tentatively negative answer to the question of whether there was at that date any distinctive Provençal cuisine. The tomato, of course, had not yet made its appearance in Europe. Olive oil certainly was used, mainly for frying, but so were nut oil and saindoux. There was a taste for garlic and a preponderance of mutton. But these and other traits which today we think of as typical of Provence were common to all the countries bordering on the Mediterranean. Stouff concludes that soup was the basic food of the peasants, artisans and simple people of Provence, as indeed it was of the mass of people in medieval Europe as a whole. Nor, for that matter, was there anything distinctively Provençal about the festival dishes or the food of the rich, for they shared in the cosmopolitan cuisine of the aristocracy throughout the medieval West. It is that to which we now turn.

THE MEDIEVAL COOKERY MANUSCRIPTS

The surviving medieval manuscripts which describe in any detail the actual cookery and recipes of the period are, needless to say, accounts of the food exclusively of the upper classes. Such manuscripts as do survive are few in number and, moreover, date from the late Middle Ages so that it is impossible to piece together any very reliable picture of change and development in cooking over the long centuries after the decline of the Roman Empire. The difficulty is compounded by the fact that the surviving manuscripts are not sources independent of each other; on the contrary, their authors seem to have copied recipes from each other or from other common sources which have since been lost. Since the same and similar recipes turn up in manuscripts in various parts of Western Europe, it seems highly probable that the food of late medieval courts was similar throughout the continent.

The four best-known cookery manuscripts from late medieval northern Italy all have many points in common with each other, and probably stem from a common source (see Frati, 1899; Guerrini, 1887; Morpurgo, 1890; Zambrini, 1863). The oldest French manuscripts in the Bibliothèque Nationale, the *Liber de cocquina* and the *Tractatus de modo preparandi et condiendi omnia cibaria* described by Mulon (1970), are also based on the same Italian sources. That is true in spite of the fact that the *Liber* at least is believed to be older than the four surviving Italian manuscripts cited. It is thought to derive from the Angevin court at Naples, possibly from as early as 1309. Scattered with French words and allusions to French practice, the *Liber* is in Mulon's words 'a sort of treaty of union between the French and Italian craftsmen . . . an edition of the ultramontane culinary literature revised and corrected to facilitate its use by the French'. The *Tractatus* too, while making reference to French usage, in no way departs from the Italian treatises. Not even the earliest culinary texts actually written in the French tongue, such as the *Enseignemenz qui enseignent à appareiller toutes manières de viandes* (Mulon, 1970: 238), are distinctively French in content.

None of these manuscripts is, however, so famous as the *Viandier* of Taillevent, or the recipe section of the treatise on household management written for his young wife by the *Ménagier de Paris*, or even the *Grand cuisinier de toute cuisine* which is known mainly through later printed editions but existed in many versions and was probably older than either the *Viandier* or the *Ménagier de Paris*. Again, the picture is of a common style of cookery, with many of the same recipes occurring with little change in several of the texts. Guillaume Tirel, called Taillevent, is believed to have lived from around 1312 to 1395, and after serving in several noble households became chief cook to Charles V in 1373 and eventually 'premier écuyer de cuisine' to Charles VI. His manuscript appears to have been compiled between 1373 and 1380. Yet the celebrated *Viandier* was by no means a collection of original dishes invented by Taillevent; it is rather a compilation of dishes gathered from earlier sources. For example, certain recipes which Taillevent gives for keeping and improving wines are found almost word for word in the earlier *Tractatus*, and indeed an earlier version of the *Viandier* as a whole has come to light (Mulon, 1970: 238).

The manuscript known as the *Ménagier de Paris* was written between June 1392 and September 1394 by an elderly townsman as guidance for the fifteen-year-old wife whom he had just married. He was a wealthy and learned man, probably an official connected with some judicial body such as the *parlement* or the Châtelet, 'obviously a member of that solid and enlightened *haute bourgeoisie*, upon which the French monarchy was coming to lean with ever-increasing confidence' (Power, 1928: 1). Quite why a man of that background had such a knowledge of cookery has never been satisfactorily explained. Though well-connected in courtly circles, he shows some caution in emulating the grandest displays of the court; he mentions such elaborate dishes as stuffed pigs, swans and herons, or peacocks cooked and then replaced within their skins and feathers, or glazed chickens and shoulders of mutton, but he does not detail how to make them, because 'it is not a work for a citizen's cook, nor even for a simple knight's and therefore I leave it' (Power, 1928: 36). Yet the recipes which the Ménagier does give are largely copied, with his own comments often added, from *Le Viandier* and from the *Grand cuisinier de toute cuisine*. Once again, then, the cookery of the upper classes is seen to be drawn from a small number of common sources.

Finally, across the Channel are found a number of English cookery manuscripts dating from the Middle Ages. Around 1390 – and thus only a decade after Taillevent and a year or two before the Ménagier set pen to paper – *The Forme of Cury* was written by the master cooks of Richard II, whom they described as 'the best and ryallest viander of all Christian kyngs'. In *The Forme of Cury* (published by Pegge, 1780, and Warner, 1791), and in several slightly later English cookery books dating from the fifteenth century, (see Napier, 1882; R. Morris, 1862; Austin, 1888), are found variations on most of the recipes listed by the *Ménagier de Paris* and by Taillevent. In short, there is abundant evidence that upper-class tables in Italy, France and England were furnished according to a common style, with dishes prepared by methods and according to recipes which were common property across the continent.

But what was the food cooked within this common tradition actually like? The first thing to bear in mind is that the cookery manuscripts deal with made dishes, but courtly meals were dominated by roast meat, to which the various savoury and sweet made dishes provided contrast and relief.[3] On grand occasions, the roast meats were served with some ceremony and skill by the far from menial carver, and eaten by the use of the hands and knife. The made dishes, very often involving sauces or gravy, appear to have been generally eaten with spoons. At any rate, it is a common characteristic that solid ingredients were ground in mortars or puréed, so that the largest pieces or gobbets were no larger than could be eaten with a spoon. Often a great variety of ingredients went into a single dish, and it appears to have been a test of a cook's ingenuity to mask or transform the flavours and textures of ingredients. Certainly a large number of highly flavoured spices are often listed as ingredients of a single dish, and colourings such as saffron (yellow), sandalwood (red), herbs (green) and mulberries (blue) were also frequently used. Sauces were thickened (again no doubt in part for convenience in eating, since food was quite generally eaten off flat trenchers of wood or of bread) by the addition of breadcrumbs, egg yolks or ground almonds – flour was not generally used for liaison until much later.

These general characteristics have often made a decidedly poor impression on later writers equipped with palates attuned to modern taste. Samuel Pegge, who first published *The Forme of Cury*, considered that the recipes it contained do not

> appear by any means to be well calculated for the benefit of recipients, but rather inimical to them. Many of them are so highly seasoned, are such strange and heterogeneous compositions, mere olios and gallimawfryes, that they seem removed as far as possible from the intention of contributing to health; indeed the messes are so redundant and complex, that in regard to herbs [in the recipe for Eourt of Flesh], no less than ten are used, where we should now be content with two or three (Pegge, 1780: xvi–xvii)

And more recently, W. E. Mead, author of a standard work on courtly feasts in medieval England, went so far as to condemn the eaters as well as the cooks:

> Fortunately for the cooks, who prided themselves upon the number of incongruous elements they could combine in one dish without making it uneatable . . . they catered for men and women who were coarse-feeders, whose palates were dulled by sharp sauces, by spiced wines and by pepper, mustard and ginger and cubebs and cardomom and cinnamon with which the most innocent meats and fruits were doctored and disguised until the cook himself could hardly determine from the taste what had entered into the composition. (1931: 60)

In the late twentieth century, familiar as we are with the food of many countries other than our own, we can more easily resist the temptation to such ethnocentric and hodiecentric comments when studying medieval recipes. For although medieval cookery was very different from modern European food, it was, as Anne Willan suggests, not entirely unlike modern Indian cookery,

> not only in its generous use of spices, but also in its habit of heightening flavour with sweet and acid ingredients. . . . Highly flavoured meat dishes were served with bland porridges, or with purées of grains and legumes, a custom also evocative of modern Indian cooking. (1977: 10–11)

In fact the cookery of the medieval upper classes appears to be most closely related to and derived from the cookery of ancient Rome, as known to us principally from the manuscript attributed to the first-century gourmet M. Gaius Apicius (published in English translation in 1936), though it actually dates from several centuries later. Something of the classical tradition is thought to have survived in monastic communities and in aristocratic courts in the more peaceful interludes of the Dark Ages (see R. W. Barber, 1973: 37–45), particularly in France and Italy; certainly copies of the Apician manuscript are known to have been made at the court of Charlemagne.[4] But the record is too sparse for us to be able to detect any definite pattern of development. The cookery recorded in the more plentiful late medieval sources shows elements both of continuity and discontinuity with that of Rome. Anne Willan, from the practising cook's point of view, sums up the continuities as follows:

> Both medieval and Roman cooks shied away from the tough meat of large animals; they had a penchant for purées, and they shared the odd (but hygienic) habit of parboiling food before roasting and part-roasting before boiling. Both set high store by songbirds and fowl of fine plumage, though these were supposed to be inferior in flavour to less showy birds like hen. For Taillevent and Apicius it was unthinkable to cook meat without honey and spices on a lavish scale, and they both loved to transform the appearance and taste of ingredients 'to make of a thousand flavours, one flavour unique', as the Roman Seneca remarked. (1977: 16–19)

However, as Willan goes on to remark, the actual seasonings used in the Apician recipes and in Taillevent's are quite different, and it is probable that what continuity there was rested not on knowledge of the rare manuscripts but on an imperfectly transmitted and slowly changing oral tradition. There is a general impression that medieval cooking had lost a good deal in subtlety compared with Roman. The relative insecurity of food supplies in the Middle Ages discussed in chapter 2, and the lack of variety associated with the disruption of trade networks, would be among the likely reasons for a coarsening and loss of subtlety in medieval food as compared with Roman.

The importance of oral tradition may also help to explain the general vagueness of medieval recipes, particularly with regard to quantities. It may be that the rare written recipes were intended as little more than *aides-mémoire* for literate and high-ranking superintendents of kitchens (such as

Taillevant and the Ménagier's young wife), while the people who did the actual cooking were expected to know by training and experience the appropriate quantities of the various ingredients. Since spices were always expensive, they were the prerogative of the prosperous, but even in their kitchens, it may be that cooks used them with much more restraint, precision and subtlety than the vague instructions to 'take cloves, ginger, pepper, cinnamon, sugar, vinegar' (or whatever) may seem to suggest. Nevertheless, there remains a clear impression that the medieval cook, in the upper reaches of society, used more strong flavourings, both in quantity and variety in a single dish, than would his counterpart in present-day England or France. The effect must often have been to mask completely the 'natural' flavour of the main ingredients, and indeed, then and later, skill in deceiving the palate appears to have been greatly valued.

The traditional explanation for the generous use of spices and other strong sweet and acid flavourings in medieval *haute cuisine* is that, given the rudimentary means of preserving food, they were essential to disguise the unpleasant taste of tainted and salted meat. That cannot be anything like the whole truth, for the use of spices began to change long before there was any significant improvement in methods of preservation. Nor is there any evidence in the surviving manuscripts that the strong flavourings were to be omitted when meat or fish was particularly fresh, which might indicate an underlying preference for the 'natural' flavour. Quite the contrary: it is clear that they were used, and expected to be used, with fresh meat too. Indeed they were used in dishes of all kinds, and for example sprinkled on 'sweet' dishes as well as 'savoury'. The temptation must be resisted to think that medieval people 'really' preferred food more or less similar to that which we eat now, but were compelled by force of circumstance (at least if they could afford it) to eat unpleasantly highly flavoured mixtures designed to obliterate basic tastes. That argument has been undermined by the discrediting of the notion that, following a sweeping autumn slaughter, there was no fresh meat to eat in winter even for the upper classes. Dyer contends that 'the explanation of the nobility's attachment to spices is more likely to be cultural – they provided a link with the sophisticated Mediterranean world' (1983: 194). In any case, as was argued in chapter 1, the idea that there are inbuilt preferences for 'natural', 'original' or '*Ur*-tastes' in food is highly implausible. The overwhelming evidence is that people come positively to like foods which developing social standards define as desirable.

The problem is not so much to explain why the upper classes in the Middle Ages liked food of this kind, but why gradually from the Renaissance onwards their tastes *changed* towards food which was generally *more* elaborate in its preparation, but less reliant on the proliferation of spices. One element in an answer to this question, I would like to suggest, may be as follows. The significance of the vague quantities and very general use of many spices in medieval recipes for dishes of all sorts may be that, however subtly they were perhaps used in the hands of the finest cooks, in general they came to be used a bit like curry powder in the inferior sort of Indian cookery today. That is to say, the dishes became rather undifferentiated and broadly 'tasted the same'. Therefore when, starting in the fifteenth century in Italy and increasingly over the next centuries elsewhere in Europe, social competition through the kitchen and the table exerted particular pressures towards the invention of an ever greater variety of made dishes, the tendency would be for the range of spices and other flavourings used in a particular dish to be smaller, and for greater restraint to be shown generally in their use. This argument would help to explain why *one* moment in the general trend of European culinary development from the Middle Ages to the present day is towards simplification of flavourings, and towards enhancement of the 'natural' and individual taste of the principal constituent of a dish. The beginnings of this manifestation of social competition now require more detailed examination.

PATTERNS OF SOCIAL EMULATION AND COMPETITION

> The struggles between the nobility, the Church and the princes for their shares in the control and the produce of the land run through the entire Middle Ages. In the course of the twelfth and thirteenth centuries a further group emerges as a partner in this play of forces: the privileged town-dwellers, the 'bourgeoisie'.

Using the sociologist's broadest brush, that is how Elias (1939: II, 3) sums up the structure of social contest in medieval Western European society. The actual course of the struggles between these major participants, and the balances of power between them, vary from country to country. But through the late Middle Ages and the Renaissance, the general trend is towards the accumulation of power by the major princes. These struggles and their outcome are eventually reflected in the cultural products of society, including how and what people ate. In detail, of course, processes of development are far more complex, and nothing complicates them more than what Elias (1939: II, 71) calls the 'polyphony of history', the much slower pace of change in one class than in another, which means that 'earlier' and 'later' characteristics in fact co-exist over long periods within a single society.

The Middle Ages can be divided broadly into what Bloch (1939: 59ff.) calls the first and second feudal ages, with the hinge between them located in the eleventh and twelfth centuries. During the first feudal age, centrifugal forces within society were in the ascendant. That is to say, a number of entangled economic, military and political forces tended to diminish the areas over which titular central lords or kings could exercise effective control. The enormous tract of Europe which constituted the Carolingian empire at the beginning of the ninth century first divided into West and East Frankish empires, and then progressively into far smaller units of effective local power;

England too became fragmented for some time into several kingdoms. The reasons are not hard to find. Kings then lacked both central administrations and central paid armies, as well as the fiscal apparatus necessary to maintain either; so even Charlemagne had to reward local subordinates with land from which they maintained themselves. During the era of the Viking invasions, and that of declining trade and increasing local economic autarky which followed, these erstwhile representatives of the central ruler repeatedly transformed themselves into hereditary and in all but name independent rulers of the lands with which they had been enfeoffed. It was an age in which the military function was the key social function, the knights the social class which fulfilled that function, and the fief of land the means by which they were enabled to fulfil it.

The first feudal age was therefore also a period in which, outside Italy, Provence and Languedoc, the knightly class became clearly differentiated from the urban population. Though they would continue to visit the town occasionally for pleasure and to fulfil political functions, a growing majority of nobles came normally to reside on their domains in the country, away from the remaining authority of kings and major magnates which tended still to be centred on the towns. Italy and southern France were an exception because they

> still bore the age-old imprint of the Mediterranean civilisations whose structure had been systematised by Rome. In those regions, each small community was traditionally grouped round a town or large village which was at one and the same time an administrative centre, a market, and a place of refuge; and consequently the normal place of residence of the powerful. These people continued as much as ever to inhabit the old urban centres; and they took part in all their revolutions. In the thirteenth century this civic character was regarded as one of the distinctive traits of the southern nobility. (Bloch, 1939–40: II, 299)

The exception is significant in view of the part which these lands, and Italy in particular, were to play in the cultural – and culinary – developments of the Renaissance. Northern Europe was very different: 'In contrast with Italy, said the Franciscan Salimbene, a native of Parma, who visited the kingdom of St Louis, the towns of France are inhabited only by burgesses; the nobility live on their estates' (Bloch, 1939–40: II, 299).

By the beginning of the second feudal age, when the process of fragmentation through the granting of fiefs had reached its limit and the first signs became evident of a reassertion of centripetal forces, the majority of the nobility were accustomed to live – and that means eat – off their own lands. And, in one manifestation of historical polyphony, this relative self-sufficiency persisted until the close of the Middle Ages and well beyond, alongside the courtly society, courtly culture and courtly cuisine which was beginning to develop. Household accounts even as late as Tudor times show the extent to which a noble household might live off the product of its own estates. Mead (1931: 35) cites the case of the Earl of Derby in 1561, who ate his own beef, mutton, venison, rabbits, game and fish, and drank his own malt and hops in his own beer. The more famous *Northumberland Household Book* (Percy, 1512) shows the same. The Percys were a major noble family in the north of England and

> The metropolis had then few of those attractions which now render it a winter residence of the great; they therefore seldom visited it, except on very particular occasions. They lived indeed with a splendour in their castles that they could maintain in no other place, and enjoyed that degree of respect upon their own domains which they could expect to receive nowhere else. (Warner, 1791: lii)

Yet their everyday fare appears to have been far from splendid – plentiful yes, but elaborate no. The Earl and Countess breakfasted, for example, on three loaves of bread (two of them admittedly were to be manchets, loaves made from the finest flour), a quart of beer, a quart of wine, and then either a chine of boiled mutton or beef, or on fast days two pieces of salt fish, six baked herrings or a dish of sprats. Dinners on fast days (about which more detailed regulations are laid down than for meat days) were not unlike these breakfasts. Capons, chickens, hens and a range of game fowl were to be bought for special occasions, but specifically only for 'my Lord's table' or for that of the steward and chamberlain. Half a century earlier still, in the latter half of the fifteenth century, we have details of the daily menus in the household of Princess Cecily, who as mother of King Edward IV can scarcely be rated as minor nobility (see Warner, 1791: xlviii–xlix). Dinner and supper normally consisted of mutton and beef, boiled or roast, replaced by salt fish, fresh fish and eggs on Fridays, Saturdays and other fast days. Bread and ale were the essential accompaniments.

These illustrations are consistent with Dyer's general conclusions from the household accounts of the large number of English lords and gentry which have now been studied by historians (1983: 191–5). Among the richest magnates, food and drink for the household could cost a third of total income, but in lesser establishments the figure might rise to a half or even two-thirds. These totals were not in the main a result of lavish expenditure on esoteric luxuries. They are largely explained by the size of household a magnate was expected to maintain[5] as much to display his rank and power as to perform domestic, religious and military functions. These provisions appear to have been based on standard allowances of bread and ale. The imported luxuries, wine and spices, accounted for a much smaller proportion of expenditure. Among the greatest magnates, the figure might be as high as 16 per cent, but was often lower. Omitting wine, the figure for spices (a category which also included rice and dried fruits) was normally no more than five per cent.[6] Probably in all but the grandest houses they were not eaten every day, and they would be reserved mainly for members of the family, guests and senior officials dining on the top table, though rules for the elaborate ceremonial of lordly dining usually specify that a sample of the finest food be passed to lower tables and to the poor.[7]

A good deal of Victorian romanticism lingers on in the popular view of the manorial community dining together in hall, like the members of an Oxbridge college, under the paternal eye of their lord.[8]

> though the fine food and spices were kept for the household at the top table, we believe the main dish – the roast beef, the boiled mutton or whatever it was – was shared pretty well throughout the hall (last come worst served). But the sending down of a serving from the top table to the lower was more than a form of patronage. It was a medieval form of supervision. The head of the household thus saw that the servants' dinner was well cooked, and the servants saw that the head *saw them well served*. If it sizzled and smelt good, the head probably directed his page to cut him a slice; and it is very reassuring to any servant to feel that, except for the flavouring and spices 'we have what they have themselves'. (Hartley, 1954: 227)

However, from about the middle of the fourteenth century, it became more common for the lord to eat in a separate chamber, vacating (except on special occasions) to the steward the high table in the hall. Langland complained about this in *Piers Plowman* (*c*. 1390: 115). This division in eating reflected the beginnings of a social division within the household, which had hitherto contained intermediate ranks of gentlemen and yeomen as well as menial servants.

> As a stronger central government produced a more law-abiding country, and as society grew more complex and full of opportunities, there was less and less reason for any but the lower social ranks to put themselves under the protection of the great by entering their service. (Girouard, 1978: 10)

The intermediate ranks gradually disappeared over three centuries or more, but the trend which originated in the mid-fourteenth century eventually led to the household of later centuries, in which the proprietor and his family were separated by a great sense of social distance and of privacy from the bulk of the servants. Even in its beginnings, the withdrawal from the hall to the chamber probably facilitated the separate development of an *haute cuisine* in the grandest households.

What then of the famous feasts? Certainly they took place, but they were by no means a frequent occurrence even in noble households. Mead (1931) rightly emphasises the *excitement* aroused by the rare event of a grand feast, in contrast to the monotony of the typical way of life even of the medieval upper class. The social functions of the grand feast on special occasions, however, were not quite so cosy as the romantic image. Henisch provides a corrective:

> In theory, a feast was the epitome of love and fellowship, and while reality often failed to mirror this ideal, a ceremonial dinner was a visible demonstration of the ties of power, dependence and mutual obligation which bound the host and guests. It was politic for the host to appear generous, because the lavishness of his table gave a clue to his resources; it was wise to be both hospitable to dependents and discriminating in the choice of guests of honour, because the number and calibre of diners in the hall

revealed his importance and his power. . . . Just as the host needed his guests, so they needed his invitation. They wished to show themselves to be a part of his family, and safely under the umbrella of his protection. To be dropped from a guest list could be very alarming. (1976: 56–7)

It is in this light that the great medieval feasts need to be viewed. They were, of course, exciting entertainments, and they were held as celebrations of special occasions of greater or lesser magnitude. The sheer number of guests and vast supplies of food assembled from great distances for the most enormous of these feasts such as the Nevill banquet at York in 1465 (Warner, 1791: 93–106, see chapter 2 above) meant that such events were scarcely commonplace. But these and many smaller-scale events were not merely entertainments and celebrations – they were a means of asserting social rank and power, and a means of doing so which was perhaps becoming more attractive and significant for the nobility as the process of internal pacification was progressively limiting their opportunities to resort to warfare as a means of establishing their standing over their fellow noble subjects of the king.[9]

In this respect, there are possibly parallels in social function between the late medieval banquets and the famous institution of potlatching among the Kwakiutl Indians of British Columbia. The Kwakiutl were a tribe remarkably preoccupied with social rank and prestige, and devoted great effort to accumulating varied goods from canoes to pots and pans, cloth, sewing machines, zinc wash-boilers and especially blankets (useful goods in themselves, but in quantities far beyond what was usefully needed), which they then gave away to their rivals and followers at ostentatious potlatch feasts. The more property they were able to shower on their rivals, the greater their prestige. Most prestigious of all were the 'grease potlatches', at which actual destruction of property occurred: tub after tub of valuable oulachen oil was poured on the fire, causing it to burn up, singeing the blankets worn by the participants and even setting fire to the roof. In due course, recipients would give a potlatch of their own in return, distributing still greater quantities of goods to reassert their own rank and prestige. Interestingly, although the potlatch had been a key Kwakiutl social institution since before contact with the white man, after contact it grew very much in scale, not only because of the opportunities which arose for accumulating manufactured goods for potlatching, but because Europeans set about suppressing warfare and violence among the Kwakiutl, and 'fighting with weapons' appears to have been replaced by the functional alternative of 'fighting with property' (Codere, 1950).

So, in a similar light, it is probable that sheer volume and indeed waste of food was inherent in and necessary to the social function of such events as the Nevill banquet. The flocks of sheep, herds of cattle, gaggles of geese, shoals of fish and schools of porpoise mustered for the occasion bore only a remote and incidental relation to the nutritional requirements and capacities of the principal guests. Rather it was almost the other way round: the number of mouths would in a sense be determined by the quantity of food it was deemed necessary to distribute. For this reason, there is little evidence that the *quality* of cooking played much part in the success of these occasions. Quantity was all. Even the banquets at the court of Burgundy in the fifteenth century are not famous particularly for the skill of the Dijon cooks but for the enormous jumbled heaps of food: the meal, we are told, 'was composed of several courses, each made up of a large number of items habitually served in a pyramid on a single great dish, among which were often found animals – pigs, calves, even oxen – roasted whole' (Gottschalk, 1948a: I, 337).

Yet the Burgundian feasts are symptomatic of the accretion of power to the major princely courts which had taken place through the reassertion of centripetal forces during the second feudal age. And, as *The Forme of Cury*, Taillevent, the *Ménagier* and other late medieval cookery manuscripts show, something like a more elaborate cookery was clearly emerging in certain courts and urban centres. How is this process of social and cultural development to be understood? That certain lords gained initial advantages in the struggle for survival over their neighbours was often no doubt due to accidents of geography and of history, including the exceptional military skills and successes of particular individuals. But the longer term trend of development from about the eleventh or twelfth centuries onwards for richer lords progressively to gain ascendancy over their smaller rivals owed a great deal to the revival of trade and markets. While minor lords continued to live off the produce of their estates and were minimally involved in the growing network of trading relationships, the growth of trade benefited the greater lords far more. It was not merely that they tended to have larger agricultural surpluses to bring to market, but that they were more closely bound up with the revival of the towns.

> the growing settlements of artisans and traders, the towns, generally attached themselves to the fortresses and administrative centres of the great dominions, and however uncertain relations between the great lords and the communes within their territory might still be, however much they wavered between mistrust, hostility, open struggle and peaceful agreement, in the end they too, and the duties flowing from them, strengthened the great lords as compared with the smaller ones. They offered them opportunities of escaping the perpetual cycle of land investiture in exchange for services, and subsequent appropriation of land by the vassal – opportunities that counteracted the centrifugal forces. At the courts of the great lords, by virtue of their direct or indirect involvement in the trade network, whether through raw materials or in coined or uncoined precious metal, a wealth accumulated that the majority of lesser lords lacked. (Elias, 1939: II, 67)

As the great feudal lords progressively emerged as the richest and most powerful men in their region, there grew both the desire and the opportunity to express this power through the splendour of their courts. For several centuries, until towards the end of the medieval period, the great feudal lords were richer not only than other knights, but also far more so than any burgher; and for this reason, the great courts had much greater cultural significance than the towns. One of the earliest manifestations of the cultural role of the courts was the emergence of the *Minnesänger* and troubadours, usually educated but poor and landless offspring of the knightly class, poets and musicians who celebrated the achievements and grandeur of their patrons (Elias, 1939: II, 66ff.) Great banquets and, at a later stage, fine food, were also a means of demonstrating the power and splendour of the court and its ruler. Knowledge of the tradition of fine cooking and eating descending from antiquity probably survived in very isolated centres, perhaps in monasteries as is often said, but there is little reason to suppose it was common even in great courts until late in the Middle Ages. For example, food at the court of Henry II, king of England and ruler of more of what is now France than were the Parisian kings in the first half of the thirteenth century, is said to have been plain and of indifferent quality (Pullar, 1970: 88–9). That is not unexpected, for even the greatest courts, though connected with the growing trade networks through the sale of surplus produce, through the levying of duties, and through the purchase of luxury goods including spices, for long still relied for the bulk of their everyday needs on the produce of their domains.

Nor, as the *haute cuisine* took hold in such courts as those of Richard II, Charles V and Charles VI, is there any reason to suppose it would have diffused very widely in society. Cultural contact between the courts of Western Europe was close (even if they were often at war with each other); the general tradition of medieval *haute cuisine* and even particular recipes were, as we have seen, common to courts in Italy, France and England. But cultural influence between court and court remained for a long time stronger than between the courtly strata and other strata within the same country. For, as Elias reminds us, the agrarian world and the minor lords or knights who ruled it remained for long little changed by the growing money economy.

> The barter sector of society which, in the Middle Ages and for long after, comprised the great majority of the people, was certainly not untouched. . . . But despite all the upheavals, the pace of real changes in it was, compared to that in other strata, very small. It is not 'without history'; but in it, for a very large number of people in the Midle Ages and for a smaller number even in recent times, the same living conditions were constantly reproduced. Here, uninterruptedly, production and consumption were carried on predominantly in the same place within the framework of the same economic unit; the supra-local integration with other regions of society is traceable only late and indirectly. (Elias, 1939: II, 71)

Nevertheless, in the late Middle Ages, there are already some signs of the social diffusion of courtly cuisine. We have already noted how the *Ménagier de Paris*'s recipes are essentially the same as those of Taillevent and other courtly cooks, and the Ménagier was not a noble but a townsman – albeit one who had strong links with courtly circles. Another sign of what the courtly nobility may have felt to be pressure from below by the emulation of courtly dishes may be the disdain for butchers' meat at the grandest banquets in the sixteenth century: if such meat had been so abundant for all classes in the previous two centuries, one aristocratic response may have been to displace it from their tables and replace it with the less easily obtained game. The social prestige of the white, wheaten, bread at first eaten only by the upper classes, can be traced back to the Middle Ages in both England and France. Finally, as was suggested in chapter 2, the sumptuary laws of the late Middle Ages may be a symptom of social 'pressure from below' in the form of the emulation of courtly eating by non-noble strata. All these are signs that by the end of the medieval period the place of princely courts as style-setting centres in matters of food, as of much else, had been established. It was to go much further in the following centuries.

4

From Renaissance to Revolution: Court and Country Food

When did the ancient tradition of medieval cooking and patterns of eating begin to give way to something more closely resembling modern tastes? How did more distinct national tastes in food begin to emerge out of the common European tradition? Was there a dramatic breakthrough, or was it altogether more gradual? Certainly the date – 1494 – at which by long convention the Middle Ages are reckoned to come to an end, and Professors of Medieval History hand over their responsibilities to the Professors of Modern History, does not mark any very apparent transformation in eating habits.

Even in the seventeenth century, upper-class banquets, such as the Star Chamber dinners described by André Simon (1959), often remained occasions for fairly unsophisticated quantitative display and for prodigious feats of meat-eating. Away from the courts and the towns, the pace of change was slow. The rural gentry both of England and France continued to live well but largely self-sufficiently from the produce of their estates, even if in the course of the sixteenth and seventeenth centuries they were gradually tied more into the money economy and thus able to purchase small quantities of exotic or luxury foods.[1]

Lower down the rural social scale change could be almost imperceptible. Apart from the adoption in some regions of new foods such as maize and the potato, the broad outlines neither of the peasants' diet nor even of their recipes seem to have changed very much between the Renaissance and the Revolution. Country dwellers in most parts of Europe continued to live principally on soup, black bread, eggs and dairy produce. Soup especially remained the staple dish of rural France. It could be a rich broth, permanently stewing with constant additions, or it could be an 'instant soup' of the sort described by a traveller in south-west France in 1789:

> the bread is all ready in a big wooden dish, with a little knob of butter, and then the boiling water is poured over it. Voila! That's the soup. A clove of garlic and a raw onion grated by the cook and sprinkled over the soup – that's the seasoning, the last word in culinary fashion. The soup is served; it's excellent. One eats it with a wooden spoon. (Vaultier, 1940: 80–1)

Philip Oyler (1950: 24) describes something only a little more elaborate than this in the Dordogne between the wars in the present century.

Soup must have once been equally widespread a dish throughout England, for Andrew Boorde (1542) writes that 'Potage is not so much used in all Chrystendom as it is used in England.' In southern England, however, soups seem to have declined in popularity by the late eighteenth century. Not that this marked an improvement in country fare, for Sir Frederick Eden in his great survey of *The State of the Poor* complained that the poorest labourers in the south were 'habituated to the unvarying meal of dry bread and cheese from week's end to week's end' (1797: I, 497). Eden bemoaned the fact that even if labourers were rich enough to afford meat once a week, they cooked it by only the very simplest methods – roasting or plain boiling – not thinking to make it into a soup which would, he considered, have been both more tasty and more nutritious. Their lack of all but the simplest facilities for cooking was not the explanation, for Eden pointed out that the rural poor of Scotland and the north of England ate better with equally simple equipment. In recommending the diet of the north for adoption (or re-adoption) in the south, he described in some detail (1797: I, 497–532) not only the broths made from a little meat, oatmeal and barley, and pot-herbs, but also a number of other simply made dishes which suggest strong continuity with the peasant food (especially *bouillies*) of medieval Europe – pease-pudding, oatmeal porridge or 'hasty-pudding', crowdie (similar, but made with water or stock), and frumenty (boiled barley with skimmed milk). These ancient dishes may not have disappeared entirely even from the south, for Thomas Hardy depicts Michael Henchard, in *The Mayor of Casterbridge* (1886) eating 'furmity', in this case made from wheat and currants and raisins boiled in milk and laced with rum, at Weydon Fair in the 1840s.

Evidence of persistence in the diet and even the recipes of the peasantry is thus plentiful in both England and France. Class differences in eating at the end of the eighteenth century would appear to have been as marked as – in certain respects possibly more marked than – they had been in the Middle Ages. For against this background of continuity, very marked changes can be traced in the *haute cuisine* of the upper and middle classes, and perhaps in the food of townspeople in general. It is generally supposed that courts in the cities of Renaissance Italy made a decisive break with the medieval style of cookery common to the whole of Western Europe; that the cooks who accompanied Cathérine de'Medici on her journey from Florence in 1533 to marry the future Henri II introduced the Italian cookery to France; and that the French rapidly raised it to new heights of elegance and assumed for themselves the culinary hegemony of Europe. A distinct and distinguished French tradition of cookery is thus traced back to the sixteenth century, while the establishment of a rather different English style is usually placed a little later, in the eighteenth century. The evidence for this time-honoured interpretation is, however, fairly slender and rather complex; the processes of culinary development appear to have been more gradual than often supposed, and explaining them is not altogether a straightforward task. In one respect, however, the end of the Middle Ages did coincide with a cultural watershed – the invention of the printed book, which had its effects in the world of cookery as in so many spheres of culture.

GUTENBERG AND THE COOK

Printing, to state the obvious, made possible a great increase in the circulation of knowledge and ideas, and was associated with a considerable extension of literacy. Already by 1500, presses had been set up in 250 European cities, and about twenty million books of all kinds had been printed at a time when the total population of Europe was only about eighty million (Burke, 1978: 250). That their readership was increasingly not confined to a tiny learned élite is evident from the small chapbooks printed by even the earliest presses, and from the burgeoning array of popular literature in the sixteenth, seventeenth and eighteenth centuries (see Davis, 1975: 189–226).

What effects did printing and literacy have in general? Anthropologists and historians (such as Goody, 1968, 1977; Eisenstein, 1968) have argued that the fixing of a text in an objective, written, form makes it available for discussion and criticism in a way that oral traditions are not. The text in question may be a scientific theory, a code of behaviour (as represented in manners books, for example), a recipe, or anything else. The process of criticism of a text is likely to bring about an accelerated rate of change and rationalisation. Printing, in turn, amplifies these effects, and enlarges the circle of potential participants in the critical process. In cooking as in the case of other social phenomena like codes of manners, fashions in clothing, or styles of eating, printing also very much facilitates the process of social emulation – of the habits, styles and interests of one class or stratum by another. Yet it should not be thought that printing led to rapid cultural homogenisation. In early modern Europe it reduced certain social divisions but enhanced others. Peter Burke (1978: 270ff.) has argued that it was one powerful force promoting the 'withdrawal' of the upper classes from popular culture. At the close of the Middle Ages, popular culture was everyone's culture, in the sense that the educated participated in it as a second culture and it was the only culture for everyone else. Peasant and priest, artisan and noble shared to a significant extent a common culture of intellectual and religious interests, moral and political assumptions, but over the next three centuries this common ground dwindled very markedly. There was a sharpening of boundaries between city dwellers and peasants, and between the educated urban élite and the illiterate urban labourer. This happened in part because the effect of wider literacy, amplified by printing, made it possible for the literate, learned culture to evolve far more rapidly than the traditional culture of the less educated classes.

European popular culture was far from static for these three hundred years, but it did not, indeed could not, change so fast. . . . [T]here were all sorts of contacts between learned culture and popular culture. . . . However, this was not enough to prevent the gap between learned and popular culture widening, for oral and visual traditions could not absorb rapid change, or, to vary the metaphor, they were resilient to change, accustomed to taking the new and transforming it into something very like the old. A rapidly changing popular culture . . . would have been impossible in early modern Europe, which lacked the institutional and economic base for it. Even if the necessary schools could have been founded and the schoolmasters paid, many craftsmen and peasants could not have afforded to do without the contributions made by the labour of their children. (Burke, 1978: 281)

What are the implications of this specifically for the world of cookery and eating? One thing is certain: cookery books feature among the earliest of printed books. The very first printed cookery book appears to have been the celebrated *Kuchenmeisterey*, published at Nuremberg in 1485 and reissued in a total of 56 editions, of which 13 were incunabula. By the mid-sixteenth century, books of cookery had been printed in most of the main languages of Western Europe. From then onwards, such books form a valuable source of information about food, eating and cookery. Yet they have to be interpreted with some caution, for the connection between what is presented in the books and what was actually happening in the kitchens and dining rooms is always problematic. In Alain Girard's opinion, 'the first century of printing did no more than increase the circulation of the manuscript texts of the previous age' (1982: 108) – even though that century is widely believed to have been one in which tastes in food at least in courtly circles began to develop markedly. In the later period of the seventeenth and eighteenth centuries, Elizabeth David believes – on the basis of far deeper familiarity with the sources than I can begin to claim – that there was typically a lag of up to four decades between changes in practice occurring in the English kitchen and their appearance in the cookery books. Yet in other cases, especially in eighteenth-century France, some of the books appear to represent the very latest culinary fashions or even to run ahead of them. One reason for uncertainty about such lags and leads is that we only imperfectly understand how early cookery books were used, and by whom. Were they, for instance, written by practising cooks for the use of fellow practitioners, or were they written as a record of high fashion by and for a literate élite who only vicariously commanded operations in the kitchen?

One clue is that most of even the earliest sources of actual recipes – both the late medieval manuscripts and then printed books – are written in the vulgar languages rather than in Latin. That is a strong hint that they were written by practitioners for practitioners. It is true that there are Latin sources which contain a good deal of information about food, but these tend to be essentially medical works and manners books. They are typified respectively by the numerous manuscript and printed versions of the *Regimen sanitatis salerni*, the Salerno school's widely influential prescriptions for good health dating originally from the eleventh century, and by Platina's *De Honesta Voluptate* (1475). The latter does contain a collection of actual recipes, but they are now known to derive from a manuscript, in Italian, by a cook named Martino. Although medical texts and manners books often contained discussions of food, from the point of view of health and of fashionable dining respectively, and although some recipe books continued for some time to include sections of medical recipes and for even longer explained to their readers the correct sequence and composition of courses, cookery books rapidly emerged as a genre distinct from books about either medicine or manners. So were they read and used by cooks themselves, or merely read by members of the gentry and high officials of noble households, who used them in order to give instructions to their cooks?

There is no reason why that question need have a clear-cut answer. Probably both things happened; and, in any case, there is very little direct evidence on which to base an answer. Indirectly, however, the growing body of historical evidence on the extent of literacy among the population at large in early modern Europe may throw a little light on the question.

Few governments before the nineteenth century collected precise statistics of literacy among their subjects, and estimates have to be inferred by such means as calculations of the ratio of signatures to marks in various official documents. The ability to sign one's name is not the same as the ability to read fluently, but it is believed that the two skills are correlated, rather more people being able to read than to write their name. Such evidence suggests that a more substantial minority of ordinary people were able to read than was once thought, and that rates of literacy increased considerably between the Renaissance and the French Revolution (Cipolla, 1969). Literacy rose rapidly at a fairly early stage in parts of Italy and in England. Lawrence Stone (1964)[2] has spoken of an 'educational revolution' in England between 1540 and 1640, and it has been estimated that by 1660 possibly between a third and a half of adult males were able to read – perhaps twice as many as a century earlier. In France, the comparable increase took place later, between 1650 and 1800 (Furet and Ozouf, 1983). At all stages it was broadly true that Protestants were more likely to be able to read than were Catholics, men more likely than women and, perhaps of particular significance for our present purposes, many more craftsmen than peasants were literate. It may therefore not be entirely coincidental that many more new cookery books were published in Italy and England than in France before 1650, that then and later they appear to have been written chiefly by working craftsman-cooks (with occasional contributions from intellectuals and courtiers), and by men rather than women (with the exception of eighteenth-century England, when women wrote the most notable books). Finally, the persistence of illiteracy in the countryside no doubt helps to explain the relative slowness with which cooking, like so much else, changed there in comparison with the pace of the courts and cities.

It remains to ask whether simply writing down recipes, and subsequently their wider dissemination through printing, have implications for the theory and practice of cookery in the same way that, it has been argued, literacy has had for other aspects of thought, custom and culture. Again, an answer must be to some extent speculative, but writers such as Girard (1982) have made suggestions which are consistent with at least the broad outlines of culinary development. The written collection of recipes, and still more the printed book, had a number of interesting possible consequences within an increasingly literate circle of professional cooks. *First* of all, they broke the absolute dependence of the transmission of culinary knowledge and skill on apprenticeship and direct personal relationship, and made possible a wider transmission of knowledge than any oral tradition of word and gesture. *Secondly*, writing down a recipe tends to enhance its prescriptive character; the imperative tone of early recipes is very striking – indeed the word 'recipe' itself, as well as some other extinct or equivalent words such as 'nym' in the north of England (see Warner, 1791: 37–49), means 'take', typically the first command in the instructions for each dish. Furthermore, with printed cookery books, recipes came to be labelled with titles more consistently than in the manuscript collections. The identity of a dish and its ingredients consequently became more firmly fixed, and the scope for idiosyncratic improvisation diminished. At a later stage more precise quantities came to be specified, thus making recipes still more imperative in character. In these ways, the written and printed collection of recipes may have exerted pressures towards conformity and thus to conservatism.

Yet there were also pressures towards innovation and change. For it must be remembered, *thirdly*, that books made possible the much more rapid accumulation and wider diffusion of a record of *successful* culinary practice and experience. While this may have led some cooks to rely conservatively on what was written down as tried and proven, the very production of recipes as written texts made them available for replication, testing and improvement within a community of cooks. The speed of culinary change in the first centuries after the advent of printing should not be exaggerated, though it gradually accelerated to the point that in eighteenth-century France the latest recipes and styles of eating had become part of high fashion. By then, cookery books record not only a constant process of refinement, sometimes of originally quite ordinary peasant dishes into dishes of great cost, subtlety and delicacy for the aristocratic table, but also processes of popularisation of aristocratic dishes for the tables of the less wealthy and less discriminating. That is to look to the future. But a *fourth* possible effect of the growth of a literate culinary culture can be discerned rather earlier. That was the increasing technical cohesion and social prestige of a professional élite of cooks in the service of members of the upper class, sharing a common repertoire of methods and even of recipes.

These developments were not, of course, all solely the consequence of the advent of books alone. The printed book itself reflected developments in the structure of Western European society. In particular, the production of printed books presupposed the emergence of publishers and booksellers, and of a market for books. That in turn was part of a complex of interrelated processes accelerating in the late Middle Ages and the early modern period – an advancing division of labour, the growth of the money economy and development of markets for all sorts of goods, these in turn in part depending on and in part facilitating the increasing strength and scope of state administration and a growth in the security of everyday life. All in all, chains of social interdependence in society were growing longer and more interwoven, and this in itself promoted the diffusion of upper-class cultural models more widely through society than had been the case in the Middle Ages. Nevertheless, the book did have subtle effects of its own both in the world of cooking, and in the wider sphere of cultural life as a whole – in which it is increasingly appropriate to include cookery.

For cooks and cooking were beginning 'to pass from the ignoble world of craft to the prestigious domain of art' (Girard, 1982). The written word eventually helped to promote a striving for 'originality' and 'personalisation' in cookery as it did in the arts generally. This is not evident so early in cookery as it is, for example, in painting. Nevertheless, its beginnings can be seen in the dedication of recipes to particular noble patrons in the seventeenth century; by the eighteenth they are beginning to be attributed by name to specific cooks; in the nineteenth, the cookery book as a work of art and record of the personal achievements of the distinguished chef becomes common.

Even if the trend towards individuality in taste and culinary creation only became very obvious in the eighteenth and nineteenth centuries, traces of it can be found much earlier, and it is not unreasonable to see it as rooted in a more general transformation of art and consciousness which began during the Renaissance. Until then, it would perhaps have been true to say of cooks even in the employ of kings and nobles that:

> Their hand is guided and held by their tradition. Their ambition is not to create a shape and a pattern which is different from those anybody has created before, but rather to create the same or almost the same shape and pattern as their ancestors and masters with particular skill and perfection. That does not mean that there is no scope at all for individual variations and certainly not that there is no sense of individual achievement. But the achievement does not consist in the assertion and representation of one's unique personality through one's work. (Elias, 1970: 8)

These words are in fact a description of West African craftsmen in the present century, and they are being contrasted with artists in more developed societies who strive very consciously to produce original works of art, shapes and patterns which are as far as possible unique and unlike any others that have been made before. Works of art are valued particularly highly if they bear the imprint of an individual personality whose distinct and personal style is easily recognisable. 'Although we may not be aware of it, this type of art shows quite unmistakably the high degree of self-consciousness with which it is produced' (Elias, 1970: 7). The beginnings of this transformation towards greater self-consciousness were traced in the art of the Italian Renaissance by Jakob Burckhardt in his classic work (1860); and it is to Renaissance Italy that the beginnings of modern cookery are also most often traced.

HAUTE CUISINE: FROM ITALY TO FRANCE[3]

The hypothesis of Italy's culinary leadership of Europe in the sixteenth century rests in good measure on the influence of Martino's collection of recipes, which appeared as a sort of appendix to *De Honesta Voluptate* (1475), the Latin disquisition on good food and sober living by Bartolomeo Sacchi, known as Platina. Martino's recipes and techniques do mark the beginnings of a break with the common European tradition of medieval cookery, and the faint origins of trends which were to become more marked later. Anne Willan summarises Martino's innovations as follows:

> Martino has little time for outmoded purées and porridges, preferring more substantial dishes containing pieces of meat or whole birds in a sauce – the ancestors of the French ragoûts. His vegetables are usually cooked whole, then sliced and served with a sprinkling of cheese or fried as fritters. The old tendency to disguise foods, whether by spicing them heavily or mixing them indiscriminately is disappearing. . . . On the contrary, Martino tries to bring out the flavour of a single ingredient by careful and moderate cooking. . . . Martino also has several soups based on a meat broth, thickened with eggs and breadcrumbs or almonds. (1977: 31)

De Honesta Voluptate was much translated over the next century, and Martino's recipes were widely copied; another collection by Giovanni de Rosselli (1513), largely based on Martino, appeared in English as *Epulario, or The Italian Banquet* as late as 1598. Yet the case for Italian culinary leadership in sixteenth-century Europe is not strong. Until half way through the century, Italian cookery books mainly demonstrate the strong influence of Martino and continuities from the fifteenth century, without there being much evidence of further development. Only in the second half of the sixteenth century are there signs of vigorous renewal and forward movement in such books as Cristoforo di Messisbugo's *Banchetti* of 1549 and particularly Bartolomeo Scappi's *Opera* of 1570. Scappi's beautifully printed manual demonstrates a considerable advance in technique – methods such as marinating, braising and poaching are prominent and 'the new interest in *stufatori* [stews], which retained the meat juices and blended the flavours by gentle cooking, was typical of a more sophisticated approach to cooking' (Willan, 1977: 37).

Generally the Italian cookery books of the later sixteenth century show more varied dishes, with a diminishing proportion of recipes concerned with meat and increasing attention paid to vegetables, fruit, pastries, charcuterie including mortadella, salcizzoni and patés, soups and *minestre*. Among the latter, pasta dishes were not new – lasagne and macaroni are recorded a couple of centuries earlier – but they underwent development. In short, Scappi and his Italian contemporaries represent not only the most elegant cuisine in Europe but one which, even before the tomato achieved its later dominance, is recognisably and distinctly Italian in style. So it is clear that Italian cooks working in Italian courts in some sense anticipated the later work of French cooks at French courts in forming an elegant courtly cuisine in a marked national style.

Yet to allow that the Italians were *pioneers* is not quite the same as saying they were *leaders*. For the works of Scappi and his contemporaries, which more decisively than Martino mark a break with the medieval past, were *not* in fact translated into other European languages. That does not mean, of course, that particular recipes were not copied and adapted in France, England and elsewhere, though if they were, there is very little evidence of it in the cookery books printed in those languages. Of the prestige of all things Italian in the countries to the north during the sixteenth century there can be no doubt; one has only to think of the influence of Italy on English art and literature in the period (see Einstein, 1902). We know too that members of Italian 'cultural élites' migrated in significant numbers to early modern France (Isakovics, 1976), and it has popularly been supposed that Cathérine de'Medici's cooks introduced Italian food to the French court and laid the foundations for the development of French cuisine out of Italian. A later Medici queen of France, Marie de'Medici, wife of Henri IV, is alternatively credited with the same achievement at the beginning of the seventeenth century. Yet there is very little firm evidence for any of this – no chefs known by name, and little or no sign of their efforts in the surviving menus of banquets, which neither in France nor for that matter in Italy reveal that the elegant cuisine of a Scappi was at all widespread. Of one Italian cook, brought to France by his employer, the Italian Cardinal Caraffa, we do have a vivid account, for Montaigne describes a conversation with him:

> I made him give an account of his responsibilities. He gave me a discourse on this science of supping with a grave and magisterial countenance, as if he were speaking of some grand point of theology. He unravelled differences in appetite for me: the appetite one has at the outset, and that which one has after the second and third courses; the means of sometimes appealing to it in simple ways, sometimes reawakening and stimulating it; the rules regarding sauces, first in general and then particularising the qualities of ingredients and their effects; the different salads according to their season, what must be served hot and what cold, and the ways of decorating and embellishing them to make them even more pleasing in appearance. After that, he embarked on the order of courses, full of important and fine considerations. . . . And all this bloated with grand and magnificent words, such as

one might use in describing the government of an empire. (Montaigne, 1595b: Book I, Essay 51)

This Italian was plainly a pioneer gastronome, and his preoccupations with order and balance anticipate the ways in which the theory of good taste eventually espoused in French gastronomy differed radically from the medieval. But it is perhaps at least as significant that Montaigne recounts the conversation in the essay entitled 'On the Vanity of Words', because we have very little evidence of native French developments before the mid-sixteenth century. Root (1958: 67) speculates from a comparison of the roughly contemporary kitchens at Fontainebleau and Hampton Court that French cooking was already far more sophisticated than English by the early sixteenth century; but this is very flimsy evidence. Cookery books are admittedly also far from conclusive evidence, but for what they are worth, French cookery books of the sixteenth century (far fewer in number than in England) continued to be versions of medieval texts like Taillevent and the *Grand cuisinier de toute cuisine*. Nor, according to Jean-Francois Revel, is there much evidence in the accounts of sixteenth-century court banquets, whether in Italy or France, of any decisive break with medieval styles and customs; all this leads Revel (1979: 151ff.) to pour scorn on what he calls *le fantôme des Medicis*. Revel probably overstates his case, but certainly it seems to be true, as Girard (1982: 11) more judiciously phrases it, that 'the impact of Italy in sixteenth-century France was limited to importing the transalpine cooks into the service of a narrow élite of the nobility and courtly circles'.

Indisputable literary evidence of the emergence of a distinctively French style of cooking is not found until the publication in 1651 of La Varenne's *Le Cuisinier François*, the cookery book which is generally accepted as first showing both a clear break with medieval food and the recognisable beginnings of the modern French cuisine.[4] Not only La Varenne's food but the format of his book set patterns for later development. It is prefaced by a 'dedicatory letter' addressed to the Marquis d'Uxelles, whom La Varenne served as *écuyer de cuisine*; its combination of cringing social humility with professional pride was to prove characteristic of later efforts in the same vein:

Monseigneur: although my condition does not fit me to aspire to the heroic spirit, it nevertheless gives me enough pride not to forget my duty. In your house I have, during ten years of employment there, discovered the secret of the most delicate preparation of dishes. I am bold enough to say that I followed this profession to great approbation from Princes, Marshals of France, and many persons of rank who have greatly admired your table in Paris and with the armies.

The book begins with tables of foods in season throughout the year, and then the first recipe given is for *bouillon* or stock which, in the hands of later cooks, was to develop into the *fonds de cuisine* fundamental to the creation of the array of sauces characteristic of classical French cuisine. La Varenne, unlike many later authors, does not have a separate section devoted specifically to sauces, but he uses his *bouillon* as the basis for 61 different soups. It is also an ingredient in many other dishes, the cooking juices of which are frequently reduced in the final stages to concentrate the flavour and form a sauce. Fairly typical is La Varenne's recipe for a dish which has remained commonplace to the present day, *boeuf à la mode* or beef pot roast: 'Pound the beef well and lard it with fat bacon, then put it to cook in a pot with good *bouillon*, a *bouquet* and all sorts of spices, and when everything is *bien consommé*, serve it with the sauce.'

Several things are worthy of note: the use of the bouquet garni to flavour the sauce; the process of reduction to concentrate the flavours implied in the words *bien consommé*; but also a certain surviving medieval imprecision in the instruction to use 'all sorts of spices'. On the whole, however, the multi-flavoured purées, as well as the penchant for exotic flesh and fowl characteristic of medieval cookery, have disappeared from La Varenne's cuisine. In contrast, he particularly favours the slow cooking in liquid of single pieces of familiar butchers' meats, and there can be seen the beginnings of the enormous array of delicately prepared French 'made dishes', which the English often referred to contemptuously as 'kickshaws' (a corruption of *quelque chose*).

La Varenne introduced – at least to the reading public for the first time – certain notable technical innovations, including the use of egg whites in clarifying consommé and the use of a roux of fat and flour to thicken a sauce. Nevertheless one should not exaggerate the suddenness or completeness of La Varenne's break with the past. Medieval survivals can be found, for example, in the spices used, and in the mixture of ingredients strange to modern palates. Both the innovations and the survivals can be seen in his recipe for *Poulets d'Inde à la framboise farcy*. The turkeys are cooked rather simply, and the sauce is thickened with a roux of pork fat and flour; but at the end he adds 'If raspberries are in season, throw a handful on top'. A mixture of tastes equally curious to later palates is seen in La Varenne's table of *entremets*, which juxtaposes meats, offal, ham, chicken, salads, vegetables, almond and lemon pastes, and *crèmes*; the single category of *entremets* was later to become much more finely differentiated.

It is not plausible to see La Varenne as an isolated revolutionary; the innovations he records must have been developing for some time in aristocratic kitchens such as that of which La Varenne had charge. Though La Varenne's book proved uniquely popular, circulating widely in numerous editions for the best part of a century and appearing in English translation as early as 1653, it was rapidly followed by others. There were Nicholas de Bonnefons's *Les Délices de la campagne*(1654), Pierre de Lune's *Le Cuisinier* (1656), *L'Escole parfaite des officiers de bouche* (1662) published by Jean Ribou, *L'Art de bien traiter* (1674) signed L.S.R., and in 1691 the first edition of Massialot's *Le Cuisinier roïal et bourgeois*. Taken together, these books make apparent certain other departures from medieval cookery. They show the rise of a butter-based cookery – butter, like other dairy produce, had not been greatly associated with the aristocratic cooking of the Middle Ages. Gradually too, fat-based sauces were displacing the acidic ones based on vinegar or verjuice which had been widely used before. There was also a gradual trend away from the use of the old strongly flavoured exotic spices, and an increased reliance on common herbs, especially parsley and thyme. Flandrin, Hyman and Hyman (1983) point to the paradox that just when the tastes and manners of the aristocracy were being strongly distanced from those of popular culture, aristocratic cooking was abandoning the spices which had hitherto been its most important distinguishing mark. The paradox was only apparent: by the seventeenth century, Portuguese and Dutch merchants had made spices accessible to the bourgeoisie, and what now came to distinguish the aristocratic table was not only the abundance and richness of dishes, but their delicacy.

Even more clearly than the recipes themselves, the prefaces to these books show clearly for the first time that people were conscious of changes taking place in culinary taste. The authors vitriolically denounce their predecessors and rivals, proclaiming the superior elegance and modishness of their own recipes. In these polemics one can discern certain strands of a new culinary aesthetic which was to be carried more fully into culinary practice in the eighteenth century. A growing diversity of dishes is favoured, but so is greater simplicity of ingredients and preparation in each. Bonnefons expresses this well:

> nothing pleases people more than diversity, and the French especially have a particular inclination towards it. That is why you should try as much as you can to diversify what you are preparing and make them distinct in both taste and appearance. Let a *potage de santé* be a good domestic broth, well enriched with good and carefully-chosen meats, and reduced into *bouillon*, with no chopped vegetables, mushrooms, spices, nor any other ingredients, but let it be simple, since it bears the description 'healthy'; and let the cabbage soup taste entirely of cabbage, a leek soup of leeks, a turnip soup of turnips, and so one, leaving elaborate mixtures of chopped meat, diced vegetables, breadcrumbs and other deceptions for the kinds of dishes which are for simply tasting rather than filling oneself up on. . . . What I say about soup I mean to apply generally as a law for everything that is eaten. (Bonnefons, 1654: 213–14)

Also prominent in this emerging aesthetic are a preoccupation with bringing order into the old and reprehensible disorder and superfluity, and a sense of the correct and incorrect, the delicate and the vulgar in the serving of dishes. All this is evident in *L'Art de bien traiter* and *Le cuisinier roïal et bourgeois*. In his preface, L.S.R. denounces the 'old authors' for their 'antique' and 'rustic' ways of preparing and serving dishes, and proclaims the superiority of the newer fashions:

> Nowadays it is not the prodigious overflowing of dishes, the abundance of ragoûts and gallimaufries, the extraordinary piles of meat which constitute a good table; it is not the confused mixtures of diverse spices, the mountains of roasts, the successive services

of *assiettes volantes*,[5] in which it seems that nature and artifice have been entirely exhausted in the satisfaction of the senses, which is the most palpable object of our delicacy of taste. It is rather the exquisite choice of meats, the finesse with which they are seasoned, the courtesy and neatness with which they are served, their proportionate relation to the number of people, and finally the general order of things which essentially contribute to the goodness and elegance of a meal. (L.S.R., 1674: 1–2)

Here, just at the time when classicism was the fashion in art and literature, L.S.R. was, as Flandrin and the Hymans observe, defining a sort of classicism in opposition to the archaic and ridiculous profusion of earlier cooks.

Among the erroneous 'old authors', L.S.R. most definitely includes the vulgar and rustic La Varenne, and lest there be any doubt, denounces him by name:

I don't believe you will find here the absurdities and the revolting instructions which M. de Varenne dares to give, and with which he has for so long deluded and bemused the foolish and ignorant populace, passing off his concoctions as if they were eternal verities and his teachings in matters of cuisine as the most approved in the world. I know that until now he has received all the glory for having laid down the rules and the methods. I know that common people, and even some of the more enlightened, have read his work as something supremely competent, sublime, and perfect; the reason for this blindness is that no-one has ever been ready to combat these errors. . . .

Doesn't it already make you shudder to think of a teal soup *a l'hypocras*, or larks in sweet sauce? Can you contemplate without horror this pottage of shin of beef *au talladin*, or that vulgar broth? That fried calve's head – doesn't it make you laugh, or rather cry with compassion? . . . Look at his shin of veal fried in breadcrumbs, his stuffed turkey with raspberries, his shoulder of mutton with olives, his ragoût of tripe, his roe deer's liver omelette, his ragoût of chicken in a bottle . . . and any number of other villainies that one would more willingly endure among the Arabs than in a gentler climate like ours, where refinement, delicacy and good taste are our most zealous concern. (L.S.R., 1674: 6–7)

The gist of this splendid invective is that less than a quarter of a century after their first publication, L.S.R. is pinpointing and deriding the medieval survivals and peasant-like elements in La Varenne's recipes.

For the social connotations of food were being made more and more explicit: not only was anything reminiscent of rusticity and the food of the peasants to be avoided, but the court and the 'best circles' were offered as models to be copied. The growing sense of 'good taste', national pride and deference to the court as the fount of all fashion are all evident when Massialot writes:

Only in Europe prevail the sense of what is proper, good taste and flair in the dressing of the foods found there; only there is justice done at the same time to the marvellous gifts provided by the bounty of other climates; and only there, and especially in France, can one take pride in our excelling over all other nations in these matters, as we do in manners and in a thousand other ways already familiar to us.

> This book can bear good witness of this. It is a cookery book which we are bold enough to describe as Royal, and not without reason, since the meals it describes for the different times of the year have all been served not long ago at the Court, or at the tables of the Princes or persons of the first rank. (Massialot, 1691: Préface)

There follow 80 pages of model meals, most of them with dates on which they were served to particular members of the high nobility. There are pull-out diagrams showing the distribution of major and minor dishes, for from 6 to 25 covers. This section certainly seems addressed to the bourgeois aspiring to live *à la mode* and in the fashion of the court. The instructions begin very simply:

> When you want to give a dinner according to the rules, you must observe the number of people in order to place your covers, and you must pay attention to the character of the dishes in order to arrange them well, avoiding having two dishes of a similar kind together without one of a different sort in between; for otherwise the thing will be done with bad grace, and could limit the choice of some of those at table, not everyone liking the same thing. (Massialot, 1691: 1–2).

After spelling out the sorts of dishes which constituted *entrées* and *hors d'oeuvres*, he specifies how a dinner for 12 people should be composed. It will consist of three services, each comprising a main central dish, four lesser dishes, and four *hors d'oeuvres*. For example, the first service might consist of two soups (one of pigeon, one of chicken and vegetables), two *entrées* (a hot partridge pie and *poularde aux truffes*), a *grande entrée* of two sorts of roast beef, and four *hors d'oeuvres* (*paupetons de pigeons*, braised quails, chickens stuffed with mushrooms, partridge with *sauce espagnole*). The second service was to comprise two roasts (turkey, served with partridges, young chicken, and woodcocks; and a large piece of lamb); four *entremets* (cream tart, two sorts of ham, and one other); and four *hors d'oeuvres* (blancmange, foies-gras, asparagus salad, and truffles in court-bouillon). The third service would consist of fruit and confectionery, but since in any socially acceptable household these would emanate from the *office*, a department separate from the *cuisine*, this is not set out in detail.

Differences in social standing were coming to be expressed not just through differences in the quantity or variety of food served at the tables of different strata, but more subtly through styles of cooking and serving. There was food to be emulated and food to be disdained. Food had become, in sociological jargon, a vehicle for anticipatory socialisation on the one hand, and for the expression of social distance on the other. 'Anticipatory socialisation', a term originated by Robert Merton (1949: 319ff.), means consciously or unconsciously adopting the ways, tastes amd manners of a social group to membership of which one aspires. Molière's Monsieur Jourdain provides a comic archetype of the process, a social climber from roughly the period of which we are speaking, and indeed in Act IV of *Le Bourgeois Gentilhomme*, the nobleman Dorante spells out the niceties of ordering a dinner in the height of fashion (Molière, 1682: 45–6) for his benefit. The penny-pinching attitude to the ordering of dinner demonstrated by Harpagon in Act III of *L'Avare* (1682: 140–1) is an equally good example of the bourgeois economising which good society disdained and distanced itself from. The bourgeois and his cook might be forced to economise, but at least they should be aware of the standards by which their efforts would be judged – as Massialot made clear:

Place and circumstance do not always permit the attainment of the very highest standards; one often has less than everything one needs, but nevertheless attempts to do the best one can. It is in this context that this book will be found not without utility in bourgeois households, where one is forced to limit oneself to a relatively few things. But even there occasions arise when one can afford – and is sometimes obliged – to give dinners of far from modest expense, when a cook can have everything he needs, and then he must know how to use it with flair so as to do it full honour. Moreover, this book shows thousands of ways with quite ordinary things like chickens, pigeons, and even butcher's meat, which can give much satisfaction in everyday meals, especially in the country and in the provinces. (Massialot, 1691: Préface)

A further stage in the break with medieval traditions and the development of the modern style of French cookery came during the eighteenth century. A change in style in courtly circles was evident immediately on the death of Louis XIV. The elegant, restrained and delicate dishes served by the Regent, the Duc d'Orléans, at his celebrated suppers are reputed to have set new standards for fashionable society (see Franklin, 1887–1902: V, 201–2; VIII, 175–222). Yet this was not immediately reflected in the publication of radically new cookery books. In fact, during the first three decades of the eighteenth century, though reprints of the classics of the previous century (especially La Varenne) circulated widely, scarcely any new cookery books appeared in France. The exception was Massialot, whose book of 1691, after being frequently reissued with minor amendments, was greatly enlarged by the addition of a second volume in 1712 and a third in 1730.

In 1733, however, there appeared the first of a new generation of cookery books. This is *The Modern Cook*, first published in English by Vincent La Chapelle, chef de cuisine to Lord Chesterfield, and in French two years later when the author had become chef to the Prince of Orange. In the by now time-honoured fashion, La Chapelle opens his book with a denunciation of a predecessor, in this case Massialot:

A cook of genius will invent new delicasies to please the palates of those for whom he is to labour, his art, like all others, being subject to change: for should the table of a great man be served in the taste that prevailed twenty years ago, it would not please the guest, however so he might conform to the rules laid down at that time. This variation in cookery is the reason for my publishing the ensuing work. The treatise of cookery entitled *Le Cuisinier Royal et Bourgeois* having been written so many years since, is not proper for present practice. T'is now upwards of thirty years since any new edition of that work appeared: however it was printed under a new title which was an imposition on the public.[6] . . . [W]ho will take the trouble to compare that piece with mine will find them entirely different. I may be so bold as to assert that I have not borrowed a single circumstance in the ensuing treatise from any author, the whole being the result of my own practice and experience.

La Chapelle's boldness provoked Philip and Mary Hyman, in a study (1979, 1981) of a depth rare in this field, to compare La Chapelle's recipes with those of Massialot. One of their first conclusions is that La Chapelle 'was one of the boldest liars in history'. They show that of the 1476 recipes in the first edition of his book, 480 – that is one third – were plagiarised directly from Massialot. Nevertheless, the Hymans conclude, when La Chapelle's recipes are subjected to minute technical examination, they do reveal certain important advances in the direction of modern culinary practice. Take, for instance, the cullis (*coulis*), a basic preparation of very rich meat and vegetable stock boiled and strained, used to thicken sauces. La Chapelle thickens his cullis with a roux made from flour, in contrast to Massialot, who still used breadcrumbs for this purpose, as they had been used in medieval times. La Chapelle also pays much attention to degreasing the cullis as it cooks. Another way in which La Chapelle anticipates later practice is his use of *sauce espagnole* as a flexible *fonds* for many other sauces; Massialot had used the name, but his was simply a single sauce among the very limited number he lists, not a general *fonds*.[7] On the other hand, La Chapelle's *espagnole* was not so elaborate and versatile as Carême's was to be. Finally, La Chapelle seems a relatively modern figure in including, especially in the fifth volume he added to his book in 1742, many foreign recipes – from German, Russian, Italian, English, even Indian sources – adapted to French taste.

Such innovations, representing only gradual advance in matters of detail over earlier practice, may seem insubstantial evidence of a culinary revolution. Nevertheless, by the late 1730s, the idea of *nouvelle cuisine* or *cuisine moderne* appears to have taken a firm hold in the public mind. In 1739 there appeared two cookery books clearly purporting to represent the new style. The first was the *Nouveau traité de la cuisine* by Menon, who was to become more famous a few years later when his *Cuisinière bourgeoise* became the most widely reprinted cookery book of the latter half of the eighteenth century. The second was *Les Dons de Comus*, attributed to François Marin who was, according to Guégan (1934: LXXIII), chef de cuisine to Mme la Duchesse de Gèsvres but on the strength of his fame subsequently became *maître d'hôtel* to the Marshal de Soubise.

Les Dons de Comus, in its original one-volume form, was not so much a cookery book as a textbook on how to *serve* food in the latest fashion. As the title-page describes it, it is

A work not only useful to those in charge of kitchens as regards their art, but principally for the use of people who are anxious to know how to give dinners and how to be served tastefully themselves, both on meat days and fish days, according to the seasons, and in the very latest taste.

A book setting out the latest fashions in food was actually more essential than cookery books, of which many already existed; even those dealing with the old cookery could still be useful, provided the cook knew his job, since the old was the basis of the new, and 'it is basically only a matter of simplifying certain things and perfecting others, to conform with the new taste' (1739: xxviii). Almost the only recipe spelled out in great detail is appropriately that for stock (*bouillon*), which Marin describes as 'the soul of sauces' and presents as the foundation for the whole edifice of the *nouvelle cuisine* (1739: 148ff.). His recipe starts with 'four to six pounds of beef, a big shoulder of veal, a hen, and an old partridge with a strong savour', stewed with celery, onions and parsley root. Having made the stock one then stews still more beef, veal, ham and so on in it to produce an extremely concentrated *quintessence ou restaurant*, which can then be used to make numerous other sauces. Marin comments that

> Many chefs would put many strongly-flavoured things into this quintessence, such as garlic, cloves, basil, mushrooms etc., but I am in favour of the simplest way, and I believe that it tastes best and it is best for health. (1739: 152)

This is a good demonstration of the process of development in taste and in technique from what Revel (1979: 206) calls a cookery of mixtures to a cookery of impregnation, a development anticipated in the seventeenth century but more clearly implemented in the eighteenth.

Much of the rest of *Les Dons de Comus* consists of annotated lists of dishes for the fashionable host to consider according to the season and the occasion. The first chapter, on soups, informs the reader that soups made with clear bouillon are most in use and lists around 50 of them. The next, on beef, gives the main cuts of carcass meat and items of offal used in cooking. It is followed by similar chapters on veal, mutton, lamb, pork, venison, poultry, game, fish, vegetables, eggs and dairy produce. This leads up to Part II of the book which is a more detailed repertoire of 'hors d'oeuvres and entremets, hot and cold and for meat days and fish days, and the little sauces which are in the very latest taste and most in use in the modern cookery' (1739: 91). One of the main hallmarks of the *nouvelle cuisine* of the 1730s and 1740s was the great variety of made dishes. Whether called *hors d'oeuvres, entrées*, or *entremets*, these were becoming as important a part of the fashionable meal as, perhaps more important than, the roasts. This can be seen in the following example (Marin, 1739: 214–16) of a supper menu for eight people, 'served according to the modern taste'.

> *Premier service*
> Un quartier de mouton en chevreuil
> Deux hors d'oeuvres:
>   Un de filet de poularde en hatereau
>   Un de pieds d'agneau en rissoles

Second service
Deux hors d'oeuvres:
Un de cuisses de poulets à l'oignon
Un de saucisse à la Sainte-Menehoult à l'oignon et anchois

Troisième service
Deux hors d'oeuvres:
Un de filet de 3 lapreaux aux morilles
Un de filet mignon, sauce à la bonne femme

Quatrième service
Deux hors d'oeuvres:
Un de filet de mouton émincé aux concombres
Un d'aîlerons de poularde à la Hollandaise

Cinquième service
Deux plats de rôts:
Un de pigeons aux oeufs
Un de trois poulets à la Reine
Une salade

Sixième service
Trois entre-mets:
Un de pois
Un d'artichaux à l'huile à la glace
Un de hâtelletes de rognons de coq

Septième service
Deux entre-mets:
Un de crêtes au vin
Un d'asperges

Huitième service
Deux entre-mets:
Un de tartelettes de pâte d'amandes, fraises et crème à la glace
Un de rôties au lard, frites à l'huile

Neuvième service
Deux entre-mets:
Un de beignets aux petits oeufs
Un de petits chous farcis

Other menus not specifically *dans le goût moderne* tend to have fewer services, each containing more dishes; but this one, though still an example of *service à la française*, since the diner has a choice of dishes within each service, has so large a number of services in sequence that it begins to resemble the *service à la russe* which was not generally adopted until more than a century later.

The original *Dons de Comus* was primarily a manual on the service of food and repertoire of dishes, but three years later Marin added to it a three-volume cookery book under the title *Suite des Dons de Comus* (1742), containing the recipes for many of the dishes which are only mentioned in *Dons de Comus*. They reveal – if there were any doubt – that Marin was a cook in the modern style of La Chapelle. For instance, he emphasises that bouillon and *jus* are to be used as *fonds*, as the bases for numerous other dishes, sauces and soups. Like La Chapelle, he instructs the reader to pay attention to skimming fat off the cullis as it cooks. Yet there are interesting throwbacks too: for instance, Marin's recipe for *coulis simple* uses bread-crumbs for thickening, and among the sauces is a section on the use of ground almonds as a liaison. Marin was evidently aware of a certain incongruity, for he justifies himself as follows:

> The old cuisine has not really been so proscribed that one does not still find traces of it in some households, where delicacy is adopted with difficulty under the name of novelty. As I am writing for everybody, I include a sample of it which can be regarded as the basis of the old gallic cuisine. (1742: 14)

This should serve as a reminder that even in a time of supposedly rapid culinary change, the break with the past is never very abrupt.

Other notable cookery books of the same period, including *Le Cuisinier Gascon* (1740) and the various works of the prolific Menon, bear out the change of fashion which Marin was so concerned to emphasise. It is perhaps not too far fetched to see in cookery, a transition in style parallel to that in architecture, from the classicised baroque of France under Louis XIV to the rococo of the age of Louis XV, the elimination of excess and the cultivation of delicacy. This transition could be seen both in the mode of service and in the recipes themselves. In chapter 2 I quoted Mercier's observation that the fashionable little dishes of the eighteenth century could cost ten times as much as those which made up the more quantitative displays of the previous century. Even so, though delicate and costly, these dishes were not so extravagantly costly as those of Carême and his followers in the next century were to be, with their constant and ostentatious use of the most expensive ingredients such as truffles and crayfish. For instance, recipes taken at random from *Le Cuisinier Gascon*, long noted as a particularly elegant collection, include cabbage with chestnuts and sausages, calves' brains *en matellotte*, and mackerel *à la Genevoise*: 'Take very clean mackerel, put them in a casserole with all sorts of fresh herbs, parsley, chives, onion, salt, pepper, cloves, and cover with water; cook them gently; when cooked, allow them to cool and serve with a cold *remoulade* or with lemon' (1740: 4). Recipes such as this could be described as delicate, but they are certainly not flashy.

Just as both the baroque and the rococo are courtly styles in art, so both the 'old' cookery of La Varenne and Massialot and the *nouvelle cuisine* of La Chapelle, Marin, Menon and their contemporaries are essentially courtly styles in cookery. The later authors did not always copy Massialot in presenting menus and recipes actually served at court on specific occasions, but titles such as Menon's *Les Soupers de la cour* (1755) and the extravagant dedications to members of the nobility which frequently prefaced the books show clearly the social circles seen as setting the standards. And it is from the seventeenth and eighteenth centuries and from aristocratic names that many familar culinary terms – béchamel, mayonnaise, soubise – derive. Such names indicate only that chefs named dishes in honour of their aristocratic patrons (or hoped-for patrons), not that aristocrats invented dishes themselves. Nevertheless, it has long been supposed that some of the leading figures in the land did actually venture into the kitchens themselves. The evidence is scattered and not conclusive. For example, the *épître dedicatoire* of *Le Cuisinier Gascon* to the Prince de Dombes bursts out:

> I can no longer keep silent: to the glory of an art which since You have exercised it has become as noble as it was already essential to the needs and pleasures of life, I shout from the rooftops that You are, Monseigneur, one of the best cooks in France. . . . I have seen you a hundred times busy in the kitchen, a hundred times have I had the honour of working under your orders. If I have acquired any reputation in my craft, I owe it even more to the emulation to which you have inspired me than to the desire I have always had of meeting your taste. Finally, the work I am taking the liberty of presenting to You is nothing more than the fruit of my reflections on your skill.[8]

Les Dons de Comus makes the same point more generally: 'We have in France several great Lords who, for their own diversion, do not disdain sometimes to talk about cookery, and whose exquisite taste contributes greatly to training excellent chefs' (1739: xxvi). Most famous of the supposed aristocrat-cooks was the Regent. In a letter referring to his skills as a cook, his mother the Princess Palatine implies that this was a part of *bon ton* which could be ranked with skills in other arts like music:

> My son knows how to cook; it is something he learned in Spain. He is a good musician, as all musicians recognise; he has composed two operas which he had produced in his chambers and which had some merit, but he didn't want them to be shown in public. (Orléans, 1855: I, 349–50)

More definite evidence of the keen interest in matters gastronomic taken by the fashionable world is contained in the long and erudite *Avertissement* which prefaced Marin's *Les Dons de Comus* and the famous controversy it provoked (discussed in detail in Mennell, 1981b). The *Avertissement*, believed to have been written by two Jesuits, discoursed learnedly on the anthropology and history of the human diet, and went on to theorise about the superiority of the *nouvelle cuisine* compared with the old. It provoked an immediate response, the pamphlet *Lettre d'un pâtissier anglois* (1739) attributed to the Comte Desalleurs, a minor courtier, who satirised the pretentiousness of the *Avertissement* and the preciousness of the *nouvelle cuisine*. This defence of the view that in food as in other things old ways are best called forth in turn the *Apologie des modernes* (1740a), in which the *littérateur* Meusnier de Querlon made it plain that the parties to this gastronomic squabble recognised its links with battles between old and new in other cultural spheres. In the same year, Meusnier satirised the voluptuous food at Versailles in *Les Soupers de Daphne*. These controversies provoked by the *nouvelle cuisine* were long remembered, though judging from Voltaire's rather confused views one may doubt whether everyone was quite clear about what constituted *nouvelle cuisine*:

I confess that my stomach cannot adjust itself to the *nouvelle cuisine*. I cannot endure calves' sweetbreads swimming in a salty sauce. . . . I cannot eat a stew composed of turkey, hare and rabbit which they try to make me take for a single meat. I like neither pigeon *à la crapaudine* nor bread without crusts. . . . As for cooks, I cannot tolerate their quintessence of ham nor the excess of morels, mushrooms, pepper and nutmeg with which they disguise dishes which are perfectly healthy in themselves. (Voltaire, 1765: LIX, 59–60)

If the cookery book writers of this period still looked to the courtly nobility for their standards, it is evident that they found their readership among the bourgeoisie as well, and to some extent they adapted themselves to this audience. Marin did so only grudgingly. *Suite des Dons de Comus* concludes with a section entitled 'Idée de la Cuisine et l'Economie Bourgeoise', directed at 'Bourgeois of modest fortune, Artisans, and other people of the Third Estate'. It contains scaled-down and less extravagant versions of the recipes he has presented earlier. One detects a certain lack of enthusiasm:

I recommend simplicity, because, without wishing to give offence to anyone, I have noticed that today many bourgeois, wishing to imitate the Great, leave the confines of their rank, spreading their table with dishes which put them to great cost without doing them any honour for want of being prepared by skilled hands. For those whose wish to cut a figure does not always match their condition or their fortune, *cuisine* ought to return to the simplicity of our fathers. Their purse and their health would be better for it. (Marin, 1742: III, 587–8)

Perhaps it is not surprising that it was not *Les Dons de Comus* which became the runaway best seller among cookery books in the later eighteenth century, but rather Menon's *La Cuisinière bourgeoise* (1746; see Girard, 1977). Menon undertook more wholeheartedly the task of enabling the bourgeoisie to participate in the culinary *grande monde*. The word *bourgeoise* in the title has the sense of 'domestic' as well as 'middle-class' and 'town-dweller'. Menon claims that many great lords, especially those concerned for their health, had asked him to produce a book of simpler and plainer cookery. Nevertheless, the gender to the word *cuisinière* gives it a quite unambiguous social meaning; only the less well-to-do members of the middle class would, by that date, make do with a woman cook in charge of their kitchen. Menon begins by setting out the personal qualities and the knowledge such a woman must have:

She must be clean in everything she does, careful with wood, coal and everything else belonging to the kitchen of which she has charge, gentle with the other servants in order to maintain peace in the household, and she must make every effort to please her Master and Mistress, serving them always at the times they have laid down.

It is necessary that she is knowledgeable about meat and how to disguise it in various ways, about fish and vegetables for fast days, about fruit and dairy produce in order to make compôtes and other things for dessert, because she takes charge both of the Kitchen and the Office[9]; women cooks who do not have these qualities must strive to acquire them, and Masters to retain in their service those who do have them. (Menon, 1746: v–vii)

Menon's book then follows the familiar layout, with chapters on foods in season, soups, the various kinds of meat, poultry, game, fish, vegetables, dairy-produce and pastries. The repertoire of recipes is very much scaled-down in comparison with Menon's earlier *Nouveau traité de cuisine*, his later *Les Soupers de la cour*, or indeed with La Chapelle's *Le Cuisinier moderne* or Marin's *Suite des Dons de Comus*. And the recipes themselves are often simplified. For example, the chapter on 'Coulis, Court-Bouillon et Sauces à la Bourgeoise' does not show how to use stock systematically to create a whole range of sauces, and the few sauces listed look more like gravies flavoured with herbs. Menon even mentions the availability of 'portable bouillon' from a shop in the Boulevard St Germain, intended for use by soldiers in the field but, for the bourgeois kitchen, no doubt as useful a short cut as the modern stock cube. Even so, though they are simplifications, Menon's simplifications are quite clearly *simplifications from courtly models*. He tells his readers to consult his three-volume *Traité*, 'obtainable from the same bookshop', for more detailed treatment of each topic.

This point is highly significant. Though the cookery book writers were, by the latter half of the eighteenth century, writing explicitly for a bourgeois audience, their food was very closely a continuation of the courtly tradition. In France, the court and the nobility still set the models for the lower orders to follow. By this date, there were already rather marked differences between English and French conceptions of 'good food', and in the social contexts within which these conceptions were rooted. So now it is time to go back and trace the rather different trajectory of culinary development in England.

COOKERY BOOKS IN ENGLAND

New cookery books were much more plentiful in sixteenth-century England than in France, where it was medieval texts which were frequently reprinted. The first English printed cookery book, which appeared in 1500 under the title *This is the Boke of Cokery*, was, it is true, also essentially medieval in character, and like its French equivalents was reprinted throughout the sixteenth century. Like the more famous *Boke of Kervynge* (1508) which detailed the rituals and vocabulary of carving at ceremonial dinners, the *Boke of Cokery* was derived from and mainly directed towards the concerns of noble households; the title-page reads: 'Here beginneth a noble boke of festes royalle and Cokery a boke for a pryncis householde or any other estates; and the makynge therof as ye shall fynde more playnly within this boke.'

However, later in the century there emerged a more distinctively English kind of book, of which Thomas Dawson's *The Good Huswifes Jewell* (1585) and Gervase Markham's *The English Hus-Wife* (1615) are typical.[10] These books appear generally to have been written for an audience not exclusively of courtly nobility concerned with the proper ways of giving dinners, but of 'housewives' or gentlewomen concerned with the practical tasks of running households – tasks in which they themselves were directly involved. Thus these books typically contain not only culinary recipes, but also discussions of 'physicke' and medical recipes for the treatment of common ailments. It is also common for them to contain sections on dairy-work and brewing, as well as on preserving, conserving and candying.[11] Markham in fact decribes his book as 'Contayning the inward and outward vertues which ought to be in a compleat woman: As, her skill in Physicke, Cookery, Banquetting-stuffe, Distillation, Perfumes, Wool, Hemp, Flax, Dayries, Brewing, Baking, and all other things belonging to an Household.'

Markham claims that he is only putting in order a manuscript which belonged to a lady of high rank – an Elizabethan countess, it is thought – but, if so, her preoccupations were ones she shared with the wives of the country gentry as a whole. The rural character of such household tasks as dairy-work, preserving and brewing is clear, and indeed *The English Hus-Wife* forms one half of a two-volume work under the title *Country Contentments* – the other volume dealing with riding, hunting, hawking and other pastimes. The recipes presented by Markham and his contemporaries for the most part also resemble what we should today think of as traditional English country cooking, including lots of pies, puddings and conserves. Some caution is required here, however: the ordinary people of the town or the country would have tasted such dishes only on very special occasions if at all. This was the food of the gentry, the nobility and probably even of the English court. For in the late sixteenth and early seventeenth centuries there is only slight evidence in England of the 'courtly' style of cuisine being developed in Italy and France.

In Markham's opening discussion of the desirable virtues of a good housewife, we encounter an early illustration of what was to become a familar theme in English cookery books: the national prejudice in favour of plain food – as the English understood it – and against foreign culinary pretensions:

> let her diet be wholesome and cleanly prepared at due hours, and cooked with care and diligence; let it be rather to satisfy nature than our affections, and apter to kill hunger than revive new appetites; let it proceed more from the provision of her own yard than the furniture of the markets; and let it be rather esteemed for the familiar acquaintance she hath with it, than for the strangeness and rarity it bringeth from other countries. (1615: 4)

The implication that his readers could be assumed to live in the country, or at the very least had large gardens in which to grow food for their households, is confirmed in Markham's second chapter, which he begins by saying that the housewife must know all about herbs, when to plant vegetables (he gives a list), and how to gather seeds for the next year.

Turning to cookery itself, Markham's book is much more highly organised than most earlier English cookery books, in which the recipes were generally jumbled together haphazardly, with no apparent rhyme or reason. But his organising principle is very different also from what was to become the standard pattern of French cookery books. Rather than dealing successively with different categories of meat or fish, Markham's chapters are arranged according to methods of cooking. First come salads and 'fricassees', then boiled meats and soups (logically considered together), next roasting and grilling, followed by baked meats and pies, and finally 'Banquetting and made dishes with other conceits and secrets'.

The word 'fricassee' (like the contemporary use by Shakespeare of 'kickshaw') implies that French culinary influence was already evident in England. Markham, however, uses the word to mean more or less any dish prepared by frying, and sometimes anglicises the word as 'fry-case'. Nowadays we might well say 'fry-up', for Markham's conception of a fricassee is as broad and unrefined as that; certainly these made dishes bear little resemblance to the ragoûts which form so considerable a part of La Varenne's book three decades later: 'Now to proceed to your fricassees, or quelque choses, which are dishes of many compositions and ingredients, as flesh, fish, eggs, herbs and many other things, all being prepared and made ready in a frying pan.' (1615: 42) Simple fricassees include that very English dish – as we think of it – bacon and eggs, the cooking of which Markham explains in some detail before moving on to 'the compound fricassees . . . which consist of many things, as Tanseys, Fritters and Pancakes, and any Quelque chose whatsoever, being things of great request and estimation in France, Spain and Italy, and the most curious[12] nations' (1615: 42–3). Tansey resembles an omelette with cream and herbs, and these are followed by fritters, pancakes, 'veale toasts' and 'panperdy' – this last, as *pain perdu*, a simple dish of bread soaked in egg yolks and fried, familiar to the medieval courts of both England and France and eaten right up to the present day under such names as 'Poor Knights of Windsor' (see Grigson, 1974: 219–21). Markham shortly loses patience, and gives a catch-all recipe for the whole category of fricassees or quelquechoses:

To make any quelquechose which is a mixture of many things together: take eggs and break them and do away the one half of the whites, and after they are beaten put to them a good quantity of sweet cream, currants, cinnamon, cloves, mace, salt, and a little ginger, spinach, endive and marigold flowers grossly chopped, and beat them all well together. Then take pigs pettitoes sliced and grossly chopped, and mix them with the eggs, and with your hand stir them exceeding well together: then put sweet butter in your frying pan, and being melted, put in all the rest, and frie it brown without burning, ever and anon turning it till it be fried enough. Then dish it up upon a flat plate and cover it with sugar and so serve it forth. Only herein is to be observed that your pettitoes must be very well boiled before you put them into the fry-case.

And in this manner as you make this Quelquechose, so you may make any other whether it be of flesh, small birds, sweet roots, oysters, mussels, cockles, giblets, lemons, oranges or any fruit, pulse, or other salad herb whatsoever. Of which to speak severally were a labour infinite, because they vary with men's opinions. (1615: 46–7)

This aleatory element is in very striking contrast with the later French cookery books, which were increasingly concerned to list and describe precisely the whole range of made dishes according with the fashions of the age. But that development lay in the future. The use of the words 'fricassee' and 'quelquechose' in early seventeenth-century England may indicate the influence of developments in French cuisine which were yet to be recorded in French books.

In this omnibus recipe, as elsewhere, the persistence of medieval ingredients and techniques in Markham's book is evident. He deals in interesting detail with boiling and with roasting, specifying the best bastings (butter and oil with cinnamon, cloves and mace) and the best dredging (*white* bread crumbs). His various sauces for different meats are all variations on simple gravy, thickened with breadcrumbs or sometimes hard boiled egg yolks and flavoured with onions, herbs, spices, oranges and lemons (1615: 60–3). Such gravies are basically medieval, but it is worth remembering that it was to sauces of this sort which Menon reverted when simplifying *haute cuisine* for the bourgeois household in the eighteenth century.

One other noteworthy aspect of Markham's survey of English cookery is his discussion of 'banquetting stuff and conceited dishes', which 'albe they are not of general use, yet in their true times they are so needful for adornation that whosoever is ignorant therein is lame, and but the half part of a compleat Housewife' (1615: 69). So of what did this 'banquetting stuff' consist? Markham's recipes for it included quince paste; quince cakes; preserved quinces; quince marmalade; hippocras (wine flavoured with spices); jelly (using calves' feet, or isinglass); leach (almond jelly with isinglass); gingerbread; jumbals (meringues, more or less); fresh cheese; spice cakes; Banbury Cake; marchpane; a general recipe for conserves; conserve of flowers; orange marmalade; baked apples, pears and wardens; and wafers. This very diverse array of dishes is not quite so incongruous as it appears at first glance when one realises that it corresponds fairly exactly to the 'dessert' sequence of dishes of a later date. They were not intended for the 'banquet' in the sense of a sumptuous formal feast. The word was also used for a very different custom that was popular in great houses in Elizabethan and Jacobean times: these assorted sweets, fruits and confectionery were often served very informally in special little rooms designed for the purpose on the roof of the house or in the grounds (Girouard, 1978: 104). Most often the 'banquet' came after the meal proper, but it could happen at any time, rather like coffee-and-biscuits, or indeed a picnic. The most general characteristic of these recipes is that the majority of them require large amounts of sugar, and would therefore be very expensive. 'Banquetting stuff' is early testimony to the English predilection and flair for puddings, pastries and other sweet dishes; by the eighteenth century their reputation in this field was well established, and the English consumed far more sugar per capita than the French. In part, however, the lack of prominence given to sweet dishes in the French cookery books in the seventeenth and eighteenth centuries is due to the division in substantial households between the departments of the *cuisine* and the *office*. What Markham calls 'banquetting stuff' would fall within the purview of the *officier*. This division was generally reflected in French cookery books: thus in addition to *Le Cuisinier françois*, there were separate books entitled *Le Confiturier françois* (*c.* 1667) and *Le Pâtissier françois* (1653) sometimes attributed to La Varenne.

Nevertheless, this division of labour, so much more marked in France than in England, is itself significant. Markham's book, like the dominant strand in English cookery books over the next two centuries, seems addressed to a strikingly different audience to that of the French books discussed above. It is addressed not to male chefs, nor to members of the nobility and *haute bourgeoisie* seeking guidance in the ordering of meals *à la mode*, but to housewives who busied themselves with all aspects of household work. Markham indeed is even more comprehensive than most of his successors, dealing in detail with the work of the brew-house, the bake-house and the dairy – the last including breeds of cow and their rearing; milking, churning, butter and cream; rennet and cheeses. All this, along with the extensive kitchen equipment implied, makes clear – even more than the discussion of 'banquetting stuff' – that the intended audience is of the country gentry. It is obvious that quite wealthy people occupied themselves with these domestic matters in a much more practical way than did the dilettante amateur cooks among the French nobility a century later.

This picture is further confirmed later in the century in another celebrated book, *The Closet of the Eminently Learned Sir Kenelm Digby, Kt, Opened* (1669).[13] Digby (1603–65) was a prominent figure at the Stuart court, and a man of many parts – qualified doctor, scientist and Fellow of the Royal Society, philosopher, soldier and privateer. He travelled widely in Europe and was Chancellor to Queen Henrietta Maria in her exile (see Petersson, 1956). He was also an avid cook, and his collection of recipes was published after his death. A large proportion of the recipes are attributed to specific friends and acquaintances, ranging from professional cooks to high-ranking members of the aristocracy, and the attributions are far more direct and concrete than anything found in the French sources either in this century or the next. *The Closet* actually opens with more than 100 pages of recipes for drinks, including 106 variations on mead, metheglin and hydromel – all made from honey and flavoured with herbs in many different ways. Sources of these recipes include Lady Hungerford, the Countess of Bullingbrook, Sir Thomas and Lady Gower (who each gave him separate and quite distinct recipes), Lord Hollis, Sir William Paston and Lady Stuart (two recipes each), Sir Baynam Throckmorton, Sir John Fortescue, Lady Vernon, Sir John Arundell, the Countess of Dorset, Lord Herbert, 'The Muscovian Ambassador's Steward', 'Hydromel as I made it weak for the Queen Mother', 'Sir Edward Bainton's Receipt which my Lord of Portland (who gave it to me) saith was the best he ever drunk', and Mr Webbe, the mead-maker to King Charles II, who made some for Digby at his house on 1 September 1663, under careful observation. Other drinks for which Digby gives recipes are ale, beer, cider, currant wine, cherry and strawberry wines. All are essentially country drinks, but apparently much in favour not merely among the country gentry but also among the highest aristocracy too.

Very much the same impression is given by Digby's recipes for the more solid branches of cookery. A few short excerpts will convey the flavour of the book:

My Lady Middlesex makes Syllabubs for little glasses with spouts, thus (p. 115)
Clouted-cream. Milk your cows in the evening about the ordinary hour (p. 117)
Wheaten Flommery. In the West Country, they make a kind of Flommery of wheat flour, which they judge to be more harty and pleasant than that of Oat-meal (p. 134)
Capon in White Broth. My Lady of Monmouth boileth a capon with white broth thus [with almonds, pistacchios and herbs] (p. 146)
My Lady of Portland's Minced Pies [with beef, veal or neat's tongues, suet, currants and peel] (p. 155)
My Lord of Denbigh's Marchpane (pp. 221–2)
My Lady of Middlesex makes excellent slipp-coat Cheese of good morning milk, putting Cream to it. A quart of cream is the proportion she uses to as much milk. (p. 226)
Apples in Gelly. My Lady Paget makes her fine preserved Pippins thus (p. 234)
My Lord Lumley's Pease-Porage (p. 142)

This last is the usual recipe for pease pudding, with some pleasant herbs added, but nothing extraordinarily epicurean from Lord Lumley, although he seems to have been regarded as a great connoisseur and was, along with Digby himself, one of the dedicatees of Robert May's book – of which more in a moment. Digby also explains how to make black puddings and various sweet and savoury boiled and baked puddings, conserves and cakes. The food he describes differs in no very marked way from that of Gervase Markham half a century earlier, but Digby by implication fills out its social context considerably. The evidence of the gentry and nobility taking an active interest in cooking is very convincing. But the dishes they make and the ingredients they use are for the most part quite ordinary, such as would be abundant on a country estate. Some of the dishes – pease pudding to name but one – are ancient staples of the peasantry; others, the sweet dishes in particular, are ones which a peasant would probably not expect to taste very often. But in Markham and Digby there is little sign of a *haute cuisine* such as was developing in France. And books of essentially the same type – addressed to housewives, containing fairly simple country recipes, and with medical receipts often mixed in with them – continued to appear very frequently in the latter half of the seventeenth century and in the eighteenth.

Yet for a relatively short period of little more than half a century, roughly from the Restoration to the death of Queen Anne, there were signs of an awareness of the emerging French courtly style co-existing with the lastingly vigorous native tradition. Several of the most notable French books were translated into English. In 1653, astonishingly quickly after the first French edition two years before, an English version of La Varenne was published under the title *The French Cook*. In 1682, Giles Rose, master cook to Charles II, published *A Perfect School of Instructions for Officers of the Mouth*, a translation (only too literally in the case of the title) of Ribou's *L'Escole parfaite* of twenty years before. In 1702 there appeared *The Court and Country Cook*, a translation of Massialot's *Le Cuisinier roïal et bourgeois* of 1691. And it should not be forgotten that much later, while he was employed by Lord Chesterfield, Vincent La Chapelle wrote the first edition of *The Modern Cook* in English before translating and expanding it into French.

More interesting than translations of French books, however, is the appearance of a small number of works by English cooks in the 'courtly' genre. Of these, the principal ones are Robert May's *The Accomplish't Cook, or the Art and Mystery of Cookery* (1660); William Rabisha's *The Whole Body of Cookery Dissected* (1661); Patrick Lamb's *Royal Cookery; or, the Complete Court Cook* (1710); Robert Smith's *Court Cookery* (1723); and Charles Carter's *The Complete Practical Cook* (1730). These books differ from the more usual English cookery books of the period, and resemble the French, in several ways. First, they are written by professional chefs and addressed primarily to other professional chefs rather than to 'housewives'. Secondly and probably in consequence, they deal more narrowly with cookery as such and avoid the common admixture of medical remedies and sections on other aspects of household management. Thirdly, their authors specifically boast of their employment in royal or noble kitchens and dedicate their books to their patrons, which to some extent justifies our labelling these as 'courtly' cookery books. Nevertheless, although they all demonstrate an awareness of the developing French style and include recipes originating in other countries too, their attitude to foreign dishes is somewhat ambivalent, and overall their food looks more like variations on traditional English cookery than an adaptation to the French model.

The careers of Robert May and William Rabisha seem to have been very similar. Both served in a number of noble households, and spent parts of their lives on the continent. May was born in 1588, his father being himself cook to Lady Dormer, who sent the son to Paris to work in a nobleman's household. He was then apprenticed to a leading London cook, before returning to join his father at Lady Dormer's. Subsequently he cooked for many other wealthy and noble employers. Of Rabisha we know less, but he tells us that he too was 'brought up in the family of an honourable lady, who spared for no cost nor charge, for my instruction in the said art, not only at home in her house, but also abroad in the late King's Court, of ever blessed memory' and that he had since 'served as Master Cook to many honourable families before and since the wars began, both in this my native country and with ambassadors and nobles in certain foreign parts'.

Both May and Rabisha dedicate their books to their patrons: to Lords Montague, Lumley and Dormer, and Sir Kenelm Digby on the one hand, and to the Duchesses of Richmond and Buckingham and three other noble ladies on the other. But though they acknowledge their employers' generous hospitality which permitted them to learn their art, they do not, unlike some of their French counterparts, write extravagant praise of their patrons' knowledgeable palates. Still more striking, their prefaces reveal nothing of the sense of rapid progress and improvement in the culinary arts which affected the French at this time. If anything, they tended to look back to noble households before the Civil Wars. The biographical note on May makes this quite explicit:

> such noble houses were then kept, the glory of that, and shame of this present age; then were those golden days wherein were practised the Triumphs and Trophies of Cookery; then was Hospitality esteemed, Neighbourhood preserved, the poor cherished, and God honoured; then was Religion less talkt on, and more practised; then was Atheism and Schism less in fashion; and then did men strive to do good rather than to seem so. (May, 1660)

Too much should possibly not be made of that, since May's book was published in the very year of the Restoration, and the future may have seemed uncertain. By the following year, Rabisha is striking a much more optimistic note – though about the prospects not so much of progress as of patronage in cookery.

> I was further encouraged in this work by seeing that happy and blessed restoration of our long-exiled Royal Luminaries, and the hopes of the benevolent influence of liberality and hospitality, which is in part the life of arts and sciences. It is indeed like the Sun in the Firmament, which keeps not his light and heat for himself, but in his gradual revolution, freely bestows himself to the giving of life, feeding and clothing the whole universe. And doth not his Representation and Production, even our Sun, our King and Nobles, do the like? Do not thousands live by their benevolence? What have they more than others, but honourable respect and attendance? As for food and rayment, they pay for, by which all men live, for all that they have comes to the purse, pocket, back and belly of all men yearly; they are like a great Wheel that moves the next, and so they move one the other, that none stands idle, the removing of which, is the destruction of the whole. (Rabisha, 1661 Preface)

Rabisha here displays a prematurely clear grasp of the multiplier principle of later economists.

May and Rabisha both make it plain that professional pride has motivated them into print. May declares that 'though I may be envied by some that only value their private interests above posterity and the public good, yet God and my own Conscience would not permit me to bury these my experiences with my silver hairs in the grave'. Rabisha is more direct, confessing that he expects to be criticised by his fellow professionals for disclosing the secrets of their craft:

I do not question but that divers Brethren of my own Fraternity may open their mouths against me, for publishing this treatise, pretending that thereby it may teach every kitchen-wench, and such as never served their times, and so be prejudicial to the Fraternity of cooks; but . . . the same may as truly be said of all the other Arts and Sciences, the Astronomer, Mathematician, Navigator, Physician, Surgeon, Farrier, and many hundred more. And what artists amongst them, make themselves perfect, as well by studying their volumes as by practice. Yet there is an evil amongst most men, when they have learned themselves by other men's light, they would extinguish that light that none may follow them, and so men monopolise all knowledge therein themselves, and condemn all those who are a guide and a light to the ignorant; there is none other but such will condemn me in what I have done. (1661, Preface)

In any case, Rabisha adds, a cookery book can only supplement, not substitute for, practical experience in the kitchen:

they are mistaken that they think a Tract of this kind can be very beneficial to any, but such as have been in some measure practitioners, and understand the nature of the ingredients proposed for the performances of any one thing; for experience shall tell all my Brethren, that it is a hard thing to teach a young practitioner to dress many hundred of the said dishes after the composition is made; nay, although they look on them, and give them direction, yet they will spoil it in the doing. Therefore I hope it will answer my end and no more, which is the instruction of young practitioners, that give their minds to the study thereof. (1661, Preface)

We could wish for no clearer statement of the intended purpose of this kind of cookery book. No doubt the same purpose motivated the professional chefs of France too, who wrote in rather larger numbers over the next decades. The resentment of fellow professionals, at which May hints and which Rabisha roundly condemns, may help to explain why more books of this sort were not written in England. I have found no evidence of this resentment in France, though it is possible that the same attitude helps to explain the long silence about French cookery which was finally broken by La Varenne.

One way in which the small number of English 'professional' books differs from the French is that May and Rabisha, and later Lamb and Smith, express much more a sense of handing down the highest skills of a traditional and relatively unchanging craft than of conveying the latest advances in technique and fashions in service. They therefore seem less than the French to be writing for the benefit of the fashionable host. Nevertheless it was only the nobility and the very rich who could afford male chefs and entertaining on the scale envisaged. The professionals were very conscious of the distance between themselves, the 'courtly' cooks, and the 'housewives' of the gentry. Yet this distance in practice never seems to have been as definite, nor to have endured so long, in England as in France. May, in fact, already writes as though extravagant noble hospitality was in decline:

Those Honourable Persons, my Lord Lumley, and others, with whom I have spent a part of my time, were such whose generous costs never weighed the experience, so that they might arrive to that right and high esteem they had of their Gustos. Whosoever peruses this volume shall find it amply exemplified in dishes of such high prices which only these Noblesses Hospitalities did reach to: I should have sinned against their several varieties, that the Reader might be as well acquainted with what is extraordinary as what is ordinary in this Art. (1660, Preface)

But, he immediately concedes, with much more grace than Marin was able to muster nearly a century later, that he also has to cater for those who cannot avoid counting the cost:

In the continuance of these my labours, I have so managed them for the general good, that those whose purses cannot reach to the cost of rich dishes, I have descended to their meaner Expences, that they may give, though upon a sudden Treatment, to their kindred, Friends, Allies, and Acquaintance, a handsome and relishing entertainment in all seasons of the year, though at some distance from Towns or Villages. (1660, Preface)

May's attitude to foreign cookery is also ambivalent, and anticipates the feelings of many later English writers. On the one hand, he acknowledges his debts:

As I lived in France, and had the language, and have been an eye-witness of their Cookeries, as well as a peruser of their Manuscripts and printed Authors, whatsoever I found good in them, I have inserted in this volume. I do acknowledge myself not to be a little beholding to the Italian and Spanish Treatises. (1660: Preface)

On the other hand his culinary patriotism is expressed in a denunciation of the French, who

by their insinuations, not without enough of ignorance, have bewitcht some of the Gallants of our nation with Epigram Dishes, smoakt rather than drest, so strangely to captivate the Gusto, their Mushroomed Experiences for Sauce rather than Diet, for the generality howsoever called A la mode, not worthy of being taken notice on. (1660: Preface)

May's very first recipe is, in fact, a version of the Spanish stew *olla podrida*, apparently favoured in England under the name of 'olio' since earlier in the seventeenth century; but the bulk of May's rather chaotically arranged recipes, despite the occasional use of foreign titles, are an enlarged and enriched range of fairly familiar English 'country' food, including a great variety of roast and boiled meat, pies, puddings and sausages (including haggis). The food in Rabisha's book, a little better arranged and organised according to method of cooking rather than category of food, is very similar.

May's book in particular has often been compared unfavourably with La Varenne's, as showing the 'awkwardness' of English cookery compared with French. Too much has been made of the antique air of his short section of 'Triumphs and Trophies in cookery, to be used at Festival Times, as Twelfth Day, etc.', in which he describes how to make ships with guns firing, egg shells filled with scented waters for the ladies to throw at each other, and pies filled with live frogs and birds – the frogs to frighten the ladies and the birds to put out the candles by their flapping – all designed to cause merriment before the dinner proper.[14] Again, May looks on these as customs of a roseate past: 'These were formerly the delights of the Nobility, before good House-keeping had left England, and the Sword really acted that which was only counterfeited in such honest and laudable exercises as these.'

Yet it is misleading to see May or Rabisha as 'behind the times'. For just as La Varenne's book is seen as the first clear evidence of a distinctively French style of cookery, so May and Rabisha are the first professional cooks to record that even in the highest reaches of society food of a fairly distinctively English style was favoured. It is true that that style represented a less clear break with the medieval past than did the French. French cookery continued to develop rather rapidly so that La Varenne was quite soon regarded as out-of-date and rustic by his successors. In England, the pace of culinary change even in courtly and noble circles appears to have been much slower.

This is evident in the books by Lamb, Smith, and Carter which effectively mark the end of whatever little native tradition England had of 'courtly' cookery books. The title-page of Lamb's *Royal Cookery* of 1710 describes it as 'containing the Choicest Receipts in all the particular branches of Cookery, now in use in the Queen's Palaces of St James, Kensington, Hampton Court, and Windsor . . . by Patrick Lamb, Esq., near 50 years Master-Cook to their late Majesties King Charles II, King James II, King William and Queen Mary, and to Her Present Majesty Queen Anne'. Robert Smith was one of Lamb's assistants for eight years in the reign of King William, and subsequently served the Dukes of Buckingham and Ormond, and the French Ambassador, the Duc d'Aumont. Charles Carter did not work at the royal court, but was 'Lately Cook to his Grace the Duke of Argyll, the Earl of Pontefract, the Lord Cornwallis, &c.'

Lamb's preface makes it clear that his is a book of food for special occasions, and that he anticipates criticism for its richness and expense:

> As for those severer Ascetics who keep Lent at Christmas, and weigh out their diet by drams and scruples, it must not be expected they should purchase a piece with so hungry a title to it, as thinking, perhaps, that luxury will thrive fast enough without study'd receipts to season and recommend it. But as a vicious palate is, by no means, a proper judge of tastes, so were it a great pity, one or two peevish cynicks should put Good eating out of countenance; especially since the author has not here undertaken

to cook out an Art of *Gluttony*, or to teach the rich and lazy how to grow fatter, by ranging Epicurism under the several heads of Jellies, Soupes, and Pottages; but his chief aim was to represent the Grandeur of the English Court and Nation, by an Instance which lay most within his view and province; the Magnificence, I mean, of those publick Regales made on the more solemn occasions of admitting Princes to their thrones, Peers to their Honours, Ambassadors to their Audience, and Persons of Figure to their Nuptial-Bed. Now, these are Solemnities which call for good Looks and better Chear than ordinary.

Bound at the back of Lamb's book are numerous fold-out diagrams, showing the lay-out on the table of dishes, many of them at meals served on particular occasions at court or in the houses of the nobility and gentry. In this, Lamb's book is strongly reminiscent of Massialot's, first published in France two decades earlier.[15]

Lamb's recipes and bills of fare contain somewhat mangled French terminology – bisque, alamode, fricassees, turkey ragoo'd, a terreyne – and his very first recipe, for Soupe Santé, is given in two variants, 'French Way, English Way'. There are also, as one might expect during the reign of King William, three recipes from Holland, 'Pike Cabilow', haddocks and 'scate or thornback', all 'Dutch Way'. Some of Lamb's favourite ingredients – lobster, venison, turkey – would have been out of the common way, but on the whole they are not very exceptional. Overall, the contents of his book are still very clearly English and not so very different from those of May or even Markham. There are lots of pies and puddings, savoury and sweet – blood puddings, Neat's Foot Pudding, Rice Pudding, Bread Pudding – and some long-term survivors from medieval times, like pain perdu and 'Sallad-Magundy'. Neither Lamb nor Smith has a section on sauces, and very few are mentioned at all; although Smith does give a not particularly extravagant recipe for cullis, they generally talk more of 'gravy'.

Lamb's disciple, Smith, in fact boasts of having put his recipes 'in plain *English* dress'. Yet Smith, no less than Lamb, sees himself very clearly as a master cook to the nobility, and indeed distances himself from the more commonplace kind of cookery-book writer when he remarks, rather snootily, that

I have not, indeed, fill'd my book with washes and beautifiers for ladies, or making of ale for country squires, all of which is foreign to my purpose; and a person that's well acquainted with cookery cannot be also acquainted in clearing the skin and the fining of ale.

In view of Smith's snobbery here and in view of the title of his book, *Court Cookery*, it is therefore a little unexpected that he shows himself very much concerned with economy and with avoiding the charge of extravagance – against which Lamb had also defended himself. Smith even casts doubt on the authenticity of some of the recipes printed in Lamb's *Royal Cookery*, partly on grounds that some of them were too costly – 'more calculated at the purses, than the *Gout* of the guests'. He says he himself has 'carefully omitted all such receipts whose extravagancy must have rendered them useless, and yet have left several valuable ones, not unworthy of the greatest prince'. Finally, he hopes that his readers will be pleased with 'the manner of performing, in a quicker and less expensive manner than hitherto' the dishes he sets out. Such an emphasis on economy was quite foreign to the spirit of the French court nobility in the seventeenth and eighteenth centuries, as we shall shortly attempt to explain, and that spirit was reflected in the writings of their cooks who make rather grudging concessions to the needs of their bourgeois readers. In contrast, Lamb appears to be a little on the defensive, anticipating charges of extravagance, and Smith positively endorses the need for economy.

Smith's book was in the event to prove almost the last by an English 'courtly' cook. Just at the time when in France very rapid development was taking place, leading up to the emergence of *nouvelle cuisine* in the works of La Chapelle, Marin and Menon, the courtly genre went into eclipse in England. A translation of Menon's *Soupers de la cour* found a market; and there appeared the occasional book by male cooks employed by the nobility, such as Charles Carter whose first book in 1730 is recognisably of the 'courtly' type – but it is significant that his second, *The Compleat City and Country Cook* published only two years later, is very different and seems to represent an adaptation to the needs and tastes of the country gentry. In any case, as we have suggested, May's and Lamb's food as a whole was never so far removed from everyday country food as was that of the French authors, even though they borrowed recipes from French sources. The eighteenth century is the age of what we now think of as English country cooking at its best, represented in cookery books written mainly by women – something unknown in France at that period. From the era of May to that of Lamb, books of the 'country housewife' genre had continued by far to outnumber the 'courtly' variety, and now there was a great efflorescence of them. By no means all were written by women: one with the precise title of *The Country Housewife* (1727–32) was produced by Richard Bradley, Professor of Botany at Cambridge, complete with brewing, wine-making, distilling and dairy-work. The first highly successful book by a woman was Hannah Wolley's *The Queen-Like Closet*, first published in 1670. But in the next century, there appeared a very large number of books by women, who often described themselves as 'housekeeper and cook' to members of the gentry. Probably the most celebrated among them are Eliza Smith's *The Compleat Housewife* (1727), Elizabeth Moxon's *English Housewifery* (1749), Elizabeth Raffald's *The Experienced English Housekeeper* (1769) and, most famous of all, Hannah Glasse's *The Art of Cookery Made Plain and Easy* (1747), which went through a phenomenal number of editions.

These authoresses were writing not for a nobleman's kitchen, but for ladies in the upper middle ranks of society in charge of their own domestic establishments and, quite explicitly by the mid-eighteenth century, their servants. Hannah Glasse, who came from a family of country gentry with houses in the north and East Anglia but through an imprudent marriage and incompetence at business experienced periods of financial difficulty, remarked that she had 'found by experience that the generality of servants are greatly wanting' in their knowledge of cookery:

therefore I have taken upon me to instruct them in the best Manner I am capable; and I dare say, that every Servant who can but read will be capable of making a tolerable good Cook, and those who have the least Notion of Cookery can't miss of being very good ones. If I have not wrote in the high, polite Stile, I hope I shall be forgiven; for my Intention is to instruct the lower Sort, and therefore must treat them in their own Way. (1747: i)

The intertwined themes of economy, plainness, and hostility to French cookery are very prominent in these books. Raffald says she has always endeavoured

to join economy with neatness and elegance, being sensible what valuable qualifications these are in a housekeeper or cook, for of what use is their skill if they put their master or lady to immoderate expense in dressing a dinner for a small company, when at the same time a prudent manager would have dressed twice the number of dishes, for a much greater company, at half the cost. (1769: iii)

French cookery was now clearly identified with extravagance, for she strikes a slightly apologetic note when she concedes that 'though I have given some of my dishes French names, as they are only known by those names, yet they will not be found very expensive, nor add compositions but as plain as the dish will admit of' (1769: ii). Hannah Glasse was far more forthright in her since much-quoted denunciation of French extravagance and duplicity:

if Gentlemen will have French Cooks, they must pay for *French* tricks. A *Frenchman*, in his own Country, would dress a fine Dinner of twenty Dishes, and all genteel and pretty, for the Expence he will put an *English* Lord to for the dressing of one Dish. But then there is the little petty Profit. I have heard of a Cook that used six Pounds of Butter to fry twelve Eggs, when every Body knows, that understands Cooking, that Half a Pound is full enough, or more than need be used: But then it would not be *French*. So much is the blind Folly of this Age, that they would rather be imposed on by a *French* Booby, than give Encouragement to a good English Cook! (1747: ii)

What these good English lady cooks really objected to was the extravagance involved in preparing the cullis or quintessence so fundamental to the sauces and indeed to the whole edifice of French cookery. The theme recurs again and again. Half a century later, Maria Rundell was still writing that

so as to unite a good figure with proper economy, she has avoided all excessive luxury, such as essence of ham, and that wasteful expenditure of large quantities of meat for gravy, which so greatly contributes to keep up the price, and is no less injurious to those who eat them than to those whose penury obliges them to abstain. (1806: iii)

The extravagance involved in making quintessence was indeed proverbial. Brillat-Savarin was to tell the story, which must already have been legendary in his own day and has often been repeated since, of the Prince de Soubise remonstrating with his steward, who proposed to use fifty hams for a single supper.

'Bertrand,' he said, 'have you gone mad? Fifty hams! Do you want to regale the whole of my regiment?'

'No, Your Highness; only one ham will appear on the table; but I shall need all the rest for my brown sauce, my stock, my garnishings, my . . .'

'Bertrand, you're a thief, and I shan't pass that item.'

'But Your Highness,' answered the artist, hardly able to contain his anger, 'you don't know our resources! You have only to say the word, and I'll take all those fifty hams you object to and put them into a crystal phial no bigger than my thumb!'

What answer could be made to so positive an assertion? The prince smiled, nodded, and the item was allowed to pass. (1826: 54–5)

The point of the story, of course, is that the great French nobleman *did* pass the item with no further question. Mrs Glasse, Mrs Raffald and Mrs Rundell would have remained unimpressed by such nonsense. All of them propose much cheaper ways of making 'gravy' – as they think of it. Raffald's substitute for cullis is eccentric, a none too attractive sounding concoction of gravy browning (caramelised sugar) and lemon pickle, which she claims 'answers both for beauty and taste (at a trifling expense) better than cullis, which is extravagant'. Glasse too inveighs against the extravagance of using a ham and a leg of veal to make a cullis, which is then used 'only to mix with other sauce', in preparing a meal for no more than ten or twelve people. Her own substitute, however, would still by modern standards be a very elaborate recipe for stock, involving as it does bacon, veal, beef, pigeon, a cock, plus carrots, herbs, spices, truffles and morels. Nevertheless, she claims a considerable saving on the ham and leg of veal, and specifies that 'if you go to market the ingredients will not come to above half a crown'. Lest that were not sufficiently cheap, Mrs Glasse then gives a still more economical recipe, which for 18*d.* 'will make as much good gravy as will serve twenty people'. When one considers that half a crown then amounted to something like half the weekly wage of a woman cook, these are still not penny-pinching recipes. Hannah Glasse was writing for an audience who had to keep a careful eye on their expenditure, and saw no shame in doing so, but who were far from penurious: the list of about 250 subscribers to the first edition of her book suggests who they might be – there were four with the title 'Lady', several doctors, a colonel and several other gentlemen holding military rank, some Esquires, but most are plain 'Mr' or 'Mrs'.

Hannah Glasse was certainly not consistent in practising what she preached. Ann Cook, a trained cook who seems to have had some personal grudge against Mrs Glasse, prefaced her own cookery book, *Professed Cookery* (1754), with a long essay in criticism of the more famous writer, and not only points out technical errors which an experienced working cook like herself would not have made, but also turns the tables on Glasse by accusing her, as she had accused the French, of reckless extravagance. As Jennifer Stead (1983) has shown, many of Ann Cook's charges were justified. Furthermore, for all her apparent culinary Francophobia, Glasse includes quite a lot of French dishes.

> I have indeed given some of my dishes French names to distinguish them, because they are known by those names. And where there is great variety of dishes and a large table to cover, so there must be variety of names for them; and it matters not whether they be called by a French, Dutch or English name, so they are good, and done with as little expense as the dish will allow. (1747: ii)

Many of what Glasse there describes as 'my dishes' were indeed not hers at all. Stead, in her study, found that 263 out of Glasse's 972 recipes had been taken from or based upon other writers' (the proportion is almost certainly actually higher, since Stead does not claim her search was exhaustive). These earlier writers include Smith and Carter among what I have called the English 'courtly' writers, who themselves show some French influence, but also La Chapelle and Massialot, the English versions of whose books had been quarried by the compiler of *The Whole Duty of a Woman* (1737) which was then requarried by Glasse. In these ways, French influences inevitably trickled down into the work of even a professed Francophobe like Glasse. So there is really no such thing as a pure-bred English cookery book. The women cooks, however, performed a service of assimilation and simplification, and the predominant impression is still of a recognisably distinct English style. Indeed, a little later, some cookery books come to segregate French recipes into a quite separate chapter; Maria Rundell (1806) does this, as does John Farley (1783).

Mention of John Farley serves as a reminder that males did continue to write cookery books in eighteenth-century England. Apart from those employed in the kitchens of the rich, whose literary output generally declined as the century proceeded, there were two other interesting categories of professional male cooks. Pastry cooks were a specialist group, and a number of them wrote books concentrating on confectionery. Of these, Edward Kidder's is particularly interesting, for it provides evidence of the early existence of cookery schools in London. *E. Kidder's Receipts of Pastry and Cookery* (*c.* 1720) is sub-titled 'for the use of his scholars', and announces that Mr Kidder teaches 'at his school in Queen Street near St Thomas Apostles on Mondays, Tuesdays and Wednesdays in the Afternoon: also on Thursdays, Fridays and Saturdays, in the Afternoon, at his School next to Furnivall's Inn in Holborn'. The title-page adds that 'Ladies may be taught at their own houses', which can probably be taken as implying that it was mainly servants who attended at his schools.

Towards the end of the eighteenth century, however, large taverns had become fashionable banquetting places for gentlemen in London. This was reflected in the publication of a number of cookery books by their chefs: John

Farley's *The London Art of Cookery* (1783), Richard Briggs's *The English Art of Cookery* (1788), and *The Universal Cook, and City and Country House-keeper* (1792) by Francis Collingwood and John Woollams. Farley was Principal Cook of the London Tavern, Briggs is described as 'many years cook at the Globe Tavern, Fleet Street, The White Hart Tavern, Holborn, and now at the Temple Coffee House', and Collingwood and Woollams were the chefs of the Crown and Anchor Tavern in the Strand. Most interestingly, none of the four claims to have learned his trade in a private household. Indeed, Farley in his Introduction says with some pride that cookery was now 'as methodically studied as the politer sciences', and that 'a regular apprenticeship is now served in it, and the professors of it are incorporated by charter, as forming one of the livery companies of London'. Farley's book is by far the most well-organised, comprehensive and systematic of English cookery books up to this time; Briggs's is largely a plagiarisation (or, more charitably, a competent revision and enlargement) of Farley's, while the most notable thing about Collingwood and Woollams is that they achieved the unusual distinction of being translated into French.

Farley's book is certainly not devoid of French influence, but overall the impression is still distinctively English. The book is divided into four parts. The first, dealing with cookery in general, is organised on the English model (but *better* organised than ever before) mainly according to *methods* of cooking rather than by principal ingredients. The chapters are as follows:

I. Introduction; II. Directions for the proper choice of different kinds of provisions; III. Boiling; IV. Roasting; V. Baking; VI. Broiling; VII. Frying; VIII. Stews and Hashes; IX. Ragoos; X. Fricassees; XI. Made Dishes; XII. Sauces for Every Occasion; XIII. Soups and Broths; XIV. Roots and Vegetables; XV. Puddings; XVI. Pies; XVII. Pancakes and Fritters.

The segregation of the most distinctively French dishes mainly into chapter XI leads to that chapter being very long (57 pages) and containing rather a jumble of dishes, starting with the predictable 'Beef à la mode' and including many typical eighteenth-century French dishes, such as 'Pullets à la Sainte-Menehout'.[16] The chapter on sauces which follows is, in contrast, not especially French in style; it contains 27 recipes, including one for force-meat balls. The sauces are basically variations on gravy, coloured with browning of caramelised sugar, with wine added; there are also several very buttery ones – melted butter was the commonest English sauce after plain meat gravy. The other chapters are predominantly English. The puddings are mainly sweet, but the chapter starts with savoury ones such as steak pudding and Yorkshire pudding; the pies are mainly savoury, but include sweet ones such as apple pie. Farley appears to have been a cook with meticulously high standards. He had almost an obsession with cleanliness, repeatedly stressing the need for saucepans to be both clean and well-tinned and he had an appendix 'on culinary poisons', particularly the risk of copper poisoning. He spelt out details not often recorded before, such as his instruction to cook vegetables in plenty of plain water, not with the meat, which will discolour them; and he warns that 'Numbers of cooks spoil their garden stuffs by boiling them too much. All kinds of vegetables should have a little crispness, for if you boil them too much you will deprive them of both their sweetness and beauty' (1783: 169). That lesson was notoriously not learned by generations of later English cooks. Briggs too is good on points like this: he emphasises the need to drain boiled vegetables very well (1788: 315), and to add such ingredients as wine or anchovy sauce some time before the dish is ready, so as to take the rawness off 'as nothing injures the reputation of a made dish worse than raw wine or anchovy' (1788: 215).

Farley is one of the first English cooks to express a clear sense – so typical of the French for more than a century – of continuing progress and improvement in the culinary arts:

> Cookery, like every other art, has been moving forward to perfection by slow degrees; and, though cooks of the last century boasted of having brought it to the highest pitch it could bear, yet we find that daily improvements are still making therein, which must be the case of every art depending on fancy and taste. (1783: Preface)

For all his French recipes and, in this case, French spirit, much else about Farley is very English. The other three parts of his book are devoted to: preserving in all its forms – pickling, collaring, potting, making hams and bacon, and preserving garden produce and fruit; to confectionery in general; and to home-made wines, cordial waters and 'malt liquors'. These concerns are reminiscent of Markham, May and Digby. Indeed, in the confectionery section, he includes a chapter containing not only 'Elegant Ornaments for a Grand Entertainment' (a few set-pieces recalling May's castles and ships) but also instructions for carving which resurrect the *Boke of Kervynge* and its elaborate ceremonial vocabulary, albeit in abbreviated and more intelligible form.

And finally, although Farley's discussion of 'marketing' (in the modern American, not British, sense) in chapter II of Part I implies that he is writing for city dwellers who buy their provisions in London's shops and markets, Parts II and IV show clearly that he is also writing very much for country dwellers who produce much of their own food and drink, and who may have difficulty in purchasing some commodities: 'As gravy beef is not always to be procured, especially by those who live in villages remote from large towns . . .' (1783: 137). All in all, though Farley is a professional cook proud of his high standards, he makes it clear that he is writing for 'housekeepers, cooks and servants' in general. There is little sign that he has any conception of a separate, élite, professional cuisine such as was already evident in France and was to develop much further in the nineteenth century. Cookery seems to have been socially stratified much less markedly in England than in France, and Farley says that:

As this work is intended for the use of all ranks in general, not only for those who have attained a tolerable knowledge of cookery, but also for those who are but young in experience, we have occasionally given the most simple with the most sumptuous dishes, and thereby directed them how properly to decorate the table of either the peer or the mechanic. (1783: Preface)

5

From Renaissance to Revolution: France and England – Some Possible Explanations

The development of cookery and conceptions of good food in France and England from the Renaissance to the late eighteenth century has been sketched, mainly with the aid of cookery books. What explanations can now be offered for the rather different courses of development observed in the taste in food of the two countries?

It needs to be said again that, when speaking of 'English cookery' and 'French cookery', we are not dealing with two entirely separate things; French cookery had an early and continuing influence on English cookery, particularly through English cooks having worked in France and French cooks working for the very wealthiest English families. Yet there is a valid contrast. The food of the English gentry and prosperous farmers, depicted in the English cookery books, enjoyed a prestige of its own to which there was no equivalent at that date in France. From the technical point of view there are clear differences between this and the French cuisine. The French developed a 'cuisine of impregnation', replacing the antique 'cuisine of mixtures'. The use of cullis as a *fonds* and the proliferation of sauces (a process carried still further in France in the next century) were precisely not the foundation of English cookery. In England, continuities from the past were much more in evidence. The old pies and joints of meat remained the centre of the English meal, whereas in France the focus of attention shifted to the delicate little made dishes.

One explanation of the differences between French and English cookery has been so often repeated that it has the force of conventional wisdom. It is that meat was so abundant and of such superior quality in England that it was not necessary to cook it with great skill, disguise its flavour, or eke it out in made dishes.[1] This story goes back, as we have seen, at least to Sir John Fortescue in the fifteenth century, and Helen Morris (1953) draws on a variety of literature and travellers' reports to show that in Elizabethan times the English were seen by continentals and by themselves as eating vast quantities of beef – 'no kickshaws, whole bellyfuls' – rather as Texans are seen today. There was undoubtedly an element of propaganda about this, but even in the nineteenth century, the great French chef Urbain Dubois (cited by Jeaffreson, 1875: II, 239) attributed the merits of English cookery to the superior quality of English meat. Yet there is contrary evidence. Arthur Young (1792–4: 306) dismissed as an 'idle prejudice' English pride in their roast beef – 'for there is not better beef in the world than at Paris'. And Drummond and Wilbraham, discussing the eighteenth century, write that

> Probably, as in earlier centuries, a good deal of the meat was tainted before it was sold. M. Grosely, a French visitor, was disappointed by the quality of the meat sold in the London shops, which apparently had a great reputation abroad. He thought it inferior, on the whole, to that sold in Paris. (1939: 227)

Certainly there is no shortage of evidence on tainting and adulteration of food in England. In any case, an explanation based on the quality of raw materials comes very close to the view (criticised in chapter 1) that human beings 'really', even innately, prefer the 'natural' taste of foods, transformed as little as possible by the culinary arts, which are thus seen as little more than a forced adaptation to circumstance. If the rich and noble in France had 'really' preferred 'plain' food, it is rather implausible that they could not have secured the high-quality raw materials they wanted. However, whatever else they show, the cookery books, their prefaces, and the gastronomic controversies which they provoke, demonstrate that powerful social forces are at work in the development of taste in food. For all its conventional wisdom I shall therefore not pursue this reductionist explanation any further, but rather concentrate on three strands of a possible explanation in social terms of the differences in the development of French and English taste in food.

The three strands are, first, the possible influence of Puritanism, or other religious differences between England and France; secondly, the role and influence of the court, and more generally differences in the distribution of power and social stratification; and, thirdly, the differing relationship between town and country on the two sides of the Channel. These are not three independent 'factors', nor three mutually exclusive explanations. They are interrelated strands of explanation. Thus the relatively high prestige of the countryside and rural ways of life in England was connected with the balances of power between various social groups. And the unfolding of balances of power within both French and English society was considerably affected by the outcome of struggles involving religious issues. That being said, the first strand, the attempt to explain differences in English and French food directly by reference to religious differences, is extremely weak.

PURITANISM AND FOOD

It has often been suggested, usually in a casual sort of way, that English attitudes to cooking and eating were deeply and lastingly influenced by

'Puritanism', though that term is not usually closely defined. The symptoms have often been supposed to be the typical modern Englishman's indifference to food, or shame at his enjoyment of it, and their aetiology has by implication been assumed to lie in religious doctrines of the distant past. Thus, in the 1930s, J. I. Davies said that: 'There was a time, not so long ago, when it was considered 'bad form' to be interested in what one ate. This was perhaps a relic of Puritanism' (*Wine and Food*, no. 4, 1934: 62). About the same time, a witty German writer in the *Berliner Bösen Zeitung* gave 'A German View of British Dietary Habits':

> The inhabitants of Puritania, generally known as England or Great Britain, are, to their sorrow, obliged to take meals at regular intervals like the people of other countries. . . . The average Englishman picks like a canary at his plate. He is ashamed of his own appetite, and where an Englishman is found who eats with apparent enjoyment, he apologises to everybody around him for behaving like a beast. . . . In reality he is anxious about having a healthy appetite. . . . The mealtime in England is a form of the high school of puritanism and renunciation of life. (translated in *Wine and Food*, no. 11, 1936: 61–3)

In fact, as discussed in chapter 2 above, the historical evidence for seventeenth-century Puritanism having instilled widespread feelings of guilt about appetite is very thin. It therefore seems even less likely that it can be convincingly credited with shaping the whole subsequent style of English cookery. Yet this is what Philippa Pullar has sought to argue. She bases her case (1970: 125–31) on Puritan denunciations of luxuries and of prolonged festivities at Christmas and other traditional holiday times, and she appears to blame the Puritan influence both for a decline in the use of spices and for a hostility towards foreign dishes. The defeat of Puritanism at the Restoration and the rather evident French influence thereafter pose a difficulty, but Pullar asserts that 'nothing was ever quite the same again', and 'the seed of Puritanism was sown'. And this, according to Pullar, was the origin of the bifurcation (which she somewhat overdraws) between French sophistication and English plainness:

> It is an interesting conjecture that had it not been for this Puritan stunting, the English tradition might have blossomed as richly as that of the French. The ingredients were as fine as any in France. . . . Where did it all go wrong? What other explanation is there than it was rusted by this Puritan mould? (1970: 130–1)

We shall look in a moment at some possible alternative explanations, but let us first look a little more closely at the argument about Puritanism and food. It is perhaps a little unfair to take Pullar herself so seriously, since she is a popular writer rather than a serious historian; nevertheless, she only makes explicit an interpretation which has been hinted at in passing by numerous writers over many years.

The 'Pullar hypothesis' (if we may so dignify it) draws too simple a picture of Puritanism in seventeenth-century England; and it also neglects the existence of comparable religious currents in France. In the first place, as Christopher Hill (1964) has argued, before 1660 very few 'Puritans' were the general killjoys of the later stereotype. The category of 'Puritan' was much more amorphous than is often supposed, but even among the rather diverse preoccupations of those who were so described, the quality of English cookery is not at all a common concern. It is true that sabbatarianism *was* a common concern and that, in promoting Sunday as a day of religious observation and rest, Puritans were also hostile to the traditional observation of numerous irregular festivals, holidays or 'feast-days'. Hill interprets this as a response to the urban and industrial way of life already emerging in England (1964: 145ff.), a recognition of the greater need for a regular pattern of work – and of rest – in commerce and industry than in agriculture. (For that reason, he argues, the cause of sabbatarianism, like Puritanism in general, was more popular in the towns than in the countryside.) In any case, it is too facile to identify feast-days with feasting as an object of Puritan antipathy. Sabbatarians opposed church-ales and other entertainments associated with the old feast-days, but they were mainly concerned with drunkenness and other diversions inimical to the proper observation of the sabbath. When food is discussed it is, as we observed in chapter 2, in the context of the sin of gluttony rather than in terms of the moral superiority of one type of cookery over another.

In the second place, just because the word 'Puritanism' is not used of France, it is a mistake to assume that there were no comparable currents of religious opinion there. Even setting French Protestantism on one side, there were elements in Tridentine Catholic theology, and especially in its Jansenistic manifestations, which produced an outlook not unlike Puritanism.[2] Just like the Puritans, and with far more vigour than many more conservative Anglicans, the Counter-Reformation Church fought in the seventeenth century to suppress church-ales and many other popular festivals it saw as relics of paganism, to enforce sobriety and regular church attendance (Delumeau, 1971: 175–8; Bossy, 1970: 60–1). No one has ever argued that post-Tridentine Catholicism or even Jansenism succeeded in making the French feel guilty about enjoying food, and it is hardly more appropriate to attribute such impact to Puritanism in England.

It was only later, according to Hill, that the Puritans 'narrowed' into the Nonconformist 'killjoy' mould, with their exclusion from the universities, politics and public life. So to attribute the style of English cookery in the eighteenth century to the effects of 'Puritanism' is to credit the Puritans with far-reaching cultural influence at a time when their influence in the more general public domain was considerably diminished. Obviously they were not entirely silenced. In the reign of William III, numerous local Societies for the Reformation of Manners were active. The manners they sought to reform were those of the lower orders, particularly aspects of behaviour like sabbath-breaking and drunkenness which might offend others, and they sought to reform them principally by better enforcement of existing legislation (see Bahlman, 1957). The members of such societies may not have had neutral feelings on the subject of luxurious food, but their feelings on the matter did not feature prominently in the Societies' propaganda. The lower orders, needless to say, did not commonly indulge themselves to excess with over-elaborate cuisine. That those who were in a better position to overindulge themselves could anticipate some criticism is indicated by such scattered evidence as the defensive note struck by Patrick Lamb when recording the food of festive occasions at court; but there is nothing to suggest that the expected attack was specifically religious in origin.

One scarcely looks to the greatest religious leader of eighteenth-century England, John Wesley, for an instance of rich living and *gourmandise*. Yet he seems to have enjoyed his own food and expected others to do the same. In his journal for 16 August 1744, he expresses some astonishment at a letter he had received from a brother clergyman which he describes as 'remarkable'. The letter reads, in part:

> Rev. Sir; I was surprised on Sunday, when you were pleased to tell me I carried things to extremes in denying the lawful pleasures in eating. All which I advance is that he who will be Christ's disciple must absolutely deny himself. It was once a great self-denial to me not to go to a play, or to other diversions; but that is now no self-denial to me at all; so that if I was now called to deny myself in these things only, I might take up with what is past, and now live an agreeable, self-indulgent life. But God forbid. I plainly see every hour produces occasions for self-pleasing. . . . At noon, I may find many pleasant things; and of this it was I said to Mr Richards, 'if there are two dishes set before you, by the rule of self-denial, you ought to eat of that which you like the least.' And this rule I desire to observe myself; always to choose what is least pleasing and cheapest; therefore I feed much upon milk. It is pleasant enough and nothing I can find is so cheap. (1829–31: I, 469)

No better example could be found of the progressive, slippery-slope, killjoy kind of self-denial. Wesley himself did not approve of it. Abstaining from pleasant food was 'the lowest kind of fasting'. He showed some preference for 'plain' food, but food was to be enjoyed: 'it is usually innocent, mixed with a little mirth, which is said to help digestion' (1829–31: V, 347; VII, 32).

The attitude that food, like sex, is something necessary, but definitely not to be enjoyed by the virtuous, is more evident in nineteenth- than eighteenth- or seventeenth-century England, and may have some affinity with later nonconformism rather than with Puritanism or early Wesleyanism. In early nineteenth-century England, in E. P. Thompson's phrase (1963: 411), an 'all-embracing 'Thou Shalt Not!'' permeated *all* religious persuasions in varying degree. The nineteenth century, however, is far too late to save the 'Pullar hypothesis', which specifically attributes to the influence of Puritanism the divergence between French and English conceptions of good food in the previous century. And even if we concede that, though Wesley for one did not wholeheartedly approve of it, the killjoy strand of self-denial among post-Restoration Puritans and their eighteenth-century successors became stronger, the hypothesis is weak on other grounds too.

Sociologists are always excited if they can trace an 'elective affinity' between a religious ethic and a pattern of attitudes to mundane behaviour, as Max Weber did between 'the Protestant ethic' and 'the spirit of Capitalism' (1904–5). It is tempting to see such an affinity between the kind of attitude expressed by Wesley's correspondent of 1744 and the supposed English preference for 'plain food' as compared with the French. As we have seen, many of the English cookery-book writers showed a concern with economy of which the unnamed clergyman would have approved, and which was foreign to most of the contemporary French writers. Yet the 'plainness' of the food of the eighteenth-century English gentry can be exaggerated: its cooking differed technically in certain ways with that developing in France, but it was plentiful and not particularly cheap. The 'Pullar hypothesis' would seem to require that the French sort of food was 'really' or inherently more pleasurable to eat than the English style, and that the gentry yet ate in the English way from a conviction that they ought to deny themselves that pleasure. A more parsimonious explanation is that they actually liked their food the way they ate it.

Besides, to point to an 'affinity' is a long way from providing an adequate explanation: as Goudsblom (1974: 188–9) has said, even Weber's *The Protestant Ethic*, 'a masterpiece of well-documented "interpretative understanding"', is hopelessly inconclusive when it comes to the problem of explaining the actual part played by Calvinism in the sociogenesis of capitalism, failing to take adequate account of the dynamics of the total social figuration within which both Calvinism and capitalism developed. In comparison, the suggested 'affinity' between Puritanism or Nonconformism and English attitudes to food and cookery is much less well documented. And, even if it were better documented, it seems to me unlikely that it would provide the basis for a satisfactory causal explanation. For the food of the eighteenth-century cookery books which Pullar takes as representative of the distinctive 'plainness' of English food was the food of the prosperous middle class, the gentry, and much of the nobility. Yet these were not the groups where the influence of Puritanism and Nonconformism were strong in the eighteenth century. After 1660, and still more clearly after 1688, there no longer existed the threat of the Catholic influence of France and Rome which had done so much to draw the gentry and Puritans together. In consequence, as Christopher Hill concludes, 'there was no need for the alliance between gentry and Puritanism after 1660: henceforth nonconformists are drawn almost exclusively from the industrious sort of people' (1964: 217). And the 'industrious sort of people' cannot plausibly be argued to have had, within the social figuration of eighteenth-century England, the power to determine for society as a whole the models of good taste in food and eating.

COURTS AND COOKING

The role and power of courts and their associated élites in determining such models of good taste requires much more attention. So do the ways in which that rôle and power differed between countries. And their power in cultural matters cannot be understood separately from the unfolding patterns of power more generally in each country as a whole.

This is a large and complicated subject which at times will appear to take us a long way from food and cooking. We shall argue that, at least after the English Civil Wars, members of the English élite were much less subject to social forces compelling them towards conspicuous consumption and the display of increasingly 'refined' tastes than were French courtiers until the end of the *ancien régime*. Furthermore, because French court-society formed a highly visible establishment whose members were much concerned to maintain its boundaries, wealthy outsiders just beyond those boundaries fought fiercely to emulate its tastes and fashions. The fashionable world of France, however, remained relatively small in relation to society as a whole. In England, in contrast, the blurred boundaries and closely packed layers of society permitted fashions to penetrate more deeply, but they were not so dominated by the tastes and preoccupations of exclusively courtly circles.

Werner Sombart, in his book on *Luxury and Capitalism* (1913), saw the papal court at Avignon in the fourteenth century as the first 'modern' court, in the sense that it was no longer simply the base of a feudal warrior nobility, but a centre which attracted a cultured and leisured élite with some expertise in the arts of consumption. It was followed by the splendours of the courts of Renaissance Italy – the papal court itself, now returned to Rome, and those of Milan, Ferrara, Urbino and elsewhere. The beginnings of the courtly way of life were to be found in Italy, according to Sombart, because it was there earlier than elsewhere that the necessary conditions developed. These conditions included 'the decline of knighthood, the urbanisation of the nobility, the creation of the absolute state, the revival of the fine arts and sciences, the cultivation of the social graces, and the accumulation of great fortunes' (1913: 3). More fully than Sombart, Alfred von Martin traced, in his *Sociology of the Renaissance* (1932), a 'curve of development' from the vigour of the early Renaissance bourgeoisie to their assimilation to a courtly aristocracy by the sixteenth century, and showed how social and political changes were reflected in the arts and intellectual life. Though it is beyond the scope of the present book to investigate closely the evolution of taste in food in Renaissance Italy, it is highly probable that the same social and political developments would be conducive to rapid development in the culinary arts too. Thus it is not at all surprising that cookery books recording the courtly cuisine of sixteenth-century Italy antedate anything comparable in France by a hundred years.

Court-Society in France

Nevertheless it was, as Sombart argues, the emergence of court-society in France that proved decisive in the history of modern court life: the French court 'from the close of the sixteenth century on through the following centuries became the unrivalled model in all things pertaining to court life' (1913: 3).[3] In comparison, Sombart considered,

> the other courts of Europe had either no significance in the cultural life of their countries, or they were mere slavish copies of the French court. This is particularly true with regard to the English court, which was not founded until the time of the Stuarts. (1913: 4)

That statement is too crude. A differentiation within élites into 'court' and 'country' groups was evident in many European states between the sixteenth and eighteenth centuries – a social and political division with powerful cultural affinities. But the development of an absolutist court-society in England was nipped in the bud in the mid-seventeenth century, while that in France continued to develop for another century and a half. This helps to explain some cultural differences between the two countries, including some of the differences between French and English food in the seventeenth and eighteenth centuries.

'Nothing', says Norbert Elias (1969: 232), 'is more fruitless, when dealing with long-term social processes, than to attempt to locate an absolute beginning.' The line of development of French court tradition can be traced back from Louis XIV through Henri IV and François I to the courts of the Capetians. Elias, however, like Sombart before him (and like Le Grand d'Aussy [1782: III, 278–9], the first serious French food-historian, long before either) recognises that the reign of François I (1515–47) marks an important stage in the growth of royal power, in the preponderance of the royal court over rival centres of prestige (such as the court of Burgundy, extinguished a generation earlier), and in the transformation of segments of the old warrior nobility into a new courtly aristocracy.

Much of France's internal history from the reign of François I to that of Louis XIV is the story of royal efforts to draw the teeth of the old nobility. This was not just a matter of the astute policies of individual kings. It was a manifestation of the longer-term process which Elias calls 'the royal mechanism' (1939: II, 161ff.). By that he means the tendency, observable in many countries of Western Europe from the Middle Ages, for the power of royal governments to grow through the kings' ability to 'play off' against each other groups which in alliance could have limited the royal power. The subjugation of the nobility's fighting capacity to royal control did not proceed smoothly, but through a series of violent contests. In the course of the process, the power of the nobleman was being undermined by the decline of their traditional social functions and by economic developments. The direct link between landholding and military service was gradually severed. Members of the *noblesse* continued to wield their *épées*, but as officers in a professional royal army, not in a feudal levy of their own. Their commands came to be obtained through patronage. In his study of *The House of Saulx-Tavanes* (1971: 8), Robert Forster observes how by the late seventeenth century, the members of this ancient Burgundian line were no longer 'winning fame and fortune as *condottieri* captains in a frontier service on behalf of an insecure monarchy', but instead, they were becoming 'domesticated' in the armies of Louis XIV. In order to participate in the scramble for prestige posts in the army – and other lucrative posts – it was necessary to live at or near the royal court. Like many other ancient families, the Saulx-Tavanes migrated from the provinces to Paris. The move proved largely successful: in the eighteenth century the Comte de Saulx-Tavanes was rewarded with the offices of Royal Bailli and commander-in-chief in Burgundy, his brother bacame Cardinal Archbishop of Rouen and a great figure at court, while his grandson rose to the rank of duke. Against this, the financial ruin of cadet members of the family scarcely mattered.

Courtly life under Louis XIV and Louis XV was the outcome of a reconstitution of the French nobility in train since the reign of François I. It involved the incorporation into a new court aristocracy of some families of bourgeois origin, but more significantly it also involved the emergence of an increasingly clear social distinction within the nobility itself between the families which belonged to the court and the now despised *noblesse campagnarde*. 'The more insignificant the traditional functions of vassal and knight became – functions which previously maintained the distance between the nobility and other classes – the more distance and prestige attached to the function of 'belonging to the court'.' (Elias, 1969: 162) Increasingly, aristocratic life centred on the royal court until, in the reign of Louis XIV, more or less continual residence at court was required of the highest-ranking aristocrats, who served their monarch in effect in the role of personal servants.

The economic forces involved in the creation of this courtly aristocracy were complex. The decline of noble fortunes has probably been exaggerated by historians in the past. The provincial nobility – and it must be remembered that the courtiers were never more than a minority of noblemen – now seem not to have been the impoverished buffoons they were often painted. In Robert Forster's study of the nobility of Toulouse (1960) or Darnton's of Montpellier (1984), they emerge as sober men, managing their estates sensibly, with incomes inadequate only to life in Paris, and leading a modest style of life not radically different from that of the more prosperous of their bourgeois neighbours. Between their style of life and that of the court aristocracy there was a much greater gap.

The threat of *dérogeance* as an obstacle to noblemen sustaining their fortunes by entering into commerce has also been overstated in the past. While it is true that in most provinces of France, unlike in England, involvement in trade traditionally did lead to the loss of noble rank, Louis XIV and Louis XV progressively removed the legal barriers to noblemen participating in trade and industry. Guy Richard has shown that in the eighteenth century, a minority of noblemen were major proprietors of ironworks, forges, mines, armaments and textile works. They seemed to presage the emergence of 'a veritable "business nobility", bourgeois in its preoccupations, feudal in its motivation' (1974: 18). That was interrupted by the Revolution, and under the *ancien régime* noble businessmen remained a small minority: most nobles had neither the taste nor the financial resources for enterprise. The mainstay of noble income remained land. In the past, historians have dwelt upon the decline of income from feudal dues and agriculture in relation to rising prices, and especially the cost of goods made in the towns (Mandrou, 1961: 104). Certainly many noble families experienced hard times – in the case of the Saulx-Tavanes it was in the mid-seventeenth century. Their impoverishment can, however, be overstated. In the eighteenth century, as Richard (1974: 27) points out, most of the lesser and middling nobility still had revenues greater than the incomes of all but the very few richest bourgeois. Noble poverty was a very relative thing – relative to the much greater cost of the style of life imposed on those who participated in court-society.

For with their exclusion from independent military and governmental power, the life of the court nobility increasingly centred on social display, elaborate ceremonial, and virtuoso consumption. Norbert Elias (1969) more than anyone else has demonstrated the essential functions within French society of the time of the superficially senseless details of courtly life. Rituals such as the king's daily *lever* and *coucher* ostensibly expressed the old nobility's bonds with the king as well as the nuances of gradation within its own ranks. They were also means of expressing the social distance from those encroaching social groups whose functions and power, unlike its own, were growing. The old nobility, as Elias shows, no longer properly had any real function from the viewpoint of the nation-state as a whole. But they had functions for the king himself. By serving him in the capacity of personal servants, they helped to set him decisively apart from the rest of society; and more important, he preserved the old nobility as a counterweight to the various bourgeois groupings. On the successful promotion of fragmentation, tension and rivalry between all other groupings in society did royal power depend.

In this context, Elias explains, the people of the court

> developed an extraordinarily sensitive feeling for the status and importance that should be attributed to a person in society on the basis of his bearing, speech, manner or appearance. The intense scrutiny of each manifestation of a person . . . to determine whether or not he is respecting traditional boundaries proper to his place within the social hierarchy, and to assess everything relating to him in terms of its social valency, its prestige value, sprang directly from the mechanism of rule in the court society and the hierarchical structure centred on the king and the court. This sensitivity formed in the ruling class as an instrument of self-assertion and defence against the pressure from those of lower rank. Accordingly, these people experienced many things that we would be inclined to dismiss as trivial or superficial with an intensity we have largely lost. (1969: 55–6)

Thus, for example, the size and architectural detail of the residences of the various grades of the nobility and the bourgeoisie followed a recognised scale, as did the number of servants – including kitchen staff – appropriate to each rank. 'The higher one went in the social scale, the more demanding the obligation of magnificence became' (Robert Forster, 1971: 114). The court-society thus entrapped its denizens in an elaborate 'system of expenses' which ruined many great families, and would have ruined more had not royal favour rescued them with pensions or lucrative court offices. The system of fine distinctions and their involvement in status contests were too closely connected with their social identity for them to be able to economise like good bourgeois. Nobles could not escape their costly way of life, because it was so absolutely linked to rank.

> What appears as extravagance from the standpoint of the bourgeois economic ethic – 'if he was running into debt why did he not reduce his expenses?' – is in reality the expression of the seigneurial ethos of rank. . . . What in retrospect generally appears to us today as a 'luxury' is . . . anything but superfluous in a society so constructed. . . . In a society in which every outward manifestation of a person has special significance, expenditure on prestige and display is for the upper classes a necessity which they can not avoid. (Elias, 1969: 53, 63)

Excursus on 'Luxury' and 'Refinement'

This points to the difficulty of defining the meaning of words like 'luxury' and 'extravagance', which it is so often tempting to use in connection with the history of *haute cuisine* and the related word 'refinement', which I have already had occasion to use in relation to food without pausing to define it. Sombart defined luxury as 'any expenditure in excess of the necessary' (1913: 59), but he immediately added that 'obviously this is a relative definition which becomes intelligible only when we know what constitutes "the necessary"', and therein lies the kernel of the problem. We may, says Sombart, define 'the necessary' either subjectively or objectively. A subjective definition would mean judging it in relation to some ethical or aesthetic standard arbitrarily chosen and imposed on the historical situation by the observer: that approach is not relevant to serious historical and sociological interpretation. Any objective measure of 'the necessary', however, is difficult to establish. One possible yardstick, at first glance especially relevant to the study of 'luxury' and 'extravagance' in food, is found in human physiological needs. Yet while there were, in European societies at the period we are discussing, many people who at least intermittently did not obtain nourishment sufficient for their basic physiological needs, and others who through lack of later dietetic knowledge and socially conditioned choice among available foods suffered physiological deficiencies,[4] sheer quantitative lack of food necessary to meet physiological needs was not a problem in the social strata who were vehicles for the development of cookery. Judged in relation to basic physiological needs, virtually the whole history of cookery would have to be considered a study of 'luxury'.

Sombart's alternative 'objective' yardstick is to judge 'the necessary' in relation not to physiological needs but in relation to cultural wants and needs[5] – which vary, as he recognises, 'according to historical period'. Luxury judged in relation to culturally defined standards of necessity, he says, has two aspects, quantitative and qualitative. Quantitative luxury is synonymous with prodigality – 'such as the keeping of a hundred servants when one would do' – while qualitative luxury is the use of goods of superior quality; the two types are in most cases found together. Here again, however, there are difficulties. A decade before Sombart, Thorstein Veblen in *The Theory of the Leisure Class* (1899) had mordantly analysed the social forces compelling the wealthy American families of the late nineteenth century towards 'conspicuous consumption'. A little later Max Weber wrote that '"Luxury" in the sense of a rejection of the purposive-rational orientation of consumption is, to the feudal ruling class, not something "superfluous" but one of the means of its social self-assertion.' (1922: II, 1106). Elias demonstrates that this is more true of the court society than of the real 'feudal ruling class'[6] (or of the age of the American 'Robber Barons'). But his real achievement is to show, far more persuasively than Veblen, Weber or Sombart, how expenditure in consumption of many kinds was a necessary expression of the seigneurial ethos of rank and how that ethos both grew out of the structure and activity of court society and was necessary for its continuation. It was a compelling necessity and not 'freely chosen'.

The reflection of the dominance of the court-society and its 'ethos of rank' can now be clearly seen in the French cookery books discussed earlier. It can be seen in the direct reference to meals at court in Massialot, in the importance attached to the correct number of dishes and courses for particular occasions and numbers of guests, in the variety expected in the repertoire of dishes (as set out, for example, in *Les Dons de Comus*). It can also be seen in the rather grudging spirit of concessions to the needs of economy, and the clear retention of the food of courtly circles as the models from which the 'more economic' recipes are derived. There is a very definite contrast of ethos with most of the English cookery books of the eighteenth century: for example, Lamb's defensive stance towards criticisms of 'luxury', and the striking declamations of bourgeois-rational, 'economic' attitudes towards cookery by Hannah Glasse, Elizabeth Raffald and many other English authors. The difference in ethos is, as we shall argue in a moment, anchored in a greater difference in the whole social figuration of the two countries than is at first superficially apparent.

But first a remark about 'refinement'. It is easy to speak of French food as becoming 'more refined' than English, but less easy to define exactly what that means. Sombart, again, perceived that the term 'refinement' was closely related to the notions of 'luxury' and 'extravagance', and raised similar problems:

> 'Refinement' is any treatment of a product over and above that which is needed to make it ordinarily useful. . . . [But] if refinement were to be understood in an absolute sense, most of our articles of use would have to be assigned to the category of refined goods, for almosty all of them gratify needs over and above our animal needs. Consequently we must . . . use the term 'refinement' merely for that degree of elegance which surpasses the prevailing standards of luxury in goods. (1913: 59–60)

So it is hard to define what constitutes refinement in cookery at a particular time yet one easily recognises it, like an elephant, when one sees it. Arthur Young, comparing ordinary meals in England and France on the eve of the Revolution, captures something of the way in which French food was more 'refined' in precisely Sombart's sense, than English:

> We have about half a dozen real English dishes that exceed anything, in my opinion, to be met with in France; by English dishes I mean a turbot and lobster sauce – ham and chicken – turtle – a haunch of vension – a turkey and oysters – and after these, there is an end of the English table. . . . The variety given by their cooks to the same thing is astonishing; they dress an hundred dishes in an hundred different ways, and most of them excellent; and all sorts of vegetables have a savouriness of flavour, from rich sauces, that are absolutely wanted to our greens boiled in water. This variety is not striking in the comparison of a great table in France with another in England; but it is manifest in an instant between the tables of a French and English family of small fortune. The English dinner, of a joint of meat and a pudding, as it is called, or *pot luck*, with a neighbour, is bad luck in England; the same fortune in France gives, by means of cookery only, at least four dishes to one among us, and spreads a small table incomparably better. (1792–4: 306)

Sombart could also have said, though he did not, that there is a 'subjective' aspect also to 'refinement'. The differentiation, elegance and variety of 'refined goods' is also associated with the development of *knowledgeable refinement* and discrimination, and with opportunities for displaying it. The connoisseur emerges in the world of food just as he does in the words of art and music. Montaigne's Italian cook is a perfect early example; while

Montaigne's mild mockery illustrates how, in a field not yet universally considered a sufficiently dignified and central concern in noblemen's lives, refinement may be seen as affectation. By the eighteenth century, however, knowledge and discrimination in culinary matters was an expected part of *bon ton* among those who constituted the *bonne compagnie* of the court and fashionable circles in Paris. Desalleurs, a minor courtier himself, poked fun at this, just as Montaigne had done, but it is clear from his *Lettre d'un pâtissier anglois* that this affectation (as he saw it) was no longer by any means confined to a few chefs, Italian or French, but had become widespread among their employers. Desalleurs catches the ethos of court-society spreading to the dining-rooms of the *monde*:

> To see in the best houses the number of people invited, let alone the order and profusion of our suppers, a foreigner would think that vanity were host, and that friendship played no part. . . . Thanks to the good taste of the century, our meals have become a school of civility and compliments, which last throughout the supper, unless cut short by learned analyses of all the dishes and all the sauces, which being so numerous it takes a long time to discuss. (1739: 9)

Another symptom of the dignity achieved by the culinary arts and the interest taken in them in courtly circles in eighteenth-century France is the association of aristocratic names with particular dishes or sauces that we noted earlier. As Brillat-Savarin was to write:

> Towards the end of the reign of Louis XIV the names of the most famous cooks were almost always coupled with those of their patrons, who took pride in the association. These twin merits were united; and the most illustrious names appeared in the cookery-books, beside the preparations they had patronised, invented, or given to the world. (1826: 261)

To understand this manifestation of social display and competition through the dining-room and kitchen it is not important to know whether a dish was created in person by the great patron whose name it bears, or invented by his or her own chef, or merely named in the patron's honour by an aspiring culinary client. That the patrons were eager to have dishes associated with their names is enough.

All the same, as we have mentioned earlier, there is some evidence that several great courtiers did dabble in the kitchen themselves, and we quoted the Princess Palatine who mentioned in the same breath the skill of her son, the Regent, both as cook and musician. It is perhaps a little puzzling that noblemen who could and did employ staffs of professional cooks should themselves have taken the trouble to become skilled cooks, or should at least have wished it to be thought that they were. The same question can be asked of the better-documented phenomenon of the aristocratic musician. It is not enough to say simply that they enjoyed music or cooking. An explanation may perhaps in part lie in the process of curialisation which had stripped the *noblesse d'épée* of independent political and administrative functions and made the skills of social display and consumption of central importance to its way of life. In these circumstances it may sometimes have seemed that the patron was more dependent on the skills of his employee than *vice versa* – that indeed is a comic theme familiar in, for example, the plays of Beaumarchais. The patron's acquisition of superior skill, to be exercised not daily as a chore but according to the caprice of the moment, or even the acquisition merely of the appearance of superior skill, knowledge and taste, would be one strategy for maintaining a favourable balance of power. The artistically accomplished amateur or dilettante is a figure who seems to appear in periods when a nobility is losing its original social functions.[7]

It is therefore rather interesting that there are far fewer signs in seventeenth- and eighteenth-century England of the dilettante nobleman-cook. The closest parallel would appear to be Sir Kenelm Digby and his circle, and that may be significant since it was under the Stuarts that England came closest to developing a court-society on the French model. Yet one has the impression that the recipes of Digby and his friends were something rather different: more rustic, much less consciously 'delicate' or 'refined', and arising directly out of practical housekeeping on modest country estates. Certainly May, Rabisha, Lamb, Smith or Carter praise their patrons only for their generosity and hospitality, not for their exquisite taste or practical knowledge. And the women writers of the eighteenth century, like Hannah Glasse and Elizabeth Raffald, appear to be writing either for housekeepers employed by members of the gentry or for gentlewomen who themselves took an active part in the supervision of relatively modest establishments. To appreciate and to explain these differences, it is necessary to say a little more about the development of English society during the period.

The Court, Noblemen, and Gentry in England

The power and structure of the English ruling class by the eighteenth century presented marked contrasts with the French. A different pattern of social and political development can be traced back a long way. Marc Bloch, in his survey of the institutions of European feudalism, spoke of 'the exceptional case of England', and went so far as to argue that: 'In the French or German sense of the word, medieval England had no nobility; that is to say that among the free men there was no intrinsically superior class enjoying a privileged legal status of its own, transmitted by descent' (1939–40: 330–1). That was not to deny that in the Middle Ages English society, like others of the time, was based on an 'extremely rigid hierarchic division', but 'the line was drawn at a lower level than elsewhere'. Bloch traces the origins of this English distinctiveness back to the thirteenth century when royal governments, aware of the increasing ineffectiveness of the old system of feudal service, ensured that henceforth the duty of military service should be based not on blood and descent, but on landed wealth whatever its nature.

The assumption of knighthood was required of all free possessors of a certain quantity of free land, and the crown abandoned all measures to prevent the buying and selling of fiefs. The long-term consequence was the formation of a much more 'open' aristocracy, with a relatively permeable boundary between the peerage and what later came to be known as the gentry Certainly the peers had privileges, but these were chiefly of an honorific and political nature (a seat in the House of Lords most obviously) rather than legally based as in France (where the most valued noble privileges included hereditary exemption from most forms of taxation).

In short, the class of nobleman in England remained, as a whole, more a 'social' than a 'legal' class. Although, naturally, power and revenues were as a rule inherited, and although, as on the continent, the prestige of birth was greatly prized, this group was too ill-defined not to remain largely open. (Bloch, 1939–40: 331)

For our limited purposes it is not necessary to become embroiled in the details of historians' debates about exactly when and how the gentry was or was not rising, or even about exactly how 'open' was the English aristocracy.[8] What is most important is that this line *was* 'drawn at a lower level than elsewhere', and that this produced differences, as compared with France, in the figuration of power and alliances. In particular, it influenced the workings of the 'royal mechanism'. Partly because of the absence of deep and unambiguous legally based fissures in the English landed classes, there was a tendency for alliances against the king to be more successful than in many other countries of Europe (see Koenigsberger, 1977). This statement must not be misinterpreted. For a long time after the Conquest, the English royal administration was a good deal stronger than the French, and through the outcome of struggles over the centuries it continued to grow. The royal mechanism can be observed at work in England, but in the end the monopoly dominance of English kings over their subjects proved to be less securely based than that of the French. Certainly a trend towards 'absolutism' has often been discerned by historians as the Tudor monarchs increasingly got the measure of the noble magnates. Under Elizabeth, the military function of the aristocracy declined, so that by the end of her reign a large proportion of peers had never seen military service (Stone, 1965: 266). Then, and particularly under the first two Stuarts can be seen the beginnings of an English court-society not unlike that developing in France. London and the court increasingly drew noblemen and other office-seekers and, like Paris and its court, impelled them to various forms of conspicuous expenditure. John Aubrey bequeathed a memorable and amusing testimony to the formation of a courtly and (in Elias's sense) more civilised way of life in his picture in *Brief Lives* of Thomas Tyndale,

an old Gentleman that remembers Queen Elizabeth's raigne and Court . . . and with much choler inveighs against things now:

Alas! O'God's will! Now-a-dayes every one, forsooth! must have coaches, forsooth! In those dayes Gentlemen kept horses for a man-at-Armes, beside their Hackney and hunting horses. This made the Gentry robust and hardy and fitt for service; were able to be their owne guides in case of a rout or so, when occasion should so require. Our Gentry forsooth in these dayes are so effeminated that they know not how to ride on horseback! (*c.* 1680: 461)

By the 1620s and 1630s, England seemed to be moving steadily nearer to a system of government modelled on that of Richelieu, with absolute authority and aristocratic privilege centred on a glittering court. Parry's account (1981) of the representation of James I and Charles I and their royal status through the art, masques and other entertainments at court brings out striking similarities to what was later to be seen at Versailles under Louis XIV, analysed in turn by Apostolides (1981). There was emerging in England, as in France, a distinction between 'court' and 'country' interest groups which was reflected not just in different political, religious and social attitudes, but in different cultural tastes. This differentiation did not, however, have a chance to proceed as far as it was to do in France. It is, for example, worth noting that the burden of status fell particularly heavily on many early Stuart noblemen, because the medieval ideal of lavish charity and keeping open house in the country persisted alongside the newer demands of conspicuous consumption fostered in the capital (Stone, 1965: 187, 583–4). It is not too fanciful to see something of this in the uneasy combination of rusticity and French-flavoured sophistication in Robert May and other English 'courtly' cookery books of the seventeenth century.

Although an English 'absolutism' had been incipient and the court in the ascendant under the Tudors and first two Stuarts, the final struggles between the crown and its subjects were to halt the process in its tracks. Whereas in France the outcome of the Wars of Religion and the Fronde had been a further shift in power-ratios towards the king, in England the outcome of the Civil Wars was to tip the scales back towards the parliament, the aristocracy and the gentry. How decisive this outcome had been was not at first absolutely clear to contemporaries (such as May and Rabisha), for after the Restoration the court of Charles II (1660–85) – where Patrick Lamb learned his trade – still dominated both politics and fashion. For all its vitality, however, the Restoration court was not comparable with Versailles. James II (1685–8) ill-advisedly made little secret of his admiration for Louis XIV, but fear of his 'absolutist' ambitions together with his own political incompetence quickly brought about his downfall. His deposition in the 'Glorious Revolution' of 1688 set the seal of final confirmation on the outcome of the Civil Wars. When finally in 1714 Queen Anne was succeeded, according to Act of Parliament, by the first of the Hanoverian kings, it could be said that the king was more dependent on the Whig aristocracy than *vice versa*. This is perhaps a rather crude summary of a complicated story and a complicated process of shifting power ratios. Plainly the courts of William and Mary, Anne, and the Georges remained appreciable centres of political influence and intrigue. What is indisputable, however, is that the English nobility and gentry cannot be said, unlike their French counterparts, to have been 'defunctionalised'. They retained independent political power well into the nineteenth century, and thus had other and more important modes of expression than competitive virtuoso consumption.

The English ruling-class in the eighteenth century was in fact strikingly different in structure to that of France. 'Landed society' was dominant, and landowners were conventionally regarded as falling into three categories: the peers, the gentry, and the freeholding farmers who constituted the successors of the 'English yeomanry' (Wilson, 1965: 15; Mingay, 1963: 6ff.). Yet these three categories did not correspond exactly to any very clear lines of social demarcation within the landowning class. There were certainly very considerable differences from the greatest landowners down to the least in social status, income, style and standard of living, but none of the sharp social divisions and rivalries that the French kings had taken such care to promote in France. There was no real counterpart in England to the division between the *noblesses d'épée* and *de robe*, nor even to the disdain felt towards the *noblesse campagnarde*. The English peers were quite small in number – around 160–70 until late in the eighteenth century. They tended to own the largest estates and have the largest incomes, though some of the wealthiest landowning families among the non-noble gentry actually outstripped the less wealthy of the peers (Mingay, 1963: 9). This overlapping of incomes had the effect of blurring social distinctions, and the peerage was closely connected with the gentry not only directly by marriage but also through the younger sons of peers who, under primogeniture, inherited neither title nor estates and themselves became members of the gentry class.

The gentry themselves were a much larger class, and less easy to define. Contemporary estimates of their numbers ranged from 8000 to 20,000 (Mingay, 1963: 6). The lower boundary of the gentry is particularly hard to draw precisely:

> The peculiar fact, in regard to the English gentry, is that it is utterly impossible to define its lines of demarcation, especially in relation to the stratum below. . . . Esquire and gentleman were general terms and designated the independent man who lived on his rents, or followed some 'respectable' occupation. . . . [I]t was always recognised . . . that a man had to command a certain income to be counted among the gentry. But the amount of such income and the definition of a 'respectable' occupation has at all times been left to 'public opinion'. (Sombart, 1913: 12)

Thus, although members of the lesser gentry might personally manage a home farm, the gentry proper were not primarily farmers, but derived their income from rents, mortgages and investments, supplemented sometimes by the profits of office or a 'respectable' profession. But, again, the lower boundary was blurred by overlapping incomes and intermarriage between gentry and farmers. Finally, another boundary more blurred in England than in France was between landed society and trade. The threat of 'derogation' had never existed in England, and landowners showed more taste for investment in trade than did their French counterparts. Similarly, while successful merchants in both countries bought land and aspired to the status of gentry or even nobility, in England the pressure to sever all links with business was not so acute (nor so damaging to commerce) as in France.

Nearly all of the English landowning class spent a substantial part of each year living on their country estates, taking part in country pursuits and in the social life of 'county' society. The majority of them were not wealthy enough to have any alternative but to live there more or less permanently, and they participated in the affairs of their county as Justices of the Peace and in other local offices. The wealthiest families – amounting perhaps to about 400 of the greatest landlords – were in the habit of spending three or four months in London in the winter and spring of each year. This annual migration to the capital, known as the 'London Season' had begun haphazardly in the early seventeenth century, and was firmly established by the eighteenth (F. J. Fisher, 1948); it was to endure throughout the nineteenth and survive into the twentieth. The great London houses maintained by these families were centres of social and political influence which rivalled, and often outshone, the royal court. For in the eighteenth century, English monarchs no longer had anything comparable to the French crown's degree of control over ascents and descents. As Mingay writes,

> it was no longer possible to hope, as in the sixteenth and seventeenth centuries, that the personal favour of the crown might lead to gifts of offices, monopolies, and lands. . . . In the eighteenth century the monarch could neither make nor unmak as hitherto, and the road to advancement lay rather through government office and ministerial patronage, or through extraordinary ability in warfare, through eminence in the law, or less commonly through trade. (1963: 27)

The London season was closely entangled with politics; Parliament was normally in session in the winter and spring months, and of course many of the gentry were members of the Commons and all the English peers sat as of right in the Lords. The London season and its expenses were also, however, essential to those who pretended to membership of the highest circles of society; the season could not be missed without risking loss of prestige and influence. The impulse towards costly ostentation was perhaps not so unchecked and unquestioned as in France, but it was there:

> Probably only a minority of landlords relished ostentation as an end in itself. The more discerning saw it to be inherent in their social position and political functions, something essential to their role in society, but also something that should be kept within bounds. It is clear that many proprietors felt the need to temper hospitality with economy. . . . But generally the size of the family and the steady flow of visitors, the need to maintain prestige, and the pressure of social conventions and responsibilites all combined to nullify moves towards household economy. (Mingay, 1963: 161)

So something akin to the compelling French 'system of expenses' did exist in England, though ranks were more blurred and exigencies which linked expenditure to rank were not so rigid or so definite. The 'bourgeois' spirit of economy, expressed in the English cookery books, was not quite so foreign to the English landowner as to the French courtier. Above all, however, the fact that the English nobility and gentry had *not* been 'defunctionalised', but continued to hold real social and political power, made them less preoccupied with the outward symbols of differences in rank which had lost their social function, and reduced the pressure towards 'ornamental' display in matters such as manners, art, architecture and food.

It would be wrong to pretend that the tight circle of the French royal court did not loosen after the death of Louis XIV. Social life was slowly decentralised from the court to the Parisian *palais* and *hôtels* of the princes and aristocracy, and by the late eighteenth century fashionable society had become still looser, to embrace financiers and rich bourgeois. Even so, the court 'merely shared its significance as a theatre of social life, a formative influence on convivial culture'; the court remained the place where 'all the threads of society ran together, from it the rank, reputation and even, to an extent, the income of court people continued to depend' (Elias, 1969: 79). The fashionable society of Paris did not regain an independent connection with the government of the country, as existed in England. Most of the *monde*, and certainly the bourgeoisie, displayed mass apathy towards politics. On the other hand, the 'feudal reaction' – the reassertion of aristocratic privilege in the decades immediately before the Revolution – seems only to have channelled the aspirations of the upwardly mobile still more towards luxury and conspicuous consumption.[9] Duclos showed great insight in contrasting the fashionable worlds of London and Paris at this period:

> Manners do in Paris what the spirit of Government does in London: they confuse and make equal in society ranks which are distinct and subordinated in the state. All the orders of society live together in familiarity in London, because all the citizens need each other; common interest brings them together.
>
> Pleasures produce the same effect in Paris; everyone enjoying himself does as he pleases, with this difference, that equality, which is a good thing when it stems from a principle of government, is a very bad thing when it comes only from manners, because that only happens through their corruption. (Duclos, 1751: 15)

Desalleurs makes a more direct connection between display through the table and the distancing of good society from the practical concerns of government, pointing to the removal of public affairs from public discussion and their replacement by affectation and ceremony:

> In place of that Gallic liberty with which [our forebears] conversed informally about their own concerns or about the political affairs of their country (quite ridiculous according to the latest fashion), in place of joking like them about our pleasures, our passions, our inclinations, the times and good taste constantly refined with luxury have taught us to make supper into a ceremonious business. (1739: 8–9)

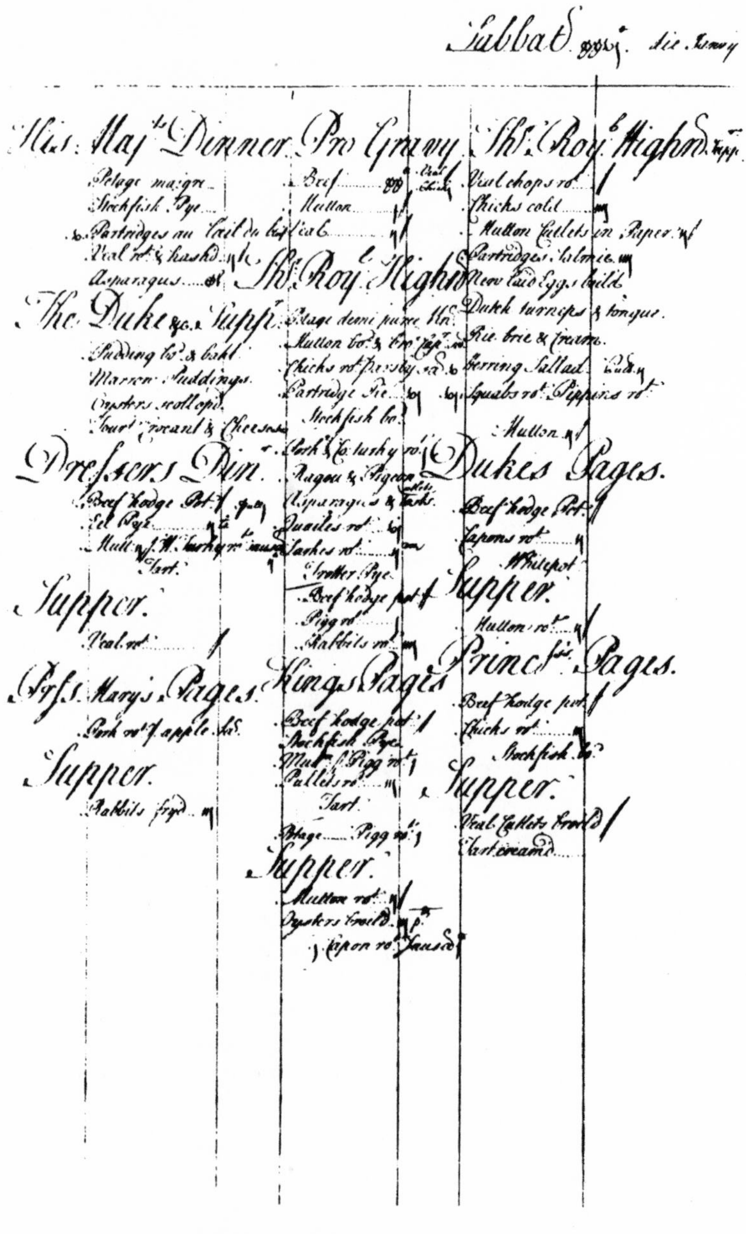
Sabbat

His Majesty Dinner
Potage maigre
Stockfish Pye
Partridges au Tail du bief
Veal rost & hash'd
Asparagus

The Duke &c. Supper
Pudding boil'd & bak'd
Marrow Puddings
Oysters scollop'd
Tourt groseil & Cheesecakes

Dressers Din.
Beef hodge Pot
Eel Pye
Mutton & Turky

Supper.
Veal rost

Princess Mary's Pages.
Pork rost & apple sauce

Supper.
Rabbits fryd

Pro Gravy
Beef
Mutton
Veal

His Royal Highness
Potage demi puree
Mutton boil'd & broth
Chicks rost Parsley
Partridge Pie
Stockfish boil'd
Pork & Co. turky rost
Ragou & Pigeons
Asparagus & Eggs
Quailes rost
Larkes rost
Tartes
Trotter Pye
Beef hodge pot
Pigg rost
Rabbits rost

Kings Pages
Beef hodge pot
Stockfish Pye
Mutton & Pigg rost
Pullets rost
Tart
Potage Pigg rost

Supper.
Mutton rost
Oysters broil'd
Capon rost sauce

His Royal Highness Supper
Veal chops rost
Chicks cold
Mutton Cutlets in Paper
Partridges salmie
New laid Eggs boil'd
Dutch turnips & tongue
Rice brie & Cream
Herring Sallad
Squabs rost Pippins rost
Mutton

Dukes Pages.
Beef hodge Pot
Capons rost
Whitepot

Supper.
Mutton rost

Princess Pages.
Beef hodge pot
Chicks rost
Stockfish boil'd

Supper.
Veal Cutlets broil'd
Tart cream

Figure 5 *Bill of Fare, St James's Palace, 31 January 1740*
Source: Public Record Office, LS.9/143

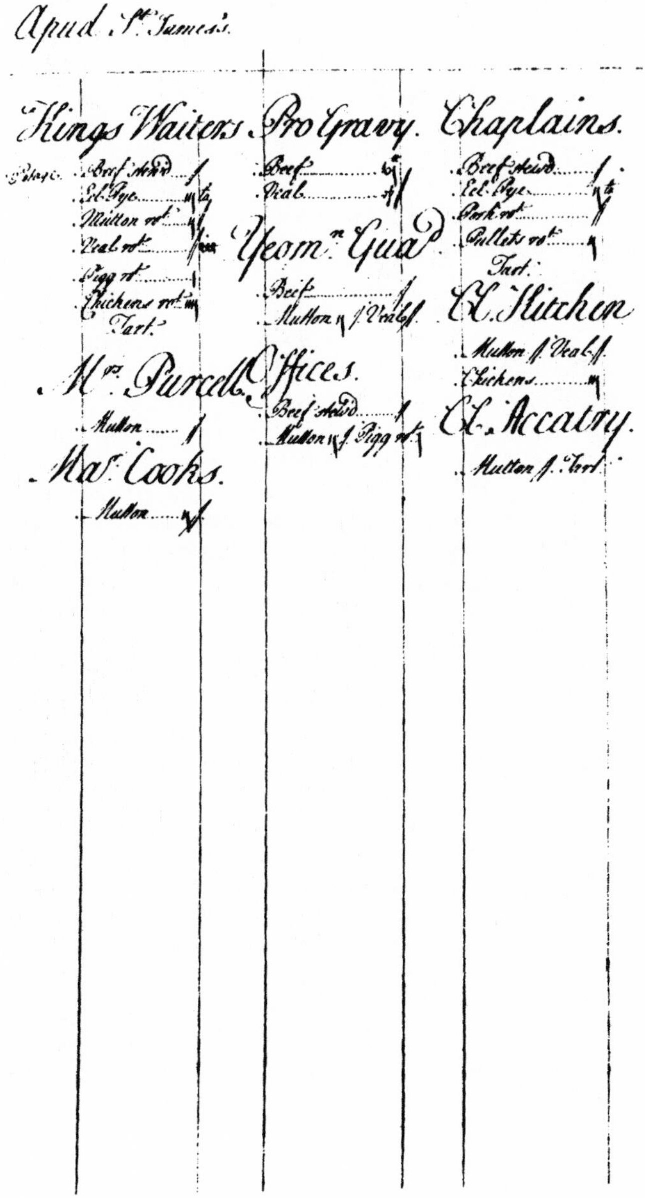

Apud St. James's.

Kings Waiters.	Pro Gravy.	Chaplains.
Potage	Beef	Beef stewed
Beef stewed	Veal	Eel Pye
Eel Pye	**Yeomn. Guard**	Pork rost
Mutton rost	Beef	Pullets rost
Veal rost	Mutton / Veal	Tart
Pigg rost	**Offices.**	**Ch. Kitchen**
Chickens rost	Beef stewed	Mutton / Veal
Tart	Mutton / Pigg rost	Chickens
Mr. Purcell.		**Ch. Accatry.**
Mutton		Mutton / Tart
Mas. Cooks.		
Mutton		

The eclipse of the distinctively 'courtly' English cookery book after Lamb (1710), Smith (1723) and Carter (1730) may seem to coincide almost too neatly with the accession of the Hanoverians in 1714 and the diminution of the political and social role of the English court to only a little more than *primus inter pares*. It would seem more reasonable to expect some measure of 'cultural lag', a delay between shifts in balances of power in society and their reflection in matters of taste such as cookery. Perhaps, however, there already *had* been a lag, for it is arguable that the court's leadership in matters of taste had begun gradually to decline much earlier. Preserved in the Public Record Office are the daily bills of fare for meals served at court virtually from the Restoration to the Regency. Until the beginning of the eighteenth century they are not sufficiently detailed to tell much about the dishes actually served, except on special occasions such as the Coronation banquet of James II in 1685, in which Patrick Lamb himself had a hand.[10] What is most striking about this vast table is that the great dishes in the centre are little different from the banquets of medieval times, and while there is considerable diversification among the lesser dishes, the food is not strikingly different from that of Gervase Markham. There is not a lot of evidence of French influence either in language or substance, and there co-exist on the same table foods such as caviare and black puddings which would later come to have very different connotations.

The ordinary daily meals at court become clearer in the reign of Queen Anne. An example chosen at random is her private dinner at St James's Palace on Sunday, 19 December, 1705.[11] It consisted of: 'Oleo, Pigeons, Sirloin of Beef rost, Venison, Chyne of Mutton, Turkey, Snipes, Ducks, Partridge'. That seems to be a large meal for a large lady, but there is little to suggest any very elaborate or refined cookery. On the same day the waiters, yeomen of the guard, chaplains and the rest of the household got at least two meats each for dinner, with the exception of the master cook who had only mutton. (The master cook, indeed, appears – implausibly! – to have lived on nothing but mutton for a whole century.) There are scattered references in this ledger to dishes such as 'henn pye' and 'tart', but no very illuminating detail.

Nothing very dramatic seems to have changed in the everyday meals of the royal household with the accession of the Hanoverians, save that garbled French is somewhat more in evidence in the following dinner served to King George I at St James's on Saturday, 1 July 1721: 'Pottage Profitrole pullet; Beef Hotch Pott; Fricandoes white; Chickens and pease; Chyne of Lamb; Capons Enfans; Squobbs Fricassy [young pigeons]; Salmon; Pullets with Eggs; Ducks and Pheasants potts.; Carpes gr'y; Artichokes; French Beans; Bacon fraize'.[12] With the exception of the chicken soup with savoury profiteroles, which is a 'refined' French dish, there is again little here which could not have appeared in the pages of Gervase Markham.

Again, in 1740, exactly when *Les Dons de Comus* had provoked fashionable debate about the *nouvelle cuisine* in Paris, King George II and his household were eating 'good plain English country fare', relished more by a little French terminology than by French technique (figure 5). The ledgers for the reign of George III (1760–1820) show slightly more signs of French (and also Italian and even occasionally Indian) influence, but the predominant style is still English, 'plain', 'traditional', 'country' food – and the rest of the household certainly ate nothing else. Here is one example of a private royal dinner, again plucked at random, from the long reign.[13]

Saturday, 1 July 1780: Kensington Palace
Their Majesties' Dinner:
Pottage vermicelly [sic]
Pullets with Rice Pillaw
Fillets of mutton and potatoes
Cold chicken and sliced tongue
Ham with pease and beans
Small turbot and small lobster
Quails
Artychokes
Cherry Tart
Lambs Sweetbreads Ragou'd
Omelettes en roulade.

These, of course, are everyday royal meals, and there was greater show for grand occasions – as Patrick Lamb considered highly appropriate.[14] Even so, what is most striking is how relatively little the food eaten by royalty differs from that eaten by a minor member of the gentry class like Parson Woodforde, the country clergyman whose diary carefully records what he eats. Thus, dining with the squire of his parish on 23 May 1788, Woodforde reports that dinner consisted of a 'fine Trout, Leg of Mutton Roasted, Beef Stakes, Pigeon Pye, hashed Calf's Head, rosted Pigeons and Asparagus and green Apricot Tart' (1926–31: III, 28). A few weeks later, entertaining neighbours in his turn, he gave them for dinner '2 Dishes of Soals fryed, ham and 3 boiled Chicken, a large piece of boiled beef, Beans, a couple of Ducks rosted and Peas, Gooseberry Pies and Currant Tarts' (1926–31: III, 35). Not so much difference, except that the number of dishes for the king and queen dining alone appears to have equalled that for Parson Woodforde when dining in company.

It is true that a minority of grandees employed French chefs, and Arthur Young claimed that 'every man in Europe that can afford a great table, either keeps a French cook, or one instructed in the same manner' (1792–4: 306). How many that really was is uncertain. Presumably the king could afford it, but meals at court scarcely reflected the latest detail of French fashion. Lord Chesterfield, as already noted, had Vincent La Chapelle as his cook for a time, and it seems likely that French cooks were particularly the prerogative of the grandest of the Whig grandees, and played a part in the development of the great London houses as centres of prestige and influence.[15] J. H. Plumb

(1952) has traced Sir Robert Walpole's graduation, as he rose from country gentleman to Prime Minister, from homely country food to (according to the satirists anyway) ostentatious and expensive French dishes and sauces, though Patrick Lamb's was the only cookery book found on his shelves. The prestige of French cookery certainly did not hold unambiguous sway, and signs of prejudice against it are very common. Joseph Addison, writing in *The Tatler*, no. 148, 21 March 1709, mocks the 'false delicates' who indulge in French food:

> They admit of nothing to their tables in its natural form, or without some disguise. . . .
>
> They are not to approve any thing that is agreeable to ordinary palates; and nothing is to gratify their Senses, but what would offend those of their Inferiors.
>
> I remember I was last summer invited to a friend's house, who is a great admirer of the *French* cookery, and (as the Phrase is) *eats well*. At our sitting down, I found the table covered with a great variety of unknown dishes. I was mightily at a loss to learn what they were, and therefore did not know where to help myself. That which stood before me I took to be a roasted Porcupine, however did not care for asking questions; and have since been informed, that it was only a larded Turkey. I afterwards passed my eye over several Hashes, which I do not know the names of to this day; and hearing that they were Delicacies, did not think fit to meddle with them. . . .
>
> I was now in great hunger and confusion, when, methought, I smelled the agreeable savour of Roast-beef, but could not tell from which dish it arose, though I did not but question that it lay disguised in one of them. Upon turning my head, I saw a noble Sirloin on the side-table, smoking in the most delicious manner. I had recourse to it more than once, and could not see, without some indignation, that substantial *English* dish banished in so ignominious a manner, to make way for *French* kickshaws.

The same prejudices emerge from Woodhouse's study of the diaries of 80 English visitors to Paris between 1660 and 1789: 'the overwhelming evidence', she writes, 'shows that English travellers returned from France better pleased with England' (1976: 193), in matters of food as of much else. One of them, Robert Poole, wrote in 1741 that

> Would you have a carp stewed, they'll bring you a dish of carp smothered over with onions, wine, herbs, etc., whereby it is become a perfect hodge-podge. . . . Hence then in regard to food in its proper taste it is far better dressed in the City of London than here [Paris]. (Woodhouse, 1976: 83)

And Mary Berry (1828: 40–1), looking back to the eighteenth century, says that French fashions appealed primarily to those Englishmen who had lived abroad a good deal, and that 'no man standing for his county [i.e. for Parliament], or desirous of being popular in it' would be wise to adopt such French ideas as three-pronged forks, or sofas – French dishes, one infers, would have been equally unpopular. Lastly, one recalls Hannah Glasse's railing against French chefs, though her hostility did not preclude her borrowing some French recipes.

It seems, then, that the fashion for French food was confined to a small circle, perhaps a very small circle, of the richest London society. The food portrayed by the English women cookery-book writers would appear to be more typical of what the majority of their prosperous fellow-citizens ate. English country notions in food seem to have had some resilience even in London and at court. If food was not the vehicle for social competition in eighteenth-century England that it was in France, the reasons included the lesser role of the English court as a style-setting centre, and that in England rivalries among the nobility and gentry could to a greater extent than in France still find expression in social functions more substantial than cuisine, fashion and social display.

TOWN AND COUNTRY

We have often spoken of the 'country' character of much English food, in contrast to the 'courtly' quality of French. Since courts (despite Louis XIV's creation at Versailles of a garden suburb before its time) are essentially urban in nature – they involve large concentrations in one place of courtiers and the many tradesmen who meet their diverse needs – this strongly implies a rural/urban contrast underlying the development of food in the two countries. This, however, needs more exploration, for England was in no simple way a more rural and less urban country than France. If anything, the opposite was the case. The scale of London and its place in English society and the British economy might lead one to expect that it would exercise a cultural dominance at least as great as that which Paris and the court enjoyed in France. It was not just a matter of the institution of the London Season: the city itself was bigger relatively to the total population of the country and by the eighteenth century bigger absolutely than Paris (see table 1).

Table 1 Approximate population of London and Paris, 1600–1800

Date	*London*	*Paris*
1600	200,000	400,000
1650	350,000	450,000
1700	575,000	500,000
1750	675,000	525,000
1800	900,000	550,000

Sources: Wrigley (1967: 215–16); Landry (1935); Hélin (1963: 249).

London grew rapidly throughout the seventeenth and eighteenth centuries, while Paris stagnated after 1700. Since the population of France was about four times as large as that of Britain, at least until the rapid increase in the British population in the latter half of the eighteenth century,

London's preponderance was even more striking: Paris accounted for about two and a half per cent of the French population in 1650 and much the same in 1750, whereas London's share of the population of England was as high as seven per cent in 1650 and had risen to about eleven per cent a century later (Wrigley, 1967: 215–16). Both Paris and London were many times bigger than any rival town in either country. F. J. Fisher (1948) has pointed to the growth of London as a centre of conspicuous consumption as a neglected factor in the development of capitalism in England; in contrast, while the importance of luxury industries in Paris has long been recognised, they were not sufficient to contribute crucially either to urban growth or the development of French capitalism in the eighteenth century.[16] Moreover, London's position in English society appears even more remarkable in the light of Wrigley's estimates of the rate of migration from the country to the capital and back. Although exact calculations are impossible, Wrigley concludes that the proportion of the total adult population of England who at some stage in their lives had direct experience of life in the great city was as high as a sixth, or even more. Thus,

> If it is fair to assume that one adult in six in England in this period had had direct experience of London life, it is probably also fair to assume that this must have acted as a powerful solvent of the customs, prejudices and modes of action of the traditional, rural England. The leaven of change would have a much better chance of transforming the lump than in, say, France, even if living in Paris produced the same change of attitude and action as living in London, since there were proportionately four or five times fewer Frenchmen caught up in Parisian life than Englishmen in London life. (Wrigley, 1967: 221)

Although the spread of fashions in food is less well documented, it is clear that other fashions, in clothes and manners for instance, did permeate from town to country. Before the eighteenth century the process was relatively slow. The country, besides lagging behind the town's fashions, also perhaps had a reluctance to abandon old forms, even including those originally adopted from the towns. In the last years of Queen Anne's reign, Addison hinted at this in *The Spectator*, when comparing the manners of the town and the country:

> Several obliging Deferencies, Condescensions and Submissions, with many outward forms and ceremonies that accompany them, were first of all brought up among the politer Part of Mankind, who lived in Courts and Cities, and distinguished themselves from the Rustick part of the Species (who on all Occasions acted bluntly and naturally) by such mutual Complaisances and Intercourse of Civilities. (1711–12: I, 135)

In the town, however, the proliferation of courteous formalities had become burdensome, and according to Addison, manners in the modish world had become more relaxed, yet the old forms persisted in the country:

> If . . . we look on the People of the Mode in the Country, we find in them the Manners of the last Age. They have no sooner fetched themselves up to the Fashion of

the Polite World, but the Town has dropped them, and are nearer to the first State of Nature than to those Refinements which formerly reigned in the Court, and still prevail in the Country. . . . A Polite Country Squire shall make you as many Bows in half an hour as would serve a courtier for a Week. (1711–12: I, 135–6)

Thus the country may have missed out on all the more fleeting of fashions, and that is a possibility to bear in mind when studying the diffusion of culinary fashions.

In the case of clothes, the diffusion of fashion from towns and courtly circles outwards into the country and down through the social scale is fairly well documented. The process was peculiar to European civilisation, for it could flourish only in a society whose upper ranks were sufficiently open to permit the necessary process of emulation. According to Harold Perkin (1969: 94), the phenomenon first emerged in the fifteenth century at the break-up of strict feudalism, with cycles of perhaps half a century. It gradually speeded up, accelerating markedly in the eighteenth century, when the cycle lasted no more than a decade. There seems an obvious parallel here with food fashions. As we have suggested, in the Middle Ages there was a vast gulf in eating between the estates, and change is only discernible from about the time of the Renaissance. Judging from the prefaces of late seventeenth- and eighteenth-century cookery books in both England and France, there was an acceleration in food fashions paralleling that in dress, even if the polemics exaggerated the pace of change in underlying techniques.

In matters of dress, what was distinctive about England was that by the eighteenth century, the following of fashion extended much further down the social scale than in other countries. Foreign visitors remarked, and the art of the period confirms, that servants and even labourers wore a conscious imitation of the dress of their immediate superiors. The reasons for this English peculiarity certainly include the size of London and extensive to-ing and fro-ing between it and the provinces, demonstrated by Wrigley. At least as important, though, was the pattern of social stratification discussed above. Perkin in particular emphasises 'the compression of the socio-economic spectrum' and 'narrowing of social distance' which had come about more in England than elsewhere in Europe. The 'closely-packed layers' of English society were especially favourable to the rapid diffusion of fashion.

The history of the fashion doll is symptomatic of differences between England and France in the eighteenth century. For 400 years dolls – sometimes life-size – were exported from France dressed to the last detail in the latest fashions of the court. One such doll is recorded as having been sent from Paris to the English court as early as 1396. By the eighteenth century they were eagerly awaited each year. Such dolls, however, were inevitably limited in their immediate influence essentially to a London élite and, for all London's dominance, relatively slow to filter through to the rest of society. During the eighteenth century, therefore, the French doll was displaced by cheap printed cardboard English substitutes, which 'dramatically exemplifies the change from fashion which was expensive, exclusive and Paris-based, to a fashion which was cheap, popular and London-based' (McKendrick *et al.*, 1982: 43). The new dolls enabled the lead of the legislators of fashion in the capital to be quickly copied by the rest of society. Significantly, towards the end of the century, the acceleration of changing fashion was such that the élite began to express its superiority not through extravagantly distinctive style but through subtleties of cut: 'although fashions changed more rapidly, there was greater social uniformity in the changes' (McKendrick *et al.*, 1982: 55). In France, in contrast, the fashionable world remained relatively small with, at this stage, a greater gulf to bridge between it and other classes. That is one reason for the relatively smaller economic significance of Paris's luxury industries than London's.

If fashions in dress spread so far and so rapidly in eighteenth-century England, it is something of a puzzle why French courtly cookery – which we know to have been the vogue in the greatest London houses – did not spread further than it seems from the evidence of the cookery books to have done. Closely related fashions, such as the times at which meals were eaten, followed a trajectory much like that for clothes. The time at which English people ate dinner had steadily become later; it had been eleven o'clock in the early sixteenth century, and slid around the dial with accelerating speed until at the end of the eighteenth century it was seven or eight in the evening. London led the way, with the provinces at first lagging many years behind the capital (Rees and Fenby, 1931; Palmer, 1952). The mere timetable of the day had connotations of rank which could be felt painfully – Jane Austen in her unfinished novel *The Watsons* (1871) depicted the embarrassment occasioned her heroines by the early hours of their relatives, humble country gentlefolk, compared with the local scions of the aristocracy.[17]

Yet in the realm of food itself, 'country' traits showed considerable resilience in England. The explanation cannot, as we have seen, lie directly in the bald economic and demographic facts, in the absolute degree of urbanisation or rurality in the two countries. Explanations must be sought in the cultural domain itself, and in particular in the higher prestige accorded the country life in England than in France. In spite of London's size, urban and rural life interlocked far more in England than in France, and this was valued: 'in contrast to the French courtier's proverbial terror of catching rusticity, the English liked to think of themselves as wedding civic to country tastes. *Rus in urbe* and *urbs in rure* were cherished ideals' (Porter, 1982: 56).

The disdain in which the *noblesse campagnarde*, roughly the equivalent of the English country gentry, were held by the court nobility has been mentioned several times already. As long as rustication from the court to his country seat was the most dreaded punishment to befall a nobleman, the prestige of country life was unlikely to be high. After the Napoleonic Wars, things were to change:

A residence at their country seats being no longer prescribed to them, under the name of exile, as a punishment in consequence of what was called disgrace at Court, a country life has become fashionable. All those possessing country houses pass many months in them, wisely taking that part of the year which is most favourable to the real enjoyment of the country; while much expense and attention are bestowed both in the ornament and the improvement of these residences. (Berry, 1828: 159)

But that lay in the future. Under the *ancien régime* there had certainly been a good deal of fashionable romanticisation of the simple country life. Classicism and aristocratic romanticism – nostalgia for the rural past expressed in art and literature – can be understood as reactions to the 'curialisation' of the old nobility (Elias, 1969: 214–67). Yet none of these cultural manifestations, nor the antics of Marie Antoinette and her ladies playing at being shepherdesses at Le Petit Hameau indicate anything about the *real* prestige of the country life. All this co-existed in the seventeenth and eighteenth century with literary satire and ridicule of the *noblesse campagnarde* (Vaissière, 1903).[18] Country pursuits were less central to the life of the French than the English social élite; few French noblemen were so practically involved in farming, and were socially far more distant from their country neighbours and tenants than their English counterparts. No doubt a few great courtiers, like Arthur Young's friend the Duc de Liancourt, took a keen interest in agriculture, but the first Duc de Saulx-Tavanes appears to have been typical of many others who visited their estates once or twice in a lifetime (Robert Forster, 1971: 104).

How might these social differences and differences in attitudes towards urban and rural life affect the development of conceptions of good food in the two countries? One effect was that the English gentleman, living at least a substantial part of the year on his estates and involved in the life of the countryside, was content to eat in great degree off the product of his land. In the eighteenth century it was customary to brew beer, make butter and cheese, and certainly bake bread at home. In the country there was inevitably less variety of produce available for purchase than could be found on the London markets, and countrymen were accustomed to eating their own produce as and when it came, not being too choosy or discriminating since there was less to choose and discriminate among. Country kitchens were necessarily offered fewer resources and less scope for an elaborate cuisine, but the quality and freshness of the produce was often better than that available in London.

Given the interlocking of urban and rural life in England, it may be that the very strength of rural traditions provided ballast even in the city for withstanding the veering about of the winds of fashion. In the manuscript recipe books of the period, there is evidence of dishes handed down in families from generation to generation. Jane Austen's letters are full of references to such recipes (though not unfortunately of the recipes themselves), and J. E. Austen-Leigh in his memoir of his aunt gives a well-balanced account of the way of life of the country gentry around the turn of the century:

The dinners too were more homely, though not less plentiful and savoury; and the bill of fare in one house would not be so like that in another as it is now, for family receipts were held in high estimation. A grandmother of culinary talent could bequeath to her descendant fame for some particular dish, and it might influence the family dinners for many generations. . . . One house would pride itself on its ham, another on its game-pie, and a third on its superior furmity or tansey pudding. Beer and home-made wines, especially mead, were more largely consumed. Vegetables were less plentiful and less various. (1871: 292–3)

Florence White (1938: 338) claims that recipes of 'good epicurean country-house cookery' had been handed down from mother to daughter in her family since Elizabethan times.

No doubt a similar inheritance of country recipes existed in France, but it was not much attended to under the *ancien régime* because of the courtiers' fashion-setting monopoly and the wider gulf separating the court and country. In 1806 Grimod de la Reynière was able to write, a shade condescendingly, of the sort of food that could be expected by guests at a French country house:

The cooking could not be other than less refined in the country than in the city; but the fare will be more abundant and wholesome there, the wines pure and plentiful. The *entremets* will consist of vegetables and creams, in the absence of pastry, as it is impossible to procure good pastry outside Paris, unless one employs a pastry-cook of one's own. The kitchen garden and the dairy will provide nearly all the dessert. Coffee and liqueurs will be served at table. (1806: 115)

The old story that English raw materials were superior to the French may well derive from comparing not factual like with like, but cultural ideal with cultural ideal – that is to say, comparing the produce available in the Frenchman's cultural ideal of Paris with the Englishman's cultural ideal of the country. At any rate, the pride of an English country gentleman in living off his own produce is well expressed, and no doubt a little caricatured, by Smollet's Matthew Bramble in *Humphry Clinker*:

At Brambleton-hall . . . my table is, on a great measure, furnished from my own ground; my five year old mutton, fed on the fragrant herbage of the mountains, that might vie with venison in juice and flavour; my delicious veal, fattened with nothing but the mother's milk, that fills the dish with gravy; my poultry from the barn-door, that never knew confinement, but when they were at roost; my rabbits panting from the warren; my game fresh from the moors; my trout and salmon struggling from the stream; oysters from their native banks. . . . My sallads, roots, and pot-herbs, my own garden yields in plenty and perfection; the produce of the natural soil prepared by moderate cultivation. The same soil affords all the different fruits which England may call her own, so that my desert is every day fresh-gathered from the tree; my dairy flows with the nectarious tides of milk and cream, from whence we derive abundance of excellent butter, curds and cheese; and the refuse fattens my pigs, that are destined for hams and bacon. (1771: 124–5)

Bramble then proceeds to make a point by point comparison with what is available in London, unfavourable in all respects to the city.

CONCLUSION

To hear him speak, or to read the diary of the real-life Parson Woodforde, one could think that little had changed between the Renaissance and the Revolution. Of course, a great deal had changed in both countries. The money economy had vastly extended, markets expanded, transport improved. In the social distribution of nourishment and in the development of cookery, the pace of change had been slow in comparison with what was to happen in the next century. Nevertheless, in these centuries there had emerged the main outlines of distinctive English and French cookery and attitudes towards food. In discussing these national differences it is easy to overstate them, and to lose sight of the fact that then, as later, the same social forces were at work in both countries even if the timing was different. Timing is important though. It was important that French *haute cuisine* continued to develop in a specifically courtly context for a century and a half longer than in England. It was important too that the English women cooks, and perhaps the male tavern cooks, played a part in the development of a simplified and more socially homogeneous style of cookery akin perhaps to that of the inventors of the cardboard fashion doll. Again, the beginnings of the same process can certainly be seen in France – less grudging in Menon's *La Cuisinière bourgeoise* than in most of his precursors – though the supremacy of courtly models remained unchallenged. That was to have important consequences for the development of French professional cuisine after the Revolution, which in turn had important consequences for English cuisine in the next century.

6

The Calling of Cooking: Chefs and their Publics since the Revolution

The Revolution has long been recognised as a landmark in the history of French eating. That is not because it destroyed the tradition of *haute cuisine* which had been developing at least since the mid-seventeenth century. It did not. However great the rupture it brought about in political authority, the persisting continuities in French cookery – as in many other aspects of French culture – from the *beau monde* of the *ancien régime* to that of the bourgeois-dominated nineteenth century are quite striking. It is arguable that the eighteenth-century tradition of English cookery was more radically disrupted by the economic and social changes in train in Great Britain than the French tradition was by the more dramatic political upheavals in France. Nevertheless, the Revolution is a culinary landmark because of the transformation which it permitted or precipitated in the cooking profession and its theatre of operations. The age of the great French restaurants is usually reckoned to date from the Revolution, and their emergence proved an immense stimulus to still more rapid development of elaborate, refined and luxurious food. In the hands of the famous cooks of the Napoleonic and Restoration periods, among whom the most celebrated of all is the name of Carême, there developed something which in retrospect has come to be known not merely as *haute*, but as *grande cuisine*. The gap between professional and domestic cookery widened, as did the related gap in prestige between male and female cooks. Parallel to the emergence of a cookery profession catering for a dining *public*, there also emerged the bourgeois gastronome – not himself a cook, but an expert in the art of eating and a leader of public opinion in matters of taste.

The nineteenth century also saw the full establishment of a French international culinary hegemony, not merely over England but over much of the rest of Europe and, by the end of the century, North America too. That of course did not mean – any more than the prestige in England of French, and French-trained, chefs in the previous century had meant – that French food was either familiar or commonplace to any but a well-to-do minority. Nevertheless, that minority grew in size, and French dishes were to be found not only at the tables of a few of the richest aristocrats and gentry, but also setting the style in London clubs, hotels and restaurants. French hegemony meant in particular hegemony within the cooking profession. English professional cooks may not always have cooked exclusively in the French model, but they were less inclined to dispute the supremacy of the French than, say, Hannah Glasse had done so chauvinistically.

One consequence of this French hegemony is seen in the cookery books of the nineteenth century. The great French chefs achieved a near-monopoly of manuals for the professional cook – the rare exceptions being by English authors working exclusively in the French tradition – and some of them also wrote books of domestic cookery too. In contrast, the best-known English cookery books, such as Eliza Acton's (1845) or Isabella Beeton's (1861), were directed exclusively to domestic kitchens.

A second consequence is that in the nineteenth century *national* differences became more nearly correlated with *class* differences. In the eighteenth century, although French influence and French prestige had been strong, it was possible to discern a fairly distinct English tradition with a prestige of its own.

A third consequence is that, while the continuity in development in French *haute cuisine* from the eighteenth century into the nineteenth is quite clear, a coarsening and decline of the great English 'farmhouse' tradition of the eighteenth century is rather apparent in the nineteenth. Quite apart from any effects which rapid industrialisation may have had in disrupting that tradition, its vitality was probably sapped by the dominance which French models enjoyed at the highest levels of society. English cookery was, so to speak, decapitated.

The *grande cuisine* codified by Carême and his contemporaries seems equally to have passed through a phase of coarsening and decline in the middle of the nineteenth century, but it was to experience renewal and revision in the hands of Georges Auguste Escoffier and his associates, and it emerged even more dominant in the world of professional cooks. The Escoffier school itself decayed in the mid-twentieth century, until the *nouvelle cuisine* movement appeared. The cycle of codification, coarsening and renewal is one of the interesting characteristics of the history of cookery since the Revolution, and appears to be associated with periods of change in the social circumstances of the catering profession.

THE REVOLUTION AND RESTAURANTS

The story of how the great Parisian restaurants arose after the Revolution is a little more complicated than how it is sometimes told. It was not simply that the cooks formerly employed in the kitchens of aristocrats who had fled abroad or perished in the Terror, finding themselves without work, were obliged to open the first restaurants. Noble emigration and the guillotine certainly did play their part in making available an increased supply of skilled manpower. Yet the first of a new form of eating-place open to the public – that which came to be known as the restaurant – made its appearance in Paris during the two decades *before* the Revolution. All the same, though it may seem paradoxical in the light of Paris's later reputation for its great restaurants, 'eating out' seems to have been more a part of the way of life of respectable gentlemen in eighteenth-century London than in Paris. (Respectable gentle*women*, of course, did not eat out in public until well on into the next century.)

In London, Paris, and every other city in Europe, it had always been possible to purchase cooked food. The restaurant could trace its ancestry back to several different kinds of institution, though none of them had quite matched the restaurant's particular combination of style and type of food, social milieu and social function. Earliest precursors of the restaurant were perhaps the cookshops described in accounts of medieval cities (such as William Fitz-Stephen's picture of London in about 1183), where townspeople could send their own meat to be cooked, or where equally they could buy a hot dish ready cooked, choosing from a wide selection of pies, puddings and joints of meat. The cookshop was particularly important to the lower ranks of citizens, for only the larger houses had adequate means of cooking (Drummond and Wilbraham, 1939: 32–3), but in its original form it was certainly not a socially exclusive gathering-place for well-to-do men about town. Cookshops existed for centuries, gradually evolving in England towards the sociable coffee-house. When Monsieur Misson wrote his well-known description of a London cookshop in the late seventeenth century, it was apparently a place where men of all social ranks, from peers and gentry to merchants and tradesmen, would take a snack together.

> Generally four spits, one over another, carry round each five or six pieces of butcher-meat, beef, mutton, veal, pork, and lamb; you have what quantity you please cut off, fat, lean, much or little done; with this, a little salt and mustard upon the side of a plate, a bottle of beer and a roll; and there is your whole feast. (Misson, 1698)

In Misson's native land, in contrast, this route of development towards the restaurant was, as we shall see in a moment, partially blocked.

The inn too, throughout Europe, had for centuries fulfilled a specific social function, but a function not quite the same as that later met by restaurants. Inns provided meals for the travellers who stayed in them, but one ate what one was given when one was given it.[1] In every country, some inns were better than others. In eighteenth-century London, many of them had a considerable reputation for their 'ordinary' – a fixed-price, fixed menu or *table d'hôte* dinner provided daily. It remained broadly true, however, that at an inn one did not choose a meal from a menu and the food was not as a rule very elaborate; nor were inns as such exactly places of fashionable resort.

As popular meeting-places, from the later seventeenth century onwards there were both in London and Paris the coffee-houses or *cafés*. The coffee-houses of Restoration London are famous as centres of political intrigue and commercial intelligence, while in Paris from the same period date such celebrated institutions as the Café Procope where literary côteries met in the eighteenth century (Fosca, 1934). By then, many of the London coffee-houses had become dining-rooms serving 'ordinaries' almost to the exclusion of coffee – but again this was a path the Parisian cafés did not follow.

Closest approximations in the eighteenth century to the later restaurants, both in their social functions and in the food they served, were the English taverns. The word 'tavern' originally signified a place where men went to drink wine, as opposed to an ale-house where beer was sold (Timbs, 1866: II, 110ff.). A tavern was thus from the beginning likely to cater for a socially superior clientèle. By the eighteenth century many taverns in the capital were noted eating-places and centres of social life. John Farley, as already mentioned, was Principal Cook at the London Tavern, Collingwood and Woollams were at the equally famous Crown and Anchor Tavern, and Richard Briggs served at The Globe in Fleet Street and the White Hart in Holborn; they are all known to us through their cookery books before any comparable Parisian figures.[2] Judging from their books, it seems probable that the London diner could make his choice from an extensive list of English fare and French dishes too. Baudrillart quotes the astonished and disdainful Marquis Caraccioli, who in his *Paris, le modèle des nations étrangères, ou l'Europe française* published in 1777 says of the English: 'Badly housed, except at their country residences, they can eat no better than at the tavern. It is there that they often take a visiting friend. . . . Is that how a gentleman should live?' (Baudrillart, 1878–80: IV, 426).

The suggestion that indifferent town lodgings of visiting country gentry contributed to their patronage of taverns is interesting. Certainly taverns must have had that advantage to a relatively modestly situated widower like Samuel Johnson. But Johnson did not see tavern life in that light. He extolled its virtues, and 'triumphed over the French' for their lack of it (Boswell, 1791: I, 650). Certainly many of those with whom in Boswell's pages we see Johnson associating in taverns were wealthy enough and of sufficient social standing for them to be there by choice, not necessity. Taverns indeed could accommodate both the exclusive dining clubs like the Sublime Society of Beef-Steaks[3] and the vast banquets beloved of the aldermen of the City of London, at which a thousand or more might sit down at once.

In Paris before the Revolution there was little equivalent to this. The first restaurants did open there in the last years of the *ancien régime*, and Grimod de la Reynière mentioned the fashion in France for all things English during the fifteen years before the Revolution as one of the reasons for their emergence as an approximate counterpart to the tavern. Beauvilliers's first great restaurant, opened in 1782 or 1786, was La Grande Taverne de Londres. Yet while it is never safe to dismiss the effects of fashion, especially when attested to by such an expert eye-witness as Grimod, it seems more relevant to ask why eating-places on the English model had not developed in France before, rather than give what must surely be undue weight to a last-minute ephemeral gust of fashion. French inns were not radically unlike English ones, serving a fixed *table d'hôte* dinner, especially for travellers. But the cookshops, which had once been very much like their English counterparts, had not developed into the same variety of chop-houses and taverns. The main obstacle to that were the rules and privileges established by the guild of *traiteurs*. The *traiteurs* had on the one hand secured for themselves an exclusive right to sell cooked meat dishes; and on the other hand they had imposed on themselves the limitation that they would sell such dishes only in quantities which contained a whole cut of raw meat, whatever it might be (Dumas, 1873: 20). In other words, a *traiteur* would not sell individual helpings of cooked dishes for consumption on his own premises, though he would sell a whole meal for a dinner party in the purchaser's own home. The *traiteurs* had in effect decided it was to their commercial advantage to be, in modern terms, something between outside caterers and a superior sort of take-away; and they were in a position to prevent others outside their own guild from meeting the rather different need which, in England, was already being met by the best taverns. Although a cooks' guild still existed in London – in the form of the Worshipful Company of Cooks which descended from original medieval companies of cookshop proprietors, piemakers and confectioners – its powers were very slight. It still attempted in the eighteenth century, but with very limited success, to enforce its right to require anyone practising as a cook in the City of London to enrol (and pay dues) as a freeman of the Company. It could not prevent anyone from trading as a cook; by tradition, in London, anyone who had served an apprenticeship and become a freeman of any of the Livery Companies could practise *any* trade, and, in addition, by the eighteenth century many 'foreigners' (people who were not citizens of London) were licensed to trade there (see Kahl, 1961). The catering profession thus represented in microcosm the differences in development between the two economies, the English already further down the road of liberalism and *laissez-faire*.[4]

Nevertheless, cracks began to appear in the monopoly of the *traiteurs* as early as 1765, the date of the celebrated Boulanger case. Boulanger was a seller of *bouillons*. While the *traiteurs* claimed the exclusive right to sell ragoûts of cooked meat, the stock or bouillon produced in the cooking had always fallen outside their monopoly, and in the 1760s was being sold under the name of *restaurant* – in the sense of restorative or 'pick-me-up', something healthy, good for the stomach. Boulanger apparently decided that the idea should be extended to cover a healthy dish of a more solid kind, and the dish he chose was sheep's feet in white sauce. The *traiteurs* not unreasonably saw this as a ragoût and took the matter to the courts. The case became something of a *cause célèbre*, and the outcome was that *parlement* changed the law, ruling that sheep's feet in white sauce did not constitute a ragoût. Boulanger's victory is one of the chestnuts of gastronomic history, and possibly rather too much has been made of it as a turning point in the rise of the restaurant in the modern sense. The case was probably more a symptom than a cause of the decline in the guild system as a whole, already in train since mid-century. In principle Boulanger made only a minor breach in the monopoly of the *traiteurs*, which survived until the Revolution swept it away along with many other guilds and their privileges. In practice, a number of restaurants opened in Paris in the years before the Revolution. Mostly they served rather ordinary food in not very elaborate surroundings, though some of them were later to be famous names. Beauvilliers, Robert, Bancelin, Meot and the 'Trois Frères Provençaux' all opened their doors before the Revolution. And the title *restaurateur* was beginning to supplant that of *traiteur* in prestige (Caillot, 1827: I, 353).

So the beginnings antedate the Revolution. But the Revolution itself had effects both on the demand for restaurants and in making it possible for supply to respond to that demand.

One source of demand much noted by contemporaries was the arrival in Paris of large numbers of revolutionary deputies from the provinces, who for the most part lodged in boarding houses and rather naturally fell into the habit of taking their meals together in the restaurants springing up in increasing numbers especially in and around the Palais Royal and the rue Richelieu. As a newly powerful group, the deputies were well-placed to set a fashion which others would follow. Thus was forged in Paris a counterpart to the connection which had long existed in London between parliamentary life and the life of the taverns and coffee-houses. The influx of provincial deputies is also, incidentally, thought to have brought to Paris many provincial dishes which were to be a fertile influence in the expanding repertoire of Parisian restaurants; for example the Frères Provençaux were especially noted, at least in the early years after the Revolution, for their provençal dishes such as Brandade de Morue and Bouillabaisse. The deputies of the Revolutionary period having helped to establish securely the fashion for eating in restaurants, people continued to follow the fashion even though in the next 80 years or so there were to be only infrequent periods of effective parliamentary life in France.

Other ways in which the social and political changes of the Revolution increased public demand for restaurants are less certain. Hayward suggested very tentatively the *nouveaux riches* preferred to eat in restaurants because

> the new patriotic millionaires, who had enriched themselves by the plunder of the church and nobility, were fearful, in those troubled times, of letting the full extent of

their opulence be known; and thus, instead of setting up an establishment, preferred gratifying their Epicurean inclinations at an eating house. (1852: 24)

Another reason for the greater proliferation of restaurants in France than in England (during the nineteenth century as a whole and not just immediately after the Revolution) has been suggested by Theodore Zeldin: 'the English, precisely because they were rich enough to entertain at home, therefore ate out less, and there were far fewer restaurants in England as a result' (1977: II, 754). At first glance, Zeldin's suggestion (as well as contrasting strongly with the Marquis Caraccioli's observations on the English in the previous century, quoted above) looks exactly contrary to Hayward's, though in fact the two are not incompatible. I suspect, however, that the connection between wealth and the fashion for eating out is not quite so direct. Possibly it is not merely differences in wealth which account for eating at home or eating out, but differences in the food that was expected, especially below the ranks of the very wealthiest. The first great chefs of the post-Revolutionary era developed an even more elaborate cuisine out of the courtly food which had already established its prestige as a model to be emulated further down the social scale and to a much greater extent than in England. It would have been difficult for any but the richest to produce a semblance of this food in their homes – it required expensive ingredients and a large kitchen staff. Grimod de la Reynière (1806: 16) argued, for instance, that a full-time specialist *rôtisseur* was essential if the highest standards were to be attained in roasting, since that required his entire attention – and a cook, whose casseroles, *marmites* and ovens required all of *his* attention could not conceivably roast as well. So, expensive as the best restaurants were, it was probably far cheaper for most of their clientèle to eat in them when they wished than to aim at such standards of hospitality at home. Furthermore, as Jean-Paul Aron (1967, 1973) shows, there developed in Paris a whole spectrum of restaurants to suit all pockets from the richest to the poorest. The sumptuousness of the food diminished with the bill but, to a much greater extent than in England, the chain of influence from the top to the bottom, though a long one, was unbroken. It is possible – and this is perhaps little more than speculation – that among the French both the fairly well-off and the less well-off had come to aspire to a cuisine a little more elaborate than they could afford to create at home.

A further clue to changing fashion in France around the time of the Revolution is unwittingly provided by Samuel Johnson's account of why taverns were already so popular in England much earlier:

'There is no private house,' said he, 'in which people can enjoy themselves so well as at a capital tavern. Let there be ever so great plenty of good things, ever so much grandeur, ever so much elegance, ever so much desire that everybody should be easy, in the nature of things it cannot be: there must always be some degree of care and anxiety. The master of the house is anxious to entertain his guests – the guests are anxious to be agreeable to him; and no man, but a very impudent dog indeed, can as freely command what is in another man's house, as if it were his own. Whereas, at a tavern, there is a general freedom from anxiety. You are sure of a welcome; and the more noise you make, the more trouble you give the more good things you call for, the welcomer you are. . . . No, Sir, there is nothing which has yet been contrived by man, by which so much happiness is produced as by a good tavern or inn.' (Boswell, 1791: I, 650)

Such a means of escape from the anxieties Johnson describes would have been quite foreign to the French courtly nobleman under the *ancien régime*. As was argued in the last chapter, anxieties of this sort and the problems of status from which they derive were so central to the way of life of the French court-society that to seek to escape them in so 'rational' a way would have been tantamount to abandoning noble status altogether. To resort to the use of taverns for entertaining in *bonne compagnie* could be seen as analogous to involvement in trade, carrying in milder form the perils of derogation. Something like this thought may have underlain the Marquis Caraccioli's astonishment at the use of taverns in the more open social world of London. At any rate, Johnson's attitude looks much more a manifestation of the ethos of bourgeois rationality than of court rationality, and similar attitudes may have appealed to the French bourgeoisie, who after the Revolution set the tone and fashions of social life far more than they had done before.[5]

None of these speculations about the growing demand for restaurants is as concrete as the effects of the Revolution on the 'supply side', in sweeping away the guilds and, especially, in closing the aristocratic kitchens and sending their cooks out to seek an alternative means of making a living. In any case, supply need not merely be a response to an existing demand: supply, through the workings of fashion, also helps to create its own demand. There is no doubt about where the supply of personnel came from: many of the restaurateurs had learned their trade in noble households. Beauvilliers left the employ of the Comte de Provence (later Louis XVIII) to open his restaurant well before the Revolution, in good time for it to be the favoured meeting place of Mirabeau and other leading figures of the Constituent Assembly (Aron, 1973: 18–21). The departure into exile of the Prince de Condé three days after the fall of the Bastille released both Robert, who opened a soon to be famous restaurant in the rue Richelieu, and Meot, whose establishment was to count the Jacobin leaders among its clientèle. And though the three brothers-in-law known as the Frères Provençaux opened a restaurant in 1786, two of them left it temporarily for experience in the kitchens of the Prince de Conti, before his flight in turn made possible their return to their own kitchens.

Whether the Revolution 'caused' the rise of the restaurant or whether, as is more plausible, it merely accelerated a trend that was already under way, there is no doubt that the advent of the restaurant marks a new stage for the cookery profession and for cookery itself. The balance of power between the chef-restaurateur and his clientèle is somewhat different from that between the cook and his aristocratic patron. The rather more equal relationship can be seen very early, with Beauvilliers swaggering among his diners wearing a sword, the mark of an erstwhile servant of the crown; and a century later when the word *patron* could be applied to the restaurateur himself, it was still more evident. Even at the beginning of the nineteenth century, the cringing, obsequious tone of the prefaces with which seventeenth- and eighteenth-century author-cooks dedicated their recipe books would have been inconceivable. There was now an alternative route to the top of the culinary profession; rather than ingratiating themselves with one of a small number of rich employers, ambitious cooks could proudly compete with each other for the custom of a much larger body of diners-out. The transformation undergone by the cookery profession was parallel to the more familiar changes in the social rôles of writers, musicians and artists during much the same period. Mary Berry did not have cooks especially in mind, but might well have had, when she wrote that in post-Revolutionary France, 'the fashionable tradespeople and professors of the arts of luxury, now feeling independent of all protection from their superiors, trusted entirely to the superiority of their talent, or their taste, for success' (1828: 148).

Abraham Hayward (1852: 22) compared cooks and writers, thinking back to Spenser waiting in Southampton's ante-room, and a time when a patron was 'almost as indispensable to an author as a publisher', in contrast to the nineteenth century when literary men depended 'almost exclusively on the public for patronage, to the manifest advantage of all parties'. A similar evolution among musicians can be seen by comparing Haydn's position as a sort of superior household servant at Esterház, with the proudly independent Beethoven making his way in the musical life of Vienna; it was Mozart's misfortune to be a transitional figure, the 'bourgeois artist in court-society'.[6] In the same way that the social rôles of composers, writers and artists were transformed by the emergence of literary and cultural publics, so was that of at least the élite of cooks by the creation of a culinary public. The culinary domain may seem of less moment but, like the intellectual salons which had emerged during the eighteenth century, the restaurant is in its way a symptom of wider shifts in social power. For, as Habermas has shown in his study of the structural development of the public sphere (1960), the growth of literary and cultural forums of opinion was an essential prerequisite for the development of a genuinely critical and political domain of bourgeois public opinion. The coffee-houses and cafés, taverns and restaurants in England and France played a key part in making possible that relatively autonomous sphere of opinion. For the culinary profession itself, however, the crucial thing was that it now had its *own* public. That marks a stage en route towards still more impersonal market-like relations between cooks and consumers with the industrialisation of the food industry in the next century. For the restaurateur, though, relations with his public remained more personal. Indeed at first, when it was common for a diner to discuss his dinner with the proprietor and order it a day in advance, the power-balance in the face-to-face relationship of restaurateur and client may have superficially seemed not greatly different to that in the equally face-to-face relationship of the head of the great household and his master-cook. But a restaurateur had many clients, not one. And to speak of a new restaurant-going public means by definition that there was now such a thing as *public opinion* in matters of culinary taste. A restaurateur could now establish a reputation which carried through the new public by word of mouth, by the new gastronomic press, and by the influence of opinion leaders.

In this new situation, the development of *grande cuisine* can be understood more in terms of competition between restaurateurs for clientèle than the more general competitive social display between rich patrons. In a competitive market, the incentives and pressures to innovation are much greater, and the pace of culinary development quickens noticeably. From the post-Revolutionary years onwards, well-authenticated examples of the creation of new dishes become increasingly common.[7] Before then, there are few if any instances of the origins of a particular dish being known; there is little besides nineteenth-century gastronomic myth and speculation, most of it quite implausible or inconclusive, about such questions as who made the first mayonnaise or béchamel. The very idea of originality in a recipe is itself almost an invention of the bourgeois age. The idea of culinary *progress* certainly appeared in the late seventeenth century, and by the eighteenth, Vincent La Chapelle was, as we have seen, claiming personal originality even if the claim is open to doubt. Before the nineteenth century, however, not only can we not say with certainty that a particular cook originated a particular dish (as opposed to printing it for the first time in a book), but it is rare for us to know cooks by name and very rare to know much more than their names. Other than their names and one or two of their employers we know next to nothing about La Varenne, May, Massialot, Lamb, La Chapelle, Marin or Menon. In the case of Menon, the most prolific and successful writer of cookery books in eighteenth-century France, we do not even know his forename – indeed even his surname is known only from the *privilège*, not the title-page, of his books. This anonymity is silent witness to the low status of cooks. Interestingly, Vatel, whose suicide in 1671 when the fish failed to arrive for a royal banquet is reported by Mme de Sévigné (1726: I, 234–6) and subsequently retailed in every gastronomic essay and history of cookery for want of any other definite names, held not the lowly office of cook, but the rather grander one of *maître d'hôtel* to the Prince de Condé. Franklin (1887–1902: III, 207) seizes on the unusual fact that the Duc de Luynes thought the death of an outstanding cook worthy of mention in his diary for 1748 as evidence that the status of cooks must by then have been rising. It probably was – but it is a rather slim piece of evidence, and we still do not know the cook's name. In contrast, even very early in the age of the restaurant, things were very different: from then we know the names and about the careers of large numbers of the greatest chefs of France, irrespective of whether they worked in restaurants or in great houses, and whether or not they wrote cookery books.

England apparently lagged behind France for some little time. Launcelot Sturgeon, writing in 1822, contrasts the recognition given cooks in the two countries as follows:

> Whatever may be the praises bestowed on a dinner, the host never thinks of declaring the name of the artist who produced it; and while half the great men in London owe their estimation in society solely to the excellence of their tables, the cooks on whose talents they have risen languish 'unknown to fame' in those subterranean dungeons of the metropolis termed kitchens. In France, on the contrary, a man's cook is his pride; he glories in his feats beyond all the exploits of his ancestors. . . . To this it is that the French are indebted for those professors of the art who have raised the national glory to that pitch which is their greatest boast; and until we imitate them in this respect we must either be content to be dependent on them for all our tolerable artists, or to put up with the plain roast and boiled, and the meagre catalogue of made-dishes of our own fat kitchen-wenches. (1822: 192–4)

Things soon changed even in England. The Duke of Cumberland, later King of Hanover, according to Hayward (1852: 17), went so far as to print on his menus against each dish the name of the cook responsible for it. And some cooks came to require appreciation: we are told that Wellington's chef resigned because the Duke showed total indifference to the quality of the food (Hayward, 1852: 16).

That serves as a reminder that in neither country was there a sudden and total switch from great chefs working in the private households of great men to working in restaurants for a public. Restaurants were a crucial development essential to the rising status of star cooks and rapid innovation in *grande cuisine*. Yet there were still great hosts famous for their lavish tables, like Napoleon's arch-chancellor Cambacérès, or Talleyrand (whose hospitality is described by Arbellot, 1940). It so happened that Carême, who more than any other single chef codified French cuisine for most of the nineteenth century, was not a restaurateur, but worked as a peripatetic celebrity for a succession of great patrons, including Talleyrand, the Prince Regent, and the Baron de Rothschild.

THE AGE OF CARÊME

Antonin Carême, born in 1784, about the time Beauvilliers first opened his restaurant and five years before the onset of the Revolution, grew up in the new gastronomic world of the Directory and Empire. From a very poor family – Carême is said to have been abandoned as a child and left to seek his own fortune – he first learned the craft of the confectioner in the fashionable *pâtisserie* of Bailly. From there he entered the kitchens of Talleyrand, working for 12 years as *pâtissier* under the Prince's chef Boucher. There he learned the arts of cookery in general, and broadened his experience further by working as an 'extra' on grand occasions under many celebrated cooks. After leaving Talleyrand, Carême worked for a dazzling list of patrons, including the Prince Regent, Czar Alexander I, the Austrian court during the Congress of Vienna, and finally he spent seven years with M. de Rothschild. Already vastly celebrated, Carême died relatively young in 1833. His fame outlived him, resting on his books: *Le Pâtissier royal parisien* (1815a); *Le Pâtissier pittoresque* (1815b); *Le Maître d'hôtel français* (1822); *Le Cuisinier parisien* (1828); and finally *L'Art de la cuisine française au dix-neuvième siècle* (1833–5). This last was unfinished at his death, and the final two of the five volumes were written by Plumerey.

'To Carême,' Montagné wrote in *Larousse Gastronomique* (1938: 212), 'money meant nothing: his art alone was important, and he prized nothing but the glory of his profession.' In this he was to set an ideological pattern as well as a culinary model for French cooks in the nineteenth century. The claim that Carême was indifferent to money cuts two ways, however. Indifferent to amassing money for himself he may have been, but his indifference also meant that he did not want to have to give it a thought when spending it on behalf of his employers. Though he claimed that *L'Art de la cuisine française* was comprehensive in scope, and contained recipes useful to all ranks in society, most of its contents are manifestly costly to prepare, and Carême warned that it was:

> an error for those of lesser station to try to pattern their tables after the rich, crowding them with badly prepared food, badly served because of inexperienced help. Better to save a simple meal, well-prepared; and not to try to cover the bourgeois table with an imitation of the rich. (1833–5: I, lviii–lvix)

From the very first, Carême's food required not merely costly ingredients but the most elaborate and therefore costly preparation. Whilst still in his teens, working as a *pâtissier* with Bailly, he came to associate confectionery with architecture, and spent much time studying and copying prints of classical architecture in order to reproduce them in the kitchen as elaborate set pieces or *pièces montées*. The architectural style was carried over into his cooking generally. Dishes were displayed on decorated bases or *socles*, and ornate carvings and statuary in lard and in spun sugar were an essential, if inedible, part of any Carême's grand dinners. Beauvilliers, who summed up his own life's work in *L'Art du cuisinier* in 1814, the year before Carême's first books appeared, ridiculed Carême's masterpieces of picturesque ruins made of lard and Greek temples in sugar and marzipan (see figure 6). Carême claimed that his art supplied food for mind and heart, and pleasurably filled the gastronome's leisure. To which Beauvilliers retorted that the cook's job was not to please the eye but the palate; not to fill one's

Figure 6 Designs by Carême

leisure but one's belly pleasurably. Not surprisingly, contemporary commentators counted Beauvilliers as leader of the 'classical' school of thought in cookery, and Carême as leader of the 'romantics' (Hayward, 1852: 25).

Yet Carême's work, like several other landmarks in the history of cookery, represents at one and the same time an advance in complication and a movement towards simplification. The complication is the more obvious, but the simplification is there too. It consists in a codification of procedures, the elimination of the merely redundant, and in the pursuit of ideal blends of flavours rather than the harsh juxtaposition of contrasts. For example, Carême established the principle of garnishing meat with meat, fish with fish, and dispensed with such things as trimmings of cockscombs and sweetbreads which had survived since the Middle Ages (Willan, 1977: 143). Carême's culinary aesthetic is caught very well in Lady Morgan's frequently quoted description of a dinner at the Baron de Rothschild's – even though she barely names a single dish on the table.

> To do justice to the science and research of a dinner so served would require a knowledge of the art equal to that which produced it; its character, however, was that it was in season, – that it was up to its time, – that it was in the spirit of the age, – that there was no *perruque* in its composition, no trace of the wisdom of our ancestors in a single dish – no high-spiced sauces, no dark-brown gravies, no flavour of cayenne and allspice, no tincture of catsup and walnut pickle, no visible agency of those vulgar elements of cooking of the good old times, fire and water. Distillations of the most delicate viands, extracted in silver dews, with chemical precision –
>
> 'On tepid clouds of rising steam' –
>
> formed the *fond* of all. EVERY MEAT PRESENTED ITS OWN NATURAL AROMA – EVERY VEGETABLE ITS OWN SHADE OF VERDURE . . . (Morgan, 1831: II, 416–17)

Lady Morgan describes the dinner as a 'specimen of the intellectual perfection of an art, the standard and gauge of modern civilisation'.

The principal locus of simplification in Carême's work lay in the sauces, already long recognised as the cornerstone of French cuisine. Carême abandoned the old and complicated cullis of the eighteenth century in favour of a triad of basic sauces – espagnole, velouté and béchamel. The preparation of each of these *fonds*, though complicated by modern standards, represented considerable simplification of earlier practice. Each would be prepared in large quantities in the professional kitchen in the age of Carême and then used, with the addition of numerous other flavourings, as bases for a whole range of 'compound' sauces for particular dishes.[8] Including the further families of egg-based sauces derived from mayonnaise and hollandaise rather than from the *fonds* and not susceptible to preparation long in advance, Carême himself used over one hundred sauces, and this total was constantly added to by his successors during the rest of the century. There was a parallel proliferation of dishes closely related to the sauces – notably soups and soufflés. (Recipes for soufflés appear in Carême's books for the first time; like the improved sauces, they were in part made possible by technological improvements, notably the closer control of heat in the kitchen range invented by an American, Benjamin Thompson, Count Rumford.) Simplification and codification were a prerequisite for this proliferation; thus simplification and differentiation are seen to be not just opposites, but dialectically entangled with each other. Together they represent a process of rationalisation in the kitchen.

Simplicity and complexity are related in another way: the most complicated processes of preparation are often directed towards an end product of apparent simplicity. Carême's cuisine could be said unconsciously to mirror the economic transformation beginning to overtake Europe during his lifetime. The lengthening chains through which the production of commodities by means of commodities is achieved under capitalism is also seen in Carême's recipes. His cookery, as Revel (1979: 300) notes, is always a multi-storey structure. It is rare for the first ingredient mentioned to be the one which gives the dish its final appearance. Almost every recipe involves the use of the sieve or cheesecloth, straining, extracting, concentrating, reducing. And every dish depends on the previous preparation of purées, essences and sauces, the composition of which is taken for granted, and which are listed among the ingredients in just the same way as a piece of celery or a chopped onion. Yet, in the end,

> Like classical art, the result of Carême's art is always very simple and extraordinarily easy to appreciate. What is complicated is the process by which it is arrived at, a process whose goal, moreover, is not to superimpose flavours but quite on the contrary to isolate them and throw them into relief. With Carême, *grande cuisine* is not, as it is too often thought to be and as it is frequently caricatured, a barbarous accumulation of ill-assorted ingredients, but rather a matter of preserving the dominant flavour into the final preparation. Carême introduced into cookery what in painting are called 'values' – that is to say, he made it understood for the first time that flavours and aromas must be judged not in isolation, but in their mutual relations. (Revel, 1979: 300)

French cooks of the nineteenth century were no less fond of comparing their craft with the sciences than with the arts. Carême may certainly be said to have established something very closely akin to an artistic style or school in cookery. His books also have some claim to embody the first paradigm, more or less in T. S. Kuhn's sense of the word, of professional French cuisine. The analogy between cookery and the sciences ought not to be driven too hard, but is none the less in some ways illuminating. Kuhn (1962) discusses the role in history of such works as Ptolemy's *Almagest*, Newton's *Principia*, Franklin's *Electricity*, Lavoisier's *Chemistry* and Lyell's *Geology* (as well as many less famous theories); they served for periods ranging from decades to millennia to define the legitimate problems of a research field for generations of practitioners. These 'paradigms', says Kuhn, shared two essential characteristics: they themselves were achievements sufficiently unprecedented to attract an enquiring group of scientists away from rival theories; and their achievement was not final – in that, while establishing major assumptions, they left countless problems for later workers to solve. Now, while there had certainly been famous cookery books before, and there were other very famous author-chefs in Carême's own lifetime, no previous work had so comprehensively codified the field nor established its dominance as a point of reference for the whole profession in the way that Carême's did. And Carême laid foundations on which others could build; just as Kuhn's 'normal scientist', working within an established scientific paradigm, 'does not aim at novelties of fact or theory and, when successful, finds none' (1962: 52), aiming rather to articulate the accepted assumptions in new situations, so until nearly the end of the nineteenth century Carême's followers – even the greatest names like Jules Gouffé, Urbain Dubois and Joseph Favre – essentially worked within the framework he had established.

There are other parallels too. Kuhn suggests that one consequence of the establishment of the first paradigm in a scientific field – the consequence of agreement on fundamentals – is the much more rapid progressive accumulation of knowledge and its extension to wider and wider territory; often this stage is associated with the establishment of the first specialist journals in that branch of a discipline, which in turn is associated with the writings of specialists becoming less and less intelligible to the general educated reader. Again, the nineteenth century did see a rapid extension of the repertoire of French professional cookery, and it did witness – though not until some decades after Carême's death – the appearance of specialist journals for professional cooks; and the gulf between the techniques of the professional kitchen and what was possible to the domestic cook did widen. Finally, Kuhn shows how in a given field scientists eventually come up against certain problems ('anomalies') which prove inconsistent with the fundamental assumptions of the paradigm in which they are working; this provokes a crisis and eventually leads to the overthrow of the old and its replacement with a new paradigm, so renewing the cycle. Carême's 'paradigm' could be said by the late nineteenth century to be showing its age and proving incapable of dealing with problems then arising. To repeat the warning, however, the scientific analogy should not be pushed too hard: the story of professional French cookery can equally be likened to the succession of schools in the history of art, beginning with vigorous working out of new ideas, followed by their routinisation and exhaustion, and eventually the resurgence of yet another new aesthetic.

The continuation of Carême's school is seen at its best in such books as Jules Gouffé's *Le Livre de cuisine* (1867), *La Cuisine classique* by Urbain Dubois and Emile Bernard (1856), and Joseph Favre's *Dictionnaire universelle de cuisine et d'hygiène alimentaire* (1883). Gouffé (1807–77) was a pupil of Carême himself; as was quite commonly possible at the time, he made his fortune as a restaurateur in a mere 15 years between 1840 and 1855, and was only tempted out of retirement a decade later by the gastronomes Baron Brisse and Alexandre Dumas *père*, who persuaded him to take charge of the kitchens of the Jockey Club. The *Livre de cuisine* is notable for Gouffé's having systematically separated the treatment of ordinary domestic cookery in the first part of the book (more than 300 pages) from the exposition of *grande cuisine* in the second part (nearly 500 pages). What may appear unusual respect and attention paid to domestic cookery by one of the élite of French professional chefs is better understood, however, as an attempt to establish domestic and professional cuisines as two quite distinct disciplines and distinct conceptions of good cooking.

> Culinary manuals generally mix up the *petite* with the *grande cuisine*, the simplest dishes with those of the most complicated type; whence stems a most deplorable amalgam, which explains how the study and practice of the culinary art have made so little progress until now. (1867: ii)

Gouffé alludes to the allegation that standards have declined since his master, 'l'illustre Carême', but affirms his faith in the 'continuing progress to which cookery is susceptible' (1867: v). His own heart is clearly in *grande cuisine*, and his dishes are elaborately designed and displayed in the manner of Carême.

Félix Urbain Dubois, sometime chef to the King of Prussia, is even more famous for his architectural creations, and his dishes were often ornamented with inedible decorations. If this ornamentation tended to reinforce the old tendency for food to be less than piping hot by the time it reached the diner's mouth, Dubois is on the other hand credited with doing something for the cause of hot food by being the prime mover in the displacement of *service à la francaise* by *service à la russe*. The former phrase means the method, dating from the Middle Ages, of serving a large number of dishes simultaneously in each course, from which the diner took his choice in the manner of a modern buffet; the latter means the modern method of service, where each dish is cut up in the kitchen and a helping served to each guest, with the meal composed of fewer dishes but more courses in sequence than under the old system. *Service à la russe* made its appearance in France and England around mid-century, but was not universally followed until the 1890s.

Though the prestige of French cooks in England long antedated the nineteenth century, French culinary hegemony across the Channel was greatly strengthened by several of the greatest names working in England after the Revolution. Carême himself, as already mentioned, cooked briefly for the Prince Regent, and Beauvilliers, too, worked in England during a period when his previous royal connections made it prudent to close his restaurant in Paris. Most prominent among the French chefs working permanently in London during the early nineteenth century was Louis Eustache Ude, Louis XVI's former cook, who spent 20 years as chef to the Earl of Sefton, and then made Crockford's Club in St James's as famous for its dining tables as its gambling tables. Ude's cookery book (1813), written in something approaching English, contains some recipes of English origin, as did that of Beauvilliers, but most of the traffic in influence and personnel was northwards. In the middle of the century Hayward (1852: 77) listed 'the most eminent cooks of the present time in England'; of the twenty-eight cooks, three *pâtisseurs* and (separately noted) four confectioners listed, only three appear to have English names. Of Hayward's other list of thirteen 'young men rising into reputation', again only three have English names. Among their employers, only two are commoners, and two are clubs: the rest are peers or sons of peers. This serves as a reminder that when we speak of 'French culinary hegemony' in England, we are still speaking of hegemony among a social élite. Nevertheless, that élite was probably somewhat wider and the hegemony a good deal stronger than it had been in the previous century, and that had consequences for English cookery beyond the élite. Its most immediate consequence was that much of English professional cookery in the nineteenth century was derivative – from French models – to a much greater degree than was, say, the work of John Farley.

By far the two most famous professional male cooks in England around the middle of the century were Alexis Soyer and Charles Elmé Francatelli. Soyer (1809–58) was a Frenchman, but passed all his adult life in England and to this day is virtually unknown in his own land; he was in many ways a more typically English figure than French. Francatelli (1805–76), on the other hand, was in spite of his name proud of being born an Englishman – but he had been a pupil of Carême in Paris. Both of them were cooks in the style of Carême, though even in their lifetimes discerning observers questioned whether their achievements reached quite the first rank.

Soyer was an extraordinary man, remembered now perhaps more as one of the great characters of Victorian England than for his cookery itself.[9] He was something of a dandy and a wit – he is caricatured as the French chef Mirobolant in Thackeray's *Pendennis* (1848–50). He was a showman, a writer of some ability, and an inventor in the best Victorian mould – of patent sauces (manufactured by his friends Messrs Crosse and Blackwell), of a great variety of novel kitchen equipment, of naval kitchens, and of widely used field-stoves. Above all, however, he remained a cook of amazing range. After working for various members of the peerage and gentry, he became chef of the Reform Club, whose celebrated kitchens he designed and presided over for many years. The Club's membership embodied the peculiar political blend of the early Liberal Party – the good living of the Whig grandees with the austerity of early capitalists, bourgeois vulgarity with social concern – and all this seems reflected in Soyer's activities in cooking.

On the one hand, at the Club, he was noted for his lavish cuisine, and once created a dish costing a hundred guineas. He also specialised in organising the vast banquets, so much part of English public life and so much despised as vulgar by gastronomic observers of the English scene. For instance he organised a banquet for Prince Albert and all the mayors in the country, and for the annual dinner of the Royal Agricultural Society at Exeter in 1850 he roasted an ox whole, by gas. The sheer scale of these occasions – the Exeter dinner was for a thousand covers – and the distribution of the leftovers to the poor, are reminiscent of the great medieval feasts. On the other hand, Soyer increasingly threw his energies into charitable work and culinary reform. At the opposite pole from his hundred-guinea dish, he invented a recipe for nourishing soup at three farthings a quart (see Soyer, 1847); Prince Albert sampled it at Soyer's soup-kitchen in Leicester Square, and in 1847 Soyer was busy establishing soup-kitchens in Ireland during the great potato famine. Back in London, the great banquets for the rich were matched by a Christmas dinner in Ham Yard for 20,000 of the city's poor. Finally, in 1855, he was sent to the Crimea by the British Government to tackle the scandalously insanitary conditions in the hospital kitchens (Soyer, 1857), contributing alongside Florence Nightingale to saving life there – but at the expense of fatally undermining his own health.

Soyer's first cookery book was *The Gastronomic Regenerator* (1846); 'a simplified and entirely new system of cookery, with nearly two thousand practical receipts suited to the income of all classes'. In fact, in the first and by far the largest section, entitled 'The Kitchen of the Wealthy', Soyer presents an essentially French and not strikingly novel cuisine in the style of Carême, complete with the most elaborate *socles*, decorative skewers, *pièces montées* in the shape of temples and pagodas, and so on. Even so, there are some signs of adaptation to English taste and, even here amongst his most flamboyant and extravagant dishes, there are frequent and rather un-Gallic hints at the desirability of economy both in cost and effort required in preparation. For example:

> *Velouté*. This sauce has stood for a century as a foundation sauce in the highest class of cookery, and may be admired for its utility and the delicacy of its flavour; but I have avoided referring to it in almost every receipt on account of the expense attached to it and its tedious fabrication. (1846: 5)

'The Kitchen of the Wealthy' concludes with a long account of the kitchens of the Reform Club (1846: 611–29), and is followed by the section entitled 'My Kitchen at Home' (1846: 631–710): 'In the department entitled my Kitchen at Home will be found the same arrangements [in the sequence of a bill of fare], and the repetition of many dishes from the Kitchen of the Wealthy, but so much simplified that the industrious classes of society may partake freely of them at very moderate expense' (1846: xi). Plans of cottage kitchens designed by Soyer are provided, and the food includes far fewer sauces and many more puddings and dishes made from leftovers, but the style of cookery is still essentially French.

Soyer wrote at greater length for the middle classes in his *Modern Housewife, or Ménagère* (1849), which sold in vast numbers in spite of being written in the curious form of letters between 'Hortense' and 'Eloise'. More remarkable still was the success of his cookery book for the working class, *A*

Shilling Cookery for the People (1854), which sold ten thousand copies in the first six weeks and more than a quarter of a million within a few years. This too was written in epistolary form. It was not, perhaps, addressed to the very poorest, for many of its recipes seem fairly complicated and costly. There are several obvious French influences, such as the recipe for Pot-au-Feu and a general prejudice in favour of soups (which the English lower orders appear to have had a matching prejudice against), but it is basically adapted to English traditions. The *Shilling Cookery* is also, as we shall see in the next chapter, a prime ethnographic source on English urban working-class cookery in the middle of the nineteenth century. For, as Soyer explained,

> whilst semi-buried in my fashionable culinary sanctorum at the Reform Club, surrounded by the *élite* of society, . . . I could not gain, through the stone walls of that massive edifice, the slightest knowledge of Cottage Life. Determined to carry out my long thought of projects, I cheerfully bade adieu to my wealthy employers . . . and, like a pilgrim of the olden time, I set forth on my journey, visiting on my route every kind of philanthropic and other useful institution, but more especially the domains of that industrial class, that backbone of every free country – the People. (1854: viii)

Alexis Soyer was a phenomenon. Judged by the heights of his *haute cuisine*, however, he was not considered in quite the highest rank of cooks by the guardians of true French standards even in his lifetime. Hayward described Soyer as

> another *artiste* and writer on gastronomic subjects, whose name has been a good deal before the public. He is a very clever man, of inventive genius and inexhaustible resource; but his execution is hardly on a par with his conception, and he is more likely to earn his immortality by his soup-kitchen than his soup. (1852: 76–7)

Jerrold, a little later, went so far as to describe Soyer as vulgar:

> M. Alexis Soyer's ground will not be trespassed upon. All his modes of regenerating the kitchen are not ours. His gastronomic phantasies and eccentricities were of a sensational kind. His 'Pagodalique' and 'Hundred Guinea' dishes are vulgarities. (1868: 2)

Francatelli, the free-born Englishman with an Italian name, fared rather better with the strict constructionist culinary francophiles. After training with Carême, Francatelli had returned to England and worked in the kitchens of various peers before succeeding to the office at Crockford's once held by Ude. From there he became, for a short time, *maître d'hôtel* and chief cook in ordinary to Queen Victoria. Later he spent seven years in Soyer's shoes at the Reform, ran the St James's Hotel, and finally ended his career at the Freemasons' Tavern.

Francatelli's *The Modern Cook* (1846) is an essentially French-style treatise, starting in systematic fashion with 104 sauces. Even the contents of the puddings section are in the French rather than the English fashion, and the whole is the product of an orthodox member of Carême's school, far more so than Soyer's works are. Yet even in Francatelli there are traces of the influence of English attitudes even if scarcely of English dishes. In the footsteps of Soyer, Francatelli wrote *A Plain Cookery for the Working Classes* (1861). As the *Dictionary of National Biography* notes with approval, 'While able to dress the costliest banquets, Francatelli was also a culinary economist.' Even in *The Modern Cook*, gestures towards parsimonious housekeeping were apparently obligatory:

Judicious economy being at all times a great consideration, the Author has studied to apply its practice in the composition of every recipe contained in this book. Many dishes are obviously expensive, and can only be indulged by the wealthy epicure; – but even here the cost may be reduced by avoiding waste, and by turning to account ingredients carefully reserved for the purpose by the aid of foresight and economical habits. In large establishments, when properly conducted, there is indeed less relative waste than in the kitchen of a small private family under the management of an ordinary cook. (1846: v)

All the same, Francatelli's concessions to English tastes were fairly minimal: he was always the pupil of Carême. He lamented that, though possessed of a great abundance of all kinds of food in excellent quality, 'our cookery in theory and practice has become a by-word of ridicule'.

By now, the advantages which London had enjoyed over Paris in its eating-places in the eighteenth century had been quite reversed. Thomas Walker (1835: 259–62) compared the intimate atmosphere of the Paris restaurants, especially their *cabinets particuliers*, with the large, high-ceilinged, cavernous London dining-rooms. Walker, like Jerrold a little later, particularly despised the vulgarity of the big public dinners to which the London taverns were still particularly adapted. Jerrold listed many taverns where 'you may have a chop broiled under your nose . . . that shall defy criticism', perfectly cooked turtle, venison and poultry, and excellent oyster houses, but anything more elaborate was a bad risk, and public dinners were invariably gastronomic failures: 'nobody for one moment would think of comparing the most carefully prepared dinner for sixty with such a menu as Francatelli prepares for half-a-dozen, in Piccadilly' (1868: 111–12). At about the same time, Jeaffreson wrote that cookery in public dining-rooms had, for want of critical diners and competent cooks, languished for half a century, 'and in the last twenty years has sunk to the low level of vulgar industry'.

To our opprobrium, it must be confessed that there is no Continental capital so poorly provided as London with establishments where the stranger may obtain a fairly good dinner for a small sum, or an excellent dinner at a great price. (Jeaffreson, 1875: II, 241–2)[10]

In London, the best eating-places were still private or semi-private. The privacy of the tables of the very wealthy was, of course, common to England and France, and in neither country very relevant to Jeaffreson's stranger seeking a good dinner. To the privacy of the London clubs – even if that privacy was shared among the fairly large number of members who were the shareholders of these 'joint-stock palaces', as Thomas Walker (1835: 252–9) called them – there was, on the other hand, little equivalent in Paris. (The Jockey-Club, at which Gouffé served as chef, was an exception modelled on its English counterpart.) A few of the London clubs at certain periods had great reputations as eating places – most notably Crockford's under Ude, the Reform under Soyer, and both later under Francatelli. Generally speaking, however, clubs provided good average rather than excellent food; one reason, it was suggested, was that working for a committee provided a chef with no clear guiding taste, nor incentive to please it. It was also suggested that the clubs, which became steadily more numerous from about 1820 onwards (Timbs, 1866), helped to undermine standards in the public eating-places. For at his club a man could enjoy for a few pounds a year facilities, comfort and food otherwise available only to the very wealthy. The stratum of moderately well-to-do bachelors and periodic visitors to town who in Paris played such a part in building up the restaurants were to a considerable extent in London siphoned off into the clubs.

So where else was good cooking to be found in London in the first half of the nineteenth century? The best, according to contemporary opinion, was to be had not in the taverns, inns, or even the clubs, but in a number of exclusive private hotels around St James's Street and Piccadilly.[11] The St James's Hotel, run for a number of years by Francatelli, was one of these. The word 'hotel' was considered rather pretentious until around 1820, having something of the French sense of an aristocratic residence. The establishments which then began to spring up bearing that title differed from the inns in that they had no common dining-room (Borer, 1972: 162). A resident took a suite and ordered meals to be served in his private sitting-room – these were the menus 'Francatelli prepares for half-a-dozen in Piccadilly'. Several of the hotels had noted French chefs, and it was their food which mainly distinguished them from the houses where a visitor to the capital could hire an apartment and keep himself. The early hotels, in other words, most closely resembled what a century later would be called service flats. They did not yet fully belong in the public sphere. For at first one had to be resident in order to dine there. Even when common dining-rooms appeared, they were not necessarily fully open to the public. In his memoirs Captain Gronow (1862: I, 54–5) speaks of Stevens's Hotel in Old Bond Street, which was popular with an exclusive set of army officers: exclusive in the most literal sense, for he relates that 'if a stranger wanted to dine there, he would be stared at by the servants and very solemnly assured that there was no table vacant'. Stevens's Hotel, in other words, was half way to being a private club. At this stage, the boundary between the public and private spheres, already very clear in France, remained rather ambiguous in England.

Not that all remained well, apparently, in France. In the middle decades of the nineteenth century it was widely charged that – as well as mediocrity persisting in London – there had been a falling off of standards in Parisian restaurants. Hayward quotes and endorses the opinion of the noted connoisseur the Comte d'Orsay that not one of the famous Paris restaurants could in 1852 serve a dinner such as were produced by Ude, Soyer or two other French chefs working for English aristocrats. Even the celebrated Véry, whose supremacy in 1814 had been marked by its catering for the Allied Sovereigns, had now sunk into d'Orsay's second division. D'Orsay's conclusion that 'the pretended French gastronomy . . . has emigrated to England', however, was no doubt a little tongue in cheek, and in any case juxtaposing the standards of the finest private chefs in London with restaurants in Paris was no longer a comparison of like with like. One reason why standards in the restaurants were falling was the excessive ease with which they could please ignorant foreigners, especially the English. Jerrold (1868: 114) complained that Paris's reputation drew many utterly undiscriminating diners to its tables, that the cheaper restaurateurs in particular lay in wait for them, and that the ease with which they could be pleased corrupted the cooks: why take the trouble when the difference will not be noticed? The other side of the coin was the inability or conservative reluctance of the uninitiated to appreciate true excellence when confronted with it. Jerrold recalled ordering dinner for a Manchester family he encountered in perplexity with the menu at Brebant's:

> I cannot call the *menu* to mind at this moment: but Madame Manchester pushed the Marennes oysters from her with disgust, vowed she could not sit in the same room with the melon; and finally, when a *foie gras aux truffes*, perfectly cooked, was put upon her plate, tasted, drew back from the table with an expression of uncontrollable disgust, saying, 'Ugh! whatever is that? I never tasted anything nastier in my life!' This family had been a fortnight in Paris, and throughout had been dining off 'a good plain joint, sir', – I think at the Hotel Byron, all the time. (1868: 116)

Both complaints – of the corrupting effect of the ignorant palate, and of the conservatism of the typical English diner – have been endlessly repeated from the nineteenth-century gourmets to the editors of today's restaurant guides.

Another reason for a fairly widespread sense of stagnation or decline was the tendency of the most prominent chefs to gild the lily – a temptation inherent in Carême's whole approach, but one which the master resisted rather more successfully than his followers. Dallas complained that 'Too much art in cookery may be as fatal as too little; and it is impossible to read some of the receipts of the master cooks without wishing that they could forget high art and come down to common sense' (1877: 4). He illustrated his point with the case of Sauce Robert, an onion sauce which is one of the oldest and simplest in the repertory. In its original and classic form, said Dallas, it could be found in Beauvilliers: made from onions, well-browned, with the addition of a little French mustard. But it was now impossible to recognise the sauce in the liquid which was now served up in its name in both Paris and London. The great chefs could not rest content with the simplicity of the old recipe. 'They glory in high art and all the wonders of science; and they have improved upon the sauce until its fine gusto is lost in a weak civilisation.' Onions were not polite enough: the quantity was reduced and sometimes they were mixed with chopped gherkins. In the original recipe there had been neither wine nor vinegar, save for a little tarragon vinegar in the mustard: now one set of chefs (Dubois, Bernard and Gouffé most notably) loaded it with wine and even ketchup, and another set (he names Francatelli) drenched it with vinegar. And there were even 'cookery books whose writers think they cannot have too much of good thing, and drown the sauce in wine and ketchup as well as vinegar' (1877: 5). Dallas also complained that, for all its pretensions, French cookery could yield monotonous results. That was particularly true of the cold buffet, where the use of aspic reduced everything to a boring repetitiveness. As an extreme example, he cited a supper menu of Francatelli's, consisting of eight *grosses pièces* and forty-eight cold entrées, every single one of which – even including the salads – used aspic (1877: 2). Nor were these complaints just a repeat of the usual English cry for 'good plain food'; Dallas was a supporter in general of French cuisine. By the late 1870s, *grande cuisine* was ripe for further reform, and the social circumstances were right too.

THE AGE OF ESCOFFIER

The transformation of French professional cookery which took place in the late nineteenth and early twentieth centuries is associated particularly with the name of Georges Auguste Escoffier (1847–1935). Escoffier achieved extraordinary celebrity in his lifetime, and his influence has endured thanks in large part to his *Guide culinaire* (1903) which acquired a biblical (or 'paradigmatic') status among chefs that even Carême and Félix Urbain Dubois had never attained. Indeed it remains a central text in the training of professional cooks to the present day. Escoffier was not, however, a unique and isolated great man who single-handedly brought about a culinary revolution. He was one of the great generation of chefs whose greatness lay in their response to new opportunities and new circumstances arising in their lifetimes. In particular, this was the age when the great international hotels sprang up. Escoffier was one of the central figures – others who may be especially mentioned include his friends and collaborators Philéas Gilbert, Prosper Montagné, and Prosper Salles – in a network of influence connecting the kitchens of leading hotels and restaurants in all the major cities of the Western world.

The great hotels which began to be built throughout Europe and America in the 1880s and 1890s were in part a slightly delayed response to the greatly increased mobility of the railway age. The well-to-do now travelled more frequently and in greater numbers across national frontiers, as well as to the capital cities, spas and resorts of their own countries. The new hotels at which they stayed were not only much larger but also quite different in character from the exclusive private hotels in London where good food was to be had in Francatelli's generation. They were more sumptuous and offered more luxuries to their residents. But they were no longer private, in the sense that one did not have to be resident in order to avail oneself of many of their facilities, and most importantly, their public dining rooms were fashionable venues. Of course, they were still exclusive, but exclusiveness now rested on their expense alone rather than on a semi-private association with a particular social circle (such as Gronow's army officers at Stevens's Hotel earlier in the century). Another novel characteristic of the new hotels was that it was now respectable for ladies to dine there in public. Restaurants in Paris and taverns in London had hitherto been largely male preserves (though Jerrold mentions the Burlington and the London Tavern as being suitable for women as early as 1868 – possibly because they had private rooms);[12] ladies had, however, dined in private apartments in the early hotels, and this carried over into the more public hotels of the late nineteenth century. The presence of women in itself changed the social character of dining rooms; Escoffier himself noted that one reason for the hotels becoming so much part of fashionable life was that 'they allow of being observed, since they are eminently adapted to the exhibiting of magnificent dresses' (1903: xi). He mentioned that, with the advent of mixed dining, late suppers at the hotels after the theatre became fashionable, and that 'the well-to-do began to flock to them on Sundays in order to give their servants the required weekly rest'.

Escoffier played a considerable part in the development of the fashionable hotel. Working as a young man in his native Provence and in Paris, he rapidly made his mark, and became associated with César Ritz in promoting new hotels first on the Riviera then in London.[13] In 1890 he took charge of the kitchens of the new Savoy Hotel in the Strand, moving in 1898 to the Carlton where he remained until his retirement in 1921. It was during this period that he accomplished a reform of the organisation of the professional kitchen which was rapidly copied throughout the industry. Escoffier ended the division of the kitchen into various more or less independent sections, a pattern going back to medieval times. We have already mentioned that in the aristocratic household of the *ancien régime*, the *office*, responsible for sweets and desserts (and also for *hors d'oeuvres*), was an entirely separate department from the *cuisine*, and this persisted some way into the nineteenth century. But quite apart from that division, within a large-scale *cuisine* there had traditionally been a number of sections, each responsible under the chef for a category of dishes but working independently of each other. Thus the same component preparation, such as a sauce, might be made quite separately by several sections of the kitchen at the same time.

Instead of this system, Escoffier organised his kitchen into five interdependent *parties*, each responsible not so much for a type of dish as for a type of operation. The *parties* were those of the *garde-manger*, responsible for cold dishes and supplies for the whole kitchen; the *entremettier*, for soups, vegetables and desserts; the *rôtisseur*, for roasts, grilled and fried dishes; the *saucier* who made sauces, and the *pâtissier* who made pastry for the whole kitchen. Herbodeau and Thalamas (1955: 79) illustrate the different *modi operandi* of the old and new regimes in the kitchen in relation to the preparation of one dish, *oeufs à la plat Meyerbeer*. Under the old system, it would have taken a single cook about fifteen minutes to prepare in its entirety; under the new, eggs were cooked by the *entremettier*, kidney grilled by the *rôtisseur*, and truffle sauce prepared by the *saucier*, and the whole assembled in only a few minutes.

The effect of Escoffier's reorganisation of the economy of the kitchen was thus to break down traditional craft demarcations, while advancing the division of labour into more rational specialisations and weaving the kitchen staff into closer interdependence with each other – in microcosm, the same trends as were unfolding in the industrialising economy at large.[14] The goal in relation to which Escoffier's reforms could be judged 'rationalisation' was, of course, the speedier service required by a less-leisured clientèle, arriving perhaps after the theatre and expecting their supper served promptly within minutes of ordering. Long gone were the days when it was common to order one's meal at a restaurant early in the day or the day before. Escoffier was very conscious of the social changes which were necessitating changes in the style of cookery as well as of service. The heavy and elaborate style previously popular was, he said, inappropriate to

> the light and frivolous atmosphere of the restaurants; was, in fact, ill-suited to the brisk waiters, and their customers who only had eyes for each other. . . . It is eminently suited to State dinners, which are in sooth veritable ceremonies, possessing their ritual, traditions, and – one might even say – their high priests; but it is a mere hindrance to the modern, rapid service. The complicated and sometimes heavy menus would be unwelcome to the hypercritical appetites so common nowadays; hence the need of a radical change not only in the culinary preparations themselves, but in the arrangements of the menus, and the service. (1903: xii)

The simplification of the menu, of its service, and of the actual cookery to which Escoffier is alluding here was the work of more hands than his alone. Escoffier himself certainly played a leading part in shaping the familiar form of the meals served in restaurants and at formal dinners down to the present day – a sequence of courses from *hors d'oeuvres* or soup through fish, meat usually with vegetables, sweet, savoury, to dessert (or more commonly a sample therefrom). In this, his model menus published as columns in journals for his fellow cooks and eventually in his *Livre des menus* (1912), were particularly influential. But such menus, and the speed of service achieved in the great new hotel restaurants, would not have been possible without the prior acceptance of *service à la russe*, first championed by Dubois in the 1860s. And as for cookery itself, it was above all Prosper Montagné (1865–1948) who campaigned against fanciful and over-elaborate dishes. He argued constantly, and eventually at length in *La grande cuisine illustrée* (1900) written jointly with Salles, that sauces and garnishes were not meant to camouflage, cover or make more acceptable the food they garnished. Their function was rather to help and not to hide, to add to the flavour, taste or consistency of the food they adorned, and to do it discreetly. There were to be no *socles*, *bordures*, *hâtelets*, no carvings in wax or mutton fat, no silver ornaments. Everything was to be edible. At first, Escoffier resisted some of Montagné's thrust towards simplification (Gottschalk, 1948b) – one of his own earliest publications was a little book about the use of wax flowers in decorating the table – but he certainly came to share these views and presented them cogently in *Le Guide culinaire*. This work, although always known simply as 'Escoffier', was in fact a collective work, largely written by him, but 'with the collaboration of MM. Philéas Gilbert, E. Fetu, A. Suzanne, B. Reboul, Ch. Dietrich, A. Caillat, etc.'. It can be fairly taken to represent not the views of one man, but an aesthetic shared by most of the leading names among French professional chefs of the period.

Although the *Guide culinaire* still represented the *fonds de cuisine* as fundamental to French professional cookery, and listed hundreds of sauces derived from them, it marked a decline in the near-universal use of the *espagnole*, *béchamel* and *velouté*, and the increased use of the lighter *fumets* – that is, much simpler essences or juices of fish, meat or vegetables. *Fumets* were used to intensify rather than conceal the natural taste of the dishes they accompanied, whereas the constant use of the strongly flavoured *espagnole* and *velouté* had gradually come to make everything taste alike (as, for example, in Francatelli's cold supper menu in which every dish used aspic). More generally, Escoffier and his associates aimed not to include a profusion of strong flavours in a single dish, but to achieve a perfect balance between a few superb ingredients. The fact that these superb ingredients might well still include expensive and 'rich' items like truffles and crayfish sometimes makes the modern reader fail to perceive Escoffier's objectives and his simplification. But his aims can be seen most perfectly in his use of only a few of the most ordinary ingredients, and in the simplest way, to create one of his most celebrated dishes, the Pêche Melba. In its final form, this involves the inspired addition, to the original peach with vanilla ice-cream, of the counter-balancing tartness of puréed raspberries.

Not that the development of taste was at any time unilinear and without counter-currents. At much the same time as Escoffier and his collaborators were producing *Le Guide culinaire*, the noted engineer, amateur cook and gastronome Ali-Bab (Henri Babinski) was producing his *Gastronomie pratique* (1907). Ali-Bab made no concessions to simplification, and championed richness and complication. His recipe for *lièvre à la royale* ran to ten pages, and the sauce contained foie gras, truffles, brandy and any number of other flavourings, so that, as Curnonsky (1958: 237) pointed out, 'the taste of the hare disappeared into the background', whereas a true *lièvre à la royale* ought to have a sauce made simply from the hare's blood, cream and garlic. Nor did the taste of the dining public move uniformly and instantly to greater simplicity; one of King Edward VII's favourite dishes consisted of pheasant stuffed with snipe, themselves stuffed with truffles, and the whole thing served with a rich sauce (Magnus, 1964: 268).

Nevertheless, greater simplicity was a dominant objective during this period, and it was then that what is now known as 'international hotel and restaurant cooking' assumed the form familiar today – a style which in the words of Waverley Root (1958: 10) 'appears all over the world on menus whose French is frequently as bad an imitation of the real thing as the cooking is likely to be'. Though nowadays one of its most familiar features is a rather pretentious routineness, it was shaped very much by the restaurant-going public's constant demand for novelty, and since the early nineteenth century the invention of new dishes has been one of the principal ways in which great chefs and restaurants competed with each other in the market.

> But novelty is the universal cry – novelty by hook or by crook! It is an exceedingly common mania among people of inordinate wealth to exact incessantly new or so-called new dishes. Sometimes the demand comes from a host whose luxurious table has exhausted all the resources of the modern cook's repertory, and who, having partaken of every delicacy, and often had too much of good things, anxiously seeks new sensations for his blasé palate. Anon, we have a hostess, anxious to outshine friends with whom she has been invited to dine, and whom she afterwards invites to dine with her. (Escoffier, 1903: xii–xiii)

Escoffier, though noted as creator of perhaps more famous dishes than any other individual chef, went on to complain of the strain and difficulty of trying to meet this demand for new dishes with a relatively limited number of raw materials and combinations. 'Personally, I have ceased counting the nights spent in the attempt to discover new combinations, when, completely broken with the fatigue of the heavy day, my body ought to have been at rest.' He and other innovating chefs of the period seem to have drawn on three rather different sources for new dishes.

First, many of them made a systematic study of earlier authors. Montagné, for example, is known to have studied not only Carême's published work, but his manuscript notes in the Talleyrand archives. Escoffier, according to Herbodeau (in his Introduction to the English translation of *Le Guide culinaire*) not only derived inspiration for his own recipes from those of Carême, Dubois and Bernard, but also found many ideas in the *Viandier* of Taillevent, a modern edition of which was published in 1897. This well demonstrates how the printed record of the past facilitates innovation.

Secondly, traditional peasant dishes were sometimes transformed into items of *haute cuisine*, the substitution of expensive ingredients for everyday ones often obliterating any hint of humble origins. Elizabeth David provides the following imaginative reconstruction of how Escoffier came to transform a very simple vegetable dish of his native Provence, sliced potatoes with artichokes baked with olive oil and garlic and scented with wild thyme, into something altogether grander.

> So rustic a dish can hardly, he realises, be offered to the fine ladies and gentlemen who frequent the elegant restaurant over which he presides. From force of habit he banishes the garlic and adds sliced truffles. It is a period in the history of cooking when the addition of truffles would make a poached mouse or a fricassee of donkey's ears acceptable to those rich and great ones who flock to eat the creations of this famous chef. They do not know that, for once, they will be eating what is almost a peasant dish. Truffles are one of the natural products of Provence. In a dish of potatoes and artichokes – another of the local products – they are by no means out of place. The olive oil of the country will not however be acceptable to the Parisians or to Londoners. Butter must be used instead. Concentrated, clear meat juice must, it goes without saying, be added. In the classic cooking of professionals meat juice or broth goes with everything, olive oil with nothing save salads, vinaigrette and mayonnaise sauces. . . . In its original form [the dish] would have made . . . an entire meal. To the customers of the renowned and glorious Auguste Escoffier potatoes, artichokes and truffles do not make even one course. They belong with a joint of meat. So Escoffier uses his vegetables as a foundation upon which to bake a choice little cut of spring lamb . . . he calls his creation *carré d'agneau Mistral*. He publishes the recipe in a book; and another of the myriad village dishes of France has entered the repertory of *la cuisine classique*. (David, 1964: 29)

A third category of new dishes, however, cannot usefully be regarded as adaptations either of peasant dishes or of older written recipes. A dish like *pêche Melba* really cannot be classed other than as an individual invention, deliberately created. It was not something gradually evolved out of an anonymous tradition. But such dishes immediately became common property: Escoffier complained that while artists, writers, musicians and inventors were protected by law, the chef had absolutely no redress for plagiary of his work (1903: xiii). Sometimes a dish has all the hallmarks of an individual and deliberate creation – Root (1958: 78) points to *crêpes Suzette* as an example – yet it has passed so thoroughly into the public domain that there is only speculation about who invented it, when and where.[15]

It is ironic that for all their inventiveness, their aiming for simplicity, their willingness to break with the past, Escoffier and his colleagues were themselves fated to establish a new orthodoxy lasting more than half a century. 'Escoffier' became a bible. Perhaps the religious image is appropriate, for there took place something analogous to what Max Weber (1922: I, 246–54) called the 'routinisation of charisma' in religious movements following the passing of their founders. Unwittingly, Escoffier had in his turn 'decreed for eternity laws that were applied blindly, sometimes with talent, too often with complete mediocrity', as Gault and Millau (1976: 148) were to phrase it. For instance, although Escoffier himself had moved away from the routine use of *espagnole* and *béchamel*, among his routine followers in international hotel and restaurant cooking there was 'no question of casting doubt on the excellence of the *fond de sauce* which, nine times out of ten, stood simmering throughout the week on the corner of the stove'. Against practices like that there has taken place since the 1960s the most recent of the successive revolutions or renewals in French professional cookery, now known as *nouvelle cuisine*.

NOUVELLE CUISINE

The label is hardly original: the same words were used in the 1740s for the new cookery of La Chapelle, Marin and Menon, and occasionally in the 1880s and 1890s for the work of the Escoffier generation. The term was applied in the 1960s by Henri Gault and Christian Millau to the new style of cookery they found in the work of such chefs as Paul Bocuse, Jean and Pierre Troisgros, Michel Guérard, Roger Vergé and Raymond Oliver. Their *cuisines* were quite diverse and individual, but Gault and Millau 'discovered the formula', which they then championed in their gastronomic guides and magazine. They pinpointed ten common characteristics (1976: 154–7). *First*, the *nouveaux cuisiniers* rejected unnecessary complication in cookery – an impulse for which there are many precedents. *Secondly*, they reduced the cooking time for most fish, seafood, game birds, veal, green vegetables and pâtés, aiming thereby to 'reveal forgotten flavours'. In this, and in the rediscovery of steaming as a method of cooking, *nouvelle cuisine* may owe something to the practice of Chinese cookery. *Thirdly*, *nouvelle cuisine* was (as the title of Bocuse's 1976 book indicated) a *cuisine du marché*. That is to say, the chefs insisted on buying the freshest ingredients available in the market each day. Many products had been bastardised and polluted by food technology and overproduction; the new chefs preferred to eliminate inferior ingredients altogether rather than mask them with aggressive sauces. *Fourthly*, in order that each dish be of a high standard, the international hotels' gigantic lists of prefabricated dishes were abandoned, and a much shorter menu presented to the customer. *Fifthly*, the new chefs abandoned strong marinades for meat and served game fresh, not 'high'. *Sixthly*, they eliminated excessively rich and heavy sauces, especially the lingering *espagnole* and *béchamel*. They had a particular horror of the use of flour roux, and made more use of good butter, fresh herbs, lemon juice and vinegar in dressing their dishes. *Seventhly*, they turned to regional dishes and away from the pretensions of Parisian *haute cuisine* as a source of inspiration for new dishes. *Eighthly*, the new chefs showed great curiosity about the most avant-garde techniques. Their kitchen equipment was ultra-modern – Bocuse made use of microwave ovens. Even their mistrust of frozen food was tempered by an interest in how to use it intelligently. *Ninthly*, they tended to have the dietetic implications of their work constantly in mind: Guérard's *La Grande Cuisine Minceur* (1976) sold hugely, both in France and in English translation. *Tenthly*, a common characteristic of the leaders of *nouvelle cuisine* was their sheer inventiveness. The Troisgros brothers' recipe for Escalopes de Saumon à l'oseille (1977: 158–9) is representative of the sort of dish which has already become an international classic. The pairing of the salmon and sorrel recalls Escoffier racking his brains for both 'new combinations' and simplicity three quarters of a century earlier.

One characteristic of the *nouveaux cuisiniers* that Gault and Millau did not include in their list is that most of them are chef-proprietors of their own restaurants, almost in the way that Beauvilliers, Véry, Legacque and the rest were after the Revolution. *Nouvelle cuisine* originated in rebellion against the Escoffier orthodoxy, particularly as stultified in international hotel cuisine. Several of its leaders were students of the great Fernand Point at the Pyramide in Vienne, and went on like him to own relatively small restaurants in provincial towns. Perhaps it was inevitable that the bureaucratic pressures and accounting preoccupations within modern hotel chains would today make them unpromising sites for cooking at the highest level, however suitable an environment they had given Escoffier. Accountancy plays little part in *nouvelle cuisine*. By its nature it is expensive: it requires the finest ingredients and is extremely labour-intensive. Like the ideas of Carême and Escoffier before it, the influence of *nouvelle cuisine* has spread around the world, to Western Europe, the USA, and even Japan. In Britain, the Roux brothers (of Le Gavroche and the Waterside Inn) and Anton Mosimann (of the Dorchester) established enormous reputations in the 1970s and 1980s. Perhaps it is unavoidable that as its ideas are adapted by lesser talents in less liberal contexts, *nouvelle cuisine* too will undergo routinisation and become a dogma. Already in the mid-1980s, some writers have detected signs of its exhaustion.

CONCLUSION

It is striking that, apart from the abandonment of the trimmings, decorations and inedible architectural fantasies of the Carême tradition, the aesthetic aims of Escoffier, Montagné, and their collaborators are in summary not unlike Carême's. The aim of achieving a perfect balance between a few well-chosen flavours is simply a development from Carême's understanding that 'flavours and aromas must be judged not in isolation, but in their mutual relation', compared by Revel to the notion of 'values' in painting. In fact, in summary, the achievements of each successive 'revolution' in the history of French cuisine – from the age of La Varenne, through Carême to Escoffier and on to the *nouvelle cuisine* of the present day – can sound remarkably similar: each of these so-called 'revolutions' involves (amongst other things) the pursuit of simplicity, the using of fewer ingredients with more discrimination, moving towards enhancing the 'natural' flavour of principal ingredients, and in the process the production of a wider range of dishes more differentiated in flavour because less masked by the use of a common cocktail of spices, or the same basic sauces. If the word 'revolution' implies a cyclical pattern in changing taste, it is the wrong word. For Escoffier and his contemporaries, what they were achieving was not the overthrowing of the past, but a further spurt forward in a longer-term process of development. 'Tastes are constantly being refined', he wrote, 'and cooking is refined to satisfy them.' The same thought perhaps underlay Paul Bocuse's advice to Gault and Millau (1976: 143) on where next to sample *nouvelle cuisine*: 'if that's your taste, if you are looking for a simplicity which is not simplification – nor indolence – . . . you must visit the Troisgros brothers'. Escoffier, at any rate, would have found it obvious to speak of a process of the 'civilising of taste', to place alongside that of the 'civilising of appetite' proposed in chapter 2. For beneath the succession of dominant styles in French professional cookery is something more complicated than random vagaries of fashion: each new spurt of development has involved not just the overthrow of some aspects of the previous one, but also the renewal of recognisably the same pursuit of refinement, simplicity, restraint, and an increasingly conscious calculation of precisely how innovations will be received by an audience.

7

The Calling of Cooking: The Trade Press

Unintentionally, by studying the tastes and styles expressed in celebrated cookery books, we may so far have conveyed a 'great man' conception of culinary development. The printed book is by far the most abundant evidence for the history of cookery, and the most significant stages in its development are marked by books written by famous chefs. Because they were famous they wrote books, or they were famous because they wrote books. The great men certainly played their part, but they did not direct the whole process of development, which was complex and largely unplanned – and a whole profession was caught up in it. Fortunately, from the late nineteenth century onwards, many journals addressed to the cooking trade appeared in both France and England. They are an antidote to history-through-cookery-books, help to show how the books came to be what they are, and remind us that the great men were only a small minority within a large profession. They also reveal a great deal about the motives and self-conceptions of the profession's members.

THE FRENCH ART OF COOKERY

The last two decades of the nineteenth century saw a sudden proliferation in Paris of journals about cooking and for cooks. They include *Le Progrès des cuisiniers* published by the cooks' *syndicat*, *La Cuisine française et étrangère* (1891–1927) and *L'Art culinaire*. The last had the largest circulation and influence, and was the most interesting. It appeared for the first time in 1883, and was published fortnightly until the First World War, when conditions caused its appearance to become rather sporadic. It resumed regular publication in the 1920s, and there are occasional references to it up to 1939, although I have been unable to examine any copies after 1931. Its position as principal trade journal of the Parisian cook, along with many of its contributors and much of its general outlook, was inherited by *La Revue culinaire*, published since 1920 by the Société Mutualiste des Cuisiniers de Paris. That still exists, though today a journal of rather different character, *Néo-Restauration* dating from 1972, circulates more widely.[1]

The Plight of the Profession

The beginnings of journals for the cooking profession in the last quarter of the nineteenth century in part reflects the general growth of newspapers and periodicals, together with the spread of literacy in France at that time (see E. Weber, 1977: 465ff.; Zeldin, 1977: II, 492ff.). More especially, however, their circulation and content reflect both the considerable size of the profession and changes in its structure at the end of the century. The great names among chefs in the first part of the century had, of course, been only the most successful few among a much larger, more anonymous and less well-paid profession. But most of them (Carême being the most notable exception) had made their reputations as the owner-chefs of celebrated restaurants. It was not unrealistic for an ambitious young cook to aspire to owning his own restaurant and to rely for success on his own individual skills as a cook. It was common for owner-chefs like Gouffé to make their fortunes in a relatively few years. By the end of the century the cooks' career structure and opportunities had changed considerably. By then, the average Paris restaurant was a bigger establishment, and most of them were owned by businessmen who did not themselves cook. By extension, most chefs were employees – the best well-paid, the majority enjoying neither high pay, nor good working conditions, nor security of employment.

A report in 1893 by the Office de Travail (cited by Linda Bishop Young, 1981: 80) asked whether, if a man managed to advance to the grade of chef, he could still hope eventually to own his own restaurant. Its conclusion was that an enterprising chef might even then have become a *patron* in the provinces or in a seaside resort, but he was unlikely to do so in Paris. The problem was not merely that hotels and large fashionable restaurants were now normally owned by businessmen or limited companies, but that in moderate and inexpensive restaurants even a chef did not earn enough to be able to save to acquire his own business, and the cost of borrowing was prohibitive. Moreover, the constant threat of unemployment also greatly jeopardised career prospects.

The same report estimated that between 10,350 and 11,000 people were employed in Parisian restaurants, hotel kitchens and *bouillons*, and 4000 cooks in private homes. Estimates were difficult to make, because of the wide variety of work and places of employment involved, and because of the instability of employment too. Unemployment tended to fluctuate seasonally: in summer, many cooks migrated to the resort areas, but flooded back to Paris in the autumn when there was severe competition for jobs at every level. Only informed guesses can be offered of typical rates of unemployment.

L. B. Young (1981: 42) cites figures for men of between 24.2 per cent and 25.3 per cent in 1896, and 33.5 per cent and 53.3 per cent in 1901. For women the corresponding figures were better but scarcely good: 6.3 per cent to 11.2 per cent in 1896, 11.3 per cent to 20.2 per cent in 1901.

For cooks who succeeded in finding employment, working conditions were generally appalling. Descriptions abound of the overheated, badly ventilated, damp and unhygienic basement kitchens, far removed in all but distance from the elegant dining rooms they served. The drink provided to cope with the heat resulted often in cooks being in a semi-permanent state of inebriation – something which Escoffier for one put an end to in his kitchens. But for many there was no improvement; George Orwell's description of the sordid conditions in a Paris hotel between the two world wars (1933: 54–74) does not differ much from reports in the nineteenth century.

The conditions and insecurity of cooks' employment led to the formation of several associations to further their interests. As early as 1840, at an open-air meeting on the pavements outside Les Halles, the Société Mutualiste des Cuisiniers de Paris was formed. It still exists today, though more as a professional association than a trade union. There were also, by the late nineteenth century, several *syndicats* organising workers in the food trades. However, the restaurant workers, because of their numerous scattered small places of employment and the high incidence of unemployment among them, were never the easiest of the food trades to organise. There never took place in restaurants anything comparable to the Parisian bakers' strikes of 1903 and 1907.

Against this background, one peculiar characteristic of the French trade journals is quite striking: the extent to which food and cookery as such remained the centre of its attention. There were articles bemoaning the status and working conditions of the profession, but the focus of attention was on recipes and menus. And indeed the pursuit of ever grander achievements in the kitchen itself was explicitly seen as the chief means of improving the humble status, poor pay, dreadful working conditions, and insecurity of employment which were the lot of most cooks. Readers were encouraged to take pride in the achievements of Carême and other famous cooks of the past, to see their own work as a source both of personal satisfaction and as a means of advancing the profession as a whole.

From a sociological point of view this is rather interesting. For the emphasis is *not* on how individual cooks with exceptional skills and creative abilities may rise to particular eminence and enjoy the fruits of success. It is not the typically middle-class concern with personal achievement and competitiveness leading to individual social mobility, based on an image of society as a ladder of open opportunity. The obvious insecurity of employment in the cooking trade, together with the diminishing chances of rising to be a self-employed proprietor (which were less obvious and probably only partly perceived), made such an image unrealistic. But still less did the journals manifest the classic proletarian 'solidaristic collectivism'.[2] In other words, however miserable the pay and conditions of the majority, the cooks, although they seem to have had a clear sense of their identity as an occupational group, showed little taste for confrontation with the employers or willingness to take industrial action. Such action was in any case manifestly difficult to organise. The peculiarity of the emphasis on the need for progress, improvement, achievement in cookery as such was that this was seen as a *collective* enterprise, something that would be achieved by collaboration among cooks proud of their art. And the result would be not individual mobility but 'stratum mobility' – the profession as a whole rising within the prestige ranking of occupations generally in society.

This strategy was perhaps most closely analogous to that of 'professionalisation', the process by which many occupations in the twentieth century have sought to improve their social ranking and pecuniary rewards by emulating the old 'liberal professions', like the law and medicine. They do so by laying claim to a systematic body of knowledge acquired through specialised training, an ethic of disinterested service to the public, and a measure of autonomous authority in their particular field (see Wilensky, 1969; and Goode, 1969). Such claims are no doubt rather far fetched in an increasingly market-oriented occupation like cookery. But however it is interpreted, the 'food-centred' strategy undoubtedly had important consequences for the development of French professional cookery, and it is the dominant theme in a journal like *L'Art culinaire*.

L'Art culinaire

The first issue of *L'Art culinaire* appeared on 28 January 1883, as a supplement to *La Petite Revue illustrée littéraire, artistique et gastronomique*, a fortnightly magazine founded the previous year by Maurice Dancourt, who was later to edit *L'Art culinaire* itself under the pseudonym Châtillon-Plessis. In fact the supplement long survived its parent, which ceased publication in 1884. *L'Art culinaire* is described as the official organ of the Union Universelle pour le Progrès de l'Art Culinaire. The contents are advertised as 'Cookery, theoretical, practical and historical; previously unpublished menus and recipes; anecdotes, gastronomy, gossip, etc., etc.'. The leading article is a long statement of 'our aim', which 'is all contained in the title of the Society of which this magazine is the organ – it is the *Progress of the Culinary Art*'. The faith of the age in the inevitability of progress in every field is well expressed in this first statement of objectives:

> With the passage of time, everything changes, is transformed and improved. Our tastes and the means we use to satisfy them closely follow this ascendant path. We don't eat and we don't cook as once we ate and cooked. . . .
>
> In this *nouvelle cuisine*, we need – to use a famous expression – new men, and a new *culinary grammar*.

> It is not that we want to foment revolution among the kitchen stoves; what we want, we cooks of Paris helped by our colleagues and friends throughout the world, is to bring the benefit of our experience, our work and our inventiveness to the public, and say to them: here is what this age and our modern taste command us to present to you. Try it and judge for yourselves.
>
> And we believe firmly that the public will give recognition to the efforts we are making. These efforts are inspired by a profound desire for progress and improvement.

The 'new men' whom the editors had in mind were no doubt principally the contributors and subscribers to the new journal. In fact the group of chefs who founded *L'Art culinaire* included many established names at the peak of their profession, but even more who were to be the outstanding names of the rising generation. Prominent from the beginning as contributor and editor was Philéas Gilbert, soon to be joined by his friend and collaborator Auguste Escoffier, writing from Nice and then for many years from London.

L'Art culinaire, like *Le Progrès des cuisiniers* and *La Cuisine française et étrangère*, always emphasised the continuity of culinary traditions from the past, carrying frequent articles about the lives and achievements of great figures both living (like Urbain Dubois) and dead (like 'l'illustre Carême'). There was a strong theme of antiquarian pedantry – speculation on probably unsolvable mysteries like the origin of the name of 'mayonnaise', or 'chaud-froid sauce'[3] which indeed continues to the present day in the *Revue culinaire*. This pride and interest in the past was, curiously enough, not merely backward looking but part and parcel of the ideology of those who looked to progress and change in cookery itself as the means of raising the status and conditions of the profession. Philéas Gilbert was the most eloquent and prolific spokesman for this dominant point of view. Writing in the third issue, he broached the question to which he was frequently to return:

> What is our true position in society? The art we profess gives us the right to everyone's respect and esteem, for cookery can and must go hand in hand with the liberal arts.
>
> But it seems that, from prejudice, the cook is brushed aside and considered a hireling, without those who brush him aside even taking the trouble to cast a glance at the man's life, a life of nothing but toil and self-sacrifice. And, sad to say, those who employ him, who should owe him their abundant encouragement, are the first not to understand, nor wish to understand. . . . Why is this disdain felt towards us?

Gilbert left that question to people more competent than he to answer it, but affirmed his belief that

> the cook will not regain the rank allotted to him in society until, through perseverance and effort, he has set his art back on its pedestal, and caused his skills to be seen as requiring intelligence equivalent to those of other professional men. That goal will be achieved when every cook, full of his own importance, aspires to a seat at the great banquet of the sciences.

Gilbert and many other contributors were to use artists, natural scientists and medical doctors indiscriminately as reference groups for the cooking profession, though art was the favourite model. From time to time, some cooks doubted whether this was realistic. For example, in 1887, one of Gilbert's articles in *Le Progrès des cuisiniers* provoked the objection that 'if cooks clung nostalgically to their image as artists' they would weaken their ability to fight as workers to end the inequalities of their condition (L. B. Young, 1981: 82). Gilbert's reply was that they were both artists and workers, and he advocated joint tribunals to mediate between workers and *patrons*.[4]

Three concrete objectives were prominent in *L'Art culinaire* in its early days: to make known the latest ideas and achievements by creating through the journal an international network of French cooks; to establish a 'professional school of cookery' in Paris; and to promote *concours culinaires* or cookery competitions.

The first of these objectives was discussed by A. Tavenet in an article in the first issue:

> Most of these inventions remain unknown outside the narrow circle in which they originate. They are accessible only to a limited number of those who have produced them or seen them produced, for want of a means of making them public, or because their excessively modest author remains satisfied by the pleasure they have given to the diners for whom his inventions were intended.
>
> That is why we had the idea of creating this professional organ. We wish that so many treasures were not lost, often forgotten even by those who discover them. We are certain that many of them, inspired as they are by devotion to the progress of their profession, would be happy for their colleagues to profit by their experience.
>
> Therefore the creation of a special journal is not only useful but necessary in response to the privations and isolation of men of genius who, until now, have been unable to fulfil themselves for lack of a common centre. Around this journal will come to group themselves all the progressive ideas and all the legitimate inspirations achieved for the profit of the art and of those who, by their hard labour, have devoted their lives to it.

That this was to be an international enterprise was clear from the beginning. In the fifth issue (25 March 1883), Gilbert presents the constitution of the Union Universelle pour le Progrès de l'Art Culinaire (founded late in 1882, just before the journal itself), the first article of which mentions links already between the Paris chapter and similar groups in other countries, naming England, the USA and Spain in particular. The rules are comprehensive, covering such matters as expulsion from membership, a provision put to almost immediate use to expel to Joseph Favre and five other colleagues 'for their hostile actions in trying to bring about a split in the society' (22 April 1883). The nature of the quarrel – whether to do with politics, personalities, differences between an older and a younger generation, or cookery itself – is unclear, but Favre established a rival *Académie culinaire*, and in spite of legal action continued to use the name of the Paris chapter. In consequence, Gilbert explained in the issue of 10 June, *L'Art culinaire* was now to be the organ of the renamed Société des Cuisiniers français pour le Progrès de l'Art Culinaire, which nevertheless remained the *section générale* in Paris of the

Union Universelle. In spite of these altercations, *L'Art culinaire* did not become a factional sheet, and by the 1890s had established itself, by then under the editorship of Châtillon-Plessis, as the leading professional culinary journal in the world, listing as contributors the most famous chefs throughout Europe and North America. By 1914 it claimed '100 collaborators, 3,000 correspondents, and 10,000 readers internationally'. By 1894, Gilbert was already feeling sufficiently confident of the standing of the profession to circulate a petition asking the French government to confer the Légion d'Honneur on Urbain Dubois, Achille Ozanne, Louis Bérenger, Charles Driessens, Auguste Escoffier, Alfred Suzanne, Marius Berte and Gustave Garbin for their services to French cookery (15 June 1894). Apparently the profession had not quite reached those heights, for the petition did not succeed, although a quarter of a century later Escoffier and Gilbert himself were in fact honoured in precisely this way.

The second objective, of founding a professional school of cookery, was also achieved within a decade, but proved sadly short-lived. The Société des Cuisiniers français painfully amassed the two or three thousand francs needed to open the school in the rue Bonaparte in 1891, but after ten years of effort the school survived only thirteen months. The professional courses of instruction alternated with that on domestic cookery by Charles Driessens – 'a veritable orator in his genre' and the school was financially supported by the Paris city council. But the school was forced to close when the council refused to renew its grant, apparently in part because 'discontented spirits undermined its success' (Châtillon-Plessis, 1894: 243). Thereafter French cooks continued to be trained as they always had been, by serving in kitchens under their seniors – and although there are now some college catering courses, that remains largely true in France to the present day, in marked contrast to England.

The third objective, the promotion of *concours culinaires*, was in fact the first achievement of the group which founded *L'Art culinaire* and antedated the journal itself by a month. The initiative to form the Union Universelle, hold the *concours*, and launch the journal was taken by 'some of the profession's dreamers under the dynamic leadership of Thomas Genin' late in 1882 (Châtillon-Plessis, 1894: 214). They must have moved fast, for the first *concours* was held on 14 December 1882. Its success led to the organisation of a second one in November 1883, and thereafter it became an annual event in January of each year; in 1885 the Minister of Commerce accorded it his patronage, and by 1894 it had so grown that Châtillon-Plessis could describe it as 'one of the annual attractions of Paris'. The idea of cookery competitions spread rapidly abroad too. A *concours* modelled on the Parisian one was held in Vienna in 1884, and in 1885 seven French chefs working in England, led by Eugène Pouard, chef to the officers of Her Majesty's Guard at St James's Palace, issued an invitation through the columns of *L'Art culinaire* to the first London culinary exhibition, held at Willis's Rooms, St James's. Brussels followed in 1887, and New York sometime before 1892.

Figure 7 Monsieur Vassant's 'Poulardes à l'anglaise', 1882

The great success of the *salons culinaires* in Paris was such that already by 1894 Châtillon-Plessis could register a complaint:

> The *concours culinaires* in Paris have served as the model for all the *concours* since established everywhere else. Unfortunately, around exhibitions in general there gravitates a multitude of bizarre personages, crooked dealers, gimmicky manufacturers and implausible tradesmen, who quickly transform an honourable affair into a business to do with money and advertising, and, in the numerous imitations of the *concours culinaires* it would be difficult to pick out those which were worthy of their model. (1894: 234–7)

In the same year, even the Paris *concours* came in for criticism from Philéas Gilbert, who complained that there were not enough entries, the jury was too large, and most of the exhibits were more pastry and confectionery than cookery as such (*L'Art culinaire*, 15 March 1894). All the same, the very appeal among professional cooks of the idea of competitive cooking, or cooking as a spectator sport, is rather interesting. It is surely not without significance that it was precisely at this period that sport itself was coming to be organised in its modern form, and the distinctions between amateur and professional players and between players and spectators taking shape, both in England and France (see Dunning and Sheard, 1979; Holt, 1981).

It would be wrong, however, to give the impression that *L'Art culinaire* was largely given over to programmatic and ideological pronouncements on the future of the profession. The most striking fact about the journal is the extent to which food itself remains the centre of attention, on a pedestal – always figuratively and sometimes literally. The bulk of its contents are menus, recipes, articles about particular foodstuffs and techniques, and reports from abroad.

As for menus and recipes, by around 1890 Escoffier had emerged as the pre-eminent spirit. From 1894 he contributed model menus to every issue, with the title 'L'école des menus: étude et composition de menus modernes à la maison, à l'hôtel, et au restaurant'. He contributed many recipes too. But his was by no means the only voice. It should not be thought that the transition to the new Escoffier style was other than slow. Older styles persisted for a long time. At the first *concours* in 1882, for example, the first three prizes were won by the chefs of leading Paris restaurants with dishes very much in the style of Gouffé. Escoffier, then at the very beginning of his association with Ritz, came fourth. The gold medal was won by M. Vassant for his *poulardes à l'anglaise* (see figure 7). There is irony in the title if *à l'anglaise* is taken to imply rather simple methods of cookery. The most English characteristic of this enormously long and costly recipe is that the end result is a piece of architecture strongly reminiscent of St Pancras station. The third prize-winner was Louis Kannengieser, for his *pains de foie gras à la française*, displayed even more elaborately on a chariot pulled by lions – but only the pear-shaped *pains* were edible, and they contained a quarter kilo of truffles as well as two kilos of foie gras and other expensive ingredients (*L'Art culinaire*, Nos. 1–3, 1883).

The transition could not be other than slow. Developments in style might now seem more than ever before to owe their origin to developments within the cookery profession, but if the balance of power between the profession and its clientèle was rather more even than a century earlier, the dining public's tastes could not be changed abruptly. As André Simon was to explain with great clarity in his preface to the biography of Escoffier:

> He was a man of faith, but he was no 'hot gospeller'. All the great improvements in the culinary art which he introduced were brought about step by step, in a progressive or evolutionary manner which avoided clashes with the protagonists of quantity and glamour in matters of gastronomy, either in the great hotel kitchens or in the houses of the great. One must bear in mind the fact that Escoffier had not merely to get his own fellow chefs to accept his culinary reforms and his new dishes; he had also to please the dining public. He never was his own master. He always had to serve, and he served loyally those who provided for him the stage upon which he could act before the great and rich of the New World and of the Old World, a fickle cosmopolitan crowd, who had to be pleased before those who needed it most could be trained to appreciate the best. (Herbodeau and Thalamas, 1955: 5)

Philéas Gilbert and Prosper Montagné were 'hot gospellers' in personal style and in cookery more than was Escoffier, but Simon's reminder of the constraints under which they worked applies to them all. Even 30 years later, when Escoffier was at the height of his fame, earlier styles survived. In 1913, when Raymond Poincaré was elected to the Elysée, two dishes named in his honour show the contrasting styles. The first, by M. F. Lemaëstre, was *escalopes de langoustes à la Poincaré* (1 March 1913), and was displayed on an elaborate *socle*, with leaping dolphins, and instructions for the decoration of the *socle* alone take up half a page of print. The edible part of the dish, the *langoustes* set in jelly, arranged amidst the leaping lard dolphins with macedoine of vegetables in mayonnaise, and trimmed with prawns and truffles impaled on *hâtelets*, is pure architecture. But by this time, the later and lighter style was more dominant, and the next issue (15 March 1913) carried Escoffier's recipe for *poularde Poincaré*. The actual cookery was more complicated, but the finished effect simpler. The chicken was braised in veal stock, while most of the effort went into the sauce, a rich cream *béchamel* with shrimps, truffles, cockscombs and parmesan cheese. The sauce was to be poured over the chicken, which was otherwise unadorned, except that one could if one wished trim it with a few 'nice big truffles'.

French cookery in the late nineteenth and early twentieth centuries, in spite of (or perhaps because of) its protagonists' sense of superiority, was more open to foreign ideas than before or since. Kouindjy (1926: 92) attributes this to diplomatic influences: each new alliance brought with it a fashion for things Russian, English, or whatever. Wars could have similar effect: *L'Art culinaire* on 15 March 1894 carried recipes with Persian and Tunisian titles, with passing reference to the colonial war then in train in North Africa. On the brink of the First World War it was carrying recipes for the apparently quite unfamiliar wiener schnitzel, and Charles Dietrich's articles on polenta and other Italian recipes (1 March 1913). The journal surveyed the culinary art worldwide, sometimes with approval, more often with disapproval, but always with interest. In the 1890s, Ernest Glass contributed regular articles from the USA. In the issue of 15 March 1894 he gave American recipes for codfish steaks, chicken hash with cream (a breakfast dish of minced chicken and potatoes on toast), and brown turkey hash (similar, using leftovers or alternatively corned beef). He comments that Americans like this very much because they are always in a hurry; there is no editorial approval or disapproval, and Escoffier follows on the next page. More overt disdain was evident in E. Raff's report on a visit to the Netherlands as a member of an official French delegation to the Amsterdam Exhibition of 1883: '"Domestic" cookery is not complicated in Holland. Tea, potatoes, gin . . . and that's all, more or less. Meat is reserved for Sundays.' He had been to an enormous restaurant, but

> A visit to the kitchens did not inspire me with enthusiasm. On this side were sixty beefsteaks prepared *in advance*, ducks and guinea-fowls the same. Over there, forty women making *sandwiches*. This system of nutrition is enough, it would seem, for foreigners who, moreover, pay through the nose for it. So much the worse for them (9 September 1883)

England, on the whole, received more respectful treatment, though mainly because so many French chefs were now finding employment there. In 1894, Alfred Suzanne (1839–1916) published *La Cuisine anglaise*, probably the only book about English cooking written by a French chef for a French audience. Suzanne himself had worked in England himself for 40 years, and in fact his book was primarily designed to help French chefs employed over the Channel who often lost their jobs through their inability to adapt to English tastes.

> The rich Englishman always has a penchant for his national cuisine which he can only ill disguise. He always makes a rule to return to it every so often, not only by taste, but also for the good reason that his robust stomach accustomed from infancy to substantial fare, adapts itself badly to an essentially French regime, with our light soups and delicate dishes. (1894: 8)

Suzanne says there are many excellent English dishes, like turtle soup, fried whitebait, sucking pig stuffed with sage and onion, beefsteak or lark pudding, York ham and Wiltshire bacon, chicken curry, or braised rabbit with capers. Even though any comparison between English and French cuisine as a whole must be to England's disadvantage, a French chef working in England must learn to appreciate these best dishes. In any case,

> After a year or two in England, French cooks know how to turn these 'good things' to their advantage, by bringing to them a refinement and the cachet of good taste which is so distinctively theirs – in short, by 'Frenchifying' them. (1894: 8)

Welcoming Suzanne's book, Gilbert (31 March 1894) commented that France was then in the grip of Anglomania, with English sports and fashions all the rage, and even English food itself enjoying a certain favour in some quarters, so it was important that the profession know how to respond to this demand.

In France itself there is no doubt that the cooking profession identified itself closely with the demand of the rich for luxurious food. Despite its concern with raising the status of cooks and its consciousness of the often meagre pay and working conditions, there are few manifestations before the First World War of any unease with, for example, the lavish use of extremely expensive ingredients. Nevertheless, in 1906 (1 March) there appeared an article entitled 'Le Luxe dans l'art culinaire'. Though it defends 'luxury' in cooking, it would appear to be a response to some underlying criticism of extravagance.

> The culinary art is full of luxury, but a luxury indispensable to its vitality. . . . It is the art of stimulating appetite, of taking exact account of every taste and of all the diametrically opposed physiological dispositions. . . . Good cooking and its comforts contribute to make men sociable who are otherwise too inclined to fight amongst themselves, or to be afflicted with a stomach in revolt due to a bad digestion. (*L'Art culinaire*, 1 March 1906)

A few years later, when Poincaré entered the Elysée, a similar defensive note was struck by Prosper Montagné (15 March 1913), who welcomed the prospect of a renewal of sumptuous entertaining there, implying that Presidential fare had been meagre over the previous decade, probably in response to public criticism of extravagance and 'luxury'. The First World War changed the tone dramatically. In 1915, only one issue of the journal appeared, and this was partly devoted to a patriotic denigration of German food. But by 1916, when quarterly issues appeared, French cuisine seemed a shadow of its former self: recipes from Escoffier included *boeuf à la bourguignonne* adapted to the trenches (or at least the reserve camp) and using lard, tinned bully beef, and biscuit crumbs for thickening. He also wrote a column under the unaccustomed title of 'life on the cheap', advocating among other things more use of rice and pasta.

La Revue Culinaire

Although *L'Art culinaire* resumed regular publication after the war, superficially with little change, it seems not to have regained its former international circulation and pre-eminence. Moreover, while still full of menus and recipes, it became less informative about the state of the culinary profession. In many respects its place was taken, from 1920 onwards, by *La Revue culinaire*, published to this day by the old-established Société des Cuisiniers de Paris, and first edited by Francis Carton who at about the same time took over the management of the Restaurant Lucas (later Lucas-Carton), the most famous Paris restaurant of the inter-war years. *La Revue* never seems to have acquired the former pre-eminence of *L'Art culinaire*, nor to have circulated much outside France; but it did acquire many of its most illustrious contributors, including Escoffier, Gilbert and Montagné, and much of the spirit of the early *Art culinaire*. The *Revue* contained general articles about the state of the profession, the culinary art, the hotel and tourist industries, as well as menus and recipes. Yet, as in *L'Art culinaire*, food itself and its history have remained the centre of attention. The continuities in flavour can be seen in articles selected at random over six decades of the *Revue*: 'What is a Salmis?' (Gilbert, February 1921); a proposal to erect a monument to Brillat-Savarin (October 1921); the origins of *Homard à l'Américaine*, or was it *Armoricaine*? (March 1938); the story of Vatel's suicide (April 1950, and again in March 1970 – a hardy perennial, that one); Taillevent (February 1970); the origins of the Société des Cuisiniers de Paris (January 1980).

The early issues of the *Revue* show that in the years after the First World War, the profession was nevertheless passing through something of a crisis. For this there appear to have been three main reasons. First, employment opportunities for French chefs abroad were declining, particularly in the United States and Great Britain, which both introduced restrictions on immigration (January and April 1921); prohibition also badly hit the restaurant trade in America (January 1921). A second reason appears to have been rather widespread criticism by 'soi-disants gastronomes' in the newspapers that standards of French cookery were in decline. Such criticism elicited several yelps of pain, and in October 1921 Gilbert and Montagné wrote a joint article, 'Sur la Critique Culinaire', complaining of the 'damage' done by criticism in the daily press by 'men of letters' (not named, but certainly meaning Curnonsky, de Croze, Des Ombiaux, and their circle[5]). They recognised the precedents for culinary criticism going back to Grimod de la Reynière, but considered the present instances to be 'ill-informed'. A note after their article stated that: 'The editors of the *Revue culinaire* fully endorse the just remarks expressed in the article above, relating to the renewed and unjustified attacks and the intrusions into the domain of culinary technique by publicists very far from qualified to make them.'

That is very reminiscent of the claims to freedom of professional judgement made by members of the liberal professions. (It could hardly offer a more striking contrast with the obsequious prefaces to cookery books under the *ancien régime*.) On the other hand, the *Revue* was far from hostile to the development of the hotel trade and tourism which the same 'publicists' were doing so much to foster. Escoffier (January 1921) wrote on the opportunities presented to the inns and small hotels of provincial France by the motor-car and growth of tourism – their food was already excellent in its simplicity, but they needed to improve their facilities, and the lavatories in particular were such as he would not care to describe. (*Plus ça change!*) Articles on, and enthusiasm for, the traditional regional recipes of France have always been more prominent in the *Revue* than they were in *L'Art culinaire*.

The third reason for the post-war crisis was more deep-seated and longer-lasting. It was economic pressures and technical change. Economic changes are reflected in an article by Maurice Graillot on 'Cuisine Commerciale' (March 1921). The term had become current in a pejorative sense, used in contrast to *cuisine artistique*, but Graillot said that since the profession now centred on hotels and restaurants rather than on the households of the rich, he could not see how cuisine could be other than commercial. Moreover, food was now too expensive for hotels and casinos to be able to run it as a loss-leader, and cooks would now inevitably have to learn to cost up their creations. Other controversies were triggered by changing technology. The early issues of the *Revue* carry advertisements for electric mixers, and given the perpetually high rates of unemployment among cooks it was not surprising that fears were expressed of the effects of machinery in displacing men. Equally unsurprisingly, this fear was often partly disguised in the argument that labour-saving machinery would also undermine standards in cookery itself. An unsigned article on 'Cuisine et Machinisme' in January 1921 argues, however, that

> Science, machines, progress that nothing can stop, will in the end increase production, speed it up and make it easier. . . . Machinery will not kill sumptuous cuisine, because it will always be impossible for machines to create individual masterpieces. Useful and necessary popularisation has never destroyed the arts. Photography has not killed painting, nor the barrel-organ killed music.

Philéas Gilbert concurred, arguing that 'nothing will halt the march of progress', quoting Carême on how cooks were killed by hard labour in the heat of kitchens, recalling how much of kitchen work was sheer hard slog, and therefore seeing much to welcome in the saving of effort made possible by machines. A few months later (October 1921), writing under the title 'La Cuisine Industrialisée', Gilbert in effect says that there is nothing new under the sun, and recalls that similar fears were being expressed in the early days of *L'Art culinaire*. Gilbert's ideology remained the same as it had been four decades earlier, and seems in fact to represent the dominant strand in the thinking of French cooks to the present day. He was not in the least Luddite; proud of the profession's past, but not backward-looking; as confident in 1921 of the inevitability of progress as in 1883, when he had upbraided a colleague who had the temerity to claim that cookery had 'reached its apogee'; and always seeing innovation and continuing improvement in cookery itself as the best means of raising the status and rewards of professional cooks.

Not that *every* innovation was seen as an improvement. In the early issues of the *Revue* there appeared a whole series of articles on frozen food, which was treated with great caution. Goose, it was said, could not be successfully frozen – it acquired 'a faint taste of old fish'. The flesh of chickens was too fat and flabby to be kept longer than a month in cold store: 'Consommateurs, abstenez-vous!' Pigeons went black in cooking if frozen for longer than six months, and only guinea-fowl among poultry seemed to freeze with some success. This caution in France towards frozen food (and other forms of preserved and processed foods) is quite striking when compared with England, and it continues in the emphasis given to fresh, high quality raw materials in the *nouvelle cuisine* of the present day. Even in the 1960s and 1970s, the *Revue culinaire* still contained very little discussion of short cuts, frozen food, mass production and so on. The April 1979 issue, for example, contains a very hostile guide to food additives. The journal was still chiefly concerned with teaching people to cook in the classical manner, even if the recipes were somewhat less free with the truffles and crayfish. It continues to lay down the rules of good culinary practice, explaining for example in February 1970 that the use of *beurre manié*[6] was classically regarded as a last resort or stopgap measure, and certainly not to be accepted as good practice.

All the same, in the 1960s one senses in the pages of the *Revue culinaire* that it is associated with an older generation, the last generation who were pupils of the great chefs of the Escoffier era, and who are now themselves reaching the end of their careers. By the 1970s there is also a sense of the exhaustion of a tradition, a certain quality of tiredness and looking backward. For example, the March 1979 issue included a long lecture by Eugène Herbodeau (Escoffier's great pupil and successor at the Carlton) on Carême, and also an article on vols-au-vent and a recipe for *tripes à la mode de Caen*, both by Philéas Gilbert, who had then been dead nearly four decades. In June 1979 a long article questioned whether there was anything new in *nouvelle cuisine*: it could all be found in Escoffier. These were typical contents. Not surprisingly there were complaints that the journal no longer had any appeal to the younger generation of French cooks. Indeed, in March 1970, a very defensive editorial on 'La Revue Culinaire et les Jeunes' had concluded weakly by quoting a letter from a young cook praising the journal – a letter received and published more than twenty years earlier in April 1949!

Néo-Restauration

In the circumstances, it is more surprising that an iconoclastic journal like *Néo-Restauration*, now the most widely circulating catering trade journal in France, did not appear far earlier than April 1972. Unlike any earlier journal in France, *Néo-Restauration* has openly looked abroad for its models – to the USA and, to a lesser extent, to Britain: it was directed, as the first issue proclaimed, to the new commercial opportunities presented by 'les cafétérias, grills, snacks, fast-foods de tous genres, coffee shops, "libre service" avec linéaire de distribution en continu ou en scramble, drugstores, quick-lunch, etc.' – in short, *cuisine à la franglais!* It is true that the French, at their cafés, always had a form of fast-food operation. But that had not appeared to deserve any journal of its own, and was certainly not mentioned in the same

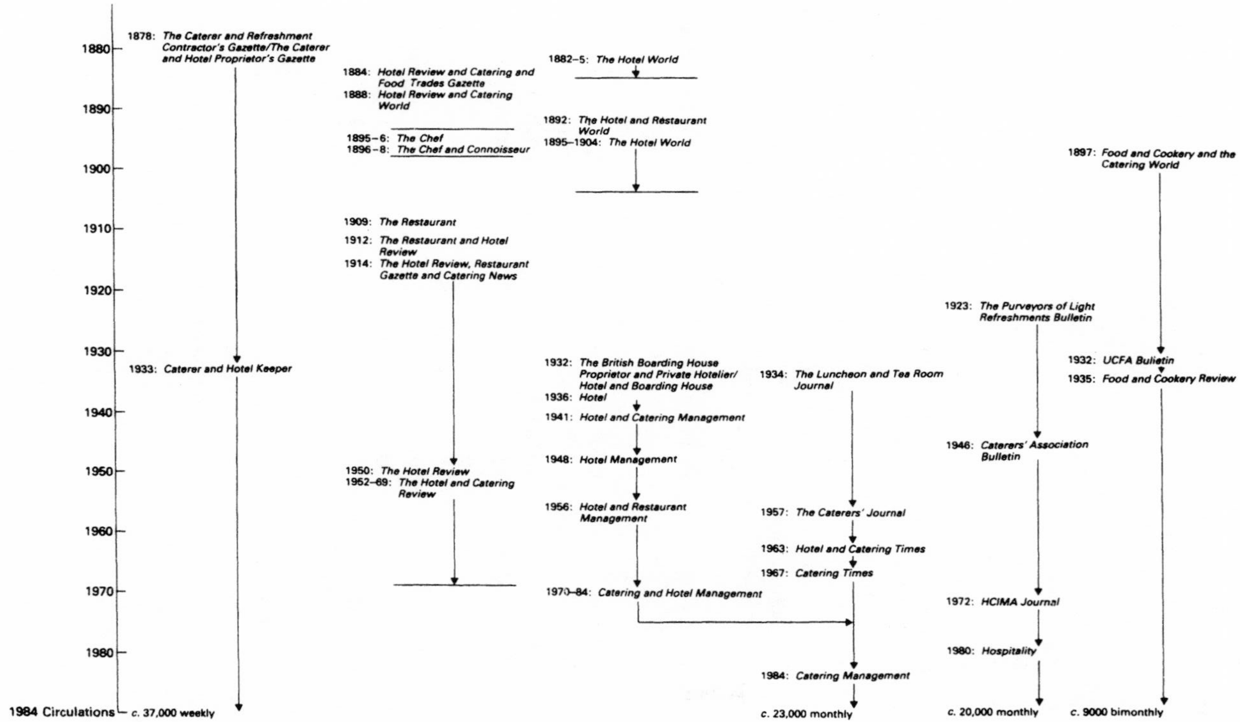

Figure 8 *The catering trade press in Britain (principal publications only)*

breath as 'cuisine'. Probably that in itself is a symptom of the universal hegemony that *cuisine classique* had enjoyed; the world of cookery was seen in terms of an unquestioned hierarchy with central standards at the top, whereas in Britain it had long been seen as a series of separate markets, or perhaps sub-cultures, none of them enjoying unquestioned dominance.

Néo-Restauration blatantly challenged the old assumptions. Its first editorial described it as: 'a monthly which brings a new image to innovative public catering, which, through its new methods, is responding to the developing needs and tastes of a clientèle of consumers whose numbers, demands and mobility are constantly growing.' The first issue had articles about government statistics showing the growth of meals eaten outside the home, on pioneering French fast-food operations, on the opportunities presented by the building of motorways in south-west France, on luncheon vouchers, hot-drinks machines and microwave ovens, and on management and training of personnel in cafeterias and fast-food establishments. In 1974, the title became *Néo-Restauration/Hôtellerie* (*Néo* for short), and the contents broadened to include hotel and kitchen equipment. So this French journal certainly looks more like its British counterparts. Yet there is a difference. Even in the early issues of *Néo-Restauration* there was a certain concern with standards of cooking, and reservations about some trends – 'Frozen food is not the panacea some people imagine it to be'. And by 1979, a quarterly supplement – 'Néo Quat'Saisons' – was appearing in the magazine, devoted to recipes from the most famous French restaurants. For example, the November 1979 issue contained Paul Bocuse's recipe for truffle soup, and a salad from the Troisgros brothers. In other words, the French tradition of putting food itself on a pedestal as the focus of attention reasserted itself, and even *Néo* seems to have moved 'up-market'.

The traditions of the profession in France remain strong. While it does not require much training to operate a microwave oven, and while there are now *écoles techniques hôtellière*, the élite are still trained by working in the kitchens of famous restaurants under great practitioners. That was well expressed by the head of a distinguished Department of Catering at a British polytechnic. Inviting me to attend an international conference on training for catering and hotel management, he regretted that no one from France was to be present. His explanation of this notable absence was that 'Oh, the French are decades behind us and the Americans in the sophistication of their catering education – they are still at the stage of just teaching people how to cook the stuff.' It is all very different in England.

CATERING, ENGLISH STYLE

The trade press in England dates from about the same time as in France, but there is a striking difference in flavour and emphasis. As figure 8 shows, the words 'catering' and 'hotel' have been predominant among the titles of the various journals published during the last century, and their contents are found to reflect the titles. 'Catering' certainly has very different connotations from 'cuisine', let alone from 'l'art culinaire'; its overtones are of supplying food to the masses – of pushing it across the counter, so to speak – rather than of an artistic response by élite cooks to the sophisticated tastes of a social élite. In fact, all the main trade papers surviving in England today trace their origins to publications concerned with food at well below the highest levels of social prestige. *Catering Management* traces dual ancestry from the *Luncheon and Tea Room Journal* and *The British Boarding House Proprietor*; the oldest surviving title, *The Caterer and Hotel Keeper*, was originally *The Caterer and Refreshment Contractor's Gazette*; while *Hospitality* stems from *The Purveyors of Light Refreshments Bulletin*.

The concern with hotels and their management also presents a contrast with France. It is true that articles on this subject appeared in *L'Art culinaire* and *La Revue culinaire*, but they were never a dominant theme. In France, there are separate, widely circulating papers like the old-established *L'Hôtellerie* (founded 1882) and *L'Industrie hôtelière de France et d'Outre-Mer* (founded 1951) which, however, are devoid of culinary interest. This separation of publications is perhaps in part a reflection of the relatively greater separation of two kinds of establishment, where a large proportion of the best restaurants are not in hotels, and where many of the lesser hotels still serve no food other than breakfast. But it is more a reflection of an attitude of mind: a greater willingness to regard cookery and hotel management, though they are related, as sufficiently separate and sufficiently important each to deserve its own specialised press. (That may be less true since the appearance of *Néo*, but it is broadly valid for the last century as a whole.)

In England, on the other hand, it never seems to have been possible to establish a large circulation paper concerned principally with 'food on a pedestal'. Several attempts seem to have been made to establish a British equivalent to *L'Art culinaire*, but without lasting success. *The Hotel Review* of 1884–8 was, in spite of its name, quite largely concerned with culinary matters. Its contents each month included menus of notable dinners; a section on 'practical gastronomy' giving recipes English and French – including in August 1886 instructions for the preparation of snails (even though they were acknowledged to be 'not very popular' in England), and bouillabaisse in July 1887; book reviews; and interviews with notable figures in the field – in November 1886 Mr A. B. Marshall, proprietor of the Mortimer Street School of Cookery, in April 1887 Mr Henry E. Maynard of the Griffin Hotel, Leeds, giving a full account and typical menus of his daily two-shilling ordinary. But this journal appears only to have survived about three years. *The Hotel and Restaurant World* was in very similar mould in the following decade: it carried a good deal of news from abroad, especially from America and France; it often quoted *L'Art culinaire*, which 'as our readers know, is the leading culinary journal of the world' (January 1898), and shared its concern with the state of the profession and with minutiae of gastronomic history. But *The Hotel World*, too, failed to survive very long. Closest of all to *L'Art culinaire* in intention was *The Chef*, founded in 1895. At first this was directed very specifically to practising chefs. On its cover page was a series of articles on celebrated chefs – Carême, Soyer, Francatelli and others – and there was a monthly menu card in colour, accounts of banquets, together with an 'employment bureau' for cooks seeking work, and correspondence columns preoccupied with the need for a chefs' union. Yet from December 1896 it was retitled *The Chef and Connoisseur*; it seems to have been trying to move up-market, seeking readers among the diners – because, one infers, it was not selling well enough among the cooks. The series on celebrated chefs was replaced by a less prominently displayed one on 'famous hotels and their managers'. By then it did not differ much from *The Hotel World* and disappeared before it. Finally, after another decade had elapsed, there appeared *The Restaurant*, proudly sub-titled 'The Only Journal Exclusively Devoted to the Restaurant Trade'. Its first issue (August 1909) declared that

> As a mere annexe to the hotel, the restaurant is already served by several periodicals of high reputation in their respective spheres. But the restaurant of today is not merely an annexe to the hotel; in ever-increasing numbers, it has an independent existence of its own, with interests which are not necessarily those of the hotel.

Yet by 1912, *The Restaurant* had become *The Restaurant and Hotel Review*, and by 1914 simply *The Hotel Review* – in which guise it did at least survive for a total of sixty years.

In sum, the English commercial environment does not seem to have been very hospitable to journals centred on food and cookery.[7]

UCFA

The principal exceptions to that statement are the publications of the Universal Cookery and Food Association (now simply the Cookery and Food Association or CFA), whose *Food and Cookery Review* claimed a circulation of 9000 in 1983, probably more than ever before. UCFA was never a very large organisation, but it was an extraordinarily interesting one because its origins were linked with those of *L'Art culinaire* in France, yet it developed a most peculiarly English slant of its own. It grew in fact out of the small group, rather informally organised but calling itself The Culinary Society, which under the leadership of Eugène Pouard organised the first Cookery Competition in Willis's Rooms, London, in 1885. The group had about two dozen members, and in 1887 organised a second competition, again very much on the model of those held in Paris by the *Art culinaire* group. On 5 December 1887, however, a special meeting was held at St James's Hall, with Mr J. Roberts in the chair, at which the Culinary Society was formed into the

Universal Cookery and Food Association. The word 'Universal' signified that this was in effect the British chapter of the Union Universelle pour le Progrès de l'Art Culinaire of which *L'Art culinaire* was the French organ. UCFA's first committee of management was dominated by French chefs working in London, including two of the three who had actually organised the 1885 competition, as well as Queen Victoria's chef, Monsieur J. Ménager. There were also several English names including that of Charles Herman Senn. Nowadays perhaps best remembered as the bowdleriser of Mrs Beeton, Senn (1864–1934) was the dominating figure in UCFA almost from its inception right up to his death.[8] The association grew rapidly: in 1892 it claimed 186 members, 917 in 1897, and more than 1200 in 1902; that was probably the peak, for in 1926 Senn was lamenting that 'membership has unfortunately not been so well maintained', and referred to 1897 as a high point.[9] Though this was scarcely a mass movement, it was too large for the dominance of French chefs to endure, and by early in the twentieth century there was a separate Association Culinaire Française in London – which, however, seems to have had cordial relations with Senn and UCFA. And UCFA continued to list among its objects the promotion of links with similar organisations on the continent (*Cookery Annual*, 1908: 66).

Senn himself never questioned the supremacy of French cooking, but perhaps for that reason seems to have steered UCFA away from any attempt to compete in that domain. The slant he gave to the association was an overriding concern with educational and charitable work. His leanings can already be seen in his account of UCFA's origins in the 1885 competition: 'The first exhibition . . . was organised with the object of making a display of essentially French cookery, which, though small, proved a *great educational success*, and did the highest credit to its promoters' (*Cookery Annual*, 1908: 63, my emphasis). But the 1887 meeting was more important: 'From that time *the work took a more practical and earnest form*' (1908: 64, my emphasis). The notion that the standing of the cooking profession can best be advanced through ever-greater achievements in *haute cuisine* for a social élite was entirely absent from UCFA's thinking. Instead, its object was 'to promote and encourage the advancement of cookery in every grade among all classes of the community' (1908: 56). How this was to be achieved was spelled out in a list of aims and activities.

First among these was the holding of exhibitions – an aim shared with *L'Art culinaire*. The UCFA organised annual cookery exhibitions in London in direct line of succession from that of 1885 until the 1930s, when the collaboration of a commercial sponsor was enlisted. Out of these exhibitions directly stem the biennial Hotelympia events of the present day, of which a *salon culinaire* still forms a small feature. It is also true that Châtillon-Plessis complained about the huge commercial success of the Paris exhibitions displacing cookery from the centre of attention. In the case of the London exhibitions, however, the aim seems to have been rather different from an early stage:

The Holding of Exhibitions periodically, at which the various branches of the culinary art are shown, and the manufacturers of food specialities and various accessories exhibit their productions and introduce novelties. At these exhibitions may be seen school children busy at work preparing simple menus, and teachers demonstrating household and artisan cookery, to show how dinners for the working classes may be prepared at a small cost. Hospital and invalid dietary also finds a place in the display of tempting and palatable dishes for the sick and suffering. Naval and marine cooks may be seen demonstrating the preparation of wholesome food for our sailors, in contrast to the 'salt junk' and ship's biscuits so frequently provided for them, while the Army cooking in barrack or camp kitchen for the preparation of our soldiers' rations is always interesting to visitors to the Association's exhibitions. (*Cookery Annual*, 1908: 58)

Second in the list of aims and activities was the provision of 'Free Lectures to Poor and middle-class housewives dwelling in crowded parishes'. Each course consisted of from ten to eighteen lectures, at the end of which a competition was held and prizes awarded (*Cookery Annual*, 1908: 58). Over 600 lectures had been given since 1887 in London and the provinces, especially in hospitals and at the 'missions' which were such a feature of middle-class charitable activitiy in the slums of late Victorian cities (*Cookery Annual*, 1908: 64, 71). Courses in 'sick-room cookery' for nurses were one of Senn's particular favourites, and UCFA was also fond of organising courses in 'nautical cookery' and cookery competitions for scouts, guides and army cooks (*Cookery Annual*, 1926: 41–48).

Thirdly, in the same vein, came 'The Publication of Economical Cookery Recipes at popular prices for the working classes.' Between 1881 and 1908, it was claimed, 'seventy thousand booklets of cheap cooking recipes have been distributed gratuitously' (*Cookery Annual*, 1908: 64). This activity stood in direct line of succesion from Soyer's work in the East End and his *Shilling Cookery*, and from Francatelli's *Plain Cookery*.

UCFA also ran an accident insurance scheme for members, an employment bureau for chefs and cooks, and a benevolent fund. These, at least, were concerned with the welfare of professional cooks. Like the *Art culinaire* group too, UCFA was interested in the training of young cooks, and with more success than the ill-fated Professional School in Paris. In 1908, it was already supporting eighteen boys at the Westminster School of Cookery, a private venture run by Miss Richards, an UCFA member. In 1910, 'largely on the initiative of UCFA' (*Cookery Annual*, 1914: 80), the London County Council opened the LCC Cookery Technical School for Boys at the Westminster Technical Institute, with Ivan Kries, another UCFA member, as its Chief Instructor and Senn on its Consultative Committee. This was the forerunner of the Westminster Hotel School, which has been one of the most important training centres for professional cooks in Britain.

The charitable, not to say do-gooding, orientation of UCFA – its declared objective of improving cookery throughout society, not of merely improving the standing of the profession – enabled it to attract the most extraordinary list of patrons. The 1908 *Cookery Annual* listed Queen Alexandra as Chief Patroness, followed by 11 other members of the royal family, 13 ordinary dukes and duchesses, the Lord Lieutenant of Ireland, the Lord Mayor and Lady Mayoress of London, and two and a half pages of other nobility and gentry in strict order of precedence. There followed another list of President (W. Burdett-Coutts MP), Vice-Presidents and Committee of Management. One interesting name was that of Mr Isidore Salmon, the Managing Director of the rapidly growing J. Lyon's catering chain. He was Vice-Chairman in 1908 and became Chairman in 1909. His presence, and that of other similar figures, is some indication of the organisation's evolution since the gatherings of working chefs in 1885 and 1887.

So also are two subsidiary organisations within UCFA, the Réunion des Gastronomes and Le Cordon Rouge. The first, despite its name, was not a gastronomic dining club, but an organisation of proprietors and managers of hotels, clubs and restaurants. Its declared objective was 'to raise the social position of the catering profession generally', but its main business appears to have been maintaining black lists and exchanging references on employees, and circulating information about fraudulent customers. Le Cordon Rouge was a sort of pretentious imitation order of chivalry, with a 'Supreme Don' and 'Brother Dons'.[10] In addition, all members of UCFA were encouraged to boast the letters MCA (Member of the Cookery Association) or GCA (Governor, or very senior member of same) after their names. All this gave UCFA a rather masonic air, which it retains within the profession to the present day.

All the same, it would be wrong to give the impression that UCFA's publications were entirely preoccupied with the internal affairs of an exclusive club. They, more than other British trade journals, remained centred on cookery itself. But the cookery they described, and the attitude towards food and cookery they represent, do not in fact seem to differ radically from those found in the rest of the British trade press.

The Extent of French Hegemony

UCFA and its publications were the main bastions (apart from the French chefs themselves) of culinary francophilia in England, yet as we have seen, that hardly remained for very long the main thrust of its concerns. The rest of the trade press shows that in the age of Escoffier when the international prestige of French cookery reached its highest, its influence in the world of English professional cooks remained ambiguous. There were frequent genuflections in the direction of Paris, but the evidence points to the real influence of France being limited both socially and geographically. Periodically there were controversies about whether even the use of French in menus should be abandoned. *The Hotel Review* of August 1886 reported that, under the influence of the Kaiser, the Germans were dropping French in their menus, and asked whether the English should follow them. In 1909, according to *The Restaurant* for October that year, the *Evening News*, having campaigned patriotically against the employment of numerous German waiters in London restaurants, was now turning its energies to a campaign against menu French. Senn himself was an exponent of the curiously chimerical franglais style: his recipes and menus boast titles like 'Fillets of Sole aux Huîtres', 'Skate au Beurre Noir' and 'Rabbit en Casserole'.[11] That practice attracted the wrath of both sides: most people were agreed at least that menus should be written either in plain English or good French.

Judging from the bills of fare for notable contemporary dinners published in the trade journals, neither the substance nor the terminology of French cookery was as common in the provinces as in the Home Counties and capital (perhaps one should say capitals, since there is some slight evidence that Edinburgh was also an outpost of French fashions). For example, the menu of the Royal Academy banquet of 1886 (given in *The Hotel Review* for June) is entirely in French (with the one untranslatable exception of 'Whitebait') and, though this disguises some English specialities like turtle soup, lamb cutlets and saddle of mutton, most of the items on the vast table appear to have been French in style as well as in title. In contrast, a big dinner given in Leeds Town Hall for one of the city's MPs (*Hotel Review*, November 1886) consisted of dishes like oxtail soup, boiled beef and dumplings, boiled mutton and caper sauce, roast beef and Yorkshire pudding, and plum pudding. *The Restaurant*, in February 1910, with an air of great daring, recommended

> in large industrial and commercial towns the introduction daily of a few exclusively foreign dishes. This will prove acceptable to many, not only to foreigners themselves, but also to those who, having resided sometimes abroad, may like to renew their acquaintance with foreign cookery.

But little had changed two decades later: *The Hotel Review* for January 1930 contains 'menus of the month' from London, Edinburgh and Ben Rhydding (near Ilkley, Yorkshire). The first was a Rotarian dinner in Lewisham (hardly, one infers, a gathering of the social *crème de la crème*), the second a coming-of-age dinner for the son of the proprietor of the Royal British Hotel; both were written wholly in French and contained some essentially French dishes. The last was a masonic dinner in honour of the Earl of Harewood, husband of the Princess Royal. The menu was written wholly in English and the food was English in substance; clear turtle soup, fillets of sole Princess Mary, roast pheasant, brussels sprouts and so on.

There were other foreign influences on English catering during this period, but they did not generate the controversy, or at least ambivalence, which attached to French food. References to curries are not uncommon, and they had been part of English cooking since the eighteenth century; English recipes for them differ from the original Indian, however, in being mainly for leftover cooked meats with the addition of curry powder. There are periodical references to Italian dishes, which usually means the use of pasta. The American influence can also be detected quite early, though it was slight in comparison with the period after the Second World War. *The Hotel Review* of 1884–8 contains recipes for fish chowder, hominy and mint julep, while *The Restaurant* in August 1909 comments that melon as an *hors d'oeuvre* is catching on rapidly from America. In February 1930, *The Hotel Review* was explaining with great solemnity that 'Hamburg Steaks are prepared from minced raw beef flavoured with salt, pepper, nutmeg, minced onion and chopped parsley. Form into small cakes, flour and fry them. Serve with good brown sauce, adding a spoonful of Heinz tomato ketchup.' One cannot imagine the need for such a detailed explanation of a hamburger in more recent years!

But what of the English culinary tradition itself, as represented in the pages of the trade press? A book review in *The Hotel Review* in April 1887 reported the view 'that the epoch of Francatelli and Soyer is past, and that an almost entirely new and a distinctly more English school has taken the place of that of which they were the most distinguished exponents'. Actually, a good deal of it seemed to consist of English dishes garnished in a French way; *The Hotel World* in December 1895 welcomed the marketing of tinned, concentrated *espagnole*, *allemande* and *italienne* sauces, by means of which 'all this luxury is to be placed within the reach of the great middle class and of the ordinary cook'. A columnist in *The Hotel World* in September 1897 in fact bemoaned the decline of English cookery; its most distinctive and distinguished characteristic had been its roast meats, but these were now disappearing as baking in closed ovens replaced true spit-roasting on open hearths. The average Englishman unconsciously came to accept this, because 'once losing touch with 'quality' the palate becomes inured to the dull uniformity of mediocrity, and soon unconsciously acquiesces in its loss of discernment'.

Plenty of distinctly English 'made-dishes', however, appear in the recipe columns. For example, *The Hotel Review* of 1886 includes instructions for boiled rice dumplings with custard sauce; purée of split pea; coffee cake; steamed peach pudding; suffolk dumplings; Sussex hard dumplings; brown bread dumplings; marrow dumplings; and 'maids of honour'. And the model menus which *The Hotel Review* provided for caterers in the 1930s are full of 'plain English fare'. Here is an example of a 2*s*.6*d*. Sunday dinner from the January 1930 issue:

Cream of Veal and Barley
Roast Loin of Lamb
Mint Sauce
Mashed Parsnips
Baked Potatoes
Orange Marmalade Pudding
Lemon Sauce
Cheese and Biscuits

Plainness must certainly have been the norm when, in the October 1930 issue, it was considered necessary to give detailed instructions for 'Buttered Cabbage' – merely boiled cabbage tossed in melted butter.

After the Second World War, French dominance was still less evident in the British trade press, though biennial reports of the *salons culinaires* at the Hotelympia exhibitions serve as a reminder that due deference was still paid to French models at the highest levels of the trade, even if they were little reflected in those magazines. Thus at the 1954 *salon* there were sculptures in spun sugar worthy of Carême – a kitten in a shoe, a New York skyscraper, and the 1953 Coronation procession. A photograph shows the judges inspecting 'a dish made from fish' – useful information, since it was so totally swamped in decoration that it looks more like yet another sugar model. These were throwbacks to the age of Urbain Dubois and Jules Gouffé, and that they were still occasionally presented to people actually to eat is suggested by HRH Prince Philip's remark at a CFA dinner a decade later:

> Speaking of the decoration of food, Prince Philip said amidst further laughter: 'I think it must be something to do with the British aptitude for gardening. I am being invited constantly to look at something which has on top of it something looking like a flower-bed – with a mass of bits and pieces on top. I suppose it looks all right, but it doesn't induce me to eat it, and I am sufficiently old-fashioned to want to eat my food and not to look at it.' (*Hotel and Restaurant Management*, April 1964)

That in post-war England lip-service to French models was expected, but that it amounted only to lip-service, is suggested by a monthly series of very brief profiles of chefs which appeared in *Hotel Management* in 1954. Of the 12 chefs featured, two were French, gave classic French dishes as their favourites, and cited Escoffier as their favourite culinary work. Of the 10 British chefs, one, in charge of food at the Royal Opera House, Covent Garden, said his favourite dish was Irish stew and his favourite book 'memory'. Of the remaining nine, four chose Escoffier and five Saulnier's *Repertoire*, which is simply an *aide-mémoire* listing hundreds of garnishings; but few of their 'favourite dishes' were clearly French – they were curry (two), roast beef, roast grouse, boiled beef and carrots, chicken Maryland, sole bonne femme, pot-au-feu and Wiener schnitzel ('escalope au viennaise' – *sic*).

COQUUS ECONOMICUS

The really striking, virtually central concern running through the British trade press for the best part of a century is with economy. It is a theme we identified even earlier, in the English cookery books of the eighteenth century, and it is one of the distinguishing marks of English culinary culture in comparison with the French.

In the first half of the twentieth century, the preoccupation is mainly with economising in the cost of ingredients, but since the Second World War the concern has been particularly with savings in the cost of labour, and thus especially with 'convenience foods'. In the earlier period, typical articles are on 'Economy in Small Things' in *The Restaurant*, September 1909, and on 'Menu Drafting and Costing' in *The Hotel Review*, July 1930. The 1909 article declares:

True economy is the soul of all business, but more so in that of a restaurant. There is perhaps no word so little understood as the word economy. I would like to see more efforts made to make the best of every scrap that comes to hand. With only a little care and taste anything can be made pretty and nice at very little cost. Many things are put into the dustbin that could be used up and made into tasty dishes. 'Waste Not' should be the maxim of every restaurant management and it is when this maxim is strictly adhered to and put into practice that a restaurant pays best.

English cooks, alleged the author, had much to learn from the French in the art of thrifty cooking: 'the materials out of which the most tempting of entrées are made are those which in [many English restaurants] would be thrown to the dogs' – such items as sweetbreads seem to be in mind here. That may have been true, but it is also true that the preoccupation with economy was almost entirely absent from the French culinary press of the time: *L'Art culinaire*'s theme was rather the pursuit of perfection, if need be at extravagant cost. The memoirs of Gabriel Tschumi, a cook in the royal kitchens at Buckingham Palace at just the same period, illustrate the contrasting attitude of the French-dominated world of élite cookery.

If a dish were hopelessly ruined . . . it was thrown away. Sometimes dozens of pheasants or soufflés in which four or five dozen eggs had been used found their way into the garbage pails. . . . No-one can learn cuisine without making a good many mistakes in the process, and it is essential that those learning have the best materials at their disposal. (1954: 50)

The two attitudes neatly represent the difference between 'bourgeois rationality' and 'court-rationality' (Elias, 1969: 110–11), the one dominant in English culinary culture, the other persisting as a strong flavour in French.

Both the cookery columns and the advertisements in the English press are full of advice on how to economise. The same 1909 article advises against excessive use of tinned vegetables when fresh ones are cheaper even if they involve more work. That suggests the relative cheapness of labour at the time. Similarly, in the December 1909 *Restaurant*, there appears an advertisement for 'Eggo', pre-Freudian dried egg powder; its use is urged on grounds of its cheapness, not convenience. By the inter-war years, even though the cost of labour had risen somewhat, the emphasis is the same. By the 1930s for example, the first instant coffee was on the market, and though the adjective 'convenient' was used, the stress was on the lack of waste – 'there are no 'grounds' left in the cup' (*Hotel Review*, February 1930). Some of the economy tips in the recipes seem penny-pinching to a bizarre degree: 'Mint Sauce: Now that good fresh mint is expensive, it is a good plan to chop it with an equal amount of watercress to make it go further' (same issue).

The most prominent concern, however, was with the use of leftovers. It would be absurd to pretend that leftovers found no use in France: Aron (1973: 198ff.) paints a revolting picture of the trade in *les restes* in nineteenth-century Paris, and Baron Brisse compiled a book (1868) of leftover recipes for the domestic cook. Yet the concern with using up surplus cooked food was slight in the French trade press (and French women's magazines) compared with their English counterparts. Every issue of *The Hotel Review* in 1930 contained a leftover recipe, some of them fairly horrific. For example, the main dish of a suggested 2*s*.0*d*. lunch in January was meat dormers:

> Boil ½lb of rice, drain it; when cold add ¼lb finely-chopped suet, 1lb of minced cooked meat [what kind is not specified], salt, pepper, bind with egg and form it into sausage shape. Flour them and fry carefully. Serve with brown onion or tomato sauce.

And in February:

> Hashed Pork: This dish is prepared from leftover pork. Mince a little onion, fry in butter. When golden, dilute with a little vinegar, add good brown sauce, and simmer a few minutes. Add the pork cut in medium-sized pieces, place in the sauce with a few sliced gherkins, and reheat but do not boil.

Other leftover meat recipes include 'Roman Pie' in July – cottage pie with macaroni on top in place of the usual potatoes – and 'Country Pie' in September – 'Pass through the mincer remains of pork with any other cooked meat *to be disposed of* . . .'[my emphasis]. Leftovers arose, of course, because of the dominance of plain roast joints in the better menus. The word 'horrific' may seem to be an unwarranted subjective judgement, but is objectively justified because many of these warmed-up meat recipes almost certainly carried a considerable risk of food poisoning.

Yet *The Hotel Review* hardly seems to have been directed at the humblest level of street-corner café. Apart from suggested menus and recipes, it contained much news of the higher reaches of the hotel trade, including a monthly column on 'Nouvelles de l'Hôtellerie Francaise' *in French*; and lunches and dinners at 2*s*.0*d*. and 2*s*.6*d*., the cheapest of its model menus, would not have been within the range of the poor – they would have been eaten by middle-class people. Although these menus have no particularly crusading air, it seems fair to infer that they were intended to be more imaginative than the average hotel of the time. Occasionally, in efforts to fancify a simple and common dish, one can hear distant echos from the world of Escoffier. For example, in February 1930 there are full instructions for 'Banana Custard': 'Slice the bananas and lay them in the bottom of a glass dish. Cover with raspberry jam, then pour over a boiled vanilla custard. Serve when cold.' That novelty, raspberry jam! – does it represent a distant memory of the inspired purée in *pêche Melba*?

After the Second World War, the concern with economy continued in much the same way. Right at the end of the period of food rationing, Mrs Robert Way was instructing the readers of *Hotel Management*, January 1954, to 'Transform your "Cinderella" Dishes', but with a slightly apologetic air:

> Extra profit . . . can be gained by the careful cooking and service of cheaper cuts and types of food. By this statement the writer does not mean 'be economical'; we must get away from that attitude if we want people to pay the right price for our food.[12]
> But some expensive ingredients such as wine and cream are, in fact, economical as only small quantities are needed to make less important items wear an air of exclusiveness.

In practice, Mrs Robert Way's notion of being 'economical' seems to work out just like the pre-war writers:

> Raised pies such as veal and ham pie or pork pie for the cold service can be made cheaper without loss of goodness by the addition of good left-over meat trimmings to the basic filling. So long as the 'named' material is recognisable, as much as a third of these odds and ends which would otherwise find their way to the stockpot can fill in with often a real advantage in flavour. There is no need to lower the standard of food; it is merely a question of using these cuts in luxurious ways.

Nevertheless, from the 1950s onwards, the concern with economy gradually acquired a new slant. Increasingly attention shifted away from leftovers, a problem stemming from the domination of menus by the traditional British roast joints, to avoiding the waste material arising in the first place. In other words, convenience foods and pre-cooked catering provisions became the centre of attention. Already in 1954 there were many advertisements for and articles on a variety of instant mixes and frozen foods. 'There's not a scrap of waste with Bird's Eye', said one advert, though Mrs Robert Way commented that 'Quick-frozen foods seem to be beyond the pockets of many caterers, but the writer thinks that too much nervousness is shown in this direction' (*Hotel Management*, February 1954).

Ten years later, very little of this nervousness had survived. In *Hotel and Restaurant Management* in the 1960s, cooking as such was much less prominent an interest altogether. The journal now contained few recipes and no menus. What it did contain was a lot of articles on 'portion-control', new equipment like microwave ovens and griddle units, and above all frozen food. It was mainly concerned with the sort of enterprise which *Néo-Restauration* sought to spread in France a decade later, though *Néo* has never become so nearly an uncritical puff for the manufacturers of food and equipment. Already in January 1964 Winifred McCullough, writing on 'The Shape of Catering to Come', looks forward to:

> The cookless kitchen . . . [in which] the staffing problem will be solved by a galley type servery using only ready-cooked deep frozen main meals, sweets and vegetables plus one or two grilled and griddled items each day. 'Top Tray' [a range of Bird's Eye products] and microwave ovens are one form of this service.

The same issue contains under the heading 'Trends at Hotelympia' articles by managers of two of the leading frozen-food manufacturers. One of them, from Bird's Eye, writes:

> One of the major food manufacturing industries in this country is also the fastest growing: namely the Frozen Food Industry.
>
> It is also the most maligned sector of the catering supply industry. Many hoteliers are frightened of admitting that they use Frozen Food at all. This situation, which is obviously both wrong and nonsensical, has been created by ill-judged attacks upon frozen food by some self-appointed and ill-informed gourmet critics.

He then proceeds to describe his own firm's Restaurant Range 'specially suitable for hotel banquets', and an adjacent advertisement shows an elegant and manifestly socially superior couple in evening dress, wine on table, looking knowledgeably and approvingly as the waiter serves helpings direct from the foil freezer trays The effect was, however, somewhat spoiled by the appearance nearby of a photograph and one of the few recipes in the paper: '½ packet frozen Skinless Beef Sausages, boiled and sliced. Added to 1 × 2½ lb pack Sliced Green Beens with horseradish sauce, milk, mustard and seasoning.'

The freezing companies were able to enlist the services and support of some prominent chefs – for example Jean Vincent, former head of the Westminster Hotel School, who by 1964 was working for Bird's Eye and writing articles emphasising that pre-frozen meals – often by now including classic French dishes – were cooked in just the same way as if they were prepared in the restaurant from fresh ingredients. No doubt that is so. Certainly it would be rash to assume that the advent of frozen food meant that food in British hotels and restaurants declined in quality overall. Possibly it did in some establishments just below the top of the range; but judging from the contents of the trade press from the 1920s to the 1950s, it is very likely that frozen dishes represented a distinct improvement on what had gone before lower down the hierarchy of professional kitchens.

The microwave oven was also just making its appearance in Britain in 1964. The freezing companies saw it as an essential adjunct to their products. They were anxious to convince the trade that deep-frozen packages could be cooked in them without prior thawing; if that were true, it would mean that waste would be still further reduced, since it would never be necessary to guess likely demand in advance. Others were more cautious, and warned of the problem of uneven cooking of food in the microwaves because of the persistence of 'cold spots'. There was also some nervousness about the safety of the early models: the story was told of the death of an employee of the manufacturers, at whose post mortem it was discovered his kidneys had been cooked inside his body by leaking microwaves (*Hotel and Restaurant Management*, February 1964). Another concern of the day was with 'call-order' cooking – fast-food operations, partly occasioned by the traditional large-scale kitchens and their ranges having become uneconomic in expensive city-centre locations. Here the concern was not so much with the cooking as with its presentation – 'its theatrical atmosphere has in itself proved an attraction to the public' according to one article. According to another, a puff for GEC call-order unit equipment, 'The chef in the white cap and coat is an exciting figure; brought to the "front of the house" he can be used in creating the right atmosphere for "positive selling"' (January 1964). And the editor of *Hotel and Restaurant Management* underlined the shift in focus from cooking food to selling it, writing in the same issue:

> Caterers must look upon themselves as salesmen as much as craftsmen. Their food is their merchandise; their surroundings their 'display aids'. Just because a caterer uses frozen foods widely, this does not mean he can afford to be lazy. A restaurateur can and must assert his personality and craftsmanship if he is to be successful. To do this he should be creative by such means as making attractive floral table settings to set off the colour in the food; in tempting *hors d'oeuvres* and in enticing sweet trolleys.

The early 1960s seem to have been a turning point in the British catering trade. The journals are strikingly different in content and attitude from those of previous decades, and the trends which began then have only been reinforced more recently. For example, in *Catering and Hotel Management* in 1979, there are advertisements for such new products as 'Bilmar Roast Turkey Breast':

> The end of the ordinary turkey. . . . With Bilmar Roast Turkey Breast you have no bones, just the pure natural meat through and through. And now, to make this delicious serving even more convenient, a ready sliced pack is available.

According to the 1984 *Good Food Guide*, more than 70 per cent of British restaurants now used pre-cooked frozen meals. What have been the implications of these profound changes for the training and the social standing of the cooking professions in England?

'THE PROFESSION' AND 'CRAFTSMAN-GRADE COOKS'

An article on 'Our Profession' in *The Hotel World*, February 1897, is as extravagant in tone and aspiration as the disquisitions that Philéas Gilbert had then been contributing to *L'Art culinaire* for a decade and a half. 'A profession', declared the anonymous author, 'is distinguished from a trade or occupation by the fact that to be a recognised member of it, the member must have passed certain examinations, and experienced certain technical training which pre-supposed him to be a person fully qualified to profess and execute the duties incumbent upon those who devote themselves to its practice'. And on those grounds, 'our profession' stood comparison with the most respected and longest established, for it

> demands more technical knowledge, more study of detail, and more continuous exertion of the intellect than that of all the so-called professions of War, Church, and

Law combined, and even in the profession of Medicine. [A member of our profession has] to attend to the care of the inner man, and cater to hygiene to such an extent that not only must he be no mean chemist, but is often a more able physician to the ailing than many of those who boast of medical diplomas.

Gilbert could have claimed no more. The difference, however, was that the English author was writing not about cooks, but about the 'profession' of hotel manager; and that difference in focus was a persistent one between England and France from the late nineteenth century onwards. There is in the English trade press an underlying disdain of cooks and cookery, of mere craftsmen; food itself is not 'on a pedestal'; prestige gravitates towards 'management'. UCFA may seem an exception, with its unusual strategy of redemption through good works but, as we have seen, that too became strongly influenced by catering management and its activities were *de haut en bas*.

The awed tone in which *Hotel World* in December 1895 described 'the lengthy and tedious process' which went into 'the making of a man cook in France' is indicative of the relative lack of training which went into making English cooks. The article described how the French apprentice learned in turn the art of larder cook, preparing vegetables, meat, fish and poultry; then the techniques of roasting, broiling, frying and baking; then the mysteries of sauces and soups; and finally served a long period with the *pâtissier* in all that concerned sweets, pastries and ices. As a result of this long culinary education

The salaries paid to many French cooks by the nobility for merely superintending the gastronomic arrangements of their establishment are considerable; five or six hundred pounds a year is very common, and frequently a thousand pounds is given.

In contrast, what often passed for the training of an English cook is described in an interview with Mr A. B. Marshall, proprietor of the Mortimer Street School of Cookery, in *The Hotel Review*, November 1886. Mr Marshall promised to turn out perfect cooks in three months of study – 'the whole thing from first to last' – for a fee of £21. But most pupils did not take the whole course, and a great many were simply sent by their mistresses to improve their knowledge in one area, such as soups and entrées, in a single day. Mr Marshall's pupils, be it noted, were all women.

Concern at the quality of training of English cooks led UCFA to take the initiative in persuading the London County Council as early as 1910 to set up what was eventually to become the Westminster Hotel School. In fact, at first glance, by the First World War there was far better *public* provision for the training of cooks in Britain than in France. The 1914 *Cookery Annual* lists the 'principal cookery schools in Great Britain', of which eighteen were in the provinces and eight in London.[13] But these apparently all trained only or mainly women. A following list names eleven 'schools of cookery for boys and men' (UCFA, 1914: 110) – but ten of these were Nautical Schools of Cookery in East London, Liverpool, and all the principal ports, leaving only the London County Council school devoted to training professional male cooks for the higher quality market. As in France, some cooks trained by apprenticeship to distinguished chefs in private or restaurant kitchens, but these lists of schools give some hint of the relatively greater dominance of women among professional cooks in England than in France.

Little changed in this picture until after the Second World War, when the public reputation of English catering probably reached its nadir, and the trade became quite suddenly conscious of its need for more and better trained cooks. The Hotel and Catering Institute (HCI) took the lead in encouraging the growth of hotel and catering training in technical colleges up and down the country, in courses which – at least at first – concentrated on teaching practical craft skills. By 1954, as many as 108 technical institutions were offering such courses, with about 7500 students in attendance – more than any other European country and 'comparing favourably with the number in the United States' (*Hotel Management*, June 1954).

The shortage of chefs and other 'craftsmen' immediately after the war was 'so acute that the industry's spokesmen tended to clamour for craft workers and somewhat underplayed the need for potential managers' (John Fuller, in *Hotel and Restaurant Management*, September 1964). However, the very marked distinction in prestige between the hotel manager and the mere cook, evident in the British trade press since the beginning, grew if anything more, not less, pronounced. Not surprisingly, it was soon manifesting itself in the training courses, within which there emerged in effect two streams – those for 'potential executives' and those for the 'craftsman grade' who were 'likely to remain specialists but potentially promotable'. Equally unsurprisingly, students of any ambition saw themselves as 'potential executives', and, possibly more decisively, their teachers also saw *themselves* as primarily concerned with training the more prestigious stream. The Scottish Hotel School, established in 1944 as the first major specialist institute in the field since the Westminster School, was from the beginning designed to recruit and educate academically well-qualified 18-year-olds who could reasonably aspire to management posts, and indeed the SHS has now become part of the University of Strathclyde. As early as 1954, John Fuller (who was later Professor both at Strathclyde and at Surrey Universities) was reporting the fear that too many students might be aiming for the higher prestige executive posts (*Hotel Management*, August 1954). At that time he was inclined to dismiss such fears, but a decade later he was close to confirming them:

> A danger which Britain may face is that the status attraction of higher level work might lead to an over-provision of attempts at top-level training which, however valuable, must be supported by strong development of courses designed to provide good staff in the lower echelons. (*Hotel and Restaurant Management*, September 1964)

The supply of committed and highly skilled British cooks can scarcely have been promoted by the view that those who actually do the cooking are the 'lower echelons' possessed of merely 'craft skills', and by the prestige accorded to 'management'. The craft skills, including a thorough grounding in Escoffier, may still be taught, but the ladder of promotion leads straight out of the kitchen. Would an English Bocuse or English Troisgros brothers be likely to see long apprenticeship and superlative and innovative achievement in the kitchen as the route to the pinnacle of their profession? As a matter of fact, some of the most notable new restaurants in Britain in the last two decades have been opened by 'amateur' cooks – or at least people outside the conventional craft training schemes. Meanwhile, the domination of the 'manager' in the trade as a whole has increased still further. In 1971, the Hotel and Catering Institute amalgamated with the Institutional Management Association (to which had previously belonged people responsible for catering in schools, hospitals, factories, leisure centres and so on). The resulting body, The Hotel, Catering and Institutional Management Association (HCIMA), is very clearly the dominant professional association in the trade, but there were immediately complaints that its activities were dominated by the ex-IMA institutional managers (*Catering and Hotel Management*, May 1974). In any case, the HCI had already by the 1950s delegated responsibility for the low prestige 'craft skills' qualifications to the City and Guilds of London Institute – the examining body for most apprenticeships in Great Britain. This was taken by some to indicate a lack of serious concern, but in fact the pages of the trade press abound with worried comment about craft standards. In January 1964, *Hotel and Restaurant Management* reported that

> The five year cook's training scheme had been found too long. . . . Lady (Gertrude) Williams, in her study of apprentice training in Europe, considered that in this country we did tend to think too much about the length of training rather than the quality.

Later that year, the Government established the Hotel and Catering Industry Training Board (HCITB), which assumed overall national responsibility for the training of cooks and others of like grade in the industry.

Yet 15 years later, there was still disquiet, and a thought-provoking piece by the then President-elect of the HCIMA, Mr M. A. Roberts, in *Catering and Hotel Management* (July 1979), could be read as meaning that the British mode of training cooks was wrong, and the French right. It was a time for everyone to realise, contended Mr Roberts,

> that the most effective contribution to maintaining and improving standards of cookery in this country ought to come from qualified and experienced chefs. Here I suggest that the qualification is a sound basic training in a good kitchen and not necessarily a certificate of any sort. My experience as a manager with busy kitchens in my last two positions has led me to the conclusion that chefs are only really made in busy kitchens. I appreciate the usefulness of some basic theory and the teaching of very basic skills but this should probably be on a day release basis. Technical colleges

simply cannot teach the handling and cookery of food on a large scale. Cooking is a craft skill rather than an academic discipline of any sort, and practice makes perfect. . . . As individuals and members of the HCIMA I find that colleagues are increasingly concerned with the quality and standards of cookery and training of chefs. We will contribute more by teaching our own apprentices properly instead of complaining about the teaching in technical colleges.

One of the best demonstrations of the truth of Mr Roberts's argument was by David Adlard at the first Oxford Cookery Symposium at St Antony's College, Oxford, in 1980. Mr Adlard, then a young and enthusiastic commis-chef at the Connaught, later to be proprietor of one of the rare British restaurants to earn a rosette from the *Guide Michelin*, had received basic training at a technical college before escaping to the very different world of the Connaught. The professional textbooks used on the course, he recalled, failed to convey any feeling for the art of cookery, and described the manipulation of the raw materials 'as if they were describing motor-car maintenance for apprentice mechanics'.

CONCLUSION

Against this background, it is hardly surprising that one sociologist, surveying the condition of British cooks in the early 1970s, felt able to speak of the 'proletarianisation' of the occupation (Chivers, 1973). He portrays them as declining both in skill and status. Now, taking a longer-term view, it would be mistaken to imagine that any but a small minority of cooks, British or French, ever enjoyed anything other than modest social status. But Chivers was undoubtedly right to point to the 'deskilling' of cooks brought about by technological changes like the advent of frozen foods, catering packs, call-order cooking, and fast-food operations. Even in the case of cook-freeze systems, where the spokesmen of the manufacturers are at pains to point out that before freezing, dishes are cooked exactly as they always were, the bulk production of a standard range of 'classic' dishes requires less skill and flair from cooks at the factory than would cooking equivalent quality food in a 'live' kitchen.

Yet technology does not seem to me to explain everything. 'Ideological' considerations also seem to have some bearing on the state of the occupation of cook in England and France. The long-standing dominance of 'management' in the English catering trade, and its disdain for the humble 'craftsman cook' appears to have facilitated the relatively more uncritical adoption of new technology in Britain than in France, and made British cooks more vulnerable to 'proletarianisation'. The contrasting French tradition portrayed earlier in this chapter equally seems at least to have helped delay and partly modify the progress of the same trends in France.

One reason for these differences between England and France is the much clearer distinction in France between professional and domestic traditions of cookery, and the virtual absence of that distinction in England. We shall examine that in more detail in the next chapter.

8

Domestic Cookery in the Bourgeois Age

In studying the world of the professional chefs and their clientèle, it is easy to lose sight of the wider world of domestic cookery – what people at large ate at home and how they prepared it. The very expression 'at home' evokes the social milieu of the bourgeois, whose residence is 'private', clearly demarcated from the public sphere in a way that a noble household was not. In the same way, the idea of 'domestic cookery' can only exist in contradistinction to a recognisably separate way of cooking, usually by professionals, in institutions – whether courts, restaurants or hospitals – which are not, or not merely, private households.

By the nineteenth century, the differentiation between professional and domestic cookery was well established, a familiar part of the experience of the well-to-do. Leadership in the development of professional *haute cuisine*, as we have seen, belonged unquestionably to the French, building on their inheritance of courtly cuisine from the *ancien régime*. In England, a process of domestication of cookery had been evident in the eighteenth century. The consequence was that, in the nineteenth century, French cookery captured the social commanding heights in England more decisively than it had in the previous century, and national differences in cuisine became entangled with class differences in Britain in even more complicated ways.

In the experience of the poor, there was still not much other than domestic cookery – unless it were in barracks or on board ship. Broadly speaking, until the nineteenth century social differences in eating had scarcely diminished since the Middle Ages (though the reliability of food supplies had improved). The most important development during the century was the beginning of the trend towards relatively greater social uniformity in food. That reflected the closer interdependence of social classes in an industrial society, and eventually it involved closer interconnections between professional and domestic cookery. In the short term, however, the two appeared to draw further apart, for the French professional chefs were at pains to differentiate their work from mere domestic cookery. Domestic cookery was in both countries seen as primarily the preserve of females, whether paid women cooks or housewives cooking for their own families.

MALE CHEFS AND WOMEN COOKS

The feminist historian Lois Banner has asked 'Why women have not been great chefs' and, after surveying a good deal of evidence that they have not, concludes that

> In the final analysis women have not been great chefs, just as they have not been great artists, or professionals, or whatever else the popular mythology would add, for a variety of complex historical, psychological, and sociological reasons. Women have written cookbooks and have created new dishes and new cuisines. They have served as cooks in well-to-do homes and in restaurants when men were not available. But throughout the ages, a status-conscious public has when possible preferred to be served by men, while male chefs themselves have not been unwilling to lessen competition and shore up their own status by denying women access to the prestigious positions in the world of cooking. In general women have not been great chefs because the rôle has not been available to them. (1973: 212)

All that is true, but as an answer it tends towards circularity and begs the main questions: why have male cooks had higher prestige, and why have they been able to deny the role of 'great chef' to women?

The kernel of any answer must lie in the very close association in most human cultures of women with ordinary domestic cooking. Whenever a technically more elaborate, socially more prestigious cuisine has begun to develop, it has necessarily involved differentiation both technical and social from the everyday cookery of the majority of the people. Since the latter is generally associated with women cooks, it is highly likely that any process of social differentiation will involve distancing from the food of the lower orders and from the women who cook it. At any rate, as Goody (1982: 101) notes, ever since Egyptian times it has been men who took over women's recipes for daily cooking and transformed them into a court cuisine. Why should this have happened so consistently? The most likely explanation lies in the origin of the social institution of the court not as a 'private' or 'domestic' household, but as a military establishment. It is probable that men always served as cooks with armies (and by extension on fighting ships), and that their function in the kitchens of the court began as an extension of that rôle. There is no reason to suppose that the food cooked by male cooks was in origin any more sophisticated than that cooked by women, but men having established their monopoly in courtly kitchens, they became the instruments of the refinement of cooking as the court itself developed as the locus of the arts of consumption. The military connections of male cooks were still perceptible in the courts of late medieval and early modern Europe: Taillevent, for example, appears to have had some function in the provisioning of armies, and La Varenne, whose title of 'écuyer' retains military connotations, speaks of cooking for his master the Marquis d'Uxelles with the armies in the field.

In the seventeenth and eighteenth centuries both in England and France, as we have seen, cookery books describing the food of the courts were written by men. Among English authors, however, that genre became extinct around 1730, and the typical English cookery books of the eighteenth century were those by women addressed to the domestic cooks of the gentry and middle class. On the whole, these books represented the cookery of the English 'farmhouse' kitchen; writers like Hannah Glasse do appear to have owed a debt directly or indirectly to French 'courtly' sources, but their role was essentially that of (in Banner's words) 'the simplifier and translator of the recipes of the classic cuisine to women with neither the training nor time to produce the original masterpieces in their own kitchens' (1973: 199). As for professional cookery specifically in the English style, as represented, for example, in the work of John Farley late in the eighteenth century, it appears to have been technically and in terms of social prestige relatively rather close to the domestic tradition. Leaving on one side (for the moment) the high prestige of specifically French cuisine and of French chefs in England at the time, the gap between professional and domestic cookery was little developed; and in consequence the gap in status between men and women cooks also seems to have been relatively slight. None the less it did exist. Discussing the position of women cooks in the servant hierarchy of the eighteenth-century English household, Hecht writes that though their responsibilities were exactly the same as those of a male cook in a household where a man was employed, yet

> however accomplished female cooks may have been, they were considered inferior in talent and knowledge to men. Contemporary advertisements furnish clear proof that this was the case, for they make it plain that preference was often given to women who had experience in assisting a man-cook. (1956: 65)

But that, Hecht implies, had a good deal to do with the much greater likelihood that a man cook was French or had received French training. Much the same continued to be true in the nineteenth century. Hayward expressed the following instance of what would later be regarded as male chauvinism:

> women make far the best English cooks, practically speaking; and the fair sex have supplied some tolerably apt pupils of the French school; but they seldom arrive at distinguished proficiency unless they are both handsome and *coquettes* – for the simple reason that no Frenchman who affects taste will take pains to teach a woman who is not able and willing to minister to the gratification of his vanity. (1852: 56–7)

A French or French-trained chef was often the highest-paid member of staff; Marcham, the Duke of Rutland's chef at Belvoir Castle was paid £147 in 1810, rising to £161. 14*s*. in 1814. In contrast, typical wages for a woman-cook in the kitchens of members of the gentry appear to have been sixteen guineas a year in 1820, £21 in 1836, and still only £22 a year in 1890 (F. M. L. Thompson, 1963: 193).

Yet within the less prestigious realm of English cookery, men and women cooks alike appear to have shared much the same humble (and perhaps declining) status. Sir Henry Thompson offered a cogent explanation of the low status of English cooks, male or female: their general lack of any systematic training, which in turn he saw as a consequence of their low status:

Once make cookery a distinct business to which the young may be trained, which it never yet has been, and the chance of now and then producing a first-rate cook, who may advance the art, is within reach. Hitherto the practice of cookery has been merely a resource for wage-getting among ignorant women, who took to it at hazard, and acquired such traditions as pertained to the kitchen they happened to enter. Still further, until it is recognised in this country as a profession which a man with some education and natural taste can exercise, we must be content to rank below other countries in rearing artists of the first order. (1880: 194)

In England, outside the highest ranks of French cookery, women cooks seem to have competed very well against men in the market for employment as domestic cooks, but against a background of what seems to be a rather well-documented decline in standards of middle-class home cooking in the Victorian era. The situation prompted Betty Wason (1962: 230) to pose the question: 'Was it because women were now serving as cooks that the culinary arts suffered? Or was it the other way round, that when cooks slipped from their place of eminence, women were finally hired to do the job?'

In France, the gap in status was much clearer, in part because it was not as in England obscured by entanglement with the differing prestige of English and French cuisine. Already by the middle of the eighteenth century, Duclos could look back to the end of the reign of Louis XIV and remark with an air almost of incredulity that male cooks had then been found only in houses of the first rank, and that 'more than half the magistrates employed only women cooks' (1772: lxi). By the nineteenth century the superior status of male cooks was taken for granted. Witness the condescending remarks of Châtillon-Plessis:

Good women cooks are not scarce today, although one may often regret the reasons of economy which in some house leads to them being substituted for male chefs. Reasons of *false* economy . . .

Quite certainly a woman cook can never give a table the attractive style that a male chef can bring to it. The profession involves fatiguing work that only a man can undertake, and elements of ingenuity which a woman will never know how to carry off. . . .

That said, nothing must prevent us paying homage to the modern Sophies who have the respect of their priests and strive with success for the triumph of their art. These Georges Sands of cookery are scarcely more numerous than the Georges Sands of literature, but they have no less right to the esteem of every connoisseur. (1894: 90–2)

Nevertheless, in the latter half of the nineteenth century, competition in France between men and women for positions as professional cooks was becoming more severe. Apart from the large numbers of women employed as cooks in middle-class households, some worked in the kitchens of the smaller and less-celebrated restaurants.[1] L. B. Young (1981: 79) quotes the 1893 report of the Office de Travail on the catering trades:

> Here . . . as in the clothing industry . . . the struggle between men and women workers, what the classic socialist works call 'the struggle of the sexes', is waged with such intensity that economists are not the only ones to recognise it. *Cuisiniers* and *cuisinières* fight for the offers of employment and in spite of the well-known superiority and inventiveness of the most renowned male chefs, in spite of the resistance to fatigue which their physical strength allows, success has gone to their female rivals.

This competition between the sexes helps to account for the continuing concern amongst French chefs to emphasise the distance between their own *grande cuisine* and the ordinary domestic cookery associated with women cooks and housewives. Occasionally voices were raised recognising that poor pay and conditions were problems common to all cooks of either sex; Thomas Genin suggested that membership of the Union Universelle pour le Progrès de l'Art Culinaire be open to professional cooks of both sexes (*L'Art culinaire*, 25 February 1883), but in the next issue the editors were at pains to emphasise, apparently in response to many expressions of alarm, that this had been only M. Genin's *personal* suggestion, and it had attracted little support. The far more general attitude was expressed in the first issue of *L'Art culinaire* (28 January 1883) by A. Tavenet, stating the policy of the new journal: 'We shall not abstain from giving recipes for simple family dinners, but without descending to what is called *la petite cuisine* or domestic cookery.' The continuing concern, discussed in the last chapter, to raise the status of the profession by means of achievements in cookery itself, involved an attempt not just by French professional cooks but specifically by French *male* professional cooks to monopolise the power of setting taste and fashion in matters of eating. How far did this monopolisation succeed, on either side of the Channel?

THE DECAPITATION OF ENGLISH COOKERY

We have already examined in the Chapters 6 and 7 how in France male chefs accomplished the transition from the private kitchens of upper-class households, rapidly developing a distinctive *grande cuisine* and successfully establishing their dominance of the more public sphere of the restaurants. What influence did their cuisine have in turn on the domestic cookery of the middle classes? Though they often affected disdain for mere domestic cookery, and were at pains to distance themselves from it, the relationship between the cookery of the restaurants and middle-class domestic cookery in France appears to have been relatively direct and simple, uncomplicated as it was in England by the pattern of culinary 'cultural dependency' – the co-existence of native and foreign styles of food with different social connotations.

In France, the channels of influence were manifold. There was, as we have noted, a continuous hierarchy of restaurants serving food varying in lavishness and expense, but essentially within a single tradition, and dining out in restaurants played a more prominent part in the way of life of the French middle classes in the nineteenth century than it did among their English counterparts. Cookery books directed at upper- and middle-class households also form a link. Many were written by famous chefs. Even Carême claimed (albeit somewhat implausibly) that his *Art de la cuisine française au dix-neuvième siècle* was suitable for use in the domestic as well as the professional kitchen, while Gouffé's *Livre de la Cuisine* was divided into sections dealing with *grande* and *petite cuisine*, the latter simplified but clearly derived from the model of the former. Probably more widely influential – in so far as cookery books do influence domestic cookery – was Viard's *Le Cuisinier impérial*, the most successful middle-class cookery book of nineteenth-century France, which went through a vast number of editions, changing its title to *Le Cuisinier royal*, *Le Cuisinier national*, and back again with each change of regime up to the Third Republic. A best seller from its first publication in 1806, by 1812 it had already reached its seventh edition – more, it was said, than any other book, literary or otherwise, of the period. The contents were laid out in the standard manner – soups, *grandes sauces* (including *espagnole* and the rest), *petites sauces*, beef, veal, and so on – the recipes clearly simplified from more elaborate models. According to the Preface,

> Some will be able to find things to criticise in this work's simplicity of style, but what else ought one to sink one's teeth into if not into a cookery book? So what! Isn't simplicity the mark of genius, and doesn't an academic style exist already for the olympians?

Even so, it is noteworthy that Viard's title was *Le Cuisinier*, in contrast to his predecessor Menon's *La Cuisinière bourgeoise* (which incidentally continued to be reprinted far into the nineteenth century). Another very popular cookery book of the century, *La Cuisinière de la campagne et de la ville* (1818), used the feminised title to signify that it was directed at middle-class households, but its author was a man, Louis-Eustache Audot.

Later on, male chefs of high professional reputation were to play a prominent part in the movement to improve domestic cookery. Henri-Paul Pellaprat was probably the only man whose name can be mentioned in the same breath as such contemporaries as Escoffier, Montagné and Gilbert who nevertheless chose to devote the bulk of his career to training women cooks – in 1902 he became head of the Cordon Bleu school in Paris (not, of course, an establishment noted for the spartan simplicity of its cookery).[2] Charles Driessens, one of the most prominent members of the Escoffier circle, gave lectures on domestic cookery for housewives in Paris in the 1890s, reports of which formed the centrepiece of the women's magazine *Pot-au-feu*. Although in both England and France the majority of cookery columns in women's magazines since the late nineteenth century have been by women for women, in France these publications have carried more articles by noted male chefs – from Driessens to Raymond Oliver – than their counterparts in England.[3] All in all, the links between élite and domestic cookery seem more direct in France than on the other side of the Channel.

In England, the picture was much more complicated. There was nothing new in a fashionable élite eating food cooked according to the French style and system, and in the nineteenth century there are signs not only of that élite growing in size, but of a French veneer being applied to basically English-style fare in the upper reaches of the middle class. There is also overwhelming evidence that average middle-class cookery (let alone that of still lower social ranks) remained largely untouched by such influences.

> On questioning the average middle-class Englishman as to the nature of his food, the all but universal answer is, 'My living is plain, always roast and boiled' – words which but too clearly indicate the dreary monotony, not to say unwholesomeness, of his daily food; while they furthermore express his satisfaction, such as it is, that he is no luxurious feeder. (H. Thompson, 1880: 62)

That attitude also seems to have formed a dyke, somewhere in the middle ranks of the social hierarchy, through which fashionable French models did not seep. An important consequence of the prestige of French cookery in the higher social circles appears to have been the 'decapitation' of English cookery. That word was used in passing in the last chapter to describe the effect on professional cookery in the English style of having the fashionable restaurants in England dominated by French-style cookery and, to a considerable extent, French chefs. 'Decapitation' also appears to have had three important consequences for English domestic cookery.

First, by the latter part of the nineteenth century, the by then largely unquestioned superiority of French cookery produced a corresponding sense of the inferiority of English cookery. Sometimes that was tinged with chauvinistic defiance, but a defiance that led to conservatism, the defiance of the bunker, rather than to innovation and development within the English tradition to rival the French. Secondly, as the word 'decapitation' implies, English-style cookery was deprived of élite models of its own to copy, and this probably contributed to the mediocrity which both contemporary and subsequent observers remarked on in English cookery in the Victorian era. Thirdly, as an extension of that, there was virtually no difference between professional and domestic cookery in the English style; there was no group of professional cooks working in their native style but seeking to distance themselves from ordinary domestic cookery, and no longer much sign of domestic cooks emulating in simplified form the models of a distinct native professional tradition.

French cuisine, until then found only in some aristocratic households and a small number of London clubs and private hotels, seems to have spread considerably between the end of the Napoleonic wars and the middle of the century. Captain Gronow, reminiscing in 1862 about the customs prevalent in the second decade of the century, recalled that:

> Even in the best houses, when I was a young man, the dinners were wonderfully solid, hot and stimulating. The *menu* of a grand dinner was thus composed: – Mulligatawny and turtle soups were the first dishes placed before you; a little lower the eye met with the familiar salmon at one end of the table, and the turbot surrounded by smelts, at the other. The first course was sure to be followed by a saddle of mutton or a piece of roast beef; and then you could take your oath that fowls, tongue and ham, would as assuredly succeed as darkness after day.
>
> Whilst these never-ending *pièces de résistance* were occupying the table, what were called French dishes were, for custom's sake, added to the solid abundance. The French, or side dishes, consisted of very mild but very abortive attempts at Continental cooking; and I have always observed that they met with the neglect and contempt they merited. (1862–6: I, 37)

It should be noted that this much-quoted passage is not just another instance of an English author prejudiced against French food – Gronow was a devotee of French cuisine and lived much of his later life in Paris; but it does indicate the relatively small penetration even of upper-class tables by French cookery around 1815. By mid century, however, it had become *de rigueur* among the fashionable, and Burnett (1966: 57) describes this as one of the most outstanding dietary changes of the period.

Yet the diffusion of French models was patchy: the two codes of cooking persisted alongside each other. Not only the 'average' middle class but many of the country gentry in particular seem to have remained conservative in taste and untouched by fashion. Pierce Synott, in an essay (1936) examining the food of farmers and gentlemen of the 1840s as portrayed in the novels of R. S. Surtees, speaks of the deliberate neglect of the 'make-up' of dishes, so that simplicity became almost monotony, in contrast to an intense concentration on materials:

> Matter was all-important; manner followed. Substance always came before style, because there was only one style, which consisted in interfering as little as possible with the raw material. Only once is a 'french dish' [*sic*] mentioned – at a supper at a pretentious inn – but the author shows his contempt, and the French dish turns out to be four greasy mutton chops. On the other hand, the attention focused on the quality of raw material was stupendous, and must have been effective. It was that kind of lynx-eyed, fidgety, impatient attention which nowadays would rightly be called greed.[4]

Sometimes the two codes co-existed in the same kitchen. The same author (Synott, 1938), studying the kitchen books for 1837–8 of the Duke of Cambridge (younger brother of George IV and William IV), concludes that under the veneer of conventional menu French the Duke's meals were dominated by traditional English roasts – 'the same dishes that Mr Pickwick would eat'. But even so, the Duke did employ a French chef (and he was the dedicatee of Soyer's *Gastronomic Regenerator*). Synott certainly overstated his case when he concluded that 'the cultural affinities that once united the upper classes of England and France had vanished.'

The expansion of French cuisine fits in closely with changes in the size and structure of fashionable Society in England during the nineteenth century. London Society, centred on the court and politics, had existed in the previous two centuries. As noted in chapter 5, the beginnings of the annual migration of leading families from their country seats to London for the Season, coinciding with the Parliamentary session, can be detected at the start of the seventeenth century. In the eighteenth century, Mingay (1963) estimates, about 400 families were involved in the Season. During the next century, numbers grew steadily and from the 1820s onwards the Season and its calendar of events became more formalised. By the end of the nineteenth century it has been estimated that as many as 4000 families were actively involved in London Society and the Season (Davidoff, 1973: 61). The number of individual members of these families was of course larger still, and it was in the course of this tenfold growth that the phrase 'The Upper Ten Thousand' came into common use to describe the social élite. In addition to London Society there were subordinate or peripheral Societies in the counties and provincial towns. Many gentle families whose resources would not stretch to participation in the London Season were nevertheless full members of County Society, leadership of which was assumed by the migrant families when resident at their country seats.

'Society' was a textbook example of status-group, a group which in Max Weber's classic definition shares a common situation in relation to the social estimation of 'honour'.

> status honour is normally expressed by the fact that above all else a specific *style of life* is expected from all those who wish to belong to the circle. Linked with this expectation are restrictions on social intercourse (that is, intercourse which is not subservient to economic or any other purpose). These restrictions may confine normal marriages to within the status circle and may lead to complete endogamous closure. (M. Weber, 1922: II, 932)

This can be seen very clearly in the case of Society in nineteenth-century England. Membership was confined (and marriages contracted among) those deemed to possess the attributes of a 'lady' or 'gentleman'. With the growing numbers of individuals involved, the required outward manifestations of gentle status became more and more formalised and elaborate. Throughout the middle part of the century, admission rituals and etiquette – introductions, the exchange of cards and formal visits, of who 'knew' whom (in a very specific sense of 'knowing'), and of 'correct' behaviour in every situation (including dining and the giving of dinners) – became ever more defined. This happened for two reasons. One was that, with the large numbers involved, it was more difficult to rely on personal knowledge and informed gossip about a person's character and standing. More importantly by far, however, was that the growing numbers claiming social recognition (as well as the political recognition more commonly discussed in the standard histories of the period) threatened to overwhelm the style of life itself. The 'established' circle, already members of the in-group, tended to adopt the no doubt largely unconscious strategy of constantly raising the requirements of the 'style of life' necessary for an 'outsider' to claim membership of Society (see Elias and Scotson, 1965).

Davidoff (1973: 13) notes how the housekeeping manuals, etiquette books and magazines of the period confirm that the standard of living expected of all upper- and middle-class groups rose considerably. As in the case of the eighteenth-century French nobility, much of the required expenditure was on matters of ceremonial display, and on the household establishment necessary to maintain the expected style of life. Again, as in that case, this expenditure can with hindsight appear 'irrational'. Yet it was experienced as highly compelling by those caught up in the system – so much so that, as Banks (1954) pointed out, many mid-Victorian middle-class families even made the moral breakthrough of adopting contraceptive methods in order to be able to uphold the necessary lifestyle. Why it was so compelling can better be understood if Society is seen as functioning as a filter, regulating the flow of people into the most significant positions in society at large. For until the latter half of the nineteenth century, posts in the army, the Church, the Civil Service, local government, and many of the professions, were acquired largely through patronage and personal acquaintance. In short, Davidoff defines Society as 'a system of quasi-kinship relationships which was used to 'place' mobile individuals during a period of structural differentiation fostered by industrialisation and urbanisation' (1973: 15). In spite of efforts by the 'established' to reduce the mesh of the filter, the social pumps forced more and more people through it.

From the late eighteenth century the landed aristocracy seems to have been conscious of the pressure from below as industrialisation created new sources of wealth and newly wealthy groups. As F. M. L. Thompson (1963: 8–9) has remarked, 'the caste-like attitude of the landed aristocracy became more pronounced at the very time that Pitt inaugurated the great expansion of the peerage'. In fact, in Pitt's time and for a long time afterwards, concern at the social dilution of the peerage was premature[5] but, as W. I. Thomas's famous dictum has it, 'if men define situations as real, they are real in their consequences.' The consequences in this case included the no doubt unplanned but impressively successful efforts of what was still in essence a landed élite to maintain its social (and political) dominance long after it had lost its monopoly control of the principal means of wealth creation.

In this, the aristocracy was assisted by the landed gentry which shared a similar life-style, albeit on a reduced scale. The gentry were in many respects fundamentally a more conservative class than the nobility (F. M. L. Thompson, 1963: 20), and that was especially true of those whose resources did not run to indulgence in the annual transhumance, and whose lives were thus circumscribed in provincial limits; their alleged tastes in cookery in the 1830s and 1840s appear to be one manifestation of this conservatism. On the other hand, the landed gentry were a much more fluid class than the nobility. They enjoyed much more latitude in contracting marriages with non-landed families of roughly equal standing. This provided a fairly broad channel of recruitment, and an effective mechanism of co-option, into Society. Those who had acquired wealth in industry or commerce could quite easily use it to buy landed estates, and in due course see their families intermarry with established gentry and, as often as not, sever connections with the business whence their wealth originally derived.

Landed and London Society remained the reference group for rising middle-class strata, and its tastes and manners were emulated widely.

> Already by the 1830s and 1840s it seems that the hard work, thrift and abstemiousness on which many of the middle classes had founded their fortunes were coming to be abandoned in favour of competitive expenditure. The new values were demonstrated in terms of houses and furnishings, horses and carriages, the lavish employment of domestic servants, dress, and – not least – in terms of food. (Burnett, 1966: 54)

Sometimes the emulation could spill over into vulgarity. Thomas Walker, protesting at over-elaborate meals and the numbers of dishes removed uneaten from the tables of some of the newly wealthy, wrote:

> I think the affluent would render themselves and their country an essential service if they were to fall into the simple, refined style of living, discarding everything incompatible with real enjoyment; and I believe, that if the history of overgrown luxury were traced, it has always had its origin from the vulgar rich – the very lowest class worthy of invitation. (1835: 227–8)

Mockery of the newly wealthy trying to emulate the longer-established élite (many of whom themselves failed to meet Walker's standards of simplicity and refinement), and still more mockery of the pretensions and anxieties of those like the Grossmiths' Mr Pooter who could not realistically expect to achieve membership of their reference group, was a stock-in-trade of Victorian humour. Yet on the whole the Victorian *nouveaux riches* did not behave as *nouveaux riches* are supposed to. They accepted the rules, they were 'neither aggressive, inept, nor ostentatious', as Girouard (1978: 268) concludes in studying their performance in their newly acquired country houses.

In spite of the success of the landed aristocracy and gentry in prolonging their social dominance, by the 1880s the basis of London Society was beginning to widen. The balance of power between landed and business interests in society at large was shifting, not only because of the growing numbers, wealth and prominence of industrialists, but also because the agricultural depression had undermined landowners' resources. The sheer numbers who now took part in the London Season led to Society's becoming less of a unity than it once had been, with a measure of segmentation taking place between social circles. Somewhat separate circles could be distinguished centring on the court, on politics and Parliament, on millionaire financiers, and on the racing set, though the circles intersected through common membership. 'Politics and public affairs came in some measure to be separated from the wider social world of Society at large, but the segregation of social spheres meant it was possible to admit and control certain elements that previously had been defined as unworthy' (Davidoff, 1973: 64).[6] This was part of a more fundamental change in the functions of Society from about the middle of the century. Its functions as a filter, in 'placing' people through a network of quasi-familial contact and patronage began to be replaced by more formal, less particularistic institutions. Commissions in the army could no longer be purchased, competitive examinations were introduced for admission to the Civil Service and many of the professions, and political office became more genuinely elective at all levels. (The 'County Sets' had centred on the county magistracy, who were largely responsible for county administration until elected county councils took over most of their functions late in the century.) And the public schools grew in numbers and importance as places where boys from the well-to-do middle class could acquire not just the increasingly necessary learning but also the tastes and manners of the older families with whose offspring they mixed early in life. In consequence of all these developments, towards the close of the century, '"Society" functions came to be regarded simply as a way of life, pleasure as an end in itself with a secondary re-emphasis on the marriage market' (Davidoff, 1973: 65). With politics and public affairs withdrawn into somewhat more restricted and 'private' circles, and with the enlargement of Society as a whole, the Season and social life of the élite took on a more theatrical air involving social display in relatively more public spheres. The rise of the great hotel restaurants from the 1880s, described in chapter 6, is to be understood as part of this development. It is striking that the partial 'defunctionalisation' of English Society was associated with a shift towards social display, just as the more thoroughgoing defunctionalisation of the French nobility had done a century and more earlier.

These, then, were some of the social forces which generated pressures towards emulation of the tastes and style of life of fashionable Society among members of the middle and upper-middle strata of Victorian England. They appear to have contributed to the 'decapitation' of English cookery in two ways: first by encouraging the somewhat wider adoption of French-style cuisine, and secondly by encouraging ladies with social pretensions to remove themselves from any practical involvement in the kitchen.

The evidence about cookery in private households is more circumstantial than that for the sphere of professional cookery discussed in the chapters 6 and 7, but it seems to point the same way – to French influence strong among the social élite, and especially in London, but patchy and superficial elsewhere. Even 'ten thousand' would represent a vast expansion of French cuisine compared with the previous century, but they were only a small island in the country as a whole. Fashion-consciousness, as we have noted, already penetrated quite deeply through the social layers of eighteenth-century England, and John Burnett has argued (1966: 2) that the further growth of town living in the nineteenth century stimulated competition and social imitation among *all* social classes, not just in the highest reaches, and that this led eventually to more sophisticated tastes and eating habits generally. He cites as outstanding examples the spread of tea and white bread, which had previously been luxuries of the well-to-do. It needs to be reiterated, however, that French cookery, though fashionable among the enlarged élite, certainly did not spread very far down society: the *average* middle-class diet remained 'plain roast and boiled'.

A growing disdain for practical work in the kitchen could perhaps be more widely and easily emulated. Very early in the century, Maria Rundell complained that among female accomplishments 'domestic occupations stand not so high as they once did' (1806: xxv). About the same time, Jane Austen made Mrs Bennet take great offence when Mr Collins enquired which of her daughters he should compliment on having cooked so excellent a meal: she 'assured him with some asperity that they were well able to keep a good cook, and that her daughters had nothing to do in the kitchen' (Austen, 1813: 57). Later, Jeaffreson claimed that 'not one young gentlewoman in a hundred can make an omelette or cook a *sole au gratin*' (1875: I, 184). In the course of the century, for the well-to-do lady, 'doing the housekeeping became little more than a daily interview with the housekeeper and the cook' (Fussell and Fussell, 1953: 185). Mrs Rundell quite explicitly blamed this trend on middle-class people's pretensions to upward mobility and what was later to be called 'anticipatory socialisation':

> The custom of the times tends in some measure to abolish the distinctions of rank, and the education given to young people is nearly the same in all: but though the leisure of the higher may be well devoted to different accomplishments, the pursuits of those in a middle line, if less ornamental, would better secure their own happiness and that of others connected with them. We sometimes bring up children in a manner calculated rather to fit them for the station we wish, than that which it is likely they will actually possess; and it is in all cases worth the while of parents to consider whether the expectation or hope of raising their offspring above their own situation be well founded. (1806: xxvi)

The cookery books of the period, as always, provide interesting evidence even though, as always, reservations have to be borne in mind about the connection between what appears in the books and what actually happened in the kitchen. Mrs Rundell's *New System of Domestic Cookery* was one of the best selling cookery books of the first half of the nineteenth century, though opinions differ about the quality of the cookery in which she was urging her middle-class readers to take a personal interest. Esther Aresty

(1965: 164) speaks of 'this undistinguished little book with its stodgy, unappetising recipes', but if in detail they were not subtle and represented no technical development her recipes were broadly similar to those of the plain English eighteenth-century tradition. French dishes were segregated into a brief 15-page chapter of their own. Not very different is another bestseller of the period, Dr Kitchiner's *The Cook's Oracle* (1817), which however did mix in some exotica – not all of them French – and some rather distinctive recipes of the Doctor's own invention. Around the middle of the century, anyone who wanted French cuisine would have had to turn to the works of Soyer or Francatelli, where it was slightly adapted to the English market, or of course, if rich enough to employ a French chef, they could use actual French cookery books. English middle-class cookery books continued, however, in basically the same English mode. What many present-day cookery experts regard as the most distinguished book of the period, Eliza Acton's *Modern Cookery for Private Families* (1845), is also built on a backbone of 'plain English' dishes, and Elizabeth David (1968) has described this book as 'the final expression, the crystallisation, of pre-Industrial England's taste in food and attitude to cookery'. Surprisingly, that even ran as far as upholding the ancient English reputation for soggy vegetables: like Mrs Beeton after her, but unlike Farley, Briggs and Rundell immediately before her, Acton disapproves of vegetables served *al dente* (1845: 299). Yet in other respects Eliza Acton, compared with her forerunners, is already more cosmopolitan in outlook, and writing for a more urban middle-class audience. While she expects her readers still to be able to pick their own fruit for jam-making, she also expects them to be able to purchase a wide range of other ingredients for French, Italian, Jewish and Indian dishes.[7]

English cookery books from the eighteenth century through Rundell and Acton to Mrs Beeton need to be read in sequence: each can appear rustic in comparison with its successors, but the growth of urban living is evident when each is compared with its predecessor. Certainly, Isabella Beeton's *Book of Household Management* (1861) merits its reputation as the first book written unambiguously for an urban middle-class audience. It was, moreover, a sufficiently lowly middle class that the wife could not escape the responsibility of supervising domestic details, and needed to be told a great deal about it. Apart from cookery, Mrs Beeton wrote at length about precisely those matters which were causes of concern and social anxiety to the aspiring middle classes – etiquette, table settings, the hierarchy of servants and how many of them were required in typical households with various incomes. Bills of fare and lists of food in season – which Eliza Acton had not thought necessary to provide, possibly assuming more of the countrywoman's knowledge of crops and seasons than Mrs Beeton did only a decade and a half later – were set out in detail. As for Mrs Beeton's cookery itself, there are superficial signs of French influence, but it is mainly 'plain English', and Aresty's retrospective judgement (1965: 179) is that 'Mrs Beeton's recipes were . . . in themselves uninspired'. Certainly there is no sense of progress and development in English domestic cookery in the middle and late Victorian period. The representative cookery book of the next generation was Cassell's gigantic but anonymous *Dictionary of Cookery* (1875). This too was apparently addressed to the lower middle class, since the introductory essay on 'The Principles of Cooking and Table Management' speaks of the typical small household consisting of husband, wife and two servants. The essay is far from systematic and certainly would not bear comparison with the expositions of the 'principles' of cookery by Carême, Gouffé or Escoffier. It proclaims 'economy to be the soul of cookery', and the depth of the French influence can be judged from the author's equation of 'entrées' with croquettes and kromeskies made from leftover cold meat, and from his advocacy of flower-shaped slices of turnip for the adornment of dishes. With the exception of Acton, it does not seem unfair to describe the food of the nineteenth-century English domestic cookery books as rather monotonous, and above all lacking in any sense of the *enjoyment* of food.

THE LOWER ORDERS

It is, however, hazardous to depict the history of middle-class cookery in the nineteenth century solely in terms of decline. Its apparent mediocrity is in part a trick of historical perspective. What may appear to be a falling away from élite standards is also to be understood as part of a broader process of improving standards of eating for a large part of the population. For the developing relationship between professional and domestic cookery and the advancing frontier of gallicisation in England were, from the point of view of most social historians, minor matters compared with the changes beginning to take place along the frontier between the food of the prosperous and the food of the poor. Not only were the numbers of the fairly prosperous – Mrs Beeton's readership – growing, but change was afoot in the food of the less than prosperous. It must always be borne in mind that for centuries, while the culinary tastes of the upper strata had been developing rapidly, the food of the majority of the people had been changing much more slowly, in an altogether different mode of historical time. At the beginning of the nineteenth century, as Marc Bloch pointed out, the gulf between the food of the poor and the prosperous was little less striking than it had been several centuries earlier; only during that century was it possible to see 'the beginning of a trend towards greater uniformity in food – speaking in very relative terms – from the top to the bottom of the social ladder' (1954: 232). That essential truth may be partly obscured by the abundance of historical evidence from the nineteenth century on which rest numerous horror stories about the food of the poor – particularly in England but also in France, particularly in the towns but also in the country.

Country Fare

Nowadays the expression 'country fare' is an advertising cliché, with nostalgic connotations of abundance, of fresh ingredients freshly cooked, and of general well-being. To anyone familiar with English cookery books, it is most reminiscent of the food of the eighteenth-century gentry. There is little evidence that the everyday food of the majority of country-dwellers ever conformed to the romantic stereotype, and contemporaries were generally not at all romantic about it.

It was the common opinion that French peasants showed far more talent for making appetising meals out of resources at hand than did their English counterparts.[8] We have already quoted Arthur Young's opinion to that effect on the eve of the French Revolution, and the same view was endlessly repeated by nineteenth-century observers. For instance, Richard Jefferies:

> In Picardy I have often dined in a peasant's cottage, and thoroughly enjoyed the excellent soup he puts upon the table for his ordinary meal. To dine in an English labourer's cottage would be impossible. His bread is generally good, certainly; but his bacon is the cheapest he can buy at small second-class shops – only soft, wretched stuff; his vegetables are cooked in detestable style, and eaten saturated with the pot liquor. Pot liquor is a favourite soup. I have known cottagers actually apply at farmers' kitchens not only for the pot liquor in which meat has been soddened, but for the water in which potatoes have been boiled – potato liquor – and sup it up with avidity. And this is not in times of dearth or scarcity, but rather as a relish. (1872: 32)

The prestige of French country cookery has derived in part from its place in the ancestry of what came eventually to be known as the 'international hotel and restaurant style' of cookery. That style had no single point of origin, geographically or in time. It assumed its modern form in the era of Escoffier, through the simplification of nineteenth-century *cuisine classique*, which had arisen out of a tradition of *haute cuisine* developing at least since the time of La Varenne. That tradition may in turn be understood as arising out of a differentiation within the butter-based cookery of northern France: it is customary to distinguish between the *haute cuisine* and *cuisine bourgeoise*, the latter in spite of the urban connotations of the name being in effect the peasant and domestic cookery of the Île de France. It seems sensible to follow Waverley Root (1958: 10) in reserving the term *cuisine paysanne* for the food of the regions of France where cookery is based either on olive oil (Languedoc and Provence) or on pork and goose fat (principally Alsace and the Massif Central).[9] Though some Provençal influences appeared in Paris after the Revolution, through such hands as those of the Trois Frères Provençaux, the *cuisine paysanne* had relatively little influence on *haute cuisine*. When it did, for example when Escoffier himself adapted dishes from his native Provence, it underwent a process of 'butterisation'. The social distance between *haute cuisine* and French domestic cookery reached its apogee in the nineteenth century. The regional names which were then sometimes used are often misleading; for instance, *sauce béarnaise* was invented in a nineteenth-century Parisian restaurant and named in honour of the memory of Henri IV who came from the Béarne – it was not in any sense a Gascon recipe. Thus the 'restaurant' style of cookery became to a great extent autonomous and international, no longer specifically linked to the domestic cookery of northern France in any real sense – though it came to feed back onto French domestic cookery, as we have seen.

By the beginning of the twentieth century, French regional cookery was being celebrated as something admirable in its own right. Newnham-Davis and Bastard, in their remarkable *Gourmet's Guide to Europe* of 1903, after an opening chapter on the Parisian restaurants, included separately one of the earliest discussions of the food of the French provinces, mentioning such subsequently famous specialities as tripes à la mode de Caen – 'a homely dish, but it is not to be despised'.

With the eclipse of the most extravagant restaurant cooking after the First World War, the less costly traditions of French regional cookery came to be more celebrated both in France and England. Yet it is easy to romanticise how well the French peasantry really ate. Zeldin (1973–7: II, 725) is certainly right to stress that most Frenchmen in the nineteenth century ate very different food from what was being concocted in Parisian restaurants, but in the light of numerous accounts of peasants' talent for making wholesome meals out of scant resources, he may well be exaggerating the awfulness of their cooking when he writes:

> In so far as peasants' cooking was influenced by ideas from outside, in the nineteenth century it conformed to the medieval school of thought. This had as its principle to mix many ingredients without much attention to quantities . . . and to add spices as liberally as possible. (1973–7: II, 728)

There is no doubt that peasant cookery in the nineteenth century was dominated by the cauldron and thus by the method of slow boiling, nor that their diet was in consequence preponderantly of soups and vegetable dishes, together with bread. Emile Guillaumin, in his reconstruction of *The Life of a Simple Man*, based on conversations with 'Old Tienon', a peasant born the son of a share-cropper in the Bourbonnais in 1823, recalls:

> We ate bread as black as the chimney . . .
>
> Soup was our chief fare; onion soup morning and evening, and at midday potato soup with haricots or pumpkin, with hardly any butter. Bacon was reserved for the summer, and for festivities; with that we had rissoles, indigestible and doughy, which stuck to our teeth, and baked potatoes and haricots cooked in water slightly whitened with milk.
>
> We regaled ourselves on cooking days, because then we had tarts and cakes, but those 'side dishes' were quickly exhausted. Ah! good things were not plentiful! (1905: 6)

This picture is borne out by Tardieu's study of the peasant way of life in the pre-industrial rural Mâconnais (1964). There, soup was typically consumed at all three meals of the day (including breakfast); they were generally vegetable, not meat, soups, with bread added for bulk. Also eaten a great deal were various *bouillies*, resembling porridge made by boiling grains in milk or water, and including a polenta-like staple made from maize. Apart from boiling and the similar process of brazing in a closed *coquotte*, only frying and cooking directly on the fire, as with skewers or grilling, were common. Vegetables, especially potatoes, roots and dried pulses, were the essential base of the everyday diet. Salads were popular, unlike in England. Fruit was seldom eaten raw, but was cooked. Some foods, though available, were not eaten; in this part of France, mushrooms were mistrusted until late in the nineteeth century. Bread was already by the nineteenth century commonly bought from a baker. Meat played a rather small part in the peasant diet, with pork and charcuterie much the most common. Every family kept its pig. Game was quite important. Fish and, more surprisingly, poultry were little eaten. In short, the peasant diet of the Mâconnais was no more exciting than Guillaumin's picture of that of the nearby Bourbonnais.[10]

A recipe book published under the auspices of the French Ministry of Agriculture in 1867, Marceline Michaux's *La Cuisine de la ferme*, was directed at improving the state of peasant cooking, and well demonstrates how country cooking then looked from the vantage point of Paris.

> Go and sit at the tables of most of our peasants and you will . . . rediscover there a primitive, traditional diet, always the same or very nearly so for generations, sometimes insipid, sometimes overspiced, and, despite that, often costing more than if the food were more varied, flavoursome and good. (1867: 1)

One might rather expect that note to be struck in England than in France.[11] On the other hand, Mme Michaux's recipes are much more varied and ambitious than anything directed at the rural poor in England, amounting in fact to a small compendium of good, simple country cooking as it was portrayed a century later by Elizabeth David.

So what is the truth about the great French peasant dishes subsequently so famous? Did they exist or did they not? The answer is probably that they did, but few people were fortunate enough to eat them all the time. As in the English countryside, some people were better off than others; and some no doubt ate the 'special' dishes more often than others. The main point, however, is that for most of the French peasantry they *were* special – the festival dishes served on special occasions in particular areas. Again, Guillaumin's old Bourbonnais peasant recalled having notable meals to mark various *rites de passage*. After his first mass in 1835: 'the meal was a liberal one: there was soup made with ham, rabbit, chicken, a very fresh wheaten loaf, cakes and buns: there was wine (I drank a whole glassful) and coffee, which beverage I had never tasted before' (1905: 37). A wedding feast:

> A great slaughter of fowls had taken place the previous evening. I had counted as many as twenty geese, ducks and chickens, exposing upon a bench their bleeding

nakedness. In another place was a quantity of meat which the butcher from Bourbon had brought in his cart. When I returned from the fields all this was being cooked in the bakehouse. I regaled myself with some giblets and rolls with fresh butter, which had a very appetising smell. (1905: 40)

And a funeral:

Some preparation had been made, wine bought, and a piece of meat for soup, and my mother added an omelette. (1905: 76)

Tardieu (1964: 104) records that in the Mâconnais beef and veal were reserved for great village occasions like the feast of its patron saint, for Christmas and Easter, and baptisms, weddings and funerals. It was at these times that beef was eaten in the form of the notable dishes like pot-au-feu and various daubes. In the countryside, the contrast between everyday and festival food always remained much more marked than in urban areas, and even today when rural eating has largely moved into line with urban ways, the Mâconnais retains the tradition of special festival dishes and menus (1964: 97, 222). Rural France has put up some resistance to the standardisation of food.

Nevertheless, from the period of French industrialisation in the latter half of the nineteenth century onwards, the trend towards relatively greater social uniformity of food can be detected even in the Mâconnais. From then onwards standards of living steadily rose, and together with improved trade and communications, this led to the area becoming less reliant on local production. A wider variety of foods, from elsewhere in France and further afield, became available for purchase. Butchers' meat came to be eaten if not daily then two or three times a week, and the consumption of pork declined relatively. The advent of manufactured stoves and ovens, supplanting cooking over the fire in the hearth, meant that the new, more varied food could be cooked more quickly and in more varied ways (Tardieu, 1964: 221–2).

In sum, it is important not to romanticise French country cooking too uncritically. For many people there, as in the English countryside, life was poor and the diet monotonous. All the same, many accounts of how peasants ate suggest a certain talent for producing tasty dishes from very little, and there may be something in Philip Oyler's contention that, 'the people themselves revel in good food, and the love of something, anything in fact, is the main requirement for producing it' (1950: 45). In contrast, descriptions of the food of the poor in the nineteenth-century English countryside paint a picture so bleak that one imagines they have lost the ability to revel in anything.

The main difference between the rural poor of France and those of England was that while most of the former were peasants, or at worst share-croppers, cultivating a little land for themselves, by the nineteenth century most of the latter were wage-labourers. In chapter 4 we cited Sir Frederick Eden's great survey of the condition of the poor at the close of the eighteenth century, including his description of the monotony of their diet especially in southern England. Their plight was the outcome of prices having risen steadily throughout the century, and wages having failed to keep pace. That was particularly serious since many of them were gradually having to purchase more of their food than in the past: the enclosures, which in many parts of the country had been taking place more rapidly than before, had deprived the poor of the real income they derived from their rights over common land. It was not just that fewer of them were able to pasture a cow or even manage to keep a pig; even the loss of rights to gather fuel contributed to making more people dependent on bread purchased from the baker, since baking at home was made more difficult – though few of the poor had ever had good cooking facilities anyway.

William Cobbett in *Rural Rides* (1821–32) confirmed Eden's observation of the dullness and inadequacy of the diet of the rural poor, and in his *Cottage Economy* (1821) set out to show them how, through better management, they could improve it. He gave 'Information relative to the brewing of Beer [his denunciation of their drinking tea is famous] making of Bread, keeping of Cows, Pigs, Bees, Goats, Poultry, and Rabbits, and relative to other matters deemed useful in the conducting of the Affairs of a Labourer's Family'. The labourer who did all that Cobbett told him would, however, need to be both very well organised and relatively well provided with the necessary facilities. Not much seemed generally to have changed half a century later when Jefferies described the Wiltshire agricultural labourers' diet, which consisted

> chiefly of bread and cheese, with bacon twice or thrice a week, varied with onions, and if he be a milker (on some farms) with a good 'tuck-out' at his employer's expense on Sundays. On ordinary days he dines at the fashionable hour of six or seven in the evening – that is, about that time his cottage scents the road with a powerful odour of boiled cabbage, of which he eats an immense quantity. Vegetables are his luxuries, and a large garden, therefore, is the greatest blessing he can have. He eats huge onions raw; he has no idea of flavouring his food with them, nor of making those savoury and inviting messes or vegetable soups at which the French peasantry are so clever. (1872: 31–2)

Again, this was in the south of England, and both income and components of the diet seem to have been better in the north. But it is generally true that 'The farm labourer was the last of all fully employed workers to make substantial gains in his standard of life – this only towards the very end of the Victorian age' (Burnett, 1981: 564).[12] Even early in the twentieth century, studies of village life by Maud Davies (1909) and by Seebohm Rowntree and May Kendall (1913) show that such things as bread and dripping, and bread and (by now cheap, manufactured) jam, were staples in labourers' families, and that only the products of their gardens made their diets nutritionally better than those of the poorest labourers in the towns.

Flora Thompson's recollections in *Lark Rise to Candleford* (1939–43) of her late-Victorian childhood in an Oxfordshire hamlet capture the rhythm of eating among the rural poor more vividly than the lists of victuals found in the social surveys, yet are largely consistent with their more systematic findings. The people of Lark Rise seem to have lived a little better than the poorest to be met in the pages of Cobbett or Eden. Most families were able to keep a pig, which kept them in bacon for at least part of the year. Fresh meat was a luxury only seen in a few cottages on Sunday – and then generally in the form of 'sixpennyworth of pieces', meaning scraps from the butcher, which were generally cooked in a boiled suet pudding called a toad. The cooking facilities were limited; in themselves they did not differ much from those found in a typical French peasant kitchen, but were used in slightly different ways. Boiling was the principal method, and the three-legged pot over the fire the principal utensil. But there is no mention of soup being eaten. The one hot meal of the day consisted of three separate components, all boiled in the pot together: a piece of bacon from the flitch, amounting to little more than a taste for each member of the family; cabbage or other green vegetables in one net, potatoes in another; and a roly-poly pudding wrapped in a cloth. On Sundays and special occasions, the boiled suet pudding would have meat in it, on other days jam or currants, but in either case was eaten first to take the edge off the appetite. By no means everyone had an oven, and bread was bought. On rare occasions when a small joint was obtained as a bargain on Saturday night when butchers disposed of their remainders, it was either roast on a piece of string directly over the fire, or, as in France, was pot-roasted. For special occasions like the feast after the pig-killing, a neighbour's bread oven could be borrowed, and then joints of pork, potatoes, batter puddings, pork pies, and sometimes a cake or two, were all baked at once.

As in France, the marked oscillation and contrast between the sparsity of everyday eating and the feasts on special occasions persisted from medieval times through to the end of the nineteenth century in rural England. Richard Jefferies described how, when the opportunity occurred, the amount of food his Wiltshire labourers would eat was astonishing:

> Once a year, at the village club dinner, they gormandise to repletion. In one instance I knew of a man eating a plate of roast beef (and the slices are cut enormously thick at these dinners), a plate of boiled beef, then another of boiled mutton, and then a fourth of roast mutton, and a fifth of ham. He said he couldn't do much to the bread and cheese; but didn't he go into the pudding! I have even heard of men stuffing to the fullest extent of their powers, and then retiring from the table to take an emetic of mustard and return to a second gorging. (1872: 32)

The Fussells vouch for having seen with their own eyes in their early twentieth-century childhood exactly the same dishes eaten in similar quantities – 'their bellies bulged' – at harvest suppers (1953: 179–80). Accounts of such occasions always mention the same foods: beef and mutton, roast and boiled, a variety of vegetables, puddings plain and plum, and apple pies and so on to finish with. The rhythm of special occasions is much the same as in France, but there seem to be fewer mentions of dishes which were special in any other sense than their infrequency. Perhaps that owed something to the attitude recorded by Flora Thompson: 'When some superior person tried to give a hint, the women used to say, 'You tell us how to get the victuals; we can cook it all right when we've got it'; and they could' (1939: 25).

By the early twentieth century, there were many signs that much of the glory of the English 'farmhouse' tradition of cookery had been lost, and that such of it as survived was under threat. At least, some people thought so. Most notable among them was Florence White, one of the first specialist cookery journalists in England. Miss White had early connections with members of the arts and crafts movement, and in her autobiography she relates how in the 1920s she was stung by abuse of English cooks and cooking in the press to set out to travel all over the country in search of traditional English cookery. She consciously compared her project with that of Cecil Sharp, who travelled the country in search of folk songs, music and dances, and alleged that in 1926 'no-one had any idea that England possessed any national cookery beyond roast beef, Yorkshire pudding, and Christmas plum pudding. It was perfectly sickening to hear nothing but these dishes mentioned as England's cooking' (1938: 316).

After a year's work, she found she had struck a rich line of research. 'We had the finest cookery in the world,' she wrote, rather overstating her case, 'but it had been nearly lost by neglect.' The task was far too big for one person, so she wrote a letter to *The Times* to enlist help, and as a result the English Folk Cookery Association was formed. Her original idea had been that the new association would be affiliated to UCFA, of which she was a member, and would form a link between it and the Folk Lore Society. It is extremely interesting that Senn (whom she does not directly name) and his organisation rejected this proposal. For all their very English devotion to good works among the poor, their underlying devotion to French cuisine was such that they were quite hostile to the notion of 'English folk cookery', and 'every obstacle was thrown in my way' (Florence White, 1938: 318). Nevertheless, Florence White and her collaborators undertook a major effort of rescue archaeology, notably in *Good Things in England* (1932), an important source of recipes that turn up in many later books on English cookery.

Why exactly did English traditional cookery need to be rescued or rediscovered? The answer seems to be that the social base carrying that tradition had become greatly attenuated, and, in addition, industrialisation and urbanisation disrupted the transmission of rural lore more seriously in England than in France.

The social base of the English country tradition of cookery had shrunk for three reasons. First, while it is certainly mistaken to imagine that there was once a Golden Age when the rural poor daily ate masterpieces of 'folk cookery', enclosures and rising prices during the eighteenth century and the first quarter or thereabouts of the nineteenth had enlarged the category of wage-labourers, and probably made more people's diet more monotonous than it had been. This nibbled away at the lower margin of the 'farmhouse tradition'. Secondly, the tradition was also eroded from above by the exit from the kitchens of the grander sort of lady and the apostasy to French food of the grandest. The older traditions were increasingly left during the nineteenth century to the lesser farmers' wives. For, as the Fussells write,

> The great lady was no longer the leading example of a country housewife. That part was left to the farmer's wife, and many of the richer farmers' wives were as good at aping the gentry as the wives of the rich manufacturers, professional men and wholesale tradesmen of the new towns. All these were astonishingly genteel. The lesser farmers' wives all over the country continued to live the life of their foremothers. They were excellent housekeepers, renowned locally for their special dishes, their dairy skill, their skill as nurse and midwife and with animals. (1953: 184)

Significantly, Florence White was first introduced to traditional English cooking not so much in her own poor suburban home, where the meals were much as in Lark Rise, but in the home of her aunts in the country at Fareham – aunts who were not wealthy, but belonged to a family in which recipes had been handed down from mother to daughter for generations.

Thirdly, during the nineteenth century, farmers and their wives were, of course, rapidly coming to form a smaller and smaller part of the population as a whole. As a proportion of the male economically active population of Great Britain, those involved in agricultural occupations declined from something of the order of 35 per cent in 1811 to about 28 per cent in 1851, then more rapidly to about 12 per cent in 1911, 6½ per cent in 1951 and around 4 per cent in recent years.[13] In contrast, France was, and indeed has remained, a more agricultural country. In 1856, of its economically active male population, about 53 per cent were in agricultural occupations; by 1901 this had fallen only to 43 per cent, and half a century later in 1954 was still as high as 26 per cent. The period of most rapid decline in the numbers occupied in French agriculture has in fact been only since the 1950s, and in 1968 agriculture still accounted for about 16 per cent of the French male labour force – a proportion roughly four times as large as in Great Britain. If it is correct to assume that farmers' wives are the principal carriers of country traditions of cooking the produce of the land, these figures point to the attenuation of the social base of English traditional cookery (in proportion to society as a whole), with particular rapidity since the mid-nineteenth century.

The growth of towns, of which the declining agricultural fraction of the labour force is one reflection, had significant effects of its own on diet and cookery. Most obviously, urban residents have always had to purchase more of their foods and to produce less for themselves than has the rural population. For the poor, in the short term, this meant that they lived less well than in the country, losing the free produce of their gardens and hedgerows; but patterns of trade and transport had always meant that a wider variety of produce was available in town markets than in the country, and with their further development the relatively poor in the towns eventually came to enjoy a more varied diet too. Less tangibly, the growth of towns probably affected cookery by disrupting the informal transmission of knowledge and tradition. In this respect, the *speed* of urbanisation is probably more relevant than its absolute extent.[14]

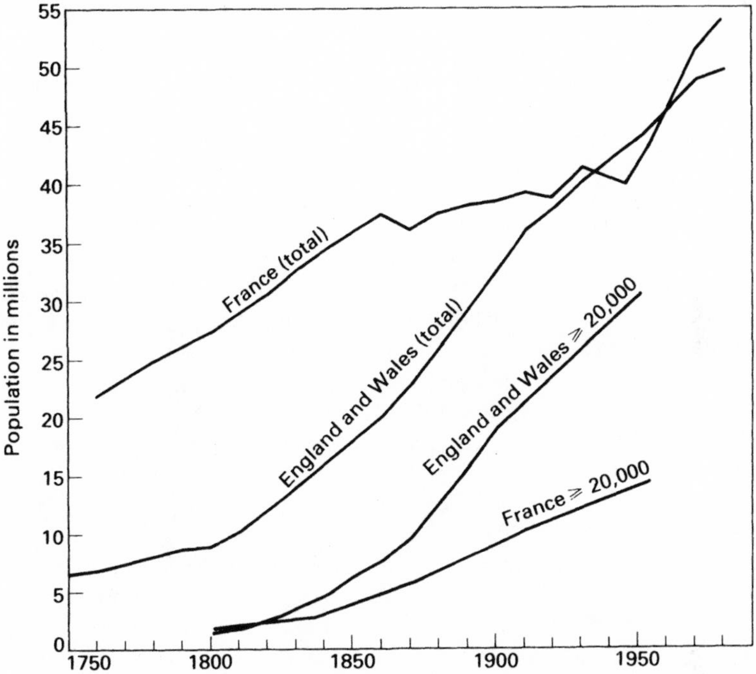

Figure 9 England and France: growth of total population and of population resident in towns of more than 20,000 inhabitants

Sources: A. F. Weber (1899); Mitchell and Deane (1962); Mitchell (1975); United Nations (1957); *Population Trends* 35, 1984; *Annual Abstract of Statistics* (HMSO, 1981).

Urbanisation went further, faster and earlier in England than in France. As can be seen from the graphs in figure 9, in 1801 nearly 17 per cent of the population of England and Wales were already living in towns of 20,000 or more inhabitants, as against less than 7 per cent in France. By 1851, the figure for England and Wales had reached 35 per cent, while France still had under 10 per cent. By 1901 nearly 60 per cent, and by 1951 nearly 70 per cent of the people of England and Wales lived in towns with more than 20,000 people. Only in 1906 did the corresponding proportion of French people reach a quarter, and it was still only one third in the early 1950s. Nor is that the whole story; figures for town-dwellers as a proportion of the total population tend to understate the contrast between England and France, for throughout the nineteenth century the French population as a whole was growing much more slowly than that of England and Wales. Rapid population growth can in itself generate both practical problems of social organisation – as it did in the cities of nineteenth-century Britain – and impose strains on the transmission of cultural traditions from generation to generation. The two processes, population growth and urbanisation, entangled together, have often created 'discontinuities of community'.[15] Such discontinuities arise not only in the cities experiencing a rapid increase in population, but also in rural areas which are losing numbers. As a matter of fact, during the first half the nineteenth century, because Britain's population as a whole was rising so rapidly, the rural population continued to grow in spite of migration to the towns, but in the second half its decline became not just proportional but absolute.

Another feature of the latter period is that by then the medium-sized towns of between 20,000 and 100,000 were growing even faster than London and the cities of more than 100,000 (A. F. Weber, 1899: 40–80). In France, because of the slower growth of total population, a measure of rural depopulation was evident at a relatively earlier stage in the urbanisation process. But there Paris and the small number of other major cities accounted for the lion's share of the urban growth, and France as a whole retained its predominantly rural character much later than did England. The very fact that the period of the most rapid urbanisation came later in France may in itself have meant that it ruptured the continuity of folk knowledge, in cookery or whatever, less than was the case in England. For when the French towns were growing fastest, the popular press and compulsory education were also developing rapidly, and to some extent may have provided more formal media to compensate for any disruption of the informal media through which knowledge and tradition had been transmitted.

Food in the Towns

It is easy to forget that even in Paris during the age of the great restaurants not everyone ate well. Benoîston de Châteauneuf remarked how distressing it was that 'even among the most prosperous nations' some people died every year not perhaps directly from starvation but none the less from the effects of inadequate nourishment (1820: 70). Workers and artisans spent the largest part of their wages on bread, 'the most indispensable food', and otherwise lived mainly on vegetables, potatoes, and fresh and salt pork. In fact many, having neither wood, nor coal, nor utensils with which to cook, bought much of their food from the *charcutier* – the strongly spiced products were to their taste, and there was no waste, but such food was not good for them. Butchers' meat was eaten only at rare intervals and, comparing figures for the city's meat supply in 1637, 1689, 1779, 1789 and 1817, Benoîston concluded that while supplies had risen gradually up to the Revolution, since then they had far from kept pace with the growth of the city's population (1820: 66). Two decades later, Villermé reported some improvement in the food of town workers. In many towns, notably Lyon, Reims and Sedan, and in several provinces such as Normandy, the consumption of meat, white bread and soups made with meat was much more common than formerly (1840: II, 7).[16]

The real horror stories came from the rapidly growing towns of industrial England. Most famous of all is Friedrich Engels's account in *The Condition of the Working Class in England in 1844*:

> The habitual food of the individual working-man naturally varies according to his wages. The better paid workers, especially those in whose familes every member is able to earn something, have good food as long as this state of things lasts; meat daily and bacon and cheese for supper. Where wages are less, meat is used only two or three times a week, and the proportion of bread or potatoes increases. Descending gradually, we find the animal food reduced to a small piece of bacon cut up with the potatoes; lower still, even this disappears, and there remain only bread, cheese, porridge, and potatoes, until on the lowest rung of the ladder, among the Irish, potatoes form the sole food. . . . But all this presupposes that the workman has work. (1845: 105)

Among the worst of all, the unemployed and the ill-paid, 'all sorts of devices are used; potato parings, vegetable refuse, and rotten vegetables are eaten for want of other food' – which all led to a multitude of diseases. The quality of the food supplied to the workers was also appalling. In Manchester,

> The potatoes which the workers buy are usually poor, the vegetables wilted, the cheese old and of poor quality, the bacon rancid, the meat lean, tough, taken from old, often diseased cattle, or such as have died a natural death, and not fresh even then, often half decayed . . . but having bought it, they must use it. (1845: 101)

Engels went on to catalogue the various ways in which many foodstuffs – butter, sugar, coffee, cocoa, tea, pepper for instance – were systematically adulterated. These practices had indeed been exposed before, notably by another German, Fredrick Accum, in his *Treatise on the Adulterations of Food and Culinary Poisons* (1820). But, as Engels wrote,

> the poor, the working-people, to whom a couple of farthings are important, who must buy many things with little money, who cannot afford to inquire too closely into the quality of their purchase, and cannot do so in any case because they have had no opportunity of cultivating their taste – to their share fall all the adulterated, poisoned provisions. (1845: 103)

There is no reason to doubt the veracity of Engels's account, which was based both on his own observation and numerous other contemporary descriptions, although he was describing the worst conditions in a bad decade. Even though conditions generally improved somewhat from about the middle of the nineteenth century, early in the twentieth the urban poor still ate rather badly. One of the fullest descriptions is found in Mrs Magdalen Pember Reeves's *Round about a Pound a Week* (1913), a report of a four-year investigation of a working-class area of Lambeth, south London, by members of the Fabian Women's Group. The families in this area were of the 'respectable' working class, the men in regular work, though humble and unskilled labourers, not artisans. They brought home, as the title of the book says, wages of about £1 a week. From among many examples, here is part of a typical week's menu. Mrs X was a 'good manager' with a husband and four children all under the age of five.

Sunday – Breakfast: One loaf, 1 oz. butter, ½ oz. tea, a farthing's worth of tinned milk, a half pennyworth of sugar. Kippers extra for Mr X. Dinner: Hashed beef, batter pudding, greens, and potatoes. Tea: Same as breakfast, but Mr X has shrimps instead of kippers.
Monday – Breakfast: Same as Sunday. Mr X has a little cold meat. Dinner: Sunday's dinner cold, with pickles, or warmed up with greens and potatoes. Tea: One loaf, marmalade and tea. Mr X has two eggs.
Tuesday – Breakfast: One loaf, 1 oz. butter, 2*d*. worth of cocoa. Bloaters for Mr X. Dinner: Bread and dripping, with cheese and tomatoes. Tea: One loaf, marmalade, and tea. Fish and fried potatoes for Mr X. (Reeves, 1913: 113–14)

The food of workers in Middlesbrough, reported in Lady Bell's *At the Works* (1907), was much the same, and so was that described in Seebohm Rowntree's famous study of York (1901).[17] Accounts like these, together with the report of the *Inter-Departmental Committee on Physical Deterioration* in 1904 prompted by the large numbers of men found physically inadequate to serve in the Boer War, led Drummond and Wilbraham to contend that 'the opening of the twentieth century saw malnutrition more rife in England than it had been since the great dearths of medieval and Tudor times' (1939: 483). This extreme claim has been disputed by Burnett (1966: 27) among others. Though there is no doubt about the poverty of the 'submerged tenth', conditions had almost certainly been worse half a century before. Since then urban living had had complicated effects on diet, not all of them deleterious.

One the one hand, in the towns more food had to be bought from bakers, butchers, grocers, greengrocers and other tradesmen, for several obvious reasons. Fewer people had gardens or patches of land on which to produce significant amounts of their own food. Since in poorer homes cooking facilities were generally limited, and since in any case with both men and women now working extremely long hours and more continually than in the countryside, convenient and quickly prepared food was favoured. Just as the workers in French towns relied on the *charcutier*, so bacon, kippers and other quickly fried foodstuffs were popular in England. From the late nineteenth century, frequent recourse to the fish and chip shop was also a feature of working-class life (see Priestland, 1972). According to Campbell (1966), these trends undermined even the hitherto healthier diet found in Scotland. The consumption of bread (never much made at home, and relative to oats little eaten previously) and of eggs (costly, but quickly cooked) rose, while the consumption of meat and of vegetable broth fell. The cuts of meat favoured in Scotland had been those requiring long cooking, and broths, whether containing meat or only vegetables and cereals, took too long to cook on work days even if the cooking facilities existed.

On the other hand, wider markets, better transport and more effective marketing methods brought about improved food supplies – meat (including tinned meat), fish and fruit all became more plentiful.[18] Increased supplies and variety brought with them the possibility of greater choice, even for the poorer groups. Whether this element of choice always led to an improvement in overall welfare is questionable – for example, cheap sweet jams and biscuits became very popular, but were not necessarily more nourishing than what had been eaten before. Now, according to the dogmas of liberal economics, any augmentation of choice represents, *ceteris paribus*, an improvement in welfare. But that dogma rests on the explicit assumption that consumers have perfect knowledge of conditions in the market, and that they are the best judges of what constitutes their own best interest. The *Report of the Inter-Departmental Committee on Physical Deterioration* questioned that assumption:

> While the greater cheapness of many articles of consumption has brought them much more widely within the reach of the poor, there has been no corresponding increase in knowledge as to the economic expenditure of money on wholesome food. (1904: 57)

That the poor spent unwisely what money they had for food, that they were furthermore ignorant of nutrition, ignorant of how best to cook their food, and generally lacking in culinary taste and imagination is the frequent lament from the mid-nineteenth to the mid-twentieth century. Alexis Soyer discussed the 'General Ignorance of the Poor in Cooking' at length in his *Shilling Cookery* (1854). He speaks for example of ox-cheeks as tasty, nutritious and very cheap, but requiring lengthy cooking.

> Frequently on my visits to the abodes of the poor, while in London last winter, I have often seen this article of food completely spoiled. On one occasion, I asked an old lady how she cooked it. 'Sure enough', said she, 'by fire'. 'But, my dear woman', I enquired, 'how long do you cook it?' 'Ah', she replied, 'sometimes as long as an hour, and boiling it like the very deuce all the time, till the water will not stand it any longer.' 'And pray', I asked, 'what do you do with the water?' 'Faith, there is no water left, but only black muck at the bottom of the pot, which I throw away', was her reply.
>
> When I found she was so ignorant, I asked her if I should come back and teach her how to cook, properly, an ox cheek. . . . I . . . put it in the pot with four quarts

of water, and four teaspoonfuls of salt, and some leaves of celery, which articles were given to her by a neighbouring greengrocer. Her fire was made up, and the pot was placed on it until boiling, and then removed to the side of it and skimmed. There I left it, and went round to pay my other visits.

At the end of three hours I returned, and, she having a large basin in the room, I put some crusts of bread in it, and poured the liquid from the pot into it, and the meat I placed on a dish, and sat down with the old dame, serving the soup out into cups with a beer-jug, having nothing better, and, to her great surprise, cut the cheek easily with a very bad knife, it being so tender. After tasting it and finding it very good, she said she would show her neighbours how to do it. (1854: 46–7)

Many others were to follow in Soyer's footsteps; we have already mentioned the missionary work of UCFA and the Fabian Women's Group. They tend to tell the same story. It is the story of amazing nutritional and culinary ignorance certainly; it is also a story of cooking facilities at least as bad as those in Soyer's tale; but it is often finally a story of people liking what they are accustomed to, and in no hurry to change. Mrs Reeves describes the typical equipment: a kettle, a frying-pan, and two saucepans, both burnt (1913: 56–9). Few people in Lambeth then had gas cookers. The Fabian ladies repeatedly explained to the women the nutritional value of porridge for breakfast. No matter how often it was explained, porridge did not find its way into the family menu. The reasons only gradually came out. With only burnt pans, it was difficult to stop the porridge 'catching' and tasting nasty. It needed constant attention, which with children milling at the mother's feet it did not receive. And, finally and fundamentally, the family did not like it: the children 'eaved at it', and one husband threatened more literally to heave it at his wife.

CONCLUSION

The advent of reforming middle-class ladies among the urban poor folds together the two sides of this diptych chapter – the solid middle-class confident of their tastes in food and skills in domestic cookery, and the working-class housewives supposedly deficient in both. George Orwell, who in *The Road to Wigan Pier* (1937) described working-class food almost as depressing as in Victorian times, had no time for do-gooding ladies:

I have heard a Communist speaker on a platform grow very angry about it. In London, he said, parties of Society dames now have the cheek to walk into East End houses and give shopping-lessons to the wives of the unemployed. He gave this as an instance of the mentality of the English governing class. First you condemn a family to live on 30/- a week, and then you have the damned impertinence to tell them how to spend their money. He was quite right – I agree heartily. (1937: 89–90)

Orwell himself recognised, as some of the good ladies did not, that the working class actually liked what they ate, but that did not prevent him from regarding it as inferior:

the English palate, especially the working class palate, now rejects good food almost automatically. The number of people who *prefer* tinned peas and tinned fish to real peas and real fish must be increasing every year, and plenty of people who could afford real milk in their tea would much sooner have tinned milk – even that dreadful tinned milk which is made of sugar and cornflour and has UNFIT FOR BABIES on the tin in huge letters. (1937: 89)

In his indignation, Orwell falls too easily – like the reforming ladies – into the assumption that poor quality tinned foods being eaten early in the twentieth century represented a decline in the standard of popular diet. Yet inferior as they might be to the food of the middle class, in longer term perspective they almost certainly represented an improvement in quality and reliability on the foods available to the poor before.

Orwell, like so many before him, compared the tastes of the English lower classes unfavourably with their French counterparts, and declared it a pity that 'merely for the lack of a proper tradition, people should pour muck like tinned milk down their throats and not even know that it is inferior to the product of the cow'. He put the blame on the industrial system for destroying the English tradition of eating:

If the English physique has declined, this is no doubt partly due to the fact that the Great War carefully selected the million best men in England and slaughtered them, largely before they had had chance to breed. But the process must have begun earlier than that, and it must be due ultimately to unhealthy ways of living, i.e. to industrialism. I don't mean the habit of living in towns – probably the town is healthier than the country in many ways – but the modern industrial technique provides you with substitutes for everything. We find in the long run that tinned food is a deadlier weapon than the machine gun. (1937: 88)

Probably the origins of discontinuity in tradition need to be placed back in impoverishment in the countryside even before rapid urbanisation; and although Orwell may have been right to exonerate town life as such, the sheer speed of urbanisation in England probably did disrupt the transmission of knowledge and tradition more than the industrialisation entangled with it (for in terms of economic growth, industrialisation in England was relatively slow when compared with subsequent industrialisations elsewhere).

In any case, the effects of industrialisation on the tastes in food of all classes in both England and France were far more complex than the simple debauchery depicted by Orwell and many later writers. Through the food manufacturing industry, and through the mass media also concomitant with industrial society, the professional and domestic traditions of cookery became more closely entangled, and national insularities were undermined. Some of these patterns of development can be seen in cookery columns in women's magazines over the last century; and it is particularly useful to study the English magazines together with the French, because the continuities in France provide a base against which to project trends in England.

9

The Enlightenment of the Domestic Cook?

Concern about inadequate diet and ignorance of cookery among the poor, leading to the missionary activities of people as diverse as Soyer, UCFA and the Fabian ladies, was part of the wider middle-class movement of reform and improvement characteristic of the later nineteenth century. The broad impulse to reform, however altruistic its conscious motivation, reflected the closer interdependence of social classes in the emerging urban-industrial societies, and was not confined to Britain. Improvements in water supply and sanitation, for one example, owed much to the recognition that cholera did not stop at the doors of the rich. For another, all but the richest had to use public transport in the growing towns, and if the middle classes could not be segregated from close contact with the less well-scrubbed and sweetly odoured they had a constant incentive to raise the standards of personal hygiene among their social inferiors (see Goudsblom, 1979; van Daalen, 1979). If efforts to improve working-class cookery are not immediately susceptible to so apparently cynical an interpretation, it has often been suggested that it sprang in part from an awareness that poorly nourished workmen were less productive workers, and a concern that women servants were such inadequate cooks.

Be that as it may, efforts to improve standards of domestic cookery were widely made in the late nineteenth century, and took official as well as voluntary forms. Many countries began to introduce cookery into their school curricula at about the same time. Apart from the improving urge, this appears to have reflected a growth of dietetic knowledge rather than any preoccupation with the aesthetic aspects of eating; and more generally it is to be understood as part of the wider tendency in industrialising societies to rely more on formal instruction in educational systems in place of informal learning in the home for the transmission of knowledge from generation to generation. The Swedes led the way, establishing a two-year course for teachers of cookery in Göteborg in 1865, and also introducing the subject into secondary schools (Kouindjy, 1926: 135ff.). The Germans followed in the 1870s, first at Karlsruhe, then elsewhere. The USA went furthest: most of the important women's colleges provided courses in domestic science and Kouindjy specifically mentions Harvard (no less), Chicago, Wheaton and Smith Colleges. The respectability of the subject at tertiary level in America was related to the institution there of the profession of dietician in hospitals and nursing homes.

In France, domestic science was introduced into the primary school curriculum under Jules Ferry in 1882. The regulation was not implemented everywhere, but by 1908 25 out of 30 schools in Paris gave cookery lessons to girls in their last year of school (Kouindjy, 1926: 145–6). Up to 1904, the concern of these courses was purely domestic and practical, but from then onwards a more scientific motivation appeared, with the study of food hygiene becoming academically respected.

In England the story is similar. The teaching of cookery in schools remained optional for a long time, but was pursued with vigour in some cities. Books of recipes used at these classes in Liverpool (1883), Manchester (1889) and London (E. Briggs, 1890) give a clear picture of what the pupils were taught and, by inference, what they were not taught. The recipes represent food very much in line with what one would expect from accounts of lower middle-class food, the trade press, cookery books and, as we shall see, cookery columns of the time. It is very English, with almost no sign of the French influence prevalent in the higher reaches of society. Cooking methods are very simple – boiling, roasting, frying, stewing. There are lots of pies, puddings and cakes. Leftover recipes are prominent – shepherd's pie, dormers, rissoles and numerous ways with stale bread and breadcrumbs. The Manchester book is simply a collection of 121 of the recipes which had been in use for some time on single sheets of paper. It is a distinctly utilitarian product, as one might expect from nineteenth-century Manchester. The spirit of Mr Gradgrind left no room for emotional involvement in cooking: there is no enthusiasm, no sense of an aesthetic dimension, and the recipes are presented as separate 'facts' to be learned, rather than forming a course of instruction in general techniques. The section on cooking vegetables reinforces a notorious English failing, advising people to boil carrots for 'about an hour', cauliflower for half-an-hour, and cabbage for up to an hour and a quarter. The London School Board's book avoids some of Manchester's faults (as they would later be considered): Miss Briggs warns against overcooking vegetables and, more generally, advises against the mere rote learning of recipes – emphasising the need for understanding through a long list of 'General Axioms for Plain Cookery'. Yet the overall impression of the books from all three cities is dull, stodgy and unimaginative, and little skill was demanded.[1] Even so the range of dishes included implied that this was directed at the moderately well off lower-middle class and artisans, since the recipes require more utensils and better cooking facilities than the poorer working-class household typically had, and more varied ingredients than they could afford.

The early cookery classes do at least appear to have been concerned with actual cooking. Just as in France and the USA, where Kouindjy noted the appearance of a more scientific slant early in the twentieth century, so in Britain the emphasis in school cookery classes appears to have shifted steadily towards the prevention of food poisoning rather than skill in cooking and enjoyment of eating. That at any rate is the impression gained from a standard modern textbook like Abbey and Macdonald's *'O' Level Cookery* (1963) or Creese's revision notes for 'O' Level cookery (1973). Their preoccupations are with the range of foodstuffs available and their nutritional properties, and with hygiene and safety in the kitchen, but the actual methods of cooking described are rather elementary.[2]

Despite cookery classes in schools most housewives, both in England and France, appear to learn most of what they know about what they like and how to cook it directly but informally from their mothers. Yet of course the mother–daughter relationship does not constitute a closed loop through which the same tastes and knowledge are transmitted from generation to generation without change.[3] Domestic cookery has changed more rapidly in the twentieth century, certainly in England and probably in France too, than ever before. What other informal channels of influence and agents of innovation come into play?

Several are obvious. First there are new foodstuffs and food products made known particularly through advertising. Secondly, there is increased contact with the foods of other countries, either directly through foreign travel or vicariously through the media, restaurants and shops. Thirdly, there is the influence of cookery writing, in books, magazines and newspapers – an influence always difficult to assess. All three are interwoven with each other, and all three are subject to the two-step or multi-step flow of communication. That is to say, as media researchers have repeatedly demonstrated, the printed and electronic media have their most direct influence on a particularly receptive minority of 'opinion leaders' among their audience, who adopt innovations, tastes and opinions themselves and then in turn influence others through informal networks of face-to-face personal contact.

The existence of such opinion leaders in the domain of food was demonstrated by Kleyngeld (1974) in a large-scale study in the Netherlands; they proved to be people distinguished mainly by their 'involvement in food', taking a special interest in food and cooking, adopting new products and serving them to friends. Perhaps that is no surprise; but it still leaves the question of where such 'food innovators' obtain their information and ideas – whether it be about new products or new ways of cooking. By the twentieth century there were many sources of influence besides the cookery book. In any case, cookery books were becoming too numerous and diverse to be easily studied as a medium of influence. Merely drawing a representative sample poses insoluble problems. Their variety and specialisation are significant facts in themselves, but it is much easier to follow trends in fashion through the cookery columns which appeared in the popular mass-circulation women's magazines in France and England.

WOMEN'S MAGAZINES

There are several reasons for choosing to study the messages about cooking transmitted by women's magazines. First of all, in the twentieth century they have achieved very large circulations. The most successful ran at their peak to several millions,[4] far more than the sales of any single cookery book (though of course books are retained much longer than a magazine). Secondly, though the various magazines differ to some extent in the social composition of the audience at which they are aimed, each of the longer-surviving magazines appears to be directed at the same sort of audience over time, so that it is possible to be fairly confident in interpreting trends in the content of cookery columns as real changes in fashion rather than as the effect of the magazine trying to move up- or down-market. Thirdly, the most successful magazines have tried to appeal to quite a wide social spectrum of readers, and, whether or not one accepts that the 'consciously classless' editorial ideology identified by Ferguson (1982) was factually well-founded in British (or French) society, this made the magazines a particularly likely medium for stimulating the processes of opinion-leadership and social emulation in matters of taste in food. Fourthly, the magazines show clearly the kind of advertising about foodstuffs, food products and cooking equipment to which housewives have been exposed at each period. Until the 1950s, the printed media were the main vehicles of advertising, and even though television has since then been more potent, there is nevertheless a high correlation between what is advertised in the electronic and the printed media.

Fifthly, it is easier to feel more confident about the connection between what appears in the cookery columns and what actually happened in the domestic kitchen than was the case with the cookery books discussed in earlier chapters. Certainly some caution is still needed, but from the late nineteenth century there is a plethora of sources which make possible informed guesses about that connection. There is a high degree of correlation between the food found in cookery columns and cookery books on the one hand, and descriptions of domestic food in contemporary literature, memoirs and journalism on the other. It appears to be broadly true that women's magazines, in cookery as in other supposedly feminine concerns (see Ferguson, 1982: 9), sought to set high standards for their readers, leading them but taking care not to run too far ahead of them – which could have demoralised the housewife and been bad for the magazines' circulation.

Sixthly and finally, there is a certain amount of direct evidence from both England and France about the use made of cookery column recipes. In surveys in London, McKenzie (1963) found that among a sample of middle-class housewives, 91 per cent of those who bought women's magazines read the recipes in it, 76 per cent had on occasion tried recipes and the same proportion had cut out and saved recipes – though only 9 per cent had tried one in the previous fortnight. The corresponding figures for a more working-class sample were slightly lower: 85, 58, 52 and 3 per cent. In France, Claudian *et al.* (1969: 1382) found that 61.5 per cent of their sample made use of recipes; the most common source was still cookery books, but magazines and newspapers came second.[5]

The history of women's magazines in Britain and France is broadly similar. There were periodicals for ladies in both countries in the eighteenth century – indeed *The Ladies' Mercury* was published in London as early as 1693 (see Cynthia White, 1970). Until the mid-nineteenth century they were addressed to the upper class – hardly surprising, since it was they who had the money, literacy and leisure necessary to buy and use such magazines. The content was not exclusively domestic. Many of these periodicals contained articles on intellectual and moral issues, and sometimes on public affairs. Only a few publications in either country espoused the cause of improving the status of women in society, though a worthy concern with improving them as individuals was more widespread. The early Victorian period, in England at least, saw a narrowing of contents, an increasing home-centredness and preoccupation with purely 'female accomplishments'. This reflected the increasing circumscription of the sphere in which it was considered proper for a respectable female to live out her life. (Something of this attitude persisted until very recent years. Until into the 1960s the popular women's magazines continued to express disapproval of wives and mothers who went out to work. By then, though, the magazines aiming at an audience further up the social scale were expecting their readers to have interests certainly, and a career possibly, outside the home.) The prominence given to social news was no exception in this context for, as we have seen, from the middle of the nineteenth century, Society was gradually becoming less intimately linked with public affairs and more a matter of a female-regulated marriage market.

The mid-Victorian period was one of transition for the women's press. Certain publishers began to recognise the potential of a wider middle-class audience, and brought out new titles to cater for it. In England the most notable was Samuel Beeton's *The Englishwoman's Domestic Magazine*, which appeared in 1852. Beeton set out to provide guidance for the social-climbing wives of business and professional men. The guidance his magazine gave in all that concerned cookery and domestic management is familiar in the form of his wife's famous *Book of Household Management* which originated as weekly contributions to the magazine. Isabella Beeton also wrote on fashion, visiting Paris twice yearly to view the latest collections (Cynthia White, 1970: 44–6). In France, a roughly comparable paper, founded in 1860 and aimed at a similar audience, was *La Mode Illustrée* (Zeldin, 1973–7: II, 557–8).

The most rapid growth of the women's press in both countries came a little later, in the last two decades of the century. Several disparate reasons combined to bring about this growth. Mass education caused a rapid growth in demand for reading matter, chiefly from social classes in which literacy had previously been far from universal. There were also several technological changes which made it possible to satisfy this demand: the mass production of cheaper paper, mechanical typesetting, and rotary presses. Developments in retail distribution, dependent on improved transport, made possible a truly national press (more strikingly in England than in France). Those same developments in transport and distribution were also affecting the food trades, and creating a need for food products to be advertised nationwide. Since, as it happened, the magazines were at the same time becoming economically more dependent on advertising, it is not only their cookery columns which are of interest from the point of view of fashions in food. Indeed, that dependence made the columns to some extent reflect the advertising.

From among the many magazines founded in this period, I chose to study closely a few which enjoyed a measure of longevity. Longevity suggests a magazine was successful in achieving mass appeal and a large circulation compared with short-lived rivals. Moreover so long as a magazine does not abruptly change its formula and target audience, longevity also makes it easier to trace changes of fashion through its contents over time. Among the French magazines I examined *Le Pot-au-Feu* and *La Femme chez elle*. The former is of particular interest because, as its name implies, it was focused principally on cookery; it survived from 1893 to 1940, with a successor of the same name enjoying a briefer life from 1949 to 1956. *La Femme chez elle* was published in Paris from 1899 to 1938. On the other side of the Channel, *Woman's Life* was a typical product of the Newnes stable, pitched at a popular market. It began in 1895 and survived until 1934 when it was amalgamated with the new *Woman's Own*.

The years between the two World Wars were again a period of rapid growth, and whereas the Society-orientated papers now declined, the circulation of those aimed at middle-class and lower middle-class readers grew hugely. In Britain, *Woman's Own* appeared in 1932 and *Woman* in 1937, both of them taking full advantage of colour printing which at that time first became technically possible for long high-speed printing runs; these two magazines have dominated the popular market since then. France was slightly behind: *Elle*, the closest equivalent to *Woman's Own* and *Woman*, appeared only after the war in 1945. Another magazine of particular interest, because it has always aimed to provide a service centring on household matters for an audience of relatively well-to-do, upper middle-class women, is *Good Housekeeping*. The independent British offspring of the American parent of the same name, this monthly first apeared in 1922. The closest French equivalent, *Femme Pratique*, arrived on the scene much later, in 1958.

LE POT-AU-FEU

The fortnightly magazine *Le Pot-au-Feu* arose directly out of the lectures on domestic cookery given in 1893 by the distinguished chef Charles Driessens for housewives in St Denis and Paris. The statement of 'our programme' printed inside the back cover of all the early issues began with a statement reminiscent of complaints in England in earlier decades.

> In recent years, women's education has made considerable progress. Law, medicine, philosophy, painting, astronomy, music, women learn everything: everything, except cookery. There are scarcely any girls who do not know how to thump away at the piano; yet most of them have no idea how to set about cooking an omelette.

Le Pot-au-Feu blamed the cookery books, all of which it said were the same – they explained nothing. They were useful only to readers who already knew all about cookery. In contrast,

> M. Driessens, in his course, explains everything. He creates the dish which is the subject of his lecture before the very eyes of his audience; he explains the whys and hows, accompanying his demonstration with often picturesque comments which imprint themselves on one's mind without one being aware of it. The cost of the dish, how much it needs to be cooked, how to serve it, the necessary seasonings and flavourings, each of these points is covered with indisputable expertise.

Le Pot-au-Feu would concern itself with *practical* cookery, it stressed, principally for the family. It was addressed to housewives, 'whatever the social circle to which they belong', and would set out to provide a useful course of instruction for young women initially learning to cook, for those who needed to know how to direct the work of their (women) cooks, and for those who themselves actually cooked for their own families. In attempting a 'classless' appeal to women of all social backgrounds through providing a service they all needed, *Le Pot-au-Feu* anticipated the ideology of many later women's magazines, especially after the Second World War. In being focused mainly on cookery, however, it was not typical of women's magazines at large, either in its own time or later.

The transcripts of Charles Driessens's lectures, the centrepiece of early issues, are lively and vivid, and they begin with quite elementary matters. Three of his first lectures discussed the relative merits of the traditional earthenware *marmite* and the new iron ones (1 May 1893), gave very precise instructions for making *pot-au-feu* (15 May), and explained the use of roux in making sauces (1 June). The latter provides a very clear example of the relationship between the professional *cuisine classique* and domestic *cuisine bourgeoise*. Driessens acknowledges that it is not feasible for most domestic kitchens to have at hand the *fonds* and *sauces mères* of the professional establishment, and that sometimes even in the best-run households meat juice and stock are unavailable, when sauces are made simply with water.

To avoid these inconveniences, I advise you, ladies, to make your 'fonds de cuisine' entirely with roux, which you can use in dishes where a professional would use espagnole or velouté; and with meat-extract, which will allow you – just like the classic meat juices – to enrich your sauces. The resulting cuisine will perhaps be a little less fine, but it has the advantage of being quick and practical. When meat-extract is good, it is always a better replacement for stock than is water. For myself, I have adopted *Liebig* [the meat extract invented earlier in the century by the scientist Baron Liebig].

For all his simplification and democratic helpfulness Driessens was, like his *Art culinaire* associates, a little obsessed with what was 'correct', and had no hesitation in legislating on the matter for his audience. In his lecture on making *pot-au-feu*, he listed precise proportions of meat, bones, water, salt, carrots, turnips, parsnips, leeks, onions and garlic. At this point, a lady in the audience interrupted to ask 'And cabbage, monsieur?' Driessens replied firmly:

Cabbage, madame, the characteristic ingredient of *croûte-au-pot*, is not found in the classic *pot-au-feu*. . . . One can, however, put in thyme and bay leaf: that is an importation from Belgium. As for parsley, I have always seen it repudiated in the great Paris restaurants.

Other contributors also explained simple dishes and techniques in early issues of *Le Pot-au-Feu*. The magazine began to suggest menus based on recipes given in each issue. The following examples of a suggested lunch and dinner (1 September 1893) are probably fairly representative of good *cuisine bourgeoise* meals of the time:

Friture de Poisson
Boeuf en Goulasch
Daube de Veau aux Carottes
Salade de Chicorée
Gâteau de Vichy

Potage à la française
Boeuf bouilli sauce tomate
Perdreaux rôtis
Laitues au Jus
Tarte aux fruits

Menus similar to these examples continue to be suggested in French women's magazines up to the present day, a striking demonstration of the continuity seen in this field in France. *Le Pot-au-Feu* itself, however, though it remained much the same in outward appearance over the years, had a tendency to gravitate towards towards slightly more sophisticated cookery. These tendencies in *Le Pot-au-Feu* are easy to understand: no doubt anyone who bothered to take a specialised magazine on cookery, even one geared to household needs, would be a more committed cook than the average. The cookery columns found in the general women's magazines, which also built their circulation on advice columns, short stories, fashion, knitting patterns and so on, were probably pitched at a more representative audience. Even so, there was not a great difference between the menus and recipes in *Le Pot-au-Feu* and those in *La Femme chez elle*. Between the French and English magazines it was much more striking.

TO THE SECOND WORLD WAR

A comparison of *Woman's Life* (1895–1934) and *La Femme chez elle* (1899–1938) is revealing. The one was weekly and the other monthly, later fortnightly, but their general contents were quite similar, and they appear to have been pitched at a similar kind of middle- or lower middle-class audience. *Woman's Life* contained popular romantic stories together with articles on fashion, sewing and household hints, and an anodyne gossip column with lots of innocuous titbits about the interests and delightful natures of the innumerable princesses of the period. There was an etiquette column, assuaging readers' anxieties about correct behaviour in circles far above most of them. *La Femme chez elle*'s contents were much the same: fashion, furniture, child-rearing, sewing, embroidery, knitting, and 'un causerie sur les devoirs mondains' resembling the etiquette column of the English magazine. There was no fiction, though there was a section on 'literature', recommending some light, popular books, and on art and piano music. The other notable difference between the two magazines was that *Woman's Life*, in its early years, made a pitch at the working woman: its cookery column was at first entitled 'The Working Woman's Cookery Column', and there was a series of articles on 'How Women may Earn a Living'.[6] *La Femme chez elle*, as its title implied, assumed its readers were full-time housewives. But in most respects the contents of *Woman's Life* and *La Femme chez elle* were much the same.

Should anyone still doubt that France and England had different styles of domestic cooking and related attitudes towards food, however, they need look no further than the cookery columns of these two magazines. In *La Femme chez elle* the cookery column on *cuisine pratique* by 'Tante Colette' was a prominent feature, often the leading item, while in *Woman's Life* the cookery column was much smaller and generally further back in the magazine. Even more striking was the enthusiasm which the French writer brought to the cookery. She 'wrote up' the food, so to speak, expecting her readers to *enjoy* thinking about food as well as actually preparing it and eating it, and she whipped up a sense of excitement and anticipation in her columns. Here is an example from only the second issue (15 February 1899):

> Today . . . I have just hit upon a recipe which I want to tell you about right away, because it is just in season. Only I had better warn you that you will need all your patience. Not because it is complicated or difficult; it just takes a long time. But I

hasten to add, so that you will take your courage in both hands, that this is going to be a real treat, a great delicacy which you are bound to enjoy and which, once you have made it, will last you two weeks, three weeks, as long as you like. . . . We are going to make galettes.

Galettes! You are disappointed. You already know two or three different recipes, and you make them every year.

Don't despair. Just see whether Tante Colette's galettes are like any others, and which are the best.

Writing to excite like this was characteristic both of *La Femme chez elle* and *Le Pot-au-Feu*. There were few examples of it in English women's magazines until well after the Second World War. The recipe for galettes, incidentally, is quite lavish: to 1 ½ kg flour it uses 1 kg butter, 1 kg sugar, ½ litre of cream, 7 egg yolks and 7 whipped egg whites. The quantities may be reminiscent of Mrs Beeton, but Mrs Beeton had become a joke for extravagance; nor would the readers of *Woman's Life* be expected to separate eggs (too fiddly) or to leave the batter to stand for 12 hours before cooking (takes up too much time).

The recipes found in *La Femme chez elle* changed very little over its whole existence – a continuity symbolised by the appearance in the issue of 1 January 1937, only a year before the magazine folded, of a recipe for galettes identical to that of 1899, except that the quantities had been cut by half. To the English reader of today, the easiest way of describing the general character of this food would be to say that it is very much the sort of French 'country' or 'provincial' food popularised by writers like Elizabeth David (1951, 1960) among the English middle classes after the Second World War. Typical recipes were: ravioles, cotelettes de mouton, sauce Soubise, oeufs au gratin, crêpelinottes (April 1899); croquettes aux oeufs, cassoulet, soufflé aux pruneaux (1 February 1922); truite à la crème, lapin sauté ménagère, canard bonne-femme (1 January 1937). Compared with their English counterparts, the recipes were lighter and more varied – English writers tended to rely for variety on ringing the changes on a huge repertoire of heavy puddings – and the general approach was distinctively French. For example, a recipe for poulet à la paysanne (June 1899) simply instructs the reader to roast the chicken in butter, and then remarks, 'While it is cooking, you will be busy making the sauce, which is the important part of the dish and requires all your attention.' The sauce was quite complicated, made from onions, bacon, butter, white wine and tomatoes, all sieved and then added to more onions, bacon and mushrooms gently cooked in butter. The reader is warned, all the same, not to be so preoccupied with the sauce that she forgets the bird, which must be basted regularly, to be golden, succulent and cooked *à point*. Other recipes casually propose, in *La Femme chez elle* as well as in the more specialised *Pot-au-Feu*, dishes involving hollandaise, without anticipating terrible panic. Here the influence of French professional cookery can be discerned.

Unlike in the professional journals, however, recipes for leftovers are common and an early issue of *La Femme chez elle* (February 1899) speaks of 'using up leftover meat, our eternal headache as housewives', but there is not the obsessive concern with economy found in England, nor is cookery assumed to be a burden. In France, the housewife seems to be assumed not only to enjoy cooking and eating, but to have inherited knowledge of certain basic skills. Significantly, from time to time it is evident that *La Femme chez elle* was consciously addressed to a more rural society that its English counterparts. As late as 1937, a recipe for poule-au-pot begins: 'We have adapted this recipe for those of our subscribers who have a farmyard and want to make use of some old hen when it has become a poor layer. So, kill an old hen . . .'. That instruction would not have been found in the English magazines even before the turn of the century, because they could already assume that the vast majority of their readers lived in towns, and also perhaps because their readers were already too squeamish.

Cookery was featured less prominently in *Woman's Life* than in *La Femme chez elle*, and tended over time to become still less prominent. It occupied half a page in most issues. Before the First World War, there was relatively little in the way of background chat introducing the suggested menus and recipes, and virtually none of the whipping-up of excitement found in the French magazine. The space is rarely spared even to suggest that a dish might appeal to a husband. None the less, the general assumptions underlying the 'Working Woman's Cookery Column' were set out in the issue of 28 December 1895:

> *Dinners for Moderate Incomes.* I propose to address myself to housewives who are able to afford between 15*s.* and £1 a week on dinners, these dinners to be suitable for three adults. Each dinner to consist of three courses – plain, yet wholesome, and as varied as the outlay will allow.

The concern with economy in English cookery writing is by now scarcely unexpected. Even though the title 'Working Woman's Cookery Column' soon disappeared, the bias towards plain, economical food persisted throughout the magazine's life. There were exceptions, indeed fluctuations. In the issues for 1906, such extravagances as lobster and asparagus make occasional appearances; and the French influence, though still slight, is detectable in recipes for 'Lyonnais potatoes' or 'Spinach à la francais'. That was the era of the *Entente Cordiale*. In the bleak wartime issues of 1916, full of discussions on such questions as whether to marry the boyfriend who was off to Flanders, the cookery columns for once are more discursive. Scottish recipes in the issues of 29 April are used as an excuse for a little fantasy, under the title 'When Tommy comes to Tea', about entertaining two Black Watch soldiers. Understandably, the main concern was then with earnest advice on how to make best use of the food available in wartime. Curiously enough, amidst the general wartime drive for economy, it was thought necessary to caution readers against too enthusiastic an indulgence in the national predilection for economical food.

I've heard several friends talking lately about keeping down the food bill, and though no-one is keener on war economy than I am I don't believe in economising too much on food. We mustn't be extravagant, but we should save in everything else possible before food, don't you think so? (20 May 1916)

Photographs had now appeared to illustrate the cookery columns and, interestingly, many of them are credited to the ubiquitous C. H. Senn. Ten years later still, the food, as well as the other contents of the magazine, are a bit more cheerful and varied, and the French influence is more evident once again. But the solid ballast of the food column was 'plain, yet wholesome' English food. What constituted the prevailing conception of wholesomeness can be gleaned from the following typical example of part of a week's menus from the issue of 28 December 1895:

Wednesday: Soup – potato soup; Meat – breast of mutton stewed with vegetables; Veg. – potatoes; Pudding – baked currant pudding.
Thursday: Fish – plaice floured and fried; Meat – steak and potato pie; Veg. – sprouts; Sweet – cornflour mould and jam.
Friday: Soup – lentil soup; Fish – boiled cod and egg sauce; Veg. – potatoes; Pudding – open jam tart.
Saturday: Fish – fish cakes, remains of cod; beef kidney stewed; Veg. – cabbage; Pudding – pancakes.[7]

The 'cornflour mould with jam' reminds one irresistibly of Mr Pooter's embarrassment at the endless reappearance on his table of the leftover blancmange (Grossmith and Grossmith, 1892: 110–11). There is a high proportion of leftover dishes in the *Woman's Life* cookery columns. The general heaviness of the food compared with that in the French counterpart is striking. Puddings were a constant feature – sweet or savoury; boiled, steamed or baked; generally with suet, sometimes with breadcrumbs or a sponge-cake mixture. The advertisements reinforced the message of the cookery columns. Atora grated suet and Bird's custard powder were advertised in nearly every issue.

For your school children – those growing boys and girls! Pudding with Hot Bird's Custard sauce is the food to sustain them through afternoon school. There's energy and warmth in Hot Bird's Custard and steamed puddings; also the material for sturdy growth. Puddings with Hot Bird's Custard cost little and nourish much, and they are within the reach of everybody. Bird's Custard hot adds zest to any pudding and takes it out of the ordinary. It doubles the nutriment and trebles the enjoyment. (27 February 1926)

A small number of very old recipes turn up repeatedly – 'pain perdu' and 'maids of honour' most notably. But whereas the fine English cookery of the eighteenth-century cookery books was butter-based, the food described in the late nineteenth- and early twentieth-century magazines is principally based on the use of suet and dripping. For example, the egg sauce to be served with cod in the menu just quoted is made with roux, stock and boiled eggs – superficially just like any French recipe, but with the striking difference that the roux was made with dripping, not butter.[8] Nor were sauces a principal and integral feature of a dish as in France – they were more commonly something separate, to be poured over something else almost as an afterthought. Indeed, one article in *Woman's Life* (27 March 1926) is entitled 'Sauce Saves the Situation'.

> My ideal cookery-book would have a 'first-aid' section in it, and it would be mostly recipes for really good sauces. Then when unexpected visitors turn up, or the housewife wanted to turn a very 'homely' meal into a much more elaborate one, she'd turn quickly to her first-aid pages, and pick out the sauce that would do the trick.

Thus the sausages and mash planned as a family meal were to be transformed into something worthy of visiting company by being served on fried bread (fried in dripping of course) and 'masked' with an onion sauce (sauce normande).

Only limited skills (as well as limited time and money) seem to have been expected of the reader of *Woman's Life*. Generally the techniques required are rather simple, and only a few operations are involved in each recipe. Of course, exceptions can be found: for example, the vegetable salad in the week's menu quoted above was to include home made mayonnaise. But an article singing the praises of a three-tier aluminium steamer (20 February 1926) shows that this was to be used much like a cauldron in Lark Rise (or the Middle Ages) to produce much the same sort of meal:

> Now that winter is really here, we can indulge ourselves with savoury meat puddings – our steamer makes the suet crust deliciously mellow and appetising – and its upper storeys cook potatoes in their jackets and a generous allowance of brussels sprouts to perfection, with a minimum of trouble on our part.
>
> Another favourite 'heavy' meal is a nice little piece of mildly-salted beef. This we put to simmer with a good plateful of neatly-cut carrots and turnips and some small, *mild* onions, the whole covered with hot water, in the ground floor of the steamer, and use the upper compartments for a couple of dishes of vegetables and a delicate steamed pudding.

In the same year, *Woman's Life* was sharing the concern of other women's magazines of the 1920s at 'the servant problem', and incidentally leaving a picture of the utter helplessness of housewives hitherto accustomed to having a cook. 'Elaborate entertaining's always difficult for the servantless woman. That's why many people have given up asking people to dinner, and are having supper parties instead' (4 September 1926). The following supper menu was proposed:

Hors d'oeuvres
Poisson en Coquilles
Veal and Ham Pie
Beetroot and Potato Salad
Gâteau de Marrons

The 'Poisson en Coquilles' was in fact cold fish with pickle and mayonnaise in a scallop shell, and the last course was simply chestnut purée. At least that suggested more initiative than did an advertisement for 'Skipper' tinned sardines: 'Oh Tomkins, this is your evening out, is it not? Just lay the table for supper and put out the tin of Skippers (there's a tin in the cupboard). We'll open it ourselves' (27 February 1926).

Overall, *Woman's Life* supplies more evidence of what we have called the 'decapitation' of English cookery. Somewhat less clearly it also shows the hesitant progress of the trend towards relatively greater social uniformity in eating of which Marc Bloch spoke. There is a little more variety in the food and methods of cookery suggested in 1926 than in 1896. Interpreting this as evidence of a real social trend is complicated by the magazine beginning to fret itself about matters such as 'the servant problem'. Did trends in its cookery column indicate simply that it was trying to move up-market, addressing a more solidly middle-class market than the lower middle-class and even reasonably prosperous working-class audience of 1896? Probably not. The general impression given by *Woman's Life* in the 1920s is that – in addition to the element of social voyeurism it had always contained – it was trying to appeal to a broad social spectrum, and doing so in a rather confused way. Its newer, colour-printed Newnes stable-mate, *Woman's Own*, into which *Woman's Life* was shortly merged, developed this broad appeal much more successfully. The food featured in the newer magazine did not represent any abrupt change.

Woman's Own was distinguished in its early days by having Florence White, under the pseudonym 'Mary Evelyn', as its cookery editor. That is a good clue to the sort of food that appeared in its columns – mainly traditional English, but the best of its kind and including a number of hitherto unfamiliar regional dishes. Miss White's column in the first issue leads off on a predictable note of economy, under the heading 'How Much Shall I Spend on Food?' It deals with stocking the store cupboard, but much of the rest of the page is concerned with home-baking of bread, which she recommends strongly in preference to buying it. Baking generally, mainly of cakes and sweet pastry, was very prominent in *Woman's Own* and other English women's magazines, reflecting that even if bread and cheese, bread and jam, bread and dripping were no longer the staples for most people, flour was a dominant element in the diet. It came into main courses too in the form of puddings and pies, but it was sweet pastry which took up most room and in which there was endless variety. In contrast, Miss White was conscious of the danger of monotony in main courses:

It might be easier to make the menus more appetising if she could spend a great deal on food, but when a penny has to do the work of twopence it calls for all the ingenuity the young housekeeper possesses. I have planned these menus for a week with an eye to economy and variety . . .

Sunday – Veal and ham pie (hot), cauliflower, sauce and baked potatoes, fresh fruit salad.

Monday – Cold veal and ham pie, mashed potatoes, baked apples.

Tuesday – Gloucester beef and vinegar stew, roly-poly golden syrup suet pudding.

Wednesday – Stew left over from Tuesday served in flan case, covered with mashed potatoes. Boiled onions and sauce. Feather pudding. . . . (12 November 1932)

In fact Florence White produced a much greater variety of recipes than this excerpt suggests – salads (regarded as expensive), jams and chutneys, potted meat and fish, soups, cakes and puddings of all sorts. In 1933 she wrote a series of simple articles explaining basic methods of cookery – roasting, baking, broiling, pastry-making and so on – skills taken for granted in *La Femme chez elle*. In general she wrote far more by way of background introduction and explanation than had been common in *Woman's Life*. Yet there is still an almost total absence of the 'sensual' quality in writing about food which was already common in France and was to become common in England too after the Second World War. In the 1930s the tone was the opposite of sensual. For instance, under the headline 'Mary Evelyn tells you how to Cook Fish Appetisingly' (2 September 1933), the article begins: 'This Food is cheap and very nourishing. It should appear on every table once or twice a week', and nothing about how good it is to eat. Things seemed to have changed three weeks later (23 September 1933) when there began a series of articles on 'The Way to a Man's Heart', a theme which was later to be a principal cliché of women's magazine cookery columns. But Miss White emphasised careful planning of menus as well as good cooking as the way for the little woman to ingratiate herself with her husband (she did go so far as to suggest tomato juice as a surprise first course). The characteristic note was struck on 7 October, when the third article was headed 'Use Up Those "Left-Overs" and You'll Find "The Way to a Man's Heart" by Keeping Down Expenses'.

Woman's Own, along with *Woman*, was later to achieve massive circulation and, probably, influence. But a much better harbinger of things to come was *Good Housekeeping*, founded a decade earlier in 1922. *Good Housekeeping* was a monthly, and directed at a readership further up the social scale than those of *Woman's Life* and *Woman's Own*. The typical *Good Housekeeping* reader, then as now, belonged to the solid professional and business middle class. The magazine was mildly progressive in its outlook, the early numbers unusual among women's magazines of the time in including articles on issues of the day by writers such as Lady Violet Bonham-Carter and Rebecca West ('the famous feminist'). 'The Reason for *Good Housekeeping*' was proclaimed in ringing tones in the first issue (March 1922):

Any keen observer of the times cannot have failed to notice that we are on the threshold of a great feminine awakening. Apathy and levity are alike giving place to a wholesome and intelligent interest in the affairs of life, and above all in the home. We believe that the time is ripe for a great new magazine which shall worthily meet the needs of the homekeeping woman of today.

There should be no drudgery in the house. There must be time to think, to read, to enjoy life, to be young with the growing generation, to have time for their pleasures, to have leisure for one's own – to hold one's youth as long as possible, to have beauty around us – line and colour in dress, form and colour in our surroundings; to have good food without monotony, and good service without jangled tempers.

Good Housekeeping set out in particular to meet the needs of the housewife in the age of domestic transition dominated by 'the servant problem', dedicating itself to providing a *service* for its readers focused especially on the latest labour-saving household equipment and on cookery.

Cookery columns in early issues declare that 'tastes differ widely – we hope to include something to please everyone', but a sense of what is better or worse, what is 'correct', often creeps in. Underlying the cookery column, as indeed the rest of the magazine, are a spirit of improvement and the pursuit of the new. In cookery, these two objectives could conflict.

The concern with 'newness' is understandable in view of the frequent references to the monotony of food in English households in the 1920s. It was mentioned in the magazine's statement of its purposes quoted above, and many times thereafter.

The motor-car, the telephone, the aeroplane, wireless, and the week-end habit, all contribute to the elimination of irksome sameness from the lives of most of us. Yet there does remain one department of modern life where unnecessary monotony is not only tolerated but persisted in by quite a large number of people, who would be the first to resent it in any other. The ever-recurring question of daily meals is answered by many in the laziest fashion possible by giving their household the same food on the same day of the week, irrespective of the time of year or of climatic change. (April 1925)

The pursuit of newness and encouraging housewives to be a little more adventurous was associated with an enormous stress on *testing* by *experts* in the *Good Housekeeping* trial kitchens. Authority spoke with a stentorian voice:

Tried and Proven. This is the motto of the Department of Cookery. We offer these pages in all confidence, as they are developed by actual experiments carried on in a fully equipped model kitchen. There need be no hesitation in using any of the recipes, success is assured if the directions are followed completely. (March 1922)

Do not be discouraged if you are a new housewife and do not know how to cook. Follow the directions we give in these pages and you will soon learn how to market and serve meals perfectly. We speak with authority, as every recipe and every statement has been proved by experience. (September 1923)

One article in October 1923 was less encouraging – perhaps it had not been cleared with the circulation manager:

> The secret of good cooking may lie, to a certain extent, in the knowledge of food values, in accurate weights and measures, and a precise regulation of heat; but this is not all that is necessary. Neither is a good recipe a guarantee that a certain dish will be a success. As an example of this, several pupils in a class will be given the same recipe and exactly the same directions, but when they attempt to make the dish no two results will be alike.
>
> There is another qualification for successful cookery that is frequently forgotten, and that is an *intuitive* sense of taste and fitness, which is *natural* to some people. It enables them to tell how a dish will taste by simply reading the recipe, and to know *instinctively* what will be the result of combining certain ingredients together. It is a streak of *genius* possessed by the fortunate few . . . [my emphasis]

Anyone lacking this streak of genius, the article continued, could only hope to approach similar results through sheer hard work. What both this article and the more typical ones stressing *tested* recipes have in common is the assumption that the typical reader is not in possession of an inheritance of skills passed down from generation to generation. Each recipe is presented in isolation, with little sense that the dish, its ingredients, and the techniques it requires are interconnected with other dishes, ingredients and techniques – a sense of interconnectedness that can be found within an inherited tradition (or within a codified system like Escoffier's).

To help remedy that deficiency, *Good Housekeeping* from time to time ran series of articles on elementary cooking techniques. The first of these, beginning in August 1925, was entitled 'The Bride's Primer of Cookery', and covered topics like making shortcrust pastry, steaming, stewing, preparing the Christmas dinner, marmalade making, making stocks and thick soups, making broths and consommés, grilling, simple cake-making, making jams and jellies, and flaky pastry. In view of the generally low level of expertise readers were assumed to have in cookery, it is a little surprising that another article, in January 1924, on 'The Right Way to Start a Small Restaurant', was entirely concerned with matters like furniture and decorations, and said nothing at all about the food, beyond this one piece of advice: 'Don't grab after the pennies and the pounds will roll in, especially if you give good food, good portions, and quick service.' There was no sign in *Good Housekeeping* in the 1920s that this was still the age of Escoffier, and little evidence of any influence from recent French professional cookery, except possibly a general tendency towards greater lightness in food. If anything, any influence was still pre-Escoffier. For instance, some articles are clear examples of what Roland Barthes (1957: 78–80) was later to call 'ornamental cookery'. One, in the 'Bride's Primer' series was entirely devoted to 'Garnishing and Decoration': 'By the judicious use of various embellishments, uninteresting and plebeian food can vie with dishes that are difficult to prepare and costly to procure' (November 1926).

If French professional cookery of the time had little overt influence in the early issues of *Good Housekeeping*, the French housewife was constantly being held up as a paragon. Under the first cookery editor, Florence Jack, there was a constant if subtle improving zeal in which French domestic cookery was often the model to be copied:

The French never season their food at table to the same extent as we do – they would consider it an insult to the cook – but each dish arrives adequately seasoned. (October, 1923)

The cooking of vegetables is a branch of cookery which receives too little attention in this country. . . . A French housewife would look with scorn on the way in which we often serve them up, cooked in water, imperfectly drained, and tumbled into a vegetable dish without further attention. (July 1922)

There is no branch of cookery so imperfectly understood by the average cook as that of soup making, and its importance as part of the everyday diet is not sufficiently appreciated in this country. In a French household, the soup forms an essential part in the day's menu, and no dinner is considered complete without it. (May 1922)

Efforts were made to improve the range of foods and dishes served. An article on seafood anticipates that the reader will be both ignorant of and slightly anxious about trying it (September 1923). Nor were readers expected to be quite *au fait* with salads and salad dressings – the classic French dressing of oil and vinegar is explained minutely as something unfamiliar, but the writer expresses a clear preference for it rather than various English concoctions of 'boiled dressing', which are described in a disapproving tone (June 1922).

This style of cookery writing did not survive very long. In September 1924 the Good Housekeeping Institute opened, which was central to the magazine's notion of providing a service to its readers. The Institute tested and reported upon household equipment (in effect performing a function similar to the Consumers' Association and *Which?* more than three decades later). The magazine's test kitchens were also moved to the Institute, and from then on the cookery columns appear under the name of D. D. Cottington-Taylor, who had previously written on household equipment. She had now become Director of the Cookery Department, and Florence Jack disappeared. From then until the Second World War the cookery columns of *Good Housekeeping* became much more conventional, concentrating on baking, confectionery and the more familiar (and heavier) English fare. D. D. Cottington-Taylor was billed as having various diplomas and certificates in domestic science and cookery. The one qualification she did not boast, but which Florence Jack did, was MCA. Remembering UCFA's essentially francophile loyalties, it is probably significant that the gallicising and improving strain in *Good Housekeeping* diminished when a member was succeeded by a non-member.

Cookery as presented in the women's magazines, it is worth repeating, is almost certainly more varied and demanding in skill than what is actually encountered in most typical homes. The reputation of English domestic cookery before, during and immediately after the Second World War for being heavy, monotonous and lacking in skill seems not to be a myth. There is testimony not just from the magazines but from numerous contemporary descriptions. An American lady, Margaret Halsey, in her book *With Malice Toward Some*, gives a skittish account of a year spent as the wife of a visiting lecturer at the then University College of the South West in Exeter in the mid-1930s. Here are her notes on a typical dinner:

> Canned grapefruit (slightly warmed). This is unusual and was probably designed as a sop to the Americans, which is exactly what it was.
>
> Soup. The soup, thin and dark and utterly savourless, tasted as if it had been drained out of the umbrella stand.
>
> Roast beef. The meat is the one bright spot in the local cuisine. It seems a shame to spoil this symmetry of criticism with a word of praise, but I do think English meat much superior to ours, finer textured and with more flavour.
>
> Boiled potatoes and Brussels sprouts. Here is a country where the soil is so fertile that if you plant an acorn in the ground, you have to jump back quickly in order not to have it hit you on the way up. And the English raise Brussels sprouts. With sometimes a flyer in cabbage. Is it pure ignorance, or some complicated form of Puritan spitefulness?
>
> Raspberry tart. It is possible to eat English piecrust, whatever you may think. The English eat it, and when they stand up and walk away, they are hardly bent over at all. It can be eaten, but it definitely does not come under the head of sensual indulgence.
>
> Savoury. This is a sardine (or, alternatively, a piece of cheese) resting on toast which sweats melted butter. It serves no discernible function except to give the maids another lap to walk. (1938: 25–6)

The Second World War and the era of continuing food rationing after it was a distinctive period in the history of British eating. It has been well documented by Raynes Minns in her book *Bombers and Mash* (1980: 85–93, 103–41). Yet it is not easy to identify any lasting effects it left on the British palate or British cookery, unless it were destroying the last vestiges of resistance to tinned and processed foods. Apart from its directly democratising effect in equalising the types and amounts of foodstuffs available to all social classes, rationing served to encourage ingenuity in cooking the limited raw materials, and forced people at least to try things they had not tasted before.

> To be English is to be notoriously conservative in taste for food. Do we deserve this character, should we be doing something about wiping it out? A hundred chances to one, you have to admit that until recently the family were scared of trying a new dish;

they would say, 'it may be all right for some people, but I am not used to it'. (*Woman's Own*, 30 October 1942)

Some adaptations to wartime adversity were exactly the same concoctions urged upon readers in peacetime as feats of adventure: 'sausages en surprise' (Minns, 1980: 113) were much the same as *Good Housekeeping*'s 'smothered sausages' of March 1922: sausages encased in mashed potatoes and recooked.

While encouraging inventiveness in cooking, wartime conditions tended to snuff out any incipient tendencies there had been towards the use of more exotic foods – in the strict sense that exotic foods are imported. On balance, the gallicising tendency was diminished, though cookery writers like Constance Spry and Ambrose Heath ransacked French domestic cookery for ways of making something tasty out of next to nothing, and there was renewed urgency in pleas on nutritional grounds to eat more soups and not to overcook vegetables. Overall, the war tended to reinforce the Englishness of English cooking – more cakes and puddings, more oatmeal, more dumplings, more leftover dishes. Some very old staples of the poor, like Hasty Pudding, reappear among wartime recipes. Above all, economy could now be urged upon the housewife all the more strongly because justified on social rather than private grounds: 'Food wasted is another ship lost.'

The battle on the kitchen front lasted long after the war, for food rationing did not end in Britain until 1954 and was indeed more severe after the war than during it. Yet it seemed more to have reinforced existing traits than to have left any really enduring legacy of its own. André Simon, surveying the state of domestic cookery in England and France at the end of rationing wrote as follows in his editorial to *Wine and Food*, 83, Autumn 1954:

This newly recovered freedom has been hailed by many joyfully and gratefully, but we very much doubt whether it has made any difference whatsoever to the standard of dullness of meals which will continue to be the rule in far too many homes of the British Isles. . . . the housewife looks upon cooking as a chore and a bore; she prepares, without any pleasure, meals which are eaten without any pleasure, without any complaints if bad and without a word of praise if good. To the average French housewife, on the contrary, cooking is a hobby and a joy; she will spend more time in her kitchen, and not grudge a minute of it: but, of course, she knows that she is cooking for people who take a keen interest in their meals: who will appreciate the trouble she has been taking for them and will tell her so.

That could have been said at any time – indeed it had been said repeatedly – during the previous hundred or so years. One might initially have viewed it with caution as a kind of folk-myth – a myth at least among gastronomic folk – but studying the women's magazines of the period seems to confirm that it was largely true. Considerable changes were, however, to unfold in the years following the end of rationing, especially in England and to a lesser extent in France.

TRENDS SINCE THE SECOND WORLD WAR

Zeldin notes that from the end of the nineteenth century, and increasingly in the period 1930–60, women's magazines in France 'provided women with reading matter which consolidated their status as a separate caste' (1977: II, 557). In other words, their contents were designed to appeal to and promote readers' common identity as females and to play down everything which separated them as members of different social classes. The British magazines attempted to do the same, though before the Second World War they seem not to have succeeded to the same degree, possibly because consciousness of the minute differentia of social rank was so much stronger in England. There were good commercial reasons for trying to create this 'consciously classless' appeal (as Marjorie Ferguson, 1982: 168, calls it). *Woman* and *Woman's Own* both reached their peak circulations, of 3,311,700 and 2,515,400 in the first half of 1962 (Cynthia White, 1970: Appendix IV). Their exact French counterpart, *Elle*, followed a very similar path (it claimed a circulation of 2,928,000 in 1967). Ferguson points to two techniques through which the sense of classlessness was promulgated:

> [The first] eschews social class differences by omission rather than inclusion, avoiding any mention of stratification as such. The other propounds a 'classless' female society by the inclusion of a 'representative' cross-section of individual occupations and social strata (in line with the magazine's readership profile), either within a given article, or across an entire issue, or both. The net effect is to suggest homogeneity within the cult [of femininity]. There is only one class of membership, that of woman, where the badge of belonging is supplied by sex and gender, not by status or income. (1982: 168)

The first technique was seen in at least one magazine's avoiding, before the 1960s, any reference to a daily bath – since in a large proportion of readers' houses that was not then a practical possibility. The second technique had been employed rather unsuccessfully in the 1920s by *Woman's Life* – unsuccessfully because a more sophisticated kind of ambiguity is required than the crude juxtaposition of articles for working women and references to 'the servant problem'. Both techniques were deployed with more success in cookery columns after the Second World War in both *Woman's Own* and *Elle*. Yet it was the cookery columns of *Elle* which provoked Roland Barthes to some sweeping assertions about different class attitudes to food in France.

Elle *and Roland Barthes*

One of the celebrated short essays which Barthes wrote between 1954 and 1956 and published under the collective title *Mythologies* was on 'Ornamental Cookery' (1957: 78–80). It was an analysis of the contrasting semiotic content, as Barthes perceived it, of the cookery columns of *Elle* and *L'Express*.

The weekly *Elle* (a real mythological treasure) gives us almost every week a fine colour photograph of a prepared dish: golden partridges studded with cherries, a faintly pink chicken chaudfroid, a mould of crayfish surrounded by their red shells, a frothy charlotte prettified with glacé fruit designs, multicoloured trifle, etc.

The principal characteristic of this 'ornamental' style of cookery was the glazing and rounding-off of surfaces, burying food under smooth coatings of sauces, creams, icings and jellies. This cookery, wrote Barthes, was intended for the eye alone, and responded to a need for 'gentility'. Its use of coatings was for ever trying to disguise the primary nature of foodstuffs, hiding the 'brutality' of meat or the 'abruptness' of seafood. 'A country dish is admitted only as an exception (the good family boiled beef), as the rustic whim of jaded city-dwellers.' With the word 'gentility' Barthes is here hinting at what Elias had more explicitly identified as part of a civilising process, the transformation of feeling reflected particularly in the tendency for whole joints to disappear from fashionable French tables in the nineteenth century.

Ornamentation, said Barthes, proceeded in two ways:

on the one hand, fleeing from nature thanks to a kind of frenzied baroque (sticking shrimps in a lemon, making a chicken look pink, serving grapefruit hot), and on the other, trying to reconstitute it through an incongruous artifice (strewing meringue mushrooms and holly leaves on a traditional log-shaped Christmas cake, replacing the heads of crayfish around the sophisticated béchamel which hides their bodies).

By the mid 1950s, *Elle* had a vast circulation and was read in many working-class homes in France. That, Barthes believed, explained the 'ornamental' cookery in its columns. The role of the magazine was to present to its working-class audience 'the very dream of smartness'. 'Ornamental' cookery was 'a cuisine of advertisement, totally magical'; because it represented a dream, and its working-class readership was not expected actually to attempt to make the recipes, *Elle* 'was very careful not to take for granted that cooking must be economical'. Therein lay the great contrast with *L'Express*,

whose exclusively middle-class public enjoys a comfortable purchasing power: its cookery is real, not magical. *Elle* give the recipe for fancy partridges, *L'Express* gives that of *salade nicoise*. The readers of *Elle* are entitled only to fiction; one can suggest real dishes to those of *L'Express*, in the certainty that they will be able to prepare them.

The brilliance of Barthes's insight and the neatness of his explanation are undeniable. But might it not be *too* brilliant and too neat?

Like other representatives of structuralist thought, Barthes shows little sense of history. He seems unaware that the 'ornamental' food he describes in *Elle* in the years when wartime shortages were finally disappearing was a degenerate survival of the haute cuisine of the Gouffé era. Then certainly it had actually been cooked, though only for an élite minority, and had persisted ever since as a cliché of the cold table at *salons culinaires*,[9] and made occasional appearances in the pages of magazines like *Good Housekeeping* which scarcely addressed themselves to a working-class audience. So a 'timeless' explanation equating 'magical' cooking with a working-class audience and a 'realistic' one with the comfortably-off middle class is at least over-simple.

That criticism would perhaps not undermine Barthes's argument fundamentally. More disturbingly, however, when one actually looks at the cookery columns of *Elle*, they prove to bear only the most tenuous resemblance to what he describes. 'Ornamental' cookery is little in evidence in *Elle* both a few years before and a few years after Barthes was writing. Even in the mid 1950s, I had to search among the considerable variety of cookery writing in *Elle* to find examples precisely corresponding to Barthes's account. There was indeed, in the issue of 17 January 1955, an article giving six recipes for cooked grapefruit – soufflés de pamplemousse, salade d'oranges et pamplemousse, pamplemousse au porto, tarte à la crème de pamplemousse – but illustrated with black-and-white not colour photographs, and the dishes were not ornamented. As for Barthes's pink chicken and the preference for pink he characterised as 'frenzied baroque', it seems to have appeared in a single article entitled 'Le souper rose' in the issue of 31 January 1955. It suggested three pink recipes for supper after a visit to the theatre: salade au paprika, crème glacée à la framboise, and chaudfroid de poulet. The last was obviously what Barthes had in mind: the chaudfroid was tinted pink and trimmed with truffles. Sheer escapism! – but the authoress, Marie-Pierre de Toulouse-Lautrec, dispelled the air of fantasy by concluding realistically that the chicken could be trimmed 'more simply with a few sprigs of cress'. In any case, articles of this sort were only a small minority of the variety of cookery writing which appeared in *Elle* at that period.

Cookery occupied very little space in *Elle* in its earliest years. The magazine first appeared in the bleak post-war winter of November 1945. The first issue contained nothing at all on food, but the second (28 November) contained recipes for 'Three Soups That Will Warm You Up'. Other signs of the hard times were a dinner menu with a croque monsieur as the main course (12 December) and, in the Christmas issue a fortnight later, instructions on how to make a turkey last over five days' dinners – dinde farcie aux marrons; abattis de dinde aux carottes et céléri; croquettes de dinde; risotto de dinde; soufflé de dinde. (In England at that time, the problem would have been getting the turkey, not making it last five days.)

By the early 1950s it was an unusual issue of *Elle* that did not contain anything about cooking, although its prominence varied considerably. Very often the cookery column was small and towards the back of the magazine, after the popular romantic stories and so on, frequently without illustrations, even more frequently with only black-and-white photographs. For a long time the nearest thing to a fixed point in every issue were the contributions by Dr Edouard de Pomiane, the medical man who ever since the 1920s had been urging the French to adopt a healthy diet. In 1952 he was prominently featured in a series entitled 'Le Cours Supérieure de Cuisine du Docteur de Pomiane', but sometimes he was cut down to a single simple recipe with no illustrations. In 1953 began a column under the title 'Manger pour Vivre, Non Pas Vivre pour Manger', written by de Pomiane in collaboration with Georges Duchêne of the Institut Scientifique d'Hygiène Alimentaire. From about this time, slimming became a regular preoccupation in the magazine, and *Elle* continued to provide healthy, unfattening recipes and menus, often with calorie counts each week until the late 1960s. Here is one example, the dinners for part of one week suggested in the issue of 25 February 1952:

Monday: Carottes râpées à la laitue; Foie aux champignons; Fromage.
Tuesday: Pamplemousse; Boeuf mode aux carottes; Crêpes.
Wednesday: Mâches et betterave; Rougets grillées; Pommes de terre vapeur; Fromage.

There is nothing very ornamental about that. Occasionally, such menus were accompanied by photographs showing the dish neatly decorated with whirls of cream, or whatever, but generally the recipe itself was entirely practical and simply did not mention the decoration. These suggested menus changed surprisingly little from the 1940s to the 1970s.

In addition to the weekly healthy eating column by Dr de Pomiane and his successors, most issues of *Elle* since the 1950s contained at least one other article on cookery, usually by a female writer. These were often presented with more exuberance, in large spreads with colour photographs (treatment which Dr de Pomiane received only occasionally). These were what Barthes seized upon. For example, in the issue of 3 January 1955, Annie Fabre wrote an article illustrated by four photographs of roast veal, each with a different and elaborate garnish. The caption read:

For a dish to be a success and do the mistress of the house honour, it must both have a delicious flavour and be prettily presented: pleasure for the taste and pleasure for the eyes. Harmonise each dish with the garnish that suits it best. To help you put this into practice, here are four ways of preparing roast veal.

These remarks could well have given Barthes his idea about appeal to the eye. But the actual recipes for roast veal are quite simple, and neither too expensive nor too complicated for the ordinary housewife to follow. She could simply ignore the ornamentation.

As it happened, in the following few weeks of early 1955, there was an unusual number of articles of the sort which Barthes focused upon, including the cooked grapefruit and the pink supper. There were also far more utterly unpretentious features about (among other things) making pancakes; salads; coffee; toffee for a children's party; recipes using tomatoes; recipes using oranges (illustrated by a colour photograph of a bowl of oranges – scarcely fitting Barthes's requirements for 'ornamental' cookery photographs). The articles which came closest to Barthes's model were those on cakes and sweets – and those dealing with food for special occasions. For a first communion lunch (2 May 1955) there are indeed highly ornamented chaudfroid dishes on a spectacular buffet, just as a similarly romantic soft-focus treatment is given to wedding breakfast in an earlier issue (11–18 May 1953). It is hardly surprising that the 'magical' properties of such special occasions were played up, and the appeal would scarcely be uniquely to the working class.

All the cookery writers in *Elle* dwelt on the sheer enjoyment of eating – even in early issues, and well before this was at all common in England. Sometimes this kind of writing could be mistakenly seen as promoting a sense of the magical. Even Dr de Pomiane, who for all his concern with 'correct' diet was the opposite of a killjoy, could conclude an article on curries with the words 'Close your eyes – you are in the Orient' (14 January 1952). Calorie-consciousness was not allowed to overshadow enjoyment: the slogan 'Manger pour Vivre . . .' was in due course replaced by the more encouraging heading 'Beauté, Santé, Diététique, Gastronomie'. An article by Margaret Duval on 'How I Balance the Menus for My Five Children' (16 February 1953) was itself nicely counterbalanced by one on the food of Alsace-Lorraine, headed 'So Much the Worse for the Figure', showing three plump ladies behind a huge choucroute garnie in the Auberge des Tanneurs, Strasbourg.

Overall, Barthes's interpretation seems to have been based on a highly selective reading of *Elle*. On the whole, the practicality of most of the cookery columns and the air of classlessness achieved through the sheer variety of the contents are striking. Barthes's comparison of *Elle* with *L'Express* was simply absurd. The difference in the context and purpose of the two magazines had a far more obvious bearing on differences in their cookery columns than did the modal social class of their readerships. *L'Express* is a weekly news magazine founded in 1953, directed at both sexes and concerned largely with current affairs. Its early issues contained nothing on cookery. Even in 1955 recipes were difficult to find: they are contained in tiny boxes on the women's pages, allowing no space for more than the tersest instructions, and none for either redundant trimmings or photographs. One column (22 January 1955) looks at ways of improving packet soups – something *Elle* would not have countenanced – but on the whole the menus and recipes are very similar to those suggested by Dr de Pomiane and his successors in *Elle*.

Trends in the women's press since he wrote his essay shed still more light on Barthes's thesis about 'ornamental cookery'. The style itself has disappeared from the magazines' pages. It was never the dominant element, but examples of it were to be found more commonly in the mid-1950s than before or since, both in France and England, and both in the women's magazines and in the trade press. One explanation may be that the style completed its slide down the social scale, from the élite of mid-nineteenth-century Paris to the readers of *Elle* in the 1950s, dropping off at the bottom when universally considered a vulgarity. More definitely, it is significant that the 1950s were a decade of stagnation in professional cookery: that could help to explain the survival of an antiquated style. The 1960s in contrast were a period of vigorous renewal in French professional cookery, which was soon evident in the cookery columns of women's magazines. Features on notable restaurants, with their chefs' recipes, had appeared from time to time in *Elle* in the 1950s, but became very common indeed in the 1960s and 1970s. Even before *nouvelle cuisine* had been so christened, its stars were appearing in *Elle*, and by the 1970s its influence was quite explicit. The issue of 3 April 1978 reported on two new restaurants in Paris, offering 'a fine, light cuisine' in which 'Flour is banned, and vinegar is king instead'. Alongside these sometimes elaborate (but *not* ornamented) dishes, many more mundane ones persisted – croquette potatoes, or rice pudding, for example. There was also an increase in the prominence of regional recipes, perhaps especially from the *cuisine paysanne*. For example, in the issue of *Elle* dated 12 August 1965, instructions for *bouillabaisse* are illustrated with a photograph of it being cooked over an open fire on the beach. This sort of thing was a regular summertime gimmick both in *Elle* and *Femme Pratique* (the cookery columns of which are remarkably similar to those of *Elle*). Did this represent the 'rustic whim of jaded city-dwellers', or more simply increased leisure and holidays further afield?

Some slight changes were also apparent by the 1960s in the advertising in *Elle*: advertisements appeared for such items as instant ice-cream mix (add milk and cream), and Mont Blanc instant desserts. Yet by the late 1970s it was surprising how little had changed in the French magazines. There is still no preoccupation with short cuts, no obsession with economy, no assumption that cooking is a time-consuming burden, and little implication that cookery is particularly difficult.

Post-War England

In contrast with the striking continuities observed in France, there were to be fairly rapid changes in cookery as represented in English women's magazines. That was not obvious towards the end of rationing: virtually nothing seemed to have changed. The columns of *Woman's Own* in 1952 were full of very 'English' food, there was little or no sign of French or any other foreign influence (save possibly a little American), and still not much suggestion that readers and their families might actually *enjoy* cooking and eating. There were still lots of leftover dishes, but the gradual lifting of rationing was marked by articles on foodstuffs newly available after long scarcity. For instance, in the issue of 4 September 1952, the cookery column was built around pork and ham, and there were recipes for 'Spicy Baked Ham' (with Worcester sauce and mustard), 'Roast Pork with Raisin Stuffing', 'Pork Chop Suey' (tomatoes, mushrooms, onion), 'Ham-Apple Bake', 'Braised Pork Steak', 'Ham Loaf', and 'Pork Dormers'. In spite of the appearance of the word 'spicy', which was to become a cliché epithet for any dish containing virtually any flavouring beyond salt and pepper, the writing in this article did nothing to excite the palate, and the illustration was one small, black-and-white, slightly blurred photograph.

Changes were soon afoot. The most immediately striking agent of change was the advent of a vast range of frozen, tinned, 'instant' and pre-cooked foods. They were not merely more 'convenient' – they also introduced many new kinds of food to the housewife, and, according to the National Food Survey Committee, considerably improved the nutrition of the British people.[10] Their impact from around 1960 in the British trade journals has already been described, and Cynthia White though not specifically studying cookery columns notes their impact on women's magazines at exactly the same time:

The magazines reflected all these changes in their cookery articles, in higher quality ingredients, in the variety and sophistication of recipes, and elsewhere in a new preoccupation with nutritional values and dietetics. More time was being spent in collecting food, but less actually preparing it, since manufacturers had reduced much of the drudgery of the kitchen by marketing pre-cleaned and prepared foods. Hence, cookery ceased to be an eternal battle to make cheap ingredients stretch and look appetising, and became an absorbing new hobby, for men as well as women, who were now willing to experiment with foreign recipes and new foods. The growing popularity of the *delicatessen* for all classes was evidence both of greater purchasing power and more catholic taste. (1970: 161)

Not surprisingly, the technological changes – the manufactured foods – were in evidence rather earlier than were changes in attitudes. The consequences of the one without the other, during what was possibly a period of transition in the history of English eating, were mordantly captured by P. D. James in the first of her detective novels, *Cover her Face*. Her policemen heros are sitting in an inn after a dinner cooked by a landlady noted for her 'good plain cooking and plenty of it' – an expression which 'had struck ominously on the ears of men whose travels had inured them to most of the vagaries of good plain English fare'.

Mrs Piggott was reputed to take some trouble with her soups. This was true in so far as the packaged ingredients had been sufficiently well mixed to exclude lumps. She had even experimented with flavours, and today's mixture of tomato (orange) and oxtail (reddish brown), thick enough to support the spoon unaided, was as startling to the palate as to the eye. Soup had been followed by a couple of mutton chops nestling artistically against a mound of potato and flanked with tinned peas larger and shinier than any peas which had ever seen pod. They tasted of soya flour. A green dye which bore little resemblance to the colour of any known vegetable seeped from them and mingled disagreeably with the gravy. An apple and blackcurrant pie had followed in which neither of the fruits had met each other nor the pastry until they had been carefully arranged on the plate by Mrs Piggott's careful hand and liberally blanketed with synthetic custard. (1962: 144)

Changing attitudes were evident in *Good Housekeeping* some years before they appeared in *Woman's Own*. If the magazine judged its more upper middle-class readership accurately, right from the end of rationing they were showing signs of an interest in more varied eating, were prepared to see cookery as an enjoyable hobby, and were sensitive to its possibilities as a weapon in competitive social display. Already in February 1954, a collection of 'recipes for special occasions' comprised blanquette de veau, pineapple suprême, crême brulée, hot chocolate soufflé, red mullet, jugged hare, filet de boeuf à la Dubarry – French vocabulary well to the fore again. The following month contained an article giving recipes by the chefs of five fashionable restaurants in London and the Home Counties: four of them were French dishes, the fifth Chinese. The same month an article on pancakes advised readers to 'Make the sauce for crêpes Suzette at the table; it's a personal and elegant touch that your guests will appreciate.' One does not need special expertise in semiotics to translate that as 'Show off: impress your guests with your superior expertise: make them feel mildly inferior.' By 1958 the phrase 'hostess cookery' had become established in *Good Housekeeping* jargon. The magazine of course continued to cover all the routine and traditional things, like pickling and jam-making, at the appropriate season each year, but even the most mundane items were now to be justified as part of the repertoire of the entertaining 'hostess':

> We have long appreciated the pork sausage as a quick and easy to prepare homely meal in itself; but with a little ingenuity and only a little trouble it qualifies for a place in hostess cookery, as our recipes on the following pages show. (January 1958)

Interestingly, this emphasis on impressing people is nothing like so prominent in the pages of *Femme Pratique*, which began publication in 1958. Not that the level of culinary expertise expected of readers of the French magazine was any lower – on the contrary, more knowledge and more curiosity in particular was taken for granted. But the difference in the cookery columns of *Femme Pratique* and *Elle*, the social distance so to speak, was much less than between *Good Housekeeping* and *Woman's Own*, and by the late 1960s was becoming hard to detect. At that time, the sensitivity to nuances of social gradation was being applied with renewed vigour to the culinary domain.

The newer attitudes appeared a little later and more hesitantly in *Woman's Own*. The impact of the technological changes in food manufacture and marketing came first. By the mid-1950s, advertisements abounded for products like 'Mary Baker Fruit Cake Mix', 'Creamola Bakewell Tarts Mixture', Symington's powdered soups (with a recipe for steak and kidney pie including a packet of oxtail soup as the star ingredient), 'Quaker Quick Macaroni' (with a ten-minute recipe for 'Quick Macaroni Fritters' by Marguerite Patten, who was later to be on the staff of the magazine itself), and, of course, tinned foods. Readers were encouraged to overcome any lingering reluctance to use the latter: 'For a bachelor girl's party – and it all comes out of tins' was the title of one article. Sausages, baked beans and sliced cooked meats were principal proposals there. By 1962, fully processed whole dishes were being advertised – such as Vesta Beef Curry ('Succulent – but not too spicy . . . all the drudgery's done for you by experienced chefs').

Alongside that trend, if not immediately so obvious, were also the signs of attitudes changing towards a greater spirit of adventure in cookery. Already by 1957, there was much more use in the cookery columns of adjectives like 'delicious', 'tasty' and 'spicy'. Greater prominence was given to ideas from abroad – notably from France, but from many other countries too. In *Woman's Own* this side of things was in the hands of Phillip Harben, then rising to the peak of his celebrity as a 'TV chef',[11] whose dynamic style did a great deal to create a sense of excitement about cookery in Britain. At first, though, even he was a little hesitant and apologetic about introducing foreign dishes. For example, he gave a recipe for 'Steak Stroganoff' (3 January 1957), but although noting that most versions of Boeuf Stroganoff involved the use of soured cream as a principal ingredient, he seemed to assume that was out of the question (possibly because elsewhere it was then often considered necessary to explain to the English reader that soured cream is not cream which has gone bad) and proceeded in his 'English reconstruction of the dish' to specify lengthy marinading in lemon juice, Worcester sauce and mustard. Even so, his version was a good deal closer to the Russian original than the slowly cooked casseroles of beef and tomatoes to which English magazines sometimes attach the name Stroganoff. A Harben recipe for 'Veal and Ham Rarebit' proved to be a version of saltimbocca alla Romana, but with the sage leaves replaced by cheese – 'anything sliceable' or even 'that convenient sliced cheese you can buy in packets' (7 March 1957). In the case of 'Ragoût of Sea Food' (23 October 1957), Harben refused to call it *bouillabaisse* on the grounds that any dish using the name without real Mediterranean ingredients was 'an impostor'. Other Harben articles that year presented Russian recipes (piroshki, borsch, 2 October), advocated the use of individual spices instead of commercial curry powder (but still used cooked rather than fresh meat for curry), and explained 'Cooking with Wine' – then still an exotic idea in England – including coq au vin (27 November).

Phillip Harben was definitely in the business of leading his readers, but took great care not to go at so brisk a pace that he got too far ahead. His colleague, Jane Beaton, continued to present the more familiar repertoire, and in 1957 was still showing a great deal of caution at using French vocabulary: her 'Cauliflower Cheese Puff' (21 March) was a soufflé, no more and no less. But by 1962 she too was reassuring her readers that 'sauce-making isn't really difficult', and explaining not only the use of roux but also how to make hollandaise (17 March 1962). There was more excitement in her writing too – 'Think of the wonderful things that can be baked in a pie' (3 February 1962).

The nearer we come to the present day, the more difficult does it become to discern any clear trends in the cookery columns. Since the 1960s there appear to have been fluctuations and even contradictory developments. Overall, the emerging pattern could be described as 'diminishing contrasts, increasing varieties'. This is more especially true in England. In France, as time went on, there was less and less to distinguish the cookery of *Femme Pratique* and *Elle*. Both showed the contrasting influences of the *nouvelle cuisine* and of convenience foods – the first more evident and the second less than in the equivalent British magazines – but both continued to expect their readers still to cook in a fairly traditional French way. The image of cookery as an enjoyable part of life at the weekend and on holiday in a more leisured society was also strong. As early as summer 1959, *Femme Pratique* was speaking of the joys of travel, discovering the local products or worming the recipe for a sauce out of the cook in some restaurant by means of a ruse or flattery. But overall, what is most striking is how relatively little the image of domestic cookery had changed in French magazines over the course of the twentieth century.

In England, the picture is more confusing, possibly in part because the mass circulation women's magazines experienced something of a crisis in the 1960s. Both *Woman's Own* and *Woman* lost over half a million readers between 1962 and 1968 (Cynthia White, 1970, Appendix IV). Though the circulations of these and other weeklies remained very large, they lost ground relatively to a a number of newer, more 'specialist' monthly women's magazines, the most successful of which in the 1970s were those centring primarily on cookery and the home (Ferguson, 1982: 33). Thus *Woman's Own* was probably experimenting, in its cookery columns as elsewhere, in an effort to rediscover the right mix to appeal to its audience. As it happened, *Good Housekeeping* also underwent a minor crisis in the 1960s, decided to concentrate more on cookery and the home, and doubled its sales during the 1970s. These market pressures have to be borne in mind when looking at the magazines' contents in the last two decades.

On the one hand, some articles had a distinctly more 'gastronomic' tone than had been common in England – a more pronounced tendency to legislate on what was right and wrong in matters of taste (laying down right and wrong in matters of *diet* became common rather earlier). Thus, in *Good Housekeeping*, January 1963, Phyllis Garbutt could write:

> Happy-go-lucky cooks who pride themselves on their inventiveness may have the time of their lives 'putting everything into the stockpot'. What emerges, though, as some sort of soup, rarely pleases the others who are asked to eat it. Soup-making is quite a precise art.

She went on to discuss the correct ingredients for *pot-au-feu* in a way very reminiscent of Charles Driessens, concluding that in its 'genuine' form the dish was only practical for a large family, and moving on to excluding cabbage from any kind of stock, distinguishing broths and consommés from purées, cream soups and bisques, before finally giving a number of 'correct' recipes for soups. The same issue gloatingly reported a 'gourmet's triumph', a food-tasting organised by Egon Ronay at which the panel had successfully discriminated between fresh and frozen foods of many kinds. But the article quoted an observer as imagining that the average housewife would not have been so successful, which 'bears out what we have found out at our own tasting panels'. *Good Housekeeping* had introduced home-freezers to its readers in February 1958, when they were very unfamiliar in Britain. In August 1963 (the same year, that is, as Phyllis Garbutt's article) several pages were devoted to an imaginary conversation with a reader on the subject of convenience foods, during which the magazine's anonymous spokesman gave her approval to among other things: boil-in-the-bag rice, rapid-cooking pasta, pizza in a bag complete with yeast, dehydrated Chinese and Indian dishes, bottled Melba sauce, garlic powder and garlic spread, and frozen food in general. That gives a reasonable impression of the state of the art in the food industry in 1963. By 1967, the convenience strain appeared to have the edge over the gastronomic element: a recipe for 'Canadian Fish Balls' reads in part: 'Make up a packet of instant potato and combine with a packet of parsley sauce-mix, made up with ¼ pint milk. Flake, and stir in, salmon from a 7¾ oz. can (drained). Season with salt, pepper, and mace.'

Regular contributions to *Woman's Own* well into the 1970s by the long-serving Jane Beaton and by Marguerite Patten ensured continuity of some time-honoured themes, like annual articles on marmalade making, and even on baking bread which enjoyed a resurgence in England at that time. Sometimes Marguerite Patten gave a whole week's menus superficially little changed in decades: 'a week of hearty meals that are economical, time-saving, tasty and guaranteed to give the family the warmth and nourishment they all need' (8 January 1972). The main feature of that week's menus was the use of one lot of provisions for two meals – for example, kippers one day, kipper paté the next – but more as an economical end-in-itself than as a necessary adaptation to leftovers as the by-product of the weekend joint. Nor did Miss Patten go in for 'doing something disgusting with a tin of soup' – everything was home made. *Woman's Own* did not, on the whole, go overboard for the deep-freeze, though it assumed the readers bought some ready-frozen foods.[12] On the other hand, an article in the issue of 31 March 1979 explained 'when it is convenient to cheat':

> Classic fish and shrimp mousse is delicious, but the recipe is a trifle long-winded. However, if you take a pack of frozen cod in shrimp sauce and liquidise it – you're half-way there! Alex Barker gives you a cheat's charter for quicker, posher nosh!

Other recipes in the article include mock zabaglione from instant custard mix, and beef in red wine pie from tinned red wine sauce. All the same, it is interesting that even when the concern is with speed and short cuts, the end is seen as 'posher nosh', and the means 'cheating'.

There was a distinctly more cosmopolitan air about *Woman's Own* by the 1970s. The annual article on pancakes for Shrove Tuesday was in 1979 entitled 'A Quick Flip Around the World' and included not just English pancakes but Breton galettes, crêpes Suzette, Russian blini, Chinese pancake rolls and American waffles. It was common for photographs of tables to have wine and glasses in the background – something rare in the 1960s and almost unheard of before then. Recipes by famous (male) chefs and restaurateurs such as Robert Carrier, long a regular feature of French magazines, became more common in *Woman's Own*. Occasionally there were articles on aspects of classic French cookery techniques – such as espagnole, velouté, and mayonnaise sauces, by Jane Beaton (11–18 March 1972). The general impression, however, is not of a movement towards French cookery as such, but at least towards a preponderance of 'made' or 'made-up' dishes, with a corresponding decline in fashion of the traditional English meat-and-veg. and pudding meal. The impression is confirmed by the readers' recipes featured in *Woman's Own* from time to time. In 1972 (15 January) prize-winning recipes from six readers included things like: 'Sardinian Spinach Special', pancakes with ham, cheese and spinach; 'Viking Veal', the veal spread with liverwurst [*sic*] and onion, wrapped around two spears of asparagus and rolled in bacon, then casseroled in a packet of mushroom soup; and 'Spicy Carrots', the carrots cooked with onions in stock with cornflour, but, despite the name, with no spices – only a little dried thyme. Whatever else they were, incidentally, these recipes were not 'ornamental' in Roland Barthes's sense – the elaboration, such as it was, was taking place in the actual cooking of the dish, not in the form of surface trimming.

Overall, there appears to be no clear trend or policy in the cookery columns of the English women's magazines. Start-from-scratch, back-to-the-farmhouse recipes alternate with others representing the most ruthless short cuts with convenience foods. Three things are clear, however. First, the sense of 'excitement' about food grew considerably in the magazines from the 1950s onwards, until they more closely resembled their French counterparts. Secondly, and linked to that, there is a more cosmopolitan feel to the magazines, and the food found in the cookery columns has become strikingly more diverse and adventurous than, say, it was in the 1930s. Convenience foods, so often seen as undermining cookery skills and traditions, have also played a vital part in committing housewives to be more adventurous and varied in their cooking. Thirdly, cookery writers appear no longer to be so consciously addressing housewives of a particular social class; the difference they bear most in mind seems to be that between those who go out to work and those who do not.

CONCLUSION: COOKING, WORK AND LEISURE

What is one to make of these diverse and even contradictory developments?

In the 1960s, when the 'embourgeoisement' thesis was much discussed among sociologists, it might have been tempting to interpret the evidence of the cookery columns as showing how housewives were coming to share a common 'middle-class' lifestyle. Part of the story would have been how the disparity between *haute cuisine* and *cuisine bourgeoise* in France – which had never lost touch with each other – had gradually narrowed. Another part would have been about how French models (along with some other foreign influences) had also gradually trickled down the English social hierarchy until the marked class divisions in cookery had been largely obliterated. Everyone would now have been seen as eating, more or less, in a 'middle-class' way.

That thesis would have chimed in with the editorial philosophy evolved by the successful women's magazines in the 1950s – a philosophy, as Ferguson (1982: 32) points out, based on beliefs about audience consensus and 'an identity of interest amongst cohesive, primarily home-based females'. Ferguson concedes that the 'embourgeoisement' thesis may have had a brief historical applicability with respect to the post-war women's magazine audience – in the period of rapidly rising material prosperity enjoyed in Britain (and also in France). But the general thesis was largely discredited by research such as that of Goldthorpe *et al.* (1968), which tended to show that in spite of their material prosperity, 'affluent workers' retained many traits quite different from middle-class lifestyles. And Ferguson points out that the attempt by the women's magazines to speak equally and simultaneously to all women was not a lasting success:

> the declining sales of magazines for 'all' women from the mid-1960s onwards offers further confirmation of the non-feasibility of class-convergence models. The patterns of class differentiation in Britain were segmenting and polarising, rather than cohering and homogenising, during the social ferment of the 1960s and the economic decline of the 1970s – if they had not before. (1982: 32)

All the same, even if the simple 'embourgeoisement' model was always too crude, the diffusion of middle-class tastes and attitudes is undoubtedly *one* element evident in the cookery columns of women's magazines. But it is entangled with some other issues much discussed by sociologists, notably the relationship of men and women, and the relationship of work and leisure in modern society. These issues come together in the question of whether domestic cookery, as part of caring for a home and family, should be regarded as constituting 'work' just as much as if it were paid employment outside the home, or whether it is a source of fulfilment, enjoyment, even excitement, and thus more a part of 'leisure'.

The answer is obviously that it is both. Housework, including domestic cooking, has never fitted easily into the work versus leisure schema. For the full-time housewife, and still more for the working wife who in practice usually still has to carry the main responsibility for feeding the family, cooking is certainly not simply part of 'free time'. It is necessary, unavoidable activity. Yet eating is generally a pleasurable activity, and cooking in anticipation of that pleasure *can* itself be pleasurable.

Much of this ambiguity is evident in the attitudes transmitted by the magazines. In all of them, the idea of cookery as an enjoyable, fulfilling part of family life in all social classes is now conveyed strongly. The theme of cookery as a burdensome, worrying chore is more prominent in the British magazines than the French, more prominent up to the 1950s than since and, not surprisingly, more prominent in the magazines whose readership extended further down the social scale.

It is easier to see why cooking should have seemed so much of an unavoidable, unenjoyable burden in the past, especially in the lower strata of society, than it is to explain why there should be differences between England and France. Witnesses before a British Government Committee in 1904 had an unflattering (and unsociological) explanation:

> If, as one witness emphatically stated, with the support more or less marked of others, a large proportion of British housewives are tainted with incurable laziness and distaste for the obligations of domestic life, they will naturally have recourse to such expedients in providing food for their families as involves them in least trouble. (Interdepartmental Committee on Physical Deterioration, 1904: 40)

This viewpoint is a valuable indication of the prevalent social attitude which made cooking a woman's obligatory duty, scarcely a source of pleasure. The Committee none the less saw fit to mention in its report the gross inadequacy of cooking facilities among the poor as a more direct cause of inadequate nourishment, and it could have mentioned the abundant evidence and consequences of shortage of money and time. Yet none of this accounts for the apparent differences with France. Part of an explanation may be that, traditionally, fewer French wives than English have gone out to work, so that the *average* reader of French magazines may simply have more time for cooking. Even allowing for that, however, French women do appear to devote more time to cooking than do equivalent English women.[13] This seems to be something with deeper historical roots. In several previous chapters we have encountered a less marked concern with economising in the kitchen among French cooks than among English, and a willingness to spend time may well be a simple extension of the same attitude – an attitude towards cookery rooted in a cultural inheritance running back into the age of court society. But it would be absurd to pretend that to all French women, all cooking is always and entirely a source of joy and pleasure. For them as much as the English it is also something they are compelled to do (see Herpin,

1980). Significantly, one of Giard's interviews with French housewives (1980) carries the title 'Basically, Cooking Worries Me'.

The idea that cooking is also enjoyable was always more familiar in the French magazines and to a lesser extent in an up-market British magazine like *Good Housekeeping*, burgeoning into everything implied in the phrase 'hostess cookery' – cooking, eating, entertaining and sociability as part of a leisured social life. Its spread in England and in the more popular magazines does not represent only the diffusion of upper-middle class attitudes, but also rising standards of living and the growth of leisure time among all ranks of the working population. It would be hazardous though, to jump to the conclusion that cooking is something that the housewife is any less compelled to do. An editorial in *Woman's Own* commented on the more abundant, varied and adventurous food making its appearance in the early 1960s:

> the kitchen has become the most important room in the house. This is the room which, more than any other, you love to keep shining and bright. A woman's place? Yes. For it is the heart and centre of the meaning of home. The place where, day after day, you make with your hands your precious gifts of love.

Amazingly unliberated though this may be by later standards, it points to compulsions on the domestic cook no less real for being unconscious and internalised. The same article also asserts that:

> To feed the hungry is a natural feminine instinct – an instict so fundamental, so deeply a part of being a woman, that we are hardly ever consciously aware of it. We certainly aren't while we're rushing around making pastry, scraping carrots, and peeling potatoes. It does explain, though, the quite disproportionate feeling of failure we all have when something goes wrong in the oven. (20 January 1962)[14]

In her pioneering book *The Sociology of Housework* (1974) Ann Oakley reported that among the housewives she studied, of all housework tasks cooking was seen as potentially the most enjoyable, challenging and creative. They would like to experiment, not always to cook the same old things. In practice, competing calls on their time – looking after children, cleaning, shopping, ironing, washing – and the sheer number of meals that had to be planned and provided, all combined to put the brakes on their enjoyment of cooking. Housewives often come to see themselves almost exclusively as suppliers of food to the rest of the family, not as consumers of it (see Sofer, Janis and Wishlader, 1964: 96). Oakley, concerned mainly to demonstrate that housework (including cooking) is *work*, is moved to criticise the women's magazines whose object, she argues,

> is not how to get the most nutritious meals prepared in the shortest possible time, but rather how to go beyond the usual range of meals with time-consuming inventiveness and culinary skill. The aim is not simple efficiency. Instead, it is an *elaboration* of the task, designed to subtract it from the category of 'work' and add it to the creative pleasure dimension. (1974: 58)

This, in my view, is an oversimplification. For one thing, as we have seen, there is considerable diversity in cookery writing in the magazines, and some of it has always been aimed at sheer speed and efficiency. More important, it is over simple to draw such a rigid and static polarity between work and leisure. For the housewife, whether or not she also goes out to work (and it is a rare household where the main responsibility for providing meals still does not fall on the female even if she is also a bread*winner*[15]), cooking shares with the rest of housework many of the characteristics of the world of paid work. It is something she is compelled to do, socially patterned by schedules and expectations. This is true of many other activities performed by both men and women in 'non-work' time. It is a mistake to imagine that there are only two strongly contrasted categories of activity: on the one hand 'work', socially highly constrained, and on the other hand 'leisure', meaning the class of mimetic or play activities – sports, arts, hobbies – in which we pursue the excitement and pleasure absent in work. There are many other kinds of activity in between. Many domestic activities – financial transactions, household maintenance, as well as housework – have to be performed whether one likes it or not and, as Elias and Dunning (1969) have pointed out, this category of 'private work and family management' tends to take up more time as the standard of living rises. Cooking does not belong exactly there. It represents catering for a biological need, fulfilment of which is pleasurable, and it can play its part in the pleasures of sociability. That does not mean that cooking can always be in itself enjoyable. Cooking, eating and drinking

> can all be, and usually are, routinised up to a point, but they can also be de-routinised from time to time in a more deliberate manner than is often the case. At the same time, they all have this in common with the mimetic class of activities: they can provide heightened enjoyment provided one is able to cater for them in a non-routine manner, such as eating out for a change. (Elias and Dunning, 1969: 57)

This provides a far better interpretation of the women's magazines since the Second World War. A period in which adequate leisure time is not the privilege of the few has not meant that cooking has been transformed into purely a hobby, a freely chosen activity; but it has meant that ways of de-routinising cooking and eating from time to time have appealed to many more. The magazines have not denied that cooking can be a burdensome routine, and they have paid attention to frozen food, microwave ovens, and other least effort, most efficient means of cooking. They have also, however, as is seen in the confusing diversity of their contents in recent decades informed their readers of a great many ways in which from time to time cooking and eating can be de-routinised for enhanced enjoyment.[16] They are not alone in this: in the next chapter we shall examine the related function performed – first for the minority, then for many more – by the gastronomes and restaurant guides.

10

Of Gastronomes and Guides

Gastronomes and their writings have been frequently mentioned in earlier chapters. Now it is time to look at them a little more closely and to examine the part they have played in shaping taste in England and France.

Precursors of the gastronome can be seen in action in the 'battle of the books', or battle of prefaces to cookery books, in the eighteenth century. But the gastronome as a distinct and recognisable figure, and gastronomic writing as a distinct genre, emerged after the French Revolution. From then onwards there has been a continuous line of development linking Grimod de la Reynière's *Almanach des Gourmands* (1803–12) to the restaurant guides of today. Gastronomy has generally been seen as the preserve of an élite, laying down canons of 'correct' taste for those who were wealthy enough to meet them. I shall argue that gastronomes have, whether they intended to do so or not, also performed a democratising function in the shaping of taste. Gastronomic writings, in common with all manners books, perform this function because the moment they are printed they disseminate knowledge of élite standards beyond the élite – and, of course, authors and publishers seek the financial rewards of sales outside the most exclusive circles. Both functions – of articulating élite standards and of democratising taste – always co-exist in gastronomy, though the balance between the two has tilted gradually during the last two centuries.

The word 'gastronomy', learnedly derived from Greek, seems to have been invented by Joseph Berchoux in 1801, who used it as the title of a poem. The term was rapidly adopted both in France and England to designate 'the art and science of delicate eating'. 'Gastronome' was a back-formation from 'gastronomy' – 'gastronomer' and 'gastronomist' were also sometimes used in English in the nineteenth century – to designate 'a judge of good eating'. The connotations of 'gastronome' partly overlap with those of the older words 'epicure' and 'gourmand', and the newer one 'gourmet'. Both 'epicure' and 'gourmand' had formerly had pejorative meanings close to 'glutton' – that is, they were applied to people who ate greedily and to excess. 'Epicure' had by the beginning of the nineteenth century, particularly in English, acquired a more favourable sense of 'one who cultivates a refined taste for the pleasures of the table; one who is choice and dainty in eating and drinking'. In France, the word *gourmand* had acquired the same favourable sense and it was in that sense that Grimod used it in the title of the *Almanach des Gourmands*. The *Oxford English Dictionary* also records 'gourmand' as acquiring that favourable sense in English in the early nineteenth century, although to the present day English writers commonly make a distinction between a 'gourmand' with the pejorative sense of glutton, and 'gourmet' in the favourable sense of a person with a refined palate. The word 'gastronome' differs from all these other words in one key respect: a gastronome is generally understood to be a person who not only cultivates his own 'refined taste for the pleasures of the table' but also, by *writing* about it, helps to cultivate other people's too. The gastronome is more than a gourmet – he is also a theorist and propagandist about culinary taste.[1]

One final distinction: Jean Conil (1962) argued that there was a difference between a gastronome and an epicure – he suggested that gastronomes were conservative, defending old standards, while epicures were adventurous innovators. Conil's usage, almost echoing Karl Mannheim's distinction between 'ideology' and 'utopia', was idiosyncratic and not adopted by anyone else. Nevertheless, it usefully points to the co-existence of the élite-defining and democratising functions in the work of those who are commonly called gastronomes.

THE FOUNDING FATHERS: GRIMOD AND BRILLAT-SAVARIN

Between them, two writers effectively founded the whole genre of the gastronomic essay. They were Alexandre-Balthazar-Laurent Grimod de la Reynière (1758–1838), and Jean-Anthelme Brillat-Savarin (1755–1826). Virtually everything of the sort written since quotes or harks back to these two authors one way or another.

Grimod de la Reynière was the son of a rich farmer-general, and already noted before the Revolution for his eccentric hospitality – such as the black-edged invitations to what purported to be his own funeral supper. In reduced circumstances after the Revolution, his genius for publicity led him to found the Jury des Dégustateurs, whose members met weekly at the Rocher de Cancale restaurant (later the similar Société des Mercredis met at Legaque's establishment) to pass judgement on the dishes before them. The ingenuity of the scheme lay in its revealing how eager were restaurateurs and food merchants of all kinds to supply their products for public evaluation by the Jury. The *Almanach des gourmands*, published annually (except in 1809 and 1811) from 1803 to 1812, was a development of the same idea. Grimod apparently expected to be adequately and regularly rewarded for the praise he bestowed on restaurants and food shops. It was not until more than a hundred years later that the leading restaurant guides in France and England managed to establish a reputation for impartial and 'objective' evaluations uninfluenced by backhanders from the evaluated.

That is not to detract from Grimod's achievement as the most important of the founding fathers of literate gastronomy – not only in the *Almanach des gourmands*, but in the *Manuel des amphitryons* (1808) and the monthly *Journal des gourmands et des belles* (1806–08). The first edition of the *Almanach* contained a comprehensive 'Calendrier nutritif' which discussed the whole range of foodstuffs in season month by month. There followed an 'Itinéraire nutritif, ou promenade d'un gourmand dans divers quartiers de Paris', which was to be the centrepiece of successive issues of the *Almanach*. It came to cover not only restaurants and cafés but *rôtisseurs* and *traiteurs*, grocers, greengrocers and florists, butchers and *tripières* – food suppliers of every kind in Paris. The *Almanach* also contained articles on varied topics of gastronomic interest: for example, the issue of 1806 holds forth (under the title 'Turtle Soups') on English cookery in general, and, in an equally superior tone, on 'Rural Hospitality'; and the 1807 issue contains a sardonic article on 'Diners about Town', full of informative social commentary. Anecdotes were also a staple ingredient: Grimod was already retailing in the *Almanach* the exploits of the Jury Dégustateur. A final ingredient of the *Almanach*, and still more of the *Manuel des amphitryons*, was authoritative advice on matters of gastronomic *savoir-faire* – the sequence and composition of courses, construction of menus, and so forth.

Unlike Grimod's writings, which have been little reprinted and thus remained rather inaccessible,[2] *La Physiologie du goût* (1826) by Brillat-Savarin has been in print ever since its first publication, and is much the most famous of all gastronomic essays. Brillat-Savarin was a lawyer from Belley in the French Alps, and a bachelor who spent most of his life in Paris eating at the best tables. His tastes were shaped by both rural and metropolitan traditions of eating, and further diversified by a brief period as an émigré which took him as far as the USA and shooting wild turkeys in New England. His book was many years in preparation and published in the last few weeks of his life. It opens with a series of aphorisms, the most quoted of which is 'Tell me what you eat: I will tell you what you are.' These are followed by the 148 'Gastronomic Meditations' in 30 chapters which form the bulk of the book. Brillat-Savarin sets out the physiological knowledge of the day, on the sense of taste, appetite, and the nutritional qualities of foodstuffs, but in a light and witty way enlivened by many anecdotes (he is the original source for many such stories as that of Bertrand and the 50 hams mentioned in an earlier chapter) and concluding with a highly speculative 'Philosophical History of Cooking' from the origins of mankind to his own day.

In France there has been a continuous line of successors to Grimod and Brillat-Savarin. To mention only some of the better-known, there were

Eugène Briffault who published *Paris à table* in 1846; Charles Monselet who revived the title *Almanach des gourmands* from 1860 to 1864; Baron Brisse, who could claim to have written the first newspaper cookery column and published *Le Calendrier gastronomique pour l'année 1867: les 365 menus de Baron Brisse*[3]; Alexandre Dumas *père*, who is said to have regarded his posthumous *Grand dictionnaire de cuisine* (1873) as the most important of his extremely numerous literary productions; and Châtillon-Plessis of the *Art culinaire* circle who wrote *La Vie à table à la fin du 19e siècle* (1894). Some of these were nearer to recipe books than the books of the twin founding fathers had been, but all were clearly in the same tradition. The tradition was vigorously renewed after the First World War by Curnonsky and his associates, and is most notably represented at the present day by Henri Gault and Christian Millau with their *Guide gourmand de la France* (1970) and annual *Guides de la France*.

In England, gastronomic writing has mainly consisted of close imitations of French models. It started quite early. An anonymous author writing from Bath published in 1814 *The School for Good Living*, a humorous but learned history of cooking and cookery books since antiquity, which appears to have owed some inspiration to Grimod though his name is not mentioned. The following year there appeared *The Epicure's Almanack*, very closely indeed modelled on the *Almanach des gourmands* but, obviously, surveying the eating places and food suppliers of London rather than Paris. Both books antedated Brillat-Savarin by more than a decade, and the pseudonymous Launcelot Sturgeon's *Essays, Moral, Philosophical and Stomachical on the Important Science of Good-Living* (1822) shows indebtedness to Grimod while developing some of Brillat-Savarin's themes *avant la lettre*. Drummond and Wilbraham (1939: 397) considered that the nearest approach to Brillat-Savarin's classic produced in England was Dr William Kitchiner's *Apicius Redivivus, or, The Cook's Oracle* (1817), which was sub-titled 'Actual Experiments Instituted in the Kitchen of a Physician' and in some sense shared the Frenchman's subsequent concern to apply the physiological knowledge of the day to cookery. But *The Cook's Oracle* (as subsequent editions were entitled) was in fact mainly a cookery book, not a gastronomic essay, even if that boundary line can sometimes be difficult to draw precisely.

Later English gastronomes, such as Abraham Hayward (*The Art of Dining*, 1852), William Jerrold (*The Epicure's Yearbook*, 1868), Eneas Sweetland Dallas (*Kettner's Book of the Table*, 1877), and Dr Gustave Strauss (*Philosophy in the Kitchen*, 1885) were mainly French-orientated. That is, they took their standards from France, and the influence of Grimod and Brillat-Savarin is very evident in their writing, although they added commentary on English food, cookery and eating places. Later still, this was all the more evident in the writings of the most prolific gastronomic writer in twentieth-century England, André Louis Simon, who was himself a Frenchman though he lived most of his life in Britain. It is arguable that the only really original English gastronome was Thomas Walker (1784–1836), who appropriately wrote a weekly paper called *The Original* in 1835. Since Walker anticipated several later trends in taste, we shall examine his views in a moment. His writings were given wider currency through Hayward's book, which grew out of review essays in the *Quarterly Review* in 1835 and 1836; Hayward not only retailed the French anecdotal repertoire, but is also the principal source for many distinctively English gastronomic chestnuts, such as accounts of the lives of Ude and Francatelli, of Parliamentary whitebait dinners at Greenwich and Blackwall, of feasting in the City of London, and reflections on the gastronomic implications of London gentlemen's clubs. But, apart from Walker and until the novel institution represented by the *Good Food Guide* since the 1950s, England produced little in the way of an autonomous gastronomic tradition with a character of its own.

GASTRONOMY AS A LITERARY GENRE

Gastronomic literature as developed mainly in France and much copied in England possesses certain characteristic themes. One frequent component is the disquisition on what constitutes 'correct' practice at the time on such questions as the composition of menus, sequences of courses, and techniques of service; the archetype of this is Grimod's *Manuel des amphitryons*, though eighteenth-century cookery books usually had a section on such matters (*Les Dons de Comus* was chiefly concerned with them), and the manuals on carving and the ceremonial of the table date from the Middle Ages.

A second component is dietetic, setting out what foods and what forms of cookery are good for one according to the prevailing knowledge of the day. This was, as we have noted, a theme in Brillat-Savarin, and it has been especially prominent in the work of the not inconsiderable number of medical men – such Edouard de Pomiane and Alfred Gottschalk – who have written on food and gastronomy. Even so thoroughly unhealthy a cookery book as Ali-Bab's *Gastronomie pratique* contained a section – an afterthought might be more accurate – on the treatment of obesity.

A third component, and one probably more central to the gastronomic literary tradition, is a brew of history, myth, and history serving as myth. The more solid kernel of this can be found in frequent potted biographies of historically famous eaters and, from the nineteenth century, cooks. Carême outstrips all others among the cooks. Only Vatel can be mentioned more often, but the story of his suicide (contained in only a few sentences of Mme de Sévigné) is used mythically to express the devotion of the cooking profession to their art. Typical of other frequently retailed stories which have an even less secure historical basis is that of the Prince de Condé, Bertrand and his 50 hams, serving much the same mythical function. Closely similar are the stories, most of them again lacking any solid foundation in history, about the origins of particular dishes, techniques, and their names. Favourites include mayonnaise (said by some to have been 'invented' by the Duc de Richelieu's cook and named in honour of his military exploits at Mahon – but there are alternative speculations), and chaudfroid sauce. A typical story to explain the latter name tells how a famous host and minister of the crown in eighteenth-century France was called away to see the king just as dinner was served, and how when he and his guests finally sat down to eat on his return hours later, the sauce was found to be as good cold as hot. That story includes two traits common in gastronomic mythology: the involvement of the famous personage, and the element of accident. The supposed involvement of the great, either as passive witnesses of or active collaborators in the discoveries of cooks well expresses the balance of power between cooks and their patrons or publics, which in the first great period of gastronomic writing in the nineteenth century was gradually shifting in the cooks' favour, though it was still unequal. The role of accident in gastronomic mythology is also interesting: just as mankind's conquest of fire, a process which almost certainly spread over hundreds of millennia, is represented in the mythologies of many cultures as a sudden event caused by the exploit of a Promethean hero, so advances in cookery are usually represented in gastronomic literature as unique individual inspirations rather than as gradual processes (see Goudsblom, 1984).

A fourth and final component of gastronomic literature is the nostalgic evocation of memorable meals. Notable menus, lovingly amplified by discussions of why such and such a dish was so remarkable, are often a staple ingredient of gastronomic writing. This is one of several respects in which the literature of gastronomy resembles that of cricket: meals in place of memorable matches, cooks and gourmets of the past in place of the batsmen and bowlers of a bygone age – 'we shall not see their like again' – and so on.

Of course, not everything which can be counted as gastronomic literature contains all of these four basic components, and the relative prominence of each varies a good deal. Within the genre, some writing is mainly historical in slant, some mainly concerned to define what is correct and in good taste, some more practically concerned to provide a critical assessment of the eating-places of the day. Moreover, there is an ill-defined margin at which the gastronomic essay gradually shades into the cookery book. The more learned sort of cookery book, such as those of Dumas and Ali-Bab, or more recently of Elizabeth David or Jane Grigson might be considered gastronomic literature as much as cookery books.[4] In either case, they seem intended to be read as literature. Significantly, the charge (if it is a charge) has been levelled both at the gastronomic essay and the 'learned' cookery book that they have an affinity with pornography. Certainly, both gastronomy and pornography dwell on the pleasures of the flesh, and in gastronomic literature as in pornography there is vicarious enjoyment to be had. In gastronomy, however, vicarious enjoyment is more definitely intended to be a prelude to, not a substitute for, direct and actual enjoyment.

Whatever the problems of defining its boundaries, the core characteristics of gastronomy as a literary genre since the early nineteenth century are easily recognisable. So what rôle has it played in the shaping of culinary taste, and in society more widely?

THE SOCIAL ROLE OF THE GASTRONOME

The rise to prominence of gastronomes and gastronomic writing was closely entangled with the emergence of restaurants after the Revolution. Grimod and his imitators played a significant part in the growth of a public for the burgeoning trade of restaurateur. Who most needed whom is, however, debatable. The rise of the restaurant had begun before 1789, and it had become part of the fashionable scene in Paris during the decade before Grimod published the first issue of the *Almanach*. A public already existed; it was not created by the gastronomes. Nevertheless, when the number of participants – in this case both restaurateurs and diners – is large and continually growing, it is arguable that an informed and coherent public opinion generally necessitates more open and formal media of communication to supplement informal networks of gossip.[5] Inevitably this brings about a differentiation within the dining public between the relatively more powerful leaders of opinion who write the gastronomic criticism and the relatively less powerful who merely read it.

The relationship between gastronomes and restaurateurs, as seen by the gastronomes, is nicely encapsulated in Grimod's story of the 'discovery' of the braised turkey (1804: 265). He tells how, with fellow members of the Société des Mercredis he conceived the idea that turkey could and should be braised. The restaurateur Legaque was horrified at the suggestion – turkeys could only properly be cooked by roasting – but he obeyed their instructions, and the result was, according to Grimod (needless to say) delightful. This story is typical of many in which gastronomes are represented (usually by themselves) as the innovating force inspiring the plodding cook. Aron (1973: 140) interprets this story as showing the power of the consumer over the restaurateur in the post-Revolutionary era, but that is a slightly oversimplified view. Over-personalised accounts of culinary innovations, of which the story of the braised turkey is only one of many, tend to understate the importance of the continuous pressure of competition among restaurateurs themselves: the whims of passing gastronomes were not the only, nor the main, source of pressure on cooks to innovate and refine their cuisine.

Nevertheless, whatever influence gastronomes had in shaping taste was exerted in a consistent direction – towards discrimination, choice and delicacy in matters of eating, which are the kernel of the gastronomic message. The social role of the gastronome is essentially 'urban' in character because it is at the opposite pole from the spirit of traditional rural self-sufficiency, eating the product of one's own land and taking it as it comes. More self-evidently, the gastronomic spirit is rare among those whose poverty allows them little choice. There must be food in abundance and variety, and of course variety and subtlety in cookery to permit gastronomes to select some things and reject others. Yet a wealthy stratum and town life are probably not sufficient conditions for the emergence of the gastronome and gastronomy: there is little sign of them in, for instance, Amsterdam at the height of its wealth in the seventeenth and eighteenth centuries. The original locus of refinement in eating, as we have argued, appears to have been court-society. Why then did the gastronome as a distinct figure appear in France *after* the Revolution? Possibly a comparison with dandyism is revealing. A dandy, 'one who studies above everything to dress elegantly and fashionably; a beau, fop, "exquisite"' (*Oxford English Dictionary*), is a figure more native to England than is the gastronome, and the word came into vogue about 1813–19 for the 'swells' of the Regency period. The dandy is to matters of dress what the gastronome is to matters of eating. In his biography of Benjamin Disraeli, Robert Blake remarks of dandyism:

> It seems to be a characteristic of an era of social flux, when aristocracy is tottering or uncertain, but when radicalism has not yet replaced it with a new set of values. It flourishes in a period when manners are no longer rigidly fixed, but have not yet degenerated into mere anarchy, so that there is still a convention to rebel against, still a world to be shocked and amused by extravagance and eccentricity. The dandy must have a framework within which to operate. The social grades must still exist, but it must be easy for those with sufficient courage, carelessness or sheer brazen determination to climb from one to another. (1966: 78)

This hypothesis seems to fit not only the 1830s and 1890s in England when, as Blake observes, dandyism was prevalent there, but also the first decades of the century in France, when the gastronomes first appeared. The provocative, somewhat exhibitionist lifestyle of Grimod and his circle in particular was strikingly parallel to dandyism, mainly differing in its use of food rather than dress as a means of display.

Of course it was not necessary that the precise social conditions which favoured the emergence of the gastronome endure for gastronomy as a literary genre to survive. Once the tradition had been created, it could persist, while changing its emphases and functions according to changing circumstances.

At first, what we have called the élite-defining function is more evident than the democratising one. It is apparent in the display of expertise. The gastronomes encouraged talk about food; without talk, critical appreciation of the cooks' achievements would be impossible, and only critical appreciation would give the cooks an incentive to compete with each other for the patronage of an informed public. Launcelot Sturgeon reports already in 1822 that

It formerly was considered well-bred to affect a certain indifference for the fare before you; but fashion has acquired more candour, and there is now no road to the reputation of a man of *ton*, so sure as that of descanting learnedly on the composition of every dish. If you have ever been in France . . . it affords you a famous opportunity to praise French cookery. (1822: 41–2)

The fashion no doubt took a long time to become universal: Harold Macmillan recalled[6] that in the British upper middle-class circles in which he grew up before the First World War it was still considered bad form to talk about food. Curnonsky (1958: 241–2), while also noting that it was once not the thing to talk about what one ate, remarks that *after* the First World War things had progressed to the point that in France it was acceptable even to discuss how much it had cost.

Another facet of the cult of gastronomic expertise, in which the function of élite-demarcation is especially noticeable, is seen in the propensity of gastronomes to lay down elaborate rules of good taste. For example Châtillon-Plessis (1894: 143–7), in discussing the correct sequence of courses, lays it down that the dinner proper ends with vegetable dishes (*entremets de légumes* – then as now often served separately in France), that cheese follows as *entremets de transition* between dinner and dessert, to be followed by dessert proper, which consists of sweets, pastries, confectionery, ices and fruit. He then even decrees the order in which these various items of dessert should be eaten, though apparently does not expect his rules to be widely followed; he concludes by saying that in the best houses there are at any rate separate menus for the dinner and for the dessert.[7] Legislation in a different key is contained in André Simon's assertion that 'the only part of the pig which is introduced into polite gastronomic society is the Ham' (1929: 102). That would be news to generations of peasants in both France and England, who knew that almost the only inedible part of a pig is the squeak (see Grigson, 1970). No doubt the association of pigs with peasants, and charcuterie with the urban poor of France, is by no means unconnected with gastronomic disdain of pork. Certainly an assertion like Simon's implies not merely discrimination – selection and rejection – but waste and social stratification among foodstuffs.

Rule-making at its seemingly most eccentric and absurd occurred in some of the many gastronomic dining clubs which proliferated in line of succesion from the Société des Mercredis and had titles such as Académie des Gastronomes, Compagnons de Cocagne, Académie des Psychologues de Goût. Writing in *Grandgousier*, September 1936, Alfred Gottschalk mocked the rules of one such society, sent to him by Austin de Croze, which both of them considered absurd. Among the rules to which they most objected were the following:

Coffee must be served *boiling* in hot cups. Gastronomes of the XXX society do not eat *hors d'oeuvres*; they accept soups only very exceptionally.

(To this, Gottschalk comments 'No one is forcing them to'!)

Meals will be served silently and quickly.

(Comment: 'Do these gentlemen regard the meal as a *corvée*?')

Foie gras must always be served at the beginning of the meal.

(Comment: 'Hot, it can belong with the entrées; or, *en croute*, after the roast'.)

Such rule-making activity ought not to be seen only as a display of the expertise of an in-group. Like the refined manners and equally absurd-seeming ceremonials of court-society, it can also be understood as part of a civilising process. Curnonsky hinted at this in a toast he quotes himself as having drunk with friends in 1903 to the French and the Chinese, the two nations who had 'invented both polished manners and a cuisine'. Gastronomes, he said, 'united these two superior forms of civilisation': 'Gourmets are, in fact, by definition nice people, good humoured and good company; gastronomy imposes the good manners without which a copious meal would risk degenerating into a dissolute orgy' (1958: 241). Here, then, we have a direct connection between what in chapter 2 we spoke of as 'the civilising of appetite' – in which gastronomes played a significant part – and the more general process of refinement of taste and manners.

On the other hand, by the inter-war years, some voices at least were being raised against rigid rule-making – as Gottschalk's sceptical interjections above illustrate. In the same article Gottschalk declared that:

> We have repeatedly protested against the ultimatum-like ukases poured out by certain gastronomic societies claiming to rule over the art of eating. In our opinion, gastronomy is a land of freedom, where everyone is free to do what he likes, on the one condition that he does not bother his neighbours.

Gottschalk's apparent assertion that 'anything goes' should not however be taken absolutely literally. It expresses a reaction against overly rigid detailed rules and excessive formality, which may be a minor facet of a more general 'informalisation process' (Wouters, 1977) in a socially relatively more equal society. This relaxation is best understood as marking not the abandonment of rules of taste and good behaviour, but the increasing expectation that people will self-regulate their own conduct without need for authoritarian and detailed decrees.[8] It can also be seen as part of a general movement towards a pattern of 'diminishing contrasts, increasing varieties', as we shall discuss in the concluding chapter.

Gastronomes and gastronomy had, in any case, also played a democratising role from the earliest stages. It has to be remembered that as a distinct figure, the gastronome appeared on the scene in the course of a general widening of the market for sophisticated cooking. When appearing to be at their most élitist, effete and exclusive, gastronomes and gastronomy were also helping to widen the circle for good eating. In a more egalitarian period, their activities in making known the pleasures of the table, and encouraging more cooks and diners to share their own interest in them, have become more evident; and in the process the gastronomic tradition has itself evolved.

GASTRONOMY AND DEMOCRATISATION

In France, the activities of Curnonsky and his circle marked an important development in the gastronomic tradition. Curnonsky ('Why-not-ski') was the pseudonym of Maurice-Edmond Sailland (1872–1956), who described himself as the 'Prince of Gastronomes' and in 1928 founded the Académie des Gastronomes modelled on the Académie Française, with forty seats, each named after one of the famous gastronomes of the past. He was thus at first glance an unlikely figure to play an important part in the democratising of fine food. But Curnonsky's princely title had in fact been conferred by democratic means – in a popular referendum organised in 1927 by the magazine *Le Bon Gîte et la bonne table* (Arbellot, 1965: 75). (The runner-up in the poll was Maurice des Ombiaux, and also-rans included Ali-Bab and Edouard de Pomiane.) Moreover, Curnonsky himself was not a Parisian but an Angevin, who speaks of having learned the pleasures of the table from his old family cook, whose cooking owed nothing to schools or books and everything to 20 generations of her peasant ancestors (1958: 177–8).

The significance of Curnonsky and his friends was that they seized the opportunity of linking gastronomy and tourism, and thus initiated a great interest in and vogue for French regional cookery. Curnonsky himself tells the story with characteristically moderate modesty:

> After the 1914–18 war, Louis Forest, Austin de Croze, Marcel Rouff, Maurice des Ombiaux and myself created the gastronomic press and, particularly in *Comoedia*, consecrated the holy alliance between tourism and gastronomy. This pioneering work benefited from two novelties: the 'democratised' motor-car and the taste for good fare which, after some years of anguish and privation, developed in France from 1919 onwards. . . . The motor-car allowed the French to discover the cuisine of each province, and created the breed of what I have called 'gastro-nomads'. (1958: 53–4)

The alliance of tourism and gastronomy was particularly to the advantage of tyre companies like Michelin and Kléber-Colombes, who began to publish their celebrated guides to the restaurants and hotels of France. Curnonsky and his friends had links with them, but also wrote their own guides. In the 1920s, with Marcel Rouff, Curnonsky planned a 32-volume series on the provinces of France entitled *La France gastronomique*. Of these, 28 were complete when Rouff died, so in 1933 Curnonsky produced with de Croze a one-volume synopsis, *Le Trésor gastronomique de France*. A by-product of their activities was the richest crop of gastronomic anecdotes since the days of Grimod and Brillat-Savarin. A typical example was the story of the perfect cassoulet they ate at Castelnaudary. The point of the tale was that good cooking takes time. Curnonsky's friends had to wait from noon one day till noon the next to eat the cassoulet prepared by Mme Adolphine (semi-retired and rather selective about whom she chose to feed). 'A cassoulet for this evening!', she greeted them. 'Where do you think you are? In Paris, where all the dishes are always ready?' (Curnonsky, 1958: 196–7). Cassoulet – a dish of beans, pork, sausages, and other meats to hand – is an archetypical peasant dish of a sort which certainly would not have appealed to fashionable Parisian diners a generation earlier.

Curnonsky advocated more simplicity and less pompous show in restaurant cooking. The majority of diners, he wrote, no longer cared whether the dish bore the name of a famous diplomat or other celebrity: they were less impressed by the 'suprêmes', 'délices', 'financières', 'mousselines', and 'all the thingummys à la royale, à l'impératrice, or à la princesse'.

> They ask simply that things taste of what they are, that a fricassée is called a fricassée, a matelote a matelote, a roast chicken a roast chicken, that nothing is substituted for butter, and that they do not have inflicted on them those abominable 'fonds de sauce' and those standardised 'ratatouilles' with which the cosmopolitan palaces and caravanserais stuff luckless tourists from Singapore to San Francisco, and from Cairo to Buenos Aires and Pernambuco. (1958: 274)

Curnonsky's advocacy of simplicity and his emphasis on the quality of raw materials points the way towards his successors Gault and Millau, who a generation later so effectively championed the *nouvelle cuisine*.[9]

In England, as we have remarked, few really original gastronomes appeared, though there were many imitators of the French. The exception was Thomas Walker, whose views make him a pioneer of simplicity, informality and even of the 'democratisation' of eating long before its time. Care must be taken with a word like 'democratisation'. Anyone who could speak, as Walker did, of the 'vulgar rich' as 'the very lowest class worthy of invitation' (quoted in chapter 8 above) was not an absolute democrat. Relatively speaking, however, Walker's conception of good taste was a striking anticipation of later trends.

> The simple style I propose is as different from the ornamental and cumbrous one now in vogue, as the present cropped, unpowdered, trousered mode of dress is from that of a gentleman's dress in the middle of the last century, when bags, swords, buckles and gold lace were universally in use, and I may be thought as much out of the way in my notions by some, as anyone would have been in the year 1750 who should have advocated the dress of 1835. But simplicity and convenience have triumphed in our dress, and I have no doubt they will equally do so in time in our dinners. (1835: 269)

Walker opposed all ornamentation and superfluity. He favoured small dinner parties, with uncluttered tables so that guests could help themselves to what they wanted. At small dinners, 'attendants are a restraint upon conversation' and upon one's ease in general' (1835: 272). Above all he was against wasteful excess, which still in Victorian England often represented a vestige of the potlatch element in entertaining.

In the first place, it is necessary not to be afraid of not having enough, and so to go into the opposite extreme, and have a great deal too much, as is almost invariably the practice. It is also necessary not to be afraid of the table looking bare, and so to overcrowd it with dishes not wanted, or before they are wanted, whereby they become cold and sodden. 'Enough is as good as a feast', is a sound maxim, as well in providing as in eating. The advantages of having only enough are these: it saves expense, trouble and attendance; it removes temptation, and induces contentment, and it affords the best chance of having a well-dressed dinner, by concentrating the attention of the cook. The having too much, and setting dishes on the table merely for appearance, are practices arising out of prejudices which, if once broken through, would be looked upon as the height of vulgarity. (1835: 272)

As to the food itself, Walker favoured simple English-style cookery for his regular meals, but 'It must be confessed that a French dinner, when well-dressed, is extremely attractive, and, from the lightness felt after a great variety of dishes it cannot be unwholesome' (1835: 286). One of the greatest luxuries, he said, was to have plenty of carefully cooked vegetables, and urged more attention be given them in England. And he urged his readers not to feel above dealing themselves directly with tradesmen (1835: 273) – that was the way to obtain the best quality raw materials, and here Walker anticipated by nearly a century and a half one of the themes of the *nouveaux cuisiniers*.

A century after Walker, the foundation of the Wine and Food Society by André L. Simon in October 1933 marked another interesting development on the English gastronomic scene. The Society has always been francophilic, and might at first glance have appeared to be merely trotting tamely in the footsteps of Curnonsky: its first activities were dinners in London devoted to the wines and dishes of specific regions of France. Yet as an organisation the Society marked an interesting transition between the small, exclusive gastronomic dining clubs of the past and the mass-readership campaigning publications like the *Good Food Guide*. Although the Society's membership appears to have been decidedly upper- and upper-middle class, it grew to be very large, with chapters in many parts of Britain, the Commonwealth and the USA. The members were held together through the medium of a quarterly journal, *Wine and Food*, the contents of which were a lively mixture of gastronomic interest – articles on the history and literature of wine and food, book reviews, accounts of notable meals past and present, critical assessment of hotels and restaurants, reports from gastronomic explorers in the unknown regions of Britain and Europe. The Society outwardly appeared little like a vehicle for 'democratisation' in matters of food. Indeed, one at least of its meetings in the 1930s was picketed by unemployed workers protesting at the luxury, waste and indulgence it represented (*Wine and Food*, 20, Spring 1939). And in the *Evening Standard*, 13 September 1935, Osbert Sitwell wrote an article entitled 'Food Snobs', a thinly disguised attack on the Society – objecting, among other things, to what he saw as the pretentiousness of talking about food at all.

Nevertheless, if he was no more a 'democrat' in any absolute sense than Walker had been, Simon was a great proselytiser in the cause of the appreciation of good food. The objectives of the Society were, he wrote,

> to bring together and assist all who, believing that a right understanding and appreciation of good food and wine are an essential part of personal contentment and health, are anxious to see a greater number of people, in England, take a more intelligent interest in what they eat and drink.

The intention was, to use once more the term employed in chapter 9, to assist people in 'de-routinising' their experience of cooking and eating. Simon continued:

> The first and foremost object of the Society is to raise the standard of cooking in the country, as a means to better health and greater contentment; as a means also to a greater number of visitors spending their holidays in England than will ever be tempted to do so so long as the present deplorable state of the majority of country inns exists. (*Wine and Food*, 1, Spring 1934)

Such trenchant views soon excited hostility from the hotel tràde. A comprehensive paper on 'The Present State of Gastronomy in England, with Some Suggestions for its Amendment' presented at a meeting of the Society surveyed the scene in some detail, spoke of 'a pretentious dullness' as the chief characteristic of food in English hotels and restaurants, and finally blamed the apathy and indifference of English diners for the indifference and laziness of its cooks. The paper provoked what can only be called a threatening letter from Sir Henry Dixon Kimber on behalf of the Hotels and Restaurants Association of Great Britain: he threatened to withdraw support from the Society if this sort of thing continued (both the paper and the letter were printed in *Wine and Food*, 1, Winter 1934). While this did not gag the Society completely, it did perhaps make it wary of indulging in blanket condemnation; and, pursuing a transparent strategy of co-option, it invited Kimber to address its Annual General Meeting the following year. His speech (in *Wine and Food*, Winter 1935) is interesting; he accused the critics of English catering of generalising too carelessly, but then in a way virtually conceded the case in the following argument:

> I think it is a mere waste of time to attempt to compare British cookery with French. The French people are, by nature, as well as by training, for the most part *instinctively* cooks, in the true sense of the word. They are, in general, natural artists in the selection and preparation of foods. The British, as a race, are not, though there are many individual exceptions. But don't forget – different nationalities have different tastes, and employ different methods. As silly is it to abuse the English for not cooking like the French, as it would be to abuse the French for not cooking like the English.

One needs no further reminder that racism was in the air of European politics in the 1930s.

The ability of gastronomy to express the spirit of the times was also evident later, in the very different atmosphere of the war and post-war years. Then, the democratic visions of a new and better world were expressed in such articles as Phillip Harben's on 'Gastronomy and Democracy' (*Wine and Food*, 41, Spring 1944), written in reaction to the United Nations Hot Springs Conference on the Food Requirements of the Nations, which laid down that all industrial workers should have the opportunity of obtaining one-third of their total necessary daily categories at a midday meal. Before the war, said Harben, too many people in Britain had lived on a diet principally made up of fish and chips, white bread, margarine (pre-war margarine contained no vitamins), jam and cheap cakes. Even if plentiful, such a diet was not healthy, which was why rickets, scurvy and ill-health generally were so prevalent. Some classes were confined to such a diet because they could only afford the kind of food which did no more than relieve the sensation of hunger. But others, said Harben, chose shoddy foodstuffs because they had come to like them. How, then, in the post-war world, were people to be persuaded to eat sensibly?

> By giving them lectures on dietetics? I don't think so. I think the solution lies in a very different direction. I believe that if people are given the best of everything, if they are obstinately and stubbornly supplied with only the very finest food to eat, they will soon come not only to like it, but to demand it.

This is a splendid manifestation of the benevolent Fabian paternalism then much in vogue. Harben saw the solution to the problem in community feeding, particularly in the publicly owned and managed British Restaurants and civic canteens which had been created to meet wartime needs. He assumed that they would continue to exist after the war, and that they could be used as the means of reforming popular taste in food. They should 'foster the attitude that food is a fine art, worth cultivating for the sake of the pleasure and the well-being that it brings; and get away from the so-common attitude of hygienic austerity and condescension' – for Harben saw the British experts' obsession with dietetics as condescending, and linked to a disdain for actual food and cookery. But he recognised difficulties in his strategy of communal feeding. Could people be induced to use the public restaurants and carry the standards back to their homes? The problem was that the British as a whole were so individualistic – against communal anything – and 'as a nation we are not much addicted to eating out'.

An equally idealistic article appeared in the next issue. John Fuller, who spent the war training RAF cooks, looked forward to 'Cooks and Cooking in Post-War England'. He emphasised the need for more training schools and higher status for cooks – in the creation of which, as events turned out, he himself was to play a prominent part. He, too, foresaw an important role for the municipal restaurants (which in the event did not long survive the war) as well as for the food industries in the future link between the country's raw materials and its people's health and happiness:

the future seems surely bringing to the professional cook an increasing share of that responsibility from the housewife, perhaps leaving for the home little more than the chance to pursue cookery as a fascinating hobby. (*Wine and Food*, 42, Summer 1944)

That remark was prescient, if a little overstated.

Fuller blamed the failings of English cookery in the past on the apathy of the typical Englishman about food. He returned to that theme three years later, emphasising how supply and demand were intricately related in a vicious circle – though the supply of good food well-cooked was small in Britain, it seemed the demand was equally minute. Tragically, the small discriminating band who created the demand for good food still tended to follow the tradition of turning to foreign craftsmen.

However, tomorrow's chef will cook for the people, we hope, and receive not decorations from archdukes but acclaim from the 'man-in-the-street'. To ensure that a demand for fine cooking is engendered in the people it will be necessary for all gastronomes to work for gastronomy in the spirit, if not by the method, that Sir Henry Wood worked for music. Music has been taken out of the orphanage in Britain, let gastronomy follow. (*Wine and Food*, 54, Summer 1947)

Such idealism did not last. John Fuller was so much the voice of the *Zeitgeist* that we have already had occasion, earlier in this book, to cite his later advocacy of cook-freeze systems.

How much power and impact did groups like the Wine and Food Society have? Probably not much. They may have had some marginal influence in some quarters of the catering trade – some independent restaurateurs were themselves keen members of the Society. On popular taste, despite the visions of people like Phillip Harben and John Fuller in the 1940s, the effect must have been negligible. But they did point the way to the restaurant and hotel guides of the post-war years, which adopted a much more aggressive stance towards the catering trade and, through their very large readerships, became a force which could scarcely be ignored.

GUIDES TO EATING

Tourist guides to hotels and restaurants are an old-established institution, and the idea of grading establishments in terms of comfort, facilities, service and cuisine was familiar long before the Second World War. Guides like Michelin, however, made – and still make – their judgements without publicly discussing the grounds for reaching them in particular cases. Even the greatest eating-places simply receive their two- or three-star listings, with at most a laconic line or so mentioning a few of the *specialités de la maison*. The more 'talkative' kind of guide-book, which describes each restaurant and comments critically on its strengths and weaknesses, its particular style and the personality of its chef, is a post-war development in both England and

France. In England the *Good Food Guide* and Egon Ronay's annual guides, and in France the Gault-Millau guide, have all appeared on the scene since the Second World War. Gault-Millau and Ronay are rather similar, in having been initially the work of campaigning individuals, but gradually growing into large organisations with trained and paid inspectors to visit and judge hotels and restaurants. The *Good Food Guide* is rather different in that it involves many hundreds of the dining public in making reports on their own experiences.

The *Good Food Guide* was founded by Raymond Postgate who did not at all fit the older stereotype of the gastronome. He was a man of the left, the brother-in-law and collaborator of the socialist historian G. D. H. Cole. The title of their well-known joint work of social history points to who was intended to benefit by his gastronomic activities – *The Common People* (1938). The *Good Food Guide* arose out of the 'Good Food Club' which Postgate started in 1949 in a short-lived magazine *The Leader*.[10] The 'Club' was something of a fiction: it had, as Postgate always emphasised, 'no organisation, funds or officers' and could not 'engage in correspondence'. That did not prevent it being an effective device in trying to improve British cooking and restaurant keeping.

> The idea was almost childishly simple. People who care about good food, good drink and courtesy – those three things only, not accommodation, which is covered by other guides – would report where they found them. They would exchange information. They would visit the places recommended by their colleagues, and report if the recommendations stood up to a test. (*Good Food Guide*, 1954: 3)

The *Guide*, of which the first edition was published in 1951, consisted of members' reports 'coordinated and revised' by Postgate himself as 'President and founder of the Club', exercising benevolent autocracy in the best Fabian tradition. As for 'membership', it was obtained simply by buying a copy of the *Guide* in a bookshop – it contained report forms which any purchaser could fill in and return to Postgate, who then arranged for second, third and subsequent opinions. He also wrote to each proprietor asking a standard range of questions about prices, opening hours, and their own opinion on what they cooked best.

'The plan,' wrote Postgate, 'got out of hand almost at once, and ever since I have been desperately trying to keep up with the enthusiasm of the members, ninety-nine per cent of whom I've never even met.' The great danger, of course, was that the system would be subverted by restaurateurs and proprietors attempting to insert puffs in the guide for their own commercial advantage. As a safeguard, every member returning a report form had to sign a declaration that he or she had no interest in the concern, and his or her name or initials were printed in the guide after the entry. Other essential rules were that the guide would accept no advertisements from the catering trade, that no member would accept complimentary meals or other forms of veiled payment, and that members would not identify themselves as such – at least until after the meal. In 1962 the *Good Food Guide* passed under the auspices of the Consumers' Association. That year for the first time, five paid inspectors were employed, but the 'members' continued to be the primary source of information: 10,229 of them had submitted reports on between 20,000 and 30,000 eating-places.

The editors of the *Good Food Guide*, and Egon Ronay too, sought to promote intelligent appreciation and criticism of eating places. But on what standards is such criticism based? By what criterion is cooking judged to be better or worse? There seems generally to have been more unspoken consensus about this in France than in England – as we have already observed in women's magazines and trade journals. The annual award of rosettes by the *Guide Michelin* has long been awaited with excitement, and while there may be disputes about whether a particular restaurant has been accurately rated, the general idea of a scale from better to worse appears unproblematic to the French. Even though Michelin is vague about its criteria – two stars 'worth a detour', three stars 'worth the journey' – a unilinear scale is understood and accepted. Gault-Millau introduced a refinement of red tocques for distinction in *nouvelle cuisine* and black tocques for outstanding *cuisine classique*, but this was not a major breach of the principle.

In contrast, the British guides took many years even to move towards a simple better/worse rating, and there were many greater problems in deciding what exactly this should mean. It was not just that there were fewer eating-places whose outstanding excellence could be taken for granted whatever the criterion used; there was also apparent a greater diversity of taste and less consensus about what constituted excellent cooking. For many years both Postgate and Ronay claimed only that each eating place they listed was 'good of its kind', which left scope for enormous confusion. By around 1970, however, things had changed sufficiently for the guides to have more confidence in rating restaurants in linear, better and worse fashion. Partly it seems to have been a matter of changes in the restaurants themselves, but also partly a matter of greater consensus about critical standards – a consensus which the Guides themselves appear to have done much to create. In 1972 Ronay wrote that:

> For fourteen years we have appraised the cooking in a restaurant according to how well it achieved what it set out to do. No comparisons were implied. But good cooking has spread spectacularly, the public's judgment has grown more sophisticated, and we find our former concept outgrown. While we still take into consideration how an establishment lives up to its self-projected image and the public's expectations, we found ourselves able to apply absolute measures more easily. The stars (and they apply only to cooking, as before) are now awarded on a comparative basis.[11]

There was much greater consensus about the faults of the establishments which would never appear in the guides. The annual prefaces in which the editors have sounded off about the evils of the trade have attracted a great deal of publicity in the national press. Indeed, the excitement generated by these jeremiads in Britain is possibly the nearest equivalent to the excitement annually felt by the French about the rosettes awarded by Michelin at the opposite end of the quality spectrum.[12]

What were the principal targets of the guide editors' criticisms? In the early years of the *Good Food Guide*, Postgate was attacking abuses which were a mixture of hangovers from wartime austerity and of sheer laziness and incompetence. They included: false pie crusts (squares of pastry baked separately from the stewed meat or fruit); mock cream sold as cream (eventually made illegal); bottled salad cream, often diluted, masquerading as mayonnaise; 'hot plating' of meals, which made meat or fish dry up; cold joints of meat sliced thinly and served with hot gravy; bad coffee; and cheeseboards comprised only of plastic cheddar, 'processed cheese' and Danish blue. Ronay's language could be even more colourful than Postgate's. Libel laws, he said in 1962, prevented him naming the main culprits of crimes against food, but 'What they do in Wales could be called gastronomic rape, except that they don't even seem to derive pleasure from it.' Ronay's targets included two forms of pretension: menus too long for anything to be done well, and the theatrical practice of flambéeing dishes at the table by waiters, who usually ruined anything the chef had achieved. That sort of criticism, however, is already noticeably at a higher level than Postgate had had to start, and indeed both guides agreed that from the early 1960s (a period, as the evidence of the trade journals and women's magazines has already shown, of rapid change in British cooking whether professional or domestic) there were some distinct signs of improvement. Both guides paid tribute to the burgeoning of small independent restaurateurs, many of them 'ex-amateurs' who had flair, imagination and enthusiasm, but no formal training in cookery; several of these received lavish praise in the *Good Food Guide* and stars from Ronay. Even some of the professionals showed some signs of reforming: a Trust House manager was reported in 1962 as having been inspired by a course to do real mayonnaise instead of bottled salad cream with the lobster.

Frozen food has been a bane of the guides. As early as 1963 Ronay reported that 'Sales talk is turning an increasing number of restaurants into heating-up houses.' According to the *Good Food Guide*, 1967–8, fresh vegetables were rare and getting rarer, though in 1969 Ronay said that more restaurants were offering only fresh vegetables in season; the two reports probably are not contradictory, but refer to different levels of the trade. Early experiments with cook-freeze systems were discussed with horror in the *Good Food Guide* also in 1967–8; by 1984 it was able to report that more than 70 per cent of British restaurants used frozen food plus a microwave oven as their mode of 'cooking'.

The effects of the large chains of hotels and restaurants in promoting standardisation and mediocrity have been a particular object of complaint in the British guides. Pioneers like Sir Isidore Salmon of J. Lyons had been treated like heroes of the age in the trade press at the beginning of the century, and certainly the initial effect of such chains seems to have been greatly to improve standards of mass catering. By the 1930s, the other side of the coin was being scrutinised from time to time in the pages of *Wine and Food*. Barry Neame, an independent restaurateur active in the Wine and Food Society from its beginnings, attributed the faults of English catering to the lack of the personal touch; that in turn was due in large part to considerable numbers of hotels being owned by railway companies, breweries and other big businesses. Managers were too beholden to their companies, and concerned mainly with selling the brewery's beer, not with good food (*Wine and Food*, Winter 1934). After the war, the trend was more pronounced. Postgate wrote in the 1963–4 *Good Food Guide* that:

> the most notable development in the catering world is one that in another world would be called gigantism. There has been a highly significant growth of half a dozen monster organisms, which have swallowed up so many smaller units that very often the first question one has to ask of an hotel or restaurant is not 'Who is the landlord?' but 'To what chain are you attached?'

His point was well taken. According to a market research survey (Acumen, 1978: 109ff.), Trust House Forte in the late 1970s owned 220 hotels and motels, more than 200 roadside cafés, several chains of restaurants and steakbars, as well as running ten motorway service areas, catering at airports and for several airlines, and holding the franchise for refreshments in the Royal Parks. It even owned several famous London restaurants, including the Café Royal and Quaglino's. Other vast organisations in the catering field included Grand Metropolitan, the Rank Organisation, EMI, Empire Catering, United Biscuits, and the Granada group. What Postgate most objected to about these giants was their 'buying up or opening inns and restaurants and pouring them into a mould out of which they come as nearly exactly alike as directors' adamancy can make them'. He was not blind to their positive achievements. They had bought up many of the 'incompetent and insolent hotels' which had in the past made British catering an international jest, and they had improved them in almost every respect except one – the food. Forte's provided 'nothing but complete dullness'; Ind Coope all the standard international items but not always cooked either imaginatively or even correctly, and Trust Houses 'an unimaginative menu' coupled with 'an exasperating habit of moving a manager elsewhere as soon as he has worked up his hotel to a high standard and become a valued citizen of the town'. Ronay repeatedly took up the same cudgel. 'Large hotel chains', he wrote in 1971, 'are turning their managers into accountants and book-keepers, pressurised to watch profit percentages and interim budgets, with little time left to actually manage their hotels in the traditional sense.' Service industries, argued Ronay, suffered by merging into large groups, especially in the hotel and catering industry, which was populated by individualists whose initiative could not blossom in a corporate atmosphere. Risk-taking became pointless, experiments suicidal. On the continent, he noted, the chains had remained smaller and more flexible.

Ronay in particular has carried his attack on other gigantic vehicles for the subversion of mass taste well beyond what is strictly required of a restaurant guide in the narrow sense. It is ironic to recall Phillip Harben's or John Fuller's visions at the end of the war of the professional chef operating paternalistically through publicly owned mass catering to lift the taste of the public at large. That is not how Ronay sees the effects of large organisations in catering, whether in the public or private sector. He has conducted surveys of catering at airports, in hospitals and on motorway service areas. Hospitals represent the largest public sector catering organisation of all in Britain: 2000 hospitals feed half a million patients, plus hospital staff, every day. Though Ronay claimed in 1973 to have applied the simplest criteria possible, and been as lenient as possible in view of the difficulties catering staff faced (including a very low per capita daily budget), he found standards of cooking and often of raw materials 'scandalously low'. A few exceptional hospitals showed what could be done on a low budget, but Ronay provides vivid illustrations of the failings of the majority. Vegetables were (by venerable English tradition) often boiled to the point of discolouring. Menu planning was sometimes disastrous, offering for example 'a choice of smoked haddock or tinned spaghetti; mashed potatoes served with a potato, onion and cheese pie; a choice of three fish dishes'. Scrambled eggs, a dish quickly made but needing careful attention and therefore quite unsuitable for mass production, were nevertheless frequently on the menu. A West Country hospital gave the recipe: 'Fresh eggs were beaten up and mixed with diluted powdered milk. This is placed in a steamer for half an hour until it sets like an egg custard, before being whisked to give it a scrambled egg appearance.' The result, commented Ronay, was 'a light coloured, rubbery texture of egg custard consistency and mild egg flavour, with no seasoning, in a container with nearly one inch of water in the bottom, the water having separated from the eggs as time passed'. It is possible that Ronay's strictures were noted, for six years later a second survey revealed considerable improvements – though not, of course, perfection.

Ronay's greatest apparent success, however, concerned motorway service areas. His first report in the 1972 guide on the 18 service areas then existing painted a fairly bleak picture: 2 were rated good, 8 acceptable, 5 poor, and 3 'appalling'. Six years later, things had deteriorated. There were then 40 service areas, many of them with 2 outlets, making 56 in all. Of these, Ronay considered only 1 good, 14 acceptable, 29 poor, and 12 appalling. The worst results were found at Trust House Forte's establishments: 11 out of the 15 were 'poor' or 'appalling'. Motorway caterers had 'an almost universal contempt for their customers' palates.' As usual, Ronay gave plenty of vivid examples to justify his conclusions.

Ubiquitous as this dish is, there is hardly a steak and kidney pie, even when home-made, which is edible. At least half the sausages are very poor: unsightly, bready, burnt, skinny and shrivelled. With a single, Scottish exception . . . all fish is frozen, often thrown straight from the refrigerator into the frying pan. Practially no decent chips can be found – they are soft, soggy, often grey. The ubiquitous peas, from poor brands, are mishandled and shrivelled, often found swimming in a livid green liquid. . . . Sausage rolls, so-called Cornish pasties and meat pies were an ordeal to taste.

The furore in the press generated by this report led to questions in Parliament and, more or less directly, to the Government setting up an official committee of inquiry into motorway service areas, under the chairmanship of Mr Peter Prior. The committee rapidly produced a report (Prior, 1978) which, if more restrained and cautious, largely substantiated Ronay's findings, even down to the steak and kidney pie:

One conclusion, to which the Committee came with reluctance, was that some MSA employees, and even some managers, were incapable of distinguishing good food from bad. Two members sampled 'steak and kidney pie' at one area which they considered to be the worst item they had tried anywhere. It tasted awful and looked awful. Later when the members disclosed their presence, the manager, in the course of a tour, indicated the pie. 'Take a look at that,' he said, with genuine pride, 'that is what Egon Ronay thought was dreadful'. (1978: 20)

Nor did the opinion surveys commissioned by the Committee reveal as much dissatisfaction among those eating at the service areas as might have been expected. Of those interviewed at the areas, 41 per cent thought the food enjoyable, and another 45 per cent found it acceptable; even allowing that 'acceptable' may have been taken to mean 'not quite bad enough to complain about', this seemed to be a fairly high level of public contentment. Figures from a survey of people interviewed at home, not actually on the service areas, however, were much lower – suggesting that the food seemed worse when recalled than it did when eaten, and/or that many people were avoiding the service areas because they disliked them so much. At any rate, in the years since the Prior Report, the chains who run virtually all the service areas have been making rather visible efforts to improve them.

Nevertheless, the discrepancy in the case of motorway service areas between the dissatisfaction of the 'experts' – Ronay's team and the Prior Committee – and an apparently fairly satisfied general public raises some awkward general questions about what it means to speak of 'better' and 'improved' catering. If people in general *like* it, does that not make it by definition 'good food'? Obviously, if food is positively unhygienic or dietetically harmful, there are 'objective' grounds for condemning it; but if it is simply a matter of aesthetic judgement, does not the majority view outweigh that of the 'refined' or expert minority? Sir Charles Forte certainly thought so. Interviewed on television in March 1980, he admitted being riled by Ronay's charges against Trust House Forte, but replied that takings were up by 19 per cent in the previous 6 months: he was giving people what they wanted.[13]

CONCLUSION

These issues are by no means peculiar to matters of eating. They have wide ramifications. The same questions arise time and time again in discussions of cultural policy, when people at large seem not to like the forms of culture that the minority of 'experts' consider they ought to.[14] The same questions arise in the problem of what is good behaviour: as Elias has shown, the definition of good manners provided at any given time by an 'expert' minority never coincides with how the majority of people then actually behaves. Gastronomes and food guide activists are comparable with such minorities. What effect overall have they had in shaping conceptions of good food and making it available to those who want it? And what is the basis – and extent – of their power?

The power of the campaigning guides today – and this includes Gault-Millau in France as much as Egon Ronay and the *Good Food Guide* in Britain – springs in principle from the same source as Grimod's at the beginning of the nineteenth century. It derives from their influence on the readers, and through them on public opinion more widely. Today that also involves organisation on a larger scale than the Jury des Dégustateurs. The guides' teams of anonymous inspectors, paid or unpaid, and still more vast numbers of people who buy and consult the publications each year, make them a force which caterers can ignore only at some cost. To the independent, up-market restaurateur, a recommendation in one of the guides whether in England or in France is worth money. Raymond Postgate, writing in the *Good Food Guide* in 1954, foresaw with his usual acumen the effects of the 'mass-observation' of eating-places he had organised.[15] With Club members travelling around and 20–30,000 eyes watching them, restaurateurs newly entering a trade could become widely known for their good food much more quickly than before. Perhaps more important, 'an hotelier whose service and cooking is going down can never be at his ease. He can never be sure which quiet customer is watching him on behalf of the Club.' For if securing an entry is worth money, the loss of it can be costly. Thus the guides engender in the restaurateur a certain watchfulness and exert a constraint towards striving always to maintain high standards.

Grimod, with only a few associates, was able to influence the relatively small number of leading independent restaurateurs in post-Revolutionary Paris. It is scarcely surprising that many more independent restaurateurs today should pay heed to the larger-scale organisations which produce the guides. The targets of the guides' most interesting campaigns nowadays, however, are themselves vast organisations. They are far more formidable adversaries, and the balance of power between the mass caterers and the self-appointed upholders of catering standards is much more complex and indeterminate. The guides have hesitated to take on neither the giant private-sector conglomerates nor the great public-sector organisations. Egon Ronay's critique of the mass-produced hospital scrambled eggs or motorway steak-and-kidney pie poses recognisably the same sort of questions as gastronomes have always asked (if usually at a more esoteric level): what constitutes a *good* pie or *true* scrambled egg? But why should mass caterers pay any attention to their complaints? Lord Forte (as he now is) can affect indifference as long as his cash registers continue to ring. Yet even the chains and public sector catering organisations like hospitals seem to have made some response to criticism: the gastronomic guides may have little financial power there, but they still have the power to cause public embarrassment and they do actively encourage their readers to complain. In short, they provide what Galbraith (1952) called 'countervailing power' on behalf of customers confronted with public or private conglomerations of power in the catering trades. It was highly appropriate that the *Good Food Guide* was taken under the wing of the Consumer's Association, publishers of *Which?* For today's gastronomic guides are part of the more general consumer movement found in most Western countries, whose successes include Ralph Nader's famous campaigns against motor manufacturers in the USA, to the highly successful Campaign for Real Ale in Britain, and campaigns against mass-produced bread in several countries. One of the general characteristics of consumer movements is that they are concerned to reverse, or mitigate the effects of, mass production.

In order to have any chance of successes in their trials of strength with the mass producers, the leaders of any consumer movement have to ensure that they are seen as the delegates or spokesman for substantial numbers of followers. Thus, like the leaders of political parties, the editors of the guides have to pay as much attention to persuading their followers as persuading the caterers that their tastes are right. For Gault and Millau or Egon Ronay, who began as campaigning individuals, that raises no ideological problems. For the editors of the *Good Food Guide*, which at least pretends to be the democratic expression of its readers' taste, it causes some qualms. Christopher Driver reflected on the problem in the 1980 edition. Given that many, probably most, people were perfectly content with mass-produced food, by what right did the *Guide* rate more highly the preferences of those who were not so content?

> Looking at the whole spectrum of more-or-less-edibles from *haute cuisine* to teenage junk food, what do you dismiss because you happen not to like it, and what are you prepared to call a bad idea, badly executed and unscrupulously priced?

The *Guide* itself, he admitted, had done at least its share in persuading the British bourgeoisie into eating more garlic per capita than the northern French did, and into eating its lamb and duck as pink as its sirloin. Most of those who made reports for the *Guide* liked their food that way – in part because the *Guide* had told them they should – but was it *objectively* better? Grimod de la Reynière would not have been troubled by such self-doubt. One reason for the doubt is that no matter what large numbers of the 'bourgeoisie' have come to share such tastes, they are manifestly a small minority of the people at large and of the market. In consequence, the outcome of trials of strength on the upper level between self-appointed leaders of culinary public opinion and the mass producers of food depends not only on the leaders carrying their followers with them, but also on the balances of power on the lower level between groups bringing to the market very different likes and dislikes.[16] In the circumstances, the guides' successes in their battles are perhaps surprisingly numerous.

11

Food Dislikes

So far this book has been mainly concerned with the development of conceptions of 'good food', and 'good taste' in all matters culinary. Yet likes are inseparable from dislikes. People's dislikes in food may take many forms – from a mild distaste which may be set aside if it would cause embarrassment to one's host at dinner, all the way through to feelings of overwhelming repugnance and revulsion at the very thought of eating a particular food. These dislikes and aversions are as much formed socially as are people's likes. They, too, are part of social standards, and they too change over time.

From time to time, therefore, it has been impossible to avoid implications about the parallel processes of development of views of what constitutes 'bad food' and 'poor taste'. For a growing sense of 'delicacy' and 'refinement' in regard to food and cooking – as in other fields of behaviour – is quite inseparable from a growing sense of dislike or aversion towards foods and dishes defined as 'indelicate' or 'unrefined'. Repugnance is merely the other side of the same coin from refinement, as Norbert Elias demonstrated in *The Civilising Process* (1939). Thus the gradual refinement of table manners, notably through the adoption of the fork, was associated with increasing feelings of aversion to touching food with the hands, and even stronger feelings of revulsion towards such practices as removing food from one's mouth and putting it back in the common bowl. And the gradually increasing control and removal behind the scenes of bodily functions such as urination, defecation and vomiting were equally associated with the growth of feelings of shame and disgust in cases when these functions were performed under the gaze of others.

In matters of food and cookery too, there was a long-term process of formulating and 'rationalising' what was correct and refined – as we have seen, gastronomic writing played a part in this comparable in some ways to Elias's manners books. This may be thought of as a process of 'civilising of taste' parallel to the 'civilising of appetite' discussed in chapter 2, and food dislikes and avoidances inevitably underwent rationalisation as much as positive preferences. The strength that such dislikes can acquire is seen when people are faced with a dearth: although, as mentioned in chapter 2, people have resorted to eating acorns or worse, and cases of cannibalism are not unknown in extreme circumstances, there are equally many cases of hungry people unable to overcome their revulsion towards foods at hand. Elias sees 'rationalisation' and the growth of feelings of repugnance as two parts of one process:

> No less characteristic of a civilising process than 'rationalisation' is the peculiar moulding of the drive economy that we call 'shame' and 'repugnance' or 'embarrassment'. Both these, the strong spurt of rationalisation and the (for a time) no less strong advance of the threshold of shame and repugnance that becomes more perceptible in the make-up of Western men broadly speaking from the sixteenth century onwards, are different sides of the same transformation of the social personality structure. (1939: II, 292)

Now it may be objected that repugnance towards certain foods is universal, found in all cultures and throughout history. Certainly, there is no absolute zero-point in this or in any other civilising process. Just as Elias points out that, while the expression of feeling by people in the Middle Ages was altogether freer and more spontaneous than later, 'it certainly did not lack social patterning and control in any absolute sense' (1939: I, 215), so it must be emphasised that food preferences and avoidances nowhere lack social patterning altogether. But has this patterning itself changed in a patterned way in historic societies? Is it possible to discern *trends*, and to speak of a *structured* process of development?

The question can be confused by the past emphases of social scientists. On the whole, they have looked most closely at food prohibitions and avoidances in 'traditional' or 'primitive' – meaning non-European – societies, while in European societies attention has been given on the contrary more to positive likings and preferences. A superficial inference might be that the path of development has been from great selectivity towards catholicity of taste. However, it is by no means so simple.

Recent theorists have, as noted in chapter 1, on the whole seen food preferences and avoidances as always socially patterned, but taken the patterning and the sense of revulsion it often entails largely for granted. In *The Powers of Horror*, an essay on 'abjection', Julia Kristeva describes very well the symptoms of psychologically deep-rooted repugnance and its physiological manifestations:

> Food loathing is perhaps the most elementary and archaic form of abjection. When the eyes see or the lips touch that skin on the surface of milk – harmless, thin as a sheet of cigarette paper, pitiful as a nail paring – I experience a gagging sensation and, still further down, spasms in the stomach, the belly; and all the organs shrivel up the body, provoke tears and bile, increase heartbeat, cause forehead and hands to perspire. (1980: 2–3)

Yet within her avant-garde psychoanalytic framework, Kristeva interprets repugnance as a problem of individual psychology, not as a question of social development. People are assumed always to have felt revulsion of this sort: if in the past they did not gag on hot milk, they gagged on something else, and the sense of repugnance was equally strong even if its objects were not always the same.

Mary Douglas in *Purity and Danger* (1966) situates the sense of defilement much more strongly in a social context. For her, defilement is connected with the boundary or margin of an order – one feels polluted and experiences repugnance when one has transgressed some socially defined and significant categorisation. This is very helpful; but again Douglas, unlike Elias, does not conceive of boundaries changing, of how the frontiers of repugance may advance in a non-random way over time in historic societies.

Plainly we are close to the troublesome anthropological notion of 'taboo'. There are great differences in what anthropologists regard as the proper meaning of taboo. To avoid 'tiresome and unprofitable debate', E. B. Ross (1978: 1) uses the word in its most general sense, to mean simply *avoidance* of certain animals or plants as a source of food. That is too simple for our purposes, however, for we are concerned not only with *behaviour* but with people's *feelings* with regard to the foods they eat. English, like other languages, contains a rich vocabulary to describe these feelings, from the neutral *avoidance* upwards in strength through *aversion* to *repugnance* and even *revulsion*. The increasing strength of the words corresponds to a rising scale of feelings associated with breaking a 'taboo'.

Paul Kapteyn (1980: 47–90) has gone further, and suggested not only that there are variations in the strength of feelings associated with breaking prohibitions, but that two different kinds of taboo need to be distinguished: what he calls 'primitive' taboos and 'civilised' taboos. The word 'taboo' was introduced into English by Captain James Cook, who described the avoidances of various sorts among Polynesians encountered on his voyages of discovery. Cook noted, however, that many of these taboos could be set aside by individuals with no personal sense of guilt, shame or revulsion; for example, Tahitians collectively avoided eating with English sailors, but often a single Tahitian woman would break this convention without guilt so long as fellow-Tahitians did not know about it. This kind of avoidance, in other words, was enforced by what Elias terms *Fremdzwang* – 'external constraints' or constraint by other people. The same word, 'taboo', was soon applied also to something which Kapteyn argues is actually quite a different concept: the changes in social personality over time that Elias calls civilising processes. A striking illustration comes from Sir Walter Scott, who describes how an aunt in her eighties asked him to send her the novels of the seventeenth-century writer Aphra Behn. She returned them, indignant at the impropriety of their contents. She had felt ashamed, *while sitting alone*, to read them; and yet, she herself reflected, 60 years earlier she had heard the same novels read out loud in the best social circles, with no one feeling any such embarrassment. The feelings of personal embarrassment she felt in old age even when alone is testimony to the growth in her lifetime of what Elias calls *Selbstzwang* or self-constraints, in this case in matters of sexual propriety.

Modern theorists from Freud in *Totem and Taboo* (1913) to Mary Douglas have tended to equate rather than distinguish the two concepts identified by Kapteyn. It is not fashionable to draw any distinction between, say, the avoidance of eating the ritual animal of one's lineage in a tribal society and, for example, the revulsion many people in Western societies now feel at the idea of eating animal brains. The dominant view might be called the 'quantum theory' of taboo. It is that all societies pretty well equally use avoidances to demarcate boundaries of various sorts. The actual patterns differ, but the principle of patterning is the same. If there are changes in the objects avoided, if a food previously eaten is now avoided, then probably there are others which once were not eaten but now are. People of all types of societies have similar capacities for repugnance, and changes in the patterning of repugance are not to be interpreted as advances or movements in any particular direction.

It has to be admitted that the 'quantum theory' is very difficult to refute: it posits that the particle of repugance jumps unpredictably. Nevertheless, while acknowledging this difficulty, it seems well worth while to look in the specific context of food and eating for evidence of structured changes in patterns of food dislike paralleling the development of notions of delicacy and refinement. We shall explore four broad reasons for food avoidances: the trained incapacity to enjoy food; fear of the after-effects of eating certain foods; fear of social derogation; and moral reasons for revulsion. These four are not intended to be exhaustive, nor even mutually exclusive.

TRAINED INCAPACITY TO ENJOY FOOD

Elias's theory gives a prima facie case for looking for signs of an increased incidence of individual fads, anxieties and neuroses about food, since pressures leading towards them can be generated within any civilising process. He explains the general principle as follows:

> sometimes the habituation to affect inhibition goes so far – constant feelings of boredom or solitude are examples of this – that the individual is no longer capable of any form of fearless expression of the modified affects, or of direct gratification of the repressed drives. Particular branches of drives are as it were anaesthetised in such cases by the specific structure of the social framework in which the child grows up. Under the pressure of the dangers that their expression incurs in the child's social space, they become surrounded with automatic fears to such an extent that they can remain deaf and unresponsive throughout a whole lifetime.[1] In other cases certain branches of drives may be so diverted by the heavy conflicts which the rough-hewn, affective and

passionate nature of the small human being unavoidably encounters on its way to being moulded into a 'civilised' being, that their energies can find only an unwanted release through bypasses, in compulsive actions and other symptoms of disturbance. In other cases again, these energies are so transformed that they flow into uncontrollable and eccentric attachments and repulsions, in predilections for this or that peculiar hobby horse. (1939: II, 243)

Also from a more or less Freudian point of view, Daniel Cappon, discussing the psychological origins of eating disorders, makes a similar point in more colourful language: 'our North American civilisation – 'overly-civilised' some would say – places a high value on a 'feast-your-eyes-but-don't-touch' mentality – in eating habits as well as in Playboy Clubs' (1973: 80). Cappon, like Elias, sees the civilising of table manners as a significant part of a process which has culminated in many individuals dissociating eating behaviour from consciousness, a feature 'shared by all gross behavioural disorders, especially in the chronic stages'.

Whether eating disorders, of the kind considered sufficiently serious today to require psychiatric treatment, have increased in incidence historically is hard to say. We mentioned in chapter 2 that it is possible that the acute eating disorder most widely discussed today, anorexia nervosa, has become much more common. In this present chapter, however, we are concerned not so much with acute disturbances of appetite in general as with faddiness, pernicketyness and anxiety towards particular foods. Of the faddy, anxious eater, Jane Austen's Mr Woodhouse – 'An egg boiled very soft is not unwholesome' – can stand as a literary archetype. Emma's father may not have been in any danger of starving himself to death, but his constant worries at the table do appear to be a case of the 'anaesthetisation' of the capacity for enjoying food. Mr Woodhouse in *Emma* is a very English figure and I have a hunch that he and his kind may in part have grown out of the 'children's food' syndrome – something very prevalent in England but not, so far as I have been able to detect, to any great degree in France.

The Nursery Food Syndrome

Early in the nineteenth century Louis Eustache Ude, we are told, blamed the lack of enthusiasm for good cooking in England on the fact that young people were 'not introduced to their parents' table till their palates had been completely benumbed by the strict diet observed in the nursery and boarding-schools' (Jeaffreson, 1875: I, 184).[2] When Victorians referred to 'nursery food' they did not mean only food for tiny infants. In upper- and upper-middle class circles, girls especially seem to have lived in the 'nursery' under the care of nannies and governesses often until well into their teens. A special kind of diet appears to have been considered appropriate for young people, not just literally in the nursery but at boarding schools and more widely, for the notion spread also to the less well-to-do homes where children were not segregated in an actual nursery. The main characteristic of the 'strict diet' to which Ude alluded was its plainness, not to say monotony and dullness.

It is tempting to see in the 'nursery-food syndrome' some special aspect of what Philippe Ariès (1960) called 'the discovery of childhood'. In the Middle Ages, Ariès showed the lines of demarcation between childhood and adulthood were more blurred than later. Nothing in medieval dress, for example, distinguished the child from the adult (though dress did express the gradations of the social hierarchy). Only by the seventeenth century did the child, or at least the noble or middle-class child, cease to be dressed like a grown-up. Children's costume, with a quite distinct character of its own, then came into use. By the period 1900–20, Ariès notes, it had become customary to prolong 'late into adolescence the special features of a form of dress confined to childhood' (1960: 48). Did a notion of a special children's food follow a similar course to that of special children's dress? It would be easier to believe so if the idea were found widely in Western Europe. But unlike children's dress, the idea of children's food seems to have been especially prominent in England, and I have found very little sign of it in France. To speculate, it is possible that the idea of serving children a different sort of food from the adults took root in England more readily because of the very old custom among upper- and middle-class families of sending their own children out to serve in other households (a peculiarity of English child-rearing long regarded as strange in the rest of Europe – see Ariès, 1960: 352; Macfarlane, 1978: 174–5).

At any rate, the notion of food especially suitable for children seems not to have been part of any special solicitude or indulgence towards children in England, but rather a matter of making them eat what was good for them whether they liked it or not. At worst, making them eat food to which they actually felt an aversion was seen as a necessary part of breaking the child's peevish will. Even though by no means everyone was as unkind as that, the widespread parental anxiety and concern about giving children only very plain, simply cooked, weakly flavoured food must easily have communicated itself to children, and led some of them to remain anxious about food as adults. In the most serious cases, it may have led to the 'anaesthetising' of the capacity to enjoy eating. I have rather pooh-poohed the role of 'puritanism', in any specifically religious sense, in English attitudes to food. Yet there is no shortage of evidence of the lack of enthusiasm, almost guilt, which many people seem to have felt towards food and eating. We have already noted in our study of women's magazines how ill-developed, in England in the late nineteenth and early twentieth centuries, was the sense of enjoyment of food compared with France. Possibly some of that enthusiasm drained away, or failed to be created, in the course of child-rearing practices.

Anxieties about what children ate seem to have been at their highest in late Victorian times, and the anxieties they produced in adults perhaps peaked a generation or two later. The doctor Sir Henry Thompson's views seem typical of his profession when he wrote in 1880 of the dire consequences of children being given the wrong fare. It happened equally among the poor and among the more indulgent of the well-to-do. Among the poor, 'the little one takes his place at the parents' table, where lack of means, as well as of knowledge, deprives him of food more suitable than the rough fare of the adult' (1880: 3). Perhaps the poor child was no worse off, though, than the child of the well-to-do who 'becomes a pet, and is already familiarised with complex and too solid forms of food . . . which custom and self-indulgence have placed on the daily table'.

And soon afterwards commence in consequence – and entirely in consequence, a fact it is impossible too much to emphasise – the 'sick headaches' and 'bilious attacks', which pursue their victim through half a lifetime, to be exchanged for gout or worse at or before the great climacteric. (1880: 4)

Gerald Hamilton, reminiscing about his Victorian upbringing in *Wine and Food*, Spring 1939, told how

As a child I was constantly forced to eat food which I disliked, because it was supposed that what one didn't like was *ipso facto* good for one. Such criminal nonsense as this played a tremendous role in a Victorian upbringing.

Hamilton survived his childhood to become a self-proclaimed gourmet, but similar views on child-rearing were still prevalent in the inter-war years. A contributor to *Good Housekeeping*, July 1927, regarded 'with some measure of consternation the modern child who won't eat this or taste that'. Such a declaration on the part of the writer's family would have produced something resembling a volcanic eruption. Eating was a habit and the human stomach could 'tolerate all sound, plain, everyday foods'. Therefore, 'Personal disinclinations have to be overcome with tact and patience, but, as a rule, a hungry child will not refuse wholesome fare. Firmness is necessary at a crisis.' Note: food is to be 'tolerated', not 'enjoyed'.

By the 1920s and 1930s, medical opinion may have been softening, but it had not changed completely. Dr Cecil Webb-Johnson, writing in *Good Housekeeping*, August 1925, damned the schools which served inferior quality food to pupils; schools where teachers indulged in fresh butter while the girls ate margarine 'should be closed, and the head mistress hanged, as a warning to others'. Even he none the less retained the fear that digestion would be ruined if children ate adult food:

The best way in which to give meat to girls is in the form of plain roast or boiled joints. Elaborate entrées, rich and stimulating sauces, and the like, may be left to tempt the jaded palates of their elders. Digestive troubles may ensue when over-rich food is given.

Dorothy Morton, writing in the UCFA *Cookery Annual* for 1928, said much the same. Indigestion was a great fear and serious symptom in growing children. In childhood:

Plainly cooked and simply served food is decidedly best at this period if indigestion is to be avoided. Elaborate entrées, rich and stimulating sauces are best left to stimulate the jaded appetite of the elders.

The same anxieties pervade the cookery columns. *Good Housekeeping*, March 1922, advised that sausages 'if not too frequently used', formed 'a perfectly healthful addition to the bill of fare for grown-ups and older children'. If mothers were not nervous about bangers before, that half-hearted reassurance would make them so. The same lukewarmth is seen in the same issue in a section of recipes for children: 'With a little thought and ingenuity, the simplest food can often be made to look both pretty and tempting; it may only be in the manner of serving or the little bit of decoration added.'

Florence White's attitude, as expressed in her columns in *Woman's Own* in the 1930s, is a little more ambiguous. She appears to expect families to have fads, which pose problems for the housewife. In the issue of 25 February 1933, she tells how to clarify fat, which a husband and family would refuse to eat and would leave on their plates – 'wickedly wasteful'.

It may be good for them to eat fat, but if they have been allowed to grow up without training them to do so, it is too late to change them when they are grown up. . . . The only thing, therefore, is to see to it that they are not given any fat to waste; just cut it off and only give them the lean they like.

Basically, however, Miss White appears to have shared the general belief of the times that children's food should be plain, wholesome and heavy. She differed from others mainly in believing that the problem of likes and dislikes would not arise if the food were more skilfully cooked:

The other day I was horrified to hear someone say she had as a child detested suet pudding; this could only have been because the pudding was badly made. Every child and most grown-up persons like every form of suet roly-poly or blanket pudding if it is light and properly served and there is nothing in the world better for children. I have never known a child dislike it. (*Woman's Own*, 26 November 1932)

Curiously enough, in view of their own 'choosiness', gastronomic writers have always tended to be hostile to all sorts of food faddiness. In their view there is a world of difference between being highly selective in obtaining the very best food for one's own *enjoyment*, and rejecting foods as part of not much enjoying eating at all. So, paradoxically, they sometimes subscribed to the make-them-eat-it school of thought about children's food:

I have absolutely no patience with faddists. . . . I do think that all children should be trained to eat a little fat with their meat, for not only is fat good for them, but to me it is positively disgusting to see a person trim off every little bit of fat and decorate the plate with it. It is bad manners to say the least. (Scotson-Clark, 1924: 19)

The key here is that to be a finnicky eater, as opposed to simply enjoying good food, seems to have become to be regarded as socially inferior. Certainly, children evacuated from urban slums in wartime, as Minns (1980) notes, would often not eat soups or vegetables, or indeed anything much beyond bread and jam and fish and chips.

In view of the much greater salience of dislikes about food expressed in books and magazines in Britain than in France, it is interesting that more systematic research on individuals' dislikes and aversions appears to have been carried out in France. Claudian *et al.* (1969: 1288–92) asked a sample of French mothers to report the foods disliked by members of their families. The number of foods said to be 'not liked' was low among children under seven, which certainly seems to demonstrate that dislikes are socially learned: Claudian *et al.* comment that 'their tastes are not yet fixed and still possess a certain plasticity'. The incidence of dislikes then rose sharply in the 7–13 age range, reaching a peak (of more than one reported food dislike per person) among females of 14–20, then falling in the 21–59 age group – dramatically among females, who then had fewer dislikes than men – and reaching its lowest point among the over-60s. This pattern does not prove much in itself, though it does suggest that even without much evidence of a 'nursery food syndrome' in France, food faddiness increases during the psychologically stressful years of adolescence, but the French tend to get over it later.

These findings from France perhaps make it unwise to put too great an emphasis on the peculiarity of the English 'nursery food syndrome'. It may in any case have been declining. Since the Second World War, informed opinion has become less anxious about children's food. By the mid 1950s, the famous paediatrician Benjamin Spock and the nutritionist Miriam Lowenberg were reporting that lists of foods 'labelled taboo' for children were growing shorter. 'We have attained a more healthy respect for the digestive system of young children than we had twenty or even ten years ago' (1955: 157). This was an American textbook for parents, but Dr Spock's books sold widely in Britain too.[3] Nevertheless, in the absence of any directly comparable data, I have the impression that faddiness is still very prevalent among English children, much more so than among French. This impression is based partly on the content of French and British books and magazines, and partly on the experience of teachers at a High School in Exeter who have long experience in organising exchange visits between their school and a French equivalent in Rennes, and who gave me access to a small number of questionnaires completed by mothers prior to their children taking part in the 1984 exchange. One teacher summed up her impressions in an anecdote about taking 50 13–15-year-olds, half English, half French, for a traditional Devonshire 'cream tea' in Bovey Tracey. The French children ate theirs with enjoyment; the English 'proved a nightmare' with their various dislikes (about the scones, clotted cream, or jam, and demanding Coca Cola instead of tea to drink).

The questionnaires provide slightly more solid evidence, though the small numbers mean that they too have to be used rather impressionistically, and cannot be regarded as a survey meeting the highest social scientific standards. The French and English children had been matched as nearly as possible by the teachers; both nationalities came mainly from working-class and lower middle-class homes, judging from their fathers' and mothers' occupations. Unfortunately, the wording of the English and French questionnaires was not identical. The Exeter mothers were asked, 'Is there any food he/she cannot eat at all?' The Rennes question was, 'Is he/she allergic to certain foods or things? If yes, which?' The reason for this discrepancy is itself interesting: the French teachers did not expect the French children to have long lists of food likes and dislikes. And in fact, of the 22 French children, not one of the mothers had recorded any food allergies, nor mentioned any difficulties about food overleaf (where they were invited to add any other comments). In contrast, of the 23 English children, 14 mothers had mentioned foods their child could not eat. Most of them stated more than one food – the 14 produced a total of 27 mentions of non-acceptable foods. Among these there was one definite allergy (but that girl's mother also mentioned a non-allergenic disliked food) and one which may have been. The mothers had been reassured beforehand at a meeting that it would not be all snails and frogs' legs when their children reached Rennes. The remarkable thing about their questionnaire responses was that it was not foreign foods that their children disliked, but very everyday English things. Tomatoes were the most unpopular item with three rejections; the list also included: salad, carrots, cabbage, sprouts, beetroot, 'most vegetables', strawberries, 'fruit', fish, pork, lamb, stew, 'meat of any kind' (a 14-year-old vegetarian in a meat-eating family), butter, custard and nuts. Again, it must be emphasised that the French questionnaire did not so directly trigger the mothers to give lists of likes and dislikes. When the French children arrived in Exeter, some of them proved to be on a *régime* – that is, they came from diet-conscious families; but that is not the same as the positive repugnance which so many of the English children felt for particular foods. The English teachers felt socially embarrassed at having to pass on their children's numerous dislikes to their French hosts; the French caused no embarrassment. It is not easy to explain these national differences, if they really do exist: it seems weak to put it down to a gastronomic culture in France which has always emphasised food as something to be enjoyed. But behind that suggestion lie many earlier discussions in this book in which we have tried to account for the development of different gastronomic cultures in England and France.

FEAR OF AFTER-EFFECTS

Dislikes and aversions are also commonly associated with fears about the after-effects of eating certain foods. Chapter 2 was concerned with one such fear, the fear of obesity. Today the fear of being grossly overweight, for both its effects on health and on undermining the socially attractive body-image, is very widespread in most prosperous Western societies. Foods known to be fattening tend to be widely liked, not disliked, so the fear of being fat does not generally stop people eating them altogether, but they often exercise restraint or feel guilty about not doing so.[4] Several other social fears have also been sources of inhibition.

Indigestion, Bad Breath, Etcetera

It is hardly surprising, if English childhood had been so pervaded by anxieties about food, health and indigestion, that this kind of fear seems to have prevented many enjoying food in adult life. It is summed up in the common saying, 'I like it, but it doesn't like me.' Apprehension at trying any new and unfamiliar foods has been widespread. Many commentators have mentioned the average Englishman's lack of the spirit of culinary adventure. The women's magazines in the past often had to adopt a wheedling, half-apologetic tone in encouraging their readers to try the unfamiliar. A good example appears in *Good Housekeeping*, September 1923, on lobster:

> It is highly esteemed by the epicure, and is looked upon as more or less of a luxury, in spite of the fact that it is somewhat indigestible. . . . The use of condiments, such as vinegar and lemon-juice, can do much to overcome this drawback.

Nor was the fear of indigestion wholly irrational. Jane Grigson hit upon a valuable insight linking this fear both with typical English diets of the past and with fears of social embarrassment. She was wondering why the leek fell out of favour in polite society for 300 years, and happened to look up what Mrs Beeton had to say about leeks. That lady gives only two leek soups, one the traditional Scots cockie-leekie, but adds a note that leeks should be 'well-boiled' – which in this historical context means thoroughly over-cooked by modern standards – 'to prevent its tainting the breath' (1861:71). This fear of bad breath – and the fear, Mrs Grigson could have added, of gaseous emissions from the other end of the alimentary canal – seems to have been behind many fussy nineteenth-century recipes for onions.

> It seems to have been a major nightmare at the time, not just a silly refinement. I remember my grandmother's obsession with her digestive system, her purges and peppermint tablets; I remember too, how constipation hung over some families like a mushroom cloud. If digestions were as bad as all this suggests, and they probably were when diets were stodgy without fruit or many vegetables, the breath must often have been bad. Anything that could have added to the social fear – leek, onion, above all garlic – was prudently avoided, or subdued by strong-arm water treatment. (Grigson, 1978: 291)

Well before Mrs Beeton, Dr William Kitchiner had urged only the moderate use of spices, on the grounds that 'constant excessive abuse of them' would lead to the epicure being 'punished with all the sufferings of incessant and incurable Indigestion' (1821: 238). Later in the century, London schoolchildren were being taught that 'if the onion is not liked it can be omitted' from gravy, and that 'great care must be taken . . . or it will be indigestible' (E. Briggs, 1890: 38).

At its most extreme, the fear of indigestion can assume the proportions of neurosis. The symptoms were described by a medical doctor, J. Browning Alexander, in a lecture reprinted in the UCFA *Cookery Annual* for 1928. There was such a thing as 'the dyspepsia of starvation', said Alexander, which was

> due to the fact that the sufferer eliminates article after article of food from his diet, until a diet of almost complete starvation is established. A vicious circle is thus produced, by which the patient is dyspeptic because he is starved, and starves because he is dyspeptic. The only way to prevent such a calamity is to pay no heed to the dyspepsia, but to stimulate the appetite so that the vicious circle may be broken.

These fears of after-effects of eating certain foods have in common that they imply foresight in avoiding dangers of various kinds. Of course, mankind has always been afraid of eating poisonous foods, but the fears just mentioned all involve a more 'civilised', acquired type of foresight: bad breath, breaking wind and obesity have been feared because people learned to anticipate social embarrassment.

FEAR OF SOCIAL DEROGATION

A third group of fears stems from the threat of social derogation which may result from being known to eat certain foods or not to eat others. In this instance there is usually nothing intrinsic in a food itself to account for its being socially valued or despised. Despised foods may be more nourishing or more digestible than others that are highly sought after, but that does not lessen the social pressures compelling people to avoid them. This aspect of the civilising of taste presents a problem not unlike the question of why certain ways of speaking – accents, vocabulary, phraseology – are considered socially superior while others come to be viewed with disdain, shame and embarrassment. Rarely is there anything intrinsic in the words themselves, as Elias points out:

> One does not say, a court lady explains, 'un mien ami' or ' le pauvre deffunct'; all that 'smells of the bourgeois' . . .
>
> The people who select in this way are neither able, nor do they attempt, to justify further why in a particular case this form of a word is pleasing and that displeasing. . . . The certitude with which they are able to say: 'This combination of words sounds well, those colours are ill-chosen', the sureness of their taste, . . . derives rather from a more or less unconsciously operating psychological self-steering agency than from conscious reflection. But it is clear, here too, how it is first of all

small circles of courtly society who listen with growing sensitivity to nuances of tone and significance to the spoken and written word, and how this sensitivity, this 'good taste', also represents a prestige value for such circles. Anything that touches their embarrassment threshold smells bourgeois, is socially inferior, and, inversely: anything bourgeois touches their embarrassment threshold. It is the necessity to distinguish themselves from anything bourgeois that sharpens this sensitivity . . . polished social conduct, that is the main instrument in the competition for prestige and favour, provides the occasion for the sharpening of taste. (Elias, 1939: II, 301)

If speech can be socially moulded, so certainly can be eating. The same considerations of sensitivity, 'good taste' and social distance enter into what is eaten. We have already encountered many instances. The bourgeoisie, when they could afford it, emulated the carnivorous tastes of the warrior class, first quantitatively, later qualitatively. Aristocracy in turn disdained the vegetables so much consumed by the peasants, and by the seventeenth century this disdain had been adopted by a figure like Pepys. One sign of its continued path down the social scale and survival even in twentieth-century France may be the finding of Claudian *et al.* (1969: 1290–2) that among a large sample of French people vegetables were far and away the category of foods most often 'not liked' – accounting for nearly 60 per cent of all reported dislikes. Still more evidence of France's cultural inheritance from court society?

The case of white bread is also familiar. From medieval times, the high prestige of white bread has been well documented in both England and France: the further down the social scale, the darker the bread. The upper classes regarded black and brown breads with aversion – it was even claimed their stomachs could not digest them – while the lower orders aspired to white or whiter bread. By the nineteenth century the aspiration had spread even to the remoter parts of rural France. In *The Life of a Simple Man* (1905: 154–5), Guillaumin describes how his old peasant had contrived, despite the opposition of his more thrifty and conservative wife, to follow his neighbours in first cutting out the bran from their flour, and then to reduce the proportion of rye. White bread having become available to all and brown bread having thus, so to speak, fallen off the bottom of the social scale, the brown reappeared towards the top. For the fashion for wholemeal bread has begun to spread downwards from the upper reaches of the social scale since the 1950s.

The potato is possibly unique in history in having first been adopted by the poor and then having spread *up* the social scale (Wiegelmann, 1967, 1974; cf. Salaman, 1949).[5] There are countless cases of foods being dropped by higher social ranks when adopted by lower. One example is sago, in 1850 a rarity and regarded as 'invalid diet', later adopted by the poorer classes and dropped by the better-off as simply being dull. Phillip Harben painted a vivid picture of the sensitivity to social nuance now quite generally expected when purchasing food, in a column he entitled 'Class War on the Fish Slab':

'Bloaters, sir?' said the order clerk at the fishmongers, and the outraged tone of her voice showed that she felt most insulted. 'Oh, no, sir, we don't sell bloaters.'

'But why ever not?', I demanded.

'Oh, but sir', she retorted, in the voice of a kindly nanny reproving a child for using a coarse word, 'West End fishmongers don't sell bloaters.' (I like the idea of London, W.2., Paddington, being 'West End'.)

In my ignorance I never realised there were these important class distinctions in food. I shall have to be more careful in future or I shall be offending people by asking for such delicacies (indeed they are) as tripe, or black pudding. (*Woman's Own*, 13 January 1962)

MORAL REASONS FOR AVERSION: THE CASE OF MEAT-EATING

The case of meat-eating draws attention to what may broadly be called 'moral' reasons for growing food dislikes, though they are very much entangled with matters of social rank too.

Before the Black Death there was, as we discussed in Chapter 3, great social inequality in the consumption of meat. The upper classes' diet tended to include a large proportion of meat. There were exceptions: certain religious orders and individual anchorites pursued extreme abstinence from meat for reasons of religious discipline. The largely vegetarian diet of the peasants was the result of compulsions of a direct physical kind – the relative shortage of meat until the later Middle Ages – not in any sense stemming either from collective social disapproval of a carnivorous diet, still less from any internalised sense of repugnance towards meat. Indeed, the association of meat-eating with the upper classes made meat all the more desirable. So, as Elias puts it,

> A medieval peasant who goes without meat because he is too poor, because beef is reserved for the lord's table, i.e. solely under physical constraints, will give way to his desire for meat whenever he can do so without external danger, unlike the founders of religious orders from the upper strata who deny themselves the enjoyment of meat in consideration of the after-life and a sense of their own sinfulness. (1939: II, 251)

From the time of the Renaissance, however, feelings towards meat-eating gradually underwent quite widespread changes, as Keith Thomas has shown in *Man and the Natural World* (1983). The dominant view among theologians at the beginning of the period was aggressively anthropocentric: animals had been created by God for the benefit of mankind, and

> In drawing a firm line between man and beasts, the main purpose of early modern theorists was to justify hunting, domestication, meat-eating, vivisection . . . and the wholesale extermination of vermine and predators. (1983: 41)

There were other elements in the Judaeo-Christian heritage more concerned with the rights of animals, and besides, as Thomas points out, people's actual feelings towards animals were always rather more complicated than the 'official' view proposed:

If we look below the surface we shall find many traces of guilt, unease and defensiveness about the treatment of animals; and many of the official attitudes . . . were remote from the practice of many people. (1983: 50)

In the long term, these gentler attitudes were to become more dominant, not just by the logical working out of the inconsistent intellectual heritage of the theologians, but as the result of social causes.

In the medieval and early modern period it was commonplace for people not only to kill and inflict pain upon animals without remorse, but for them to enjoy watching pain inflicted. In France it was one of the festive pleasures of Midsummer Day to throw cats onto a great public bonfire, and to torture cats in the course of local charivari, for the crowds' amusement at the cats' shrieks (Darnton, 1984: 83; Elias, 1939: I, 203–4). Thomas shows the prevalence of cruelty towards animals in England too. Pastimes such as bull-baiting were not only fun, but justified on gastronomic grounds – the meat was supposed to be more tender and taste better if the animal had been tormented before dying. For the same reason it was considered good practice to whip pigs or sheep to death, and, if that were somewhat too laborious, a good butcher when slitting a pig's throat took care that the victim should not die too quickly: a good long bleeding improved the meat.

There were always some implicit patterns of avoidance – there was no zero-point here any more than in other aspects of behaviour. Although Renaissance England had a remarkably catholic taste in meat, carnivores, dogs, horses and insects were among the potential sources of protein that were generally avoided. Many explanations of these avoidances in rational terms have been offered – avoidance of creatures which themselves ate carrion, for example, and avoidance of eating indispensable working beasts – but if the explanation fits one country, exceptions can always be found in other countries or cultures. What is quite clear though is that dislike of cruelty to animals played little or no part in food avoidances in medieval and modern Europe. But there is no doubt that gradually since the Renaissance Europeans generally have become less tolerant of cruelty towards animals. Thanks to Thomas's work, the transition in feeling is particularly well-documented in England. What social changes can help to account for these changing attitudes?

Thomas particularly emphasises the rise of natural history undermining the anthropocentric view of nature; the systematic observation of animals helped to make them seem less utterly different from humans in their capacity to suffer. This was part of the overall process to which sociologists often attach the ugly word 'scientification'; the development of natural history was, in its way, comparable to the Copernican revolution: heliocentrism had also served to undermine man's image of himself as the unique centre of all creation. But Thomas may be mistaking two strands of development for cause and effect. These intellectual developments were most directly felt only by an intellectual minority. Their wider impact on attitudes towards cruelty were entangled with those of other long-term processes of social development, notably urbanisation, industrialisation, and the civilising of behaviour generally.

According to Thomas, the triumph of the new attitudes towards animals was associated with 'urban isolation from animals'. The argument needs to be handled with care. Working animals remained a feature of the urban scene until well into the twentieth century, but long before that, says Thomas, 'animals became increasingly marginal to the processes of production' and 'most people were working in industries powered by non-animal means' (1983: 182). Yet the transformation of feelings began earlier still, when 'urban isolation from animals' was not a matter of *physical* but of *social* distance, for agitation against cruelty to animals did not begin among butchers or farmers or those who handled working animals. Grooms, cab-drivers and other servants did not own the animals themselves, and were usually concerned to get a job done as quickly as possible, by abusing their charges if necessary. No,

> The new sentiment was first expressed either by well-to-do townsmen, remote from the agricultural process and inclined to think of animals as pets rather than as working livestock, or by educated country clergymen, whose sensibilities were different from those of the rustics among whom they found themselves. (1983: 182–3)

Reform movements for the abolition of cruel sports were firmly based in the towns. Thomas cites Pepys's dislike of hunting and huntsmen as early as the seventeenth century. Nor was hostility to hunting simply urban: it was also a sentiment of the professional middle-class people who were 'unsympathetic to the warlike traditions of the aristocracy' (1983: 183), since hunting was notoriously a training ground for the military skills of cavalry. Thus the development of opposition to cruelty to animals can be seen to be very much bound up with parallel aspects of the civilising of behaviour discussed especially in chapter 5 above.

Agitation culminated in the foundation in 1824 of the Society (later Royal Society) for the Prevention of Cruelty to Animals, and the enactment by Parliament of a series of laws – against cruelty to horses and cattle (1822), against cruelty to dogs (1839 and 1854) and against baiting and cock-fighting (1835 and 1849). The SPCA, as Thomas points out, can be seen as: 'Yet another middle-class campaign to civilise the lower orders. In the early years those whom it prosecuted for cruelty to animals sprang almost exclusively from the working classes' (1983: 186). The working classes were not alone in retaining a more robust attitude to the sufferings of animals. The same allegation could be levelled at chefs and gastronomes. Hayward wrote that 'A true gastronome is as insensible to suffering as is a conqueror' (1852: 112). He defended such practices as whipping pigs to death and nailing geese by their feet to boards in front of roaring fires to be force fed for *foie gras*. And he quoted with no more distaste Ude's recommendation that live eels be thrown direct onto the fire before skinning, a procedure which Ude believed to make them more digestible. Both Hayward and Ude anticipated, however, that some of their readers would find such practices objectionable.

Although it was not much reflected in the mainstream of gastronomic and cookery writing, there was a fairly vigorous vegetarian movement in England from the late eighteenth century. Indeed, according to Thomas (1983: 289), as early as the middle of the seventeenth century there were individuals who adopted a vegetarian diet not for the variety of biblical and philosophical reasons always cited by a minority of religious ascetics, but on the novel grounds that they simply believed it wrong to kill animals at all.

> By the beginning of the eighteenth century . . . all the arguments which were to sustain modern vegetarianism were in circulation: not only did the slaughter of animals have a brutalising effect upon the human character, but the consumption of meat was bad for health; it was physiologically unnatural; it made men cruel and ferocious; and it inflicted untold suffering upon man's fellow-creatures. By the end of the century these arguments had been supplemented by an economic one; stock-breeding was a wasteful form of agriculture compared with arable farming, which produced far more food per acre. (Thomas, 1983: 295)

From the end of the eighteenth century, the vegetarian movement attracted some highly articulate spokesmen, most notably the poet Percy Bysshe Shelley, whose *Vindication of a Natural Diet* was published in 1813. The *Lectures on the Science of Human Life* (1839) by the American Sylvester Graham were particularly influential. The first Vegetarian Society in England was founded at Manchester in 1847 (McLaughlin, 1978: 45). In the twentieth century, vegetarianism has grown into a sizeable minority movement in many Western countries: it has many variants, several of them inspired by exotic ideas from the East; and the 'health food' shop has become a familiar feature of the High Street, patronised by many who themselves do not adopt a vegetarian diet.

If vegetarianism has remained a minority movement, other feelings of more restricted repugnance towards the slaughtering of animals for food have come to be much more widely shared. In particular, many who continue to eat meat want to have nothing to do with slaughtering it themselves, and wish to see nothing that will remind them of what that involves. This is part of a more general trend over time for 'the animalic human activities [to be] progressively thrust behind the scenes of men's communal life and invested with feelings of shame' (Elias, 1939: II, 230). In this context, killing counts as an 'animalic' activity along with intimate acts like defecation, urination or copulation. There had always been some who felt revulsion at the sight of animals suffering in the shambles (there are precursors of every movement of feeling); Thomas cites John Foxe, author of the *Book of Martyrs* in the sixteenth century. But in the towns of medieval and early modern Europe, the slaughtering of animals took place under the public gaze just as it did in the countryside.

Only gradually in Britain in the course of the nineteenth century were slaughterhouses carefully hidden from view. Often the overt motivation of legislation and regulation was concern about public health and hygiene, but growing feelings of repugnance also played their part. The concealment of slaughterhouses had, as Thomas puts it, 'become a necessary device to avoid too blatant a clash between material facts and private sensibilities' (1983: 300). These feelings grew slowly. Again, Thomas (1983: 299) cites the case of Gilbert White, author of *The Natural History of Selborne* who, though happy enough to shoot small birds in pursuance of his activities as a natural historian, in 1765 planted a row of lime trees 'to hide the sight of blood and filth' in the neighbouring butcher's yard. The public killing of animals persisted longer in the country than in the town. We have already mentioned Flora Thompson's account of the pig-killings in Lark Rise in the late nineteenth century – she was ahead of her neighbours, adult and child, in feeling 'sorry for the pig'. Nancy Mitford, in her semi-autobiographical novel *The Pursuit of Love* describes what must be typical twentieth-century feelings on holiday visits as a child to an aunt whose house adjoined a farmyard:

> Here the slaughtering of poultry and pigs, the castration of lambs and the branding of cattle took place as a matter of course, out in the open for whoever might be passing by to see. Even dear old Josh made nothing of firing, with red-hot irons, a favourite horse after the hunting season.
>
> 'You can only do two legs at a time', he would say . . . 'otherwise they can't stand the pain.'
>
> Linda and I were bad at standing pain ourselves, and found it intolerable that animals should have to lead such tormented lives and tortured deaths. (1945: 20)

Today most townspeople would go some distance out of their way to avoid seeing what goes on in abattoirs (the French word now serving as something of a euphemism in English). Their feelings are only reinforced by the efforts of those who, like Upton Sinclair in his novel of the Chicago stockyards *The Jungle* (1905), are determined that they *should* know what goes on.

One way in which these feelings were reflected in the gastronomic sphere proper was a tendency to disguise the more recognisable hunks of animals when serving them at table. In the early modern era, as Elias notes, it was still not felt to be repugnant to carve dead animals at table. Then,

> with the slow rise of the bourgeois classes, in whom pacification and the generation of inner constraints by the very nature of their social functions is far more complete and binding, the cutting up of dead animals is pushed back behind the scenes of social life (even if in particular countries, particularly England, some of the older customs survive incorporated in the new). . . . Sensitivity in this direction grows. (1939: II, 299)

Elias is right that the cutting up of joints at table has persisted more strongly in England than in France. The 'made-dishes' that were the lynchpins of French cookery from La Varenne onwards had always, will-nilly, served to mask the identity of their components. By 1830, Lady Morgan could point to the element of disguise as one of the great characteristics of Carême's style of cookery:

> Cruelty, violence and barbarism were the characteristics of the men who fed upon tough fibres of half-dressed oxen; humanity, knowledge, and refinement belong to the living generation, whose tastes and temperance are regulated by the science of such philosophers as Carême. (Morgan, 1831: II, 417)

Later in the century, Châtillon-Plessis put the point even more directly, in words which could almost have been written by Elias.

> Much could be said on the 'civilising' role of cookery.
>
> Through concealing by clever decoration or sophisticated cooking techniques the *cruel* appearance of cuts of meat, the art of cookery certainly contributes to the softening of manners.
>
> Compare what I would call the *bleeding dish nations* with the *sauce nations*, and see whether the character of the latter is not more civilised. (1894: 61)

No doubt Châtillon-Plessis had the English in mind among the 'bleeding dish nations', with their continued preference for unconcealed and unadorned joints. Even in England, the phrase should not be taken too literally: oddly enough, whereas in the seventeenth century the English had eaten their meat rarer than the continentals, by the nineteenth century the roles were reversed, with the English eating their meat well done and finding repugnant the French taste for the *saignant* steak (Thomas, 1983: 290). And with the adoption of the *service à la russe*, the whole joint tended no longer to be quite the focus of attention it had once been: James Austen-Leigh could already look back to 'when our dinners began to be carved and handed round by the servants, instead of smoking before our eyes and noses on the table' (1871: 292). The element of disguise also seems to have entered into English cookery, not so much by sophisticated technique and decoration, as by further dismemberment of meat:

> In the past it had been customary to serve pigs, calves, hares and rabbits at the table with their heads attached, but around the end of the eighteenth century there seems to have been a growing tendency to conceal the slaughtered creature's more recognisable features. (Thomas, 1983: 300)

Even so, England seems in this respect to have lagged behind France. For instance, Dallas (1877: 99) observed that calf's head was in his day still served in recognisable form in England,[6] boiled and either whole or in halves, whereas in France it was boned and served in unidentifiable pieces – except for the ears, kept whole as the choicest morsels. On the other hand, since then, calf's head has disappeared entirely from the English table, whereas in its more disguised form it has survived on many French menus. Today I have the impression that the French tend to be less squeamish in these matters than the English. *Elle* published instructions for rillettes de lapin (4

November 1965) showing the housewife skinning the rabbit, removing its head, liver and kidney, with the animal lying recumbent and recognisable on the kitchen table – a task I imagine few readers of *Woman's Own* would now undertake without repugnance.[7] Possibly it is significant that in England it was the urban middle classes which led the transformation of sensitivity in this field, while in France the cultural legacies of the peasantry on the one hand and the courtly nobility on the other have remained stronger. Far more research is needed, however, on the question of national differences (and differences between strata within countries) in feelings of repugnance.

The whole question of the threshold of repugnance towards eating meat is quite complicated. On the whole, England and France both seem to have been moving in the direction of more 'civilised' feelings in the matter, but at differing speeds and to some extent focusing on different objects: different objects in the most literal sense. For, to many people today, the most acute sensations of repugnance are felt not towards meat-eating in general but towards that large assortment of comestible objects known as offal.

EXCURSUS ON OFFAL

Offal is a good example of the changeability of objects of repugnance, and the interaction of 'moral' and social grounds for food avoidance.

The word 'offal' is used here in the sense it has in the butchery trade in Britain, a sense stated precisely by the *Oxford English Dictionary*: 'the parts which are cut off in dressing the carcass of an animal killed for food; in earlier use applied mainly to the entrails; now, as a trade term, including the head and tail as well as the kidneys, heart, tongue, liver and other parts'. The word, however, has other less neutral meanings, which the dictionary records equally: it can mean 'the parts of a slaughtered or dead animal unfit for food; putrid flesh; carrion', and more generally it can have the sense of waste or refuse (it is related etymologically to the German *Abfall*). In American English, these pejorative senses prevail most strongly, and to use the word 'offal' in connection with food is itself repugnant to many Americans.

In French, the semantic field is rather different. The term exactly corresponding to the butcher's use of 'offal' in British English is *abats*, with *abattis* used for the equivalent parts of poultry. *Abats* and *abattis* are specifically culinary words; for the meaning of waste, refuse or garbage, which 'offal' can have in English there are in French quite separate words like *déchets*, *ordures*, *détritus*.

These semantic differences happen, perhaps accidentally, perhaps not, to bear some relationship between actual differences in feelings towards offal between France, England and the USA. The French, on the whole, are more robust than the Americans about eating not just the notorious snails and frogs' legs but also brains and many other kinds of offal. The British fall somewhere in between. So, at least, it has been suggested.[8]

It is beyond the scope of this book to investigate American eating habits in detail, but the transatlantic leg of this hypothetical tripod appears to be quite strong. Marshall Sahlins discusses the American food system rather amusingly in *Culture and Practical Reason*, and records:

> During the meteoric inflation of food prices in the Spring of 1973, American capitalism did not fall apart – quite the contrary; but the cleavages in the food system did surface. Responsible government officials suggested that the people might be well-advised to buy the cheaper cuts of meat, such as kidneys, heart, or entrails – after all, they are just as nutritious as hamburger. To Americans, this particular suggestion made Marie-Antoinette seem like a model of compassion. (1976: 172)

Sahlins points out that there is more steak to the cow than there is tongue, but steak remains the more expensive because demand for it is so much higher, and that, he argues, is thanks to steak having symbolic connotations of wealth and virility.[9] Cheaper cuts and offal are associated with the poor and with ethnic minorities ('soul food'). Already before the Second World War, a sample of 693 students at American universities rated offal very high amongst the foods they most disliked (Hall and Hall, 1939), and the trend seems to be for this aversion to increase. Schwabe (1979: 407) notes that while in 1908–9 the American *Good Housekeeping* magazine gave 11 recipes for liver, 6 for heart, 3 for tripe, 2 for sweetbreads, and 1 for kidneys (making more than 25 per cent of all recipes), the issues of 1968–9 included only 5 for liver and *none* for any other visceral organ (less than 3 per cent of recipes). Recently, the US Congress has given legal authority to the national prejuduce against at least some forms of offal by exercising its constitutional powers over inter-State commerce effectively to ban the sale of lungs, spleen, and certain other organs.

I myself was able to gather some evidence of national differences in feelings of repugnance by very informal observation and conversation among the cosmopolitan clientèle dining at St Antony's College, Oxford. Certainly there were many North Americans (i.e. Canadians included) who expressed their digust at being expected to eat braised tongue, let alone brains or tripe. The Europeans, and certainly the French, tended to be more willing to eat such things even than the English. In fact it seems possible to construct a scale of feelings about offal, with objects in ascending order of repulsiveness running from liver through kidneys, tongue, sweetbreads, brains and tripe to testicles and eyes – or something like that. The Belgian sociologist Léo Moulin found very much the same thing when he questioned, in a slightly more formal and structured way, the students from many parts of Western Europe studying at the Collège d'Europe in Bruges (1975: 129–30). Social psychologists would probably succeed in Guttman-scaling[10] attitudes towards offal, with Americans showing higher repugnance (feeling antipathy towards kinds of offal lower in the scale), the English somewhere in the middle, and the French showing lowest repugnance (being happy to eat all but the items highest in the ranking).

Yet is this all not simply a matter of *chacun à son goût*? Are there not *other* foods eaten by Americans or the British that the French would view with a reciprocal repugnance? Perhaps; but apart from a hint of French revulsion at the thought of suet pastry, I have found little sign of this – the French seem to feel repugnance only at the general mode of cookery in England, not what is cooked there!

If we accept that there are, at the present day, cultural differences in feelings of repugnance towards offal, the question remains whether there is any *historical* pattern in this? How did these feelings develop, if they *did* develop and have not always been just as they are today?

One thing is fairly certain: the association of offal with the food of the poor is fairly antique. There seems to have been from very far back a custom of the internal organs of newly slaughtered animals being given away to the lower orders. A possible reason is that, unlike carcass meat, most offal cannot be kept long, and had to be eaten immediately. The story of 'umble-pie' is also well known. Jeaffreson (1875: II, 52–5) asserts (on no very clear authority) that umbles, strictly speaking the internal organs of deer, were a greatly prized food in the Middle Ages, but that in the Tudor period they came to be regarded 'with qualified disdain, as meat fit for the inferior boards of noble banquets, but inappropriate to the higher tables'. Thus 'to eat umble-pie' came to mean much the same as 'to eat below the salt', and by extension and a convenient confusion with the word 'humble' from a different root, has passed into modern English as a phrase for any humiliating experience. By the seventeenth century, recipes such as that in John Murrell's cookery book of 1631 recommended making humble-pie out of sheep's head and pluck. 'Henceforth the common pasty of the lower table seldom contained anything better than livers and hearts of oxen. More often than not, its thick, heavy crust covered an omnium-gatherum of scraps and bones and other refuse of the previous week's dinners, recooked with potatoes and slices of pumpkin' (Jeaffreson, 1875: II, 55).

The cookery books tell a somewhat more complicated and less clear story. The 'courtly' cookery books of seventeenth-century England seem on the whole to contain fewer recipes for offal than their French counterparts. May (1660) gives one for haggis (minced sheep's pluck in a sheep's stomach) but few others. Rabisha (1661) mentions rather more – tongues, feet, heads, kidneys, sweetbreads, but no liver – without them being very prominent. Patrick Lamb's recipes (1710) include 'Pullets in Bladders', 'Patty of Calves' Brains' and black puddings, and 'Umble Pyes' feature in his menus, but again these dishes form a small minority of the contents. Writing later for possibly a socially less exalted audience, Hannah Glasse (1747), on the other hand, gives a great many offal recipes, most especially in chapter II on 'Made-Dishes' where the French influence is strongest. Half a century later still, Mrs Rundell's *New System of Domestic Cookery* is notable for its directions for carving, which imply that the frontier of repugnance had not advanced as far as it has today.[11] Calf's head for example: 'Many like the eye; which you must cut out with the point of your knife and divide in two' (p. xlvii). Or a hare:

> When everyone is helped, cut off the head; put your knife between the upper and lower jaw, and divide them, which will enable you to lay the upper flat on your plate; then put the point of your knife into the centre, and cut the head into two. The ears and brains may be helped then to those who like them. (p. lii)

All the same, there are hints here that many people might *not* like the eye, ears or brains, which perhaps helps substantiate Thomas's view that a transition in feelings about such things was in train around 1800. The evidence of the cookery books remains difficult to interpret, however. Offal recipes are not very prominent in either Eliza Acton (1845) or Isabella Beeton (1861), but they are there. Acton gives recipes for beef palates, tongues, oxtails, heart and kidney, and calves' heads, sweetbreads, liver and – one mention – brains and ears. Beeton gives recipes for beef heart, kidney, oxcheek, cowheel, oxtails and tongue, sheep's kidneys, brains, head, trotters and sweetbreads. There is possibly some sign that recipes for items nearer the top of the scale of repugnance hypothesised above were becoming less numerous; on the other hand, Mrs Beeton's book contains several drawings of calves' heads sitting very recognisably on the serving dish, so it is perhaps safer to infer that in the nineteenth century England in some respects lagged behind France in the growth of these sensibilities.

Florence White (1938: 68–9), in describing how a sheep's head and pluck (including tongue, brains, heart, lights and liver) could be had for 9*d.* and made to yield five meals for the family as well as one for the chickens, implies that in the late nineteenth century this was food for the very poor. But she does not hint at any feelings of repugnance, even looking backwards from old age. That such feelings were growing there is nevertheless little doubt. Such foods featured less and less in typical twentieth-century cookery books. Ambrose Heath, writing in *Wine and Food*, 20, Spring 1939, said:

> There are a great many parts of an animal that are not ordinarily considered appropriate for the table proper, and are usually eaten by their devotees with a feeling of apology. . . . Lamb's tails, for example, make an extremely delicious if a little muttony pie, and really delicious stew can be made of other parts of this small creature, the exact nature of which is better kept hid. But these are country joys unknown, for the most part, to the townsman.

Delicacy prevented Heath from spelling out that he was referring to 'lambs' stones', the testicles of castrated lambs. He also, in the same article, said that brains, ears, feet, heads, lights ('yes, even lights') and tripe were delicacies no longer considered quite polite.

In France, the story of attitudes towards offal is even more complicated. The complication appears to arise from two forces pulling in opposite directions: on the one hand, the association of offal with poor people's food; on the other, the usefulness of offal in creating the wide variety of ragoûts demanded in an increasingly sophisticated cookery. (The latter gives point to the modern American euphemism for offal: 'variety meats'.)

Taillevent used an extensive range of offal, and there was little sign of change during the Renaissance. Le Grand d'Aussy (1782: I, 323–5) draws on the sixteenth-century Latin text, *De Re Cibaria* (1560) by La Bruyère-Champier, physician to François I, for evidence of what parts of animals were then regarded with liking or disdain. Some surprising items, such as pig's lights (lungs), then seem to have found favour in courtly circles, although those of beef or veal were considered food for the poor. La Varenne (1651) made extensive use of offal in his recipes – heads, feet, tongue, liver, sweetbreads, tail – particularly in his section on dishes suitable for preparation in camp with the army. A quarter of a century later, L.S.R. in his *Art de bien traiter* (1674) was, as noted in chapter 4, scornful of La Varenne's rusticity and vulgarity. Among the recipes he particularly ridiculed were several offal dishes – ragoût of gras double, and roe deer's liver omelette, for example. His own recipes are mainly for carcass meat, but they do include dishes of tongue, liver, sweetbreads and 'abattes d'agneau'. The tone of L.S.R.'s preface is hostile to anything smacking of the peasantry and common people, and many forms of offal appear to have shared that association in his mind.

But the trend was against him. The usefulness of offal in creating the sheer range of distinctive made-dishes then becoming central to French cookery put it at a premium; it is known that offal fetched high prices in the markets of late seventeenth-century Paris. The cookery books of the mid eighteenth century give great prominence to offal dishes, including those made from items very high on our hypothetical scale of repugnance. Marin's *Les Dons de Comus* lists the parts of each animal that were used in cooking. Of the cow: 'the head, of which the brains are used separately; the tongue, eyes and palate; the tail; the liver; the heart; the lungs; the spleen; the intestines, large and small; the tripes in general; the kidneys' (1739: 9). The intestines were used by the *charcutier*, and of the various tripes, only the *gras double* was commonly used in the kitchen. Brains were served marinated in lemon, fried, in a terrine or a matelotte, or *en croutes*. Eyes were braised and served with a vinegar sauce. *Le Cuisinier Gascon* (1740) gives a recipe for stuffed calves' eyes *au gratin*. Menon, in *La Cuisinière bourgeoise* (1746), gives an even longer list of parts used by '*bourgeois* and people who keep a good table', adding to Marin's list, for example, sheep's 'animelles' or 'rognons extérieures', and he gives several different ways of serving calves' eyes. There is certainly no sign of repugance towards any form of offal in any of these books, even if Marin does make it clear that carcass meat is 'much more essential for cookery' (1739: 12).

The first sign of any rising sensitivity in these matters that I have been able to trace in France comes in the *Almanach des gourmands* for 1806. Grimod tells his readers where they may obtain 'ram's *animelles*, formerly so sought after, but which, fortunately for the propagation of the mutton species, have entirely passed from fashion' (1806: 269). And, as we have already noted, French ways of cooking and serving food as they developed in the nineteenth century involved increasing disguise of the more overtly animal-like qualities of ingredients. In that respect France may have run ahead of England, though the element of ornamentation and decoration in fashionable cookery has since declined. Today one has the impression that offal, both in quantity and variety, is eaten more in France than England: certainly one sees brains and sweetbread, spleen and the like on public display in the ordinary butcher's shop more frequently in France than England. It is true that among the sample questioned by Claudian *et al.* in 1969, *abats* were the most frequently mentioned dislike among meats; but with 4.10 per cent of total reported dislikes (and about the same proportion of respondents) they were by no means so frequently disliked as celery (8.0 per cent), carrots and turnips (7.8 per cent) or vegetables in general (a towering 59.3 per cent).[12]

Feelings with regard to offal certainly appear to be correlated with the developments traced by Elias and Thomas. People's increasing ability to identify themselves with animals would help to explain their growing sense of repugnance in knowingly eating brains, eyes or testicles. Yet I would be cautious about advancing this as a complete explanation. It is not utterly obvious that the various sorts of offal are inherently more likely focuses for the growth of repugnance, because inherently *looking* like parts of animals (or parts of humans), than many kinds of carcass meat. The social connotations of various items of food also play an indispensable part in the growth of feelings of repugnance. In England and France (and probably more in the former), various kinds of offal have long been viewed as poor people's food. That is not the case in all cultures. Among the Yoruba, offal is more valued than carcass meat, and is offered to honoured guests in preference to steak.[13] On the other hand, once the various sorts of carcass meat and offal have been shaken into some rough order of prestige value – which happened at a very early stage in England and France – then the virtuosos of taste can consciously or unconsciously progressively refine and rationalise the distinctions between what is delicate and what is repugnant. One element in this over time has been a strengthening of feelings of repugnance towards items of offal which, psychologically more than merely visually, raise the problem of identification with animals most acutely – brains, eyes, testicles again. But it is not the only element, and can be overridden by other forces of social fashion. It was overridden in eighteenth-century France by the then stronger social pressure for fashionable tables to contain a great variety of made-dishes.

It has also been overridden in limited manner and in limited social circles in the twentieth century, in a way which at first glance may make the growth of feelings of repugnance seem to follow a cyclical rather than linear path. Ambrose Heath noted it when he observed, in *Wine and Food*, 20, Spring 1939, that sweetbreads had by then been 'promoted to the highest rank', unlike the many other kinds of offal increasingly despised and regarded with aversion. Another more recent case is that of tripe: its popularity, especially in the north of England where it was once much eaten, has greatly fallen since the Second World War. No longer is it much eaten in Yorkshire homes cold with salt, pepper and vinegar, or in Lancashire stewed in milk as 'tripe and onions'; but one is quite likely to find it being eaten in pricey London restaurants as tripes à la mode de Caen or trippa alla Romana. The same goes for brains – in England no longer much eaten on toast in poorer homes, but highly regarded in gourmet circles as cervelles au beurre noire.

CONCLUSION

Much of this chapter has had to be unapologetically speculative. Patterns of dislike, aversion and repugnance towards food, and how they have developed over time, are both less studied and less easy to study than the development of notions of good taste in food. Yet the two subjects are essentially one: the sense of repugnance is inseparable from the sense of delicacy or refinement. We have glimpsed this in earlier chapters where 'good taste' was so often seen to be defined by distinction from bad taste. The present chapter has looked at some reasons why foods are disliked and avoided. These were a trained incapacity for enjoying food, including inhibitions communicated (especially in England) through anxieties about children's food; the fear of various after-effects, including those which cause social embarrassment; and the fear of social derogation through eating or not eating foods with particular social connotations. The dialectic of delicacy and repugnance in relation to eating meat, and especially offal, has also been explored. Although the evidence is complex, it points both to an advancing frontier of repugnance and processes of rationalisation of dislikes and aversions.

12

Diminishing Contrasts, Increasing Varieties

We have looked at the development of food habits, cookery and taste in England and France from several different angles and over a very long period of time. What long-term patterns of development can be discerned, and how can they best be summarised? And how is the present most adequately to be interpreted in the light of the past?

Interpreting the present is hardest of all, because the world in which we are ourselves involved is the most difficult to view with detachment. People feel strongly about what they eat. Their food is bound up with their personal identity and social origins – 'Tell me what you eat: I will tell you what you are.' Without benefits of a long-term perspective, and especially if the spotlight is shone on certain facets to the exclusion of others, people find themselves either passionately defending or passionately attacking present-day food, cooking and eating. Critics see contemporary eating as sharing all the virtues or, more frequently, all the vices of consumer society. We have all along treated the way a society eats as an important part of its culture, so let us now examine the possibility of interpreting modern trends in cooking and eating in the light of theories of "mass culture".

THE CRITIQUE OF CONSUMER SOCIETY

The concept of mass culture has been used by both conservative and radical critics to express disquiet at the state of the arts and of culture generally. Both groups share the view that the twentieth century has witnessed the collapse of an informed and critically independent public into an unstructured, amorphous and largely apathetic mass. The mass laps up mediocre, ephemeral, mass-produced culture, whether it be literature, music or visual arts, and cultural creation of any lasting value is threatened. The conservatives and radicals differ in where they see the threat originating.

For conservative, 'aristocratic' critics like José Ortega y Gasset in *The Revolt of the Masses* (1930) or T. S. Eliot in *Notes Towards a Definition of*

Culture (1948), the threat came 'from below': the rising power of the masses jeopardised culturally creative élites. Eliot even mentioned as one symptom of the decline of culture in Britain specifically an 'indifference to the art of preparing food'. The catering trade journals and women's magazines from the 1920s to the 1950s suggest he had a point! But I do not believe that a convincing parallel can be made between cookery and the other arts from the point of view of critics like Eliot or Ortega. Perhaps they would like to argue, as indeed gastronomes did from time to time, that the incursion of the ignorant, too easily pleased *nouveaux riches* into Paris and London restaurants undermined the standards of cooking, and was the first sign of the collapse of the informed gastronomic public opinion within which critical consensus once existed. Perhaps they would see the eclipse of the *grande cuisine* after the First World War as marking the demise of the great creative culinary artists. And they could point to the contemporary mass taste for convenience and 'junk' food bringing about the deskilling of the honest artisan cook. They could argue all this, but their case would be weak. To counter it, one could point to the *nouveaux cuisiniers* and many other cooks of today as artistically creative as any in the past, and one could caution against a 'great man' conception of history which exaggerated how 'creative' any but a tiny minority of cooks had ever been in the past.

For the radical critics, the threat to the quality of contemporary culture comes not from below but from above. It comes from the capitalist 'culture industry'. The members of the Frankfurt School preferred to speak of the 'culture industry' rather than of 'mass culture', because they wished to avoid any suggestion of it originating spontaneously within the masses (see especially Adorno and Horkheimer, 1944). The atomised mass was at the mercy of the interests controlling the culture industry. Through the profit-seeking capitalist mass media their very tastes, wants and needs could be manipulated. Several ideas advanced by members of the Frankfurt School with reference to the arts and culture in general suggest thought-provoking parallels with particular details of modern trends in cooking and eating.

Walter Benjamin, in his influential essay 'The Work of Art in the Age of Mechanical Reproduction' (1936), argues that mass reproduction destroys the 'aura' of a work of art as something unique, authentic and individual. The production of copies by the hundred thousand – prints of the Mona Lisa for instance – 'detaches the reproduced object from the domain of tradition' and leads to 'a tremendous shattering of tradition'. There are problems in drawing an analogy between a great dish and a great work of art – fond as chefs have been of the idea – because dishes, being constantly eaten, have *always* had to be constantly reproduced. Queen Victoria's chef M. Ménager used to say that though the cook has as difficult a task as anyone who created beauty from wood or stone, there were no memorials to his art: his triumph was a momentary one, between the serving of the dish and the minute when the last few mouthfuls were eaten (Tschumi, 1954: 66). So a dish, even one of the few whose first creator is known, possesses the quality of uniqueness only in a very limited way. All the same, Benjamin's essay does throw light on the significance of mass-produced tinned or frozen 'gourmet dishes', which like a print of a famous painting may not only be a poor representation of the original but may be experienced in the purchaser's own situation, probably quite incongruous with their original context and tradition.

Benjamin was to some extent more 'optimistic' than his Frankfurt School colleagues. He saw film as a novel kind of work of art, pointing the way to a new collective mode of artistic production and new aesthetic. It might be tempting to try to find an analogy in Escoffier's reform of the professional kitchen, in which more closely interdependent sous-chefs constructed a culinary masterpiece a little like the numerous specialists in a production team create a film. But that line of thought leads equally to the modern mass-production, high technology kitchen, carrying with it the deskilling and proletarianisation of the cook. This is more in line with the general pessimism of other members of the Frankfurt School.

Theodor Adorno, distinguished musicologist as well as sociologist, depicted two afflictions of musical life brought about by the workings of the culture industry: a kind of 'fetishism', and the 'regression of listening'. The characteristic of fetishism developed in music through the growth of 'a pantheon of best-sellers':

> The programmes shrink, and the shrinking process not only removes the moderately good, but the accepted classics themselves undergo a selection that has nothing to do with quality. In America, Beethoven's Fourth Symphony is among the rarities. This selection reproduces itself in a fatal circle: the most familiar is the most successful and is therefore played again and again and made still more familiar. (1938: 276)

It is very inviting to see a fetishistic character in food produced by the operation of the food industry, parallel to that which according to Adorno is created in music by the culture industry. There are certainly some forces at work tending towards the standardisation of a limited repertoire of dishes. A market research report on British catering confirmed that: 'In the case of multiple catering organisations, menus are planned at head office level and are more or less standard for all outlets with slight variations to allow for regional food preferences, etc.' (Acumen, 1978: 18).

Then there is the effect of a firm like Alveston Kitchens, who produce frozen 'gourmet dishes' widely used in British hotels. Large as is the Alveston range, it is very small compared with the repertoire found in the pages of Escoffier or Elizabeth David. There must be many great dishes which suffer the fate of Beethoven's Fourth. At a less grand level, the fashions of the supermarket shelves may have a similar effect: packets of cheesecake mix drive out the vast array of English puddings. Another example is the effect of mass production on English cheeses: from the late nineteenth century dozens of local and regional cheeses ceased to be made until in the early 1950s only about half a dozen cheeses could be found.[1] (In more recent years, many old cheeses have been revived and, as in France where variety always survived, new ones have been developed.)

The second link in Adorno's critique of modern musical culture was 'the regression of listening'. It was not the individual listen*er*, but contemporary listen*ing* which had been 'arrested at the infantile stage'. The regression was not to an earlier musical era, but rather to an infantile state in which the listener was docile and afraid of anything new. The regressed listener would 'stubbornly reject' new musical experience (1938: 286). Explaining Adorno's argument, Martin Jay in his history of the Frankfurt School actually makes the comparison with eating:

> Like children who demand only food they would have enjoyed in the past, the listener whose hearing had regressed could respond only to a repetition of what it had heard before. Like children who respond to bright colours, he was fascinated by the use of colourative devices that gave the impression of excitement and individuality. (Jay, 1973: 190)

Adorno, were he alive today and following the food scene, might well look to junk food as an instance of the regression of eating. It comes from America, like the jazz he so much disliked. Or he could instance the ornamental cookery *sometimes* found in cookery columns, where – as in jazz – very simple basic themes are endlessly reiterated with trimmings. He could point to the way that food manufacture makes it possible for people, if they so wish, to eat the same few favourite foods all the year round just as they can endlessly play the same pop record. And he would expect them so to wish: stubbornly to reject a richer and more diverse experience, the culinary parallel to *le refus ouvrier* in cultural life generally. He would perhaps argue that they had been 'forcibly retarded' by the food industry and be quite unsurprised by George Orwell's contention (1937: 89) that 'the English palate, especially the working class palate, now rejects good food almost automatically'.

At this point, Adorno's specific argument about musical life merges with the Frankfurt School's more general thesis about culture in a capitalist society. They opposed the view common among American sociologists that contemporary mass culture is a response through the market to what people want, that in its diversity it meets the demands of all tastes.[2] Adorno, together with Max Horkheimer, Herbert Marcuse, and other Frankfurt School colleagues rejected the liberal notion of individual 'taste'; it had been completely undermined by the gradual liquidation of the autonomous subject in modern society. In modern capitalism, people were manipulated down to their very instincts, their very 'needs' were moulded by the culture industry.[3]

This argument has an exact counterpart in the domain of food. Arnold Bender, a distinguished nutritionist who worked for many years in industry, asserted simply that 'the manufacturer makes what the public wants' (in

Yudkin and McKenzie, 1964: 109). We have also quoted Lord Forte's declaration that his catering empire gives people the food they like, and that his turnover proves it.

There is no need to question the sincerity of such statements. They are perfectly true, though they do not explain very much. The problem with the use of words like 'manipulation' by the Frankfurt School and other critics is that it suggests that those in powerful positions in industry – the culture industry or the food and catering industries – *consciously* and with malevolent intent set out to persuade people that they need and like products of inferior or harmful quality. It fails to draw attention to the unplanned, unintended, vicious spiral through which supply and demand are usually linked. It is now widely accepted in medical circles that many chemicals finding their way into manufactured food are harmful in large quantities. It is also becoming clear that the Western diet, too high in sugar, salt and fat, deficient in fibre, is a major cause of degenerative diseases in Western societies. That does not prove that manufacturers cynically set out to do harm. When biscuits and jams containing cheap sugar proved popular and profitable in the late nineteenth century, the harmful effects of sugar were not understood. Equally, when roller milling made possible flour with less fibre than ever before, the public's taste for white bread was well established, but its potential harmfulness was unknown. All the same, these things set in motion a compelling, self-reinforcing process which on the one hand shaped popular taste, and on the other hand established vested interests which the industry has been known to defend ruthlessly even in the light of more recent nutritional knowledge (see Walker and Cannon, 1984).

The critique we have been imagining the Frankfurt School might have made of contemporary culinary culture has some valid points. It is true that people cannot 'need' or want what they have not experienced, and that there are some forces at work tending to create concentrations of power capable of limiting and standardising some aspects of the range of experience available. Yet multinational food manufacturing conglomerates and gigantism in the hotel trade are only part of the picture. Overall the trend is towards more people in England and France having the opportunity for *more* varied experience in eating and to develop *more* varied tastes. Anyone who wishes to maintain that we are witnessing the 'regression of eating' had better remember the difficulty Adorno faced in arguing for the regression of listening. He had to recognise that 'the millions who are reached musically for the first time by today's mass communications cannot be compared with the audience of the past'. No matter how much the gastronome accustomed to the most refined cookery may deplore modern mass food, taking the long-term perspective there is no doubt that – in Western countries but not yet in the world as a whole – more varied cookery as well as more plentiful food is more widely available than ever before. If commercial interests serve to make people's tastes more standardised than they conceivably could be in the past, they impose far less strict limits than did the physical constraints to which most people's diet was subject for most of the period we have studied. And if in the concert halls of the late twentieth century Beethoven's Fifth is still played more than the Fourth, there are also more opportunities than ever before to hear Schoenberg and Stockhausen (or, for that matter, less familiar masters of the past like Josquin des Pres and Buxtehude).

So a longer-term perspective is needed: underneath the many swirling cross-currents, the main trend has been towards *diminishing contrasts* and *increasing varieties* in food habits and culinary taste. One trend, not two: for in spite of the apparent contradiction between diminishing contrasts and increasing varieties, these are both facets of the same processes, as will become clear if we look at each in turn.

DIMINISHING CONTRASTS

In the Middle Ages, at the very beginning of the long period we have studied, there were very great social inequalities in the distribution of nourishment. Differences in diet between the estates of society were more striking than the differences between various countries of Western Europe. The upper classes appear generally to have eaten more, in purely quantitative terms (as judged by modern nutritional studies of their food intake) than the lower orders. The upper classes also ate a far larger proportion of meat for much of the medieval and early modern period, though in this there were fluctuations: between the Black Death and about 1550 butchers' meat seems to have been relatively plentiful for all. Inequalities in nourishment diminished only gradually, these too fluctuating according to economic conditions. Descriptions of the diet of the poorest people of the towns and countryside in the eighteenth and nineteenth centuries can still horrify the modern reader. Slowly too, there has developed greater sensitivity of feeling towards inequalities in nourishment, as towards social inequalities generally. At some stage in the last 400 years it has become inconceivable for popes or kings to mount magnificent banquets in the midst of famine. Identification with the lot of one's fellow men, *qua* fellow men, has gradually become stronger, associated with the ties of interdependence between higher and lower social groups becoming closer and balances of power between them somewhat more equal; though even at the beginning of the twentieth century Rowntree and Kendall could report from the English countryside a farmer's complaints about workers becoming discontented and unwilling to work so hard, and they reflected:

> But we could hardly help thinking that he would have been rather sorry to measure his own needs by the needs of his men. He took it for granted that he and they represented two different types of being, and thus he failed to grasp their point of view. (1913: 316–17)

By the late twentieth century, however, it was generally considered good form to express and even to feel shock and horror at hunger not only in one's own society but in the Third World too.

In medieval and early modern Europe, the insecurity of food supplies affected both the highest and the lowest, but bore most heavily on the lower orders. The consequences of harvest failures and famines became notably less serious in France and England, with improving social and economic organisation, only from the late seventeenth and eighteenth centuries. We argued in chapter 2 that, closely connected with the increasing security of food supplies and the more equal social distribution of nourishment, there has taken place a 'civilising of appetite'. It was seen in an increased pressure towards self-control over eating, manifest initially only in the higher social circles to whom alone at first was the fear of obesity realistic, but gradually spreading (like so many other facets of the civilising of behaviour) down through the social ranks until the concern with 'weight-watching' is very widespread.

Another, but related, set of contrasts which have become less marked are those between the seasons, and between festival and everyday eating. Special food for special occasions such as Christmas or the family *rites de passage* has by no means disappeared entirely, and studies have shown, for example, that 'festival' dishes endure more in the French countryside than in the towns. But the strong rhythm of eating imposed by the seasons has markedly declined. Shops are equally full all the year round. Furthermore, advancing techniques of food processing and preservation mean that people can increasingly choose the *same* foods irrespective of season; this can mean choosing the same few favourite or most palatable foods. As Yudkin and McKenzie (1964: 18) pointed out, in some cases this can lead to a nutritionally undesirable restriction of the diet – though the more general effect of advancing technology has been to diversify diets.

The steadily spreading network of trade and transport has also served to diminish contrasts between the food of the town and the country. Historically towns have enjoyed a much greater diversity of foods in their markets than was available in the countryside. Since the nineteenth century this difference has become much less marked, though surveys (such as Claudian *et al.*, 1969) show that in the countryside restrictions of supply can still limit the contents of the shopping basket. Of course, some of the worst pictures of the food of the poor came from the towns, not the countryside; but again, the evidence is of improved trade, transport and marketing greatly benefiting the diet of the urban poor towards the end of that century.

Longer chains and denser networks of interdependence are not only a matter of geography but also of technology. Manufactured foods have formed a steadily growing part of the diet in England and – with slightly more resistance – in France. Tinned, frozen, instant and pre-cooked foods are often decried, but the National Food Survey Committee (notably in its

1960 report) has emphasised the part they have played in improving the nutritional value of the average British diet in the course of the twentieth century. Moreover, *all* social strata use convenience foods. There are minor differences related to income and occupation, but 'the gradation in expenditure was less steep for convenience foods than for all other foods' (NFSC, 1967: 2).

We have, however, in this book been less interested in the nutritional than in the aesthetic aspects of food, cooking and eating. It is one demonstration of the 'polyphony of history' that the development of *haute cuisine* served for some centuries to *increase* rather than diminish contrasts, and the curve turned downwards relatively recently. The late medieval *haute cuisine* seen in manuscripts like Taillevent and the *Forme of Cury* seems to have been confined to a few exceptional centres, and probably to special occasions too. For the rest, although the upper strata ate quantitatively more, contrasts in styles and techniques of cookery were not large: even among the rich and powerful simple roasting and boiling seem to have been the dominant methods. At the base of society, the tempo of change in cooking methods remained slow to non-existent, very much a domain of the *longue durée*. The cookery of the courts, however, underwent increasingly rapid elaboration. Printing probably helped accelerate this development: Peter Burke (1978) has argued that in medieval Europe there was a popular culture in which in some measure all ranks of society participated, but that printing helped sunder the popular and the literate culture. Something parallel probably happened in the sphere of cookery. Perhaps the common participation of all social ranks in modern mass catering, convenience and fast foods, can be seen as restoring only in the very recent past some semblance of the medieval culinary unity.

At any rate, 'refined' food became one vehicle for the expression of the superiority of upper circles. Such progressive refinement, in cookery as in manners, is accelerated by pressure 'from below'. There is *always* pressure from below though its strength varies, always social competition though its fierceness fluctuates. Elite characteristics are adopted by the rising outsider groups; established and outsider groups repeatedly merge (mixing elements of style originating in both), to form new establishments which in turn are pressured 'from below' by new outsider groups (Elias, 1939: II, 251ff.). In the history of 'refined' cookery, courtly circles played a prominent part, and continued to do so for rather longer in France than in England. Already in the mid-eighteenth century, writers like Hannah Glasse can be seen producing a style of cookery which blends elements of the French courtly style with the 'country' cookery of the English gentry. In France, in the following century, elements of the courtly tradition can be seen persisting and undergoing development in the cuisine of the restaurants, themselves essentially part of the bourgeois way of life.

Reflecting on changes since the Middle Ages, Richard Warner at the end of the eighteenth century identified a long-term trend; he put his finger on the connection between relatively more equal power ratios in society and a decline in ostentation and superfluity in cooking and eating:

> when we contemplate the vast magnificence of the baron in the romantic ages of chivalry, and . . . the halls of the great filled with the poor, we are apt, at first glance, to draw conclusions very erroneous and comparisons very unfavourable to present times and present manners. But when we consider . . . that we have exchanged this barbaric magnificence for simple elegance, unmeaning pomp for substantial comfort, ill-judged hospitality for an active industry which enables the larger part of the community to live independent of the precarious bounty of the great, and undiscriminating charity for certain and established regulations which amply provide for the children of poverty and distress, we then find reason to congratulate ourselves on this change and improvement in manners and opinions; and gladly give up the unwieldy grandeur of former ages for the blessings, conveniences and refinements of the present time. (1791: lvii)

The grandiose ostentation of professional cookery in the age of Carême, Gouffé and Dubois rather obscured any movement towards 'simple elegance', and it was the best part of a century before the truth of Warner's insight was readily apparent. Yet the nineteenth century produced such dissimilar spirits as Thomas Walker and Escoffier, both of whom in their different ways campaigned for greater simplicity and against the surviving potlatch element in meals. Just before the First World War, signs of unease at luxurious eating were to be found even in *L'Art culinaire*. The war itself was a watershed. The recollections of Gabriel Tschumi (1954) show vividly how the spirit of economy, avoidance of waste and ostentation, and a more democratic and informal air spread finally even to the British royal household, so that the food eaten by royalty after the war resembled that of their middle-class subjects much more closely than it had in the reigns of Queen Victoria or King Edward VII. In France too, according to Kouindjy, after the First World War the meals of the well-to-do became simplified and 'democratised'. Until then their diet had been too much dominated by 'the fantasies of cooks, by fashion, and by the vanity of gourmets' (1926: 161), and had paid far too little heed to what was healthy. From then onwards writers like Edouard de Pomiane and numerous successors campaigned for a healthier diet, urging their readers to eat less meat and more vegetables, and using scientific knowledge to make the case for greater self-restraint and selectivity in eating.

The contrast between élite professional cookery and everyday cookery has diminished, after the long period culminating in the nineteenth century when it steadily widened. Several elements contributed to the narrowing of the gap. Even in the nineteenth century, through the process of 'butterisation' some of the dishes of the French peasantry were being absorbed into the repertoire of *haute cuisine*. More important, from around the turn of the century and especially after the war, was the popularisation among the well-to-do of French regional and 'country' cuisine itself – without any preliminary 'butterisation', although it was the peaks and not the troughs of the peasant diet which appealed. The decisive changes which the First World War confirmed both in England and France made the old *grande cuisine* far too expensive for the market now to stand, but the process should not be thought of as simply a narrowing of the market for fine food. The gastronomes and guides, cookery books and columns have also done a great deal, especially in England since the Second World War, to spread appreciation of good cookery to *wider* audiences than before.

The growth and successive transformations of the hotel and restaurant trade have played a part too in diminishing social contrasts. In looking at the fashionable hotels and restaurants of the late nineteenth century it is easy to forget that they were perversely already a step ahead on the road to culinary democracy, since they were far more public and less exclusive places than any from which the finest food could have been obtained a century or so earlier. Nor should the contribution of chain caterers such as J. Lyons, which emerged in the early twentieth century in Britain, in making available a better standard of meal to a wider clientèle be lightly dismissed. The process has gone much further since. Of course, eating out is still related to class and income, especially in Britain, but less so than it was. The social stratification of eating-places has become still more blurred in the late twentieth century. The editor of *Hotel and Restaurant Management* made a telling point in the January 1964 issue:

> Chi-chi writers sneering at caterers who provide simple inexpensive meals at the expense of traditional haute cuisine underestimate both public demand and changing taste. The brightly-lit classless popular catering establishment is rapidly replacing the old dirty dingy 'café round the corner'. These writers would not dream of giving the old establishment consideration; but the modern popular rendezvous demands – and gets – their attention.

There is plainly a problem of perspective here. For a person accustomed to eating the most refined cooking, 'popular' food will seem tasteless and inferior; for those who are not, a Berni Inn or a similar chain restaurant may seem a distinct improvement over unenterprising menus of the sort for middle-class establishments seen in the British trade journals in the 1930s or 1950s. In the same way but a little higher up the market it is easy to sneer at the rather standardised offerings of 'international hotel cuisine', but what went before it in the same class of establishment for the same sort of clientèle would probably be judged less skilled and less enterprising.

Finally, looking at the social connotations of particular foods, with many exceptions and cross-currents the curve of contrasts seems first to rise and then to diminish. At the Coronation banquet of James II, for example, we noted adjacent dishes of foods like caviare and black puddings which subsequently came to have very different social connotations. By the late nineteenth century, *haute cuisine* was setting such store by the use of certain very expensive foods such as caviare, crayfish and truffles that they became clichéd. At the same time, the disdain felt by upper circles for some foods came to be shared by lower circles: the fate of tripe. In the opposite direction, formerly lower-class dishes have been taken up in higher circles: cassoulet, tripe again. Modern technology and accountancy have produced some quirks of this sort. *Catering and Hotel Management*, March 1979, reported how traditional leftover dishes, particularly English puddings, were no longer appearing on many menus because they were too labour-intensive. For that very reason, though, these old 'utility' dishes were being transformed into up-market frozen products. The classic case was bread-and-butter pudding,

> one of the successes of the Top Choice list. This is predominantly aimed at the higher price market because both the butter and its spreading contribute notably to the cost and so does the lattice-work which can be applied only by hand.

Other examples of dishes enjoying upward social mobility were *bread* pudding, bubble and squeak, and (not frozen, but processed) quick-soak mushy peas. Their appeal rested on nostalgia (always a potent force in food advertising) and 'inverted snobbery'.

INCREASING VARIETIES

In describing several components of a trend towards diminishing contrasts, we have been looking only at one side of a coin. A trend towards increasing varieties can be seen within the very same processes.

Variety and differentiation are, of course, intrinsic to the development of any kind of *haute cuisine*. It is not only a question of the proliferation of dishes and sauces which gathered pace particularly in France from the late seventeenth to the late nineteenth century. It was also a matter of the differentiation of the social contexts which fostered this proliferation: the differentiation of public restaurants from private households; then the differentiation of many kinds of restaurant; and the creation of a competitive market which did so much to quicken the pace of culinary change and innovation.

Yet that is increasing variety at only a fairly superficial level. For a long time the pattern was still strongly hierarchical, with one dominant style serving as an accepted yardstick. This is plainest in France, where cooks and gourmets deferred to courtly cookery in the eighteenth century and to the *grande cuisine* of the restaurants in the nineteenth. In England the story of the growth of French hegemony was a little more complicated, but there too the *grande cuisine* had effects (notably through what we have called the decapitation of English cookery) out of proportion to the number of diners who actually sampled it regularly.

During the twentieth century this prestige hierarchy has become less marked, though it still persists more in France than in Britain. Perhaps in Britain the catering profession always tended to see itself as meeting the differing needs of a series of distinct markets rather than unambiguously deriving its standards from one ultimate central model. French cuisine cast a long shadow, but was in a sense regarded as *hors concours*, setting standards too high to take much account of. In France, *haute cuisine* was and still is bound up with the national *gloire*. Even there, the advent in the 1970s of a brash magazine like *Néo* signalled that many were willing to look at catering mainly in terms of marketing, technology and throughput, though a sense of the national tradition did in time reassert itself in *Néo*'s pages.

Signs of the decline of rigid stylistic hierarchy can be traced quite far back. Just as London Society widened in the later nineteenth century with the differentiation of overlapping social circles (centred on politics, finance, the sporting scene), so a little later emerged a pluralism in the world of eating. Just as people of more ambiguous social backgrounds gained an entrée, so did entrées of questionable origin. Curnonsky (1958: 188–90) wittily caught the flavour of the pluralism which emerged in his lifetime in his account of parties in gastronomy. He distinguished five, ranging from extreme right to extreme left. The devotees of the *grande cuisine* were now to be counted as the extreme right. Their kind of learned, *recherché*, complicated cuisine required a great chef, and materials of the very finest quality; it was now to be found mainly in embassies and palaces – in hotels it was often only a parody.

The right was represented by traditional cookery: its adherents believed one ate well only at home, ate dishes cooked slowly over a wood fire by an old woman-cook who had served the family 30 years, and their cellars were full of pre-phylloxera wines and brandy laid down by a great-grandfather.

The gastronomic centrists were those whose taste ran to the good *cuisine bourgeoise* of France; they were happy to admit that one could still eat well in a restaurant; they demanded that 'things taste of what they are' and be never adulterated or fussy; they were guardians of the great regional dishes.

The left were those who advocated cookery with no frips or frills, even quick snacks and doing what one could with the minimum of time and whatever was to hand. They were quite content with an omelette, a chop, or a steak, or indeed with a slice of ham or a sausage. They did not ban the use of tinned food; they declared a good sardine in oil had its charms, and that such and such a make of tinned beans was at least as good as fresh ones. They looked for modest little restaurants where the proprietor did the cooking himself, and they recommended simple country cooking.

Finally, there was the extreme left:

> the eccentrics, the restless, the innovators, those whom Napoleon called ideologues. Always in quest of new pleasures and untried sensations, curious about all exotic cuisines, all foreign or colonial specialities, they want to taste the dishes of every country and every age.

Above all, they love to invent new dishes; and some were anarchists without bonds, who sought the overthrow of all out-of-date dishes.

This culinary pluralism is the counterpart of something which is more familiar in the arts: the loss of a single dominant style. Styles like the baroque and rococo enjoyed virtually unchallenged dominance in their age, more unchallenged indeed than the aristocratic upper classes with which they were associated. In a more problematic way so did Romanticism dominate an age and spread across the range of the arts. During the last hundred years or more, however, this stylistic unity has been lost. There is a greater diversity of tastes co-existing and competing at one time – competing more equally, again like classes and interests in society. There is a rapid succession of fashions in artistic styles. And the mixture of elements deriving from several styles is common: the label *kitsch* is often applied to at least some such mixtures.[4]

Stylistic mixtures in menus and in individual dishes are commonplace. Perhaps the most striking single example in my own experience was a smoked-reindeer pizza eaten in Finland. Rapidly fluctuating fashions have been observable since the turn of the century, when diplomatic events made things English, Russian or Moroccan successively fashionable in Paris. The wavelength has since become shorter and the amplitude wider. Christopher Dilke (in *Wine and Food*, 17, Spring 1938) described the waves of fashion which had hit London in the 1930s. First Dublin Bay prawns 'ignited by an under-waiter with the aid of some cheap brandy' and grandly termed *scampi vênitiens*. Then everything transfixed on a skewer and called *shashlyk caucasien*. Finally, at the time he was writing, French regional cookery was all the rage: Dilke compared it with Parisian society going crazy over Lancashire hotpot. 'From Stratton Street to Soho Square *le chichi régional* is supreme.' He mentioned as specially prominent cassoulet, 'slices of old sausage heated up with beans', and even *couscous*. With the exception of the last, which, originating in French colonial spheres of interest, has never become common in England although it is everywhere in France, all these fashions and many more reappeared in England after the war and spread beyond London to humble provincial eating places.

Since the Second World War there have been four major waves of foreign influence in British catering: in rough chronological order, the Italians, the Chinese, the Indians, and the Greeks and Turks.[5] To these must be added the profound and continuing American influence, especially in the hamburger bars and other fast food operations which are themselves subject to waves of fashion. Italian, Chinese, Indian and Greek/Turkish restaurants, along with American-style businesses, spread to every part of the British Isles, and mostly catered for the less expensive end of the market. As each wave of fashion succeeded the last, the effects of the previous ones did not vanish. Numbers of Italian, Chinese or Indian restaurants may have eased back slightly, but broadly speaking each has remained as a lasting presence on the British catering scene.[6]

In France, by contrast, although Chinese and Indo-Chinese restaurants are a common sight and North African food has made some headway – food follows the flag – the national traditions have held their own better than the English. France has found plenty of scope for the play of fashion *within* French cuisine. In British catering it is noteworthy that French restaurants, even counting everything from the most expensive to the humblest bistro, form a minuscule part of the trade. Of course, French cookery always had an 'ideological' sway in England out of all proportion to the numbers of establishments where it could be eaten. Nowadays surveys show that the younger age groups have a particular liking for oriental cooking – for one thing they are more familiar with it than with French dishes. The hegemony of French cuisine among the knowledgeable is, however, still quite strong. Among London restaurants with distinct national styles recommended by Egon Ronay each year from 1971 to 1979, the French have a place out of proportion to their numbers.[7]

Increasing variety is not to be seen only in the professional catering world. By the twentieth century it was no longer possible either in England or France to point to one or two cookery books which defined a dominant style of domestic cooking. Variety is also the most striking feature of women's magazine cookery columns in recent decades. Just as foreign cuisines have made fewer inroads among restaurants in France than in England, so they have invaded French magazines rather less. None the less, in both countries, while the contents of the mass-circulation and the more up-market magazines have become more alike, the food they all discuss has become more diverse and cosmopolitan. Passing fashions are reflected in their pages too.

The ever-closer interdependence of professional and domestic cookery is a prime source of change and variety. Some of the links between them are old, some newer, but all are becoming more closely interwoven. One old link is through eating out. Although eating out is still correlated with occupational rank and income, it is part of the experience of a larger part of the population than ever before. In France, where cafés and restaurants had for a long time played a part in social life more akin to the pub in England, the greatest growth in the 1960s and 1970s was in lunches eaten during working hours, in staff canteens and elsewhere. In England, social strata which had previously rarely eaten out for pleasure began to do so, especially at the less expensive eating places where the cooking was often in foreign styles. Longer holidays, increasingly spent abroad, and the growth of tourism also served to broaden ordinary people's experience of hitherto unfamiliar food.

Still more important, because they pervade people's own kitchens every day, are the links between the professional and the domestic cook created by advances in food technology and marketing. They have given the professional cook an increasing share of the responsibility, as John Fuller phrased it, for what is eaten at home. For all that they are criticised, manufactured foods of all kinds have undeniably introduced a variety to ordinary people's tables which hardly bears comparison with the monotonous diets of the less well off before the present century. Interestingly, Kleyngeld's study (1974) of housewives most likely to be among the first to adopt new manufactured food products (albeit in the Netherlands, not Britain or France), suggests that this characteristic is not strongly related to class or income, but depends specifically on their degree of 'food involvement' – how interested they are in cooking and eating.

This brings us to a final area of increasing variety: a growing diversity of motivation. Eating, needless of say, has since the dawn of human society been both a necessity and a pleasure. Yet while everyone has to eat to live, not everyone has had equal opportunities to live to eat. Cooking, on the other hand, has always been mainly work for those who actually had to do it (whether housewife or professional), even if some have always been able to draw satisfaction from a job well done. One facet of greater social equality in the twentieth century is that very few households in England and France can now employ a professional cook, so that nearly all families have to cook for themselves. For a social minority cooking has become part of necessary work, as it has always been for the majority. On the other hand, many more people have the chance from time to time to experience eating and even cooking as something out of the routine. Eating out as a species of entertainment now finds a place in the spare-time spectrum for more people, as does cooking at home for special occasions. It would be naive, nevertheless, to imagine that cookery is now a realm of pure freedom. One has only to remember the undertones of cookery columns – the implications of the phrase 'hostess cookery' for example – to realise that pressures to keep up culinary appearances are not now felt only by a few Society hostesses.

CONCLUSION

There is broader significance in characterising as 'diminishing contrasts, increasing varieties' the overall direction of development of cooking and eating in England and France. For, as Elias (1939: II, 252–6) suggests, it is one of the peculiarities of Western society that the reduction of contrasts in culture and conduct has been meshed with the co-mingling of traits deriving initially from very different social levels. In the conduct of workers can still be seen in England traces of the manners of the landed gentry and prosperous merchants, in France the airs of courtiers and a bourgeoisie brought to power by revolution. Yet equally, though work was once an attribute of the lower classes, virtually every able person is now expected to earn a living. In the history of cooking and eating we have seen something similar. Conceptions of good and bad food have developed through many successive rounds of social contest. Food favoured by some groups of people always has been and no doubt always will be disapproved of by other groups. Likes and dislikes are never socially neutral, but always entangled with people's affiliations to class and other social groups. Higher social circles have repeatedly used food as one of many means of distinguishing themselves from lower rising classes. This has been manifested in a succession of styles and attitudes towards food and eating. The tensions and competition have always been too strong in the end for establishment groups to maintain their culinary exclusiveness, and as each round led to ever-greater complexity and the rise of broader and broader classes, so a cultural and culinary blending has produced many varieties and nuances of cuisine. That same process also means that social contrasts can in long-term perspective be seen as well to have become more subtle and complex. They have diminished but by no means disappeared. Hierarchical standards have ways of being constantly transformed, surviving in new forms in a seemingly more egalitarian world. Conventional survey techniques of the sort so often favoured by sociologists will continue to show up very effectively the differences between social groups or classes at a moment in time. Such 'snapshot' methodology, however, reveals little about how much they have changed in the past or about their potential for change in the future. The risk is that sociologists exaggerate the fixedness and determinacy of social traits, and suppress the flux and movement in social life. That is what this book has tried to avoid, by consciously adopting a developmental or 'figurational' approach, by covering a very long span of time, and also by comparing two countries.

In both France and England, two neighbouring countries sharing so much history and cultural heritage, the same long-term social processes – the division of labour, urbanisation, industrialisation, civilising processes – have been at work. Thus in the broadest terms the social history of eating has been quite similar in both. Yet there have been important differences between them too, in the timing and outcome of some of the major social contests, for example. We hope we have succeeded in using the similarities and the differences to show both the broad forces shaping taste in food in France and England, and also the fluidity and indeterminacy which has permitted the emergence and development of distinctive culinary cultures.

Afterword

This second edition of *All Manners of Food* affords me an opportunity to admit that, although an historian by inclination, I am a sociologist by profession. The original publishers forbade me to make any mention of the dreaded word 'sociology', whether in the book's title or in the author's biographical details – on the grounds that it would certainly glue copies to the shelves in the bookshops. Perhaps they were right, for the book sold far better and attracted more widespread notice than the typical work of sociology. Even so, the theoretical disputation in chapter 1 was enough to put off some readers, including one whose judgment I would have greatly valued. The late Jane Grigson, who had not herself been so deterred, told me the comic but sad story of how the book came not to be reviewed in the *Times Literary Supplement:* it seems the book was sent for review to the great Elizabeth David, who opened it at pages 8–9, saw Lévi-Strauss's culinary triangle, and, without noticing my own low opinion of that idea, declined to write a review.

I intended *All Manners of Food* to be not just a book about the popular subject of food but also a contribution to the upsurge of historical sociology which has taken place over the last fifteen years or so, when the writings of – among others – Michel Foucault, Fernand Braudel, E. P. Thompson, Charles Tilly, and, of course, my own mentor Norbert Elias[1] found a wide audience. Fortunately, one no longer needs to dissemble about which side of the largely abstract boundary between history and sociology one stands on, and still less to apologise for writing about food. Sociologists, especially, used to regard eating as a rather frivolous topic for research, but not anymore.[2] Since I finished the first edition of this book late in 1984, many countries and many disciplines have contributed to a flood of serious and fascinating research on food in its social and historical context. In this Afterword, I want to sketch some of the later work that is most relevant to reading *All Manners of Food* more than a decade later, and also to glance beyond England and France to suggest how 'culinary cultures' have developed elsewhere, especially in other European countries and in the United States.

MORE THEORETICAL FUN: FISCHLER, HARRIS, MINTZ, AND FINKELSTEIN

The onslaught on structuralism has continued; I suppose no fashion is more dead than a dead Parisian intellectual fashion, unless it be a *passé* Parisian style of cookery. In his major book *L'Homnivore,*[3] even Claude Fischler, whose earlier work was much influenced by structuralism, joins in the criticisms levelled at that tradition. Like Jack Goody (1982: 29),[4] he finds the attempt to define biological factors out of the explanation of social patterns the least satisfactory part of the legacy of Durkheim; for him, 'nature/culture' is a 'false dilemma'.[5] As a sociologist deeply immersed in empirical data on French eating habits over the last two decades, Fischler is highly conscious of change and the necessity of explaining it sociologically. In this respect, like me, Fischler is somewhat critical of Bourdieu[6] for the rather static image imparted by his stress on the determination of taste by the 'cultural capital' people possess by virtue of their social class.

In long-term perspective, Fischler speaks of a contrast between the *mangeur éternel* and the *mangeur moderne;* the species *Homo sapiens* is 'an omnivore whose biological characteristics, forged through evolution by shortage and uncertainty, a few decades of abundance have not yet been able to modify'.[7] Fischler speaks of 'the omnivore's paradox' and the resulting 'omnivore's anxiety'. The paradox is that the biologically rooted human character of omnivorousness implies autonomy, freedom, and adaptability: 'Unlike specialised eaters, an omnivore has the invaluable ability to thrive on a multitude of different foodstuffs and diets, and so to adapt to changes in its environment'.[8] Unlike specialised eaters, however, an omnivore cannot obtain all the nutrients it needs from one food – it has an absolute need of some minimum variety. Thus,

> on the one hand, needing variety, the omnivore is inclined towards diversification, innovation, exploration and change, which can be vital to its survival; but, on the other hand, it has to be careful, mistrustful, 'conservative' in its eating: any new, unknown food is a potential danger.[9]

From this stems 'the omnivore's anxiety'. That anxiety, or ambivalence between 'neophilia' and 'neophobia', is of course a powerful force behind the development of the many diverse systems of culinary rules in human cultures, the systems of rules on which structuralists have focused their attention.

In shorter-term perspective, however, rapid changes in eating habits have produced what Fischler, in a much-cited essay,[10] called 'gastro-anomie'. The very codes or structures governing eating habits that the structuralists pursued, particularly since the 1960s, have been undergoing a process of 'destructuration'.[11] Fischler's *L'Homnivore* represents a summation of his own extensive writings and an end point to the structuralist dominance over the sociology of food and eating in France, for it shows a marked convergence with the more developmental perspectives emerging in Anglo-Saxon sociology and anthropology during the 1980s.

Marvin Harris's *Good to Eat*[12] and Sidney Mintz's *Sweetness and Power*[13] have something in common with my own viewpoint: we all try to account for aspects of present-day eating habits through the study of long-term developmental processes. Harris, however, prefers to describe himself as a 'materialist' rather than a 'developmentalist'. The very title of his book is an allusion to Lévi-Strauss's famous dictum that some foods are 'good to think'; Harris contends that 'whether they are good or bad to think depends on whether they are good or bad to eat'. Every human group has patterns of preference and aversion, but how are these to be explained? Anthropological orthodoxy is that the connection between food objects and their meanings is arbitrary; therefore no instrumentalist explanation of food avoidances can be valid. Harris sets out to challenge this view by calculating the practical costs and benefits which, in broad ecological context, underlie some of the most perplexing food preferences and avoidances:

> Each puzzling food item has to be seen as part of a whole system of food production, a distinction must be made between long- and short-term consequences, and one must not forget that food is often a source of wealth and power for the few as well as of nourishment for the many.[14]

One of the puzzles Harris tackles is the sacred cow in India. While not doubting its symbolic power, Harris questions how the ban on slaughter arose. He points out that in the Rig Veda, the sacred texts of early Hinduism, the slaughter and sacrifice of cattle were central activities. Harris argues that with a rapidly rising population – itself made possible by the spread of agriculture using the ox-drawn plough – cattle slaughter could no longer be sustained. Eating beef became increasingly the privilege of the Brahman priestly and Kshatriya warrior castes, while peasants and tradespeople increasingly ate grain, legumes, and dairy products. Long before modern nutritional knowledge, people must have been aware of the inefficiency of meat production compared with grain production as means of generating nourishment for humans: if grain is consumed by cattle, nine out of ten of the calories in the grain and four out of five grams of protein are lost for human consumption. In the face of this, there arose popular religious movements like Buddhism and Jainism totally opposed to killing cattle. In the ensuing conflict of religions, Hinduism eventually triumphed – Buddhism disappeared from the subcontinent by the eighth century A.D. – but not before the Buddhist and Jain opposition to eating meat had been adopted by the high castes. The nutritionally more efficient use of dairy produce survived in all castes, as did the essential use of the ox by the peasant.

Harris's explanation is thus implicitly developmental, even, in a sense, evolutionary. Solutions that 'fit' a particular ecological context are hit upon, usually less by rational deliberation than through unplanned social conflict. The mechanisms generating a range of possible solutions may be in part random, but the mechanism through which one solution emerges is not random, involving as it does selection for an ecological context, which must be understood to include the prevailing social as well as physical circumstances. Once outcomes are established, they are perpetuated by powerful symbolism and internalised repugnances. The symbolism may seem arbitrary now but was not so in its origins.

Harris also offers explanations for a number of other cases, such as the Jewish and Islamic taboos on pork, the eating and non-eating of horse flesh, dogs and other pets, and milk avoidance (for example, in China). It is fair to say that his views are controversial among anthropologists.

Underlying Mintz's *Sweetness and Power,* a study of the growth of both the supply of and the demand for sugar, is yet another theoretical orientation, that of world-system theory;[15] but the outcome has much in common with Harris, Goody, and me. Mintz, too, is critical of structuralism, arguing that meaning is not simply to be 'read' or 'deciphered' but arises from cultural applications. Meaning is the consequence of activity, and 'not to ask how meaning is put into behaviour . . . is to ignore history again'.[16] He traces the development of European sugarcane plantations in the West Indies and elsewhere from the early sixteenth century – involving indentured labour and slaves, and the rise of factory-like time-discipline in the colonies possibly before it arose in the home economies – and the creation of a mass market for sugar in Britain, the Netherlands, and especially the United States. 'Sugar surrendered its place as a luxury and rarity and became the first mass-produced exotic necessity of a proletarian working-class'. The consumption of sugar per capita in Britain increased 25 times between 1700 and 1809, and five times more in the nineteenth century. For all the evidence of humans' innate liking for sweetness, Mintz demonstrates that this increase can only be explained in terms of the interaction through time of economic interests, political power, nutritional needs, and cultural meanings.[17] Interestingly, in view of the prominence of social competition and emulation in the work of Goody and me, Mintz argues that the adoption of sugar and sweet manufactured foods by the working class in the nineteenth century had little to do with imitation but arose in a different context, from the pursuit of calories, not of display.

Another book with theoretical fish to fry is Joanne Finkelstein's *Dining Out.*[18] She views dining out 'as a means by which personal desires find their shape and satisfaction through the prescribed forms of social conduct' and thus as an example of 'how human emotions become commodified'. Even a family visit to McDonald's is promoted as offering the experience of 'a sense of occasion', while at more exclusive venues, 'pleasure may accrue from the diner's use of the event to suggest the personal possession of culturally valued characteristics such as wealth, fine taste and *savoir faire*'. Choice of a restaurant and choice of what one eats there are commonly seen as expressions of an individual's particular tastes, yet, argues Finkelstein, 'the styles of interaction encouraged in the restaurant produce an uncivilised sociality. . . . The artifice of the restaurant makes . . . us . . . act in imitation of others, in response to fashions, out of habit, without need for thought and self-scrutiny'.[19] If this is true – and it represents the continuation of a long line of social theorists' thinking about the 'inauthentic' experience of the self in modern society, from Georg Simmel through Herbert Marcuse to Jean Baudrillard, proponent of the 'postmodernist' view of contemporary social life – then it is not uniquely true of dining out. But this line of thought has always been contested by other sociologists, and it is beyond my scope here to explore theories of the self which (rather than restaurants *per se*) are Finkelstein's central concern.

MORE ON APPETITE AND ANOREXIA

Nowhere are the pressures connecting eating with self-perception more evident than in the area of appetite, dieting, and eating disorders. When I first formulated my thesis about 'the civilising of appetite' (see chapter 2), I felt more confident in tracing the general historical trend towards increasing pressure for self-constraint over appetite and the avoidance of obesity than I did in connecting this trend with the recent prevalence of eating disorders such as anorexia nervosa and bulimia.[20] Medical historians were not unanimous about whether the incidence of anorexic eating disorders is a characteristic exclusively of the last hundred years or so, or whether they have always existed but only in recent times been more reported and studied. The attention they are now receiving is undeniable: something like 300 articles are now being published annually in medical, psychological, and sociological journals on these illnesses alone. Good historical research is scarcer, partly because of the inherent difficulty of gathering and evaluating the evidence. The most comprehensive study is Joan Brumberg's *Fasting Girls: The Emergence of Anorexia Nervosa as a Modern Disease;*[21] the balance of evidence now seems to support my hunch that what was involved was not simply a matter of medical fashion but a real increase in the incidence of eating disorders in the course of roughly the last hundred years.

However, the aetiology – especially the historical aetiology – of these 'slimmer's diseases' needs to be studied in the broader context of the development of the pressure towards self-constraint over food intake – the 'civilising of appetite' – among the 'normal', nonpathological, majority of the population. Even the 'normal' level of expected restraint is harmfully severe in medical terms – at least for women. Men, too, are subject to social pressure at a minimum to avoid obesity (even the incidence of anorexia among young men is increasing), though the pressures are undoubtedly much greater on women. More women than at any other time are becoming increasingly preoccupied with their weight and size and are routinely plagued by food. Research such as that of Button and Whitehouse has established that the majority of women in western countries – probably as many as between 80% and 90% – constantly monitor their daily calorie intake and eat less than is required to prevent them feeling hungry.[22] In a social climate in which thinness is synonymous with female beauty, the majority of women report that they would like to be thinner and therefore attempt to restrict their food intake in response to social pressures.[23] Taking exercise, sometimes to extremes, is another common response: Jean-Jacques Courtine has written bitingly of 'The Stakhanovites of Narcissism', discussing bodybuilding and 'ostentatious puritanism' in American body culture.[24]

From time to time, stirrings of rebellion are heard. Susie Orbach has written two books from a feminist perspective urging rejection of the thin ideal.[25] And early in 1994, the idea 'bigger is better' enjoyed an outing in American newspapers and talk shows. This seems to me, however, to be little more than a counterpoint to the main theme. Bodily ideals are not easily changed by propaganda; it must be remembered that males' conceptions of what constitutes a sexually attractive female body are just as much culturally conditioned through a largely unplanned social process as are females' conceptions. The two sexes are thus to some extent entrapped in a double bind from which escape through the strength of individual resolve is seldom possible.

ENGLAND AND FRANCE REVISITED

So far, I have been speaking of broad trends across the Western world. But has anything happened to change the picture I painted of culinary culture in England and France? On the whole, one's impression is that the convergence between the two countries that became evident around the 1960s has continued with the spread of fast food and convenience food in France but also with the rise of greater interest in England in eating as a pleasurable social activity. Yet the differences in cultural emphasis that I depicted, and for the origins of which I tried to account, still persist – not least in the angles taken in research on contemporary eating habits in the two countries. In France, aesthetic concerns are still prominent; in England, food is mainly investigated as nutrition, as something unequally distributed, and as a problem – especially a problem for women.

Nickie Charles and Madeleine Kerr, in a study of aspects of food provision in families in the north of England, dwell upon the contradictory and problematic relationship of women to food.[26] Women are expected to deny themselves food in order to remain slim and, therefore, sexually attractive; at the same time, they have to feed their partners with healthy and nutritious meals. Men received larger portions, especially of more expensive cuts of red meat; the working-class men in the sample consumed greater amounts than middle-class men, whereas little class difference was evident among the women. These inequalities were apparently related to the nature of the men's and women's employment, to their relative control over money, and to the way the actual labour of food preparation was embedded in the power relationships within the family. The convention in wage economies that men are the breadwinners and women the homemakers dies extremely hard; reading Charles and Kerr makes one think of Maud Pember Reeves's observations in *Round About a Pound a Week* (see chapter 8) on families in London before the First World War.

Meat avoidance generally is reported to be more common nowadays among women than men, with half of all British women claiming to be 'eating less meat'.[27] Some of these differences in consumption are also found in France, but Bourdieu characteristically gives them a deeper and more aesthetic interpretation:

> the whole body schema, in particular the physical approach to the act of eating, governs the selection of certain food. For example, in the working classes, fish tends to be regarded as an unsuitable food for men, not only because it is light food, insufficiently 'filling', . . . but also because, like fruit (except bananas) it is one of the 'fiddly' things which a man's hands cannot cope with and which make him childlike (the woman, adopting a maternal role, . . . will prepare the fish on the plate or peel the pear); but above all, it is because fish has to be eaten in a way which totally contradicts the masculine way of eating, that is, with restraint, in small mouthfuls, chewed gently . . . (because of the bones). The whole masculine identity – what is called virility – is involved in these two ways of eating: nibbling or picking, as befits a woman, or with wholehearted male gulps and mouthfuls.[28]

The concern with the aesthetics of food can also be seen in the geographer Jean-Robert Pitte's survey of the whole range of French gastronomy.[29] Pitte, like many other gastronomic writers, takes a disapproving view of trends in French eating since the Second World War. It is therefore valuable to have a more detached and factual account of recent trends from sociologists. Claude and Christiane Grignon use secondary analysis of statistical data, questionnaire surveys, and interview materials to distinguish several alternative working-class food patterns and to show how they are related to different subgroups and subcultures.[30] Like Bourdieu, they emphasise the strong persistence of cultural tradition and its connection with social class, as a counterweight to the view that popular lifestyles lack autonomy and amount to little more than clumsy and delayed imitations of a dominant elite lifestyle. Pascale Pynson, on the other hand, documents the rapidity of change in French culinary culture over the quarter-century 1960–86 under the contradictory impacts of fast food, culinary multiculturalism, *nouvelle cuisine,* medical opinion and the tyranny of the dietary *régime,* and the parallel growth of the food industry and distrust of its products.[31] It is, of course, easy to make a discussion of persistence versus change resemble an argument about whether a glass of water is half full or half empty: precise measurement requires good historical data.

OTHER EUROPEAN COUNTRIES

The culinary histories of other European countries are also now being much studied, and some of the trends found in France and/or England have also been observed elsewhere in Europe.

Belgium and the Netherlands offer a most striking parallel to France and England and perhaps the best chance of a kind of independent test of the explanation I offered of the origins of culinary-cultural differences between the two sides of the Channel.[32] Belgian cookery is not just more like French, and Dutch cookery more like English, in overall stylistic impression, but the underlying attitudes the people of the two countries bring to their enjoyment of food also seem to differ in a similar way to Anglo-French differences. In this case, given that religious conflicts are historically the most salient reason for these being politically separate states, it is even more tempting to appeal to Protestantism and Catholicism in explaining the differences in culinary culture. However, it must also be remembered that in the Austrian Netherlands court society remained a powerful cultural influence throughout the seventeenth and eighteenth centuries, while in the Dutch Republic the French-influenced court circles around the Stadhouders in Den Haag and Leeuwarden were small and less powerful as model-setting centres than the merchant Regenten class of Amsterdam and Rotterdam. Anneke van Otterloo's investigation of differences in the development of culinary cultures in the mainly Protestant north and the mainly Catholic south also fails to find much evidence for the independent causal influence of religion, even though it intermingled in a more local way with other elements.[33]

In her book *Eten en eetlust in Nederland, 1840–1990,*[34] Van Otterloo shows how in the Netherlands sheer quantitative inequalities between social strata persisted strongly until the turn of the century; since then, qualitative differences have gradually become more salient. Indeed, at the present day in the Netherlands (as in many similar countries), the working class, far from lacking sufficient nutrition, is less successful than the middle class in controlling weight, among women especially but also among men and children. Dutch domestic cookery, reflecting the social dominance of a class of prosperous merchants, shows an emphasis on thrift and simplicity more reminiscent of England than of France or Belgium.

Van Otterloo notes particularly the activities of middle-class cookery teachers from the late nineteenth to the mid-twentieth centuries in reforming the cookery of their own class and, especially, of working-class housewives. This movement was part of a more general attempt at 'organised virtue' or 'civilising offensives' conducted *de haut en bas.* (These are reminiscent of, though more effective and widespread than, the campaigns in England by Alexis Soyer, the Universal Cookery and Food Association [see pp. 184ff.] or Reeves's Fabian ladies.) Van Otterloo traces the mechanisation and 'chemicalisation' of the Dutch food industry; the growing interdependence between it and the domestic cook; the simultaneous rise of health food movements of an élite character around 1900 but gaining more widespread popularity in the 1970s, many of them vegetarian and all embodying suspicion of the industry and its products; and the effect of immigration and the advent of 'world cuisine'.

Germany too offers interesting comparisons and contrasts with Britain and France. The historic political fragmentation of the German-speaking lands makes it difficult to speak of any single German national culinary culture.[35] Quite apart from Austria and Switzerland, where French influences penetrated more deeply, in Germany proper the best-known dishes are regional rather than national specialities. From the seventeenth century, the numerous noble courts of Germany were Francophone and Francophile, and thus open to the influence of French chefs and their cookery. But they were model-setting centres for the wider society to a much lesser degree than in France, and middle-class domestic cookery developed in Germany in a manner more reminiscent of England, with its emphasis on simplicity and thrift, though without suffering the coarsening witnessed there in the late nineteenth and early twentieth centuries. Significantly, the views expressed in the major classic of German gastronomic writing, *The Essence of Cookery,*[36] by Karl Friedrich von Rumohr (1785–1843) – a younger contemporary of Grimod de la Reynière and Brillat-Savarin – are more like those of Thomas Walker (see pp. 277–8) than of the more famous Frenchmen. Rumohr favours simplicity and moderation, and both his writing and his recipes are less florid than the French. The persistence of regional folk traditions in Germany today is charted by Horst Scharfenberg in his cookery book *The German Kitchen,*[37] which provides a 'culinary atlas of Germany's historic regions'. Thomas Kutsch uses more conventional sociological data to document the continuing importance of regional culinary preferences in the formation of social identities in contemporary Germany.[38]

THE CULINARY HISTORY OF THE UNITED STATES OF AMERICA

The United States too was outside the scope of the first edition of *All Manners of Food,* but its culinary history is abundantly documented and, besides the still readable and valuable *American Heritage Cookbook,*[39] there have been several important and more recent studies that invite comparison with the evidence from England and France.

The European origins of the United States, as Harvey Levenstein notes at the beginning of *Revolution at the Table,*[40] were evident as much in its culinary culture as in its political institutions. The British-American culinary heritage remained remarkably little changed until well into the nineteenth century. 'British-American culinary conservatism', observes Levenstein, 'can hardly be ascribed to the universally high regard with which British cuisine has been held, even by the British'.[41] Although the early settlers necessarily followed the Indians in using certain native foodstuffs such as corn and pumpkins, other foods native to the New World, such as potatoes and tomatoes, were adopted no sooner in America than they were in Europe – in both cases, only in the late eighteenth and early nineteenth centuries. True, by the eighteenth century Americans ate more pork and molasses than the British. Yet the only marked non-British early influences on American cuisine were Dutch and German (habitually lumped together, as in 'Pennsylvania Dutch'). Cookery books published in America were copies or adaptations of British ones, and even Amelia Simmons's *American Cookery*[42] – in 1796 the first cookbook to claim autochthony in its title – borrowed considerably from contemporary British books but also included self-evidently American vernacular recipes. The nineteenth century saw the publication of much more definitely American books on cookery and housekeeping, notably those by Lydia Child, Catharine Beecher and Harriet Beecher Stowe, Sarah Hale, and Fannie Farmer.[43] Yet even to mention these authors draws attention to the fact that, as in England, this was a tradition of women writing for women about domestic cookery. The very title of Child's book, *The American Frugal Housewife,* recalls the English (and also Dutch) theme of thrift in the kitchen (despite her insistence that this was a book for American conditions and quite different from *The Frugal Housewife* written by Susannah Carter and first published in London in 1795). Moreover, Beecher, Stowe, Hale, and Farmer all disapproved of extravagant and 'dainty' eating – perhaps more than did their English contemporary Mrs. Isabella Beeton.[44]

These authors had something of which to disapprove, for French cuisine had colonised the social heights of the great cities of the eastern seaboard just as it did London society in the nineteenth century. As I mention in passing in chapter 7, the international web of élite French chefs with *L'Art culinaire* at its centre spread to the United States as well as to the main cities and courts of Europe. French chefs had reached America long before that. Perhaps the close connection between that newly independent country and *ancien régime* France on the eve of its eclipse helped to forge the link; at any rate, that great man of the Enlightenment and considerable gourmet, Thomas Jefferson, had been ambassador to Versailles and installed a French chef at the White House. But probably there were more substantial social forces later inclining the rich in the Gilded Age towards French cuisine.

From the 1820s onwards, successive waves of poor European immigrants – beginning with the British and Irish but, more important for the future of American eating, followed by Germans, Italians, Jews, Poles, Hungarians, and many others – arrived in New York, Boston, Philadelphia, and other major cities. They brought with them what would later be called 'ethnic cuisines' that in due course were to have very considerable influence on 'mainstream' American eating. But to begin with, their tastes, like themselves, were very much looked down upon by the middle and upper classes. As in Europe, cookery schools for ladies were founded in the 1870s, and there were widespread attempts (also as in the Old World) at culinary do-gooding. Levenstein, in *Revolution at the Table,* stresses particularly how the campaigns of middle-class food reformers from the late nineteenth century combined in their propaganda the findings of the rising nutritional sciences with an essentially nativist disapproval of migrants' cuisines. These campaigns – like other forms of 'civilising offensive' – are a sure symptom of the unease of social superiors contemplating their inferiors. The United States may have had nothing like a royal court, but patterns of intense social competition not unlike those of the *ancien régime* or of the rapidly inflating London society of the nineteenth century can be easily discerned. In a novel like Edith Wharton's *Age of Innocence* (1920), the Eurocentric leading lights of the New York social establishment in the 1870s are portrayed as fully conscious of a rising 'pressure from below'. These were circumstances favourable to French culinary hegemony; perhaps those outsiders most immediately beating on the door for admission to the establishment were even more likely converts to French eating than the establishment proper. One early sociologist, Thorstein Veblen, observed the consequences of this social contest at the time and wrote about them in *The Theory of the Leisure Class* (1899). At any rate, we know that the (Swiss, but for our purposes Francophagic) Delmonicos opened their first restaurant in 1832 and that it rose to international fame over the succeeding decades. Great hotels, the environment for great chefs, spread in the United States at the same time as they did in Europe. And upper-class, domestic dining in late nineteenth-century America has been well documented in volumes by Susan Williams and Kathryn Grover.[45]

Yet the dominance of French cuisine in America was in retreat in the 1920s. Partly this must have been a consequence of the same economic forces that forced change even in France, as seen through the trade press in chapter 7. However, tastes in eating, it seems to me, reflected broader changes in social power ratios, here as in other times and places. It was not just that restaurateurs found that dishes sold better if listed in English rather than menu French but that the very same 'ethnic' styles formerly despised were becoming incorporated into and helping to shape tastes in general. 'Trickle up' of cultural traits is often a sensitive indicator of the increasing power potential of the social groups with which they were associated. What Robert Dahl called the 'ex-plebs', newly prospering ethnic communities who had once been outsiders despised by nativist Americans,[46] could now eat their own food and persuade others to eat it in the name of American patriotism. The rise of the United States to world dominance has had a global culinary impact too; the geographer Richard Pilsbury's *From Boarding House to Bistro*[47] charts the spread of the chain restaurant and the fast food outlet across America before they conquered the world.

Let us remember, however, that this is not a process of unmitigated decline in standards. Rather, it is another instance of the Janus-faced process of 'diminishing contrasts, increasing varieties' (see chapter 12). Gary Alan Fine's studies of cooks who work the upper range of American restaurants serves as a reminder. He describes the aesthetic satisfaction and pride they often feel:

> Although cooking is an industrial occupation, part of the 'hospitality industry', it is also intimately connected with aesthetic evaluation. Food must not merely be edible and nutritious, but also look, smell, taste and feel 'good'. This poses particular challenges for cooks, who must be not only labourers, but also 'artists'. . . . Yet, unlike the image of artists who specialise in the fine arts, these workers do not have control of their own time, their equipment, and their product. Craftsmen might be a better analogy for what these cooks are.[48]

This aesthetic sense and pride are reminiscent of the *Art culinaire* network in the late nineteenth and early twentieth centuries: cooks learned their skills through traditional apprenticeship in the kitchen, often working under terrible conditions for low pay, yet the feeling that they were artists with an aesthetic sensibility was central to their occupational identity.

AND THE FUTURE: DOES IT WORK?

At the close of the twentieth century, it makes diminishing sense to treat the culinary cultures of particular countries as if they could be explained purely by the internal dynamics of nation-states in isolation from one another. I caution at several points in *All Manners of Food* that English and French traditions have never been entirely separate things, but today we are perhaps seeing the emergence of a global cuisine, or at least one in which culinary traditions influence each other over distances much greater than the width of the English Channel. As always with long-term social processes, it is impossible to identify a precise starting point. Pitte, among others, dates some of the failings of *nouvelle cuisine* – including an emphasis on visual presentation sometimes at the cost of sustenance – from the Tokyo Olympic Games of 1964, when several leading French chefs saw Japanese cooking firsthand.[49]

But rather than reverting to the Great Man theory of culinary history, I think it makes better sense to continue – as I have in this book – to try to understand the creation of tastes and the diffusion of food traits and attitudes in relation to power struggles and shifting power ratios. Now some of the power struggles and changing power ratios are on a world scale. For instance, the economic miracle of Japan and of East Asia generally since the 1970s does seem to have been reflected in international culinary culture, with or without the Olympic Games. And in some parts of the world, especially postcolonial societies, nationalism may be expressed through a rejection of the food of the past and indeed the identification of nationality with non-national or multicultural cuisine. In Australia in the early 1990s, I observed that the food columnists in the newspapers verged on regarding it as politically incorrect for a restaurant to serve up a dish of unadulterated European antecedents without any admixture of Asian influence.[50] Sometimes the results of cultural hybridisation in the kitchen are magnificent, but sometimes – if I may reveal my own prejudices – they are appalling. My personal prize for the creation of kitsch in the kitchen goes to a firm of caterers in the Netherlands who once served me chicken breast garnished with a slice of Brie cheese, accompanied by sauerkraut mixed with mangoes and lychees!

Notes

CHAPTER 1 INTRODUCTION

1 Alan Watkins, *Observer*, 5 November 1978.
2 This particular experiment is very old: it is cited by Renner (1944: 18–19) from von Skramlik (1926). I chose it for its simplicity. Later research has become far more sophisticated in experimental design, but tends to point the same way. For a survey of more recent research on taste perception, see Bolles (1983).
3 See O'Mahony and Thompson, (1977); O'Mahony and Muhiudeen (1977); O'Mahony and Alba, (1980); O'Mahony and Tsang (1980).
4 These are Goudsblom's terms (1960: 69–70).
5 F. J. Simoons (1961) is the most detailed study of the geographical distribution of the principal meat avoidances and of the consumption of meats commonly avoided in the USA.
6 For a discussion of Lévi-Strauss's work as a whole, see Leach (1970) or, more briefly, Mennell (2nd edn, 1980: 125–31).
7 Principal figures in French 'Marxist structuralism' were Louis Althusser and Nicos Poulantzas, although Althusser, like so many others, eventually disavowed the label 'structuralist'. For a brief discussion of Althusser, see Mennell (1980: 86–91).
8 'Habitus' is as obscure a word in French as in English. The *Oxford English Dictionary* defines it as generally meaning the same as 'habit', but in a medical sense as a disposition to a disease.
9 The German word *Zustandsreduktion* more vividly expresses Elias's meaning, but proved impossible quite to capture in English.
10 Douglas's distinction between knowledge of hygiene and respect for conventions in the context of dirt is exactly homologous with her distinction between the nutritional and aesthetic aspects of food (mentioned above). In both cases she appears to regard developments in scientific knowledge or 'rational understanding' as the principal sources of change.
11 On the problem of 'cultural needs', see Mennell (1979).

CHAPTER 2 THE CIVILISING OF APPETITE

1 Henri IV was one culprit (Franklin, 1887–1902: III, 115), and in February 1558, the Pope gave a banquet while people were dying of hunger in Rome (Eugen Weber, 1973: 194).

2 Although this is true, it should also be noted that historians no longer believe that noble households had to exist throughout the winter on salt meat following the 'autumn slaughter' at Martinmas: some meat was salted, certainly, but some fresh meat was also generally available (see Dyer, 1983: 193). Again, however, the extent of autumn slaughter would probably be related to the success or failure of the harvest.

3 For more details of the cycle of feasts in medieval and early modern Europe, see Burke (1978: 194–6, Coulton (1926: 28–30), and Henisch (1976: 50–1).

4 See, for example, Bloch (1939–40: I, 73 and II, 411) and Huizinga (1924: ch. 1).

5 For a recent study of local famines in north-west England, see Appleby (1978).

6 See B. Behrens, in Rich and Wilson (1977: V, 604–5); and Abel 1(935: 252ff.) on 'The Historical Context of Pauperism'.

7 So equally, as Jacques Le Goff (1964) has argued, were the countering themes of the *mythes de ripaille* ('myths about having a good blow-out') found in early peasant folklore, becoming by the thirteenth century a literary theme in the French fable *Cocaigne* and the English poem *The Land of Cockaygne*, and the food miracles which multiplied about many saints. Nor should it be thought that fantasy was always necessarily very distant from reality: at least some incidents of cannibalism in time of famine seem reasonably well-authenticated – see Curschmann (1900: 59–60).

8 Certainly, they were by no means observed in all. Accounts abound of monastic gluttony. See Alfred Gottschalk (1948a: I, 343), who quotes St Bernard's denunciation of monks' gluttony.

9 Jack Goody makes the point in a wider comparative context when he writes:

> The other side of hierarchical cuisine was the extended notion of the fast, a rejection of food for religious, medical or moral reasons. . . . Abstinence and prohibition are widely recognised as ways of attaining grace in hierarchical societies such as China and India. . . . Such a philosophy of rejection could develop only within the context of hierarchical cuisine since abstention only exists in the wider context of indulgence. (Goody, 1982: 116–17).

There was always a tension in the Church's teaching: it taught that food was essentially good, but equally that abstention from it at certain times and for certain groups was good for the soul, and there was always a risk of this being distorted, as among the Cathars, one element in whose heresy was that their *parfaits* no longer ate meat, and that after the *consolamentum* (an equivalent of last rites) believers were expected to starve themselves to death even if their illness took a more favourable turn (Ladurie, 1978).

10 See St Augustine's remarks on the subject in *The Fathers of the Church*, 1948– :I, 366–7; XVI, 397–422; XXI, book 10, chapter 31; XXXVIII, 85–92.

11 See Eli Hecksher on the Swedish nobility, cited by Glamann, in Rich and Wilson (1977: 195).

12 See, for example, Hecquet (1709) and Cheyne (1724, 1733).

13 See, for example, Thomas Hardy (1874); Philip Oyler (1950); E. Guillaumin (1905); S. Tardieu (1964).

CHAPTER 3 POTTAGES AND POTLATCH: EATING IN THE MIDDLE AGES

1 'Maslin' means a mixed grain, especially of wheat and rye; on the composition of bread in English history, see Sir William Ashley (1928).

2 Dorothy Hartley has argued that the cauldron was potentially capable of producing far more than simple soups, broths and *bouillies*, and that 'because there was only one cauldron on the fire, there was not only one thing for dinner'.

> The popular idea that the huge cauldron cooked nothing but large joints of meat in a swim of broth is quite wrong. Deep, strong earthenware jars were filled and sunk into the boiling water, puddings were wrapped in linen and suspended in it. An entire dinner could be cooked in one iron pot. (1954: 36)

She had seen this system in operation on a canal-boat in Yorkshire in the early twentieth century. Flora Thompson (1939–43) describes similar methods in late Victorian rural Oxfordshire. Whether the cauldron's potential for variety was fully exploited by the average cook in the more remote past is more questionable.

3 The absence of instructions for the roasting of meat misled Samuel Pegge, the earliest commentator on *The Forme of Cury*, into believing that 'these bulky and magnificent dishes must have been the product of later reigns, perhaps of Queen Elizabeth's time, since it is plain that in the days of Richard II our ancestors lived much after the French fashion' (Pegge, 1780: xxi).

4 In addition to monasteries serving as little freezers, Byzantium was a giant freezer of Roman customs, preserving them in modified form until they were 'rediscovered' in the West in the late Middle Ages. There is little concrete evidence of the culinary influence of Byzantium, however, though it is thought that a Greek princess who married a Doge of Venice in the eleventh century was responsible for introducing the fork to Italy.

5 According to Dyer (1983) a duke or earl would have a household of over 100, a baron or bishop between 20 and 80, and so on. These figures are much in line with Girouard's account (1978).

6 The *Northumberland Household Book* (Percy, 1512) gives an inventory listing stock of pepper, mace, cloves, ginger, prunes, sugar, liquorice, saffron, dates, ground almonds and raisins, but these do not appear to have amounted to major items of expenditure.

7 See M. Girouard (1978: 30ff.) for a clear discussion of the rules drawn up by Bishop Grosseteste for the Countess of Lincoln in the thirteenth century and those in the Harleian MS for a fifteenth-century earl.

8 Cf. Benjamin Disraeli, *Coningsby* (1844), book IX, chapter 1, in which Eustace Lyle's revival of supposed medieval customs at St Geneviève is a classic instance in fiction of Victorian romanticism.

9 In consequence, the 'medieval feast' as a spectacular way of marking a great event lasted long after the Middle Ages. For example, when the Duke of Rutland came of age in 1799:

> weeks of preparations culminated in three days of feasting and display, which must have marked indelibly on the minds of the revellers a vivid impression of the magnificent munificence and grandeur of the owner of Belvoir. . . .
>
> The feasting, naturally enough, was notable for the large quantities of food and drink consumed. There were six whole oxen, twelve sheep and twenty-one pigs to keep the turn-spits busy, and the equivalent of at least a hundred sheep came dressed from the butchers. Beside this the fish and fowl, twenty-three turkeys, one hundredweight of cream cheese, and the solitary stuffed peacock for the high table seem unimportant. The quality drank two pipes of port and forty-six and a quarter gallons of brandy; they also shared with the more superior tenants twenty-three gallons of rum and four hogsheads of Lisbon wine.

There is no tally of the beer drunk on the occasion, but one brewer had brewed for thirty-four weeks in order to provide sufficient and had used over thirty quarters of malt, enough for several thousand gallons. Replete, surrounded by flags and bunting, the guests of all degrees . . . no doubt marvelled at the wealth and openhandedness of a man who could command such an entertainment. (F. M. L. Thompson, 1963: 77–8)

In every detail – the duration of the feast, the vast numbers of guests of every rank, the menu and its social gradations, not to mention its probably conscious function of demonstrating rank, wealth, and power – this stands comparison with its medieval precursors.

CHAPTER 4 FROM RENAISSANCE TO REVOLUTION: COURT AND COUNTRY FOOD

1 Good accounts of rural self-sufficiency among the relatively prosperous in mid sixteenth century are found in Barbara Winchester's study (1955) of John Johnson, a merchant of the Staple at Calais with a country estate in Northamptonshire; and in Emmanuel Le Roy Ladurie's essay (1972) on Gilles de Gouberville, one of the minor rural nobility of the Cotentin peninsula.

2 See also Stone (1969); and Schofield (1968).

3 An earlier version of parts of this section formed the Introduction to my edition of *Lettre d'un pâtissier anglois et autres contributions à une polémique gastronomique du XVIIIe siècle* (1981).

4 In their introduction (1983) to *Le Cuisinier François*, Jean-Louis Flandrin and Philip and Mary Hyman provide an outstanding discussion of the French cookery books of the second half of the seventeenth century.

5 *Assiette volante*: a selection of several articles on one plate, or a course consisting of a large number of assorted items; sometimes also used to refer to a dish passed from hand to hand without being placed on the table.

6 The 1712 edition of Massialot was entitled *Le* Nouveau *Cuisinier royal et bourgeois*.

7 Massialot's index in fact lists only 16 sauces: 'Sauces à l'Espagnol, blanche, brune, de bécasse, de brocher, d'Allemagne, à l'Anchois, à la Carpe, au Jambon, Robert, pour Viande froide et grillade, douce, remoulade, qui se servir au Rôti, nouvelle et toujours prête ou Sauce à tous mets.'

8 The extravagant tone has led to the belief that the author of this elegant little book was none other than the Prince de Dombes himself.

9 In any larger establishment at this date, the *cuisine* and the *office* were separate departments, under a *chef de cuisine* and a *chef d'office* (or *officier*) respectively, the latter being responsible for desserts, pastries, sweet dishes, etc.

10 See Oxford (1913: 4ff.) for a fairly complete bibliography of English cookery books of the period in chronological order of publication.

11 'Physicke' was associated with preserving, conserving and candying, through the 'still-room', which was the particular responsibility of the mistress of the house. Girouard (1978: 208) explains that still-rooms first appeared in English country houses in the sixteenth century and became common in the seventeenth. Stills were used to distil medicines, scent, and the cordial waters used for banquets; distilling was considered a skill proper to ladies, who also concerned themselves with the sweets and conserves which constituted 'banquetting stuff' (see below).

12 *Curious*: an obsolete use of the word, meaning 'careful as to standards of excellence; difficult to satisfy; nice, fastidious . . . especially in food, clothing, matters of taste' (*OED*).

13 On the significance of the word 'closet' and its connection with the phenomenon of the 'virtuoso', see Girouard (1978: 172ff.)

14 Christmas crackers are perhaps the last faint echo of such customs.

15 Here is one of Lamb's bills of fare, in this case for August:

FIRST COURSE

Westphalia Ham and Chickens
Bisque of Fish
Haunch of Venison roasted
Venison-pasty
Roasted Fowls aladobe
Umble Pyes
White Fricassées of Chickens
Roasted Turkeys larded
Almond Florentines
Alamode Beef

SECOND COURSE

Dish of Pheasant and Partridges
Roasted Lobsters
Broil'd Pike
Creamed Tart
Rock of Snow and Sullebubs
Dish of Sweetbreads
Sallad-Magundy

16 Mrs Rundell (1807), whose book is organised mainly according to principal ingredients, overcame the problem posed by a separate 'French' chapter by replicating in that chapter the pattern of the book as a whole – fish, meat, poultry, vegetables, etc.

CHAPTER 5 FROM RENAISSANCE TO REVOLUTION: FRANCE AND ENGLAND – SOME POSSIBLE EXPLANATIONS

1 The most elegant statement of this view was by Sir Henry Thompson in *Food and Feeding* (1880: 82–4), who argued that 'two distinct systems have been produced . . . dominating the treatment of flesh provisions particularly, on principles widely opposed to each other. . . . Both are rational – each system, perhaps, the better of the two in its own place'. Thompson was thus a functionalist *avant la lettre*.

2 For a clear exposition of the similarities between Puritanism and Jansenism, see J. Delumeau (1971: 99–128).

3 The influence of the French court on the courts of Russia, Sweden, Germany and even the Netherlands in the eighteenth century is traced by Baudrillart in his *Histoire de Luxe* (1878–80: IV, Chapter VIII).

4 Stone (1965: 562) estimates that at least one in six of the English aristocracy in the period 1558–1641 suffered from 'the stone', a disease thought to have resulted from deficiencies which eating more vegetables could have remedied.

5 For a discussion of the problems of identifying 'cultural needs' in contemporary (twentieth-century) society, see Mennell (1979).

6 Thanks to Max Weber's use of the confusing 'ideal-type' method, there is often an imprecision in his work about the precise historical reference of a term such as 'feudal ruling class'.

7 This problem was, in fact, drawn to my attention by my colleague Peter Wiseman, Professor of Classics at Exeter, who is interested in the Roman aristocracy of the first and second centuries AD – the age of Apicius.

8 See L. and J. F. Stone (1984) for a discussion of this.

9 On the political inactivity of the French bourgeoisie, and on the closing off of mobility opportunities in army, Church and State, see Elinor Barber (1955: 70–1 and 98ff.).

10 PRO: LS.9/49. *The History of the Coronation of King James II and Queen Mary* (London, 1687) records that Patrick Lamb, described as 'The King's Master Cook', made a 'messe of dillegroute' (a pottage) for the king on this occasion. For more detail of the material available in the Public Record Office, see Mennell (1984).

11 PRO: LS.9/106.

12 PRO: LS.9/123.

13 PRO: LS.9/201.

14 It may be that there was a greater difference between everyday food and festival or ceremonial food at the English court than at the French, for in French court-society there was not the clear demarcation between private and public occasions taken for granted in bourgeois society (Elias, 1969: 53). The French king ate ceremonially and alone at every meal, right up to the Revolution (see Arthur Young's comments, 1792–4: 15). Even in England, however, persons of quality were admitted to observe the royal family at table well into the reign of George III.

15 André Simon in *Wine and Food*, no. 28 (Winter 1940) mentions Lords Chesterfield, Lytton and Sandwich, and the Duchess of Devonshire – 'goddess of the Whig Party' – as among the great hosts and hostesses.

16 It is now thought that the French economy as a whole grew in the eighteenth century at much the same rate as England's, but it started from a much lower plane, and did not attain the necessary 'critical mass' until the next century (see F. Crouzet, 1966).

17 This episode was, as so often, based on Jane Austen's own experience; in 1798 she wrote as follows from Steventon to her sister, Cassandra, who was staying with their rich relatives at Godmersham Park: 'We dine now at half after Three, and have done dinner I suppose before you begin – We drink Tea at half after six – I am afraid you will despise us' (Austen, 1932: 39).

18 As Raymond Williams (1973: 18–22) has shown, the sense of a lost rural community can be traced back in English literature as far as the Middle Ages; but this is something quite different in tone and in social origin to the French 'aristocratic romanticism', tending rather to confirm the continuing real prestige of the country in England.

CHAPTER 6 THE CALLING OF COOKING: CHEFS AND THEIR PUBLICS SINCE THE REVOLUTION

1 Erasmus left a memorable picture of the mixing of all social ranks, and particularly of the take-it-or-leave-it service and indifferent food of the inns of Renaissance Germany:

> At last, in comes the Wine, and Wine that for the sharpness and subtlety of it, is fitter for a Schoolman than the Traveller. . . . But if a body should privately offer a piece of mony to get a Can of better Wine, somewhere else, they'll give you a look, without speaking a word, as if they would murther ye. If you press it further, they'll tell you presently, here have been such and such Counts and Marquises, that found no fault with this Wine; if you don't like it, y'ad best mend yourself elsewhere. . . . By this time, comes in a Morsel to pacifie a barking Stomach; and after that, in great Pomp, follow the Fishes. The first, with sippets of Bread in Flesh Porridge; or if it be a fish day, in a Soupe of Pulse. After that comes in another Soupe, and then a service of Butcher's Meat, that has been twice boyl'd, or of Salt meats twice heate; and then Pulse again, or perhaps a more substantial Dish: When ye have taken the edge off your Appetite, they bring us either Roast Meat, or Stew'd Fish (which is not amis) but they are sparing on't, and t'is quickly taken away again. (Erasmus, 1518: 64–5)

2 The London Tavern, in Bishopsgate Street, was opened in 1768 and survived until the late nineteenth century. It was noted for its vast dining room and for its live turtles swimming in vats (Timbs, 1866: II, 274). The Crown and Anchor in the Strand, was in Collingwood and Woollams's time 'a nest of boxes, each containing its own Club, and affording excellent Cheer', though latterly it had been 'desecrated by indifferent dinners and very questionable wine' (1866: I, 165). The Albion in Aldersgate Street was also noted for the 'recherché character' of its cuisine; it was there that most Corporation banquets took place and that, by tradition, farewell dinners for Governors-General of India took place (1866: II, 283).

3 The Sublime Society of Beef-Steaks was established in 1735 by Henry Rich, of Beggar's Opera fame, and met for many years at Covent Garden Theatre, then in various taverns (Timbs, 1866: I, 131), finally becoming extinct in 1867 (Jeaffreson, 1875: II, 38).

4 As early as 1614, Chief Justice Coke had suppressed a charter which conferred on the Cooks' Company unlimited right to search for and seize unwholesome victuals and dispose of them for its own benefit; the Lord Mayor and Court of Aldermen had protested this right was open to abuse, and Coke upheld their complaint, in line with his general assault on the granting of monopolies (Phillips, 1966: 22). In contrast, where the guild system was well entrenched (as in Paris) it remained strong in France until its rapid decline after 1750. But as Crouzet (1966: 157) points out, the system was never general in France, did not apply in the greater part of industry, and was unknown in many towns such as Lyon.

5 Grimod (1807: 46) also suggested that the post-Revolutionary *nouveaux riches*, being 'less credulous, less polite, less trusting' than their predecessors, and more conscious of the value of money than the value of praise, were less tolerant of the hangers-on who ingratiated themselves and made themselves *habitués* at rich tables: if so, that was another category of people who might now have to buy their own dinner in a restaurant.

6 This is Norbert Elias's phrase; it is the title of his unpublished extended study of Mozart.

7 Thus cookery achieved a form of existence equivalent to that of 'autonomous' or 'high' art, which Iván Vitányi (1983: 12) characterises as the type of art 'when the work of art turns into a final and unalterable "opus", carrying the name of its author and sounding his praises, created by professional artists . . . who live by this activity (selling their artistic products as commodities) and constitute a distinct layer in society'.

8 Montagné, in *Larousse Gastronomique*, defines *sauce espagnole* as a brown sauce based on meat stock, vegetables and brown roux (well-cooked butter and flour); *velouté* is made from white (chicken or veal) stock and a white roux; *béchamel* was formerly a velouté with cream blended into it, but later came to be made by stirring milk into white roux, sometimes with veal or chicken added to it. Terms shifted somewhat in meaning during the nineteenth century. For instance, *sauce allemande* was originally considered one of the basic sauces, but Montagné considered it a compound sauce, a velouté thickened with egg yolks.

9 See Helen Morris's biography of Soyer, *Portrait of a Chef* (1938).

10 The view that some of the soundest eating places in England were the least pretentious was often expressed. For instance, F. D. Byrne wrote in *The Restaurant* in October 1909:

> There is a charm about these dear old chop houses which one fails to find in the glamour and glitter of the ambitious restaurants which heralded in the twentieth century. 'Restaurants' they are not; there is nothing 'Frenchy' about them and never could be; but they restore the jaded human energies in the best sense of the word. To feel the reposeful influence at its best one must choose an hour when the bulk of the customers have departed, when a light or two has been lit and the fire settled down from its almost white heat to a sober crimson glow. Then place me in a comfortable bay of the old wooden partition; set before me my generous, yet homely steak – for, believe me, it is the excellence of its steak, and not of its chops, which is the glory of the true old chop-house; flank the dish with potatoes, floury, firm and dry, cooked as they only are cooked (outside Ireland) in City chop and boiled-beef houses; then crown the banquet with pickwickian port and leave me to forget the rush and sickening grind of life beneath the soothing influence of a good cigar.

Or, even later, compare this description of the George and Vulture, London, by Raymond Postgate in the 1957–8 *Good Food Guide*, p. 328:

> This is an old City chophouse back as once it was in its old glory. . . . You pick your own chop or steak and it is grilled in front of you; you may take a good roast duck or such, or fish. In 1956 a grilled steak, potatoes, bread and a tankard of beer cost a member 10/-; there was good cold beef and salmon (but not mayonnaise) and fine cheese. Very good draught Bass. You sit in pew seats, as in Dickens's day, and finish off with a glass of port – a large wine glass full up to the brim, and good port too.

Nothing much would appear to have changed from what Monsieur Misson described at the close of the seventeenth century.

11 Gronow (1862–6: I, 53–4) describes the Clarendon as the only *public* hotel in London in 1814 'where you could get a genuine French dinner'; it was kept by a chef named Jacquiers who had served Louis XVIII in exile. The other public hotels (including Limner's, 'the most dirty hotel in London', yet patronised by 'many members of the rich squirearchy') apparently served only plain English fare.

12 Some of the more traditional eating places remained male preserves until much later; a pamphlet sketching the history of Stone's Chop House (1963) notes that women were admitted there only in 1921, and a men-only dining room at Simpson's in the Strand existed until the sex equality legislation of the 1970s.

13 For further information about Escoffier, both biographical and culinary, see E. Herbodeau and P. Thalamas (1955); on Ritz, see Marie Louise Ritz (1938).

14 Escoffier was a contemporary of Frederick Winslow Taylor, and, as Herbodeau and Thalamas (1955: 79) comment in passing, 'Unconsciously . . . he was the promoter of Taylorisation' in the kitchen.

15 Jane Grigson (1982: 269) very tentatively attributes *crêpes Suzette* to the chef Henri Charpentier in the 1890s; her version of the story involves a culinary accident and the presence of a famous person (Edward VII in this instance), both recurrent elements in gastronomic mythology.

CHAPTER 7: THE CALLING OF COOKING: THE TRADE PRESS

1 Through trial and error I concluded that it was best to study one year's issues of the trade journals at intervals of one decade. Reading continuous runs of the journals served only to obscure the trend of changes taking place, while an interval longer than a decade could result in missing important events or new trends. Gaps in library holdings, however, sometimes forced me to accept longer intervals; and, conversely, where there were developments of particular interest I sometimes examined several years together of a journal. This policy was followed also with respect to the women's magazines discussed in chapter 9.

2 The attitude dominant in the journals was even further away from the 'instrumental collectivism' identified by Goldthorpe *et al.* (1968) among their 'affluent workers', to whom work was simply a means of earning money, a means to an end rather than a source of satisfaction in itself, and whose membership of a union was simply a means of raising living standards.

3 In the second issue of *L'Art culinaire* (11 February 1883), Monsieur A. Tavenet deplored the confusion surrounding the names of dishes, and announced the magazine's intention of trying to standardise such nomenclature by carrying out research into the origins of dishes and the etymology of the words used to describe them. This programme is not unlike the efforts often made by gastronomes and gastronomic societies to 'legislate' on what is correct in matters of the table (see chapter 10 below). Standardisation of terminology was in effect one of the major consequences of the authoritative, paradigmatic status achieved by Escoffier's *Guide culinaire* in the twentieth century.

4 This idea is symptomatic of the guild socialism prevalent in France at this time and later taken up by Emile Durkheim. In 1910, Escoffier himself published an outline of a *Projet d'Assistance Mutuel*.

5 See chapter 10 below.

6 *Beurre manié*: a blend of flour and butter used as a quick liaison to bind certain sauces and stews.

7 Since 1983, a supplement for chefs, called *Chef*, has been distributed free of charge four times a year with *The Caterer and Hotel Keeper*.

8 See *The Times*, 19 October 1934, for Senn's obituary. On what he did to Mrs Beeton, see Elizabeth David (1961).

9 These figures are taken from various issues of the *Cookery Annual and Year Book of the Universal Cookery and Food Association*. Most of the information on the early history of UCFA is taken from the 1908 *Annual*, which happened to be the earliest available in the Bodleian Library, but many of the contents were reprinted in later issues.

10 Membership of Le Cordon Rouge was open to:

1. Ladies who managed their own establishments and were noted for the excellence of their social and gastronomic entertainments – in other words, Society hostesses.
2. Cooks of distinction, of both sexes.
3. 'Authors, lecturers and scientists who have contributed to the knowledge of food and cookery.'
4. Proprietors and managers of hotels and restaurants.
5. Persons who had invented any article of food.
6. Persons who manufactured or provided same.

As recently as 1955, the UCFA *Member's Handbook* reported the reinstitution of the Cordon Rouge on exactly the same lines as before.

11 These particular examples are drawn from Senn's article on 'Cuisine Bourgeoise: Recipes for Good French Home Cooking' in the *Cookery Annual* for 1928, which contains a rather odd list of dishes as instances of the notion of *cuisine bourgeoise*.

12 Apparently the British public was then unwilling to pay 'the right price', since in the same issue Charles Taylor, MP for the resort town of Eastbourne, is quoted as saying: 'Sooner or later we have got to educate the public to be prepared to pay a bit more for the service and food they get in hotels. The price of food in restaurants and hotels in this country is far lower than anywhere else in the world.' That was certainly no longer true 30 years later.

13 The eight in London included the National Training School of Cookery and Other Branches of Domestic Economy, Buckingham Palace Road (established in 1873), whose diplomates were prominent among teachers and writers in the women's press; and Battersea Polytechnic Training School of Domestic Economy, which was eventually to evolve into the University of Surrey's distinguished Department of Hotel and Catering Management.

CHAPTER 8: DOMESTIC COOKERY IN THE BOURGEOIS AGE

1 An exception was at Lyons, whose noted restaurants were dominated by a number of celebrated women chefs such as la Mère Fillioux.

2 Pellaprat's main work was *L'Art culinaire moderne* (1936a). For an example of Pellaprat at his simplest, see his *Traité de la cuisine familiale* (1936b); the recipes are extremely brief and lucid, but the layout of the book and, for example, the repertoire of sauces, clearly mark its affiliations to the professional tradition.

3 Symptomatically, in a series of photo-strips instructing women how to cook various dishes which appeared in the magazine *La Femme chez elle* in 1922, the hands of the headless cook in the photos were the hands of a *man*.

4 The policy of interfering as little as possible with the 'natural flavours' did not apply only to the traditional favourites; it went also for relatively unfamiliar foodstuffs. When tomatoes first became more widely eaten later in the century,

there was at first a crop of recipes for serving them stuffed in various elaborate ways; soon, however, there was a reversion to the norm. Sir Henry Thompson (1880: 107) asserted that tomatoes were best when least meddled with, and *The Hotel World* (December 1895), noting that 15 years earlier English cookery books had scarcely mentioned the tomato, warned:

> But now that whole fields of the vegetable are in cultivation all over the country, the cookery books give many recipes dealing with it, most of them, unfortunately, erring grievously on the side of elaboration. Like the oyster, the tomato has a natural flavour so distinctive and so delicious, that anything beyond the simplest cooking must rob it of some of its gustatory value. To stuff a tomato with mushrooms, as recommended in more than one recipe, is to prove oneself destitute of a refined and cultivated palate.

5 Such was the strength of the gentlemanly ideal and the notion that substantial landed wealth was necessary to support an hereditary title that very few of the new creations went outside the old landed class – the vast majority of recipients, rewarded for distinction in the services, politics or the law, were holders of existing Scots or Irish titles, younger sons or members of cadet branches of existing noble families, or at least substantial landowning commoners. As late as the 1860s and 1870s, the introduction of even second-generation businessmen into the gatherings of Society – let alone into the peerage – was still problematical. In the 1880s and 1890s businessmen, as well as artists, Americans and other outsiders became socially acceptable. It was then, not before, that industrialists began to receive peerages in greater numbers; among them, however, were quite a few members of old landed families ennobled for their achievements in industry and commerce (Davidoff, 1973: 59–60).

6 The 'Game Models' used by Elias (1970b: 71–103) illustrate in a more general way the problems (among other things) of social organisation in situations where the number of participants is increasing. Segmentation, and differentiation into two or more strata, are typical adaptations, and as Elias points out they usually result in participants having the illusion of greater control over events.

7 In her Preface Eliza Acton is optimistic about the future of English cookery:

> until within very recent years, [English] cookery has remained far inferior to that of nations much less advanced in civilisation; and foreigners have been called in to furnish to the tables of our aristocracy, and of the wealthier orders of the community, those refinements of the art which were not to be obtained from native talent.
>
> Our improvement was for a long time opposed by our own strong and stubborn prejudice against innovation in general, and the innovations of strangers in particular; but these, of late, have fast given way before the more rational and liberal spirit of the times: happily for ourselves we have ceased to be too bigoted, or too proud to profit by the superior information and experience of others upon any subject of utility. (1845: vii)

She goes on to assert that 'The details of domestic economy, in particular, are no longer sneered at as beneath the attention of the educated and accomplished.' If so, things had apparently changed since the davs of Maria Rundell. There is not much evidence for any major change of attitude, however, though possibly the readership of cookery books had grown amongst those whose resources did not allow them to sneer at domestic responsibilities.

8 It is significant that one cannot accurately speak of the English 'peasantry', since by the eighteenth and nineteenth centuries of course the bulk of the rural

population were wage-labourers. Indeed Alan Macfarlane has argued in his admittedly very controversial book *The Origins of English Individualism* (1978) that England had never since the late Middle Ages possessed a true peasantry on the continental model.

9 For detailed maps of the geographical distribution of cooking fats, according to surveys in 1914, 1936 and 1952, see Hémardinquer (1961).

10 Roger Magraw, in a survey of recent research (1983: 109–10), points out that a more encouraging picture of diet in the French countryside can be drawn in the less remote areas where commercial agriculture was developing from quite early in the nineteenth century. But he admits that it remained bleak in the remoter parts – Brittany, the Massif Central, the Pyrenees, and the Alps: 'meat-eating was a northern and urban luxury, providing under 3 per cent of the calorie intake in the Alps'.

11 Mme Michaux concludes with a section on 'service de la table', in which she sets out not only the correct sequence of courses (down to coffee, which is '*de rigueur*'), but how to serve them – ladies first, starting on the host's right; the host must not comment on the dishes, nor offer them twice. Formerly, she says, no copious dinner ended without singing, but today that is not allowed except on such occasions as weddings, and even then it can cause 'difficulties'. In short, 'there are laws of savoir-faire, and the table, even in our countryside, cannot escape them' (1867: 167). *La Cuisine de la ferme* appears to form one small conscious part of the process of civilising a 'country of savages' vividly depicted by Eugen Weber in his *Peasants into Frenchmen* (1977).

12 See Burnett's article (1981) for a survey of trends in country diet in the Victorian age based on far more sources than it is possible to cite here.

13 These figures, derived from Mitchell and Deane (1962: 60) and Mitchell (1975: 163, 171) include those employed in forestry and fishing, but the distortion of the trend is not serious, especially as they are in any case subject to problems relating to the census classifications of occupations over more than a century.

14 As argued in chapter 5, the relationship between styles of cookery and the absolute degree of urbanisation does not ever appear to have been simple and direct.

15 The phrase is William Kornhauser's, in his book *The Politics of Mass Society* (1960), but the general idea has been widely discussed by sociologists.

16 For further sources on food in nineteenth-century French towns, see G. Thuillier, 'Note sur les Sources de l'Histoire Régional de l'Alimentation pour la France du XIXe Siècle', in J.-J. Hémardinquer, ed., *Pour une histoire de l'alimentation* (1970: 212–27); and J.-P. Aron, *Essai sur la sensibilité alimentaire à Paris au XIXe siècle* (1967: 111ff.).

17 For a thorough discussion of many more sources, see D. J. Oddy, 'A Nutritional Analysis of the British Working-Class Diet, 1880–1914', chapter 18 in Oddy and Miller (1976), as well as Burnett (1966).

18 See J. M. Blackman, 'Changing Marketing Methods and Food Consumption', B. McNamee, 'Trends in Meat Consumption', W. H. Chaloner, 'Trends in Fish Consumption', and A. Torode, 'Trends in Fruit Consumption', all in Barker, McKenzie and Yudkin (1966).

CHAPTER 9: THE ENLIGHTENMENT OF THE DOMESTIC COOK?

1 Jill Stone points out that this remark requires qualification in light of the skills needed simply to manage the stoves of the time, and some of the other equipment which was complicated to use and required maintenance and cleaning 'quite beyond our experience'. On this neglected side of the history of the kitchen, see Caroline Davidson, *A Woman's Work is Never Done* (1982).

2 Whatever the examination syllabus may impose on them, it is possible that the teachers' hearts are in actual cookery. That is one possible interpretation of the fact that the *Cookery Book* published in numerous editions since 1921 by the Association of Teachers of Domestic Science contains mainly recipes: they occupy 90 per cent of the 1973 edition, and cover the full range of English cookery without showing the slightest French influence.

3 Claudian, Serville and Tremolières (1969: 1380–2) asked their large sample of French housewives whether they cooked the same way as their mothers. As many as 63 per cent said no, 'thus demonstrating a desire to break with tradition'; that 37 per cent answered yes to such a sweeping and unspecific question surely indicates a considerable amount of momentum in tradition too.

4 For details of the circulations of the principal British women's magazines from 1938 to 1968, see Cynthia White (1970), Appendices IV and V.

5 Giard (1980) reports more detailed interviews with a small number of French housewives. One of them specifically mentions keeping cuttings from *Elle*, and also using a cookery book by Mapie de Toulouse-Lautrec, one of its cookery editors.

6 The occupations suggested in the first volume were the Civil Service, compositor, conjurer, nurse, librarian, piano-teacher, private secretary, professional singer, stewardess, typewriter [*sic*], miniature painting – and butterfly mounting! The list points to the limited range of work then considered appropriate for respectable ladies, and several, especially the last, are ways of making pin-money rather than earning a fully independent living. For the rest, there seemed to be an element of vicarious participation or voyeurism in these career articles, just as there was, more obviously, in the etiquette and gossip columns.

7 A comparison between this model menu and the actual food described by Mrs Reeves (see above) a few years later would confirm that *Woman's Life* was pitched at housewives rather better-off than the labourers' wives she visited; but there are some general similarities, and one suspects that the magazine was already leading its readers, presenting them with food a little more varied and imaginative than most of them would in practice achieve.

8 The London School Board recipe book (Briggs, 1890: 19) even gives a recipe for seed cake using dripping, not butter.

9 Patience Gray, writing on 'Decorated Food' in *Wine and Food*, no. 100 (Winter 1958), describes the exhibits in the *salon culinaire* at the Hotel and Catering Exhibition, Olympia, 1958, with considerable distaste, as survivals from the age of Urbain Dubois.

10 Cited in *Good Housekeeping*, May 1961. Creese's *Revision Notes* (1973: 66–7) includes among the advantages of convenience foods: 'Better than poor cooking'. The other advantages listed are: 'Often easy to carry home and easy to store'; 'Save time'; 'More variety in meals'; and 'No waste'. Disadvantages listed were: 'Often expensive' and 'Temptation to use them always, instead of fresh foods'.

11 Phillip Harben, probably still the most famous 'TV chef' Britain has produced, was not the first of the species; before the war, Marcel Boulestin, French proprietor of a famous restaurant in Covent Garden, had appeared regularly on the BBC's pioneering television service from Alexandra Palace. But Boulestin's fame and influence could hardly rival those of Harben, who appeared on TV just when the medium was spreading to the majority of households in the country.

12 *Good Housekeeping* by the 1970s had a weekly column on freezing. In 1974 a specialist monthly, *Home and Freezer Digest* began publication to serve those who made a hobby of freezing food. For statistics of the growth of actual consumption of frozen food in Britain during the period 1949–62, see G. E. Graham (1964: 132–3). Graham observes that there was marked hostility towards frozen food when it was first marketed in 1949, and this had been overcome by steady persuasion by one firm. In France, the hostility to frozen foods persisted far longer (just as earlier the French had been slow to adopt tinned products), and in 1964 they had 'so far made little headway'. On French attitudes to manufactured foods, see Claudian *et al.*, 1969: 1310ff. They may have put up sterner resistance than the British, but casual observation in French supermarkets in the 1980s suggests the progress of *produits surgelées* is inexorable there too.

13 The French sample in Szalai's study (1972) spent more time *eating* than did people in any of the other 11 countries (of which Britain was unfortunately not one), though French housewives appeared to spend *less* time than most others in cooking. Data for Britain analysed by Gershuny and Thomas (1980) suggest that the British spent less time cooking than Szalai's French sample but it is difficult to be confident that the data are exactly comparable.

14 Two decades later, a successful BBC television comedy series (*Butterflies*) used the wife's constant failures in the kitchen as a symbol of the comic malaise of her marriage.

15 It is often said that more men are taking an interest in cooking: there are now annual 'Man in the Kitchen Competitions'. Unless they are professional cooks or living alone, however, for men cooking is much more likely to be almost purely a hobby than it can be for their wives.

16 Thus a pink supper after the theatre need not be interpreted as escapist fantasy for the working class!

CHAPTER 10: OF GASTRONOMES AND GUIDES

1 This is my own interpretation of how the word 'gastronome' has come to be used; unlike the previous definitions which were quoted from the *Oxford English Dictionary*, this sense is implicit in usage but not explicit in any dictionaries.

2 Excerpts from the 1803 *Almanach* and the *Manuel des amphitryons* were, however, issued in a cheap paperback, *Grimod de la Reynière: Ecrits gastronomiques* (see Grimod de la Reynière, 1978).

3 The contents of the 365 menus have been analysed in detail by Jean-Paul Aron in an appendix to his *Essai sur la sensibilité alimentaire à Paris au XIXe siècle* (1967).

4 M. F. K. Fisher is another modern writer who straddles the boundary. Many of her books, such as the five published collectively under the title *The Art of Eating* (1954) might be described as gastronomy-with-recipes.

5 More exactly, this is a special case of the general exigency on growing and increasingly 'opaque' networks to develop institutions capable of introducing at least the semblance of greater 'transparency' – see Elias (1970b: 85ff.). This usually involves some differentiation between 'leaders' and 'followers', the more and the less powerful, as it did indeed in the case of gastronomes, diners and restaurateurs. On the sociological significance of gossip, see Elias and J. L. Scotson (1965).

6 The former British Prime Minister was speaking in an interview on BBC television on 20 October 1983.

7 Something of this can be seen in the practice, now mainly confined to Oxford and Cambridge colleges, of adjourning after dinner to a separate room for port and dessert.

8 Elias argues that informalisation is as much part of a continuing civilising process as formalisation.

9 Curnonsky also ridiculed the pretentious menu written in the French equivalent of Olde English, and the puffing up of each dish with extravagant epithets:

> Et, transportés au septième ciel de la gastronomie, vous dégusterez: *La tarte aux douceurs de la cousine Adelaide*, à moins que vos Seigneures ne préfèrent se sucrer les papilles gustatives avec: *Les savoureuses et onctueuses crêpes de Rigadon*, suivant le concept de nostre Grand Chef Anatole. (1958: 229)

That does not translate easily, but it is recognisably similar to a style prevalent in many English and American restaurants in the 1960s and 1970s, which Anthony Burgess mocked in *The Times*, (7 August 1982):

> two freckle-shelled eggs laid at dawn this very day in our own country hen-runs, scrambled with fresh farm butter to a golden ambrosia, served with crisp crackly crunchy nutty bacon slices cured in the Kentucky hills over fragrant hickory smoke.

10 Christopher Driver, who succeeded Postgate as editor of the *Good Food Guide* in 1970, describes its history and the post-war British gastronomic scene in general in *The British at Table 1940–1980* (1983).

11 Following the adoption of 'absolute' standards in Ronay's main guide, however, he branched out into separate guides for food in other sections of the market, with the annual *Just A Bite* ('for gourmets on a family budget'), the *Pub Guide*, and, from 1975, the *Egon Ronay Guide to Transport Cafées* – all possibly inspired by the *Guides des Relais Routiers*.

12 Postgate went so far, in his preface to the 1959–60 *Good Food Guide*, as to propose the urgent need for a *Bad Food Guide*. This humorous suggestion was apparently taken quite literally by Derek Cooper, who a few years later published a book with precisely that title (Cooper, 1967).

13 Sir Charles Forte, interviewed by Fyfe Robertson on BBC television, March 1980.

14 In Europe during the 1970s it was common for cultural policy-makers to advocate the fashionable notion of 'cultural democracy' (thus denying their intention of imposing 'high culture' on people from above) and, at the same time, to deplore the effects of the culture industries in debauching mass tastes. These two views were typically reconciled by adhering to the forlorn hope that if people's tastes were manipulated neither by proponents of high culture nor by big business, with only the neutral help of cultural midwives called *animateurs*, there would be a spontaneous blooming of a rich and diverse culture. See Mennell (1976).

15 In using this term, Postgate was tacitly comparing his organisation with the Mass Observation movement set up for social scientific purposes by Tom Hopkinson and Charles Madge in 1937.

16 See note 6 to chapter 8 above.

CHAPTER 11: FOOD DISLIKES

1 See Elias and Dunning's hypothesis, mentioned in the conclusion to chapter 9, of the need for periodic 'de-routinisation' of cooking and eating in order to renew excitement and enjoyment.

2 E. M. Forster depicted a central feature of the English character as follows:

> it is not that the Englishman can't feel – it is that he is afraid to feel. He has been taught at his public school that feeling is bad form. He must not express great joy or sorrow, or even open his mouth too wide when he talks – his pipe might fall out if he did. He must bottle up his emotions or let them out only on a very special occasion. (1920: 5)

3 The gulf between adult and children's food in America may have declined because, as has often been suggested, American adults have increasingly adopted what were once seen as children's particular predilections ('teenage junk food', etc.). Schwabe, in his book *Unmentionable Cuisine* (1979) discusses at length the very considerable narrowing of the range of meats eaten by Americans in the course of the twentieth century (little lamb or mutton, few rabbits, little game, almost no offal etc.).

4 Another increasingly common fear is that of the effects on health caused by the mass processing of food, especially by the very numerous chemical additives now permitted. This is not a new subject. As early as 1820 Fredrick Accum caused a scandal in England with his *Treatise on the Adulterations of Food and Culinary Poisons*. With the advancing technology of the food manufacturing industry since the Second World War, and its coming to encompass the food of all social classes, numerous books have expressed concern at its consequences – see Bicknell (1952); Huxley (1965); Turner (1970); Walker and Cannon (1984); Courtine (1969); Cohen and Lourbet (1976). In France particularly fears on this subject appear to have become widely shared. Large-scale opinion surveys carried out for the Fondation Française pour la Nutrition (1978) showed very widespread mistrust of manufactured foods. The French were concerned that foods be pure, natural and fresh-tasting, and as many as four out of ten believed that these qualities had been worsened by processing and 'treatment' during the previous half-decade. Their fears were vague and imprecise, not based on exact knowledge of the hormones, chemical colourings, emulsifiers, preservatives and flavourings now so widely used, but no less real for that: the fear of cancer was frequently mentioned. Fear of the effects of food additives does not yet appear to be so widely shared in Britain, although 'health foods' have a strong minority following. So pervasive is manufactured food today, however, that avoiding its possibly harmful effects is extremely difficult for any individual person.

5 The case of the potato is not just exceptional among foods, for the 'trickle *down* effect' is the prevalent pattern among many other kinds of fashion too – see Fallers (1954).

6 This is confirmed by drawings in Mrs Beeton's *Book of Household Management* (1861).

7 At the opposite pole, the anonymous minced beef of the hamburger, which now accounts for 40 per cent of all beef eaten in the USA (Schwabe, 1979: 407), may be symptomatic of the high level of repugnance there towards too recognisable hunks of animal.

8 Notably by Norbert Elias, in discussion at a conference on 'The Civilising Process and Figurational Sociology' held at Balliol College, Oxford, 5–6 January 1980. It was he who first suggested I look for trends over time in feelings of repugnance towards certain foods and that offal would be a likely area in which to look for them. Mary Douglas, on the other hand, told me (in private correspondence) that she would not expect to find any 'general theory' about offal. In the sense of a 'theory' valid for all cultures and all times, she is no doubt right; but that was not what Elias expected to be able to discover anyway.

9 The symbolic connection between steak and virility is not of course unique to America: Roland Barthes also pointed to it as a French national characteristic in his essay 'Steak and Chips' in *Mythologies* (1957: 62–4).

10 Guttman-scale: a form of attitude-scale used by social psychologists, also called a 'cumulative scale', in which a person's responses to a series of questions measure a single dimension of attitude or aptitude. Thus arithmetic ability might be measured by a series of mathematical problems of varying difficulty. A person who solved the most difficult problem correctly would be likely to solve all the less difficult ones too, and thus achieve the maximum score. A person who could not solve the most difficult, but who managed the second most difficult, would be likely also to solve the third and subsequent easier problems, and so on. In our context, I am suggesting that someone who willingly ate eyes would also be likely to eat all subsequent sorts of offal. Someone who could not eat eyes, but who would knowingly eat (say) testicles, would be likely also to eat tripe, kidneys, liver and so on. I am suggesting that attitudes towards these items are likely to form a unidimensional scale of repugnance. The actual order of items would of course have to be determined by preliminary research – the order in which I have tentatively placed them is only a hunch. Another hunch is that, although I would not expect such a scale to be valid across all human cultures, it probably does hold good for European and North American cultures – but with different nationalities and different categories of people in each country having different average scores on the scale.

11 These instructions do not appear in the first edition of 1806; they are quoted from the 1824 edition and are thought to have been inserted by the publisher to Mrs Rundell's disapproval.

12 Nor were they anywhere near so unpopular as in Hall and Hall's American study of thirty years earlier, when 27.4 per cent of respondents said they disliked 'organs' (brains scored 39.8 per cent in that study).

13 This point was made by a participant, herself a Yoruba, in a seminar based on an early version of part of this chapter which I gave at the Institute of Social Anthropology, Oxford, on 27 February 1981.

CHAPTER 12 DIMINISHING CONTRASTS, INCREASING VARIETIES

1 On the decline of farmhouse cheese-making in England and its effects, see Hartley (1954: 483–4), and Richard C. Stone, 'The Triumph of Stilton', *Wine and Food*, 77, Spring 1953.

2 For an example of this point of view, see Gans (1974).

3 For a much fuller discussion of the Frankfurt School's views as they bear on the idea of cultural 'needs', see Mennell (1979).

4 In an early essay (1935), Norbert Elias uses the word *kitsch* more widely than is usual – indeed he applies it to our whole artistic epoch; and he relates this to a social structure in which social classes and groups are more tightly and equally interdependent with each other (a situation of 'functional democratisation'), so that power chances are less unequally distributed.

5 Many other national cuisines apart from these four are now to be found in restaurants in England, particularly in London. There are also sub-varieties. 'Indian' is an omnibus term for cuisines from several parts of the sub-continent, and some of these restaurants specialise in cooking in a *tandoor*. Most Chinese restaurants in Britain provide a large but rather standardised range of Cantonese food; Pekinese cuisine arrived later and is still more common in London and the Home Counties than elsewhere.

6 The estimated division of the British retail catering market in 1977 is shown in the following table:

Type of outlet	*Nos*	*Total turnover (£m)*
Fast-food operations	1500–1550	148–51
Hot Anglo/American take-away	800–900	35–6
Sandwich bars	800	20
Fish and chip shops	10,500–11,000	275
Cafés, snack bars, etc.	20,000–22,000	475
English restaurants/steak bars	1800–2000	257–62
Chinese restaurants	1600–1800	55–9
Take-aways	2200–2400	46–50
Indian/Pakistani restaurants	1950 +	62–4
Take-aways	50 +	1
Greek/Turkish restaurants	1075	38
Take-aways	125	4
Italian restaurants	1500	70
French restaurants	500	38
Other "foreign" restaurants	600–700	35–7
Bakery shops	4000	143–5
Department stores	750–800	150
Variety stores	300	33
Other retail outlets	250–300	1
Pubs	40,000	375–80
Wine bars	500–600	15–18

Type of outlet	*Nos*	*Total turnover (£m)*
Hotels	2500	175–8
Clubs/entertainment centres	30,000+	1000
TOTALS	123,500–126,650	3455–3481

Source: Acumen Marketing Group Ltd (1978).

7 The following table shows the mean number of London restaurants with distinct national cuisines recommended by the *Egon Gonay Guides,* 1971–9 (to the nearest whole number; scores of less than 1 are not shown in the table).

French		42	English	15
Italian		30	Japanese	9
Chinese:			Greek	5
Canton	17		Jewish	2
Peking	12		Indonesian	2
Others	1		Norwegian	2
Total		30	Spanish	1
Indian		24	Middle Eastern	1

AFTERWORD

1 See Stephen Mennell, *Norbert Elias: An Introduction* (Oxford: Blackwell, 1992; published in 1989 as *Norbert Elias: Civilisation and the Human Self-Image).*

2 For a survey of recent research in the sociology of food, see Stephen Mennell, Anne Murcott, and Anneke van Otterloo, *The Sociology of Food: Eating, Diet and Culture* (London: Sage, 1992).

3 C. Fischler, *L'Homnivore: Le goût, la cuisine et le corps* (Paris: Éditions Odile Jacob, 1990).

4 Where a book or article is cited by its year and page numbers, it will be found in the original bibliography; details of new references, on the other hand, are given in the notes to this Afterword.

5 Fischler, *L'Homnivore,* pp. 122ff., 48–59. See also C. Fischler, 'Food Habits, Social Change and the Nature/Culture Dilemma', *Social Science Information,* vol. 19, no. 6, 1980, pp. 937–53.

6 Fischler, *L'Homnivore,* pp. 17–9. Since I compiled the main bibliography, the book by Pierre Bourdieu most relevant to the sociology of food has been published in English translation: *Distinction: A Social Critique of the Judgment of Taste,* trans. Richard Nice (London: Routledge, 1984).

7 Fischler, *L'Homnivore,* p. 11.

8 C. Fischler, 'Food, Self and Identity', *Social Science Information,* vol. 27, no. 2, 1988, pp. 275–92.

9 Ibid., p. 278.

10 C. Fischler, 'Gastro-nomie et gastro-anomie: Sagesse du corps et crise bioculturelle de l'alimentation moderne', *Communications,* vol. 31, 1979, pp. 189–210. See also Fischler, 'Food Habits, Social Change and the Nature/Culture Dilemma'.
11 Fischler, *L'Homnivore,* pp. 203–7.
12 Marvin B. Harris, *Good to Eat: Riddles of Food and Culture* (New York: Simon & Schuster, 1986).
13 Sidney Mintz, *Sweetness and Power: The Place of Sugar in Modern History* (New York: Viking, 1985).
14 Harris, *Good to Eat,* p. 17.
15 'World-system theory' is associated with the work of Immanuel Wallerstein and his colleagues: see Wallerstein, *The Modern World-System,* 3 vols. (New York: Academic Press, 1974–89).
16 Mintz, *Sweetness and Power,* p. 14.
17 Ibid., pp. 46, 67, 73. A similar awareness of the interaction through time of the economic, political, cultural, and nutritional is shown in relation to another commodity, salt, in S. A. M. Adshead, *Salt and Civilization* (New York: St. Martin's Press, 1992). Adshead's book, however, is less overtly a contribution to theoretical debates among social scientists.
18 J. Finkelstein, *Dining Out: A Sociology of Modern Manners* (Oxford: Polity Press, 1989).
19 Ibid., pp. 4–5.
20 See Stephen Mennell and Katherine Simons, 'Die Soziologie der Bulimie', in A. Kämmerer and B. Klingenspor, eds., *Bulimie: Zum Verständnis einer geschlechtsspezifischen Eßstörung* (Stuttgart: Kohlhammer Verlag, 1989): pp. 11–30.
21 Joan Jacobs Brumberg, *Fasting Girls: The Emergence of Anorexia Nervosa as a Modern Disease* (Cambridge: Harvard University Press, 1988).
22 E. J. Button and A. Whitehouse, 'Subclinical anorexia nervosa', *Psychological Medicine,* vol. 11, 1981, pp. 509–16.
23 In their study ('Cultural Expectations of Thinness in Women', *Psychological Reports,* vol. 47, 1980, pp. 483–91) D. M. Garner, P. E. Garfinkel, D. Schwartz, and M. Thompson found a significant increase in the proportion of space given to material about diet and slimming in six major women's magazines between 1969 and 1979 compared with the previous ten years. They also studied *Playboy* magazine Playmate centrefolds and contestants and winners of the Miss America Pageant from 1959 to 1978 as examples of ideal feminine beauty. In both groups of women they found that mean weights were significantly less than corresponding population means published by the Society of Actuaries for each year. In addition, within each of the two groups weight declined across the 20-year period which was studied. Therefore, not only were those women selected as ideal body types consistently thinner than the actual means for comparable women in the population, but also these ideal body types became thinner over time. These findings cannot be explained simply as a reflection of a decrease in average body weights over the 20-year period because the comparison of actuarial norms from 1959 with those of 1979 shows that the average weight of women under 30 (the age group from which *Playboy* playmates and Miss America contestants are most likely to come) was consistently several pounds heavier in 1979 than in 1959. In other words, the average

weight of the population was increasing at the same time that pressures to be slim were growing and the size of the ideal body image was diminishing.

24 Jean-Jacques Courtine, 'Les Stakhanovistes du Narcissisme: Bodybuilding et puritanisme ostentatoire dans la culture américaine du corps', *Communications,* vol. 56, Sept. 1993, pp. 225–51.

25 S. Orbach, *Fat Is a Feminist Issue* (London: Paddington Press, 1978); and Orbach, *Hunger Strike* (London: Faber & Faber, 1986).

26 N. Charles and M. Kerr, *Women, Food and Families* (Manchester: Manchester University Press, 1988). See also Charles and Kerr, 'Eating Properly: The Family and State Benefit', *Sociology,* vol. 20, no. 3, 1986, pp. 412–29; and 'Food for Feminist Thought', *Sociological Review,* vol. 34, no. 1, 1986, pp. 537–72.

27 Nick Fiddes, *Meat: A Natural Symbol* (London: Routledge, 1991): p. 29. See also Colin Spencer's ambitious general history of vegetarianism, *The Heretic's Feast* (London: Fourth Estate, 1993).

28 Bourdieu, *Distinction,* pp. 190–1.

29 J.-R. Pitte, *Gastronomie française: Histoire et géographie d'une passion* (Paris: Fayard, 1991).

30 Claude Grignon and Christiane Grignon, 'Styles d'alimentation et goûts populaires', *Revue française de sociologie,* vol. 21, no. 4, 1980, pp. 531–69. See also Grignon and Grignon, 'Pratiques alimentaires et classes sociales: Des différences importantes', *Problèmes politiques et sociales,* vol. 544, 1986, pp. 22–7; and 'Alimentation et stratification sociale', *Cahiers de nutrition et de diététique,* vol. 16, no. 4, 1986, pp. 207–17; and Claude Grignon, 'Hierarchical cuisine or standard cooking?', *Food and Foodways,* vol. 3, no. 3, 1989, pp. 177–83.

31 P. Pynson, *La France à Table, 1960–86* (Paris: Belfond, 1989).

32 Stephen Mennell, 'Voorspel: Eten in de Lage Lande', in *Smaken Verschillen* (*All Manners of Food*) (Amsterdam: Uitgeverij Bert Bakker, 1989): pp. 15–29.

33 Anneke van Otterloo, 'Over culinaire culturen in Noord en Zuid: Enkele opmerkingen bij de sociogenese van nationale stijl en regionale variaties in Nederland', *Groniek: Gronings Historisch Tijdschrift,* vol. 95, 1986, pp. 36–55.

34 A. H. van Otterloo, *Eten en eetlust in Nederland, 1840–1990* (Amsterdam: Uitgeverij Bert Bakker, 1990).

35 See Eva Barlösius, 'Soziale und historische Aspekte der deutschen Küche', in Stephen Mennell, *Die Kultivierung des Appetits* (*All Manners of Food*) (Frankfurt am Main: Athenäum, 1988): pp. 423–44.

36 K. F. L. F. von Rumohr, *The Essence of Cookery* (London: Prospect Books, 1993). The original German title was *Geist de Kochkunst;* the book was published in 1822 – *before* Brillat-Savarin's book.

37 H. Scharfenberg, *The German Kitchen* (New York: Poseidon Press, 1989).

38 Thomas Kutsch, 'Ethnic food, cuisines régionales, gruppen-und landschaftstypische Küchen: Essen als Teil der sozialen Identität', *Ernährungs-Umschau,* vol. 37, 1990, pp. 29–37.

39 *American Heritage Cookbook and Illustrated History of American Eating and Drinking* (New York: Simon & Schuster, 1964).

40 Harvey Levenstein, *Revolution at the Table: The Transformation of the American Diet* (New York: Oxford University Press, 1988). See also Levenstein, *Paradox of Plenty: A Social History of Eating in Modern America* (New York: Oxford University Press, 1994).

41 Levenstein, *Revolution at the Table,* p. 4.
42 Amelia Simmons, *American Cookery* (Hartford, Conn., 1796).
43 Lydia M. Child, *The American Frugal Housewife,* 8th ed. (Boston: Carter & Hendee, 1832); Catharine Beecher, *A Treatise on Domestic Economy for the Use of Young Ladies at Home and School* (Boston: T. H. Webb, 1843); Catharine Beecher and Harriet Beecher Stowe, *The American Woman's Home* (New York: J. B. Ford, 1869); Sarah Hale, *Mrs. Hale's New Cook Book* (Philadelphia: T. B. Peterson, 1857); Fannie Farmer, *Boston Cooking-School Cook Book* (Boston: Little Brown, 1896).
44 Isabella Beeton, *Beeton's Book of Household Management* (London: S. Beeton, 1861).
45 Susan Williams, *Savoury Suppers and Fashionable Feasts: Dining in Victorian America* (New York: Pantheon, 1985); Kathryn Grover, ed., *Dining in America, 1850–1900* (Amherst: University of Massachusetts Press, 1987).
46 Robert Dahl, *Who Governs?* (New Haven: Yale University Press, 1961).
47 R. Pilsbury, *From Boarding House to Bistro: The American Restaurant Then and Now* (Boston: Unwin Hyman, 1990).
48 Gary Alan Fine, 'Working Cooks: The Dynamics of Professional Kitchens', *Current Research on Occupations and Professions,* vol. 4, 1987, pp. 151–2. See also Fine, 'The Culture of Production: Aesthetic Choices and Constraints in Culinary Work', *American Journal of Sociology,* vol. 97, no. 5, 1992, pp. 1268–94.
49 Pitte, *Gastronomie française.*
50 See Michael Symons, *The Shared Table: Ideas for Australian Cuisine* (Canberra: Australian Government Printing Service for the Office of Multicultural Affairs, 1993). See also Symons, *One Continuous Picnic: A History of Australian Eating* (Adelaide: Duck Press, 1982), which vividly depicts the British culinary legacy earlier in Australian history.

Bibliography

NOTE: As far as possible, reference dates in the text are to the date of first publication. When use has been made of an edition other than the first, or of a translation, the original date of publication is given in this bibliography in square brackets, followed by details of the actual edition from which page references or quotations are taken.

English translations in the text of works cited in the bibliography in French (and occasionally other languages) are by the author unless otherwise stated. Where a published English translation is cited in the bibliography, quotations in the text are from the published version, although minor corrections have been made in a few cases.

Anon. [*c.* 1390] *The Forme of Cury*, in C. B. Hieatt and S. Butler, eds, *Curye on Inglysch*. Oxford, Oxford University Press, 1985, pp. 93–145.

Anon. [*c.* 1400] *Sir Gawain and the Green Knight*. Harmondsworth: Penguin, 1974.

Anon. 1485 *Kuchenmeisterey*. Nürnberg: J. Zeninger.

Anon. 1500 *This is the Boke of Cokery*. London: Richard Pynson.

Anon. [1508] *Here Begynneth the Boke of Kervynge*. London: Early English Text Society, 1868.

Anon. [*c.* 1542] *Le Grand Cuisinier de toute Cuisine*. Paris: J. Bonfons.

Anon. [1562] *Certain Sermons or Homilies Appointed to be Read in Churches in the Time of Queen Elizabeth of Famous Memory*. London: George Wells, 1687.

Anon. 1687 *The History of the Coronation of King James II and Queen Mary*. London.

Anon. 1737 *The Whole Duty of a Woman*. London: T. Read.

Anon. 1740 *Le Cuisinier Gascon*. Amsterdam.

Anon. 1797 *On the Conduct of Men to Inferior Animals*. Manchester.

Anon. 1814 *The School for Good Living, or, A Literary and Historical Essay on the European Kitchen*. London: H. Colburn.

Anon. 1815 *The Epicure's Almanack*. London: Longman, Hurst, Rees, Orme & Brown.

Anon. 1875 *Dictionary of Cookery*. London: Cassell.

Abbey, P. M. and Macdonald, G. M., 1963 *'O'-Level Cookery*. London: Methuen.

Abel, Wilhelm [1935] *Agricultural Fluctuations in Europe from the Thirteenth to the Twentieth Centuries*. 3rd edn, London: Methuen, 1980.

—— 1937 'Wandlungen des Fleischsgebrauchs und Fleischsverorgung in Deutschland seit dem ausgehenden Mittelalter', *Berichte über Landswirtschaft*, new series, vol. XXII, no. 3, pp. 411ff.
Accum, Fredrick, 1820 *Treatise on the Adulterations of Food and Culinary Poisons*. London.
Acton, Eliza, 1845 *Modern Cookery for Private Families*. London: Longman, Brown, Green & Longman.
Acumen Marketing Group Ltd, 1978 *A Study of the British Retail Catering Market*. London.
Addison, Joseph [1709] *The Tatler*, in *The Works*. Birmingham: Tonson, 1761.
—— [1711–12] *The Spectator*. 4 vols, London: J. M. Dent, 1907.
Adorno, Theodor W. [1938] 'On the Fetish-Character in Music and Regression of Listening', in A. Arato and E. Gebhardt, eds, *The Essential Frankfurt School Reader*. Oxford: Blackwell, 1978, pp. 270–99.
Adorno, Theodor W. and Horkheimer, Max [1944] *Dialectic of Enlightenment*. London: New Left Books, 1979.
Ali-Bab (Henri Babinski), 1907 *Gastronomie pratique: Etudes culinaires suivies du traitement de l'obésité des gourmands*. Paris: Flammarion.
Apicius, M. Gaius (attr.) [1936] *Cookery and Dining in Imperial Rome*. London: Constable, 1977.
Apostolides, Jean-Marie, 1981 *Le Roi-Machine: Spectacle et politique au temps de Louis XIV*. Paris: Le Minuit.
Appleby, A. B., 1978 *Famine in Tudor and Stuart England*. Liverpool: Liverpool University Press, 1978.
Arbellot de Vacqueur, Simon, 1940 'Le prince de Talleyrand', *Grandgousier*, 7e année, no. 3, pp. 35–41.
—— 1965 *Curnonsky: Prince des gastronomes*. Paris: Production de Paris.
Aresty, Esther B., 1965 *The Delectable Past*. London: George Allen and Unwin.
Ariès, Philippe [1960] *Centuries of Childhood*. Harmondsworth: Penguin, 1973.
Aron, Jean-Paul, 1961 'Biologie et Alimentation au XVIIIe Siècle et au Debut du XIXe Siècle', *Annales E-S-C*, vol. 16, no. 2, pp. 971–7.
—— 1967 *Essai sur la sensibilité alimentaire à Paris au XIXe siècle*. Paris: Armand Colin.
—— 1973 *Le Mangeur du 19e siècle*. Paris: Laffont.
Ashley, Sir William, 1928 *The Bread of Our Forefathers*. Oxford: Clarendon Press.
Association of Teachers of Domestic Subjects, 1973 *The ATDS Cookery Book*. London: Methuen Educational.
Aubrey, John [*c.* 1680] *Brief Lives*. Harmondsworth: Penguin, 1962.
Audot, Louis-Eustache, 1818 *La Cuisinière de la campagne et de la ville*. Paris: Audot.
Augustine, St [*c.* 400] *The Fathers of the Church: A New Translation*. New York: CUA, 1948– .
Austen, Jane [1813] *Pride and Prejudice*. London, Nelson, n.d.
—— [1871] *Lady Susan, The Watsons, Sanditon*. Harmondsworth: Penguin, 1974.
—— [1932] *Jane Austen's Letters to her Sister Cassandra and Others*. 2nd edn, London: Oxford University Press, 1952.
Austen-Leigh, J. E., [1871] 'A Memoir of Jane Austen', in Jane Austen, *Persuasion*. Harmondsworth: Penguin, 1965, pp. 271–391.

Austin, Thomas, ed., 1888 *Two Fifteenth-Century Cookery Books*. London: Early English Text Society.

Bahlman, D. W. R., 1957 *The Moral Revolution of 1688*. New Haven: Yale University Press.

Baldwin, F. E., 1926 *Sumptuary Legislation and Personal Regulation in England*. Baltimore: Johns Hopkins Press.

Banks, J. A., 1954 *Prosperity and Parenthood*. London: Routledge & Kegan Paul.

Banner, Lois W., 1973 'Why Women Have Not Been Great Chefs', *South Atlantic Quarterly*, vol. 72, no. 2, pp. 193–212.

Barber, Elinor G., 1955 *The Bourgeoisie in Eighteenth-Century France*, Princeton, N.J.: Princeton University Press.

Barber, Richard W., 1973 *Cooking and Recipes from Rome to the Renaissance*. London: Allen Lane.

Barker, T. C., McKenzie, J. C., and Yudkin, J., eds, 1966 *Our Changing Fare: Two Hundred Years of British Food Habits*. London: MacGibon & Kee.

Barthes, Roland [1957] *Mythologies*. London, Granada, 1973.

——— [1961] 'Toward a Psychosociology of Contemporary Food Consumption', in R. Forster and O. Ranum, eds, *Food and Drink in History*. Baltimore: Johns Hopkins University Press, 1979, pp. 166–73.

Baudrillart, Henri, 1878–80 *Histoire de luxe privé et publique depuis l'antiquité jusqu'à nos jours*. 4 vols, Paris: Hachette.

Beauvilliers, A. B., 1814 *L'Art du cuisinier*. Paris: Pillet aîné & Colnet, Lenoir.

Becker, Howard S. [1953] 'Becoming a Marijuana User', in *Outsiders*. New York: Free Press, pp. 41–58, 1963.

Beeton, Isabella, 1861 *Beeton's Book of Household Management*. London: S. Beeton.

Bell, Florence, 1907 *At the Works: A Study of a Manufacturing Town*. London: Edward Arnold.

Benjamin, Walter [1936] 'The Work of Art in the Age of Mechanical Reproduction', in *Illuminations*. London: Fontana, 1973.

Bennett, H. S., 1937 *Life on the English Manor: A Study of Peasant Conditions, 1150–1400*. Cambridge: Cambridge University Press.

Benoîston de Châteauneuf, L. F., 1820 *Recherches sur les consommations de tout genre de la ville de Paris en 1817, comparées à ce qu'elles étaient en 1789*. Paris: chez l'auteur.

Berchoux, Joseph de, 1801 *La Gastronomie, ou l'homme des champs à table, poème didactique en quatre chants*. Paris: Giguet.

Berry, Mary [1828] *A Comparative View of the Social Life of England and France*. London: Longman, Rees, Orme, Brown & Green, 1831.

Bicknell, Franklin, 1952 *The English Complaint*. London: Heinemann.

Blake, Robert, 1966 *Disraeli*. London: Eyre & Spottiswoode.

Bloch, Marc [1939–40] *Feudal Society*. 2 vols, London: Routledge & Kegan Paul, 1961.

——— [1954] 'Les Aliments de l'Ancienne France', in J. J. Hémardinquer, ed., *Pour une Histoire de l'Alimentation*. Paris: A. Colin, 1970, pp. 231–5.

Blumer, Herbert [1955] *Symbolic Interactionism: Perspective and Method*. Englewood Cliffs: Prentice-Hall, 1969.

Bocuse, Paul, 1976 *La Cuisine du marché*. Paris: Flammarion.

Bolles, Robert C., 1983 'A 'Mixed'' Model of Taste Preference', in R. L. Mellgren, ed., *Animal Cognition and Behaviour*. Amsterdam: North Holland, pp. 65–82.

Bonnefons, Nicholas de [1654] *Les Délices de la table*. Paris: chez Pierre Des-Hayes, 1662.

Boorde, Andrew [1542] *A Compendyous Regyment or A Dyetary of Health*. London, Early English Text Society, 1870.

Borer, Mary C., 1972 *The British Hotel through the Ages*. Guildford and London: Lutterworth Press.

Bossy, John, 1970 'The Counter-Reformation and the People of Catholic Europe', *Past and Present*, vol. 47, pp. 51–70.

Boswell, James [1791] *The Life of Samuel Johnson, LLD*. 2 vols, London: Odhams Press, n.d.

Boucher d'Argis A.-G. [1765] 'Lois Somptuaires', in D. Diderot, ed., *Encyclopédie*. Neufchâtel: Samuel Faulche, 1751–80, vol. IX, pp. 672–75.

Bourdieu, Pierre, 1979 *La Distinction*. Paris: Le Minuit.

Bradley, Richard, 1727–32 *The Country Housewife and Lady's Director*. London: D. Browne.

Braudel, Fernand 1961 'Vie Matérielle et comportements biologiques—Bulletin No. 1'. *Annales E-S-C*, vol. 16, no. 3, pp. 545–9.

——— [1967] *Capitalism and Material Life, 1400–1800*. London: Fontana, 1974.

Bretherton, R. F., 1931 'Country Inns and Alehouses', in R. Lennard, ed., *Englishmen at Rest and Play: Some Phases of English Leisure, 1558–1714*. Oxford: Clarendon Press, pp. 147–201.

Briffault, Eugène, 1846 *Paris à table*. Paris.

Briggs, E., 1890 *Cookery Book and General Axioms for Plain Cookery*. London: School Board for London.

Briggs, Richard, 1788 *The English Art of Cookery*. London: G. G. J. & J. Robinson.

Brillat-Savarin, J.-A., 1826 *La Physiologie du goût*. Paris: A. Sautelet.

Brisse, Baron, 1867 *Le Calendrier gastronomique pour l'année 1867: les 365 menus de Baron Brisse*. Paris: Bureau de la 'Liberté'.

——— 1868 *Recettes à l'usage des ménages bourgeois et des petits ménages, comprenant la manière de servir à nouveau tous les restes*. Paris: Donnaud.

Bruch, Hilde, 1974 *Eating Disorders: Obesity, Anorexia nervosa and the Person Within*. London: Routledge & Kegan Paul.

Burckhardt, Jakob [1860] *The Civilisation of the Renaissance in Italy*. London: Phaidon Press, 1944.

Burke, Peter, 1978 *Popular Culture in Early Modern Europe*. London: Temple Smith.

Burnett, John, 1966 *Plenty and Want*. London: Nelson.

——— 1981 'Country Diet', in G. E. Mingay, ed., *The Victorian Countryside*. London: Routledge & Kegan Paul, vol. II, pp. 554–65.

Caillot, A., 1827 *Mémoires pour servir à l'histoire des moeurs et usages des Français*. 2 vols, Paris: Dauvin.

Campbell, R. H., 1966 'Diet in Scotland: an Example of Regional Variation', in T. C. Barker *et al.*, eds, *Our Changing Fare*. London: MacGibon & Kee.

Cappon, Daniel, 1973 *Eating, Loving and Dying: A Psychology of Appetites*. Toronto: University of Toronto Press.

Carême, Antonin, 1815a *Le Pâtissier royal Parisien ou Traité élémentaire et pratique de la pâtisserie ancienne et moderne*. 2 vols, Paris: J.-G. Dentu.

——— 1815b *Le pâtissier pittoresque*. Paris: au dépôt de la Librairie.
——— 1822 *Le Maître d'hôtel français ou parallèle de la cuisine ancienne et moderne*. Paris: l'auteur.
——— 1828 *Le Cuisinier Parisien*. Paris: l'auteur.
——— [1833–5] *L'Art de la cuisine française au dix-neuvième siècle*. 5 vols, Paris: au Comptoir des Imprimeurs-Unis, 1847.
Carter, Charles, 1730 *The Complete Practical Cook*. London: W. Meadows, C. Rivington & R. Hett.
——— 1732 *The Compleat City and Country Cook*. London: A. Bettesworth, C. Hitch *et al.*
Châtillon-Plessis (pseud. of Maurice Dancourt), 1894 *La Vie à table à la fin du 19ᵉ siècle*. Paris: Firmin-Didot.
Chaucer, Geoffrey [*c.* 1386] *The Canterbury Tales*. Baltimore: Penguin, 1952.
Cheyne, George, 1724 *An Essay of Health and Long Life*. London: G. Strachan.
——— 1733 *The English Malady*. London: G. Strachan.
Chivers, T. S., 1973 'The Proletarianisation of a Service Worker', *Sociological Review*, vol. 21, no. 4, pp. 633–56.
Cipolla, Carlo M., 1969 *Literacy and Development in the West*. Harmondsworth: Penguin.
Claudian, Jean and Serville, Yvonne, 1970 'Aspects de l'Évolution Récente du Comportement Alimentaire en France: Composition des Repas et "Urbanisation"', in J.-J. Hémardinquer, ed., *Pour une histoire de l'alimentation*. Paris: A. Colin, pp. 174–87.
Claudian, J., Serville, Y. and Tremolières, F., 1969 'Enquête sur les Facteurs de Choix des Aliments', *Bulletin de l'INSERM*, vol. 24, no. 5, pp. 1277–390.
Cobb, Richard, 1970 *The Police and the People: French Popular Protest, 1789–1820*. Oxford: Clarendon Press.
Cobbett, William, 1821 *Cottage Economy*. London: T. Davies.
——— [1821–32] *Rural Rides*. Harmondsworth: Penguin, 1967.
Codere, Helen, 1950 *Fighting with Property: A Study of Kwakiutl Potlatching and Warfare, 1792–1930*. Seattle: Washington University Press.
Cohen, A. and Lourbet, F., 1976 *Bon Appetit, Messieurs!* Paris: Balland.
Cole, G. D. H. and Postgate, Raymond, 1938 *The Common People*. London: Methuen.
Collingwood, Francis and Woollams, John, 1792 *The Universal Cook, and City and Country Housekeeper*. London: J. Scatcherd & J. Whitaker.
Combe, Andrew, 1846 *The Physiology of Digestion, considered with Relation to Dietetics*. Edinburgh: Maclachlan & Stewart.
Conil, Jean, 1962 *The Epicurean Book*. London: George Allen & Unwin.
Cook, Ann, 1754 *Professed Cookery*. Newcastle: J. White.
Cooper, Derek, 1967 *The Bad Food Guide*. London: Routledge & Kegan Paul.
Coulton, G. G., 1926 *The Medieval Village*. Cambridge: Cambridge University Press.
Courtine, Robert J., 1969 *L'Assassin est à votre table*. Paris: La Table Ronde.
Cranmer, Thomas, 1846 *Miscellaneous Writings and Letters*. Cambridge: Cambridge University Press for the Parker Society.
Creese, Angela, 1973 *Revision Notes for 'O'-Level and CSE Cookery*. London: Allman.
Crouzet, François [1966] 'England and France in the Eighteenth Century: a Compara-

tive Analysis of Two Economic Growths', in R. M. Hartwell, ed., *The Causes of the Industrial Revolution in England*. London: Methuen, 1970, pp. 139–74.
Curnonsky (pseud. of Maurice-Edmond Sailland), 1958 *Souvenirs*. Paris: A. Michel.
Curnonsky and de Croze, Austin, 1933 *Le Trésor gastronomique de France*. Paris: Librairie Delagrave.
Curnonsky and Rouff, Marcel, 1921– *La France gastronomique: Guide des merveilleuses culinaires et des bonnes auberges françaises*. Paris: F. Rouff.
Curschmann, Fritz, 1900 *Hungersnöte im Mittelalter*. Leipzig: B. G. Teubner.
van Daalen, Rineke, 1979 'Ongewenste ontmoetingen in de Amsterdamse tram: Klachten aan de Gemeente Tram Amsterdam in het begin van de twintigste eeuw'. *Amsterdams Sociologisch Tijdschrift*, 6, 3, pp. 449–73.
Dallas, Eneas Sweetland, 1877 *Kettner's Book of the Table*. London: Dulau.
Darnton, Robert, 1984 *The Great Cat Massacre and Other Episodes in French Cultural History*. London: Allen Lane.
David, Elizabeth, 1951 *French Country Cooking*. London: John Lehmann.
——— 1960 *French Provincial Cooking*. London: Michael Joseph.
——— 1961 'Isabella Beeton and her Book', *Wine and Food*, no. 109, pp. 3–8.
——— 1964 'French Provincial Cooking', *Wine and Food*, no. 121, pp. 28–31.
——— 1968 'Introduction', to E. Ray, ed., *The Best of Eliza Acton*. London: Longmans, Green.
Davidoff, Leonore, 1973 *The Best Circles: Society, Etiquette and the Season*. London: Croom Helm.
Davidson, Caroline, 1982 *A Woman's Work is Never Done: A History of Housework in the British Isles, 1650–1950*. London: Chatto & Windus.
Davies, Maud F., 1909 *Life in an English Village*. London: T. Fisher Unwin.
Davis, Natalie Zemon, 1975 *Society and Culture in Early Modern France*. London: Duckworth.
Dawson, Thomas, 1585 *The Good Huswifes Jewell*. London, Edward White.
Delumeau, Jean [1971] *Catholicism between Luther and Voltaire: A New View of the Counter-Reformation*. London: Burns & Oates, 1977.
Desalleurs, Roland P., Comte, 1739 *Lettre d'un pâtissier anglois au nouveau cuisinier françois*. Paris.
Digby, Sir Kenelm, 1669 *The Closet of the Eminently Learned Sir Kenelm Digby, Kt, Opened*. London: H. Brome.
Disraeli, Benjamin, 1844 *Coningsby*. 3 vols, London: Henry Colborn.
Douglas, Mary, 1966 *Purity and Danger: An Analysis of the Concepts of Pollution and Taboo*. London: Routledge & Kegan Paul.
——— 1972 'Deciphering a Meal', *Daedalus*, vol. 101, no. 1, pp. 61–81.
——— 1974 'Food as an Art Form', *Studio International*, September, pp. 83–8.
——— 1978 'Culture', in *Annual Report 1977–78 of the Russell Sage Foundation*, New York, pp. 55–81.
Douglas, Mary and Nicod, Michael, 1974 'Taking the Biscuit: the Structure of British Meals', *New Society*, vol. 30, no. 637, pp. 744–7.
Driver, Christopher, 1983 *The British at Table, 1940–1980*. London: Chatto & Windus.
Drummond, Sir Jack C. and Anne Wilbraham, 1939 *The Englishman's Food*. London: Jonathan Cape.
Dubois, Félix Urbain and Bernard, Emile, 1856 *La Cuisine classique*. 2 vols, Paris: les auteurs.

Duby, Georges, 1961 'La Seigneurie et l'Economie Paysanne, Alpes du Sud, 1388', *Etudes rurales*, 2, pp. 5–36.

Duclos, Charles P. [1751] *Considérations sur les moeurs de ce siècle*, in *Oeuvres complètes* 9 vols., Paris: Janet & Cotelle, 1820.

—— [1772] *Mémoires sur la vie de Duclos, écrits par lui-même*, in *Oeuvres complètes*. 9 vols, Paris: Janet & Cotelle, 1820.

Dumas, Alexandre, *père*, 1873 *Le Grand Dictionnaire de cuisine*. Paris: Alphonse Lemerre.

Duncan, T. C., 1878 *How to Become Plump, or, Talks on Physiological Feeding*. London.

Dunning, Eric and Sheard, Kenneth, 1979 *Barbarians, Gentlemen and Players*. Oxford: Basil Blackwell.

Dyer, Christopher, 1983 'English Diet in the Later Middle Ages', in T. H. Aston, P. R. Coss, C. Dyer and J. Thirsk, eds, *Social Relations and Ideas: Essays in Honour of R. H. Hilton*. Oxford: Past and Present Society, pp. 191–216.

Eden, Sir Frederick, 1797 *The State of the Poor*. 3 vols, London: various publishers.

Einstein, Lewis, 1902 *The Italian Renaissance in England*. New York: Columbia University Press.

Eisenstein, Elizabeth L., 1968 'Some Conjectures about the Impact of Printing on Western Society and Thought: a Preliminary Report', *Journal of Modern History*, vol. 40, no. 1, pp.1–56.

Elias, Norbert, 1935 'Kitschstil und Kitschzeitalter', *Die Sammlung*, vol. 2, no. 5, pp. 252–63.

—— [1939] *The Civilising Process*, vol. I: *The History of Manners*. Oxford: Basil Blackwell, 1978. Vol. II: *State Formation and Civilisation*. Oxford: Basil Blackwell, 1982.

—— 1962 'The "Break with Traditionalism" and the Origins of Sociology', *Transactions of the Fifth World Congress of Sociology, Washington DC, 1962*. Louvain: International Sociological Association, vol. III, pp. 51–3.

—— [1969] *The Court Society*. Oxford: Basil Blackwell, 1983.

—— 1970a *African Art from the Collection of Norbert Elias*. Exhibition catalogue, Leicester: City of Leicester Art Gallery.

—— [1970b] *What is Sociology?* London: Hutchinson, 1978.

Elias, Norbert and Dunning, Eric, 1969 'The Quest for Excitement in Leisure', *Society and Leisure*, vol. 2, pp. 50–85.

Elias, Norbert and Scotson, John L., 1965 *The Established and the Outsiders*. London: Frank Cass.

Eliot, T. S., 1948 *Notes Towards a Definition of Culture*. London: Faber and Faber.

Engels, F. [1845] *The Condition of the Working Class in England in 1844*. London: Granada, 1969.

Erasmus, Desiderius [*c.* 1518] *Twenty Select Colloquies of Erasmus*. London: Chapman & Dodd, n.d.

Escoffier, Georges Auguste [1903] *A Guide to Modern Cookery*. London: Hutchinson, 1957.

—— 1910 *Projet d'Assistance Mutuel*. Paris.

—— 1912 *Le Livre des menus*. Paris: Flammarion.

Fallers, Lloyd A., 1954 'A Note on the "Trickle Effect"', *Public Opinion Quarterly*, vol. 18, no. 3, pp. 314–21.

Farley, John, 1783 *The London Art of Cookery*. London: J. Fielding, J. Scatcherd & J. Whitaker.

Favre, Joseph, 1883 *Dictionnaire universelle de cuisine et d'hygiène alimentaire*. Paris: les libraires.

Ferguson, Marjorie, 1982 *Forever Feminine: Women's Magazines and the Cult of Femininity*. London: Heinemann.

Fisher, F. J., 1948 'The Development of London as a Centre of Conspicuous Consumption in the Sixteenth and Seventeenth Centuries', *Transactions of the Royal Historical Society*, 4th series, vol. 30, pp. 37–50.

Fisher, M. F. K., [1954] *The Art of Eating*. London: Picador, 1983.

Fitz-Stephen, William [*c.* 1183] 'A Description of London', in F. M. Stenton, ed., *Norman London*. London: Historical Association, 1934, pp. 25–35.

Flandrin, J.-L., Hyman, P. and Hyman, M., 1983 'La Cuisine dans la Littérature de Colportage', Introduction to *Le Cuisinier françois*. Paris: Montalba, pp. 11–99.

Fondation Française pour la Nutrition, 1978 *Les Français et leur alimentation*. Paris: FFPN.

Forster, E. M. [1920] 'Notes on the English Character', in *Abinger Harvest*. London: Edward Arnold, 1936, pp. 3–14.

Forster, Robert [1960] *The Nobility of Toulouse in the Eighteenth Century: A Social and Economic Study*. New York: Octagon Books, 1971.

——— 1971 *The House of Saulx-Tavanes: Versailles and Burgundy, 1700–1830*. Baltimore: Johns Hopkins Press.

Fortescue, Sir John [*c.* 1471] *The Gouvernance of England*. London: Oxford University Press, 1885.

Fosca, Francois, 1934 *Histoire des cafés de Paris*. Paris: Firmin-Didot.

Francatelli, Charles Elmé, 1846 *The Modern Cook*. London: Richard Bentley.

——— [1861] *A Plain Cookery for the Working Classes*. London: Routledge, Warne & Routledge.

Franklin, Alfred, 1887–1902 *Vie privée d'autrefois, 12ᵉ à 18ᵉ siècles*. 27 vols, Paris: Plon.

Frati, L. ed., 1899 *Libro di cucina del sec. XIV*. Livorno: R. Giusti.

Freud, Sigmund [1913] *Totem and Taboo*. London: Hogarth Press, 1950.

Furet, François and Ozouf, Jacques, 1983 *Reading and Writing: Literacy in France from Calvin to Jules Ferry*. Cambridge: Cambridge University Press.

Fussell, G. E. and K. R. Fussell, 1953 *The English Countrywoman*. London: Melrose.

Galbraith, John Kenneth, 1952 *American Capitalism*. London: Hamish Hamilton.

Galton, Sir Francis, 1884 'The Weights of British Noblemen during the last three Generations', *Nature*, vol. 29, pp. 266–8.

Gans, Herbert, 1974 *Popular Culture and High Culture*. New York: Basic Books.

Garine, Igor de, 1980 'Approaches to the Study of Food and Prestige in Savannah Tribes – Massa and Mussey of Northern Cameroon and Chad', *Social Science Information*, vol. 19, no. 1, pp. 39–78.

Gault, Henri and Millau, Christian, 1970 *Guide gourmand de France*. Paris: Hachette.

——— 1976 *Gault et Millau se mettent à table*. Paris: Stock.

Gershuny, J. J. and Thomas, G. S., 1980 *Changing Patterns of Time Use: Data Preparation and Some Preliminary Results, UK 1961–1974/5*. Brighton: Science Policy Research Unit, University of Sussex.

Giard, Luce, 1980 'Faire-la-cuisine', in L. Giard and P. Mayol, *L'Invention du quotidien, 2: Habiter, Cuisiner*. Paris: Union Générale d'Editions.

Girard, Alain, 1977 'Le Triomphe de *La Cuisinière Bourgeoise*: Livres Culinaires, Cuisine et Société en France aux XVIIe et XVIIIe siècles', *Revue d'histoire moderne et contemporaine*, vol. XXIV, pp. 497–523.

——— 1982 'Du manuscrit à l'imprimé: le livre de cuisine en Europe aux 15e et 16e siècles', in J.-C. Margolin and R. Sauzet, eds, *Pratiques et discours alimentaires à la Renaissance*. Paris: G.-P. Maisonneuve & Larose, pp. 107–17.

Girouard, Mark, 1978 *Life in the English Country House*. New Haven: Yale University Press.

Glasse, Hannah, 1747 *The Art of Cookery Made Plain and Easy*. London.

Goldthorpe, J. H., Lockwood, D., Bechofer, F. and Platt, J., 1968 *The Affluent Worker: Industrial Attitudes and Behaviour*. Cambridge: Cambridge University Press.

Goode, W. J., 1969 'The Theoretical Limits of Professionalisation', in A. Etzioni, ed., *The Semi-Professions and their Organisation*. New York: Free Press.

Goody, Jack R., ed., 1968 *Literacy in Traditional Societies*. Cambridge: Cambridge University Press.

——— 1977 *The Domestication of the Savage Mind*. Cambridge: Cambridge University Press.

——— 1982 *Cooking, Cuisine and Class*. Cambridge: Cambridge University Press.

Gottschalk, Alfred, 1939 'L'Appetit de Louis XVI au Temple', *Grandgousier*, vol. 6, no. 4.

——— 1948a *Histoire de l'alimentation et de la gastronomie, depuis la préhistoire jusqu'à nos jours*. 2 vols, Paris: Editions Hippocrate.

——— 1948b 'Prosper Montagné, 1865–1948', *Wine and Food*, vol. 60, pp. 190–3.

Goubert, Pierre, 1960 *Beauvais et le Beauvaisis de 1600 à 1730*. 2 vols, Paris: Imprimérie Nationale.

Goudsblom, Johan [1960] *Nihilism and Culture*. Oxford: Basil Blackwell, 1977.

——— [1974] *Sociology in the Balance*. Oxford: Basil Blackwell, 1977.

——— 1979 'Zivilisation, Ansteckungsangst und Hygiene', in P. R. Gleichmann, J. Goudsblom and H. Korte, eds, *Materialien zu Norbert Elias's Zivilisationstheorie*. Frankfurt: Suhrkamp, pp. 215–53.

——— 1984 'The Domestication of Fire as a Civilising Process', paper presented at a conference on 'Civilisation and Theories of Civilising Processes', Bielefeld, 15–17 June 1984.

Gouffé, Jules, 1867 *Livre de la cuisine*. Paris: Hachette.

Graham, G. E., 1964 'The Food Manufacturer in a World of Economic Reality', in J. Yudkin and J. C. Mackenzie, eds., *Changing Food Habits*. London: MacGibon & Kee.

Graham, Sylvester, 1839 *Lectures on the Science of Human Life*. Boston: Marsh, Capon, Lyon & Webb.

Grigson, Jane, 1970 *Charcuterie and French Pork Cookery*. Harmondsworth: Penguin.

——— 1974 *English Food*. London: Macmillan.

——— 1978 *Jane Grigson's Vegetable Book*. London: Michael Joseph.

——— 1982 *Jane Grigson's Fruit Book*. London: Michael Joseph.

Grimod de la Reynière, A.-B.-L., 1803–12 *Almanach des gourmands*. Paris.

——— 1808 *Le Manuel des amphitryons*. Paris: Capelle & Renaud.
——— 1978 *Grimod de la Reynière: Ecrits gastronomiques*. Paris: Union Générale d'Editions.
Gronow, Captain Rees [1862–6] *The Reminiscences and Recollections of Captain Gronow*. 2 vols., London: John C. Nimmo, 1900.
Grossmith, George and Weedon [1892] *The Diary of a Nobody*. Harmondsworth: Penguin, 1945.
Guégan, Bertrand, 1934 *Le Cuisinier français*. Paris: Emile Paul Frères.
Guérard, Michel, 1976 *La Grande Cuisine minceur*. Paris: R. Laffont.
Guerrini, O., ed., 1887 *Frammento di un libro di cucina del sec. XIV*. Bologna.
Guillaumin, Emile [1905] *The Life of a Simple Man*. London: Selwyn & Blount, 1919.
Habermas, Jürgen, 1960 *Strukturwandel der Öffentlichkeit*. Neuwied: Luchterhand.
Hall, I. S. and C. S., 1939 'A Study of Disliked and Unfamilar Foods', *Journal of the American Dietetic Association*, vol. 15, pp. 540–8.
Halsey, Margaret, 1938 *With Malice Toward Some*. New York: Simon & Schuster.
Hardy, Thomas, 1874 *Far from the Madding Crowd*. London.
——— 1886 *The Mayor of Casterbridge*. London.
Hartley, Dorothy, 1954 *Food in Britain*. London: Macdonald.
Hayward, Abraham, 1852 *The Art of Dining: or, Gastronomy and Gastronomers*. London.
Hecht, J. J., 1956 *The Domestic Service Class in Eighteenth-Century England*. London: Routledge & Kegan Paul.
Hecquet, P., 1709 *Traité des dispenses du carême, dans lequel on découvre la fausseté des prétextes qu'on apporte pour les obtenir, les rapports naturels des alimens maigres avec la nature de l'homme et par l'histoire, par l'analyse et par l'observation leur convenance avec la santé*. Paris: F. Fournier.
Hélin, Etienne, 1963 *La Demographie de Liège aux XVIIe et XVIIIe siècles*. Bruxelles: Académie Royale de Belgique.
Hémardinquer, Jean-Jacques [1961] 'Les Graisses de Cuisine en France: Essais de Cartes', in Hémardinquer, ed., *Pour une histoire de l'alimentation*. Paris: A. Colin, 1970, pp. 254–71.
Henisch, B. A., 1976 *Fast and Feast: Food in Medieval Society*. University Park and London: Pennsylvania State University Press.
Herbodeau, E. and Thalamas, P., 1955 *Georges Auguste Escoffier*. London: Practical Press.
Herpin, Nicolas, 1980 'Comportements Alimentaires et Contraintes des Emplois du Temps', *Revue française de sociologie*, vol. 21, no. 4, pp. 599–628.
Hill, Christopher, 1964 *Society and Puritanism in Pre-Revolutionary England*. London: Secker & Warburg.
Holt, Richard, 1981 *Sport and Society in Modern France*. London: Macmillan.
Hoskins, W. G., 1964 'Harvest Fluctuations and English Economic History, 1480–1619', *Agricultural History Review*, vol. 12, pp. 28–46.
——— 1968 'Harvest Fluctuations and English Economic History, 1620–1750, *Agricultural History Review*, vol. 16, pp. 15–31.
Huizinga, Johan [1924] *The Waning of the Middle Ages*. Harmondsworth: Penguin, 1972.

Huxley, Elspeth, 1965 *Brave New Victuals: An Inquiry into Modern Food Production*. London: Chatto & Windus.

Hyman, Philip and Hyman, Mary, 1979–81 'La Chapelle and Massialot: an Eighteenth-Century Feud', *Petits Propos Culinaires*, vol. 2, pp. 44–54; vol. 8, pp. 35–40.

Interdepartmental Committee on Physical Deterioration, 1904 *Report*. Cd. 2175, House of Commons Sessional Papers, vol. XXXII, London: HMSO.

Isakovics, Alois von, 1976 'The Migration of Italian Cultural Elites to Early Modern France'', PhD, Boston University Graduate School.

James, P. D. [1962] *Cover her Face*. London: Sphere, 1974.

Jay, Martin, 1973 *The Dialectical Imagination*. London: Heinemann.

Jeaffreson, John C., 1875 *A Book about the Table*. 2 vols, London: Hurst & Blackett.

Jefferies, Richard [1872] 'Wiltshire Labourers', in *Landscape with Figures: An Anthology of Richard Jefferies's Prose*. Harmondsworth: Penguin, 1983.

Jerrold, William B., 1868 *The Epicure's Yearbook and Table Companion*. London: Bradbury, Evans.

Jones, C. D. H. and Sonnenscher, M., 1983 'The Social Functions of the Hospital in Eighteenth-Century France: the Case of the Hôtel-Dieu of Nîmes', *French Historical Studies*, vol. 13, no. 2, pp. 172–214.

Kahl, William F., 1961 'The Cooks' Company in the Eighteenth Century', *Guildhall Miscellany*, vol. II, pp. 71–81.

Kapteyn, Paul, 1980 *Taboe, Macht en Moraal in Nederland*. Amsterdam: De Arbeiderspers.

Kidder, Edward, *c.* 1720 *E. Kidder's Receipts of Pastry and Cookery for the Use of his Scholars*. London.

Kitchiner, Dr William, 1817 *Apicius Redevivus, or, The Cook's Oracle*. London: S. Bagster.

——— 1821 *The Art of Invigorating and Prolonging Life, or, The Invalid's Oracle*. London: G. B. Whittaker.

Kleyngeld, H. P., 1974 *Adoption of New Food Products: An Investigation into the Existence and the Character of Food Innovators*. Tilburg: Tilburg University Press.

Koenigsberger, H. G., 1977 '*Dominium regale* or *dominium politicum et regale?* Monarchies and Parliaments in Early Modern Europe', in P. R. Gleichmann, J. Goudsblom and H. Korte, eds, *Human Figurations: Essays for Norbert Elias*. Amsterdam: Amsterdams Socioligisch Tijdschrift, pp. 293–318.

Kornhauser, William A., 1960 *The Politics of Mass Society*. London: Routledge & Kegan Paul.

Kouindjy, E., 1926 *Recherches historiques sur l'enseignement de l'hygiène alimentaire*. Paris: Norbert Maloine.

Kristeva, Julia [1980] *Powers of Horror: An Essay on Abjection*. New York: Columbia University Press, 1982.

Kuhn, T. S., 1962 *The Structure of Scientific Revolutions*. Chicago: University of Chicago Press.

La Bruyère-Champier, J., 1560 *De Re Cibaria*. Lyon: S. Honoratum.

La Chapelle, Vincent, 1733 *The Modern Cook*. 3 vols, London.

Ladurie, Emmanuel Le Roy [1966] *The Peasants of Languedoc*. Urbana: University of Illinois Press, 1974.

——— [1972] 'In Normandy's Woods and Fields', in *The Territory of the Historian*. Brighton: Harvester Press, 1979, pp. 133–71.

——— [1978] *Montaillou*. Harmondsworth: Penguin, 1980.

Lamb, Patrick, 1710 *Royal Cookery; or, the Complete Court Cook*. London: Abel Roper.

Landry, Adolphe, 1935 'La Démographie de l'Ancien Paris', *Journal de la Société Statistique de Paris*, vol. LXXVI, pp. 34–45.

Langland, William [*c.* 1390] *Piers the Ploughman*. Harmondsworth: Penguin, 1959.

La Varenne, François Pierre de, 1651 *Le Cuisinier François*. Paris: chez Pierre David.

——— (attr.) 1653 *Le Pâtissier françois*. Paris: chez Jean Gaillard.

——— (attr.) *c.* 1667 *Le Confiturier françois*. Troyes: chez Jacques Febvre.

Leach, Edmund, 1970 *Lévi-Strauss*. London: Fontana.

Le Goff, Jacques, 1964 *La Civilisation de l'Occident Médiéval*. Paris: Arthaud.

Le Grand d'Aussy, P.-J.-B. [1782] *Histoire de la vie privée des Francois*. 3 vols., Paris: Laurent-Beaupré, 1815.

Le Magnen, J., 1972 'Regulation of Food Intake', in F. Reichsmann, ed., *Advances in Psychosomatic Medicine*, Vol. 7, *Hunger and Satiety in Health and Disease*. Basel: S. Karger, pp. 73–90.

Lévi-Strauss, Claude [1958] *Structural Anthropology*. Garden City, N.Y.: Doubleday, 1967.

——— [1965] 'The Culinary Triangle', *Partisan Review*, vol. 33, pp. 586–95.

——— [1964] *The Raw and the Cooked*. London: Jonathan Cape, 1969.

——— [1968] *The Origin of Table Manners*. London: Jonathan Cape, 1978.

Liverpool School Board, 1883 *The Rudiments of Cookery, with Some Account of Food and its Uses: A Manual for Use in Schools and Homes*. Liverpool.

L.S.R., 1674 *L'Art de bien traiter*. Paris: Jean du Puis.

Lune, Pierre de, 1656 *Le Cuisinier*. Paris: chez Pierre David.

Macfarlane, Alan, 1978 *The Origins of English Individualism*. Oxford: Basil Blackwell.

McKendrick, N., Brewer, J. and Plumb, J. H., 1982 *The Birth of a Consumer Society: The Commercialisation of Eighteenth-Century England*. London: Europa Publications.

McKenzie, J. C., 1963 'Recipes and the Housewife', *Home Economics*, vol. 9, no. 3, pp. 16–17.

McLaughlin, Terence, 1978 *A Diet of Tripe: The Chequered History of Food Reform*. Newton Abbot: David & Charles.

Magnus, Philip, 1964 *King Edward VII*. London: John Murray.

Magraw, Roger, 1983 *France 1815–1914: The Bourgeois Century*. London: Fontana.

Manchester School Board, 1889 *Cookery Classes, Day and Evening Schools: Recipes used at the Classes*. Manchester.

Mandrou, R. [1961] *Introduction to Modern France, 1500–1600*. London: Arnold, 1975.

Marin, François, 1739 *Les Dons de Comus, ou les délices de la table*. Paris: chez Prault fils.

——— 1742 *Suite des Dons de Comus ou l'art de la cuisine reduit en pratique*. Paris: chez la veuve Pissot; Didot; Brunet fils.

Markham, Gervase, 1615 *The English Hus-Wife*. London: Roger Jackson.

Martin, Alfred von [1932] *Sociology of the Renaissance*. London: Kegan Paul, Trench, Trubner, 1944.
Massialot, 1691 *Le Cuisinier roïal et bourgeois*. Paris: chez Charles de Sercy.
May, Robert, 1660 *The Accomplish't Cook, or the Art and Mystery of Cookery*. London: Nathaniel Brooke.
Mead, W. E., 1931 *The English Medieval Feast*. London: George Allen & Unwin.
Ménagier de Paris, Le [*c.* 1394] *The Goodman of Paris*, ed. Eileen Power. London: George Routledge, 1928.
Mennell, Stephen, 1976 *Cultural Policy in Towns*. Strasbourg: Council of Europe.
——— 1979 'Theoretical Considerations on the Study of Cultural 'Needs'', *Sociology* vol. 13, no. 2, pp. 235–57.
——— 1980 *Sociological Theory: Uses and Unities*. 2nd edn, Walton-on-Thames: Nelson.
——— 1981a 'Montaigne, Civilisation and Sixteenth-Century European Society', in K. C. Cameron, ed., *Montaigne and His Age*. Exeter: University of Exeter, pp. 69–85.
——— 1981b *Lettre d'un pâtissier anglois et autres contributions à une polémique gastronomique du XVIIIe siècle*. Exeter: University of Exeter.
——— 1984 'Food at the Late Stuart and Hanoverian Courts', *Petits Propos Culinaires*, vol. 17, pp. 22–9.
Menon, 1739 *Nouveau traité de la cuisine*. 2 vols, Paris: chez Michel-Etienne David.
——— 1746 *La Cuisinière bourgeoise*. Paris: Guillyn.
——— 1755 *Les Soupers de la cour*. 4 vols, Paris: Guillyn.
Mercier, Louis-Sebastien, 1783 *Tableau de Paris*. Amsterdam.
Merton, Robert K. [1949] *Social Theory and Social Structure*. 3rd edn, New York: Free Press, 1968.
Messisbugo, Cristoforo di, 1549 *Banchetti compositioni di vivande, et apparechio generale*. Ferrara: Giovanni de Buglhat & A. Hurcher.
Meusnier de Querlon, Anne-Gabriel, 1740a *Apologie des modernes*. Paris.
——— 1740b *Les Soupers de Daphne*. Paris: Oxford.
Michaux, Marceline, 1867 *La Cuisine de la ferme*. Paris: Librairie Agricole de la Maison Rustique.
Mill, John Stuart, 1859 *On Liberty*. London: Parker.
Mingay, Gordon E., 1963 *English Landed Society in the Eighteenth Century*. London: Routledge & Kegan Paul.
Minns, Raynes, 1980 *Bombers and Mash: The Domestic Front 1939–45*. London: Virago.
Misson, H. [1698] *M. Misson's Memoirs and Observations on his Travels over England*. London: D. Browne, 1719.
Mitchell, B. R., [1975] *European Historical Statistics 1750–1975*. London: Macmillan, 2nd rev. edn, 1981.
Mitchell, B. R. and Deane, P., 1962 *Abstract of British Historical Statistics*. Cambridge: Cambridge University Press.
Mitford, Nancy [1945] *The Pursuit of Love*. Harmondsworth: Penguin, 1949.
Molière, J.-B. P. [1682] *The Miser and Other Plays*. Harmondsworth: Penguin, 1953.
Monselet, Charles, 1860–4 *Almanach des gourmands*. Paris.
Montagné, Prosper [1938] *Larousse gastronomique*. London: Hamlyn, 1961.

Montagné, Prosper and Salles, Prosper, 1900 *La Grande Cuisine illustrée*. Paris: Flammarion.

Montaigne, Michel de [1595a] *Essays*. Harmondsworth: Penguin, 1958.

——— [1595b] *Oeuvres complètes*. Paris: NRF, 1962.

Morgan, H. Gethin, 1977 'Fasting Girls and Our Attitudes to Them', *British Medical Journal*, vol. 2, pp. 1652–5.

Morgan, Lady Sydney, 1831 *France in 1829–30*. 2 vols, London: Saunders & Otley.

Morpurgo, S., ed., 1890 *Ricette d'un Libro di Cucina del buono secolo della lingua*. Bologna.

Morris, Helen, 1938 *Portrait of a Chef*. London: Cambridge University Press.

——— 1953 'No Kickshaws, Whole Bellyfuls', *Wine and Food*, vol. 78, pp. 95–8.

Morris, R., ed., 1862 *Liber Cure Cocorum*. *Transactions of the Philological Society*, Supplement.

Moulin, Léo, 1975 *L'Europe à table: Introduction à une psychosociologie des pratiques alimentaires en Occident*. Paris: Elsevier-Sequoia.

Moxon, Elizabeth, 1749 *English Housewifery*. Leeds: James Lister.

Mulon, Marianne, 1970 'Les Premières Recettes Médiévales', in J.-J. Hémardinquer, ed., *Pour une histoire de l'alimentation*. Paris: A. Colin, pp. 236–40.

Murrell, John, 1631 *Murrells Two Bookes of Cookery and Carving*. London: John Marriot.

NFSC (National Food Survey Committee), 1960 *Domestic Food Consumption and Expenditure*. London: HMSO.

——— 1967 *Household Food Consumption and Expenditure*. London: HMSO.

Napier, Mrs Alexander, ed., 1882 *A Noble Boke of Cookry*. London.

Newnham-Davis, N. and Bastard, A., 1903 *The Gourmet's Guide to Europe*. London: Grant Richards.

Oakley, Ann, 1974 *The Sociology of Housework*. London: Martin Robertson.

Oddy, D. J. and Miller, D. S., eds, 1976 *The Making of the Modern British Diet*. London: Croom Helm.

Office of Population Censuses and Surveys, 1984 *Population Trends*. London: HMSO.

O'Hara-May, Jane, 1977 *The Elizabethan Dyetary of Health*. Lawrence, Kansas: Coronado Press.

O'Mahony, M. and Alba, M. del C. M., 1980 'Taste descriptions in Spanish and English', *Chemical Senses*, vol. 5, no. 1, pp. 47–62.

O'Mahony, M. and Muhiudeen, H., 1977 'A Preliminary Study of Alternative Taste Languages using Qualitative Description of Sodium Chloride Solutions: Malay versus English', *British Journal of Psychology*, vol. 68, no. 3, pp. 275–8.

O'Mahony, M. and Thompson, B. 1977 'Taste Quality Descriptions: Can the Subject's Response be Affected by Mentioning Taste Words in the Instructions?', *Chemical Senses and Flavour*, vol. 2, no. 3, pp. 283–98.

O'Mahony, M. and Tsang, T., 1980 'A Preliminary Comparison of Cantonese and American-English as Taste Languages', *British Journal of Psychology*, vol. 71, no. 2, pp. 221–6.

Orléans, 1855 *Correspondance complète de Madame la Duchesse d'Orléans*. 2 vols., Paris: Charpentier.

Ortega y Gasset, José [1930] *The Revolt of the Masses*. London: Allen & Unwin, 1960.

Orwell, George [1933] *Down and Out in Paris and London*. Harmondsworth: Penguin, 1974.

—— [1937] *The Road to Wigan Pier*. Harmondsworth: Penguin, 1962.

Owst, G. R. [1933] *Literature and Pulpit in Medieval England*. Oxford: Basil Blackwell, 1966.

Oxford, A. W. [1913] *English Cookery Books to the Year 1850*. London: Holland Press, 1977.

Oyler, Philip [1950] *The Generous Earth*. Harmondsworth: Penguin, 1961.

Palmer, Arnold, 1952 *Moveable Feasts*. London: Oxford University Press.

Parry, Graham, 1981 *The Golden Age Restor'd: The Culture of the Stuart Court, 1603–42*. Manchester: Manchester University Press.

Pegge, Samuel, ed. 1780 *The Forme of Cury*. London: J. Nichols, printer to the Society of Antiquaries.

Pellaprat, Henri-Paul, 1936a *L'Art culinaire moderne*. Paris: Comptoir Français du Livre.

—— 1936b *Traité de la cuisine familiale*. Paris: Flammarion.

Percy, Thomas, ed. [1512] *The Regulations and Establishment of the Household of Henry Algernon Percy, the Fifth Earl of Northumberland at his Castles of Wresill and Leckinfield in Yorkshire. (The Northumberland Household Book)*. London: William Pickering, 1827.

Perkin, Harold, 1969 *The Origins of Modern English Society 1780–1881*. London: Routledge & Kegan Paul.

Petersson, R. T., 1956 *Sir Kenelm Digby*. London: Jonathan Cape.

Phillips, F. T., 1966 *A Second History of the Worshipful Company of Cooks, London*. London: Cooks' Company.

Piozzi, H. L., 1785 *Anecdotes of the Late Samuel Johnson*. London.

Platina, *c.* 1475 *De Honesta Voluptate*. Venice.

Plumb, J. H., 1952 'Sir Robert Walpole's Food', *Wine and Food*, no. 74, pp. 64–8.

Pomiane, Edouard de, 1922 *Bien manger pour bien vivre: essai de gastronomie théorique*. Paris: A. Michel.

Porter, Roy, 1982 *English Society in the Eighteenth Century*. Harmondsworth: Penguin.

Power, Eileen, 1928 Introduction to *The Goodman of Paris*. London: George Routledge.

Prick, J. J. G., 1977 'Quelques Aspects de l'Anthropologie de l'Olfaction Gustative: les Bienfaits Spécifiques du Vin français', *Evolution psychiatrique*, vol. 42, no. 3–2, pp. 861–76.

Priestland, Gerald, 1972 *Frying Tonight: The Saga of Fish and Chips*. London: Gentry Books.

Prior, Peter (Chairman), 1978 *Report of the Committee of Inquiry into Motorway Service Areas*. London: HMSO.

Pullar, Phillipa, 1970 *Consuming Passions*. London: Hamish Hamilton.

Rabisha, William, 1661 *The Whole Body of Cookery Dissected*. London: Giles Calvert.

Raffald, Elizabeth, 1769 *The Experienced English Housekeeper*. Manchester.

Rees, R. N. K. and Fenby, Charles, 1931 'Meals and Meal-Times', in R. Lennard, ed., *Englishmen at Rest and Play: Some Phases of English Leisure, 1558–1714*. Oxford: Clarendon Press, pp. 147–201.

Reeves, M. P. S., 1913 *Round about a Pound a Week*. London: G. Bell.

Renner, H. D., 1944 *The Origin of Food Habits*. London: Faber & Faber.

Revel, Jean-François, 1979 *Un festin en paroles*. Paris: J.-J. Pauvert.

Ribou, Jean, 1662 *L'Escole parfaite des officiers de bouche*. Paris: chez la Veuve Pierre David.

Rich, E. E. and Wilson, C. H., eds, 1977 *Cambridge Economic History of Europe*, vol. v. Cambridge: Cambridge University Press.

Richard, Guy, 1974 *Noblesse d'affaires au XVIIIe siècle*. Paris: A. Colin.

Ritz, Marie Louise, 1938 *César Ritz: Host to the World*. London: Harrap.

Rogers, Thorold, 1866 *Six Centuries of Work and Wages*. London.

Root, Waverley, 1958 *The Food of France*. London: Cassell.

Ross, E. B., 1978 'Food Taboos, Diet and Hunting Strategy', *Current Anthropology*, vol. 19, no. 1, pp. 1–36.

Rosselli, G. de [1516] *Epulario, or The Italian Banquet*. London, 1598.

Rowntree, B. Seebohm, 1901 *Poverty: A Study of Town Life*. London: Macmillan.

Rowntree, B. Seebohm and Kendall, May, 1913 *How the Labourer Lives: A Study of the Rural Labour Problem*. London: Nelson.

Rudé, George, 1964 *The Crowd in History*. London: Wiley.

Rundell, Maria Elizabeth [1806] *A New System of Domestic Cookery*. London: John Murray, 1807.

Sahlins, Marshall, 1976 *Culture and Practical Reason*. Chicago: University of Chicago Press.

Salaman, Redcliffe, 1949 *The History and Social Influence of the Potato*. Cambridge, Cambridge University Press.

Salerno School [*c.* 1100] *Regimen sanitatis salerni*. London: 1528.

Saulnier, L., 1923 *Le Répertoire de la cuisine*. Paris and London.

Schofield, R. S., 1968 'The Measurement of Literacy in Pre-Industrial England', in J. Goody, ed., *Literacy in Traditional Societies*. Cambridge: Cambridge University Press.

Schwabe, Calvin W., 1979 *Unmentionable Cuisine*. Charlottesville: University Press of Virginia.

Scotson-Clark, George F., 1924 *Eating without Fears*. London: Jonathan Cape.

Sévigné, Marie de Rabutin-Chantal, Mme de [1726] *Correspondance*. 3 vols, Paris: Gallimard, 1972–8.

Shelley, Percy Bysshe, 1813 *Vindication of Natural Diet*. London.

Simon, André L. [1929] *The Art of Good Living*. London: Michael Joseph, 1951.

——— 1959 *The Star Chamber Dinner Accounts*. London.

——— 1969 *In the Twilight*. London: Michael Joseph.

Simoons, Frederick J., 1961 *Eat Not This Flesh: Food Avoidances in the Old World*. Madison: University of Wisconsin Press.

Sinclair, Upton, 1905 *The Jungle*. New York: Vanguard.

Skramlik, E. von, 1926 *Handbuch der Physiologie der niedern Sinne*. Leipzig: G. Thieme.

Smith, Eliza 1727 *The Compleat Housewife*. London: J. Pemberton.

Smith, Robert, 1723 *Court Cookery*. London: T. Wotton.

Smollet, Tobias [1771] *Humphry Clinker*. London: Signet, 1960.

Sofer, C., Janis, I. and Wishlade L., 1964 'Social and Psychological Factors in Changing Food Habits', in J. Yudkin and J. C. Mackenzie, eds, *Changing Food Habits*. London: MacGibon & Kee.
Sombart, Werner [1913] *Luxury and Capitalism*. Ann Arbor: University of Michigan Press, 1969.
Soyer, Alexis, 1846 *The Gastronomic Regenerator*. London: Simpkin Marshall.
——— 1847 *Charitable Cookery, or The Poor Man's Regenerator*. London.
——— 1849 *The Modern Housewife, or Ménagère*. London: Simpkin Marshall.
——— 1854 *A Shilling Cookery for the People*. London: George Routledge.
——— 1857 *Soyer's Culinary Campaign*. London.
Spock, Benjamin and Lowenberg, Miriam E. [1955] *Feeding Your Baby and Child*. London: New English Library, 1969.
Stead, Jennifer, 1983 'Quizzing Glasse: or Hannah Scrutinised', *Petits Propos Culinaires*, vol. 13, pp. 9–24; vol. 14, pp. 17–30.
Steiner, J. E., 1977 'Facial Expressions of the Neonate Infant Indicating the Hedonics of Food-related Chemical Stimuli', in R. Weiffenbach, ed., *Taste and Development: The Genesis of Sweet Preference*. Bethesda: DHEW Publication.
Stone, Lawrence, 1964 'The Educational Revolution in England, 1540–1640', *Past and Present*, vol. 28, pp. 41–80.
——— 1965 *The Crisis of the Aristocracy*. Oxford: Clarendon Press.
——— 1969 'Literacy and Education in England, 1640–1900', *Past and Present*, vol. 42, pp. 69–139.
Stone, Lawrence and Stone, Jeanne Fawtier, 1984 *An Open Elite? England 1540–1880*. Oxford: Oxford University Press.
Stone's Chop House, 1963 *A History of Stone's Chop House*. London: Stone's Chop House (London) Ltd.
Stouff, Louis, 1970 *Ravitaillement et alimentation en Provence aux 14ᵉ et 15ᵉ siècles*. Paris: Mouton.
Strauss, Gustave L. M. (pseud.: 'An Old Bohemian'), 1885 *Philosophy in the Kitchen: General Hints on Foods and Drinks*. London: Ward & Downey.
Sturgeon, Launcelot, 1822 *Essays, Moral, Philosophical and Stomachical on the Important Science of Good-Living*. London: G. & B. Whittaker.
Suzanne, Alfred [1894] *La Cuisine anglaise et sa pâtisserie*. Paris, L'Art culinaire, 1904.
Synott, Pierce, 1936 'Mr Jorrocks's Table Tour', *Wine and Food* no. 9, Spring, pp. 14–22; no. 10, Summer, pp. 3–12.
——— 1938 'The Duke of Cambridge's Menus', *Wine and Food*, no. 20, pp. 351–3.
Szalai, Alexander, ed., 1972 *The Use of Time: Daily Activities of Urban and Suburban Populations in Twelve Countries*. The Hague and Paris: Mouton.
Taillevent, Guillaume Tirel *dit*, [*c*. 1380] *Le Viandier*. Paris, 1897.
Tardieu, Suzanne, 1964 *La Vie domestique dans le Mâconnais rurale pré-industriel*. Paris: Université de Paris.
Taylor, Jeremy, 1854 *The Whole Works of the Rt Rev. Jeremy Taylor, DD*. 10 vols, London: Longmans.
Thackeray, William Makepeace, 1848–50 *Pendennis*. 2 vols, London.
Thomas, Keith, 1971 *Religion and the Decline of Magic*. London: Weidenfeld & Nicolson.

——— 1983 *Man and the Natural World: Changing Attitudes in England, 1500–1800*. London: Allen Lane.

Thompson, E. P. [1963] *The Making of the English Working Class*. Harmondsworth: Penguin, 1968.

——— 1971 'The Moral Economy of the English Crowd in the Eighteenth Century', *Past and Present*, vol. 50, pp. 76–136.

Thompson, Flora [1939–43] *Lark Rise to Candleford*. Harmondsworth: Penguin, 1973.

Thompson, F. M. L., 1963 *English Landed Society in the Nineteenth Century*. London: Routledge & Kegan Paul.

Thompson, Sir Henry [1880] *Food and Feeding*. 6th edn, London: Frederick Warne, 1896.

Thuillier, Guy, 1970 'Note sur les Sources de l'Histoire Régionale de l'Alimentation pour la France du XIXe siècle', in J.-J. Hémardinquer, ed., *Pour une histoire de l'alimentation*. Paris: A. Colin, pp. 212–27.

Tilly, Charles, 1975 'Food Supply and Public Order in Modern Europe', in Tilly, ed., *The Formation of National States in Western Europe*. Princeton: Princeton University Press, pp.380–455.

Timbs, John, 1866 *Club Life of London*. 2 vols, London: Richard Bentley.

Troisgros, Jean et Troisgros, Pierre, 1977 *Cuisiniers à Roanne*. Paris: Robert Laffont.

Tschumi, Gabriel, 1954 *Royal Chef: Recollections of Life in Royal Households from Qeeen Victoria to Queen Mary*. London: W. Kimber.

Turner, J. S. [1970] *The Chemical Feast: The Ralph Nader Study Group Report on Food Protection and the Food and Drug Administration*. Harmondsworth: Penguin, 1976.

Ude, Louis Eustache, 1813 *The French Cook; or The Art of Cookery Developed in all its Branches*. London: Cox & Baylis.

United Nations, 1957 *Report on the World Social Situation*. New York: United Nations.

Vaissière, Pierre de, 1903 *Gentilhommes campagnardes de l'ancienne France: étude sur la condition, l'état social et les moeurs de la noblesse de province du XVIe au XVIIe siècle*. Paris: Perrin.

Vaultier, Roger, 1940 'La gastronomie Régionale en France Pendant la Révolution', *Grandgousier*, 7e année, no. 4, pp. 79–87.

Veblen, Thorstein, 1899 *The Theory of the Leisure Class*. New York: Macmillan.

Viard, A. [1806] *Le Cuisinier impérial*. 7th edn, Paris: Barba, 1812

Villermé, L. R., 1840 *Tableau de l'état physique et moral des ouvriers employés dans les manufactures de coton, de laine et de soie*. 2 vols., Paris: Académie des Sciences.

Vitányi, Iván, 1983 *Multiple Perspectives of the Sociology of the Arts*. Budapest: Institute for Culture.

Voltaire, François Marie Arouet de [1765] *Correspondence*. 107 vols, Geneva: Institut et Musée Voltaire, 1953–65.

Walker, C. and Cannon, G., 1984 *The Food Scandal*. London: Century.

Walker, Thomas, 1835 *The Original*. London: H. Renshaw.

Warner, Richard, ed., 1791 *Antiquitates Culinariae*. London: R. Blamire.

Wason, Betty, 1962 *Cooks, Gluttons and Gourmets: A History of Cookery*. New York: Doubleday.

Waugh, Evelyn [1942] *Put Out More Flags*. Harmondsworth: Penguin, 1978.
Weber, Adna Ferrin, 1899 *The Growth of Cities in the Nineteenth Century*. New York: Macmillan.
Weber, Eugen, 1973 *A Modern History of Europe*. London: Robert Hale.
——— 1977 *Peasants into Frenchmen*. London: Chatto and Windus.
Weber, Max [1904–05] *The Protestant Ethic and the Spirit of Capitalism*. London: Allen & Unwin, 1930.
——— [1922] *Economy and Society*. 2 vols., Berkeley: University of California Press, 1978.
Wernham, R. B., ed., 1968 *The Cambridge Modern History*, vol. III. Cambridge: Cambridge University Press.
Wesley, John, 1829–31 *Works*. 3rd ed.n 14 vols, London: Mason.
White, Cynthia, 1970 *Women's Magazines 1693–1968*. London: Michael Joseph.
White, Florence, 1932 *Good Things in England*. London: Jonathan Cape.
——— 1938 *A Fire in the Kitchen: The Autobiography of a Cook*. London: J. M. Dent & Sons.
Wiegelmann, Günter, 1967 *Alltags- und Festspeisen*. Marburg: N. G. Elwert Verlag.
——— 1974 'Innovations in Food and Meals', *Folk Life*, vol. 12, pp. 20–30.
Wilensky, Harold, 1964 'The Professionalisation of Everyone?', *American Journal of Sociology*, vol. 70, no. 2, pp. 137–58.
Willan, Anne, 1977 *Great Cooks and their Recipes: From Taillevent to Escoffier*. London: Elm Tree Books.
Williams, Raymond [1973] *The Country and the City*. London: Granada, 1975.
Wilson, Charles, 1965 *England's Apprenticeship, 1603–1763*. London, Longman.
Winchester, Barbara, 1955 *Tudor Family Portrait*. London: Jonathan Cape.
Wolley, Hannah, 1670 *The Queen-Like Closet*. London: R. Lowndes.
Woodforde, James, 1926–31 *Diary of a Country Parson*. 5 vols, London: Oxford University Press.
Woodhouse, Felicity Anne, 1976 'English Travellers in Paris, 1660–1789: a Study of Their Diaries', PhD Stanford University, Calif.
Wouters, Cas, 1977 'Informalisation and the Civilising Process', in P. R. Gleichmann *et al.*, eds, *Human Figurations: Essays for Norbert Elias*. Amsterdam: Amsterdams Sociologisch Tijdschrift, pp. 437–53.
Wrigley, E. A. [1967] 'A Simple Model of London's Importance in Changing English Society and Economy, 1650–1750', in P. Abrams and E. A. Wrigley, eds, *Towns in Societies*. Cambridge: Cambridge University Press, 1978, pp. 215–43.
Young, Arthur [1792–4] *Travels in France during the years 1787, 1788, 1789*. London: George Bell, 1889.
Young, James Harvey, 1970 'Historical Aspects of Food Cultism and Nutrition Quackery', in G. Blix, ed., *Food Cultism and Nutrition Quackery*. Uppsala: Symposia of the Swedish Nutrition Foundation, VIII, pp. 9–21.
Young, Linda Bishop, 1981 'Mobilising Food: Restaurant and Café Workers in Paris: A Case Study of "Direct Action" Syndicalism, 1900–14', PhD, New York University.
Yudkin, J. and McKenzie, J. C., eds, 1964 *Changing Food Habits*. London: MacGibon & Kee.
Zambrini, ed., 1863 *Il Libro della cucina del sec. XIV*. Bologna.

Zeldin, Theodore, 1973–7 *France 1848–1945*. 2 vols, Oxford: Oxford University Press.

PERIODICAL PUBLICATIONS CONSULTED

L'Art culinaire. Paris: 1883–1939.

Catering and Hotel Management. London: 1970–83 (for antecedent titles from 1932 see figure 8).

The Chef. London: 1895–8.

Cookery Annual and Year Book of the Universal Cookery and Food Association. London: 1905–32.

Elle. Paris: 1945– .

L'Express. Paris: 1953– .

La Femme chez elle. Paris: 1899–1938.

Femme pratique. Bruxelles/Paris, 1958– .

Good Food Guide. London: 1951– .

Good Housekeeping. London: 1922– .

Hotel Review and Catering and Food Trades Gazette. London: 1886–8.

Hotel World. London: 1895–1904.

Néo-Restauration. Paris: 1972– .

Le Pot-au-Feu. Paris: 1893–1940.

Hotel and Catering Review. London: 1952–69 (for antecedent titles from 1909, see figure 8).

Members' Handbook. London: UCFA, 1951–5.

La Revue culinaire. Paris: 1920– .

Egon Ronay's Guide (various sub-titles and sponsors). London: 1959– .

Woman's Life. London: 1895–1934.

Woman's Own. London: 1932– .

Index

UNIVERSITY OF ILLINOIS PRESS
1325 SOUTH OAK STREET
CHAMPAIGN, ILLINOIS 61820-6903
WWW.PRESS.UILLINOIS.EDU